Chemistry

Richard Harwood

CAMBRIDGE
UNIVERSITY PRESS

PUBLISHED BY THE PRESS SYNDICATE OF THE UNIVERSITY OF CAMBRIDGE
The Pitt Building, Trumpington Street, Cambridge CB2 1RP, United Kingdom

CAMBRIDGE UNIVERSITY PRESS
The Edinburgh Building, Cambridge CB2 2RU, United Kingdom
40 West 20th Street, New York, NY 10011-4211, USA
10 Stamford Road, Oakleigh, Melbourne 3166, Australia

© Cambridge University Press 1998

First published 1998

Printed in the United Kingdom at the University Press, Cambridge

Typeset in Sabon 11.5pt

A catalogue record for this book is available from the British Library

ISBN 0 521 57628 8 paperback

Designed and produced by Gecko Limited, Bicester, Oxon

Front cover photograph: False-coloured satellite image of tropical storm,
NASA/Science Photo Library

Back cover photographs: False-colour image of a snowflake, Scott Camazine/
Science Photo Library; Antibiotic pills, James King-Holmes/Science Photo
Library; Satellite map of the 'hole' in the ozone layer over Antarctica,
NASA/Science Photo Library

Notice to teachers
It is illegal to reproduce any part of this work in material form (including
photocopying and electronic storage) except under the following circumstances:
(i) where you are abiding by a licence granted to your school or institution by
the Copyright Licensing Agency;
(ii) where no such licence exists, or where you wish to exceed the terms of a
licence, and you have gained the written permission of Cambridge University Press;
(iii) where you are allowed to reproduce without permission under the provisions
of Chapter 3 of the Copyright, Designs and Patents Act 1988.

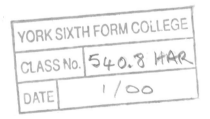

Contents

Extension material is in *italics*

1 Planet Earth   1

The Earth and its origins   1
1.1   'Chemistry without walls'   1
1.2   The Big Bang and the origin of
        the elements   1
1.3   The structure of the Earth   3
1.4   Rocks and the rock cycle   8
1.5   Shaping the landscape   10
1.6   The life history of a planet   11

The Earth's resources   15
1.7   The Earth's atmosphere   15
1.8   The water planet   17
1.9   The Earth's resources   17

Environmental management   20
1.10 The Earth seen from space   20
1.11 Atmospheric pollution   21
1.12 Water pollution   23

2 The nature of matter   27

Separation, purification and identification   27
2.1   The states of matter   27
2.2   Changes in physical state   28
2.3   Pure substances   29
2.4   Types of mixture   31
2.5   Separating and purifying substances   34
2.6   Solubility   38

Atoms and molecules   44
2.7   Elements and compounds   44
2.8   Chemical reactions and physical changes   44
2.9   Atomic theory   45
2.10 The kinetic theory of matter   46
2.11 Diffusion in fluids   48
2.12 Atoms and molecules   49

The structure of the atom   52
2.13 Atomic structure   52
2.14 Atomic number and mass number   54
2.15 Isotopes   55
2.16 Relative atomic masses   55

2.17 Radioactivity   57
2.18 The uses of radioactivity   58
2.19 Electron arrangements in atoms   59

3 Elements and compounds   64

Classifying the elements   64
3.1   The Periodic Table   64
3.2   Metals and non-metals   65
3.3   Groups and periods in the Periodic Table   66
3.4   Electron arrangement and the
        Periodic Table   66
3.5   Patterns in the Periodic Table   67
3.6   Trends across a period   68
3.7   New elements and versions
        of the Periodic Table   69
3.8   The position of hydrogen in
        the Periodic Table   70

Chemical bonding in elements and compounds   72
3.9   Chemical bonding in the elements   73
3.10 Chemical bonding in compounds   75
3.11 The physical properties of
        ionic and covalent compounds   78
3.12 The chemical formulas of
        elements and compounds   78
3.13 'What's in a name?' – naming chemical
        compounds   80

Molecular shape   *84*

The structure of materials   87
3.14 Basic physical properties   87
3.15 Exploring physical structure by
        X-ray diffraction   88
3.16 Metal crystals   89
3.17 Alloys   90
3.18 Ionic crystals   90
3.19 Giant molecular crystals   92

Allotropy   *94*

Simple molecular structures   *95*

Trends across the Periodic Table   *96*

Glasses and ceramics   *96*

Contents

4   Chemical change   100

Chemical reactions and equations   100
4.1   Physical and chemical change   100
4.2   Equations for chemical reactions   101
4.3   Types of chemical reaction   103

A closer look at reactions, particularly redox reactions   109

Electrolysis   112
4.4   Conductivity in solids   112
4.5   Conductivity in liquids   113
4.6   Electrolysis of molten compounds   115
4.7   Electrolysis of solutions   116

A closer look at electrode reactions   123

5   Acids, bases and salts   126

An introduction to acids and alkalis   126
5.1   What is an acid?   126
5.2   What is litmus?   127
5.3   The pH scale   128
5.4   The ionic nature of acid and alkali solutions   128
5.5   The importance of water   129

The chemical reactions of acids and bases   132
5.6   Acid reactions in everyday life   132
5.7   Alkalis and bases   133
5.8   Characteristic reactions of acids   134
5.9   Acids and bases in chemical analysis   136

Salts and their preparation   138
5.10   The importance of salts   138
5.11   The solubility of salts   139
5.12   Water of crystallisation   140
5.13   Preparing soluble salts   141

More about salts   144
5.14   *The preparation of insoluble salts*   144
5.15   *Making salts by direct combination*   145
5.16   *Efflorescence and deliquescence*   145

The ionic nature of acids, bases and salts   146
5.17   *Strong and weak acids*   146
5.18   *Strong and weak alkalis*   147
5.19   *Dynamic equilibria in solutions of weak acids and weak alkalis*   147
5.20   *pH and the ionic balance in water*   148
5.21   *What happens to the ions in neutralisation?*   148

5.22   *The 'basicity' of acids*   150
5.23   *The pH of salt solutions*   150
5.24   *Following neutralisation: the end point*   151
5.25   *Neutral and amphoteric oxides*   152

6   Quantitative chemistry   156

Chemical analysis and formulas   156
6.1   Chemical 'accountancy'   156
6.2   Compound formation and chemical formulas   159
6.3   Reacting amounts of substance   159

The mole and chemical reactions   162
6.4   *The mole – the chemical counting unit*   162
6.5   *Calculations on the mole*   163
6.6   *The mole and chemical equations*   165
6.7   *Calculations involving gases*   167

Moles and solution chemistry   171
6.8   *The concentration of solutions*   171
6.9   *Acid–base titrations*   172
6.10   *Solubility curves*   173
6.11   *Calculations in electrolysis*   174

7   How far? How fast?   178

Energy changes in chemical reactions   178
7.1   The reaction between methane and oxygen   178
7.2   The reaction between nitrogen and oxygen   179

Heat of reaction   180
7.3   *Experimental thermochemistry*   180

Rates of reaction   185
7.4   Factors affecting the rate of reaction   185
7.5   Catalysts   188

Surface catalysts and collision theory   193
7.6   *Photochemical reactions*   195

Reversible reactions and chemical equilibria   197
7.7   The reversible hydration of salts   198

Reversible reactions and chemical equilibria   199

8 Patterns and properties of non-metals 205

Hydrogen and water 205
8.1 Hydrogen 205
8.2 The chemistry of hydrogen 205
8.3 *The 'hydrogen economy'* 207
8.4 Water 208
8.5 The water cycle 209
8.6 Domestic and industrial water supplies 210
8.7 Water as a solvent 212
8.8 Chemical and physical tests for water 213

Oxygen and sulphur 217
8.9 The air as a resource 217
8.10 Oxygen 217
8.11 The fire triangle 218
8.12 Combustion and respiration 218
8.13 Sulphur 219
8.14 The chemistry of sulphur and its oxides 220
8.15 Sulphuric acid and sulphates 221

Carbon and silicon 225
8.16 Carbon molecules in space 225
8.17 The carbon cycle 225
8.18 The oxides of carbon 227
8.19 Carbonates and hydrogencarbonates 228

Metal hydrogencarbonates 231
8.20 *Hard and soft water* 231
8.21 *Silicon and silica* 234

Nitrogen and ammonia 236
8.22 Nitrogen 236
8.23 The nitrogen cycle 237
8.24 Ammonia 237
8.25 Nitric acid 239

Chlorine and the halogens 242
8.26 The family likeness 243
8.27 The chemical reactivity of the halogens 244
8.28 The uses of the halogens 245

The noble gases 247
8.29 Helium 247
8.30 The other noble gases 248

9 Patterns and properties of metals 250

The alkali metals 250
9.1 The reaction of the alkali metals with water 251
9.2 Flame tests for the metals 251
9.3 Compounds of the alkali metals 252

Calcium, magnesium and other Group II metals 253
9.4 Trends in reactivity 254
9.5 The reactions of burning magnesium 255
9.6 Uses and importance of magnesium and calcium 255
9.7 The limestone cycle 256
9.8 Reactivity in groups of metals 256

Aluminium 258
9.9 Aluminium's protective oxide layer 259
9.10 The thermit reaction 259
9.11 The analytical test for aluminium ions 260

The transition elements 261
9.12 Coloured compounds 262
9.13 Variable valency 263
9.14 Catalytic properties 263
9.15 Magnetic properties 263

The reactivity of metals 267
9.16 An overview of reactivity 267
9.17 The extraction of metals 268
9.18 Reactions of metals with air, water and dilute acids 269
9.19 Metal displacement reactions 269
9.20 Other redox competition reactions 269
9.21 Thermal decomposition of metal compounds 270

Electrical cells and energy 273
9.22 *Electrochemical cells* 273
9.23 *Portable power* 273
9.24 *Oxidation and reduction in power cells* 274
9.25 *Fuel cells* 275

10 Industrial inorganic chemistry 278
Chemical extraction of metals 278
10.1 Iron and steel 278
10.2 The production of iron in the blast furnace 278
10.3 Steel-making 279
10.4 The rusting of iron 280

Contents

The extraction of zinc, lead and copper 284
10.5 *The extraction of zinc and lead* 284
10.6 *The extraction of copper* 284

Electrolytic extraction of metals 286
10.7 The extraction of aluminium 286

Further industrially important processes 288
10.8 *The extraction of sodium and magnesium* 288
10.9 *Other industrial electrolytic processes* 289

Manufacturing economically important compounds 291
10.10 Ammonia and nitric acid 291
10.11 Ammonium nitrate and other fertilisers 293
10.12 Explosives 295
10.13 Sulphuric acid production 295
10.14 The chlor–alkali industry 295
10.15 Limestone 296
10.16 Direct uses 296

Resources, industry and recycling 300
10.17 Minerals and ores 300
10.18 Siting a chemical plant 300
10.19 The environmental costs of industry 301
10.20 Recycling 301

11 Organic chemistry 305

Hydrocarbons 305
11.1 Molecular ancestors 305
11.2 The unique properties of carbon 305
11.3 Alkanes 306
11.4 Alkenes 308
11.5 *Isomerism* 309
11.6 *Alkynes* 310
11.7 Chemical reactions of the alkanes 310
11.8 Chemical reactions of the alkenes 311

Alcohols 315
11.9 Making ethanol 315
11.10 The reactions of ethanol 316
11.11 Alcohol and health 316

Organic acids and esters 320
11.12 *Carboxylic acids* 320
11.13 *Ethanoic acid as a weak acid* 320
11.14 *Esterification* 321
11.15 *Soaps and detergents* 321

12 Petrochemicals and polymers 327

Crude oil and other fossil fuels 327
12.1 Crude oil 327
12.2 Alternative transport fuels 330
12.3 Coal and biogas 331

Polymerisation 335
12.4 Addition polymerisation 335

Condensation polymers and plastics 337
12.5 *Condensation polymerisation* 337
12.6 *The re-use, recycling and disposal of plastic waste* 339

Biological polymers 340
12.7 *Proteins* 341
12.8 *Enzymes* 342
12.9 *Carbohydrates* 343
12.10 *Food* 344

13 Chemical analysis and experimentation 348

Analytical chemistry 348
13.1 Inorganic analysis 348
13.2 Organic analysis 353

Medicinal chemistry 357
13.3 *Pharmaceuticals, drugs and medicines* 357
13.4 *Vitamins and minerals* 359

Experimental design and hypothesis testing 360
13.5 The scientific method 360
13.6 Revolutions in science 361
13.7 Experimental design 362
13.8 Sources of error in experiments 364
13.9 Medical screening and experimental controls 365

14 Study and revision skills 368

General techniques 368
14.1 Organisation of study time 368
14.2 Organisation of revision study 369
14.3 Strategies of study 369
14.4 Words are important 373
14.5 Examination skills 373

Multiple-choice questions   374
14.6   Multiple-choice *not* multiple-guess!   374

Short-answer questions   378
14.7   Thinking clearly   378

Data-handling and comprehension questions   385
14.8   An eye for detail   385

Answers to questions   395

Glossary of important chemical terms   401

Index   411

Acknowledgements

1, STSI/NASA/Science Photo Library; 8*tl*, David Weintraub/Science Photo Library; 8*tr*, *br*, 100, 101, 103, 105, 126, 136, 206, 213, 220, 222, 245, 250, 251, 254*tl*, *ttc*, *b*, Andrew Lambert; 11, Tony Moran; 20, NASA GSFC/Science Photo Library; 46, IBM Corporation, Research Division, Almaden Research Center; 89*br*, Science Source/Science Photo Library; 104, figure from *Chemistry and Chemical Reactivity*, Third Edition by John C. Kotz and Paul Treichel, Jr., copyright © 1996 by Saunders College Publishing, reproduced by permission of the publisher; 156, Courtesy of International Business Machines Corporation – unauthorized use not permitted; 208, B. Murton/Southampton Oceanography Centre/Science Photo Library; 210, Emma Lee/Life File; 212, Mike Evans/Life File; 219, Peter Dunkley/Life File; 232, Sheila Terry/Science Photo Library; 247, Dan Flavin, *Untitled 1970*, blue and red fluorescent light/photo credit: Cathy Carver/Courtesy Dia Center for the Arts, New York/© ARS, NY and DACS, London 1998; 248, Alexander Tsiaras/Science Photo Library; 254*tr*, from *Life Science Library: Matter*, photo by Albert Fenn, © Time-Life Books Inc.; 260, D.J. Dennis; 262, Stuart Norgrove/Life File; 263l, Reproduced by kind permission of the Dean and Chapter of York Minster; 263r, Ed Young/Science Photo Library; 264, Andrew Ward/Life File; 267, Michael Holford; 286, Ben Johnson/Science Photo Library; 291, courtesy of Deutsches Museum von Meisterwerken der Naturwissenschaft und Technik; 293*t*, Malcolm Fielding/Johnson Matthey PLC/Science Photo Library; 293*b*, Nigel Cattlin/Holt Studios International

Examination questions

The examination questions have been reproduced by kind permission of Edexcel Foundation, the Midland Examining Group, the Northern Examinations and Assessment Board, the Northern Ireland Council for the Curriculum Examinations and Assessment, the Southern Examining Group, the University of Cambridge Local Examinations Syndicate and the Welsh Joint Education Committee. Any answers or hints on answers are the sole responsibility of the author and have not been provided or approved by the examining boards.

1 Planet Earth

The Earth and its origins

This section covers the following ideas:

- the origin of the Universe in the Big Bang
- the formation of the elements by nuclear fusion in the centre of large stars
- the formation of our Solar System
- the structure of the Earth in terms of its core, mantle and crust
- the evidence for that structure from earthquakes and volcanoes
- plate tectonics and continental drift
- the rock cycle
- erosion and the formation of soil.

1.1 'Chemistry without walls'

The proper setting for the study of chemistry is the entire material universe, living and non-living. Chemistry involves laboratory-based experiment and analysis, but it is much more than that. It affects our understanding of all that happens around us. Everything is chemistry. There is no change that occurs in our material Universe that does not involve chemical processes. Whatever we may feel about the direction of change in the modern world and the problems we face, an understanding of chemistry will help us to respond to them appropriately.

Later chapters look at chemistry based in the laboratory. This chapter looks at chemistry in a wider context, and how it can help us to understand more about the Universe and our own planet, the Earth.

1.2 The Big Bang and the origin of the elements

It is thought that the Universe was born in a blistering cosmic fireball called the **Big Bang**. About 15 billion years ago, our Universe erupted out of nothing in a huge explosion. Everything – all matter, energy, even space and time – began to exist at that instant. Since then, the stuff of the Universe

has been expanding and cooling. In the earliest moments of time, the Universe occupied a tiny volume and was unimaginably hot. It was a searing fireball of radiation and **primitive particles**. As the Universe cooled, these particles assembled to form atoms. Gradually these clumped together due to the action of gravity and formed billions of **galaxies**, vast islands of stars. The Milky Way, our own galaxy, is only one of these.

Recently, amazing pictures from the Hubble Space Telescope have given us images of the huge scale of these galaxies (figure 1.1). In 1992, NASA's Cosmic Background Explorer (COBE) satellite detected slight 'ripples' in the **background radiation** of the Universe. These are seen as evidence that structures were beginning to form some 300 000 years after the Big Bang. The cold spots, where regions of the Universe were slightly denser than average, were the 'seeds' from which great galaxies were formed. This news from COBE was strong evidence for this picture of the origin of the Universe.

Particle accelerations and high-energy collisions

There seems to be an infinite variety in the world around us, but beneath it there is a small number of basic building blocks. The original primitive particles were the **quarks** and **leptons** (of which the electron is one) that inhabited the high-energy Universe just fractions of a second old. From these particles, protons, neutrons and then atoms are

Figure 1.1 A cloud of dust and gas where stars are forming, as seen by the Hubble Space Telescope. The area shown in this picture is about 4000 000 000 000 km across, and is just a tiny part of the Eagle nebula.

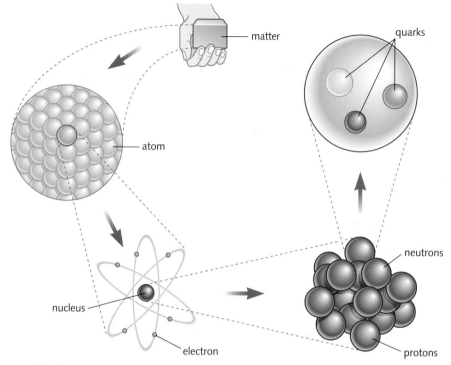

Figure 1.2 The particle round-up: from macroscopic to microscopic worlds.

oxygen, were created much later, in the nuclear furnaces deep inside stars (figure 1.3).

The first stars began as hydrogen. Within them helium and the heavier elements were formed by **fusion** processes. Atomic nuclei fuse together, giving out energy; for example

$$4\,^1H \rightarrow\,^4He + energy$$

In larger stars, some of the energy released cannot escape from the surface of the star. This energy can then cause further nuclear processes to occur; for example

$$3\,^4He \rightarrow\,^{12}C + energy$$

$$^{12}C +\,^4He \rightarrow\,^{16}O + energy$$

$$2\,^{16}O \rightarrow\,^{28}Si +\,^4He + energy$$

assembled (figure 1.2). Evidence for these particles and their interactions comes from their brief creation after collisions in particle accelerators. The use of accelerators allows scientists to 'run the clock backwards' to trace the likely events that occurred a tiny fraction of a second after the Big Bang.

During the earliest times of the Universe, **matter** and **antimatter** created in the Big Bang collided and annihilated each other. The collisions produced energy in the form of radiation. The balance between matter and antimatter in the early Universe was not even, and so the material world came into existence. Although we do not normally find antimatter in our part of the Universe now, we are able to create antiparticles in particle accelerators and learn about the conditions in which they were formed and how they behave. The first anti-matter element, anti-hydrogen, was synthesised at CERN in 1996.

The origin of the elements

About 100 seconds into the life of the Universe, the temperature had fallen to a mere 100 billion kelvins. Protons and neutrons began to collect together, making the light atomic nuclei of hydrogen, helium and lithium. However, the building of atoms did not progress beyond these light elements at this stage. The Universe's heavier elements, such as carbon and

These processes eventually stop at iron because the iron nucleus is the most stable of all. The star develops iron in its core and begins to cool. It eventually collapses inwards violently and then explodes in a **supernova**. Material from exploding stars is spread throughout interstellar space. The debris of earlier stars can collect together to form second-generation stars. Our Sun is a second-generation star and so it and the planets around it

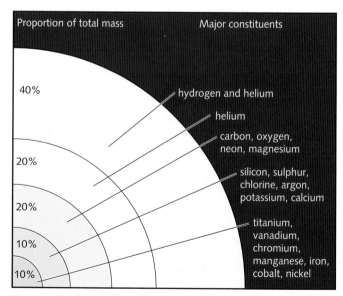

Figure 1.3 The 'shell' structure of a heavy star, just before its explosion in a supernova. The diagram shows the relative mass of each shell, not their size. The inner shells are much denser.

are enriched in the heavier elements. Elements are recycled throughout the Universe. We are a product of the ashes of long-dead stars.

The Solar System

The Sun was formed about 4500 million years ago. Figure 1.4 shows how it is thought that our Solar System was formed from its original dust cloud or **nebula**. The fact that all the major planets orbit the Sun in the same direction fits with the idea that they all formed from one nebula.

The major planets can conveniently be divided into two groups. Closest to the Sun are the rocky or **terrestrial planets**, so called because of their similarity to the Earth. This group is made up of Mercury, Venus, Earth and Mars. The second group are the **gas giants**, which lie beyond Mars. This group is made up of Jupiter, Saturn, Uranus and Neptune. There are arguments that Pluto (which is further away than Neptune) is not a major planet but a large asteroid.

1.3 The structure of the Earth

Our understanding of how the Earth works has undergone a major change. The Earth is not just a dead lump of rock in space, the victim of random unexplained events such as mountain building and climate change. What we see on the surface is the product of vigorous motions deep in the Earth. These are slow changes in terms of our lifespan, but fast when compared with the Earth's lifetime.

Evidence shows that the **Earth** is made up of several **layers** (figure 1.5 on page 4).

- The **core** consists mainly of iron and nickel and is responsible for the Earth's magnetic field. The inner core is solid and surrounded by an outer core of molten metal. This is the densest part of the Earth (density, $12.3\,\mathrm{g/cm^3}$).

- The **mantle** surrounds the core and is a thick layer of cooler, less dense rock. This rock is mainly silicates. It is partially molten and there are convection currents within it. It represents about 85% of the Earth's volume.

- The **crust** is a thin, less dense, solid outer layer. It is not a single continuous layer but is subdivided into plates of continental and oceanic crust.

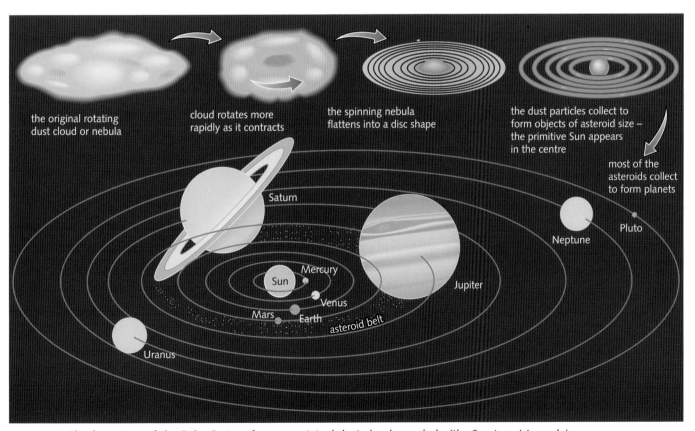

the original rotating dust cloud or nebula

cloud rotates more rapidly as it contracts

the spinning nebula flattens into a disc shape

the dust particles collect to form objects of asteroid size – the primitive Sun appears in the centre

most of the asteroids collect to form planets

Saturn

Mercury

Sun

Venus

Mars   Earth

asteroid belt

Jupiter

Neptune

Pluto

Uranus

Figure 1.4 The formation of the Solar System from an original dust cloud or nebula (the Sun is not to scale).

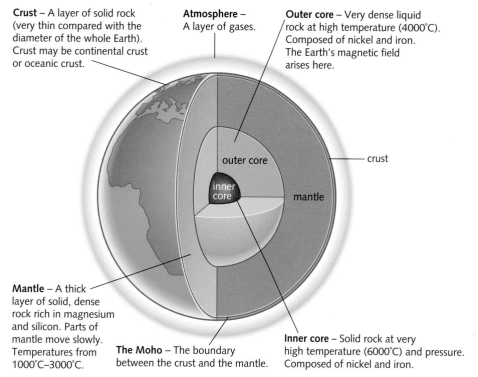

Crust – A layer of solid rock (very thin compared with the diameter of the whole Earth). Crust may be continental crust or oceanic crust.

Atmosphere – A layer of gases.

Outer core – Very dense liquid rock at high temperature (4000°C). Composed of nickel and iron. The Earth's magnetic field arises here.

Mantle – A thick layer of solid, dense rock rich in magnesium and silicon. Parts of mantle move slowly. Temperatures from 1000°C–3000°C.

The Moho – The boundary between the crust and the mantle.

Inner core – Solid rock at very high temperature (6000°C) and pressure. Composed of nickel and iron.

Figure 1.5 The structure of the Earth.

Evidence on the structure and composition of the Earth comes from several sources.

- *Earthquakes*

There are some 500 000 earthquakes each year. Only about 1000 are strong enough to cause damage, and a few lead to serious devastation and death. Earthquakes that occur in oceanic crust can be even more devastating because they can cause **tidal waves.**

The point at which the earthquake occurs within the crust is called the focus. The point on the surface of the Earth directly above the focus is called the epicentre. The energy released in an earthquake travels through the Earth in a series of **shock waves.** Geologists can record these shock waves using a series of seismic stations. The tremors produced at these stations are recorded on a **seismogram** (figure 1.6). Three types of waves are produced. Their behaviour allows the interior of the Earth to be mapped.

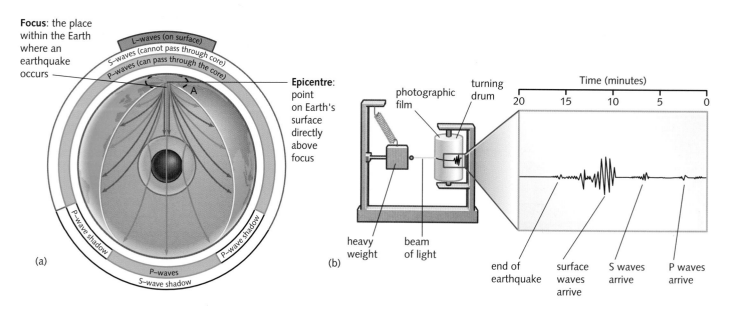

Figure 1.6 (a) Cross-section through the Earth showing the paths of the shock waves from an earthquake. The S and P waves are refracted (bent) as they pass through the Earth. A seismometer at A records the trace shown in (b). The position and size of the 'shadows' gives evidence for the Earth's internal structure.
(b) The shock waves sent out by an earthquake are detected by a seismometer.
The P-waves arrive first, as they travel fastest through the mantle. The S-waves then arrive and cause a second set of tremors. Lastly the L-waves arrive and cause the main shock.

Types of shock waves

Primary waves (P-waves) are produced by pushing and pulling forces. These can travel fastest and pass through both solids and liquids. These shock waves can pass through the core and be detected on the opposite side of the Earth from the sight of the earthquake. However, P-waves are refracted (bent) at the boundaries within the Earth, and produce a shadow.

Secondary waves (S-waves) are slower transverse waves (shaking waves) and cannot pass through liquids. The fact that they are not detected on the opposite side of the Earth shows that the core is molten. This produces a large shadow where S-waves cannot be received.

Long waves (L-waves), or surface waves, travel only through the crust. They are responsible for the largest land movements and therefore the most damage.

The sizes and positions of shadow regions where the different types of waves cannot be received helped geologists to work out the existence and size of the inner and outer core.

- *Volcanoes*
  Volcanoes are the most obvious source of information on material from inside the Earth. They give information about the crust and upper mantle where lava is produced. Plotting the location of volcanoes gives information about the regions within the Earth where most heat is being generated.

- *Meteorites*
  Geologists believe that meteorites, a few of which reach the Earth's surface, may be samples of planetary material dating from the formation of the Solar System.

- *Magnetism*
  The Earth's magnetic field is evidence for the presence of iron

in the core. In addition, analysis of the magnetic field recorded in rocks cooling on the ocean floor has given evidence of how the ocean floor is expanding in some regions.

The Earth's crust

The crust is not uniform in thickness. The oceanic crust is thinner (5–10 km thick) than the continental crust (25–50 km thick). They are also made of different materials. The oceanic crust is made mainly of basalt, while the upper continental crust has a high proportion of granite rocks (figure 1.7). The **Moho** (the Mohorovicic discontinuity) is the boundary between the crust and the mantle. Detailed descriptions of the layered structure at the surface define the **lithosphere** as the crust together with the layer of mantle immediately beneath the crust.

The outer layer of the lithosphere is not continuous. It is made of separate solid pieces called **plates**. There are seven major plates, eight intermediate plates and many smaller ones (figure 1.8 on page 6). The study of these plates and their use to explain observed features is called **plate tectonics**. Most, but not all, of the world's volcanic and earthquake activity occurs at the edges of the plates (figure 1.8 on page 6), and is caused by the movement of the plates against each other.

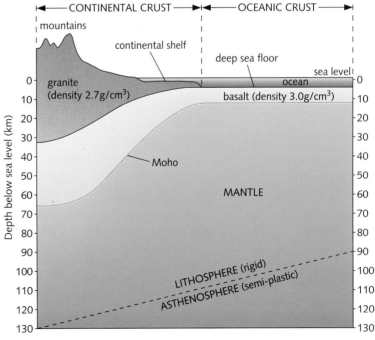

Figure 1.7 The structure of the Earth's crust, showing the oceanic crust and the thicker continental crust.

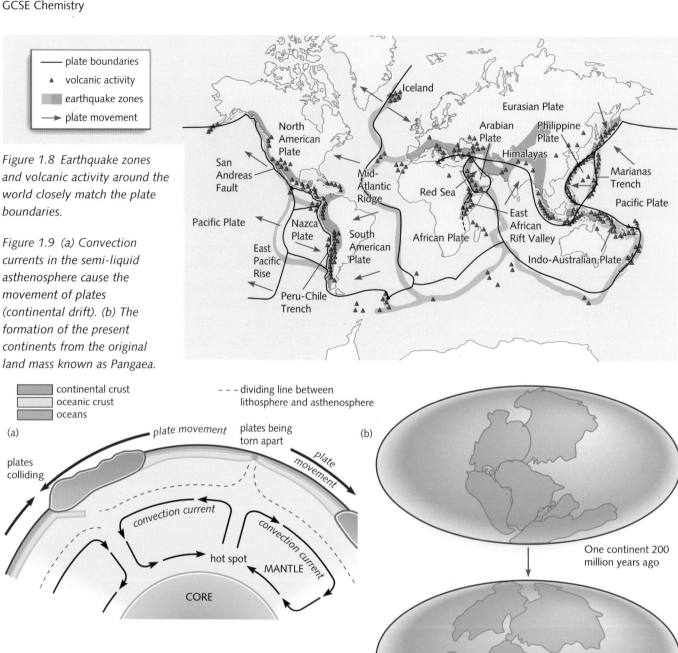

Figure 1.8 Earthquake zones and volcanic activity around the world closely match the plate boundaries.

Figure 1.9 (a) Convection currents in the semi-liquid asthenosphere cause the movement of plates (continental drift). (b) The formation of the present continents from the original land mass known as Pangaea.

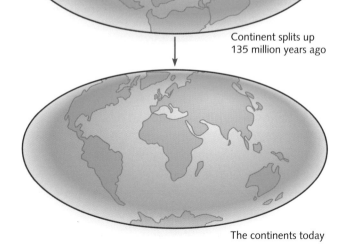

One continent 200 million years ago

Continent splits up 135 million years ago

The continents today

Convection currents in the semi-molten mantle move the plates at the surface as if they were huge rafts (figure 1.9a). The process is called **continental drift**. The movement is slow, just a few centimetres a year. But the consequences are very dramatic in the long term (figure 1.9b). Plates can move apart at ridges, or move together at trenches, or slide past each other horizontally on long straight faults (table 1.1). The most famous fault is the San Andreas Fault in California.

It is possible that, after many millions of years, an ocean will close up altogether. All the mud and silt that has formed on the ocean bottom gets squashed and folded into a thick pile of sedimentary rocks (page 9). The two continents collide, forcing these

Table 1.1 The different types of plate boundary

	Type of plate boundary	Resulting stress	Description of changes	Earthquake/ volcanic activity	Example
A	Constructive margins	tension	two plates move away from each other – new oceanic crust appears, forming mid-ocean ridges with volcanoes	gentle volcanic and earthquake activity	Mid-Atlantic ridge, e.g. Iceland
B(i)	Destructive margins	compression	oceanic crust moves towards continental crust and sinks beneath it – subduction occurs, forming deep-sea trenches	violent volcanic and earthquake activity	Nazca and South American plates
B(ii)	Collision zones	compression	two continental crusts collide – neither can sink, so fold mountains are forced up	earthquake activity, but no volcanic activity	Himalayas formed as Indian plate moved north into Eurasian plate
C	Conservative margins	shear	two plates move sideways past each other – land is neither formed nor destroyed	can be violent earthquake activity (no volcanic activity)	San Andreas Fault, California

rocks to buckle and fold upwards into mountains. This is how the Himalayas were formed. India's continental crust is still moving northwards and the Himalayas are still rising higher each year.

Evidence for plate motion

There are several pieces of evidence for continental drift that confirm the basis of the theory. The jigsaw-like fit of the present continents suggests that they were once joined. Examine the outlines of South America and Africa in figure 1.9b, for instance. It seems reasonable to think that they were once part of the same land mass. This is supported by the good match between the fossil records of each continent before they began to separate. The fossil record also suggests that land that is now quite northerly and temperate once had a tropical climate.

Volcanic **hot spots** also provide evidence of drift. The Hawaiian Islands are a famous hot spot. They were formed as the Pacific Plate moved over a stationary area of rising magma in the mantle (figure 1.9a). As the plate moved, a chain of volcanic islands has been formed.

It is believed that, about 200 million years ago, all the present-day continents were part of a single land mass, known as Pangaea (figure 1.9b).

Volcanoes

Volcanoes are among the most dramatic features of the Earth. They are breathtakingly spectacular but devastatingly violent. They pour out molten rock (lava), ash and poisonous gases such as sulphur dioxide. There are three locations where volcanoes are likely to occur.

- At *mid-oceanic ridges* The rising convection currents in the mantle cause the melting of upper mantle rocks. The molten rock rises and breaks through to the surface. This process mostly happens under water, but in some places, like Iceland, it can be observed on land. When the molten magma solidifies, it forms basalt.

- At *subduction zones* (the 'ring of fire') Volcanoes are common on the landward side of the trenches surrounding the Pacific Ocean. As the oceanic plate moves down below continental crust into the mantle, friction between the two causes the plate to melt. Rocks in the lower part of the crust melt too, and the lava that is formed is much stickier than that found at ridges or hotspots. Gases are also trapped which makes these volcanoes much more explosive. A good example of this was the volcano Mount St Helens which exploded in 1980 (figure 1.10).

Figure 1.10 *The second eruption of Mount St Helens in 1980. The first eruption in May had blasted away most of its north face.*

- At *hot spots* Some volcanoes occur in the middle of plates. They occur because they are above 'hot spots' in the mantle. Plumes of hot rock rise deep in the mantle and melt the rock above. As the oceanic plate moves over the hot spot, the position of the volcano changes creating a track of extinct volcanic islands.

1.4 Rocks and the rock cycle

The three main types of rock are formed in different ways.

- **Igneous rocks** have solidified from molten rocks, either in volcanoes or inside the crust.
- **Sedimentary rocks** are laid down (deposited) under water as a sediment. They are made from fragments worn away from older rocks, or from the remains of living organisms. They can appear on the surface after being forced upwards by movement of the Earth's plates.
- **Metamorphic rocks** are rocks that have been changed by heat or pressure, or both. They could originally have been either igneous or sedimentary rocks.

Igneous rocks

Sometimes enough heat is generated in the Earth's crust and upper mantle to melt rocks. This molten rock is called **magma**. Igneous rocks are formed when this magma cools and hardens. There are two main types of igneous rock: intrusive and extrusive.

- **Intrusive igneous rock** forms when the magma crystallises while it is still underground. Granite is a typical intrusive igneous rock (figure 1.11a). It is formed from high-viscosity magma that has cooled slowly at depth to give large crystals of light-coloured minerals.
- **Extrusive igneous rock** forms when the rising molten rock breaks through to the surface as **lava**. The lava cools and crystallises at the Earth's surface. Basalt is an example of this type of rock (figure 1.11b). It is formed from low-viscosity magma that has cooled rapidly to give small crystals of mainly dark-coloured minerals. Good examples are the towering columns of crystalline basalt on the island of Staffa off the Scottish coast and at the Giant's Causeway in Northern Ireland.

Both types of igneous rock are **crystalline**. This is particularly obvious in granite, where the interlocking crystals can be seen by eye. The deeper in the Earth's crust that the magma cooled, the longer the crystals in the granite took to form. The slower the crystallisation process, the larger the crystals in the rock. Intrusive rock can be found as sills and dykes formed within the crust (figure

Figure 1.11 *(a) The crystals in granite can be seen by eye and are interlocking. (b) The crystals in basalt are very small and must be viewed through a microscope.*

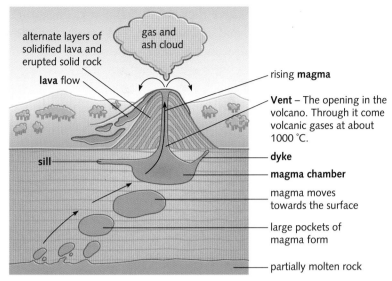

Figure 1.12 *Intrusive igneous rocks are formed when magma crystallises before it reaches the surface, forming features such as sills and dykes. Extrusive igneous rocks are formed when magma crystallises on the surface.*

1.12). Lava flows form alternating layers of solidified lava and erupted rock and ash.

Sedimentary rocks

Sedimentary rocks are made up of fragments of older rock or the remains of living organisms.

Sedimentary rocks are named after the size of fragments from which they are made:

- a rock made from pebbles is called **conglomerate**,
- a rock made from sand is simply called **sandstone**,
- a rock made from fine mud is called a **mudstone**, though if it is flaky and breaks easily it is called **shale**,
- a rock made from the shells and skeletons of organisms that lived in water is called **limestone**.

All rocks exposed on the Earth's surface are worn away by weathering and erosion. This material is transported by gravity, wind, ice, rivers and seas.

In the geological past, these sediments were forced close together and became compacted into rock as more and more material was deposited. The pressure of the material above compressed the sediment into rock. In some cases other minerals seeped between the fragments and solidified, holding (or cementing) the deposit together like a 'glue'. These sedimentary rocks formed layers or **strata**.

Metamorphic rocks

Metamorphic rocks are formed when rocks that originated beneath the Earth's surface are altered by the action of great heat and pressure. Such conditions occur at subduction zones or where plates collide. *Marble* is a metamorphic rock formed by this type of action on limestone. *Slate* is metamorphosed mudstone or shale. Any fossils that may have been present in the sedimentary rock are obliterated.

The features of the main rock types are summarised in table 1.2.

The rock cycle

The different types of rock undergo changes that occur over a long timescale. Rocks are slowly transformed (changed) in type by weathering and sedimentation or by conditions of intense heat and pressure. These changes by which rocks are

Table 1.2 Features of the different rock types

Rock type	Features
Igneous rocks	have no fossils have an interlocked crystal structure are usually hard
Sedimentary rocks	may have layers visible have separate grains may be quite soft, and disintegrate on rubbing could contain fossils if calcium carbonate is present in the rock, will fizz when added to acid
Metamorphic rocks	may be hard, though may be split along a cleavage plane may be banded or streaked may contain mica flakes in streaks or layers may have a crystalline appearance contain no fossils if marble, will fizz with dilute acid

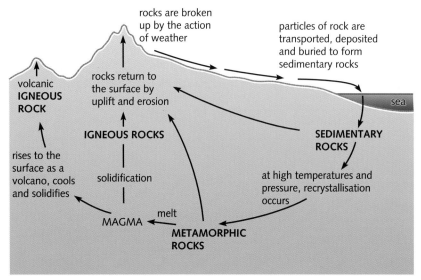

Figure 1.13 The rock cycle.

recycled from one form to another are known as the **rock cycle** (figure 1.13). In this cycle the rocks that are exposed on the surface are weathered. The particles are carried away by erosion and deposited as sediment. Eventually these deposits become sedimentary rock, which may then be brought back to the surface by movement of the Earth's crust. Alternatively, that sedimentary rock may be crushed and heated to form metamorphic rock. In turn, this rock may be melted deep in the crust to form magma, which is then squeezed to the surface. Here, on cooling, it forms igneous rock, and the cycle may begin again.

1.5 Shaping the landscape

We tend to think of the landscape as unchanging. However, it is slowly and continuously being reshaped.

The eruption of volcanoes can produce high mountains. Earthquakes send shock waves through the strata of the crust, causing cracks and faults. Less violent movement of the plates produce regions where parts of the crust are pushed together, others

where they are pulled apart. The strata bend and form folds. A good example of folded strata can be seen on the south coast of England at Lulworth Cove, Dorset. The dome of the fold is called an **anticline**, and the depression between is known as a **syncline**. Figure 1.14 shows how the chalk hills of south-east England were pushed into shape at the time the Alps were being formed elsewhere in Europe.

Weathering

Exposure to wind, rain and frost causes rocks to break apart and crumble. This is known as **weathering**. There are two main types of weathering: physical and chemical.

- *Physical weathering*
  Physical weathering includes the actions of wind, water and temperature. Rain water can collect in cracks in the rocks and freeze as the temperature drops. This causes expansion as the ice forms, forcing the crack apart. When the temperature rises, the ice melts, and again water fills the crack. This process of freeze–thaw weathering can be repeated over time, making the crack steadily wider until a boulder falls. Temperature changes also produce stresses in the rock because the different minerals present expand (in hot sunshine during the day) and

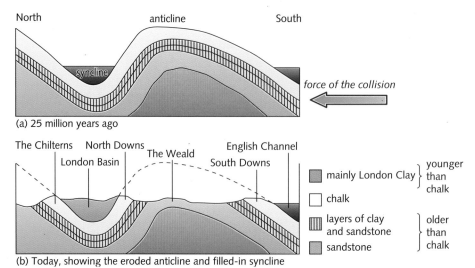

Figure 1.14 (a) The chalk hills of south-east England were pushed into shape when the Alps were formed. (b) The rocks at the top of the anticline were weathered and worn away. The London Basin was filled in with newer material.

contract (in the shade and at night) at different rates. Rocks and boulders will detach from a slope, causing **scree** (figure 1.15).

- *Chemical weathering*
Natural rain water contains dissolved carbon dioxide and is therefore slightly acidic. This rain water will very slowly dissolve rocks such as limestone (figure 1.16):

limestone + rain water
→ calcium hydrogencarbonate

$$CaCO_3(s) + H_2O(l) + CO_2(aq)$$
$$\rightarrow Ca(HCO_3)_2(aq)$$

This process will be increased by 'acid rain', which contains dissolved pollutants such as sulphur dioxide and oxides of nitrogen. Some minerals take up water and become hydrated. This causes expansion, and therefore stress, in rock formations. Fragments of rock are again broken off.

The material broken from rock structures by weathering can then be carried away by erosion.

Erosion

Erosion involves the transport of weathered material. Wind, glaciers, rivers and seas all play a part in moving rocky debris and soil. They are called carriers. The material being transported can also cause further erosion by **abrasion** (rubbing).

Eventually the eroded material is deposited as pebbles, sand or mud. This happens as a result of

Figure 1.16 *This limestone pavement at Malham Cove, Yorkshire, was chemically weathered by rainfall.*

gravity when the carrier slows down. As the wind drops, for instance, the dust settles. Rock debris will be eroded, transported or deposited by a river depending on the different speeds at which the river is flowing. For example, coarse sand will be eroded by a fast-flowing river. It will be transported by a slow-flowing river, and deposited by a very sluggish river. Rivers deposit sand and gravel when they lose speed:

- on the inside curves of rivers, and
- when a river flows into a lake or the sea.

Soil

One useful product of reshaping the landscape is **soil**. Soil is formed from fine particles of eroded debris mixed with humus. **Humus** is decayed organic material from plants and animals. It takes about 400 years to produce 1 cm of soil. Most soils are a mixture of particles of different sizes. They vary in the amounts of **salts**, water and humus present. The types of soils range from sandy to clay soils (table 1.3 on page 12).

1.6 The life history of a planet

Geologists have been able to build up a picture of how rock formations and land masses have changed from the Earth's origin to the present. Evidence from the fossil record links this to the

Figure 1.15 *This scree slope at Gordale Scar, Yorkshire, was formed by physical weathering.*

development of life on Earth. The fossil record allows geological time to be divided into three eras (the Palaeozoic, Mesozoic and Cenozoic eras). A fourth era (the Pre-Cambrian era) comes before these. During the Pre-Cambrian era the Earth's crust was forming, the oceans and atmosphere developed, and the first living organisms appeared.

Table 1.3 Different soil types

Sandy soils	Loams	Clay soils
large particle size	ideal for agriculture	small particle size
lack humus	sufficient sand for good drainage	slow draining
nutrients drain away easily	sufficient clay to hold nutrients	poor aeration

Summary of core material

You should know that:

- current evidence and theory suggest that the Universe began in a Big Bang about 15 billion years ago
- the lighter chemical elements, hydrogen and helium, were formed soon after the Big Bang, but the heavier elements were made later in the centres of large stars
- the Sun is a secondary star, and our Solar System is made up of planets of two broad types – the rocky, inner planets and the gas giants
- the Earth has a structure made up of a core, mantle and crust
- the core contains mainly the elements iron and nickel and is responsible for the Earth's magnetic field
- the mantle consists of mainly silicates and is semi-liquid
- the outer layer of the Earth is not uniform, but is divided into oceanic crust and continental crust
- the crust is divided into tectonic plates, which move slowly, driven by convection currents in the semi-liquid mantle
- these plates can move against each other in several different ways
- these plate movements can cause earthquakes and volcanic activity

- molten rock, magma, can rise to the surface during volcanic activity
- when magma solidifies, it can form igneous rocks, of which basalt and granite are examples
- there are other types of rock – sedimentary rock and metamorphic rock
- the different types of rock are linked together in the rock cycle
- sedimentary rocks are produced from fragments of other rocks (for example sandstone) or the bodies of dead sea creatures (for example limestone) compacted by the pressure of successive layers over long time periods
- metamorphic rocks (for example marble) are produced by the action of heat and pressure on igneous or sedimentary rocks
- the formation of the landscape is produced by folding and faulting of the rock strata
- rocks are also affected by the processes of weathering and erosion
- soil is a mixture of material produced by these processes and dead organic matter (humus)
- different types of soil occur depending on the nature of the mixture – some soils are sandy, others contain a high proportion of clay
- loamy soils are the most suitable for agriculture.

1.1 During an earthquake, three types of shock wave travel out from the epicentre. These are known as S-, P- and L-waves.

Following an earthquake, these waves can be detected by seismometers at recording stations. The graph below shows the speed that S-waves travel at various depths within the Earth.

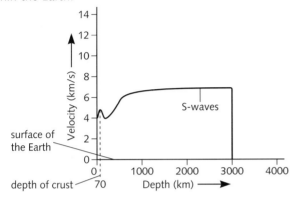

S-waves are transverse waves and make the rocks shake at right angles to the direction of movement of the wave. They travel only through solids.

(a) (i) State what happens to the waves at a depth of 3000 km. [1]

(ii) Explain what happens to the waves at this depth. [1]

(b) The outer crust of the Earth is composed mainly of granite (density 2.7 g/cm^3) and basalt (density 3.0 g/cm^3). The overall density of the Earth is about 5.5 g/cm^3. Explain the difference in density between the crust and the overall density. [2]

(ULEAC, 1995)

1.2 The diagram shows the layered structure of the Earth and its atmosphere. An earthquake occurring at X, directly below the epicentre (A), is detected at location B. Shock waves arrive at B over a period of 15 minutes.

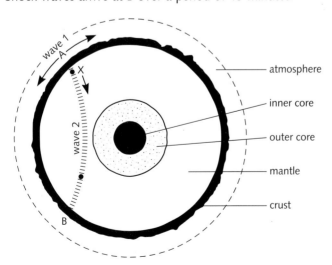

(a) (i) What name is given to point X? [1]
(ii) Which wave is a P-wave? [1]
(iii) Which wave is an L-wave? [1]

(b) An earthquake occurs when forces inside the Earth cause large masses of rock to fracture and move. Waves from the earthquake travel through the Earth and along the crust.
(i) Explain why the wave travelling through the Earth takes a curved path. [1]
(ii) Give *two* reasons why waves travelling along the crust take longer to reach location B than those travelling through the mantle. [1]
(iii) Would you expect earthquakes to originate below a depth of 1000 km? Explain your answer. [2]

(c) Suggest *one* result of a major earthquake occurring beneath the sea. [1]

(d) Give *two* pieces of information which suggest that the Earth has a core containing iron. [2]

1.3

(a) The labels show four parts of a volcano.

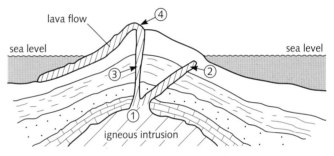

(i) At which point 1, 2, 3 or 4 will the cooling be the fastest? [1]
(ii) At which point 1, 2, 3 or 4 will the largest crystals be formed when the molten rock cools? [1]
(iii) Make a copy of the diagram and mark an X on it where a metamorphic rock is likely to be formed. [1]
(iv) Give two conditions under which sedimentary rocks are likely to be changed to metamorphic rocks. [2]

(b) Earthquakes and volcanoes often occur near plate boundaries.
(i) What causes an earthquake? [1]
(ii) What instrument is used to detect earthquakes? [1]

(c) Heat is generated inside the Earth by nuclear reactions. Some of the energy is released in volcanoes. Give two other effects that this thermal energy has on the inside of the Earth. [2]

(d) Scientists studied rocks on part of the ocean floor. The studies showed a pattern of 'magnetic stripes' on either side of what is called a spreading ridge.

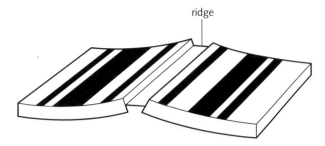

ridge

(i) Make a copy of the diagram and put an arrow labelled Y on it to show where you would find the youngest rock. [1]

(ii) Put an arrow labelled O on your diagram to show where you find the oldest rock. [1]

(iii) It is thought that the spreading of the ridge is caused by convection currents in the magma. Draw arrows on your diagram to show the direction of these convection currents. [1]

(SEG, 1995)

1.4 Below is an incomplete diagram of the rock cycle.

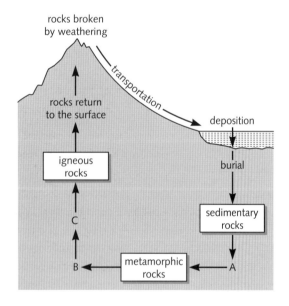

rocks broken by weathering

transportation

rocks return to the surface

deposition

igneous rocks

burial

C

sedimentary rocks

B

metamorphic rocks

A

Use the diagram to help you answer the following questions.

(a) What *two* words should be used at A to show how sedimentary rocks are converted into metamorphic rocks? [2]

(b) How are metamorphic rocks converted into solid igneous rock by processes B and C? [2]

(MEG, 1995)

1.5

(a) (i) Why are basalt and granite referred to as igneous rocks? [1]

(ii) Explain why crystals in basalt are smaller than crystals in granite. [1]

(b) Water may collect in small cracks in the surface of rocks. At times it will freeze, thawing again when the temperature rises. Explain how this freezing and thawing process causes weathering of rocks. [2]

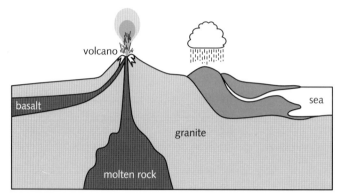

volcano

basalt

sea

granite

molten rock

(c) (i) Give an example of a sedimentary rock. [1]

(ii) Using the diagram above to help you, explain the process by which sedimentary rocks form. [3]

(MEG, part question, 1995)

1.6 The diagram shows how a line of underwater mountains is forming in the middle of the Atlantic Ocean. This is called a mid-ocean ridge.

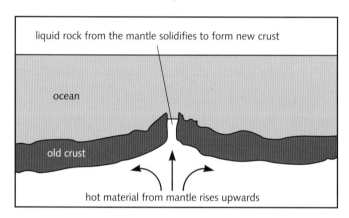

liquid rock from the mantle solidifies to form new crust

ocean

old crust

hot material from mantle rises upwards

(a) Solid rock forms when the liquid rock from the mantle layer reaches the water.

(i) Which *one* of the following is the type of rock that will form? [1]

igneous   metamorphic   sedimentary

(ii) Explain why the crystals formed in this rock are very small. [2]

(b) Europe and North America are at opposite sides of the Atlantic Ocean. Explain why Europe and North America move a little further apart each year. [2]

(c) Not all mountains are formed as mid-ocean ridges. The Alps and the Himalayas were formed in a different way. Suggest and explain a different way in which mountains can be formed. [3]

(MEG, 1995)

1.7 A, B and C represent plates of the Earth's crust moving in the directions of the arrows.

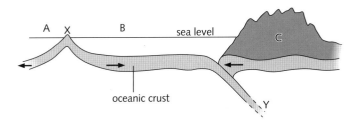

(a) (i) Give *one* natural occurrence, often disastrous, which can happen at plate boundaries. [1]
(ii) Why would you expect igneous rock to form at plate boundary X? [3]
(iii) Metamorphic rock forms at Y. Give *two* conditions which must exist at Y. [2]

(b) Explain how igneous rocks can form sedimentary rocks (in a different place). [4]

(ULEAC, 1996)

The Earth's resources

This section covers the following ideas:

- the origin of the Earth's atmosphere
- water as a major feature of the Earth's surface
- renewable and non-renewable resources
- an introduction to the recycling of resources
- alternative energy resources.

The living world, or **biosphere**, stretches around the Earth like a thin film. At 100 km down beneath our feet, the mantle is well over 1000 °C. Thirty kilometres up above our heads, the air is too thin and cold for survival. In between, the temperature and atmosphere are suited to life. The more we explore our Solar System, the more remarkable we understand our world to be. Comparison with our neighbouring planets shows how distinctive the conditions on Earth are. The mixture of atmospheric gases is completely different from those of Venus and Mars. What has made the Earth's atmosphere so different?

The answer must clearly be that *life* made the difference. The conditions on Earth were suited to the appearance and evolution of life. These circumstances have been humorously referred to as the Goldilocks phenomenon – 'Venus is too hot, Mars is too cold, but the Earth is just right!'

1.7 The Earth's atmosphere

The atmosphere of the Earth has not been constant over its history. As the planet formed by cooling, and its crust solidified, the Earth's first atmosphere formed. This **primary atmosphere** was largely hydrogen and helium. However, under intense solar activity, these lighter gases were removed from the primary atmospheres of the Earth and other planets near the Sun. They were replaced by gases produced by immense volcanic activity (figure 1.17 on page 16). This volcanic 'out-gassing' produced a **secondary atmosphere** rich in ammonia, nitrogen, water vapour, carbon monoxide and dioxide, hydrogen chloride, sulphur dioxide and hydrogen sulphide. As the Earth cooled below 100 °C (by about 3800 million years ago), the water vapour condensed and fell as rain. The oceans were formed and the soluble gases dissolved in them. The water of the oceans reacted with the land mass to produce soluble minerals.

A further dramatic change in the atmosphere occurred with the evolution of life – a change which began the transformation to present conditions. Living things need energy so that they can grow, and most now use oxygen in respiration to release that energy. In the early atmosphere there was little oxygen because it would have combined with other gases. For example, carbon monoxide burns in oxygen to make carbon dioxide, and methane burns in oxygen to form carbon dioxide and water.

The earliest living things, bacteria, released the energy they needed by **reducing** (see page 106) sulphates to sulphides or fermenting sugars to ethanol. About 3 billion years ago the first living things appeared that could make their own food using energy from sunlight. They could break the food down later to release energy for growth. These livings things were also bacteria but they contained a pigment which traps the energy from sunlight. The most important of these were the blue-green bacteria (cyanobacteria) because they used the energy trapped from light to combine carbon dioxide and water to produce sugar (food) and oxygen. This process is known as **photosynthesis** and occurs in all green plants today.

The blue-green bacteria reduced the level of carbon dioxide in the Earth's atmosphere and increased the level of oxygen. This made it possible for all life that we see today to evolve. The carbon trapped as sugars by photosynthesis in plants and bacteria passes to the animals which eat them. This is part of the **carbon cycle** which is discussed in more detail in section 8.17 on page 225.

Without photosynthesis, the Earth's atmosphere would still have high levels of carbon dioxide, like those of Venus and Mars.

Reactions involving oxygen and ultra-violet radiation produced a protective layer in the upper atmosphere. Ultra-violet (u.v.) light breaks down some oxygen molecules:

$$\text{oxygen molecules} \xrightarrow{\text{u.v. light}} \text{oxygen atoms}$$

$$O_2(g) \rightarrow 2O(g)$$

Some of these highly energised oxygen atoms (**free radicals**) react with other oxygen molecules to form ozone (O_3):

$$\text{oxygen atoms + oxygen molecules} \rightarrow \text{ozone molecules}$$

$$O(g) + O_2(g) \rightarrow O_3(g)$$

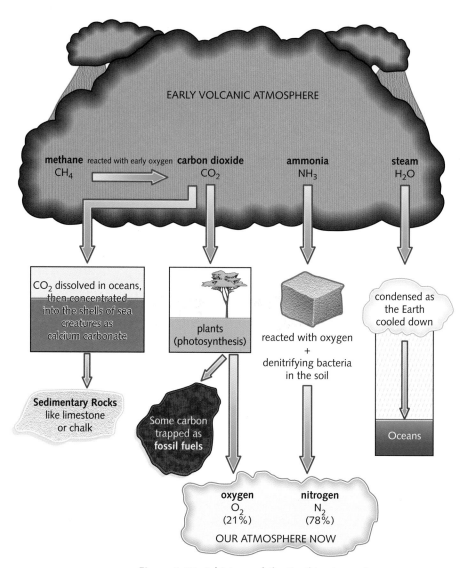

Figure 1.17 A history of the Earth's atmosphere.

Ozone is an unstable molecule, which is continually being broken down. However, it is rapidly re-formed again, so a protective layer is maintained.

The **ozone layer** prevents harmful ultra-violet radiation from reaching Earth. It protected the early Earth as plants evolved and generated more oxygen in the air. Organisms also evolved that could make use of the oxygen. They adapted to use it, with carbon from their food, in a process known as **respiration**.

The gases in the atmosphere form an envelope around the Earth, held there by gravity. The atmosphere is 80 km thick and divided into four layers (figure 1.18). Seventy-five per cent of the mass of the atmosphere is found in the layer near the Earth (the troposphere). Beyond that, it thins out, becoming extremely thin in the mesosphere.

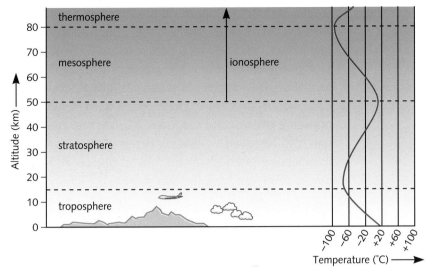

Figure 1.18 The layers of the Earth's atmosphere.

1.8 The water planet

The presence of water is an important feature of the Earth. It was necessary for life to develop on the planet, and clouds of it protect the planet from some of the heat of the Sun. During an average year, enough precipitation (rain, snow, hail and sleet) falls on the continents of Earth to cover all land to an average depth of more than 75 cm (2.5 feet). Thankfully it does not all fall at once! The wettest place on Earth is Mount Waialeale on Kauai, Hawaii, where the average rainfall is about 11.7 m (460 inches) a year! In contrast, over a 59-year period, Arica, Chile, averaged only 0.75 mm (0.03 inches) per year. It didn't rain at all for 14 of those years!

Very little of the world's water is fresh water (2.6%) – most of it (97.4%) is in the oceans. Most of the fresh water (76%) is frozen in glaciers and in the polar ice-caps (figure 1.19). Only a tiny fraction (0.01%) is available for human use. This small amount of accessible water is repeatedly recycled. It is not available evenly all over the world, and it could become a source of international tension. Boutros Boutros-Ghali warned in 1985, when he was Egyptian Foreign Minister, that: 'The next war in the Middle East will be fought over water, not politics'. Availability is not the only problem. Water, supposedly the source of life, kills at least 25 million people a year in the developing nations – 60% of them children – because it is involved in the transmission of about half of the world's major diseases. Providing clean, adequate supplies of water and the safe disposal of human waste are two of the most urgent problems facing the developing world.

The **water cycle** is one of the major cycles that support life on Earth. Other important cycles are the carbon cycle, phosphorus cycle, nitrogen cycle and oxygen cycle. (These are discussed in later chapters.) Life depends on the one-way flow of energy from the Sun and the cycling of these crucial 'elements', including water, in the ecosphere. Gravity, which keeps atmospheric gases from escaping into space, is a further important factor.

1.9 The Earth's resources

In human terms, **resources** are materials we get from the environment to meet our needs. Some are the basic material resources we and other organisms need to keep alive. Others are materials from which we obtain energy or substances useful for our civilised way of life. Chemistry helps us to understand how the

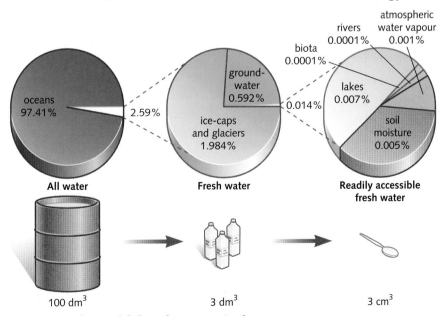

Figure 1.19 The availability of water on Earth.

basic resources sustain our life. It also provides the methods of extraction and use of other resources. Figure 1.20 summarises the major types of material resources. It subdivides them into renewable, potentially renewable and non-renewable resources, based on our short human timescale.

- **Non-renewable resources** are those which exist in a fixed quantity in the Earth's crust. They were formed over geological periods in time (millions of years) and, over a shorter timescale, are being depleted faster than they are formed.
- **Renewable resources** are those which essentially will never run out (are inexhaustible). **Potentially renewable resources** can be renewed rapidly, but they can become depleted if we over-exploit them.

More and more, we are becoming aware of the need to **conserve** and **recycle** some of these resources.

Recycling resources

Non-renewable mineral resources can be conserved by recycling. Recycling involves collecting and reprocessing a resource into new products.

The recycling of aluminium has proved a spectacular case for the benefits of recycling. Aluminium is an expensive metal to extract from its ore. The major cost in the extraction is the electrical energy needed to electrolyse molten aluminium oxide. Recycling can save up to 95% of these energy costs as well as conserve the mineral resource. Money and resources can also be saved by finding better alloys and engineering methods so that metal objects can work as efficiently and yet use less material.

Makers of beer and soft-drink containers in the USA produce 300 million aluminium cans each day. Reducing the can's mass by 1% will save about $20 million a year in aluminium. Manufacturers have reduced the mass by 20% since the 1960s; the current aim is to reduce the mass by a further 20%. The engineering problem is to maintain the strength of the can while doing this.

Steel, paper, glass and plastics are other materials that are being increasingly recycled.

Alternative energy resources

Fossil fuels are examples of non-renewable resources. For example, it is estimated that the known reserves of crude oil will be exhausted in about 60 years if used at the current rate. However, new reserves are being found, and we can become more efficient at using them. The quantity of uranium in the Earth and oceans is fixed. Thus, nuclear power is also a non-renewable form of energy. Modern 'fast breeder reactors' allow us to use the uranium fuel much more efficiently, and to reprocess (or recycle) used (spent) fuel. With such reactors, the world's uranium could be used to generate electricity for another 1000 years. Various countries have developed different policies on nuclear power. In Europe, France generates more than 70% of its electricity in nuclear power stations.

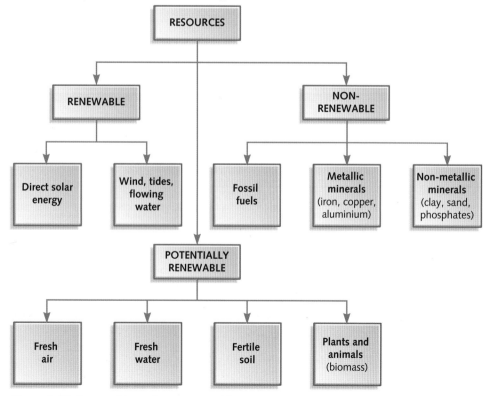

Figure 1.20 Renewable and non-renewable resources.

It is important to develop and exploit renewable, alternative sources of energy. Renewable energy resources do not have the limitations of fossil fuels and uranium. Hydro-electricity (electricity generated from the flow of water) is a common form of renewable energy in mountainous regions. A great deal of research has been carried out in recent years into other ways to obtain renewable energy. Some of these methods are attractive and can provide energy at a cost that competes with other fuels. Some are more useful in certain geographical locations than others. Figure 1.21 shows our dependence on fossil fuels for commercial energy use (in 1991), and the range of alternative possibilities for generating energy.

(a)

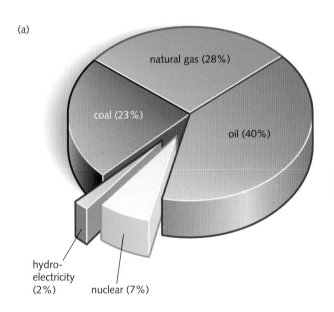

(b)

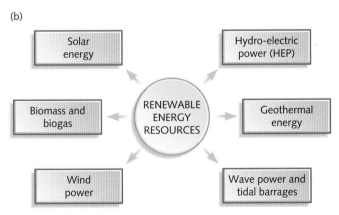

Figure 1.21 (a) World energy sources – the numbers show the importance of fossil fuels. (b) Renewable energy resources suitable for development to reduce our dependence on fossil fuels.

Summary of core material

You should know that:

- the Earth's early atmosphere was largely made up of gases produced by volcanic activity
- radical changes were produced in the atmosphere by the emergence of life on the Earth
- the neighbouring planets, Mars and Venus, still have atmospheres that are mainly carbon dioxide
- the oxygen in the Earth's atmosphere was produced by the process of photosynthesis in microbial and plant life
- the Earth's atmosphere is layered, with most of the gases being present in the lower region, the troposphere
- there is a layer of ozone in the upper atmosphere produced by the action of ultra-violet radiation on oxygen – this layer protects us from the most harmful effects of u.v. radiation
- liquid water is another major feature of the surface of the Earth – the vast majority being present in the oceans
- energy from the Sun is absorbed into the ecosystem by a number of elementary cycles, for example the carbon cycle
- the resources of the Earth can be divided into renewable, potentially renewable and non-renewable resources
- the recycling of resources, particularly those which are non-renewable, is of economic and long-term importance
- we are heavily dependent on fossil fuels for our energy needs, but a number of alternative forms of renewable energy are available to be exploited.

1.8

(a) The early atmosphere of the Earth may have contained methane and carbon monoxide but very little oxygen. At that time the temperature was high and there were many electrical storms in the atmosphere. Why is it unlikely that oxygen would have been present in large amounts if methane and carbon monoxide were present? [1]

(b) As early plant life began to develop, the amount of oxygen in the atmosphere tended to increase.
　(i) Name the process by which plants add oxygen to the atmosphere. [1]

(ii) What gas is removed from the atmosphere by the same process? [1]

(c) What temperature conditions must have existed on Earth when the oceans began to form? Explain your answer. [2]

(ULEAC, 1996)

1.9

(a) Name *two* renewable energy sources used to produce electricity. [2]

(b) You can calculate how long reserves of a fossil fuel will last by dividing the known reserves of the fuel by its annual production.
  (i) Calculate the *R/P* ratio for natural gas from the table. [1]
  (ii) Using oil as your example, suggest two reasons why the *R/P* ratio may give a misleading idea of how long a fuel will be available to people. [2]

Fuel	Known reserves, *R*	Annual production, *P*	*R/P* ratio (whole years)
Coal (million tonnes)	1 040 000	4400	236
Natural gas (billion cubic metres)	142 000	2100	
Oil (million tonnes)	137 000	3200	43

Environmental management

This section covers the following ideas:

- atmospheric pollution
  - acid rain
  - global warming
  - ozone depletion
  - photochemical smog
  - carbon monoxide and lead compounds
- water pollution.

1.10 The Earth seen from space

Finally it shrank to the size of a marble, the most beautiful marble anyone can imagine.

Astronaut James Erwin, 1969

Only a few men and women have seen the Earth from the same vantage point as James Erwin. But many have seen the spectacular photographs taken from space. Because we have seen the Earth from 'outside', we can judge the value of our planet in a different way from previous generations. Observations from satellites have also given us detailed information on the state of the planet. The detailed evidence for the depletion of the ozone layer in the upper atmosphere has been very disturbing. But the view from space has also shown up other problems. Figure 1.22 shows the extent to which we are burning away vegetation, particularly in tropical areas. In late 1997, forest clearing by burning produced huge dust clouds over eastern Asia. The climate of a vast area was affected for months.

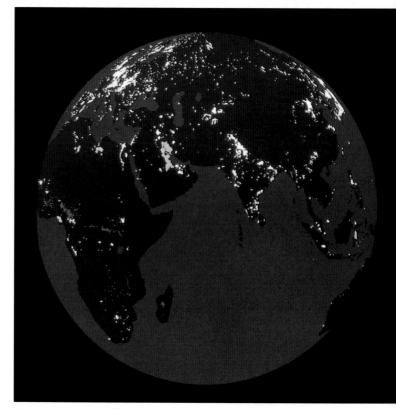

Figure 1.22 A satellite view of the dark (night) side of the Earth. The white lights of towns and cities and the yellow flares of oil fields show up clearly. The red lights show where vegetation is being burnt away.

1.11 Atmospheric pollution

There are a range of atmospheric pollution problems currently threatening the Earth's general environment. These are summarised in figure 1.23, together with some of their major causes.

Acid rain

This problem arises from the acidic gases produced by burning fossil fuels in a number of different

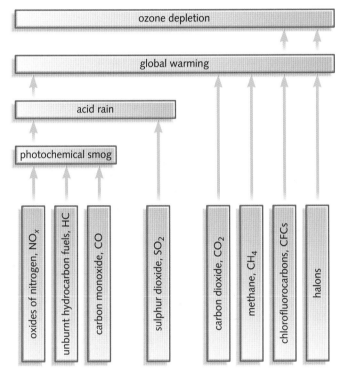

Figure 1.23 A summary of various atmospheric pollution problems caused by human activity.

situations. The majority of power stations in industrialised countries burn coal or oil. Both these fuels are contaminated with sulphur, which produces sulphur dioxide when it burns:

sulphur + oxygen → sulphur dioxide

$$S(s) + O_2(g) \rightarrow SO_2(g)$$

Oxides of nitrogen (NO_x) (for example nitrogen dioxide, NO_2) are also produced when air is heated in furnaces or in vehicle petrol engines. These gases dissolve in rain water to produce 'acid rain' (figure 1.24).

There are numerous effects of **acid rain**, for example:

- limestone buildings, statues, etc., are worn away.

- lakes are acidified, and the presence of metal ions (for example Al^{3+} ions) leached (washed) out of the soil damages the gills of fish. The fish can die.

- nutrients are leached out of the soil and from leaves. Trees are deprived of these nutrients. Aluminium ions are freed from clays as aluminium sulphate and damage tree roots. The tree is unable to draw up enough water through the damaged roots, and it dies.

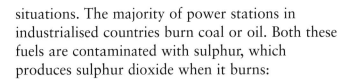

Figure 1.24 The formation of acid rain.

The wind can carry acid rain clouds away from the industrialised centres, causing the pollution to fall on other countries. In Europe, this tends to drive the problem towards Scandinavia and Germany, because the wind often blows in that direction.

Remedies for the effects of acid rain are limited. Lime can be added to lakes and the surrounding land, to decrease the acidity.

Methods of prevention are expensive, but they are more useful and beneficial in the long term. Petrol (gasoline) for cars has now been made almost free of sulphur. Fuel for power stations could be desulphurised further. Flue-gas desulphurisers can be fitted to power station and factory chimneys to reduce the levels of sulphur dioxide given off.

Global warming and the 'greenhouse effect'

The presence of water vapour, carbon dioxide (CO_2) and other gases in the air has served the planet well. The 'trapping' of heat by the atmosphere has kept the Earth warm (figure 1.25). Without this **greenhouse effect**, the average temperature of the Earth's surface would be $-18\,°C$, rather than $15\,°C$. However, higher levels of certain gases produced by human activity are increasing this heating effect and producing global warming.

The 'greenhouse gases' that produce this warming include water vapour, carbon dioxide, methane, the oxides of nitrogen and CFCs (chlorofluorocarbons). These gases absorb heat from the Sun that is reflected from the Earth's surface. They prevent this heat from being re-radiated back into space. So the Earth's surface becomes warmer. Our dependence on fossil fuels for energy and transport means that

the levels of carbon dioxide released into the atmosphere are very high (about 5000 million tonnes per year). Large-scale deforestation, particularly of the tropical rainforests, to provide land for agriculture, also increases the level of carbon dioxide in the air because it removes trees which absorb the gas for photosynthesis.

The effects of global warming are complex. The polar ice-caps would begin to melt as the temperature rose. The increase in sea level would threaten low-lying lands. Extensive climate change is possible but is difficult to predict. In some regions the effects may be good; but others may suffer long droughts. There could be major shifts in desert and fertile regions. Tropical storms could increase in their intensity.

There is evidence, from dying corals to an increase in warm-water fish in the North Sea, to show that global warming *is* taking place. Whether this is due to increased carbon dioxide levels remains to be proved. Certainly the concentration of CO_2 in the Earth's atmosphere has increased over the last century (in 1850 it was 0.027%, and in 1993 it was 0.036%). At the 'Earth Summit' held in Rio de Janeiro in June 1992, it was suggested that, by the year 2000, countries should aim to stabilise production of CO_2 at 1990 levels. Some atmospheric scientists say that a reduction of 30–60% in CO_2 is needed to keep the present temperature balance.

Ozone layer depletion

A protective layer of ozone in the stratosphere prevents harmful ultra-violet radiation reaching the Earth's surface. However, research has shown that this **ozone layer** has been depleted, particularly over Antarctica. The ozone hole has grown larger over recent years. CFCs and other halogen compounds are thought to cause the damage. International agreement has been reached on restricting the use of these compounds (the Montreal Protocol). If the situation were allowed to grow worse, exposure to higher levels of ultra-violet radiation could cause more cases of skin cancer in humans, and cause damage to crops.

Local atmospheric pollution

There are various types of pollution that occur over smaller, local areas. These usually occur in

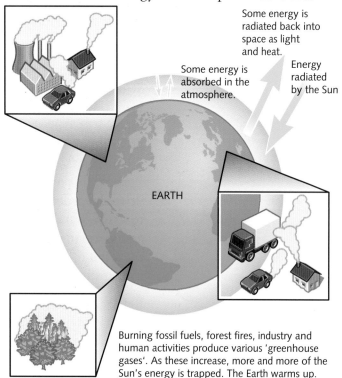

Some energy is radiated back into space as light and heat.

Some energy is absorbed in the atmosphere.

Energy radiated by the Sun

EARTH

Burning fossil fuels, forest fires, industry and human activities produce various 'greenhouse gases'. As these increase, more and more of the Sun's energy is trapped. The Earth warms up.

Figure 1.25 The greenhouse effect.

large cities, where there is heavy use of motor cars. These forms of pollution are:

- photochemical smog,
- high levels of carbon monoxide, and
- high levels of lead compounds.

Photochemical smog is formed in regions where there is a large amount of traffic. It was first identified in Los Angeles, and forms only under certain conditions. Severe photochemical smog often occurs in cities located in valleys, or surrounded by hills or mountains. On sunny, windless days, oxides of nitrogen are trapped by the hills in air that is close to the ground. A complicated series of reactions takes place and ground-level ozone is one of the products. In these circumstances ozone is harmful, particularly for asthma sufferers.

Carbon monoxide is the most common air pollutant in the industrialised world. It is produced when hydrocarbon fuels are incompletely burnt. Carbon monoxide is poisonous at levels of only 0.1%. Oxygen is very important to living things. In our bodies it is carried round the body attached to haemoglobin in our red blood cells. Carbon monoxide is attracted to haemoglobin over 200 times more strongly than oxygen. In the blood, carbon monoxide prevents haemoglobin from carrying oxygen. This leads to dizziness and headaches. Prolonged exposure to carbon monoxide causes death.

Lead compounds are the most toxic heavy-metal pollutants in the air. Lead compounds form part of the 'urban dust' that forms in a city atmosphere. People living next to busy roads can have high levels of lead in their blood. This has been linked with nervous disorders and with learning disabilities in children. The increased moves to use unleaded petrol are reducing this health hazard.

1.12 Water pollution

Water is another major resource that is essential to our life. However, as with the atmosphere, we are continually guilty of polluting the rivers and oceans. Industrial waste has been pumped into rivers in spite of legal restrictions. Many pollutants are involved, but among the most dangerous are the heavy metals such as cadmium and mercury. These can have disturbing effects on living things even at very low levels. They can also pass from one living thing to another along the **food chain** and affect life at various levels in the chain.

Industries and power stations use water from rivers as a coolant. When this water is returned to the river at a higher temperature, it causes *thermal pollution*. Less oxygen can dissolve in this warmer water, so that plants and animals in the water have greater difficulty breathing.

Sewage, detergents and run-off from fertilised fields can all reach rivers and cause damage to plant and aquatic life (figure 1.26). The beaches of Italian resorts in the Adriatic have in the past been troubled by a green slime. This slime was due to the flow of effluent (waste) from the delta of the river Po.

Figure 1.26 A lake ecosystem can become overloaded by nutrients. The growth of plants and algae increases. They die and are decomposed by aerobic bacteria. Oxygen levels in the lake drop and plants and animals in the water die as a result.

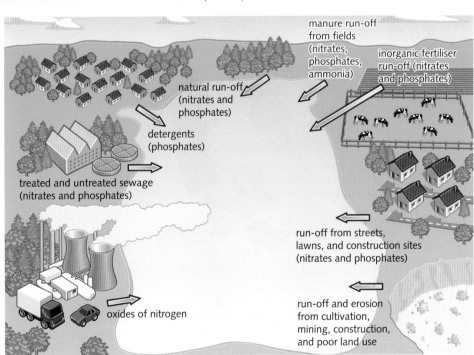

manure run-off from fields (nitrates, phosphates, ammonia)

inorganic fertiliser run-off (nitrates and phosphates)

natural run-off (nitrates and phosphates)

detergents (phosphates)

treated and untreated sewage (nitrates and phosphates)

run-off from streets, lawns, and construction sites (nitrates and phosphates)

oxides of nitrogen

run-off and erosion from cultivation, mining, construction, and poor land use

Pesticides also pose problems, as they can be concentrated through the food chain in fish. Apart from dangers to fish stocks, the concentration of possible cancer-causing chemicals at stages in the food chain is a source of great concern (figure 1.27).

There have been several major oil spills at sea, with the release of thousands of tonnes of crude oil into the marine ecosystem. You may have seen pictures of spills in Milford Haven, in west Wales, and in the Shetlands, north of mainland Scotland. The immediate effect of the oil on bird life is distressing, but the oil continues to do more unseen damage after being broken up into small droplets. These are absorbed by shellfish and micro-organisms and so enter the food chain. The ecology of a region may well be damaged for many years. The detergents used to break up surface oil slicks used to cause as much or more environmental damage than the oil itself. Although ways of treating oil spills have improved, prevention is better than cure. Modern oil tanker ships are now being built with double-skin hulls so that the chances of oil escaping after a collision are reduced.

Summary of core material

You should know that:

- human activities pollute the environment in a number of ways
- there are a number of atmospheric pollution problems
  - acid rain
  - global warming
  - ozone depletion
  - photochemical smog, carbon monoxide and lead compounds
- the pollution of rivers and oceans is caused by a range of effluents and spillage from agriculture, industry and shipping.

1.10 The map below shows an area of countryside where a small town has just been developed.

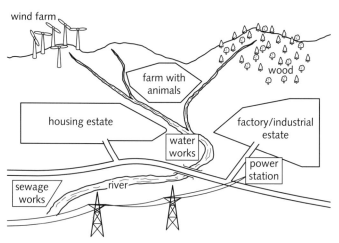

Use information from the map to answer the following questions.

(a) Identify *three* possible sources of pollution of the air. [3]

(b) Identify *three* possible sources of pollution of the river. [3]

(ULEAC, 1995)

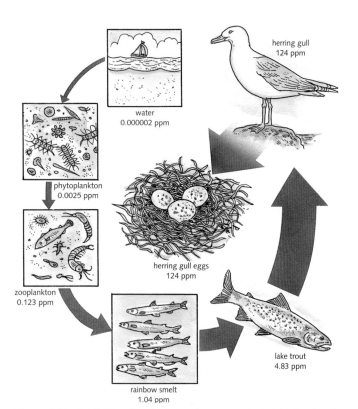

Figure 1.27 Pesticide chemicals can be concentrated in the food chain. This example is for PCBs (polychlorinated biphenyls). PCBs have been banned in Canada and the USA since 1976.

1.11

(a) Copy the diagram below and use it to describe how the greenhouse effect is caused. You may add both arrows and words to your diagram to help you. [3]

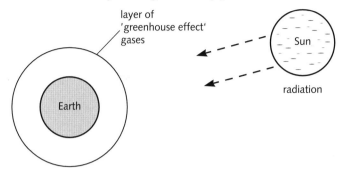

(b) The table below shows a range of 'greenhouse effect' gases, their abundance in the troposphere and their 'greenhouse effect' factors. The troposphere is the bottom 15 km of the atmosphere around the Earth. The 'greenhouse effect' factor is a measure of the 'greenhouse effect' of the gas relative to carbon dioxide.

'Greenhouse effect' gas	Abundance in the troposphere (%)	'Greenhouse effect' factor
Carbon dioxide	0.035	1.0
Dinitrogen oxide	0.00003	160.0
Methane	0.00017	30.0
Chlorofluorocarbons	0.00000004	23000.0
Water vapour	1.0	0.1
Ozone	0.000004	2000.0
Oxygen	20.0	negligible

Use the data in the table to work out which *two* gases have the most powerful 'greenhouse effect' in the troposphere. Show your working. [4]

(c) Describe *one* possible sequence of events that could be caused by an increased 'greenhouse effect'. [3]

(d) Suggest *two* ways in which 'greenhouse effect' gases could be reduced. [2]

(ULEAC, 1994)

1.12 Read the passage below and answer the questions which follow.

Ozone is a form of oxygen that has three atoms per molecule. It occurs naturally in the upper atmosphere, where the ozone layer blocks most of the harmful ultra-violet radiation from the Sun. At ground level, ozone can be produced as one component of 'photochemical smog' caused by reactions between pollutants from car exhaust fumes and atmospheric gases. Ground-level ozone is itself a pollutant, which can cause damage to trees and animals. It is a very reactive gas.

Recently, studies by scientists have shown that, while levels of ozone at ground level are increasing, the amount of ozone in the upper atmosphere is dropping. One factor that is thought to be partly responsible for this drop in ozone is the widespread use of chemicals called CFCs (chlorofluorocarbons). Following release into the atmosphere, CFCs break down and release chlorine, which reacts with ozone in the upper atmosphere.

In September 1987, the UK Government signed the Montreal Protocol, agreeing to reduce the use of CFCs by 50% by the end of the century. Some scientists believe that this will not be enough to prevent large-scale damage to life on Earth.

(a) (i) What is the molecular formula of 'normal' oxygen? [1]
    (ii) What is the molecular formula of ozone? [1]

(b) Name *one* other gas that is present in photochemical smog. [1]

(c) Give *three* common uses of CFCs. [3]

(d) Describe *one* possible consequence for humans of increased exposure to harmful ultra-violet radiation. [1]

(e) Suggest reasons for the following:
    (i) levels of ozone at ground level are increasing. [1]
    (ii) ozone produced at ground level does nothing to restore the ozone layer. [1]

1.13 The graph shows what happens to the levels of oxygen, microbes, ammonium compounds and nitrates in a river at various points below where a sewage pipe empties into the river.

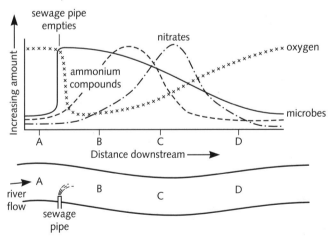

(a) Explain why the level of oxygen falls when sewage empties into the river. [2]

(b) Fish like trout need lots of oxygen.
    (i) At which points (A, B, C or D) would you expect to find trout living in the river? [2]
    (ii) A lot of waterweed is growing at point C. Explain why. [1]

(NEAB, 1995)

1.14 There is a lot of concern about pollution levels in the sea. The map shows the major water movements in the North Sea.

Key

Rivers

| 1 Tyne | 3 Thames | 5 Meuse + Rhine | 7 Weser |
| 2 Humber | 4 Scheldt | 6 Ems | 8 Elbe |

⟶ Direction of water movements

Bar charts A and B show the nitrogen and pesticide inputs into the North Sea from the eight rivers numbered on the map.

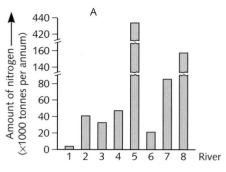

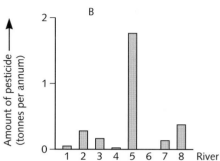

(With acknowledgements to D. Applin, *The Environment*, Blackwell Modular Science KS4, Basil Blackwell (1991).)

(a) (i) Why is pollution more of a problem in the North Sea than the Irish Sea? [1]

(ii) Use the map and bar charts A and B to explain why water pollution is a problem which affects many countries. [3]

(b) What farming methods can farmers use to reduce the levels of pesticides entering rivers? [2]

(ULEAC, 1995)

The nature of matter

Separation, purification and identification

This section covers the following ideas:

- the three states of matter, and changes of state
- the effect of impurities on melting and boiling points
- heating and cooling curves
- homogeneous and heterogeneous mixtures
- separating and purifying substances
  - filtration
  - use of separating funnel
  - evaporation and crystallisation
  - distillation
  - chromatography
- solubility and solubility curves.

Saturn is perhaps the most beautiful of the planets of the Solar System. It has fascinated astronomers because of its mysterious rings. The golden globe of this gas giant is circled by rings containing thousands of dark, closely spaced lines. The Pioneer and Voyager space-probes sent back a great deal of information on the nature of the rings and the mass of Saturn itself.

Detailed analysis shows that each ring is made up of many small rings (ringlets) packed close to each other. Each ringlet consists of a stream of icy particles, following each other nose-to-tail around the planet. The particles can be of widely varying sizes. The rings resemble a snowstorm, in which tiny snowflakes are mixed with snowballs up to the size of a house. The large icy chunks continually break and re-form under the influence of the planet's gravity. The ice that makes up one of the most spectacular features of our Solar System is made of water – the same substance (with the same formula) that covers so much of the Earth's surface.

The planet of Saturn is made of gases, mainly hydrogen and helium. Deep in the centre of these lightweight gases is a small rocky core, surrounded by a liquid layer of the gases. The inner parts of the planet's deep 'ocean', nearest to the core, are squashed together (compressed) so much that the liquid hydrogen behaves like a metal. Huge electric currents flow through this 'metallic' hydrogen, creating the planet's magnetic field. Study of Saturn's physical structure emphasises how substances that we know on Earth can exist in different physical states in different environments in other parts of the Universe. In the case of hydrogen, it begins to show some unexpected properties!

How do changing conditions affect the appearance, properties and behaviour of different substances? We shall look at the answers.

2.1 The states of matter

There are many different kinds of **matter**. The word is used to cover all the substances and materials from which the Universe is composed. Samples of any of these materials have two properties in common. They each occupy **space** (they have **volume**) and they have **mass**. Mass is what gives an object the properties of weight and inertia:

- the heavier an object, the more mass it has.
- the more inertia an object has, the more mass it has.

We say that matter is anything that has mass. This means that it has inertia and requires a force to get it moving or to stop it once it is moving. Chemistry is the study of how matter behaves, and of how one kind of substance can be changed into another.

Whichever chemical substance we study, we find it can exist in three different forms (or physical states) depending on the conditions. These three different states of matter are known as **solid, liquid** and **gas**. Thus we usually think of hydrogen as a gas. But under the conditions of temperature and pressure in the centre of Saturn, it exists as a liquid.

The different physical states have certain general characteristics that are true whatever chemical substance is being considered. These are summarised in table 2.1.

Matter is defined as anything that has mass and takes up space. There are three physical states:

- solid,
- liquid,
- gas.

The three physical states show differences in the way they respond to changes in **temperature** and **pressure**. All three show an increase in volume (an **expansion**) when the temperature is increased, and a decrease in volume (a **contraction**) when the temperature is lowered. The effect is much bigger for a gas than for either a solid or a liquid.

The volume of a gas at a fixed temperature can easily be reduced by increasing the pressure on the gas. Gases are easy to 'squash' – they are easily **compressible**. Liquids, on the other hand, are only slightly compressible, and the volume of a solid is unaffected by changing the pressure.

2.2 Changes in physical state

Large changes in temperature and pressure can cause changes that are more dramatic than expansion or contraction. They can cause a

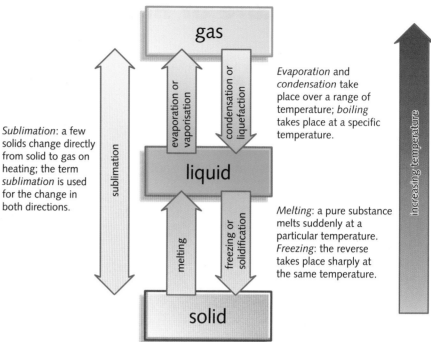

Sublimation: a few solids change directly from solid to gas on heating; the term *sublimation* is used for the change in both directions.

Evaporation and *condensation* take place over a range of temperature; *boiling* takes place at a specific temperature.

Melting: a pure substance melts suddenly at a particular temperature. *Freezing*: the reverse takes place sharply at the same temperature.

Figure 2.1 *Changes of physical state and the effect of increasing temperature.*

substance to change its physical state. The changes between the three states of matter are shown in figure 2.1. At atmospheric pressure, the changes shown can be brought about by raising or lowering the temperature of a sample of the substance.

Melting and freezing

The temperature at which a pure substance turns to a liquid is called the **melting point** (m.p.). This always happens at one particular temperature for each pure substance (figure 2.2). The process is reversed at precisely the same temperature if a liquid is cooled down. It is then called the **freezing point** (f.p.). The melting point and freezing point

Table 2.1 Differences in the properties of the three states of matter

Physical state	Volume	Density	Shape	Fluidity
Solid	has a fixed volume	high	has a definite shape	does not flow
Liquid	has a fixed volume	moderate to high	no definite shape – takes the shape of the container	generally flows easily*
Gas	no fixed volume – expands to fill the container	low	no definite shape – takes the shape of the container	flows easily*

*Liquids and gases are called fluids.

of any given substance are both the same temperature. For example, the melting and freezing of pure water take place at 0 °C.

Sublimation

A few solids – carbon dioxide ('dry ice') and iodine, for example – do not melt when they are heated. Instead they turn directly into gas. This change of state is called **sublimation**: the solid sublimes. Like melting, this also happens at one particular temperature for each pure solid.

Evaporation, boiling and condensation

If a liquid is left with its surface exposed to the air, it evaporates. Splashes of water evaporate at room temperature. After rain, puddles dry up! When liquids change into gases over a range of temperature, the process is called **evaporation**. Evaporation takes place from the surface of the liquid. The larger the surface area, the faster the liquid evaporates.

The warmer the liquid is, the faster it evaporates. Eventually, at a certain temperature, it becomes hot enough for gas to form within the liquid and not just at the surface. Bubbles of gas appear inside the liquid. This process is known as **boiling**. It takes place at a specific temperature, known as the **boiling point** (b.p.) for each pure liquid (figure 2.2).

The reverse of evaporation is **condensation**. This is usually brought about by cooling. However, we saw earlier that the gas state is the one most affected by changes in pressure. It is possible, at normal temperatures, to condense a gas into a liquid by increasing the pressure, without cooling. Sometimes the word **vapour** is used for a gas that can be compressed into a liquid without cooling. Normally, though, we use the words *gas* or *vapour* when talking generally about the gas state.

The boiling point of a liquid can change if the surrounding pressure changes. The value given for the boiling point is usually stated at the pressure of the atmosphere at sea level (**atmospheric pressure** or **standard pressure**). If the surrounding pressure falls, the boiling point falls. The boiling point of water at standard pressure is 100 °C. On a high mountain it is lower than 100 °C. If the surrounding pressure is increased, the boiling point rises. In a pressure cooker, the boiling point of water is raised to around 120 °C and food cooks more quickly at this higher temperature. The autoclave, which is used for sterilising surgical instruments, works in a similar way. Any bacteria on the instruments are killed more efficiently at the higher temperature.

2.3 Pure substances

A **pure substance** consists of one substance only: there is nothing else in it – it has no contaminating impurities. A pure substance melts and boils at definite temperatures. Table 2.2 on page 30 shows the melting points and boiling points of some common substances at atmospheric pressure.

The values for the melting point and boiling point of a pure substance are precise and predictable. This means that we can use them to test the purity of a sample. They can also be used to check the identity of an unknown substance.

The position of the melting and boiling points in relation to normal room temperature (taken as 20 °C) determines whether a substance is usually seen as a solid, liquid or gas. For example, if the m.p. is below 20 °C and the b.p. is above 20 °C, the substance will be liquid at room temperature.

The effect of impurities

Sea water is impure water. You can show this if you put some sea water in an evaporating dish and boil away the water because a solid residue of salt is left behind in the dish. Sea water freezes at a temperature well below the freezing point of pure water (0 °C) and boils at a temperature above the boiling point of pure water (100 °C). Other impure substances behave in a similar way.

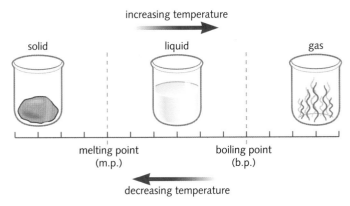

Figure 2.2 The relationship between the melting point and boiling point of a substance.

Table 2.2 The melting and boiling points of some common chemical substances

Substance	Physical state at room temperature (20°C)	Melting point (°C)	Boiling point (°C)
Oxygen	gas	−219	−183
Nitrogen	gas	−210	−196
Ethanol (alcohol)	liquid	−117	78
Water	liquid	0	100
Sulphur	solid	115	444
Common salt (sodium chloride)	solid	801	1465
Copper	solid	1083	2600
		Sublimation point (°C)	
Carbon dioxide	gas	−78	

The presence of an **impurity** in a substance:

- *lowers* the melting point, and
- *raises* the boiling point of the substance.

In addition, the impurity also reduces the 'sharpness' of the melting or boiling point. An impure substance melts or boils over a range of temperature, not at a particular point.

Heating and cooling curves

The melting point of a solid can be measured using the apparatus shown in figure 2.3. A powdered solid is put in a narrow melting-point tube so that it can be heated easily. An oil bath is used so that melting points above 100°C can be measured. We can follow the temperature of the sample before and after melting. These results can then be used to produce a **heating curve** (figure 2.4).

Figure 2.4 shows how the temperature changes when a sample of solid naphthalene (a single pure substance) is heated steadily. The solid melts precisely at 80°C. Notice that, while the solid is melting, the temperature stops rising. It will only begin to rise again when all the naphthalene has melted. Generally, the heating curve for a pure solid always stops rising at its melting point. The heating curve for wax, which is a mixture of substances, shows the solid wax melting over a *range* of temperatures.

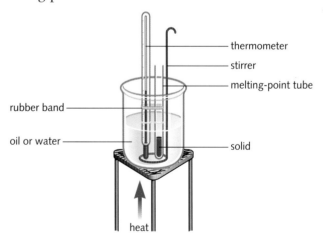

Figure 2.3 Apparatus for measuring the melting point or following the heating curve of a solid. A water bath can be used for melting points below 100°C and an oil bath for those above 100°C.

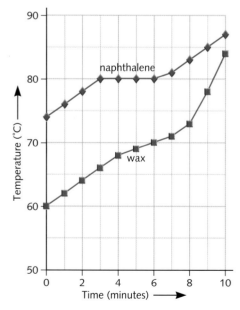

Figure 2.4 The heating curves for naphthalene (a pure substance) and wax (a mixture of substances).

It is possible to heat a liquid in the same apparatus as shown in figure 2.3 until its boiling point is reached. Again, the temperature levels out until all the liquid has boiled. The reverse processes can be shown if a sample of gas is allowed to cool. This produces a **cooling curve** (figure 2.5). The level portions of the curve occur where the gas condenses to a liquid, and then the liquid freezes.

> When a solid is melted, or a liquid is boiled, the temperature stays constant until the process is complete. The same is true in reverse when a gas condenses or a liquid freezes.

These experiments show that heat energy is needed to change a solid into a liquid, or a liquid into a gas. During the reverse processes, heat energy is given out.

2.4 Types of mixture

Our world is very complex, owing to the vast range of pure substances available, and to the variety of ways in which these pure substances can mix with each other. In everyday life we do not 'handle' *pure* substances very often. The air we breathe is not a single, pure substance – and we could not live in it if it were! Water would be rather tasteless if we drank it distilled – indeed, some companies do market distilled water that has had salts added back to it.

Each mixture must be made from at least two parts, or **phases**, which may be solid, liquid or gas.

There are a number of different ways in which the three states can be combined. In some, the states are completely mixed to become one single state or phase – 'you cannot see the join'. This is a **homogeneous mixture**. Technically, the term 'solution' is used for this type of mixture. Solid salt dissolves in liquid water to produce a liquid mixture – a salt solution (figure 2.6). In other types of mixture, the states remain separate (a **heterogeneous mixture**). One phase is broken up into small particles, droplets, or bubbles, within the main phase (see examples in table 2.3 on page 32).

Solutions and homogeneous mixtures

Table 2.3 shows us some of the ways in which substances in different states can combine. Perhaps the most important idea here is that of one substance dissolving in another – the idea of a **solution**. We most often think of a solution as being made of a solid dissolved in a liquid. Two-thirds of the Earth's surface is covered by a solution of various **salts** in water. The salts are totally dispersed into the water and cannot be seen. However, other substances that are not normally solid are dissolved in sea water. For example, the dissolved gases, oxygen and carbon dioxide, are important for life to continue in the oceans.

Less obvious perhaps, but quite common, are solutions of one liquid in another. Alcohol mixes (**dissolves**) completely with water. Beer, wine and whisky do not separate out into layers of alcohol and water (even when the alcohol content is quite

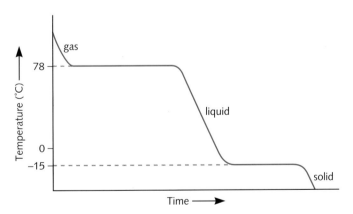

Figure 2.5 The cooling curve for a substance. The temperature stays constant while the gas condenses, and while the liquid freezes. A cooling mixture of ice and salt could be used to lower the temperature below 0 °C.

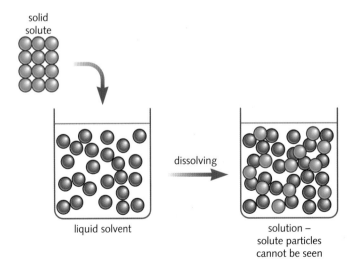

Figure 2.6 When a solute dissolves in a solvent, the solute particles are completely dispersed in the liquid.

Table 2.3 Important examples of different types of mixture

Type of mixture	Mixture	Description	Examples
Homogeneous mixtures (solutions)	*Solution** of solid in liquid	transparent solution of solid dissolved in liquid	sea water, sugar in water, salt solutions
	*Solution** of two miscible liquids	single layer of transparent liquid	vodka (alcohol and water), two-stroke motor oil (petrol and oil)
	*Solution** of gas in liquid	transparent solution of gas dissolved in a liquid	mineral and soda waters, champagne, 'fizzy' soft drinks
	Mixture of gas in gas	transparent mixture of two or more gases	air
	Alloy of two solid metals	solid, evenly spread mixture of two metals	brass, bronze
Heterogeneous mixtures	*Suspension* of solid in liquid	cloudy mixture of solid particles suspended in a liquid	river water carrying mud and silt, flour in water, kaolin indigestion medicine
	Gel	jelly-like mixture of solid and liquid, liquid trapped in the solid	fruit jelly, agar gel
	Emulsion of two immiscible liquids	cloudy mixture of tiny drops of one liquid suspended in another liquid	skin cream, milk, salad dressing, mayonnaise
	Aerosol of either a liquid or solid in a gas	small droplets of liquid, or particles of solid, dispersed in a gas	*liquid-in-gas*: mist, clouds, paint spray *solid-in-gas*: smoke, dusty air
	Foam of gas in liquid	many small bubbles of gas trapped in liquid	washing lather, froth or 'head' on beer, shaving foam
	Solid foam of gas in solid	many small bubbles of gas trapped in a solid	polystyrene foam, foam rubber, bread, sponge cake

*These solutions are particularly important in chemistry.

high). Alcohol and water are completely **miscible**: they make a solution.

Technically the air itself could be described as a solution of several gases in nitrogen, though this would be an unusual everyday use of the term. However, it is interesting to note that different gases *always* mix completely with each other. Likewise, alloys are homogeneous mixtures of metals, though we do not usually call them solutions. They are made by mixing the liquid metals together (dissolving one metal in the other) before solidifying the alloy.

Suspensions and heterogeneous mixtures
There are a great number of combinations of substances that do not mix: solids that do not dissolve in water; liquids that do not mix with

each other (they are **immiscible**). Flour does not dissolve in water but forms a slurry or **suspension**. The particles of solid are simply dispersed (spread) throughout the water and will eventually settle out if left to stand. Sand does not dissolve in water either. The ocean tides shift and deposit it on beaches and sandbars throughout the world. The great estuaries such as the Nile or Mississippi deltas are silted up by suspended soil deposited from the river.

Oil and water do not mix. Salad dressing made from olive oil and vinegar (a mixture of ethanoic acid and water) will settle out into two layers. When shaken, it forms an **emulsion** with droplets of oil suspended throughout the vinegar. Unlike pure liquids, emulsions are cloudy (opaque) so you cannot see through them. To stop an emulsion, such as mayonnaise, separating out into layers, an **emulsifier** is added. This prevents the small droplets of oil coming together to form larger droplets and then a separate layer. In traditional mayonnaise the emulsifier is egg yolk, which contains lecithin. Other food products contain other emulsifiers. In the European system for labelling food additives, emulsifiers are given E numbers from E322 to E494. E322 is lecithin.

The world of cosmetics is full of examples of emulsions. Skin moisturising creams are emulsions of oils in water; the oils prevent the skin from drying out. It is possible to switch the balance of the two phases in a cosmetic preparation. Cold cream and cleansing cream are emulsions of water in oils. They have a more oily 'feel' or texture than hand or face creams.

There are two ways in which mixtures can be formed between different substances:

- **homogeneous mixtures**, where the substances are totally mixed together and are indistinguishable – examples include solutions of salts and sugars in water.
- **heterogeneous mixtures**, where the substances remain separate and one substance is spread throughout the other as small particles, droplets, or bubbles – examples include suspensions of insoluble solids in water.

EXTENSION

Colloids and suspensions

The heterogeneous mixtures listed in table 2.3 can be divided into two types – suspensions and colloids. The difference depends on the size of the particles suspended, or dispersed, in the surrounding medium.

- **Suspensions** contain relatively large particles (over 1000 nm, where 1 nm = 10^{-9} m) of an insoluble solid, or droplets of an insoluble liquid. In time, the particles or droplets settle out.
- **Colloids** contain smaller particles (1–1000 nm) and take various forms. Emulsions, sols, gels, aerosols and foams are all examples of colloids. The particles of a colloid are too small to be seen by eye, but they do scatter light.

Colloids fill an important place in our lives. Our blood contains proteins spread throughout a watery medium; milk is a complex colloid containing fat droplets and proteins dispersed in water. We also manufacture a large number of colloids to serve a wide range of purposes. 'Emulsion' paint is an example of a colloidal system. In white 'emulsion' paint, the dispersed particles are solid (for example titanium(IV) oxide particles), mixed up in water but not dissolved in it. A true emulsion is made from one liquid dispersed in another. 'Emulsion' paint is not in fact a true emulsion. Nor is the photographic 'emulsion' coated on films. The light-sensitive layer of a film consists of fine crystals of silver bromide trapped in a gelatine gel.

Every **colloid** has at least two parts (table 2.4):

- the **dispersed phase** is split into very small particles – for example the fat in milk or the water droplets in mist.
- the **continuous phase** contains the dispersed phase spread throughout it – for example the water in milk or the air in mist.

Table 2.4 The dispersed and continuous phases of different types of colloid

Dispersed phase	Continuous phase	Type of colloid	Example
liquid	gas	aerosol	mist
solid	gas	aerosol	smoke
gas	liquid	foam	shaving cream
liquid	liquid	emulsion	face cream
solid	liquid	sol	paint
gas	solid	foam	sponge
liquid	solid	gel	butter

2.5 Separating and purifying substances

To make sense of the material world around us, we need methods for physically separating the many and varied mixtures that we come across. Being able to purify and identify the many substances present in these mixtures not only satisfies our curiosity but is crucial to our well-being and health. A range of physical techniques are available to make the necessary separations (table 2.5). They all depend in some way on a difference in the physical properties of the substances in the mixture.

The most useful separation method for a particular mixture depends on:

- the type of mixture, and
- which substance in the mixture we are most interested in.

Separating heterogeneous mixtures

In some ways these are the easier mixtures to separate. Quite often, just leaving them to stand helps with the separation. This is often the first stage in separating mixtures of immiscible liquids. It is also often used to separate solid-in-liquid suspensions if the particles of solid are large enough. Once the solid has settled to the bottom (**sedimented**), the liquid can be carefully poured off (this is called **decantation**).

A more generally useful method than decantation for separating solids from liquids is **filtration** (figure 2.7a). Here the insoluble material is

collected as a **residue** on filter paper. Filtration is useful because both phases can be obtained in one process. The liquid phase is collected as the **filtrate**. The process can be speeded up by using a vacuum pump to 'suck' the liquid through the filter paper in a **Buchner funnel** and flask (figure 2.7b). Various large-scale filtration methods are used in industry. Perhaps the most useful of these are the filter-beds to purify water for household use.

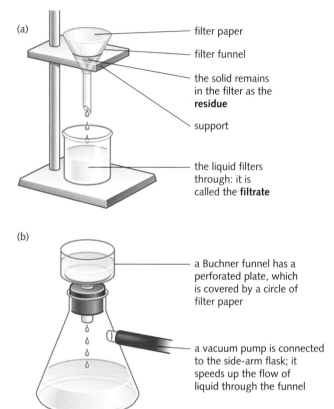

(a)
- filter paper
- filter funnel
- the solid remains in the filter as the **residue**
- support
- the liquid filters through: it is called the **filtrate**

(b)
- a Buchner funnel has a perforated plate, which is covered by a circle of filter paper
- a vacuum pump is connected to the side-arm flask; it speeds up the flow of liquid through the funnel

Figure 2.7 Filtration separates an insoluble solid from a liquid.

Table 2.5 Methods of separating substances from mixtures

Type of mixture	Mixture	Method of separation
Heterogeneous	Solid + solid (powdered mixture)	use some difference in properties, e.g. density, solubility, sublimation, magnetism
	Suspension of solid in liquid	filtration or centrifugation
	Liquid + liquid (immiscible)	use a separating funnel or decantation
Homogeneous	Solution of solid in liquid	to obtain solid: use evaporation (crystallisation) to obtain liquid: use distillation
	Two (or more) liquids mixed together (miscible)	fractional distillation
	Solution of two (or more) solids in a liquid	chromatography

Another means of separating an insoluble solid from a liquid is **centrifugation** where the mixture is spun at high speed in a centrifuge. Here, it is no longer the force of gravity on the solid particles that causes settling. Instead, there is a huge centrifugal force acting on the particles due to the high-speed spinning of the samples. This causes the solid to be sedimented at the bottom of the centrifuge tube. The liquid can be decanted off carefully.

Mixtures of two immiscible liquids can be separated if the mixture is placed in a **separating funnel** and allowed to stand. The liquids separate into different layers. The lower, denser layer is then 'tapped' off at the bottom (figure 2.8). This type of separation is useful in industry. For example, at the base of the blast furnace the molten slag forms a separate layer on top of the liquid iron. The two can then be 'tapped' off separately. The method is also very useful in organic chemistry as part of a process called 'solvent extraction'.

The separation of a solid from a mixture of solids depends largely on the particular substance being purified. Some suitable difference in physical properties needs to be found. Usually it helps if the mixture is ground to a powder before any separation is attempted.

- *Separations based on differences in density*
  'Panning' for gold is still carried out in the search for new deposits. In Amazonia, river-beds are mechanically sifted ('vacuum-cleaned') to collect gold dust. These methods depend on the gold dust being denser than the other substances in the river sediment. This type of method is also used in purifying the ores of zinc and copper, although in these cases the metals are less dense than the ores and so float on the surface.

- *Separations based on magnetic properties*
  Magnetic iron ore can be separated from other material in the crushed ore by using an electromagnet. In the Amazonian gold diggings, magnets are used to clean away iron-containing, red-brown dust from the powdered gold. In the environmentally and economically important processes of recycling metals, iron objects can be picked out from other scrap metal using electromagnets.

- *Separations based on differences in solubility*
  One very useful way of separating a soluble substance from a solid mixture is as follows. The mixture is first ground to a powder. A suitable liquid solvent (see page 38) is added. The solvent must dissolve one of the solid substances present, but not the others. The solvent is often water, but other liquids can be useful. The mixture in the solvent is then warmed and stirred. Care must be taken at the warming stage when using solvents other than water. The warm mixture is then filtered. This gives the insoluble substances as a residue on the filter paper, which can be dried. The soluble substance is in the liquid filtrate. Dry crystals can be obtained by evaporation and crystallisation (see next section). The gold prospectors in Brazil and Zimbabwe still use an immensely dangerous version of this method to extract the gold from other substances. The solvent they use is *mercury*, which dissolves the gold. The gold is then recovered from solution by evaporating off the mercury with a blowtorch. The unwanted residues, contaminated with mercury, are thrown into the rivers. Damage to the environment from this activity is very likely because mercury is poisonous to living things.

- *Separations based on sublimation*
  A solid that sublimes can be separated from others using this property (figure 2.9 on page 36).

Separating homogeneous mixtures

The separation of homogeneous mixtures is often slightly more complicated because there is no

1 The mixture of immiscible liquids settles into two layers, as the liquids do not mix

2 The tap is opened to let only the bottom layer run into the beaker

3 The tap is closed and the beaker is changed. The tap is opened to let the top layer run out

Figure 2.8 A separating funnel can be used to separate two immiscible liquids.

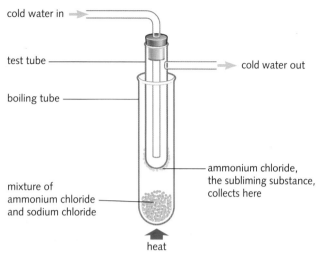

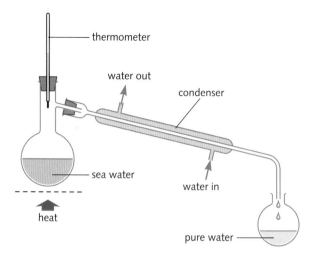

Figure 2.9 Ammonium chloride can be separated from a mixture because it sublimes. The crystals condense on the cooled surface.

Figure 2.11 The distillation of sea water.

physical separation of the phases in the original mixture. The methods of separation usually depend on solubility properties or on differences in boiling point.

Separating a solid from solution in a liquid can be carried out by **evaporation** or **crystallisation**. Evaporation gives only a powder, but crystallisation can result in proper crystals. Both processes begin by evaporating away the liquid but, when crystals are needed, evaporation is stopped when the solution has been concentrated enough. Figure 2.10 shows how this can be judged and done safely. The concentrated solution is allowed to cool slowly. The crystals formed can then be filtered off and dried.

Separating a liquid from a solution is usually carried out by **distillation** (figure 2.11). The boiling

point of the liquid is usually very much lower than that of the dissolved solid. The liquid can easily be evaporated off in a distillation flask. It is condensed by passing it down a water-cooled condenser, and then collected as the **distillate**.

Separating the liquids from a mixture of two (or more) miscible liquids is again based on the fact that the liquids will have different boiling points. However, the boiling points are closer together than for a solid-in-liquid solution and **fractional distillation** must be used (figure 2.12).

For example, ethanol boils at 78 °C whereas water boils at 100 °C. When the mixture is heated, ethanol and water vapours enter the fractionating column. Glass beads in the column provide a large surface area for condensation. Evaporation and

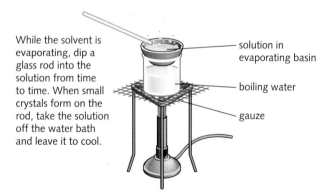

Figure 2.10 An evaporation method. This method should not be used if the solvent is flammable. Instead, use an electrical heating element and an oil or water bath.

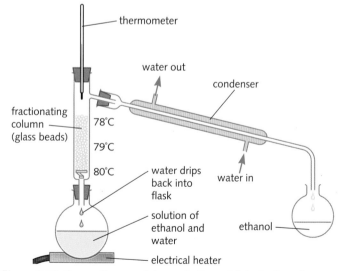

Figure 2.12 Separating a mixture of ethanol (alcohol) and water by fractional distillation.

condensation take place many times as the vapours rise up the column. Ethanol passes through the condenser first as the temperature of the column is raised above its boiling point. Water condenses in the column and flows back into the flask because the temperature of the column is below its b.p. of 100 °C.

The temperature on the thermometer stays at 78 °C until all the ethanol has distilled over. Only then does the temperature on the thermometer rise to 100 °C and the water distils over. By watching the temperature carefully, the two liquids (**fractions**) can be collected separately.

> **Fractional distillation** is used to separate any solution containing liquids with different boiling points. It can be adapted as a continuous process and is used industrially to separate:
>
> - the various fractions from crude oil (page 328),
> - the different gases from liquid air (page 217).

Separating two or more dissolved solids in solution can be carried out by **chromatography**. There are several types of chromatography, but they all follow the same basic principles. Paper chromatography is probably the simplest form to set up and is very useful if we want to analyse the substances present in a solution. For example, it can tell us whether a solution has become contaminated. This can be very important, because contamination of food or drinking water, for instance, may be dangerous to our health.

A drop of concentrated solution is usually placed on a *pencil* line near the bottom edge of a strip of chromatography paper. The paper is then dipped in the solvent. The level of the solvent must start below the sample. Figure 2.13 shows the process in action.

Many different solvents are used in chromatography. Water and **organic solvents** (carbon-containing solvents) such as ethanol, ethanoic acid solution and propanone are common. Organic solvents are useful because they dissolve many substances which are insoluble in water. When an organic solvent is used, the process is carried out in a tank with a lid to stop the solvent evaporating.

The substances separate according to their solubility in the solvent. As the solvent moves up the paper, the dyes are carried with it and begin to separate. The substance that is most soluble moves fastest up the paper. An insoluble substance would remain at the origin. The run is stopped just before the solvent reaches the top of the paper (the **solvent front**).

The distance moved by a particular spot is measured and related to the position of the solvent front. The ratio of these distances is called the R_f **value**. This value is used to identify the substance:

$$R_f = \frac{\text{distance moved by the substance}}{\text{distance moved by the solvent front}}$$

Originally, paper chromatography was used to separate solutions of coloured substances (dyes and pigments) since they could be seen as they moved up the paper. However, the usefulness of chromatography has been greatly increased by the use of **locating agents** (figure 2.14 on page 38). These mean that the method can also be used for separating substances that are *not* coloured. The paper is treated with locating agent after the chromatography run. The agent reacts with the samples to produce coloured spots.

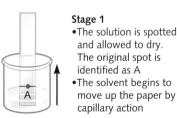

Stage 1
- The solution is spotted and allowed to dry. The original spot is identified as A
- The solvent begins to move up the paper by capillary action

Stage 2
- Solvent moves up the paper taking different components along at different rates

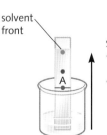

solvent front

Stage 3
- The separation of the mixture is complete
- The different components string out along the paper like runners in a race

Figure 2.13 Various stages during paper chromatography. The sample is separated as it moves up the paper.

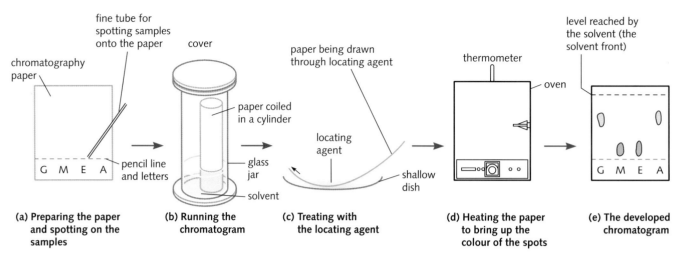

Figure 2.14 Chromatography using a locating agent to detect the spots on the paper. Alternatively the locating agent can be sprayed on the paper.

Chromatography has proved very useful in the analysis of biologically important molecules such as sugars, amino acids and nucleotide bases. In fact, molecules such as amino acids can be 'seen' if the paper is viewed under ultra-violet light.

The purity and identity of substances

Paper chromatography is one test that can be used to check for the *purity* of a substance. If the sample is pure, it should only give *one* spot when run in several different solvents. The *identity* of the sample can also be checked by comparing its R_f value to that of a sample we know to be pure. Probably the most generally used tests for purity are measurements of melting point or boiling point. As we saw earlier, impurities would lower the melting point or raise the boiling point of the substance. They would also make these temperatures less precise. These temperatures have been measured for a very wide range of substances. The identity of an unknown substance can be found by checking against these measured values for known, pure substances.

Other separation methods are also used to check whether purification has been successful. Samples obtained by distillation can be re-distilled. The purity of crystals can be improved by recrystallisation. A water sample can be tested for the amount of dissolved material by evaporating a known amount of water to dryness. The solid residue can then be weighed. This would give the amount of dissolved solid in the water.

The process of purification is of crucial importance in many areas of the chemical industry. Medicinal drugs (pharmaceuticals) must be of the highest possible degree of purity. Any contaminating substances, even in very small amounts, may have harmful side-effects. Coloured dyes (food colourings) are added to food and drinks to improve their appearance. The colourings added need to be carefully controlled. In Europe the permitted colourings are listed as E100 to E180. Many dyes that were once added are now banned. Even those which are permitted may still cause problems for some people. The yellow colouring tartrazine (E102) is found in many drinks, sauces, sweets and snacks. To most people it is harmless, but in some children it appears to cause hyperactivity and allergic reactions, for example asthma. Even where there is overall government regulation, individuals need to be aware of how particular foods affect them.

2.6 Solubility

The solubility of solids in liquids

Probably the most important and common examples of mixtures are solutions of solids in liquids.

Such a **solution** is made up of two parts:

- the solid that dissolves is known as the **solute,**
- the liquid in which it dissolves is called the **solvent.**

Water is the commonest solvent in use, but other liquids are also important. These other solvents are generally organic liquids such as ethanol, propanone and trichloroethane. These **organic solvents** are important because they will often dissolve substances that do not dissolve in water. If a substance dissolves in a solvent, it is said to be **soluble**: if it does not dissolve, it is **insoluble**.

These organic solvents (non-aqueous solvents) are present in various commercial household articles such as glues, paints, varnishes and aerosols, and this is a source of danger. Inhaling these solvents can give people a 'high'. Interest in the sensation produced can develop into the dangerous habit of 'solvent abuse'. This results in symptoms similar to alcohol abuse, producing disorientation and unconsciousness, and even death. Importantly, continuously inhaling small amounts of these solvents can cause permanent damage to the lungs and liver. More generally, a number of these solvents are flammable and can form explosive mixtures with the air. This is why they should always be used in a well-ventilated place.

If we try to dissolve a substance such as copper(II) sulphate in a fixed volume of water, the solution becomes more concentrated as we add more solid. A *concentrated* solution contains a high proportion of solute; a *dilute* solution contains a small proportion of solute. The **concentration** of a solution is the mass of solute dissolved in a particular volume of solvent, usually $1\,dm^3$ (1 litre).

Suppose we wanted a solution of copper(II) sulphate in water with a known concentration of $10\,g/dm^3$. This is what we would do.

1 Take a graduated flask and approximately half-fill it with distilled water, the solvent.

2 Weigh out 10.00 g of copper(II) sulphate, the solute.

3 Carefully add the solute to the solvent in the flask.

4 Gently shake the flask to dissolve all the solute.

5 Add more distilled water to make up the volume of the solution to exactly the $1.00\,dm^3$ mark on the neck of the graduated flask.

If we keep adding the solid, a point is reached where no more will dissolve at that temperature.

At this concentration, the solution is **saturated**. To get more solid to dissolve, the temperature must be increased. The concentration of solute in a saturated solution is the **solubility** of the solute at that temperature. Solubility is measured as the mass of solute that will saturate 100 g of water at a particular temperature.

Solubility curves

Curves showing how the solubility of a solid changes with temperature are known as **solubility curves**. The curves in figure 2.15 show how the solubility of several salts changes with temperature (see section 5.8 on page 134 for more about salts). You can see that the solubility of most solids increases with temperature. The increase for sodium chloride is very small. The process of crystallisation depends on these observations. When a saturated solution is cooled, it can hold less solute at the lower temperature and some solute crystallises out.

The solubility of gases in liquids

Unlike most solids, gases are less soluble in water as the temperature rises (figure 2.16 on page 40). The solubility of gases from the air in water is quite small, but the amount of dissolved oxygen is enough to support fish and other aquatic life. Interestingly, oxygen is more soluble in water than nitrogen. So when air is dissolved in water the proportions of the two gases become 61% nitrogen and 37% oxygen. There is an enrichment in life-supporting oxygen compared to air (79% nitrogen and 20% oxygen).

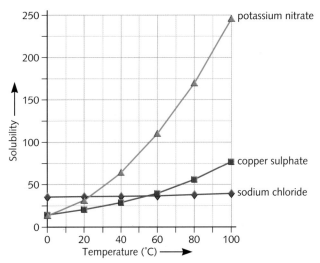

Figure 2.15 Solubility curves for three solids in water (solubility measured in grams of solid per 100 g of water).

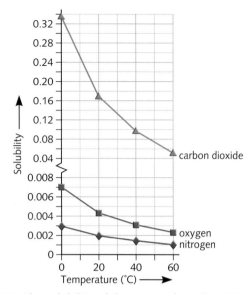

Figure 2.16 *The solubility of three gases from the air in water (solubility measured in grams of gas per 100g of water).*

The solubility of gases increases with pressure. Sparkling drinks contain carbon dioxide dissolved under pressure. They 'fizz' when the pressure is released by opening the container. They go 'flat' if left to stand open; even more so if left to stand in a warm place.

A deep-sea diver may suffer the consequences of the above properties of gases. A diver coming up too rapidly may suffer from the 'bends'. The pressure increases as you go deeper, and at the bottom it is several times greater than at the surface. If the diver is breathing a mixture of nitrogen and oxygen, more nitrogen dissolves in the diver's blood than at the surface. If the diver rises too quickly, the pressure falls rapidly. The nitrogen 'boils' out of the blood, stopping blood flow and affecting nerves. To reduce the problem, scuba tanks are often filled with helium–oxygen mixtures. Helium has a much lower solubility in blood than nitrogen does.

You will notice in figure 2.16 that carbon dioxide is more soluble than either nitrogen or oxygen. This is because it reacts with water to produce carbonic acid. This shows that the world is not chemically static. Substances are not only *mixing* with each other, but also chemically *reacting*. This produces a world that is continuously changing. To gain a better understanding of this, we need to look more deeply into the 'make-up' of chemical substances.

Summary of core material

You should know that:

- there are three different physical states in which a substance can exist
- changes in state can be made by changing the temperature and/or the pressure
- sublimation is a change of state in which the liquid phase is by-passed
- pure substances have precise melting and boiling points – their sharpness can be taken as an indication of the degree of purity of the substance
- the processes of melting and boiling require energy – when heating a substance, the temperature stays constant during these processes
- a wide variety of types of mixture are possible between substances
- some of these are homogeneous mixtures (solutions) in which the phases cannot be identified separately
- the most common solutions are those involving a liquid solvent such as water
- the solubility of most solids increases with rising temperature, whereas gases are less soluble at higher temperatures
- heterogeneous mixtures can be formed between different substances, with one phase being dispersed as small particles or droplets in the other
- suspensions are heterogeneous mixtures where the dispersed particles are large enough to settle out eventually
- in colloids the dispersed particles are so small they cannot be seen by the eye, but they do scatter light so they look cloudy
- a range of separation methods exist to purify one substance from a mixture, for example
  - filtration separates an insoluble substance from suspension in a liquid
  - distillation separates a liquid from the solutes dissolved in it
  - fractional distillation separates liquids that mix but have different boiling points
  - chromatography separates substances, particularly coloured dyes, by differences in their solubility in a solvent.

2.1

(a) Use the data given for the substances listed below to decide which of them will be solids, liquids or gases at a room temperature of 25 °C. [4]

Substance	Melting point (°C)	Boiling point (°C)
Lead	317	1744
Radon	−71	−62
Ethanol	−117	78
Cobalt	1492	2900
Nitrogen	−210	−196
Propane	−188	−42
Ethanoic acid	16	118
Benzamide	132	290

(b) Which substance is a liquid over the smallest range of temperature? [1]

(c) Which *two* substances are gaseous at −50 °C? [2]

(d) Which substance has the lowest freezing point? [1]

(e) Which substance is liquid at 2500 °C? [1]

(f) A sample of ethanoic acid was found to boil at 121 °C. Use the information in the table to comment on this result. [2]

2.2 The graph below shows the heating curve for a pure substance. The temperature rises with time as the substance is heated.

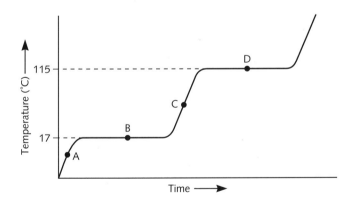

(a) What physical state(s) is the substance in at points A, B, C and D? [4]

(b) What is the melting point of the substance? [1]

(c) What is its boiling point? [1]

(d) What happens to the temperature while the substance is changing state? [1]

(e) The substance is not water. How do we know this from the graph? [1]

2.3

(a) The graph shows the temperature of a sample of phenyl benzoate (in a test tube) as it cools.

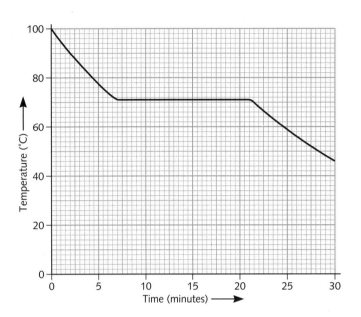

Describe the physical state(s) of the phenyl benzoate in the tube after 5, 15 and 25 minutes. [3]

(b) Another sample of phenyl benzoate was contaminated with a small amount of a different compound (with about the same melting point). A smaller sample of this impure phenyl benzoate was allowed to cool from 100 °C in the same test tube under the same conditions. Copy the graph (above), and draw on it the curve you might expect to get if you measured the temperature against the time. [3]

(c) State and explain *one* practical application of any aspect of the behaviour shown above. [2]

(ULEAC, 1995)

2.4 The table on page 42 shows some examples of mixtures. In these mixtures some substances are dispersed in another called the continuous medium.

(a) You have been given a suspension and a solution. How could you tell the difference between them by their appearance? [2]

(b) Paints often need to be stirred thoroughly before use. Suggest why. [1]

(c) Cream is whipped before it is used in cakes and desserts. Suggest why. [1]

(d) Butter is an example of one type of mixture. Name the type of mixture. Give a reason for your choice. [2]

Name	Dispersed substances	Continuous medium	Examples
Suspension	solid	liquid	paints, milk of magnesia
Emulsion	liquid	liquid	milk, mayonnaise
Gel	liquid	solid	jellies, agar
Foam	gas	liquid	whipped cream, froth
Solid foam	gas	solid	expanded polystyrene, cork

(NEAB, 1995)

2.5 Propanone is a liquid which mixes in all proportions with water. 50 cm³ of a mixture of propanone and water was placed in a flask fitted with a fractionating column and condenser as shown in the diagram below.

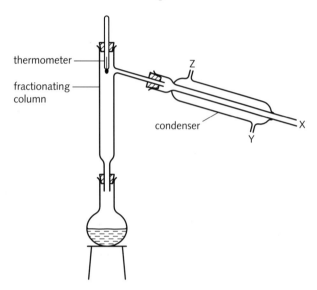

(a) (i) With what would the fractionating column be packed in order to improve its efficiency? [1]
(ii) Should the cooling water enter the condenser at Z or Y? [1]

The flask was heated, and a distillate was collected at X. The temperature was noted when the total volume of distillate collected was 5 cm³, 10 cm³, 15 cm³ and 20 cm³.

(b) What piece of apparatus would be used to measure these volumes of distillate? [1]

The diagrams below show part of the stem of the thermometer as each temperature reading was taken.

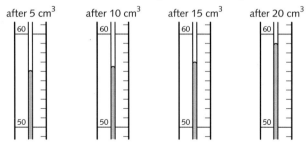

after 5 cm³   after 10 cm³   after 15 cm³   after 20 cm³

(c) Copy the table below. Read and record the temperatures in your table, and suggest values which would have been obtained when the total volume of distillate collected was 25 cm³ and 30 cm³. [4]

Volume of distillate (cm³)	5	10	15	20	25	30
Temperature (°C)						

(d) Copy the axes below on graph paper. Plot these results on your axes, and draw the graph which best fits them. [4]

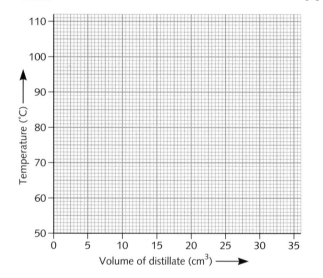

(e) Deduce from your graph the boiling point of propanone. [1]

(f) Suggest what volume of propanone was present in the original mixture of propanone and water. [1]

(IGCSE, 1988)

2.6 Chromatography is used by the 'Horse Racing Forensic Laboratory' to test for the presence of illegal drugs in racehorses.

A concentrated sample of urine is spotted onto chromatography paper on the start line. Alongside this, known drugs are spotted. The chromatogram is run using methanol as the solvent. When finished, the paper is read by placing under ultra-violet light. A chromatogram of urine from four racehorses is shown.

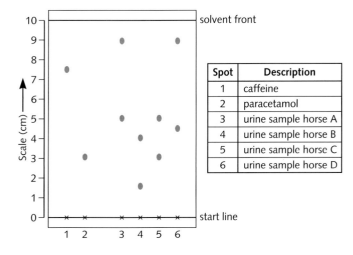

Spot	Description
1	caffeine
2	paracetamol
3	urine sample horse A
4	urine sample horse B
5	urine sample horse C
6	urine sample horse D

(a) The results for known drugs are given as 'R_f values'.

$$R_f \text{ value} = \frac{\text{distance travelled by the substance}}{\text{distance travelled by the solvent}}$$

Calculate the R_f value for caffeine. [2]

(b) Explain the meaning of the word 'solvent'. [1]

(c) State *two* factors which determine the distance a substance travels up the paper. [2]

(d) From the results, the sample from one horse contains an illegal substance.
(i) State the horse, and the drug present. [1]
(ii) Give a reason for the use of this drug. [1]

(e) It is usual for at least one horse to be tested after every race. In big races, such as the Derby, the first three horses will be tested. Only nine out of 5000 tests carried out on horses in this country have proved positive. Why are all racehorses not tested? [1]

(MEG, 1993)

2.7 Some solids dissolve easily, others do not.

(a) (i) What is the name given to liquids which dissolve solids? [1]
(ii) What is the name of the clear liquid formed when a solid dissolves in a liquid? [1]

(b) Temperature change affects the solubility of substances in water.
(i) How does the solubility of most solids change as the temperature of the water increases? [1]

(ii) How does the solubility of a gas change as the temperature of the water increases? [1]

(c) Describe how dry solid can be obtained from the liquid in which it is dissolved. [2]

(d) The graph shows how the solubility of ammonium sulphate in water changes with temperature.

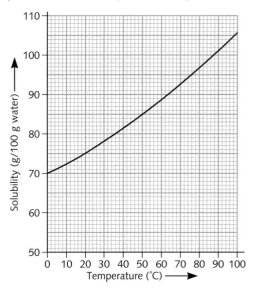

100 g of ammonium sulphate was heated in 100 g of water until it all dissolved. Use the graph to answer the following. [4]
(i) What is the lowest temperature at which the water will dissolve all the ammonium sulphate?
(ii) What mass of solid will crystallise from the liquid when it is cooled to room temperature?
(iii) This solid is filtered off at 20°C. What will you see if the remaining liquid is then cooled to 15°C?
(iv) What word is used to describe a liquid which cannot dissolve any more solid at a given temperature?

(ULEAC, 1995)

2.8 The table below shows how many grams of five different solids dissolve in 100 g of the solvents water, alcohol and trichlorethene (all at 20°C).

(a) Which solid dissolves best in water at 20°C? [1]

(b) Which is the best solvent for iodine? [1]

(c) Which solid is insoluble in all three solvents? [1]

Solvents	Solids				
	Salt	Sugar	Iodine	Chalk	Urea
Water	36.00	204.00	0.03	0.00	100.00
Alcohol	0.00	0.00	20.00	0.00	20.00
Trichlorethene	0.00	0.00	3.00	0.00	0.00

(NEAB, 1995)

Atoms and molecules

This section covers the following ideas:

- elements and compounds
- chemical reactions and physical changes
- atomic theory
- the kinetic theory and changes of state
- diffusion
- the gas laws
- the formation of molecules.

2.7 Elements and compounds

Earlier in this chapter you were introduced to pure substances, and to ways of purifying and identifying them. But what are 'pure substances'?

There are two types of **pure substance**, elements and compounds.

- **Elements** are substances that cannot be chemically broken down into simpler substances. An element cannot be decomposed by passing an electric current through it.
- **Compounds** are pure substances made from two, or more, elements chemically combined together.

Figure 2.17 summarises what we now know about matter.

Elements are the 'building blocks' from which the Universe is constructed. There are over a hundred known elements, but the vast majority of the Universe consists of just two. Hydrogen (92%) and helium (7%) make up most of the mass of the Universe, with all the other elements contributing only 1% to the total. The concentration, or 'coming together', of certain of these elements to make the Earth is of great interest and significance. There are 94 elements found naturally on Earth altogether, but eight account for more than 98% of the mass of the Earth's crust. Two elements, silicon and oxygen, which are bound together in silicate rocks, make up almost three-quarters of the crust. Only certain of the elements are able to form the complex compounds that are found in living things. For example, the human body contains 65% oxygen, 18% carbon, 10% hydrogen, 3% nitrogen, 2% calcium and 2% other elements.

2.8 Chemical reactions and physical changes

Substances can mix in a variety of ways, and they can also react chemically with each other. Indeed they can be encouraged to react, by heating for instance. In a reaction, one substance can be transformed (changed) into another. Copper(II) carbonate is a green solid, but on heating it is changed into a black powder. Closer investigation shows that the gas carbon dioxide is also produced. This type of chemical reaction, where a compound breaks down to form two or more substances, is known as **decomposition**.

Decomposition can also be brought about by electricity. Some substances, although they do not conduct electricity when solid, *do* conduct when they are melted or in solution. In the process of conduction, they are broken down into simpler substances. Thus, lead(II) bromide, which is a white powder, can be melted. When a

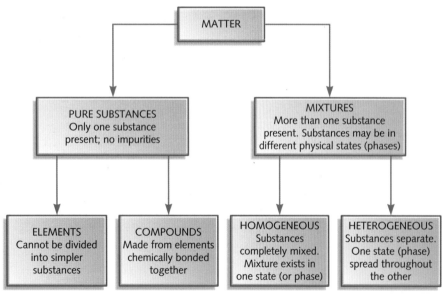

Figure 2.17 Schematic representation of the different types of matter, including elements and compounds.

current is passed through molten lead(II) bromide, a silver-grey metal (lead) and a brown vapour (bromine) are formed. Neither of these products can be split into any simpler substances.

The opposite type of reaction, where the substance is formed by the combination of two or more other substances, is known as **synthesis**. For example, if a piece of burning magnesium is plunged into a gas jar of oxygen, the intensity (brightness) of the brilliant white flame increases (see figure 4.1 on page 100). When the reaction has burnt out, a white ash remains. The ash has totally different properties to the original silver-grey metal strip and colourless gas we started with. A new compound, magnesium oxide, has been formed from magnesium and oxygen.

Although many other reactions are not as spectacular as this, the burning of magnesium shows the general features of chemical reactions.

In a **chemical reaction**:

- new chemical substance(s) are formed,
- generally the process is not easily reversed,
- energy is often given out.

These characteristics of a chemical reaction contrast with those of a simple physical change such as melting or dissolving. In a **physical change** the substances involved do not change identity. They can be easily returned to their original form by some physical process such as cooling or evaporation. Sugar dissolves in water, but we can get the solid sugar back by evaporating off the water.

Another synthesis reaction takes place between powdered iron and sulphur (see figure 4.5 on page 103). The two solids are finely ground and well mixed. The mixture is heated with a Bunsen burner. The reaction mixture continues to glow after the Bunsen burner is removed. Heat energy is given out. There has been a reaction and we are left with a black non-magnetic solid, iron(II) sulphide, which cannot easily be changed back to iron and sulphur. This example also illustrates some important differences between a mixture (in this case the powders of iron and sulphur) and a compound (in this case the final product of the reaction). The general differences between making a mixture of substances and forming a new compound are shown in table 2.6.

2.9 Atomic theory

Elements and compounds mix and react to produce the world around us. They produce massive objects such as the 'gas giants' (the planets Jupiter and Saturn), and tiny highly structured crystals of solid sugar. How do the elements organise themselves to give this variety? How can any one element exist in the three different states of matter simply through a change in temperature?

Our modern understanding is based on the **atomic theory** put forward by John Dalton in 1807. His theory re-introduced the ideas of Democritus (460–370 BC) and other Greek philosophers who suggested that all matter was infinitely divided into very small particles known as **atoms**. These ideas were not widely accepted at the time. They were only revived when Dalton developed them further

Table 2.6 The differences between mixtures and pure compounds

When a mixture forms ...	When a compound forms ...
the substances are simply mixed together; no reaction takes place	the substances chemically react together to form a new compound
the composition of the mixture can be varied	the composition of the new compound is always the same
the properties of the substances present remain the same	the properties of the new compound are very different from those of the elements in it
the substances in the mixture can be separated by physical methods such as filtration, distillation and magnetic attraction	the compound cannot easily be separated into its elements

and experimental science was able to back them up with practical observation.

Dalton suggested that:

- a pure element is composed of atoms,
- the atoms of each element are different in size and mass,
- atoms are the smallest particles that take part in a chemical reaction,
- atoms of different elements can combine to make **molecules** of a compound.

Certain parts of the theory may need changing as a result of what we have discovered since Dalton's time. However, Dalton's theory was one of the great leaps of understanding in chemistry. It meant that we could explain many natural processes. Whereas Dalton only had theories for the existence of atoms, modern techniques (such as scanning tunnelling microscopy) can now directly reveal the presence of individual atoms. It has even been possible to create an 'atomic logo' (figure 2.18), and it may soon be possible to 'see' a reaction between individual atoms.

A chemical language

Dalton suggested that each element should have its own **symbol** – a form of chemical shorthand. He could then write the formulas of compounds without writing out the name every time. Our modern system uses letters taken from the name of the element. This is an international code. Some elements have been known for a long time and their symbol is taken from their Latin name.

The symbol for an element consists of one or two letters, the first of which must be a capital. Where

Table 2.7 The symbols of some chemical elements

Element	Latin name	Symbol
Hydrogen		H
Helium		He
Carbon		C
Calcium		Ca
Copper	cuprum	Cu
Chlorine		Cl
Nitrogen		N
Sodium	natrium	Na
Phosphorus		P
Potassium	kalium	K
Iron	ferrum	Fe
Lead	plumbum	Pb
Silver	argentum	Ag
Gold	aurum	Au

the names of several elements begin with the same letter, the second letter of the name is usually included (table 2.7). As more elements were discovered, they came to be named after a wider range of people, cities, countries and even particular universities. We shall see in chapter 3 how useful it is to be able to use symbols, and how they can be combined to show the formulas of complex chemical compounds. A full list of the elements and their symbols is found in the Periodic Table (figure 3.1 on page 65).

2.10 The kinetic theory of matter

The idea that all substances consist of very small particles begins to explain the structure of the three different states of matter. The kinetic theory of matter describes these states, and the changes between them, in terms of the movement of particles.

The main points of the **kinetic theory** are:

- all matter is made up of very small particles (different substances contain different types of particles – such as atoms or molecules),
- the particles are moving all the time (the higher the temperature, the higher the average energy of the particles),
- heavier particles move more slowly than lighter particles at the same temperature.

Figure 2.18 An 'atomic logo' produced by xenon atoms on a nickel surface using scanning tunnelling microscopy.

Figure 2.19 is a summary of the organisation of the particles in the three states of matter, and helps to explain their different overall physical properties. The highly structured, ordered microscopic arrangements (**lattices**) in solids can produce the regular crystal structures seen in this state. The ability of the particles to move in the liquid and gas phases produces their fluid properties. The particles are very widely separated in a gas, but are close together in a liquid or solid.

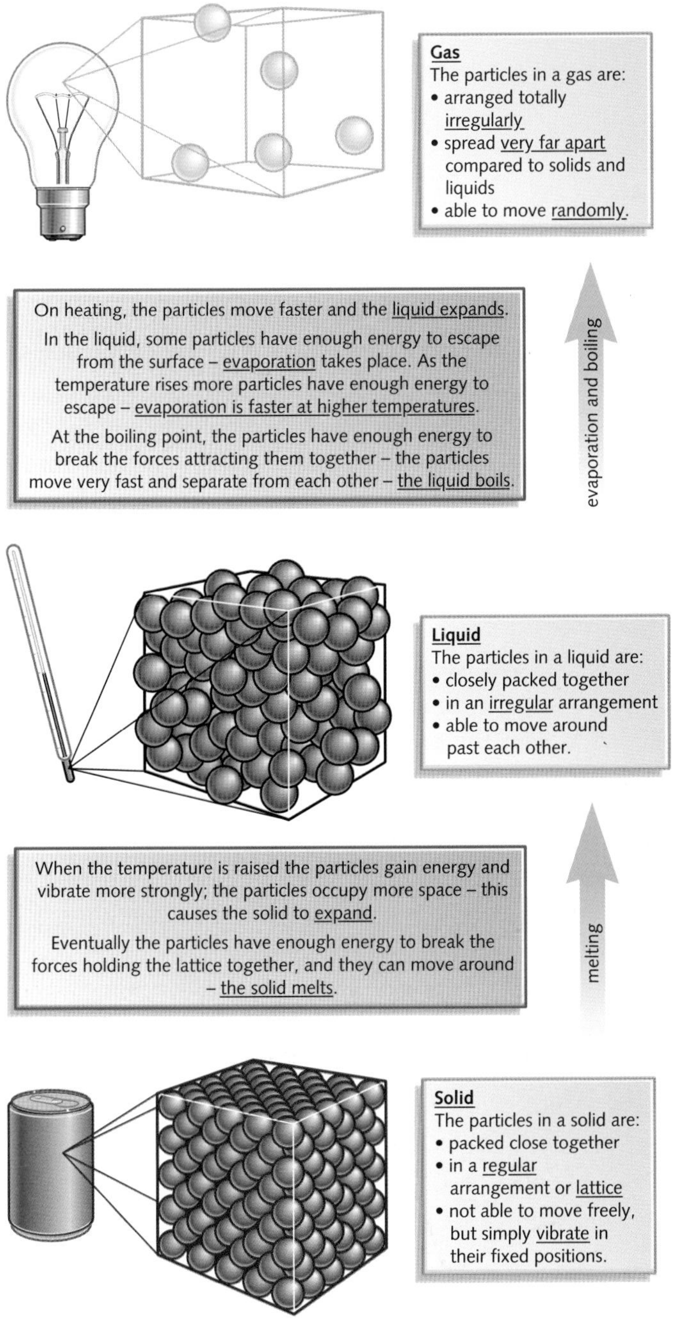

Gas
The particles in a gas are:
• arranged totally <u>irregularly</u>
• spread <u>very far apart</u> compared to solids and liquids
• able to move <u>randomly</u>.

On heating, the particles move faster and the <u>liquid expands</u>.
In the liquid, some particles have enough energy to escape from the surface – <u>evaporation</u> takes place. As the temperature rises more particles have enough energy to escape – <u>evaporation is faster at higher temperatures</u>.
At the boiling point, the particles have enough energy to break the forces attracting them together – the particles move very fast and separate from each other – <u>the liquid boils</u>.

evaporation and boiling

Liquid
The particles in a liquid are:
• closely packed together
• in an <u>irregular</u> arrangement
• able to move around past each other.

When the temperature is raised the particles gain energy and vibrate more strongly; the particles occupy more space – this causes the solid to <u>expand</u>.
Eventually the particles have enough energy to break the forces holding the lattice together, and they can move around – <u>the solid melts</u>.

melting

Solid
The particles in a solid are:
• packed close together
• in a <u>regular</u> arrangement or <u>lattice</u>
• not able to move freely, but simply <u>vibrate</u> in their fixed positions.

Figure 2.19 *Applying the kinetic theory to changes in physical state.*

The space between the particles can be called the **inter-molecular space** (IMS). In a gas, the inter-molecular space is large and can be reduced by increasing the external pressure – gases are **compressible**. In liquids, this space is very much smaller – liquids are not very compressible.

The way the particles in the three states are arranged also helps to explain the temperature changes when a substance is heated or cooled. Figure 2.20 summarises the energy changes taking place at the different stages of a heating curve or cooling curve experiment.

We are aware of these changes in our everyday life. Sweating helps to cool the body. Sweat is a liquid and energy is needed before it can evaporate. The energy comes from the heat of the body, and so the body cools down. Another example is refrigeration. The invention of efficient ice-making and refrigeration was a major breakthrough in the transportation and storage of food. Refrigerators use the energy changes involved in changing state to provide a cold environment. (Use figure 2.20 and the list on page 48 to help you understand these changes.)

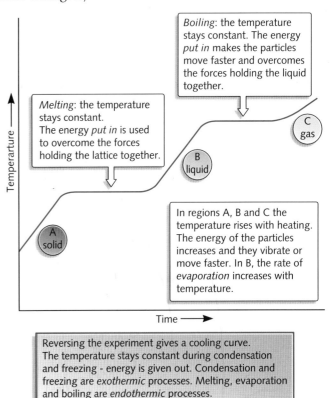

Boiling: the temperature stays constant. The energy *put in* makes the particles move faster and overcomes the forces holding the liquid together.

Melting: the temperature stays constant. The energy *put in* is used to overcome the forces holding the lattice together.

C gas

B liquid

A solid

In regions A, B and C the temperature rises with heating. The energy of the particles increases and they vibrate or move faster. In B, the rate of *evaporation* increases with temperature.

Temperature →

Time ⟶

Reversing the experiment gives a cooling curve. The temperature stays constant during condensation and freezing - energy is given out. Condensation and freezing are *exothermic* processes. Melting, evaporation and boiling are *endothermic* processes.

Figure 2.20 *The energy changes taking place during heating and cooling.*

1 The refrigerator is controlled by a thermostat. When it warms up inside, the pump is switched on.

2 The pump compresses the coolant which is a gas so that it condenses to a liquid. This gives out energy, so the liquid gets hot.

3 The liquid is cooled down by the air outside as it passes through fins at the back of the refrigerator.

4 The liquid passes through the refrigerator where it warms up and becomes a gas again. This takes in energy, so the inside of the refrigerator cools down.

2.11 Diffusion in fluids

The idea that fluids are made up of moving particles helps us to explain processes involving diffusion.

Dissolving

A copper(II) sulphate crystal is placed at the bottom of a beaker of water. It is then left to stand. At first the water around the crystal becomes blue as the solid dissolves. Particles move off the surface of the crystal into the water. Eventually the crystal dissolves completely and the whole solution becomes blue. The particles from the solid become evenly spread through the water.

Whether a solid begins to break up like this in a liquid depends on which combination of solid and liquid is taken. But the spreading of the solute particles throughout the liquid is an example of **diffusion**. Diffusion in solution is also important where the solute is a gas. This is especially important in breathing! Diffusion contributes to the movement of oxygen from the lungs to the blood, and of carbon dioxide from the blood to the lungs.

- **Diffusion** involves the movement of particles from a region of higher concentration towards a region of lower concentration. Eventually the particles are evenly spread – their concentration is the same throughout.
- Diffusion does not take place in solids.
- Diffusion in liquids is much slower than in gases.

The diffusion of gases

A few drops of liquid bromine are put into a gas jar, and the lid is replaced. After a short time the jar becomes full of brown gas. Bromine vaporises easily and its gas will completely fill the container. Gases diffuse to fill all the space available to them.

Diffusion is important for our 'sensing' of the world around us. It is the way smells reach us, whether they are pleasant or harmful. Not all gases diffuse at the same rate. This is shown by the experiment in figure 2.21. The ammonia and hydrochloric acid fumes react when they meet, producing a white 'smoke-ring' of ammonium chloride. The fact that the ring is not formed half-way along the tube shows that ammonia diffuses faster.

The speeds of gas atoms or molecules are high. We are being bombarded constantly by nitrogen and oxygen molecules in the air which are travelling at about 500 m/s (1800 km/h). However, these particles collide very frequently with other particles in the air (many millions of collisions per second), so their path is not particularly direct (figure 2.22a)! These very frequent collisions slow down the overall **rate of diffusion** from one place to another.

The movement of individual gas particles in the air cannot be seen: the particles are far too small. However, the effect of their presence and motion can be shown using a smoke cell (figure 2.22b). The smoke particles are hit by the invisible molecules in the air. The jerky, random motion produced by these hits can be seen under a microscope. This is known as **Brownian motion**. A similar effect can be seen using pollen grains sprinkled on the surface of water. The pollen grains move randomly. This motion is the result of the pollen grains being unevenly bombarded by the much smaller water molecules.

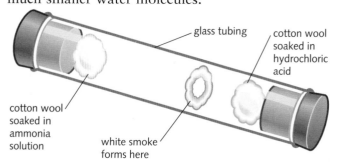

Figure 2.21 Ammonia and hydrochloric acid fumes diffuse at different rates.

EXTENSION

The absolute scale of temperature

The behaviour of gases as explained by kinetic theory led Lord Kelvin to define a new temperature scale in 1850.

Two important points derived from kinetic theory are relevant here:

- the pressure of a gas is the result of collisions of the fast-moving particles with the walls of the container,
- the average speed of the particles increases with an increase in temperature.

If the temperature of a gas in a container of fixed volume is raised, the speed of the particles will increase. This means that the particles will collide with the wall more frequently, so the pressure of the gas will increase. If a similar experiment is done where the pressure of the gas is kept constant, then as the temperature of the gas is increased so the gas expands. This is because the increasing temperature gives the gas particles more energy so they move faster and collide more frequently and generally occupy more space. Hot-air balloons work on this principle, rising and falling as the temperature of the gas in the balloon rises and falls.

If you plot a graph of volume against temperature for a particular gas, you will get a straight line. This shows that volume is proportional to temperature. However, the volume of the gas is not zero at 0 °C. In fact, the volume of the gas reaches zero at −273 °C.

A graph of pressure against temperature for a gas shows a similar straight line, as the pressure of a gas is proportional to the temperature and is zero at −273 °C. Since gas pressure is produced by the particles colliding with the container walls, we can conclude that at −273 °C the particles are not moving. At this temperature, the particles have no energy. This temperature is known as **absolute zero**. It is impossible to get colder than absolute zero. The **absolute scale** of temperature (or **Kelvin scale** – named after Lord Kelvin) starts at 0 K (zero kelvins). On this new scale the freezing point of water is 273 K, and its boiling point is 373 K (both at atmospheric pressure). Note that the unit of temperature on the Kelvin scale is just 'kelvin'. It is *not* 'degrees kelvin'.

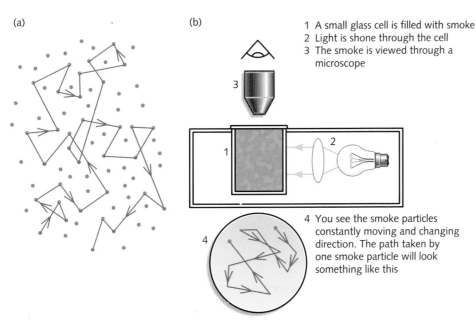

(a)

(b)

1 A small glass cell is filled with smoke
2 Light is shone through the cell
3 The smoke is viewed through a microscope

4 You see the smoke particles constantly moving and changing direction. The path taken by one smoke particle will look something like this

Figure 2.22 (a) Diffusion of a gas particle; the particle collides with many others, deflecting its path. (b) Demonstrating Brownian motion using a smoke cell; the smoke particles show a random motion.

2.12 Atoms and molecules

The kinetic theory explains how gases are the least dense and by far the most compressible of the three states of matter. This gives us confidence that the idea that matter is made up of small particles is reliable. But what of the nature of these particles? What are atoms, and how do they combine to make molecules? Some early ideas on this problem can be found by looking more closely at the speeds of various particles in gaseous elements.

The most massive objects in the galaxies are not the stars but huge clouds of interstellar gas and dust called giant molecular clouds. These clouds are often up to 200 light-years across. They are made almost entirely of two gases, hydrogen and helium, the two simplest elements in the Universe. These clouds are extremely cold (about 10 K) and the elements exist in their most stable form. The hydrogen atoms link in pairs to form molecules (H_2). However, the helium atoms stay single.

Both hydrogen and helium normally exist as gases on Earth. But they differ considerably in their properties. The particle speeds of hydrogen, helium and other gases can be compared (table 2.8). Looking at the table we can make two deductions.

> Generally, when comparing the **rates of diffusion** of gases:
>
> - the lower the molecular mass of a gas, the faster it will diffuse,
> - hydrogen, having the lightest molecules, will diffuse faster than any other gas.

Scientists analysing figures like those in table 2.8 realised that the particles in a sample of hydrogen gas do not move fast enough to be single, individual atoms. The atoms are combined to form **molecules**. In the case of hydrogen, these molecules consist of two atoms chemically bonded together (H_2). In contrast, helium atoms are found normally as individual atoms, not as molecules. This means that they are **stable** as single atoms.

Hydrogen is just one of several gaseous elements that are made up of **diatomic molecules** (molecules consisting of two atoms) and not of single atoms.

Table 2.8 The average speeds of some gas molecules at 25 °C

Name of gas	Formula	Relative formula mass	Average speed at 25 °C (m/s)
Hydrogen	H_2	2	1920
Helium	He	4	1360
Water vapour	H_2O	18	640
Carbon dioxide	CO_2	44	410

Oxygen (O_2), nitrogen (N_2) and chlorine (Cl_2) are other examples of diatomic gases. These substances are *not* compounds, since the atoms combined are of the same element.

These elements contrast with the stable gases such as helium (He), neon (Ne) and argon (Ar) which exist as single atoms. They also differ from metallic elements. In metals, for example copper (Cu), layers of individual atoms are stacked on top of each other to form a regular crystal lattice.

We have seen that some *elements* are made up of molecules. But, as we discussed on page 46, Dalton had originally introduced the idea of molecules to explain the particles making up *compounds* such as water, carbon dioxide and methane. Molecules of these compounds consist of atoms of *different elements* chemically bonded together. Water is made up of two atoms of hydrogen bonded to one atom of oxygen, with formula H_2O. Methane (CH_4) has one atom of carbon bonded to four atoms of hydrogen; and hydrogen chloride (HCl) has one atom of hydrogen and one atom of chlorine bonded together. Models of these are shown in figure 2.23.

 Water, H_2O

 Methane, CH_4

 Hydrogen chloride, HCl

Figure 2.23 Simple compounds consist of molecules made up of atoms of (two) different elements.

Summary of core material

You should know that:

- elements are the basic building units of the material world – they cannot be chemically broken down into anything simpler
- compounds are made from two or more elements chemically combined together

- the properties of a compound are very different from those of the elements it is made from
- chemical reactions produce new substances and involve energy changes
- each element is made from atoms
- the atoms of each element can be represented by a chemical symbol
- atoms can join together to make the molecules either of an element or of a compound
- the particles (atoms, molecules or ions) of a substance are in constant motion – the kinetic theory
- the nature and amount of motion of these particles in a solid, liquid or gas is different
- an understanding of the kinetic theory explains the processes involved in changing state and diffusion.

2.9 The diagram shows an experiment using the gases hydrogen and carbon dioxide. At the start, gas jar A was full of carbon dioxide and gas jar B was full of hydrogen.

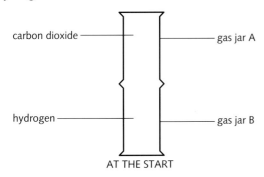

AT THE START

What will be in gas jar A after a few minutes? [1]

Choose from: carbon dioxide only
                 hydrogen only
                 a mixture of carbon dioxide and
                 hydrogen

(NEAB, 1995)

2.10

(a) Hydrogen is used in weather balloons.
   (i) Explain what happens to the volume enclosed by the balloon if you add more hydrogen. [2]

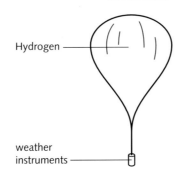

(ii) Explain what happens to the volume of gas in the balloon if the air temperature falls. [2]

(b) Hydrogen and chlorine react when mixed to form hydrogen chloride.

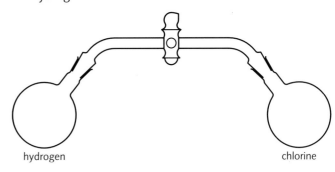

hydrogen   chlorine

Explain how the gases mix when the tap is opened. [2]

(c) In sodium street lamps the metal is used in the form of a gas.

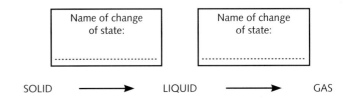

Name of change of state:	Name of change of state:
----------------------	----------------------

SOLID ⟶ LIQUID ⟶ GAS

(i) Copy and complete the diagram by naming each change of state as sodium changes from a solid to a vapour (gas). [2]
(ii) Give *two* different ways of making liquid sodium change into sodium vapour. [2]
(iii) What are the correct words to complete the following sentences. [2]
When a gas becomes liquid the change of state is called ....

The opposite of melting is ....

(SEG, part question, 1995)

2.11

(a) A tanker was used for transporting liquid sulphur.

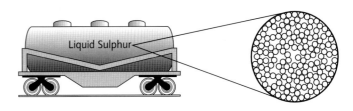

Liquid Sulphur

(i) In this diagram a sulphur molecule is shown as ○. How can you tell that the sulphur is liquid? [2]

(ii) Draw a diagram to show how the sulphur molecules ◯ are arranged in solid sulphur. [2]

(b) Look at the information on the table.

Substance	Melting point (°C)	Density (g/cm³)
Iron	1535	8
Sulphur	113	2
Water	0	1

(i) State *two* advantages of transporting sulphur as a liquid. [2]

(ii) Give *two* disadvantages of transporting a metal, such as iron, as a liquid. [2]

(c) When iron ● and sulphur ◯ are mixed and then heated, they form iron sulphide.

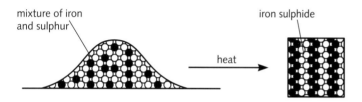

(i) A mixture of iron and sulphur was shaken with water and left to settle. The iron and sulphur formed separate layers. Explain why.

(ii) Some iron sulphide powder was shaken with water and left to settle. The iron and sulphur did not form separate layers. Explain why. [2]

(SEG, part question, 1995)

2.12 The following table gives information about three solids: cobalt, iodine and sulphur. Use the information to answer the questions.

Solid	Attracted by a magnet	Solubility in ethanol
Cobalt	yes	insoluble
Iodine	no	soluble
Sulphur	no	insoluble

(a) Suggest how a mixture of cobalt powder and sulphur powder could be separated. [2]

(b) Suggest how a pure sample of iodine could be obtained from a mixture of iodine and sulphur. [4]

(IGCSE, 1996)

The structure of the atom

This section covers the following ideas:

- atomic structure and sub-atomic particles
- the nucleus of an atom
- atomic number and mass number
- isotopes
- relative atomic mass
- radioactivity – alpha (α), beta (β) and gamma (γ) radiation
- uses of radioactivity
- the arrangement of electrons in atoms.

2.13 Atomic structure

How can atoms join together to make molecules? What makes certain atoms more ready to do this? Why do hydrogen atoms pair up, but helium atoms remain single? To find answers to questions like these, we need first to consider the structure of atoms in general. Dalton thought they were solid, indivisible particles. But research since then has shown that atoms are made up of various sub-atomic particles. By 1932, it was clear that atoms consisted of three sub-atomic particles – **protons**, **neutrons** and **electrons**. These particles are universal – all atoms are made from them. The **atom** remains the smallest particle that shows the characteristics of a particular element.

Measuring the size of atoms

Modern methods such as scanning tunnelling microscopy have allowed us to see individual atoms in a structure. However, atoms are amazingly small! A magnification of 100 million times is necessary to show the stacking pattern of the individual atoms that make up a gold bar.

A single atom is so small that it cannot be weighed on a balance. However, the mass of one atom can be compared with that of another using a **mass spectrometer**. The element carbon is chosen as the standard. The masses of atoms of all other elements are compared to the mass of a carbon atom. This gives a series of values of **relative atomic mass** for the elements. Carbon is given a relative atomic mass of exactly 12, which can be written as carbon-12.

Table 2.9 gives some examples of the values obtained for other elements. It shows that carbon atoms are 12 times as heavy as hydrogen atoms, which are the lightest atoms of all. Calcium atoms are 40 times as heavy as hydrogen atoms.

Sub-atomic particles

Evidence for the structure of the atom came from studying:

- the nature of rays produced in discharge tubes (for example cathode ray tubes),
- the light given out by excited gases,
- the nature of radioactivity.

J. J. Thompson (in 1897) found that cathode ray tubes (the early ancestors of television tubes) produced beams of small particles that could be deflected (bent) by an electric field (figure 2.24). He found that these rays were beams of negatively charged particles, which were named **electrons**. Using a different type of discharge tube filled with a small amount of hydrogen, Thompson also discovered a positively charged particle, the **proton**. Then, in 1932, Chadwick discovered a neutral particle, the **neutron**, by bombarding metal targets with radiation from radioactive material.

Dalton had suggested that atoms were solid particles. But crucial experiments carried out in Rutherford's laboratory in 1909 showed that an atom is largely empty space. Thin gold foil was bombarded with α-particles (see page 57) emitted by radioactive material (figure 2.25).

Table 2.9 The relative atomic masses of some elements

Element	Atomic symbol	Relative atomic mass
Carbon	C	12
Hydrogen	H	1
Oxygen	O	16
Calcium	Ca	40
Copper	Cu	64
Gold	Au	197

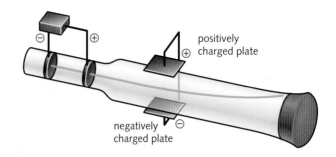

Figure 2.24 A cathode ray tube produces a beam of particles that are deflected towards a positive plate. The beam is made up of electrons.

The results of this experiment were staggering at the time. Most of the α-particles went straight through the gold foil without being deflected, and some were deflected by a small amount. But the most dramatic result was that a small number of α-particles were deflected *backwards*. α-particles have a positive charge so they must have been repelled by something dense and positively charged within the gold atoms. Rutherford calculated that an atom is mostly space occupied by the negatively charged electrons surrounding a very small, positively

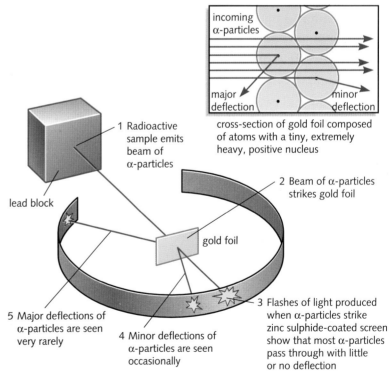

Figure 2.25 Summary of the bombardment experiment carried out by Geiger and Marsden in Rutherford's laboratory in Manchester, UK, in 1909.

charged **nucleus**. The nucleus is at the centre of the atom and contains almost all the mass of the atom. It is made up of the protons and neutrons.

To get some idea of *how* small the nucleus is in comparison to the rest of the atom, here is a simple comparison. If the atom were the size of a football stadium, the nucleus (at the centre-spot) would be the size of a pea!

When studied further, protons and neutrons were found to have almost the same mass. Electrons were found to have virtually no mass at all ($\frac{1}{1840}$th of the mass of a proton). The other important feature of these particles is their electric **charge**. Protons and electrons were found to have equal and opposite charges, while neutrons are electrically neutral (have no charge). The characteristics of these three sub-atomic particles are listed in table 2.10.

A single atom is electrically neutral (it has no overall electric charge). This means that in any atom there must be equal numbers of protons and electrons. In this way the total positive charge on the nucleus (due to the protons) is balanced by the total negative charge of the orbiting electrons. The simplest atom of all would have one proton in its nucleus. This is the hydrogen atom. It is the only atom that has no neutrons; it consists of one proton and one electron. Atoms of different elements are increasingly complex.

The next simplest atom is that of helium. This has two protons and two neutrons in the nucleus, and two orbiting electrons. The next, lithium, has three protons, four neutrons and three electrons. The arrangements in the following atoms get more complicated with the addition of more protons and electrons. The number of neutrons required to hold the nucleus together increases as the atomic size increases. Thus an atom of gold consists of 79 protons (p^+), 118 neutrons (n^0) and 79 electrons (e^-).

2.14 Atomic number and mass number

Only hydrogen atoms have one proton in their nuclei. Only helium atoms have two protons. Indeed, only gold atoms have 79 protons. This shows that the number of protons in the nucleus of an atom decides which element it is. This very important number is known as the **atomic number** (or proton number, given the symbol Z) of an atom.

Protons alone do not make up all of the mass of an atom. The neutrons in the nucleus also contribute to the total mass. The mass of the electrons can be regarded as so small that it can be ignored. As a proton and a neutron have the same mass, the mass of a particular atom depends on the total number of protons and neutrons present. This number is called the **mass number** (or nucleon number, given the symbol A) of an atom.

For **atomic number** and **mass number** we have:

- atomic number (Z) = number of protons in the nucleus,
- mass number (A) = number of protons + number of neutrons.

The atomic number Z and mass number A of an atom of an element can be written alongside the symbol for that element, in the general way as $^A_Z X$. So the symbol for an atom of lithium is $^7_3 Li$. The symbols for carbon, oxygen and uranium atoms are $^{12}_6 C$, $^{16}_8 O$ and $^{238}_{92} U$.

If these two important numbers for any atom are known, then its sub-atomic composition can be worked out.

These two relationships are useful:

- number of electrons = number of protons = atomic number,
- number of neutrons = mass number – atomic number = $A - Z$

Table 2.10 Properties of the sub-atomic particles

Sub-atomic particle	Relative mass	Relative charge	Location in atom
Proton	1	+1	in nucleus
Neutron	1	0	in nucleus
Electron	$\frac{1}{1840}$ (negligible)	−1	outside nucleus

Table 2.11 The sub-atomic composition and structure of certain atoms

Atom	Symbol	Atomic number Z	Mass number A	Inside the nucleus: Protons (Z)	Inside the nucleus: Neutrons $(A-Z)$	Outside the nucleus: Electrons (Z)
Hydrogen	H	1	1	1	0	1
Helium	He	2	4	2	2	2
Lithium	Li	3	7	3	4	3
Beryllium	Be	4	9	4	5	4
Carbon	C	6	12	6	6	6
Oxygen	O	8	16	8	8	8
Sodium	Na	11	23	11	12	11
Calcium	Ca	20	40	20	20	20
Gold	Au	79	197	79	118	79
Uranium	U	92	238	92	146	92

Table 2.11 shows the numbers of protons, neutrons and electrons in some different atoms. Note that the rules apply even to the largest, most complicated atom found naturally in substantial amounts.

2.15 Isotopes

Measurements of the atomic masses of some elements using the mass spectrometer were puzzling. Pure samples of elements such as carbon, chlorine and many others were found to contain atoms with different masses even though they contained the same numbers of protons and electrons. The different masses were caused by different numbers of neutrons in their nuclei. Such atoms are called **isotopes**.

- **Isotopes** are atoms of the same element with different mass numbers.
- They have the *same* number of protons and electrons in each atom, but *different* numbers of neutrons in the nucleus.

The isotopes of an element have the same chemical properties because they contain the same number of electrons. It is the number of electrons in an atom that decides the way in which it forms bonds and reacts with other atoms. However, some physical properties of the isotopes *are* different. The masses of the atoms differ, and therefore other properties, such as density and rate of diffusion, also vary. The modern mass spectrometer (figure 2.26 on page 56) shows that most elements have several different isotopes that occur naturally. Others, such as tritium – an isotope of hydrogen (table 2.12 on page 56) – can be made artificially. Tritium and carbon-14 illustrate another difference in physical properties that can occur between isotopes as they are **radioactive**. The extra neutrons in their nuclei cause them to be unstable so the nuclei break up spontaneously (that is, without any external energy being supplied), emitting certain types of radiation. They are know as **radio-isotopes**.

- **Isotopes** of an element have the same chemical properties. They differ in a few physical properties such as density.
- Some isotopes have unstable nuclei; they are radio-isotopes and emit various forms of radiation.

2.16 Relative atomic masses

Most elements exist naturally as a mixture of isotopes. Therefore, the value we use for the atomic mass of an element is an average mass. This takes into account the proportions (abundance) of all the naturally occurring isotopes. If a particular isotope is present in high proportion, it will make a large contribution to the average. This average value for

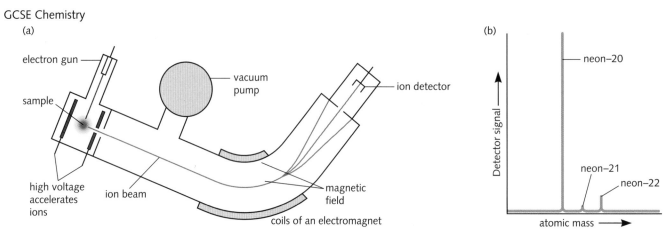

Figure 2.26 *(a) Diagram of a mass spectrometer. The atoms of the element are changed into positive ions (see page 73). The beam of positive ions is accelerated by an electric field, and then bent by a magnetic field. The amount of deflection depends on the mass of the ions. The lighter ions are deflected most and measured first. (b) A mass spectrometer trace (a mass spectrum) showing the isotopes of neon.*

the mass of an atom of an element is known as the **relative atomic mass** (A_r).

> The **relative atomic mass** (A_r) is the average mass of an atom of an element, taking account of its natural isotopes and their percentage abundance.

Because there are several isotopes of carbon, the standard against which all atomic masses are measured has to be defined precisely. The isotope carbon-12 is used as the standard. One atom of carbon-12 is given the mass of 12 precisely. From this we get 1 atomic mass unit (a.m.u.) = $\frac{1}{12} \times$ mass of one atom of carbon-12.

Table 2.12 Several elements that exist as mixtures of isotopes

Hydrogen	hydrogen (99.99%)	deuterium (0.01%)	tritium*
	$_1^1\text{H}$	$_1^2\text{H}$	$_1^3\text{H}$
	1 proton	1 proton	1 proton
	0 neutrons	1 neutron	2 neutrons
	1 electron	1 electron	1 electron
Carbon	carbon-12 (98.9%)	carbon-13 (1.1%)	carbon-14* (trace)
	$_6^{12}\text{C}$	$_6^{13}\text{C}$	$_6^{14}\text{C}$
	6 protons	6 protons	6 protons
	6 neutrons	7 neutrons	8 neutrons
	6 electrons	6 electrons	6 electrons
Neon	neon-20 (90.5%)	neon-21 (0.3%)	neon-22 (9.2%)
	$_{10}^{20}\text{Ne}$	$_{10}^{21}\text{Ne}$	$_{10}^{22}\text{Ne}$
	10 protons	10 protons	10 protons
	10 neutrons	11 neutrons	12 neutrons
	10 electrons	10 electrons	10 electrons
Chlorine	chlorine-35 (75%)	chlorine-37 (25%)	
	$_{17}^{35}\text{Cl}$	$_{17}^{37}\text{Cl}$	
	17 protons	17 protons	
	18 neutrons	20 neutrons	
	17 electrons	17 electrons	

*Tritium and carbon-14 atoms are radioactive isotopes because their nuclei are unstable.

The existence of isotopes also explains why most relative atomic masses are not whole numbers. But, to make calculation easier, in this book they are rounded to the nearest whole number. There is one exception, chlorine, where this would be misleading. Chlorine contains two isotopes, chlorine-35 and chlorine-37, in a ratio of 3:1 (or 75%:25%). If the mixture were 50%:50%, then the relative atomic mass of chlorine would be 36. The fact that the lighter isotope predominates moves the value lower than 36. The actual value is 35.5. The relative atomic mass of chlorine can be calculated by finding the total mass of 100 atoms:

$$\text{mass of 100 atoms} = (35 \times 75) + (37 \times 25)$$
$$= 3550$$

Then,

$$\text{average mass of 1 atom} = \frac{3550}{100} = 35.5$$

Thus, for chlorine:

$$A_r(\text{Cl}) = 35.5$$

2.17 Radioactivity

The decay of unstable radio-isotopes

Some elements have unstable isotopes, such as tritium and carbon-14. The extra neutrons in their nuclei cause them to disintegrate or **decay** spontaneously. This is known as **nuclear fission**. The result of these disintegrations is the release of heat energy and various forms of radioactive radiation. The heat produced by the decay of radioactive material deep in the Earth keeps the outer core molten. It provides the energy for all volcanic activity and produces the convection currents in the mantle that power continental drift.

There are three types of **radioactivity**:

- alpha radiation (α-radiation),
- beta radiation (β-radiation), and
- gamma radiation (γ-radiation).

Each radioactive isotope decays at its own rate. It is a completely random process and is unaffected by temperature or whether the isotope is part of a compound or present as the free element.

Radioactive decay is a **nuclear process** and not a chemical reaction. The type of radioactivity emitted depends on the radio-isotope involved. Radioactive isotopes with atomic numbers below 83 usually emit β-**radiation** when they decay. Isotopes with atomic numbers higher than 83 usually emit α-**radiation**. Studies on the nature of α- and β-radiation have shown that they are *particles* 'thrown out' or ejected from the unstable nuclei. In contrast, γ-radiation is a form of high-energy *electromagnetic radiation*. It is not emitted on its own, only in addition to α- or β-radiation. The different types of radiation behave differently in electric and magnetic fields (figure 2.27). These differences helped scientists to show what the different types of radiation were made of (table 2.13 on page 58).

Penetrating power

The three types of radioactive emission vary in their ability to pass through materials. This has important consequences for handling radioactive substances safely. These differences in **penetrating power** are summarised in table 2.13 on page 58.

All these forms of radioactive emission can affect the atoms or molecules of any material they pass through. The radiations knock electrons out of atoms to produce positive ions and so are sometimes called **ionising radiations**. Ionising radiations are dangerous to life because they affect the atoms and molecules in living cells. If they affect the DNA molecule in a cell (which controls all the processes for life) the cell can die or become cancerous, growing out of control.

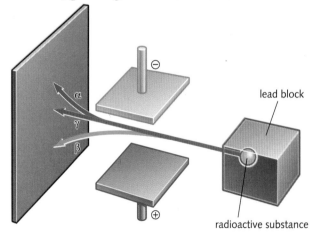

Figure 2.27 The effect of an electric field on the different radioactive emissions.

Table 2.13 Comparison of the different types of radioactive emission

Radiation	Isotopes involved	Nature	Distance travelled in air	Penetration of:		
				paper	thin aluminium	thick lead
Alpha (α)	atomic number usually >83	α-particles (helium nuclei – positive charge)	a few centimetres	no	no	no
Beta (β)	atomic number usually ≤83	β-particles (electrons – negative charge)	a few metres	yes	no	no
Gamma (γ)	only occurs with one of the other forms of radiation	electromagnetic waves	many kilometres	yes	yes	no

Gamma radiation requires thick lead and/or concrete shields to stop it. It can penetrate skin and bone and can cause burns and cancer. Beta radiation can also pass through the skin and cause illness and changes in a cell's DNA. Alpha radiation cannot pass through the skin and is, therefore, less dangerous. However, α-emitting substances can damage the skin and can cause serious damage if swallowed or breathed. This is because α-particles are strongly ionising over short distances.

2.18 The uses of radioactivity

Radioactive dating

Each radioactive isotope decays at its own rate. However, the time taken for the radioactivity in a sample to halve is constant for a particular radio-isotope. This time is called the **half-life**. Some isotopes have very short half-lives of only seconds: for example oxygen-14 has a half-life of 71 s. Other half-lives are quite long: for example carbon-14 has a half-life of 5730 years.

One important use of half-life values is in radioactive dating. **Radiocarbon dating** (which uses carbon-14) can be used to date wooden and organic objects. The decay of other elements can be tracked to give estimates of the age of rocks. The oldest rock so far dated was found in northern Canada and is 3.96 billion years old. Radioactive dating of meteorites and of rocks from the Moon suggests that all the Solar System was formed at the same time – about 4.6 billion years ago.

Industrial uses of radio-isotopes

Despite the need to handle them with strict safety precautions, radioactive isotopes are widely used in industry and medicine. Their ease of detection gives rise to several of their uses, and in medicine some of their most dangerous properties can be turned to advantage.

Industrial uses of radio-isotopes include using γ- and β-radiation to monitor the level of filling in containers, to check the thickness of sheets of plastic, paper, or metal foil (for example aluminium baking foil) during continuous production, and to detect leaks in gas or oil pipes (figure 2.28). Radioactive tracing can be used to check the effectiveness of an oil in stopping engine wear. This wear results in the release of microscopic metal shavings into the lubricating oil. The pistons of the engine are irradiated, making some of the metal atoms radioactive. After the engine has been run, the oil is checked for the presence of radioactivity. The lower the radioactivity, the more effective the lubricating oil has been in reducing wear.

Medical and food safety uses of radio-isotopes

Several medical uses of radiation depend on the fact that biological cells are sensitive to radioactive emissions. Cells that are growing and dividing are particularly likely to be damaged. Cancer cells are cells that are growing out of control so they are more easily killed by radiation than are healthy cells. Penetrating γ-radiation from the radio-isotope cobalt-60 is used to treat internal cancer tumours. Skin cancer tumours can be treated with

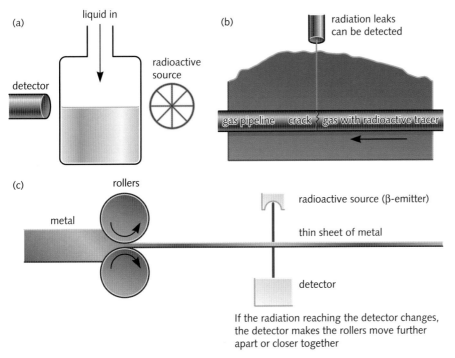

Figure 2.28 Uses of radioactivity: (a) detecting the level of liquid in a container; (b) detecting leaks in underground pipes; and (c) controlling the thickness of metal sheets.

can tell whether the thyroid is functioning properly.

Food treatment is another area where γ-radiation is used to kill bacteria and other micro-organisms such as moulds and yeasts. The presence of these micro-organisms causes food spoilage. Some bacteria also produce waste products that can be toxic and result in food-poisoning. Other bacteria, such as *Salmonella* and *Clostridium*, are disease-carrying. All these micro-organisms can be successfully killed using appropriate doses of γ-radiation. In a wide range of cases, the treatment results in no damage to the food itself.

less-penetrating β-particles. This is done by strapping sheets containing phosphorus-32 or strontium-90 to the affected area of the skin.

Bacterial cells grow and divide rapidly. They are particularly sensitive to radiation. Medical instruments, dressings and syringes can be sterilised by sealing them in polythene bags and exposing them to intense doses of γ-radiation. This has proved a very effective method of killing any bacteria on them.

Remember that the chemical properties of a radio-isotope are no different to those of the stable isotopes of the same element. This means that we can make molecules which are found in living tissue using a radio-isotope and follow how those molecules are used normally in the body. Tritium and carbon-14 are commonly used instead of hydrogen and carbon-12 to **label** biological molecules. For example, this method played a crucial part in working out how DNA is exactly copied when a cell divides. Another example is radioactive iodine-131 which can be used to check that a person's thyroid gland is working properly. The thyroid uses iodine and patients are given a very small dose of iodine-131. By measuring how much radioactive iodine is taken up by the gland, doctors

So, despite the strict safety precautions necessary, we have found a wide range of uses for radioactive isotopes. In addition to these uses, the study of radioactivity has provided some of the major breakthroughs in our understanding of atomic structure.

2.19 Electron arrangements in atoms

Radioactivity is a property of the nucleus and its study led to a greater understanding of the atom. But what of the 'orbiting' electrons? In a complex atom, how are these particles arranged? What are the consequences of that arrangement for the properties of the atom?

Radioactive emissions are described as **ionising radiations**. They are capable of ripping electrons away from atoms to form positively charged particles known as **positive ions**. High in the upper atmosphere (above 80 km), radiation from the Sun produces a similar effect. The result can be seen at certain times of the year in both the Northern and Southern Hemispheres as the spectacular coloured lights of the Aurora Borealis or Aurora Australis. These occur when streams of electrically charged particles, formed from the Sun as the 'solar wind', ionise the gases of the upper atmosphere. These effects can be reproduced in the laboratory, using less energy, and they can give clues to the organisation of electrons in atoms as described below.

Flame tests, neon lights and atomic spectra

If a clean nichrome wire is dipped into a metal compound and then held in the hot part of a Bunsen flame, the flame can become coloured. This is the basis of the **flame test** for certain metal ions (see chapter 9). It is also the source of the different colours produced by fireworks. Sodium compounds colour a Bunsen flame yellow. The yellow sodium street lights produce their colour when electricity is passed through sodium vapour. Atoms of non-metals such as neon also emit light under similar circumstances. The neon lights of advertising signs are the product of 'dancing' electrons in energised atoms.

A closer look at the light given out by gases gives us clues on the organisation of electrons in atoms. The light is analysed by passing it through a prism to produce a spectrum. The simplest spectrum is that of hydrogen, the simplest atom (figure 2.29). Scientists such as Niels Bohr were able to show that electrons exist in different **orbits** in an atom. These orbits are arranged in **shells** at different distances from the nucleus of the atom. The lowest energy shell lies closest to the nucleus, with higher energy shells further out from the centre of the atom. The light emitted by an energised hydrogen atom comes from an electron moving out to a higher energy shell than normal. This is an unstable situation. The 'excited' electron then falls back to a lower shell, giving out its extra energy as light (figure 2.30). Different changes in electron position produce light with different energy and wavelength (and therefore different coloured lines). Hydrogen produces the simplest spectrum because there is only one electron in each atom.

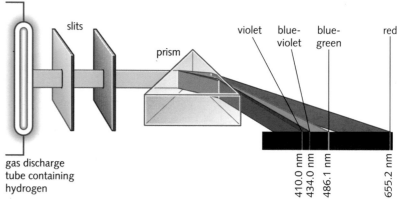

Figure 2.29 Excited hydrogen atoms produce a particular spectrum of light.

Electrons in orbit

From measurements of the wavelengths of the lines of light in the hydrogen spectrum Niels Bohr was able to calculate the **energy levels** of the electron shells in the hydrogen atom. Bohr showed that the organisation of other atoms is similar. His theory on the arrangement of electrons in the different shells in an atom is summarised opposite.

There is further evidence that the electrons in atoms are arranged in this way. This is obtained by measuring the amount of energy needed to remove electrons from them. There are 11 electrons in a sodium atom, for example. The amount of energy needed to remove the electrons from a sodium atom one by one have been measured. The first electron can be removed quite easily, suggesting that it is in the outer shell. The next eight are more difficult to remove. The final two electrons are very

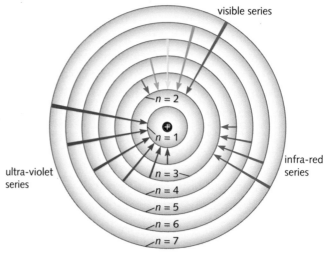

Figure 2.30 The spectra produced by energised atoms are caused by excited electrons falling back to lower energy levels in the atom. Lines are produced in the infra-red and ultra-violet as well as the visible region.

Bohr's theory on the arrangement of electrons in an atom can be summarised as follows.

- Electrons are in orbit around the central nucleus of the atom.
- The electron orbits are grouped together in shells; a shell is a group of orbits with similar energy.
- The shells distant from the nucleus have higher energy than those close to the nucleus.
- Electrons fill the shells starting with the first shell, which is the closest to the nucleus.

- Each shell can only hold a certain number of electrons (this maximum number is $2n^2$, where n is the number of the shell from the nucleus).
- The first shell can only contain up to 2 electrons. The second shell can contain a maximum of 8 electrons. The third shell can contain up to 18 electrons; but for small atoms (those with up to 20 electrons altogether) the third shell will not hold more than 8.
- The outer electrons of some atoms can be removed fairly easily to form ions.
- Chemical bonding between atoms to form molecules involves the electrons in the outer shell only.

strongly held by the nucleus in the inner shell. This analysis confirms the organisation of the electrons in a sodium atom into three shells, with the arrangement 2,8,1. (This means that there are two electrons in the first shell, eight electrons in the second shell, and one electron in the third shell.)

The number and arrangement of the electrons in the atoms of the first 20 elements are shown in table 2.14.

Table 2.14 The electron arrangements of the first 20 elements

Element	Symbol	Atomic number, Z	First shell	Second shell	Third shell	Fourth shell	Electron configuration
Hydrogen	H	1	●				1
Helium	He	2	●●				2
Lithium	Li	3	●●	●			2,1
Beryllium	Be	4	●●	●●			2,2
Boron	B	5	●●	●●●			2,3
Carbon	C	6	●●	●●●●			2,4
Nitrogen	N	7	●●	●●●●●			2,5
Oxygen	O	8	●●	●●●●●●			2,6
Fluorine	F	9	●●	●●●●●●●			2,7
Neon	Ne	10	●●	●●●●●●●●			2,8
Sodium	Na	11	●●	●●●●●●●●	●		2,8,1
Magnesium	Mg	12	●●	●●●●●●●●	●●		2,8,2
Aluminium	Al	13	●●	●●●●●●●●	●●●		2,8,3
Silicon	Si	14	●●	●●●●●●●●	●●●●		2,8,4
Phosphorus	P	15	●●	●●●●●●●●	●●●●●		2,8,5
Sulphur	S	16	●●	●●●●●●●●	●●●●●●		2,8,6
Chlorine	Cl	17	●●	●●●●●●●●	●●●●●●●		2,8,7
Argon	Ar	18	●●	●●●●●●●●	●●●●●●●●		2,8,8
Potassium	K	19	●●	●●●●●●●●	●●●●●●●●	●	2,8,8,1
Calcium	Ca	20	●●	●●●●●●●●	●●●●●●●●	●●	2,8,8,2

After the first 20 elements, the organisation of the electrons becomes increasingly complicated. The third shell ($n = 3$) can be occupied by a maximum of 18 electrons ($2n^2 = 2 \times 3^2 = 18$). However, a temporary stable state exists when there are eight electrons in this shell. The next two electrons go into the fourth shell before the third is then completely filled. At this stage you will not be asked to work out electron arrangements beyond element 20 (calcium), but you should be able to understand structures involving more electrons (for example bromine with the arrangement 2,8,18,7).

When the two essential numbers describing a particular atom are known, that is the numbers of protons and neutrons, a sub-atomic picture can be drawn. Figure 2.31 shows such a picture for perhaps the most versatile atom in the Universe, an atom of carbon-12. Studying the organisation of the electrons of an atom is valuable. It begins to explain the patterns in properties of the elements that are the basis of the Periodic Table. This will be discussed in the next chapter.

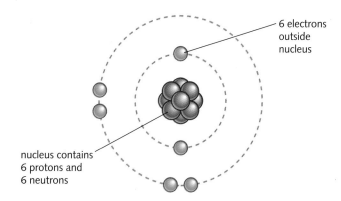

6 electrons outside nucleus

nucleus contains 6 protons and 6 neutrons

Figure 2.31 Possibly the most versatile atom in the Universe – the carbon-12 atom.

Summary of core material

You should know that:

- the atoms of the elements are made up of different combinations of the sub-atomic particles – protons, neutrons and electrons
- each element is made from atoms that contain a characteristic number of protons and electrons
- the number of protons and electrons in any atom is always the same, and defined by the atomic number (Z) of the element

- in any atom the protons and neutrons are bound together in a central nucleus; the electrons 'orbit' the nucleus in different shells (or energy levels)
- the mass of an electron is negligible compared to that of a proton or neutron, which have approximately equal mass
- the mass number (nucleon number, A) defines the total number of protons and neutrons in any atom
- isotopes of the same element can exist that differ only in the number of neutrons in their nuclei
- some isotopes of many elements have unstable nuclei and this makes them radioactive
- there are three types of ionising radiation emitted by radio-isotopes – α, β and γ
- these different types of radiation have different properties
- the different forms of radiation from radio-isotopes have scientific, industrial, medical and food safety uses
- the electrons in atoms are arranged in an organised way in different shells
- these electron shells have different energies and are at different distances from the nucleus of the atom
- electrons are placed in the shells closest to the nucleus first, and each shell has a maximum number of electrons that it can contain
- the electron arrangement of an atom – particularly the number of outer electrons – plays an important part in deciding the chemistry of the element.

2.13 Here is the symbol for a nitrogen atom: $^{14}_{7}N$

(a) What is the name given to the number of protons in the nucleus of an atom? [1]

(b) What is the name given to the number of protons plus the number of neutrons in the nucleus of an atom? [1]

(c) In the nitrogen atom shown above, calculate how many protons, neutrons and electrons there are in the nucleus of one atom. [3]

(NEAB, 1995)

2.14 Uranium-238 is a radio-isotope found in the Earth. It has a proton (atomic) number of 92 and a mass number of 238.

(a) Give the number of protons, neutrons and electrons in an atom of uranium-238. [3]

(b) Uranium-238 atoms split up to give a different element. This has a proton (atomic) number of 90 and a mass number of 234. What is the symbol for this new element? (Use the Periodic Table on page 65 to help you.) [1]

(c) Why do uranium-238 atoms split up? [2]

(NEAB, 1995)

2.15 The table gives some information about radiation from radioactive substances.

Type of radiation	Percentage of radiation which can pass through different materials		
	Paper	Aluminium sheet	Lead sheet
Alpha	0	0	0
Beta	80	20	5
Gamma	98	70	20

The element americium exists as different isotopes. Americium-241 emits mainly alpha radiation, and is used in smoke alarms. The alarm only sounds when smoke stops the alpha radiation reaching a detector in the alarm.

(a) What are isotopes? [2]

(b) Suggest why it is not hazardous to use the radioactive isotope americium-241 in a smoke detector. [2]

(c) Suggest *two* reasons why the radioactive isotope cobalt-60, which emits gamma radiation, is not used in a smoke detector. [2]

(MEG, 1995)

2.16 In 1986, an explosion at Chernobyl in Russia released a radioactive cloud. The main radioactive isotopes released were:

Element	Nucleon (mass) number
Strontium	90
Iodine	131
Caesium	137

Use the Periodic Table (there is one in figure 3.1 on page 65) to answer the following questions.

(a) (i) How many electrons are there in one atom of strontium-90? [1]
    (ii) How many protons are there in one atom of iodine-131? [1]
    (iii) How many neutrons are there in an atom of caesium-137? [1]

(b) The air around Chernobyl became polluted. What is a pollutant? [2]

(c) In Sweden, caesium-137 built up in small plants called lichen. These plants were eaten by reindeer and gave rise to radioactive meat.
    (i) If radioactive caesium was reacted with chlorine, would you expect the caesium chloride produced to be radioactive? Explain your answer. [2]
    (ii) State a beneficial use in industry of a radioactive isotope. [1]
    (iii) State a medical use of a radioactive isotope. [1]

(IGCSE, part question, 1992)

2.17 Which *one* of the following pairs represents two atoms with the same number of neutrons?

A $^{12}_{6}C$ and $^{24}_{12}Mg$ B $^{19}_{9}F$ and $^{20}_{10}Ne$

C $^{23}_{11}Na$ and $^{39}_{19}K$ D $^{59}_{27}Co$ and $^{59}_{28}Ni$ [1]

(NEAB, 1993)

2.18 Many power stations convert heat to electrical energy. In a nuclear power station the heat comes from the fission of uranium.

(a) Copy and complete the table by correctly adding the missing information for the uranium-238 isotope. [2]

Isotope	Symbol	Number of protons	Number of neutrons	Number of electrons
Uranium-235	$^{235}_{92}U$	92	143	92
Uranium-238		92		92

(b) The control rods in a nuclear reactor often contain boron. Natural boron contains about 20% boron-10 ($^{10}_{5}B$) and 80% boron-11 ($^{11}_{5}B$).
    (i) Give the electronic structure of a boron atom. [1]
    (ii) Explain why the relative atomic mass of boron is 10.8. [3]

(SEG, part question, 1988)

3 Elements and compounds

Classifying the elements

This section covers the following ideas:

- the Periodic Table, its historical development and its present form
- the division of the elements into metals and non-metals
- the arrangement of the elements into groups and periods
- the relationship of electron arrangement to position in the Periodic Table
- patterns and organisation of the Periodic Table
- the properties of certain groups in the Periodic Table
- the position of hydrogen in the Periodic Table.

3.1 The Periodic Table

Building up the modern **Periodic Table** has been a major scientific achievement! The first steps towards working out this table were taken long before anyone had any ideas about the structure of atoms. The number of elements discovered increased steadily during the nineteenth century. Chemists began to find patterns in their properties. Dobereiner, Newlands and Meyer all described groupings of elements with similar chemical and physical characteristics. But, although they were partly successful, these groupings were limited or flawed. The breakthrough came in 1869 when Mendeleev put forward his ideas of a periodic table. In his first attempt he used 32 of the 61 elements known at that time.

He drew up his table based on atomic masses, as others had done before him. But his success was mainly due to his leaving *gaps* for possible elements still to be discovered. He did not try to force the elements into patterns for which there was no evidence.

Mendeleev's great success lay in *predicting* the properties of elements that had not yet been discovered. He predicted the discovery of ten elements. He then put forward detailed ideas on the particular properties of four of these elements. Remarkably, when the elements gallium and germanium were discovered, their properties were very similar to his predictions. Table 3.1 shows the predicted and actual properties of gallium – the metal that melts in your hand! In Mendeleev's periodic table, there was a space for this element below aluminium. He called the missing, unknown, element eka-aluminium.

This success convinced chemists that there were repetitive patterns to the characteristics of the elements. All modern versions of the Periodic Table are based on the one put forward by Mendeleev. An example is given in figure 3.1. To make our calculations easier, in this book the relative atomic masses are rounded to the nearest whole number. There is one exception, chlorine, where this would be misleading as discussed in section 2.16.

In the **Periodic Table**:

- the elements are arranged in order of increasing atomic number,
- the vertical columns of elements with similar properties are called **groups**,
- the horizontal rows are called **periods**.

Table 3.1 The predicted and actual properties of gallium

Property	Eka-aluminium (predicted)	Gallium (actual)
Atomic mass	about 68	70
Density (g/cm^3)	5.9	5.94
Melting point (°C)	low	30.2
Formula of chloride	EaCl$_3$	GaCl$_3$
Formula of oxide	Ea$_2$O$_3$	Ga$_2$O$_3$
	oxide would be amphoteric*	oxide is amphoteric*

* This term is explained in section 5.25.

Key:
$$\boxed{\begin{array}{c} a \\ X \\ \text{Name} \\ b \end{array}}$$ a = relative atomic mass
X = symbol
b = atomic number

	Group I	Group II												Group III	Group IV	Group V	Group VI	Group VII	Group 0
Period 1								1 H Hydrogen 1											4 He Helium 2
Period 2	7 Li Lithium 3	9 Be Beryllium 4												11 B Boron 5	12 C Carbon 6	14 N Nitrogen 7	16 O Oxygen 8	19 F Fluorine 9	20 Ne Neon 10
Period 3	23 Na Sodium 11	24 Mg Magnesium 12												27 Al Aluminium 13	28 Si Silicon 14	31 P Phosphorus 15	32 S Sulphur 16	35.5 Cl Chlorine 17	40 Ar Argon 18
Period 4	39 K Potassium 19	40 Ca Calcium 20	45 Sc Scandium 21	48 Ti Titanium 22	51 V Vanadium 23	52 Cr Chromium 24	55 Mn Manganese 25	56 Fe Iron 26	59 Co Cobalt 27	59 Ni Nickel 28	64 Cu Copper 29	65 Zn Zinc 30		70 Ga Gallium 31	73 Ge Germanium 32	75 As Arsenic 33	79 Se Selenium 34	80 Br Bromine 35	84 Kr Krypton 36
Period 5	86 Rb Rubidium 37	88 Sr Strontium 38	89 Y Yttrium 39	91 Zr Zirconium 40	93 Nb Niobium 41	96 Mo Molybdenum 42	– Tc Technetium 43	101 Ru Ruthenium 44	103 Rh Rhodium 45	106 Pd Palladium 46	108 Ag Silver 47	112 Cd Cadmium 48		115 In Indium 49	119 Sn Tin 50	122 Sb Antimony 51	128 Te Tellurium 52	127 I Iodine 53	131 Xe Xenon 54
Period 6	133 Cs Caesium 55	137 Ba Barium 56	La to Lu	178 Hf Hafnium 72	181 Ta Tantalum 73	184 W Tungsten 74	186 Re Rhenium 75	190 Os Osmium 76	192 Ir Iridium 77	195 Pt Platinum 78	197 Au Gold 79	201 Hg Mercury 80		204 Tl Thallium 81	207 Pb Lead 82	209 Bi Bismuth 83	– Po Polonium 84	– At Astatine 85	Rn Radon 86
Period 7	Fr Francium 87	Ra Radium 88	Ac to Lr																

139 La Lanthanum 57	140 Ce Cerium 58	141 Pr Praseodymium 59	144 Nd Neodymium 60	– Pm Promethium 61	150 Sm Samarium 62	152 Eu Europium 63	157 Gd Gadolinium 64	159 Tb Terbium 65	163 Dy Dysprosium 66	165 Ho Holmium 67	167 Er Erbium 68	169 Tm Thulium 69	173 Yb Ytterbium 70	175 Lu Lutetium 71
– Ac Actinium 89	– Th Thorium 90	– Pa Protactinium 91	– U Uranium 92	– Np Neptunium 93	– Pu Plutonium 94	– Am Americium 95	– Cm Curium 96	– Bk Berkelium 97	– Cf Californium 98	– Es Einsteinium 99	– Fm Fermium 100	– Md Mendelevium 101	– No Nobelium 102	– Lr Lawrencium 103

Elements in Groups I to 0 are sometimes known as the **main-group elements**

☐ The **reactive metals**: Group I – the alkali metals; Group II – the alkaline earth metals

☐ The **transition elements**: hard, strong and dense metals

☐ The '**poor**' metals

☐ The **metalloids**: includes semiconductors, e.g. silicon and germanium

☐ The **non-metals**: includes Group VII – the halogens

☐ The **noble gases**: very unreactive

Figure 3.1 The Periodic Table, showing the major regions. (Except for chlorine, the relative atomic masses are given to the nearest whole number.)

The broadest distinction in the table is between **metals** and **non-metals**. Metals are clearly separated from non-metals. The non-metals are grouped into the top right-hand region of the table, above the thick stepped line in figure 3.1. One first use of the Periodic Table now becomes clear. Although we may never have seen a sample of the element hafnium (Hf), we know from a glance at the table that it is a metal. We may also be able to predict some of its properties.

3.2 Metals and non-metals

There are 94 naturally occurring elements. Some are very rare. Francium, for instance, has never been seen. The radioactive metals neptunium and plutonium, which we make artifically in quite large amounts, only occur in very small (trace) quantities naturally. Most of the elements (70) can be classified as metals. Together they form a group of elements whose structures are held together by a particular type of bonding between the atoms. The metals have a number of physical properties that are broadly the same for all of them (table 3.2 on page 66).

The chemical properties of metals and non-metals are also very different, as is the type of bonding present in their compounds. The distinction is therefore a very important one.

The Periodic Table does not list substances such as steel, bronze and brass, which in everyday terms we call metals and which share the properties listed for metals. They are *not* elements! They are in fact **alloys**, mixtures of elements (usually metals) designed to have properties that are useful for a particular purpose. Alloys are discussed in more detail in section 3.17 on page 90.

Non-metals are a less uniform group of elements. They show a much wider range of properties. This reflects the wider differences in the types of structure shown by non-metals.

Table 3.2 Comparison of the physical properties of metals and non-metals

Metals	Non-metals
They are usually *solids* (except for mercury, which is a liquid) at room temperature. Their melting and boiling points are usually high.	They are *solids* or *gases* (except for bromine, which is a liquid) at room temperature. Their melting and boiling points are often low.
They are usually hard and dense.	Most non-metals are softer than metals (but diamond is very hard). Their densities are often low.
All metals are good conductors of electricity*.	They are poor conductors of electricity (except graphite, a form of carbon); they tend to be insulators.
They are good conductors of heat.	They are poor thermal conductors.
Their shape can be changed by hammering (they are *malleable*). They can also be pulled out into wires (they are *ductile*).	Most non-metals are brittle when solid.
They are grey in colour (except gold and copper). They can be polished.	They vary in colour. They often have a dull surface when solid.
They make a ringing sound when struck (they are *sonorous*).	They are not sonorous.

*Electrical conductivity is usually taken as the simplest test of whether a substance is metallic or not.

- A **metal** is an element that conducts electricity and is malleable and ductile.
- A **non-metal** is an element that does not conduct electricity well and is neither malleable nor ductile.

The change from metallic to non-metallic properties in the elements is not as clear-cut as suggested by drawing the line between the two regions of the Periodic Table. The elements close to the line show properties that lie between these extremes. These elements are now often referred to as **metalloids** (or **semi-metals**). Such elements have some of the properties of metals and others that are more characteristic of non-metals. There are eight elements which are called metalloids (see figure 3.1). They often look like metals, but are brittle like non-metals. They are neither conductors nor insulators, but make excellent semiconductors.

3.3 Groups and periods in the Periodic Table

The Periodic Table allows us to make even more useful subdivisions of elements than simply deciding which are metals and non-metals. The elements present in Groups I to 0 of the table are sometimes known as the **main-group elements**.

These vertical groups show most clearly how elements within the same group have similar chemical and physical properties. Some of these groups have particular names as well as numbers. These are given in figure 3.1; Group VII elements are known as the **halogens**, for example.

Between Groups II and III of these main groups of elements are a block of metals known as the **transition elements** (or **transition metals**). The first row of these elements occurs in Period 4. This row includes such important metals as iron, copper and zinc.

The noble gases, in Group 0 on the right-hand side of the table, are the least reactive elements in the table. However, the group next to them, Group VII which are also known as the halogens, and the group on the left-hand side of the table, Group I or the alkali metals, are the most reactive elements. The more unreactive elements, whether metals or non-metals, are in the centre of the table.

3.4 Electron arrangement and the Periodic Table

When the first attempts were made to construct a Periodic Table, nobody knew about the structure of the atom. We can now directly link the properties of an element with its position in the

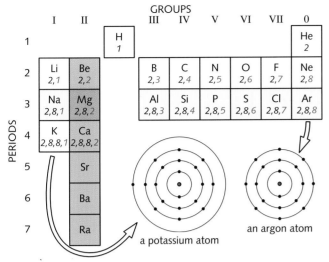

Figure 3.2 *There is a relationship between electron arrangement and position in the Periodic Table for the main group elements. The elements in* Group II *have two outer electrons. The elements in* Period 3 *have three shells of electrons. A magnesium atom has two electrons in its third, outer, shell, and is in Group II. An argon atom has an outer shell containing eight electrons – a very stable arrangement – and is in Group 0. A potassium atom has one electron in its outer shell, and is in Group I and Period 4.*

table and its electron arrangement (figure 3.2). The number of outer electrons in the atoms of each element has been found. Elements in the same Group have the same number of outer electrons. We also know that, as you move across a period in the table, a shell of electrons is being filled.

It is the outer electrons of an atom that are mainly responsible for the chemical properties of any element. Therefore, elements in the same group will have similar properties.

The **electron arrangements** of atoms are linked to position in the Periodic Table.

- Elements in the same group have the same number of electrons in their outer shell.
- For the main-group elements, the number of the group is the number of electrons in the outer shell.
- The periods also have numbers. This number shows us how many shells of electrons the atom has.

Certain electron arrangements are found to be more **stable** than others. This makes them more difficult to break up. The most stable arrangements are those of the **noble gases**, and this fits with the fact that they are so unreactive.

3.5 Patterns in the Periodic Table

There are links between the organisation of particles in the atom and the regular variation in properties of the elements in the Periodic Table. This means that we can see certain broad trends in the table (figure 3.3). These trends become most obvious if we leave aside the noble gases in Group 0.

The Periodic Table shows **patterns**:

- atomic size increases going down a group, but decreases across a period,
- elements become more metallic as we go down a group and to the left of a period,
- in the metallic groups, reactivity increases down a group,
- the most reactive metal is at the bottom of Group I,
- non-metals are found at the right of a period,
- in a group of non-metals, the most reactive element is at the top of a group,
- the most reactive non-metal is at the top of Group VII.

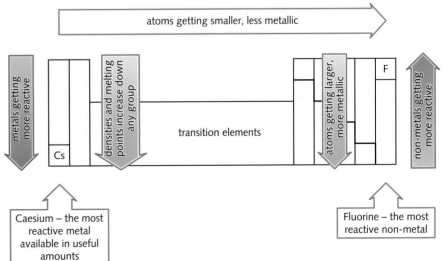

Figure 3.3 *General trends in the Periodic Table, leaving aside the noble gases in Group 0.*

The link between an element's position in the Periodic Table and the electron arrangement in its atoms helps to explain the trends we see. Individual groups show certain 'family characteristics'. These properties can be assembled into family profiles for particular groups.

'Family profiles' for Groups I, VII and 0

The metals in Group I are often called the **alkali metals**. They are soft solids with relatively low melting points and low densities. They are highly reactive and are stored in oil to prevent them reacting with the oxygen and water vapour in the air. When freshly cut with a knife, all these metals have a light-grey, silvery surface, which quickly tarnishes (becomes dull). Reactivity increases as we go down the group, so you might predict that francium, at the bottom of Group I, would be the most reactive of all the metals. However, it is highly radioactive and very rare because it decays with a half-life of 5 minutes. It has been estimated that there are only 17 atoms of francium in existence on Earth at any one moment in time.

The most reactive non-metals are the **halogens** in Group VII of the table. In contrast with Group I, here reactivity decreases down the group. For example, fluorine is a dangerously reactive, pale yellow gas at room temperature. There is a steady increase in melting points and boiling points as we go down the group and the elements change from gases through to solids with increasing atomic number. Interestingly, the lowest element in this group is also a highly radioactive and rare element, astatine. The actual properties of astatine remain a mystery to us, but we could make a good guess at some of them.

When Mendeleev first constructed his table, part of his triumph was to predict the existence and properties of some undiscovered elements. However, there was no indication that a whole *group* of elements (Group 0) remained to be discovered! Because of their lack of reactivity, there was no clear sign of their existence. Also, no link between the Periodic Table and sub-atomic structure had yet been made, which would have predicted their existence. However, analysis of the gases in air led to the discovery of argon. There was no suitable place in the table for an individual element with argon's

properties. This pointed to the existence of an entirely new group! In the 1890s, helium, which had first been detected by spectroscopy of light from the Sun during an eclipse, and the other **noble gases** in the group (Group 0) were isolated. The radioactive gas, radon, was the last to be purified, in 1908. One man, William Ramsay, was involved in the isolation of all the elements in the group. He was awarded the Nobel Prize for this major contribution.

All the noble gases are present in the Earth's atmosphere. Together they make up about 1% of the total, though argon is the most common. These gases are particularly unreactive. They were sometimes referred to as the **inert gases**, meaning they did not react at all. However, since the 1960s some compounds of xenon and krypton have been made and their name was changed to the *noble gases*. The atoms of these elements do not combine with each other to form molecules or any other form of structure. Their melting points and boiling points are extremely low. Helium has the lowest melting point of any element, and cannot be solidified by cooling alone (pressure is needed also). All these properties point to the atoms of the noble gases being particularly stable.

Put more precisely:

- the electron arrangements of the atoms of the noble gases are very stable,
- in many situations where atoms of other elements bond or react chemically, they are trying to achieve that stable arrangement of electrons found in the noble gases.

The elements of Group 0 are a 'valley of stability' between the two most reactive groups of elements (Groups I and VII). Indeed, it is their closeness to this region of stable electron arrangements that makes the alkali metals and the halogens so reactive. They can fairly easily achieve a noble-gas electron structure. The Group VII elements *gain* or *share* electrons and the Group I elements *lose* electrons to reach a noble-gas electron arrangement.

3.6 Trends across a period

The vertical groups of elements show similar properties, but following a period across the table highlights the trend from metallic to non-metallic properties. This can be explored by looking across a period. The first period of the table contains just two elements, hydrogen and helium, both of which are distinctive in different ways. The final period in the table is as yet incomplete. Each of the five remaining periods of elements starts with a reactive alkali metal and finishes with an unreactive, non-metallic, noble gas. In Period 3 for example, from sodium to argon, there appears to be a gradual change in physical properties across the period. The change in properties seems to centre around silicon; elements before this behave as metals and after as non-metals (figure 3.4).

The changeover in properties is emphasised if we look at Group IV as well. As we go down this group, the change is from non-metal to metal. The metalloids, silicon and germanium, are in the centre of the group (figure 3.4). The trends in structure that we see would seem to be linked to the changes in atomic size. This in turn controls how easy it is for atoms to lose their outer electrons to make chemical bonds. This is more difficult in smaller atoms and shows how important the outer electrons are in deciding the properties of an element.

3.7 New elements and versions of the Periodic Table

Star Trek's Captain Kirk boldly moved into controversial realms of science fiction when the Starship *Enterprise* met an alien craft that was difficult to defeat. He claimed that the hull of the spaceship was made of an unknown element with unusual properties. However, the structure of the Periodic Table convinces us that such a discovery is just about impossible. The table progresses in the order of the atomic numbers (Z) of the elements, which must be whole numbers. There are no gaps and it seems that every stable element in the Universe has been discovered.

However, this may not be completely true. Over the past 30 years scientists (mainly in America, Germany and Russia) have been able to create artificial elements that are extremely heavy. The heaviest atom made so far has an atomic number of 112. These heavy elements are extremely unstable and highly radioactive. They are made in particle accelerators by collisions between fast-moving atoms. If a collision is successful, the atoms merge and, for a fleeting fraction of a second, stay together to form an atom of a new element. Part of the purpose of producing these atoms is to improve our understanding of the structure of the nucleus. Such studies show the combinations of protons and neutrons that are stable. Calculations suggest that there might be an 'island of stability' around atomic number 114. Atoms in this region may be relatively more stable than many with lower atomic numbers. Indeed, such **super-heavy elements** might be formed naturally in the processes of nuclear synthesis that occur in supernovas. Such elements are likely to be of limited use because of their radioactivity. The atoms of these new 'stable' elements may only last for a few months.

If the Periodic Table included these new elements, it would have to be extended at the lower end. Until recently, the naming of elements 104 onwards was controversial. However, names have now been agreed for the elements up to atomic number 109. These names usually recognise the achievements of famous scientists: Rutherfordium (104), Seaborgium (106), and Bohrium (107), for example. Newer versions of the Periodic Table include these elements and also have the groups renumbered (as Groups 1 to 18) to include the transition elements which were previously unnumbered.

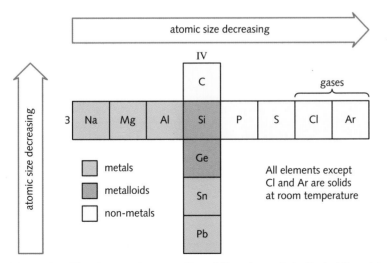

Figure 3.4 The changes in properties of the elements in Period 3 and in Group IV of the Periodic Table.

Table 3.3 A comparison of hydrogen atoms with those of lithium (Group I) and fluorine (Group VII)

Lithium	Hydrogen	Fluorine
solid at room temperature	gas	gas
metal	non-metal; forms diatomic molecules (H_2)	non-metal; forms diatomic molecules (F_2)
has one electron in outer shell	has one electron in outer shell	has seven electrons in outer shell
can lose one electron to achieve a noble-gas arrangement (forms a positive ion)	can form *either* a positive or a negative ion; can gain one electron to achieve a noble-gas arrangement, or lose its only electron	can gain one electron to achieve a noble-gas arrangement (forms a negative ion)

3.8 The position of hydrogen in the Periodic Table

Hydrogen is difficult to place in the Periodic Table. Different versions place it above Group I or Group VII. More often, in modern tables, it is left by itself. This is because, as the smallest atom of all, its properties are distinctive and unique. It does not fit easily into the trends shown in any one group (table 3.3). The unusual properties of hydrogen show themselves in various ways. Normally, for instance, we regard it as a non-metallic gas. However, liquefied under immense pressures at the centre of Saturn or Jupiter, it behaves as a molten metal.

Summary of core material

You should know that:

- the Periodic Table lists the elements of the Universe in order of increasing atomic number
- the Periodic Table has a structure that provides useful information and the elements are grouped so that certain patterns of properties repeat themselves

- the elements are broadly divided into metals and non-metals
- the metals have certain characteristic properties, the most important being that they conduct electricity and are malleable and ductile
- the Periodic Table is divided into vertical groups and horizontal periods
- there is a close relationship between the electron arrangement of an element and its position in the Periodic Table
- certain groups of elements have specific names, for example the alkali metals, and show 'family' properties
- there is a trend from metallic to non-metallic properties as you go across the Periodic Table
- the heavier elements in the Periodic Table, beyond plutonium ($Z = 94$), are artificial and often very unstable.

3.1

(a) The table below lists the properties of five elements. The letters used are *not* the symbols for the elements.

Element	Solubility in water	Melting point (°C)	Electrical conductivity of the solid	Thermal conductivity
A	insoluble	113	does not conduct	poor
B	insoluble	−157	does not conduct	poor
C	reacts	39	good	good
D	soluble	−101	does not conduct	poor
E	insoluble	−39	good	good

(i) Which of the elements are metals? [1]
(ii) Which of the non-metals are gaseous at room temperature (25°C)? [1]
(iii) Which of the elements is mercury? [1]
(iv) Give *two* differences between metals and non-metals other than those mentioned in the table. [2]

(b) (i) Which non-metallic element conducts electricity? [1]

(ii) Name *one* semi-metal (metalloid). [1]

3.2 Some elements in the Periodic Table are represented by the letters **A** to **E** and are contained in the simplified table below.

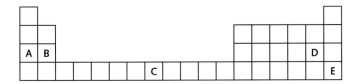

Choose, from **A** to **E**:

(a) a noble gas,

(b) a halogen,

(c) the most reactive metal,

(d) the most reactive non-metal. [4]

(ULEAC, 1993)

3.3 This question is about the Periodic Table of the elements. The letters shown in the table are *not* the symbols of the elements. You will need to use these in some of your answers. Each letter may be used once, more than once or not at all.

(a) How many protons does an atom of element **L** contain? [1]

(b) Which element shown forms ions with a single negative charge? [1]

(c) Which metallic element is more reactive than **R**? [1]

(d) Which element has its electrons arranged in four shells? [1]

(e) How many neutrons are there in an atom of element **M** (mass number 19)? [1]

(f) The table below gives data about three additional elements from one group of the Periodic Table.

Physical state at room temperature	Colour
gas	yellow/green
liquid	red/brown
solid	grey/black

What group are these three elements in? [1]

(g) What is the electron arrangement of the atom J? [1]

(ULEAC, part question, 1991)

3.4 This question refers to the Group VII elements (the halogens). Copy out and fill in the gaps in the table below. [5]

Name of element	Symbol	State at room temperature and pressure	Reaction with hydrogen
Fluorine	F		very fast
Chlorine	Cl	gas	fast
	Br	liquid	slow
Iodine	I	solid	very slow
Astatine			

(SEG, 1993)

3.5 Mendeleev said that the properties of unknown elements could be worked out by looking at the properties of other elements in the same Group or Period of the Periodic Table. Using the Periodic Table and the idea of Group trends, answer the following questions about the element strontium, Sr.

(a) (i) In which Group of the Periodic Table is strontium placed? [1]
(ii) Write the symbol of the strontium ion. [1]
(iii) Write the formula of strontium oxide. [1]

(b) Strontium reacts with water.
(i) State *one* observation you would expect to make when a small piece of strontium is added to water. [1]

(ii) Name the *two* products formed in the reaction. [2]
(iii) Write an equation to represent the reaction between strontium and water. [2]

(c) Name, or give the symbol of, an element in the same Group as strontium which is more reactive than strontium. [1]

(NEAB, part question, 1992)

3.6 Read the following passage about 'Virginium'. Answer the questions which follow with the help of the Periodic Table. In 1930 the existence of an element virginium was predicted. The following entry appeared in *Universal Knowledge*, published by Odhams Press.

> **Virginium** — a chemical element predicted in 1930, by Dr F. Allison of Alabama, to exist in pitchblende, lepidolite and certain other minerals; it was named in honour of the State of Virginia. Symbol, Vi; atomic number, 87; atomic weight, about 223.

This element was eventually discovered in 1939, and given a different name. It has no stable isotope and there is only one natural radio-isotope. This has a half-life of 21 minutes and a mass number of 223.

(a) What is the present symbol for this element? [1]

(b) In which Group of the Periodic Table is it placed? [1]

(c) State the number of protons, neutrons and electrons in one atom of this element. [2]

(d) Explain why this element is more reactive than the other elements in the Group. [2]

(e) What is meant by the term *radio-isotope*? [1]

(f) Suggest *one* reason why this element was one of the last to be found. [1]

(g) Suggest *two* difficulties which scientists would have to overcome when carrying out experiments with this element. [2]

(NEAB, part question, 1991)

3.7

(a) Use the Periodic Table to write down the chemical symbol of:
 (i) a semi-metal (an element that has the properties of both a metal and a non-metal); [1]
 (ii) an element in the third period; [1]
 (iii) the element which has four electron shells and five electrons in the outermost shell. [1]

(b) Predict *two* chemical properties or reactions of the element caesium (Cs) which is element number 55. [2]

(c) Use the Periodic Table to help you describe the structure of an atom of sulphur that has a mass number of 31. (A labelled diagram may help your explanation.) [5]

(SEG, 1994)

Chemical bonding in elements and compounds

This section covers the following ideas:

- the different types of chemical bonding in elements
 – metallic bonding
 – covalent bonding
- chemical bonding in compounds
 – covalent bonding
 – ionic bonding
- writing chemical formulas for ionic and covalent compounds
- the naming of chemical compounds
- the shape of covalent molecules
- inter-molecular forces
- the oxidation states of elements in compounds.

We live on the water planet. The surface of the Earth is distinctive because so much of it is covered with water. From space, it is the blue colours of water in seas and oceans and the white of the moisture-laden clouds that distinguish the Earth from other planets. The Earth is unique in being the only planet in our Solar System where conditions allow water to exist in all three states of matter. Another 'blue planet' exists in the Solar System – Neptune – but its structure is very different. There is a vast layer on Neptune consisting of water, methane and ammonia 'ices' thousands of kilometres deep surrounding a rocky core.

Simple compounds such as water, ammonia and methane begin to show the variety that can be achieved when the atoms of elements combine together. Water is formed from hydrogen and oxygen. Each water molecule contains two hydrogen atoms bonded to an oxygen atom. In fact, the formula of water (H_2O) is so well known that it was used in Britain in a national advertising campaign for the privatisation of the water supply: 'The A_2Z of H_2Ownership'.

Bonding involves the outer electrons of each atom. As we examine a range of substances, we shall see that, whatever type of bonding holds the structure together, it is the outer electrons that are used. The diversity of the material world is produced by the different ways in which atoms can join together.

3.9 Chemical bonding in the elements

Earlier we saw that some elements are not simply made up of separate atoms individually arranged. Elements such as oxygen (O_2) and hydrogen (H_2) consist of **diatomic molecules**. Indeed the only elements that are made up of individual atoms moving almost independently of each other are the noble gases (Group 0). These are the elements whose electron arrangements are most stable and so their atoms do not combine with each other.

Most of the elements *do* form structures. Their atoms are linked by some type of **bonding**. Most elements are metals. The structures in this case are held together by **metallic bonding**. The non-metallic elements to the right of the Periodic Table are held together by **covalent bonding**. Both these types of bonding use the outer electrons in some way. (There is a visual summary of bonding later in figure 3.13 on page 77.)

> **Bonding in the elements:**
>
> - **metallic** elements are held together by *metallic bonding*, which results in *metallic lattices*,
> - **non-metallic** elements are held together by *covalent bonding* or exist as *separate atoms* (the noble gases). Covalent bonding results in *simple molecules* or *giant molecular lattices*.

Bonding in metals

Metal atoms have relatively few electrons in their outer shells. When they are packed together, each metal atom loses its outer electrons into a 'sea' of **free electrons** (or mobile electrons). Having lost electrons, the atoms are no longer electrically neutral. They become positive **ions** because they have lost electrons but the number of protons in the nucleus has remained unchanged.

Therefore the structure of a metal is made up of positive ions packed together. These ions are surrounded by electrons, which can move freely between the ions. These free electrons are **delocalised** (not restricted to orbiting one positive ion) and form

> - An **ion** is a charged particle made from an atom by the loss or gain of electrons.
> - Metal atoms most easily lose electrons, so they become *positive ions*. In doing so they achieve a more stable electron arrangement, usually that of the nearest noble gas.

a kind of electrostatic 'glue' holding the structure together (figure 3.5). In an electrical circuit, metals can conduct electricity because the mobile electrons can move through the structure carrying charge. This type of bonding (called **metallic bonding**) is present in alloys (see page 90) as well. Alloys, for example solder and brass, will conduct electricity.

Bonding in non-metals

Hydrogen, which makes up the vast majority of the Universe, normally exists in the form of diatomic molecules (H_2). Two atoms bond together by sharing their electrons. The orbits overlap and a molecule is formed (figure 3.6 on page 74).

Through this sharing, each atom gains a share in two electrons. This is the number of electrons in the outer shell of helium, the nearest noble gas to hydrogen. (Remember that the electron arrangement of helium is very stable; helium atoms do *not* form He_2 molecules.) Sharing electrons like this is known as **covalent bonding**. It has been shown that in a hydrogen molecule the electrons are more likely to be found between the two nuclei. The forces of attraction between the shared electrons and the nuclei are greater than any repulsive forces. The molecule is held together by the bond.

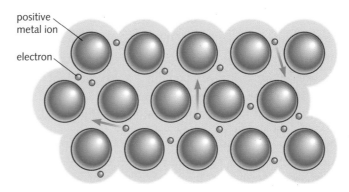

Figure 3.5 Metallic bonding – the metal ions are surrounded by a 'sea of mobile electrons'.

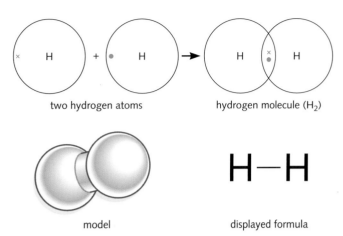

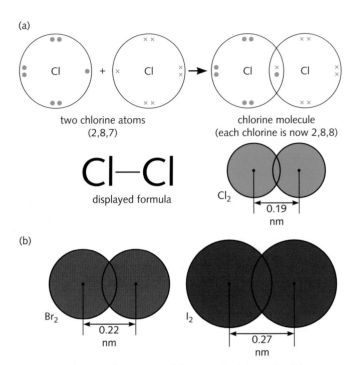

H–H

Cl–Cl

displayed formula

model   *displayed formula*

Figure 3.6 *The hydrogen molecule is formed by sharing the electrons from the atoms. A space-filling model can be used to show the atoms overlapping.*

Figure 3.7 *(a) The formation of the covalent bond in chlorine molecules (Cl$_2$). Each atom gains a share in eight electrons in its outer shell. The diagram can be drawn showing the outer electrons only because the inner electrons are not involved in the bonding. (b) Molecules of Br$_2$ and I$_2$ are formed in the same way. They are larger because the original atoms are bigger.*

The features of **covalent bonding** are:

- the bond is formed by the sharing of a pair of electrons between two atoms,
- each atom contributes one electron to each bond,
- molecules are formed from atoms linked together by covalent bonds.

Many non-metallic elements form diatomic molecules. However, in all other cases they bond in order to gain a share of eight electrons in their outer shells. This is the number of electrons in the outer shell of all the noble gases other than helium. Thus the halogens (Group VII) form covalent molecules (figure 3.7). Molecules of hydrogen and the halogens are each held together by a single covalent bond. Such a **single bond** uses two electrons, one from each atom. The bond can be drawn as a single line between the two atoms.

When molecules of oxygen (O$_2$) or nitrogen (N$_2$) are formed, more electrons have to be used in bonding if the atoms are to gain a share of eight electrons. These molecules are held together by a **double bond** (O$_2$) or a **triple bond** (N$_2$) (figure 3.8).

Phosphorus (P$_4$) and sulphur (S$_8$) form the most complicated simple molecules. These are held together by single covalent bonds. In the case of P$_4$, the atoms are arranged in a tetrahedron and there are six single covalent bonds linking the atoms. For

S$_8$, the atoms form a 'crown-shaped' ring with eight single covalent bonds between the atoms.

The non-metals in the middle of the main-group elements, for example carbon and silicon, do not form simple molecules. They exist as **giant molecular structures** held together by single covalent bonds (see section 3.19 on page 92). In these structures, the atoms are joined to each other in an extensive **network** or **lattice**. Such structures are very strong because all the atoms are inter-linked by

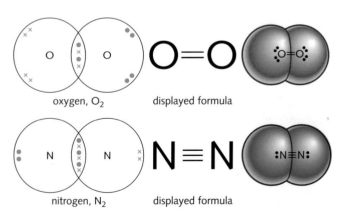

O=O

N≡N

oxygen, O$_2$ *displayed formula*

nitrogen, N$_2$ *displayed formula*

Figure 3.8 *The structures of oxygen (O$_2$) and nitrogen (N$_2$) molecules involve multiple covalent bonding.*

strong covalent bonds. The structure of the carbon atoms in diamond is shown later in figure 3.24 on page 92. A similar structure exists in silicon, which is an important element in the electronics industry.

3.10 Chemical bonding in compounds

Different elements combine together to form the vast range of compounds that make up our world. They vary from inert and heat-resistant ceramic materials to high explosives, and from lethal poisons to the molecules of life. All depend on the means of chemical bonding. Two major types of bond hold compounds together. The first is **covalent bonding**, which, as we have seen, involves sharing electrons between atoms. However, the behaviour of metal plus non-metal compounds arises from a different type of bonding. Here electrons are transferred from one atom to another. These compounds are held together by electrostatic forces between separate ions: **ionic bonding**. (There is a visual summary of bonding later in figure 3.13 on page 77.)

Covalent compounds

In covalent compounds, bonds are again made by sharing electrons between atoms. In simple molecules, the atoms combine to achieve a more stable arrangement of electrons, most often that of a noble gas. The examples shown in figure 3.9 illustrate different ways of representing this sharing. They also show how the formula of the compound corresponds to the numbers of each atom in a molecule.

In each case, the atoms achieve a share in the number of electrons present in the noble gas nearest to that element. In all but the case of hydrogen, this means a share of eight electrons in their outer shell.

Recall that multiple covalent bonds can exist in molecules of the elements oxygen and nitrogen. They can also exist in compounds too. The carbon dioxide molecule is held together by double bonds between the atoms (figure 3.10 on page 76).

Bonding in compounds:

- **non-metal plus non-metal** compounds are held together by *covalent bonding*, which results in *simple molecules* or *giant molecular lattices*,

- **metal plus non-metal** compounds are held together by *ionic bonding*, which results in *giant ionic lattices*.

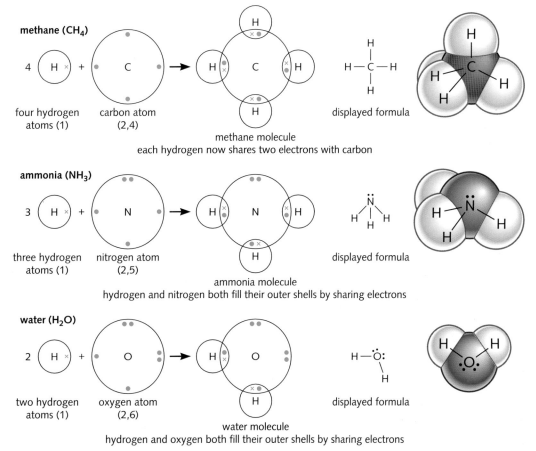

Figure 3.9 *Examples of the formation of simple covalent molecules. Again, only the outer electrons of the atoms are shown.*

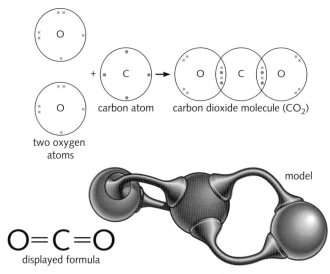

O=C=O
displayed formula

Figure 3.10 The formation of the carbon dioxide molecule, showing the outer electrons only. A ball-and-stick model can be used to show the structure.

The grains of sand on a beach show a structure that is very hard and has a high melting point. Sand and quartz are made of silicon(IV) oxide (silicon dioxide or silica, SiO_2), which has a giant molecular structure similar to that of diamond. The whole structure of silicon and oxygen atoms is held together throughout by strong covalent bonds.

Ionic compounds

Compounds of a metal plus a non-metal generally adopt a third type of bonding. This involves the

---

There are certain features common to **ionic bonding:**

- metal atoms always lose their outer electrons to form positive ions,
- the number of positive charges on a metal ion is equal to the number of electrons lost,
- non-metal atoms, with the exception of hydrogen, always gain electrons to become negative ions,
- the number of negative charges on a non-metal ion is equal to the number of electrons gained,
- in both cases the ions formed have a more stable electron arrangement, usually that of the noble gas nearest to the element concerned,
- ionic (electrovalent) bonds result from the attraction between oppositely charged ions.

---

transfer of electrons from one atom to another. This transfer of electrons results in the formation of positive and negative ions (figure 3.11). The oppositely charged ions are then attracted to each other by electrostatic forces.

Ionic compounds (such as sodium chloride) are solids at room temperature. The ions arrange themselves into a regular lattice. In the lattice each ion is surrounded by ions of the opposite charge. The whole **giant ionic lattice** is held together by the electrostatic forces of attraction that occur between particles of opposite charge. The arrangement in sodium chloride is shown later in figure 3.22 on page 91.

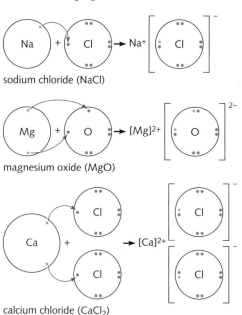

sodium chloride (NaCl)

magnesium oxide (MgO)

calcium chloride (CaCl$_2$)

Figure 3.11 Diagrams showing the formation of ionic bonds in sodium chloride, magnesium oxide and calcium chloride. Again, only the outer electrons are shown.

Polyatomic (compound) ions

The ionic compounds mentioned so far have been made from simple ions, for example Na^+, K^+, Mg^{2+}, Cl^-, O^{2-}. However, in many important ionic compounds the metal ion is combined with a negative ion containing a group of atoms (for example SO_4^{2-}, NO_3^-, CO_3^{2-}). These **polyatomic ions** (or **compound ions** or **groups**) are made up of atoms covalently bonded together. These groups have a negative charge because they have gained electrons to make a stable structure. Examples of such ions are shown in figure 3.12. In addition to these negative compound ions, there is one important polyatomic ion that is positively charged, the ammonium ion, NH_4^+ (figure 3.12). Table 3.4 gives a summary of some simple and polyatomic ions.

CO_3^{2-} : *one* carbon + *three* oxygens, with overall charge of 2–

NO_3^- : *one* nitrogen + *three* oxygens, with overall charge of 1–

SO_4^{2-} : *one* sulphur + *four* oxygens, with overall charge of 2–

NH_4^+ : *one* nitrogen + *four* hydrogens, with overall charge of 1+

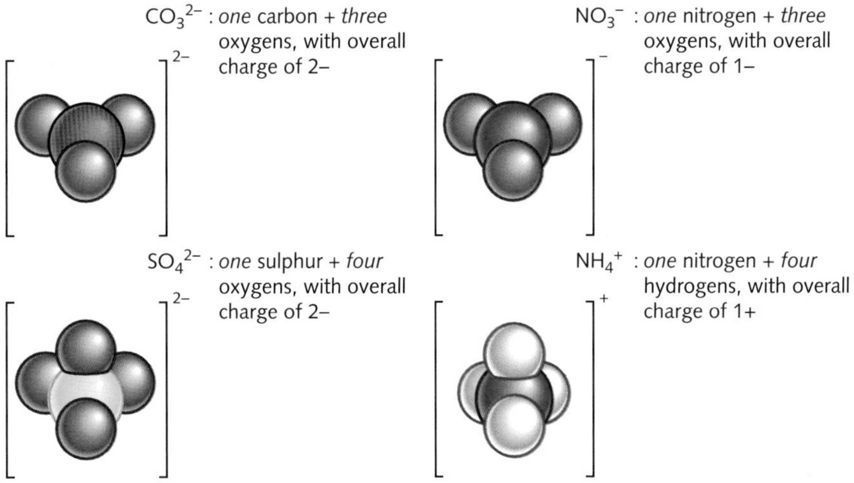

Figure 3.12 Three examples of negatively charged polyatomic ions and a positively charged polyatomic ion. The numbers of atoms and the overall charge carried by the group of atoms are shown.

Table 3.4 Some common simple and polyatomic ions

Valency	Simple metal ions (+ve)	Simple non-metallic ions		Polyatomic (or compound) ions	
		(+ve)	(–ve)	(+ve)	(–ve)
1	sodium, Na^+ potassium, K^+ silver, Ag^+ copper(I), Cu^+	hydrogen, H^+	hydride, H^- chloride, Cl^- bromide, Br^- iodide, I^-	ammonium, NH_4^+	hydroxide, OH^- nitrate, NO_3^- hydrogencarbonate, HCO_3^-
2	magnesium, Mg^{2+} calcium, Ca^{2+} zinc, Zn^{2+} iron(II), Fe^{2+} copper(II), Cu^{2+}		oxide, O^{2-} sulphide, S^{2-}		sulphate, SO_4^{2-} carbonate, CO_3^{2-}
3	aluminium, Al^{3+} iron(III), Fe^{3+}		nitride, N^{3-}		phosphate, PO_4^{3-}

Through our discussion of elements and compounds we have seen that there are **three major types of chemical bonding:**

- metallic bonding
- covalent bonding
- ionic bonding.

The types of structure based on these methods of bonding are summarised in figure 3.13.

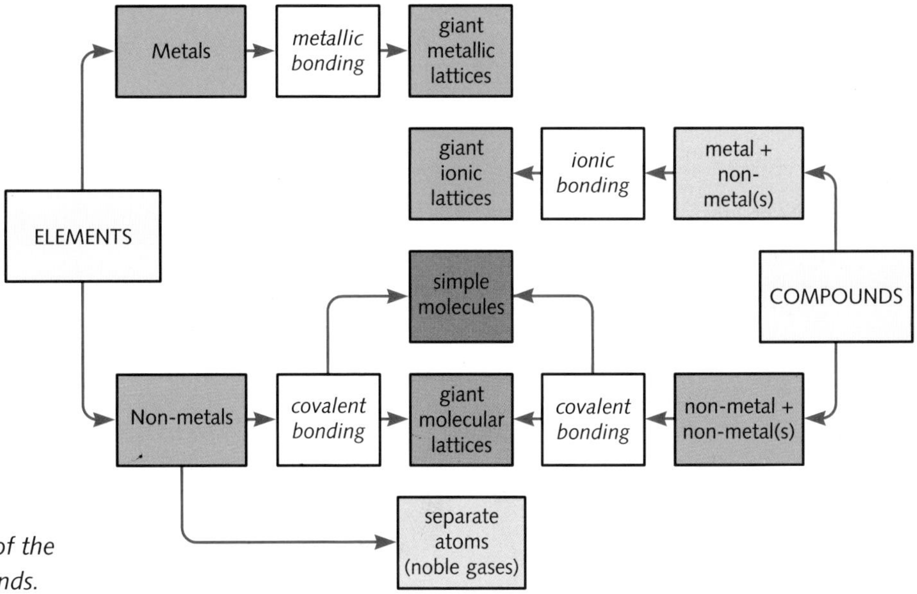

Figure 3.13 An overall summary of the bonding in elements and compounds.

3.11 The physical properties of ionic and covalent compounds

Knowledge of how atoms combine to make different types of structure helps us begin to understand why substances have different physical properties. Table 3.5 shows the broad differences in properties of ionic and simple covalent compounds.

3.12 The chemical formulas of elements and compounds

The chemical 'shorthand' of representing an element by its symbol can be taken further. It is even more useful to be able quickly to sum up the basic structure of an element or compound using its **chemical formula**.

The formulas of elements

Those elements which are made up of individual atoms or small molecules (up to three atoms covalently bonded together) are represented by the formula of the particle present (figure 3.14). Where elements exist as giant structures, whether held by metallic or covalent bonding, the formula is simply the symbol of the element (for example Cu, Mg, Fe, Na, K, etc., and C, Si, Ge). For convenience, the same applies to elements such as phosphorus (P) or sulphur (S). In these cases, the molecules contain more than three atoms.

The formulas of ionic compounds

Ionic compounds are solids at room temperature and their formulas are simply the whole-number ratio of the positive to negative ions in the structure. Thus, in magnesium chloride, there are two chloride ions (Cl^-) for each magnesium ion (Mg^{2+}):

ions present	Mg^{2+}	Cl^-
		Cl^-
total charge	2+	2−

The formula is $MgCl_2$. The overall structure must be neutral. The positive and negative charges must balance each other.

Table 3.5 The properties of ionic and simple covalent compounds

Properties of typical ionic compounds	Reason for these properties
They are crystalline solids at room temperature.	There is a regular arrangement of the ions in a lattice. Ions with opposite charge are next to each other.
They have high melting and boiling points (also high heats of fusion and evaporation).	Ions are attracted to each other by strong electrostatic forces. Large amounts of energy are needed to separate them.
They are often soluble in water (not usually soluble in organic solvents, e.g. ethanol, methylbenzene).	Water is a polar solvent. Charged ions can move about in it. Many ionic solids dissolve.
They conduct electricity when molten or dissolved in water (not when solid).	In the liquid or solution, the ions are free to move about. They can move towards the electrodes when a voltage is applied.
Properties of simple covalent compounds	**Reason for these properties**
They are often liquids or gases at room temperature.	These substances are made of simple molecules. The atoms are joined together by covalent bonds.
They have low melting and boiling points (low heats of fusion and evaporation).	The forces between the molecules (inter-molecular forces) are only very weak. Not much energy is needed to move the molecules further apart.
They are soluble in organic solvents such as ethanol or methylbenzene (very few are soluble in water).	Covalent molecular substances dissolve in covalent (non-polar) solvents.
They do not conduct electricity.	There are no ions present to carry the current.

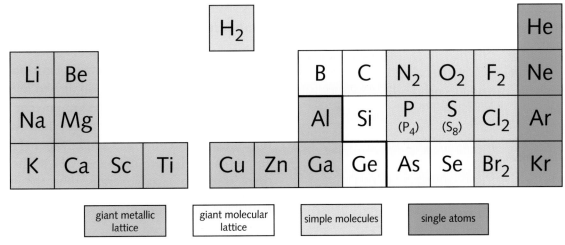

Figure 3.14 *The formulas of the elements are linked to their structure and their position in the Periodic Table.*

The size of the charge on an ion is a measure of its **valency**, see table 3.4 on page 77, or **combining power**. Mg^{2+} ions can combine with Cl^- ions in a ratio of 1:2, but Na^+ ions can only bond in a 1:1 ratio with Cl^- ions. This idea of valency can be used to ensure that you always use the correct formula for an ionic compound. Follow the examples of aluminium oxide and calcium oxide (below), and make sure you understand how this works.

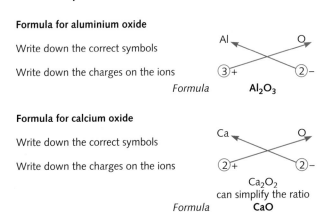

The same rules apply when writing the formulas of compounds containing polyatomic ions because each of them has an overall charge (see table 3.4 on page 77). It is useful to put the formula of the polyatomic ion in brackets. This emphasises that it cannot be changed. For example the formula of the carbonate ion is always CO_3^{2-}. Work through the examples for sodium carbonate and ammonium sulphate below.

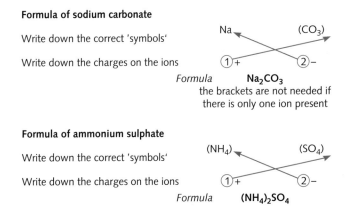

Table 3.6 summarises the formulas of some important ionic compounds.

The formulas of covalent compounds

The idea of an atom having a valency, or combining power, can also be applied to working out the formulas of *covalent* compounds. Here the valency of an atom is the number of

Table 3.6 The formulas of some ionic compounds

Name	Formula	Ions present (ratio)		
Sodium chloride	NaCl	Na^+	Cl^-	(1:1)
Ammonium nitrate	NH_4NO_3	NH_4^+	NO_3^-	(1:1)
Potassium sulphate	K_2SO_4	K^+	SO_4^{2-}	(2:1)
Calcium hydrogencarbonate	$Ca(HCO_3)_2$	Ca^{2+}	HCO_3^-	(1:2)
Copper(II) sulphate	$CuSO_4$	Cu^{2+}	SO_4^{2-}	(1:1)
Magnesium nitrate	$Mg(NO_3)_2$	Mg^{2+}	NO_3^-	(1:2)
Aluminium chloride	$AlCl_3$	Al^{3+}	Cl^-	(1:3)

covalent bonds an atom can form. The 'cross-over' method for working out chemical formulas can be applied to covalent compounds in two cases:

- simple molecules with a central atom, for example water, methane, carbon dioxide and ammonia,

Formula of ammonia

Write down the symbols
                     N   H

Write down the valencies   ③   ①

                    Formula   **NH_3**

Formula of carbon dioxide

Write down the symbols   C   O

Write down the valencies   ④   ②

                         C_2O_4

                      can simplify

              Formula   **CO_2**

- giant covalent molecules, where the formula is simply the whole-number ratio of the atoms present in the giant lattice, for example silica (see section 3.19 on page 92).

The valency of an element in the main groups of the Periodic Table can be worked out from the group number of the element. The relationship is as follows:

> - for elements in Groups I–IV,
>   valency = group number
> - for elements in Groups V–VII,
>   valency = 8 – group number
> - elements in Group 0 have a valency of 0.

For example: carbon is in Group IV, so its valency = 4; oxygen is in Group VI, so its valency = 8 – 6 = 2.

Examples of writing formulas

The method for working out formulas above does *not* work for the many covalent molecules that do *not* have a single central atom, for example H_2O_2, C_2H_6, C_3H_6, etc. The formulas of these compounds still obey the valency rules. However, the numbers in the formula represent the actual number of atoms of each element present in a molecule of the compound (figure 3.15).

3.13 'What's in a name?' – naming chemical compounds

Giving a name to a compound is a way of classifying it. Not all names are as informative as others, but modern systems do aim to be consistent. Some common and important compounds have historical names that do not seem to fit into a system, for example water (H_2O), ammonia (NH_3) and methane (CH_4). These apart, there are some basic generalisations that are useful.

- If there is a metal in the compound, it is named first.
- Where the metal can form more than one ion, then the name indicates which ion is present; for example iron(II) chloride contains the Fe^{2+} ion, while iron(III) chloride contains the Fe^{3+} ion.
- Compounds containing two elements only have names ending in ...*ide*; for example sodium chloride (NaCl), calcium bromide ($CaBr_2$), magnesium nitride (Mg_3N_2). The important exception to this is the hydroxides, which contain the hydroxide (OH^-) ion.
- Compounds containing a polyatomic ion (usually containing oxygen) have names that end with ...*ate*; for example calcium carbonate ($CaCO_3$), potassium nitrate (KNO_3), magnesium sulphate ($MgSO_4$), sodium ethanoate (CH_3COONa).
- The names of some compounds use prefixes to tell you the number of that particular atom in the molecule. This is useful if two elements form more than one compound. For example: carbon *mono*xide (CO), carbon *di*oxide (CO_2); nitrogen *di*oxide (NO_2), *di*nitrogen *tetra*oxide (N_2O_4); sulphur *di*oxide (SO_2), sulphur *tri*oxide (SO_3).

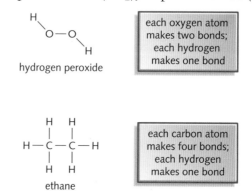

Figure 3.15 The structures of hydrogen peroxide (H_2O_2) and ethane (C_2H_6), showing the bonds made.

The names commonly used for the important mineral acids are *not* systematic and must be learnt; for example, sulphuric acid (H_2SO_4).

Two important oxidising agents (see page 106) contain polyatomic negative ions involving metal and oxygen atoms. Their modern names (potassium manganate(VII) ($KMnO_4$) and potassium dichromate(VI)($K_2Cr_2O_7$)) include the oxidation state of the metal. At this stage you will not need to write equations using these compounds, but you will need to recognise their names and formulas.

Summary of core material

You should know that:

- the structures of all substances are made up of either atoms, ions or molecules

- there are three main types of chemical bonding that hold these structures together – metallic, ionic and covalent bonding

- metallic bonding involves the closely packed atoms losing their outer electrons into a mobile 'sea of free electrons'

- covalent bonding occurs in some elements and non-metallic compounds, and involves the 'sharing' of electrons between atoms to form stable molecules

- two types of covalent structure can be formed – simple molecules and giant molecular (macromolecular) structures

- compounds of a metal plus a non-metal involve ionic bonding in which positive and negative ions are held together by strong electrostatic forces

- the physical properties of a substance are related to the type of bonding present

- each chemical compound has a particular name and can also be represented by a chemical formula that summarises the atoms or ions present.

3.8 The diagrams show an atom and an ion.

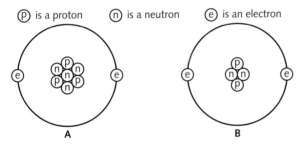

ⓟ is a proton   ⓝ is a neutron   ⓔ is an electron

A   B

(a) Explain which structure, **A** or **B**, represents an atom. [2]

(b) Why are the electronic structures of both **A** and **B** said to be stable? [1]

(c) Name the elements represented by **A** and **B** in the diagram. [2]

(d) Complete the following sentence by copying it and writing in the missing words. [2]

At the centre of an atom is the .... which contains .... and neutrons.

(e) Copy and complete the following table by correctly adding the missing information. [3]

Particle	Relative charge	Relative mass
Proton	+	
Neutron	0	
Electron		$\frac{1}{1840}$

(SEG, 1990)

3.9 Look at the table at the top of page 82. Use the information to answer the questions.

(a) Choose *one* substance at room temperature (20 °C) that is a
   (i) solid,
   (ii) liquid,
   (iii) gas. [3]

(b) (i) Which substance is an ionic compound? [1]
   (ii) Give a reason for your choice. [1]

(c) Which substance is made of molecules that change to ions when dissolved in water? [1]

(d) (i) Which *two* substances could be metals? [2]
   (ii) Give a reason for your choice. [1]

Substance	Electrical conductivity when			Melting point (°C)	Boiling point (°C)
	Solid	Molten	In water		
T	good	good	does not dissolve	1540	2760
U	poor	poor	does not dissolve	115	444
V	good	good	melts, fizzes and the solution formed conducts	98	890
W	poor	poor	poor	0	100
X	poor	good	good	808	1465
Y	poor	poor	good	−114	−85

(e) (i) Which substance could be an element from Group I of the Periodic Table? [1]

(ii) Explain the reason for your choice. [1]

(SEG, 1990)

3.10 The diagram shows the arrangement of the outer electrons only in a molecule of ethanoic acid.

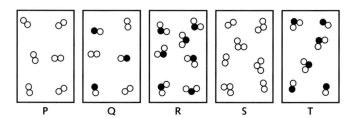

P   Q   R   S   T

(a) Copy and complete the table below by choosing the code letter for the diagram which best matches the description given in the first column. [2]

The atoms are arranged to make	Code letter
one compound only	
a mixture of an element and a compound	

The table below gives some of the properties of four elements. The letters are *not* the chemical symbols of the elements.

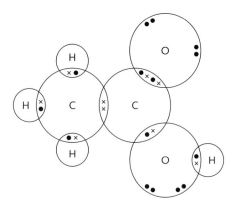

(a) Name the different elements found in this compound. [1]

(b) What is the total number of atoms present in this molecule? [1]

(c) Between which two atoms is there a double covalent bond? [1]

(d) How many covalent bonds does each carbon atom make? [1]

(e) Would you expect this compound to be a solid or a liquid at room temperature? Give a reason for your answer. [2]

(f) Ethanoic acid will dissolve in methylbenzene. Would you expect the solution to conduct electricity? Give a reason for your answer. [2]

3.11 Atoms are the basic building blocks of elements. The diagrams show a variety of ways in which two different atoms can combine.

Element	A	B	C	D
Boiling point (°C)	−246	59	1317	1322
Electrical conductivity				
when solid	none	none	good	good
when molten	none	none	good	good
when put in water	none	fair	reacts	reacts

(b) Which *two* are most likely to be metals? Give *two* reasons for your choice. [3]

The diagram shows part of the Periodic Table with information about two elements enlarged.

(c) Sodium is in Group I of the table. What can you say about the rest of the elements in this group? [1]

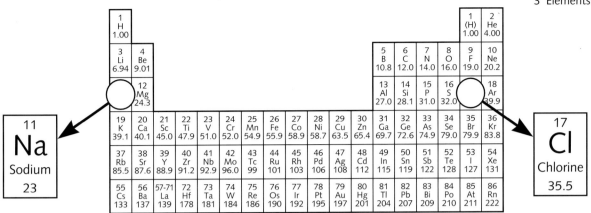

(d) (i) How many protons does an atom of sodium have? [1]
   (ii) How many electrons does an atom of chlorine have? [1]
   (iii) As well as electrons and protons, most atoms contain a third kind of particle. What is its name? [1]

(e) When sodium forms compounds it usually does so as a positive ion with one unit of charge.
   (i) What change in electron structure occurs when a sodium atom becomes a sodium ion? [1]
   (ii) What change, if any, occurs in the nucleus when the ion is formed? [1]

(f) When chlorine forms an ionic compound it gains one electron. What symbol is used to represent the chloride ion formed in this way? [1]

(g) Explain why the formula for the compound formed when sodium and chlorine react is NaCl and not $NaCl_2$. [2]

(h) What does the information given below tell you about the structure of each substance? [4]

   Chlorine melts at $-101\,^{\circ}C$. Sodium chloride melts at $801\,^{\circ}C$.

   (SEG, 1995)

3.12

(a) How many atoms of the different elements are there in the formulas of the compounds given below:
   (i) sodium hydroxide, NaOH
   (ii) ethane, C_2H_6
   (iii) sulphuric acid, H_2SO_4
   (iv) copper nitrate, $Cu(NO_3)_2$
   (v) sucrose (sugar), $C_{12}H_{22}O_{11}$ [5]

(b) What are the names of the following compounds, whose formulas are:
   (i) KBr   (vi) HNO_3
   (ii) $Al(OH)_3$ (vii) $SiCl_4$
   (iii) $CuCO_3$ (viii) $FeSO_4$
   (iv) Mg_3N_2 (ix) CH_4
   (v) PCl_3 (x) H_2SO_4 [10]

(c) Give the formulas for the following compounds:
   (i) potassium sulphate   (vi) ammonia
   (ii) aluminium fluoride   (vii) hydrochloric acid
   (iii) iron(III) oxide   (viii) copper(II) sulphate
   (iv) calcium nitrate   (ix) sulphur trioxide
   (v) zinc chloride   [9]

3.13 A bottle of Natural Mineral Water has the following details on its label:

Ion	Concentration (mg in 1 litre)	Ion	Concentration (mg in 1 litre)
Ca^{2+}	7.2	HCO_3^-	433.0
Mg^{2+}	87.0	Cl^-	33.8
Na^+	14.8	F^-	0.1
K^+	1.5	NO_3^-	4.5
		SO_4^{2-}	7.5
No other ions are present in this water			

(a) Which negative ion is present in the lowest concentration? [1]

(b) Several different salts are present in the water.
   (i) Give the formula of the salts named below. The first one has been done for you. [2]
      potassium chloride   KCl
      sodium fluoride
      magnesium nitrate
   (ii) Apart from the salts named in (i) give the names of *two* other salts that could be present in the Natural Mineral Water. [2]

(c) (i) How might you be able to tell from the boiling point that the Natural Mineral Water is not pure? [1]
   (ii) Describe how you could try to find the total mass of dissolved salts in 1 litre of this Natural Mineral Water. [5]

   (SEG, 1989)

EXTENSION

Molecular shape

One important feature of covalent molecules is that they have a specific shape. The sharing of a pair of electrons between two particular atoms gives a 'fix' on these electrons. The bonds or pairs of electrons around each atom then act on each other. They repel each other. These repulsions give the molecule its shape. The pairs of negatively charged electrons push each other as far apart as possible.

The carbon atom in methane has four pairs of outer electrons around it. The bonds arrange themselves *tetrahedrally* (figure 3.16).

Ammonia and water molecules have the same number of **electron pairs** around the central atom. However, some pairs are not shared with hydrogen atoms. From figure 3.16 we can see why the ammonia molecule is pyramid-shaped and why water is V-shaped. The shape of covalent molecules is of great importance in a wide range of situations. It is of particular importance in biological systems, because it affects the way different molecules can interact with each other, making some interactions possible and others impossible.

Forces between molecules

Covalent bonds are strong and hold the atoms *in* a molecule together. However, simple molecular compounds tend to have low melting points and low boiling points. This is because the forces *between* molecules are quite weak. It is these weak **inter-molecular forces** which pull the molecules together to form liquids and solids, but which are relatively easily disrupted by raising the temperature.

In a water molecule, for example, the bonding electrons are not equally shared between atoms. They are pulled more towards the oxygen atom than towards the hydrogens. This means that the oxygen atom is slightly negative ($\delta-$), and the hydrogen atoms are slightly positive ($\delta+$) (figure 3.17). Water is a **polar molecule**. A positive region of one molecule weakly attracts the

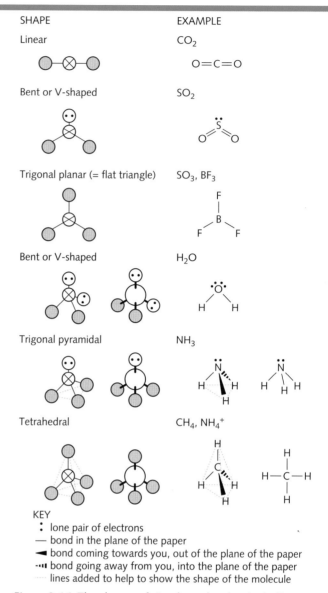

KEY
- ⦙ lone pair of electrons
- — bond in the plane of the paper
- ◀ bond coming towards you, out of the plane of the paper
- ⦙⦙⦙ bond going away from you, into the plane of the paper
- ⸱⸱⸱ lines added to help to show the shape of the molecule

Figure 3.16 *The shapes of simple molecules, including those where not all the outer electrons of the central atom are used in bonding.*

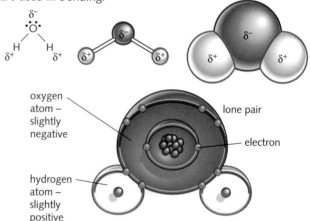

Figure 3.17 *The anatomy of a water molecule, showing the unequal sharing of the electrons making the bonds between the oxygen and hydrogen atoms.*

negative region of another. So water molecules attract each other in the liquid state. These forces also hold the structure of ice together. When heat is supplied, these weak forces can easily be broken; so the melting point and boiling point of water are low compared to substances, such as metals or graphite, which are held together by stronger forces.

Oxidation states

In many molecules the bonding electrons are not equally shared. This fact has led to the idea of oxidation states. The idea is linked to those of valency and the charges on ions. All atoms in a substance, whether part of an ion or a molecule, are given a notional charge or oxidation state.

> The **oxidation state** of an atom is decided as follows:
>
> - for a simple ion, it is the actual charge on the ion,
> - for an atom in a polyatomic ion or in a molecule, it is the charge it would have if all the bonds were broken; the electrons in a bond are given to the atom that has the strongest attraction for them.

We can see how oxidation states are worked out by considering how some examples would be split according to these rules.

Molecule	Oxidation states	Explanation
sodium chloride	Na^+ and Cl^-	it is already ionic
hydrogen chloride	H^+ and Cl^-	because chlorine attracts electrons more strongly than hydrogen
chlorine	Cl^0 and Cl^0	the atoms are not charged because both attract electrons equally

So the oxidation numbers in these examples are:

+1 Na in NaCl and H in HCl

0   Cl in Cl_2

−1 Cl in NaCl and in HCl

Some elements can have more than one oxidation state in their compounds (figure 3.18). The most obvious example of this is probably iron, which can form more than one positive ion (Fe^{2+} and Fe^{3+}). Here, and in other cases, the oxidation number of an element is included in the name of the compound. For example:

iron(II) chloride	$FeCl_2$	iron present as the Fe^{2+} ion
iron(III) chloride	$FeCl_3$	iron present as the Fe^{3+} ion
potassium manganate(VII)	$KMnO_4$	oxidation state of Mn is +7

Oxidation numbers are not only important in naming certain compounds. They can also be very useful in deciding whether oxidation or reduction (see page 106) has taken place during a particular reaction. This is because if the oxidation number of an element increases during a reaction, then that element is oxidised during that reaction. However, if the oxidation number decreases then the element is reduced.

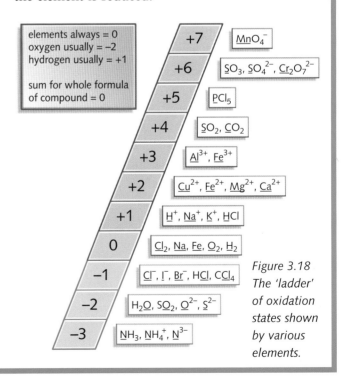

Figure 3.18 The 'ladder' of oxidation states shown by various elements.

Summary of extension material

You should know that:

- one important aspect of covalent molecules is that they have a particular shape – water molecules are V-shaped, methane molecules tetrahedral, etc.

- the forces between simple covalent molecules are quite weak

- one feature of the bonding in a substance is the oxidation state of an element in the substance

- oxidation states can be useful in naming compounds and in deciding whether substances have been oxidised or reduced in certain chemical reactions.

3.14 Titanium is a metal in the fourth period of the Periodic Table.

(a) How many uncharged particles are there in one atom of $^{48}_{22}Ti$? [1]

(b) How many more electrons are there in one atom of titanium than in an atom of argon? [1]

(b) Use your answer to (b) to predict the highest oxidation state of titanium. [1]

(IGCSE, 1992)

3.15

(a) Atoms combine with each other to form molecules. Using lines to represent chemical bonds, copy and complete the following examples to show the structures of the molecules formed.

(i) 3 atoms of hydrogen + 1 atom of nitrogen → 1 molecule of ammonia: [1]

      N   H →

  H   H

(ii) 2 atoms of hydrogen + 1 atom of oxygen → 1 molecule of water: [1]

      H

  H   →

      O

(iii) 2 atoms of carbon + 6 atoms of hydrogen → 1 molecule of ethane: [1]

      C   C

H   H   H   →

    H   H   H

(b) Atoms can lose or gain electrons when they combine with each other.

(i) Explain, in terms of electrons, what happens when an atom of sodium combines with an atom of chlorine. [2]

(ii) What is the name given to the type of bond formed? [1]

(c) Atoms can share electrons to form bonds.

(i) Explain how chlorine atoms share electrons to form a molecule. [2]

(ii) What is the name given to the type of bond formed? [1]

(IGCSE, 1993)

3.16 The table below shows the elements in the second period of the Periodic Table and a selection of their common oxidation states.

(a) What does it mean when the only oxidation state of an element is zero? [1]

(b) Explain why these elements have different oxidation states. [3]

(IGCSE, 1993)

Element	Li	Be	B	C	N	O	F	Ne
Number of electrons in outer shell	1	2	3	4	5	6	7	8
Oxidation state	+1	+2	+3	+4	−3	−2	−1	0

The structure of materials

This section covers the following ideas:

- the basic physical properties of materials
- X-ray diffraction of crystals
- the structure of crystals
  - metal crystals
  - alloys
  - ionic crystals
  - giant molecular crystals
- the allotropy of elements
- simple molecular structures
- trends in bonding across the Periodic Table
- glasses, ceramics and composite materials.

The hexagonal shapes of snowflake crystals demonstrate how simple molecules can combine to produce complex and beautiful solid structures. The regularity of a snowflake suggests that the water molecules it contains are arranged in an organised way. In general, there are three basic units from which solids are constructed – atoms, ions and molecules. These different particles produce a range of structures in the solid state, which can be classified into four broad types.

The four different types of **solid physical structures** are:

- **giant metallic lattices** – a lattice of positive ions in a sea of electrons,
- **giant ionic lattices** – a lattice of alternating positive and negative ions,
- **giant molecular lattices** – a giant molecule making the lattice,
- **simple molecular lattices** – simple molecules in a lattice held together by weak forces.

Structures of these types surround us in the real world. In some cases we use and adapt their physical properties to engineer materials to suit a particular purpose.

3.14 Basic physical properties

What are the basic physical properties that affect how we use a particular natural material? What are the properties we are looking to control when we devise an alloy or a composite material? We shall now look at these properties.

Melting point

This controls the physical state of a material under working conditions. It limits the temperature range over which the material remains solid and is structurally useful.

Density

This is the property that reflects the mass of the basic units from which the material is constructed, and the closeness with which they are packed together. It is calculated from the equation

$$\text{density} = \frac{\text{mass}}{\text{volume}}$$

and is usually measured in grams per cubic decimetre (g/dm^3) or grams per cubic centimetre (g/cm^3).

Hardness

This is a measure of the strength and rigidity of the bonding in a structure. It controls how easily the structure breaks when a force is applied. A hard material will dent or scratch a softer material. A hard material will withstand impact without changing. It is difficult to measure hardness directly but easy to compare two different materials. **Moh's scale of hardness** is based on scratching one material with another (table 3.7 on page 88). Diamond, the hardest natural material, is given a value of 10 on this scale.

Toughness

This is a measure of the energy needed to break the material. Typical tough materials have a high breaking stress and do not break in a brittle way. Materials such as glass, or ionic solids, may be hard but brittle.

Flexibility and tensile strength

Materials used in construction often have to withstand being stretched or compressed. When a material is being bent, one region of the structure is being stretched, while another is being compressed. Metals are usually strong when they are bent and stretched; we say that they are **malleable** and

Table 3.7 The hardness of some materials measured on Moh's scale

Relative hardness	Material	Uses
10	diamond silicon carbide (carborundum)	cutting tools abrasives
9	tungsten carbide	drills
8		
7	quartz	sandpaper
6	steel*	car bodies, buildings, bridges
5	glass concrete	containers, windows building materials
4	brass	decorative metal
3		
2	wood graphite	furniture, timber frames pencils, lubricant
1	talc	

* Different types of steel are found in the range from 5 to 8 on this scale.

ductile. The bonding in metals is quite flexible. The layers of positive ions in a metal can slide over each other without the metallic bonds breaking. The ions are still held together by the 'electrostatic glue' of the mobile electrons.

Some materials are able to return to their old shape after stretching; they are **elastic materials**. When you pull an elastic substance it increases in length. On release, it returns to its original length. There are limits to this ability; each elastic material has its own **elastic limit** beyond which it cannot return to the original length.

Electrical and thermal conductivity

The conduction of electricity through a solid depends on there being 'free' electrons able to move through the structure. This ability is restricted to the metallic elements, alloys and graphite (one form of carbon). Metals will also conduct electricity in the liquid state, for example mercury.

Certain compounds can conduct electricity, but *not* in the solid state. Ionic compounds do this, but they must be molten or dissolved in water to do

so. This is because the electrical charge is carried by the movement of the ions present.

Metals are very good conductors of heat because the mobile electrons can transfer heat energy through the structure very quickly. However, giant molecular covalent structures can also conduct heat well. Diamond conducts heat better than any other material, including metals, because all the atoms are linked together by rigid covalent bonds. The increased vibration caused by heat can quickly be passed through the whole structure.

Solubility in solvents

Different liquids will dissolve different types of substance. This depends on the type of particle present in the substance. Ionic compounds tend to dissolve well in water and not in covalent organic liquids. In contrast, covalent elements and compounds made up of simple molecules tend to dissolve better in organic solvents than in water. Elements and compounds with giant molecular structures are insoluble in any solvent.

3.15 Exploring physical structure by X-ray diffraction

Knowledge of the particles involved in a structure can give us clues as to how they are bonded together. But how do we gather evidence on their arrangement in the structure? In some cases we can gain further clues from the actual shape of the crystals (a **macroscopic** view). Different crystals of the same substance usually have the same shape. Crystals of common salt (sodium chloride) are cubic, whereas quartz crystals (silicon oxide) are hexagonal. If the substance forms such definite shapes, then it suggests that the particles are arranged in a regular way (at the **microscopic** level). X-rays can be used to investigate the way the particles are packed together in a crystal.

Looking at a small light bulb through a piece of stretched cloth (figure 3.19a) gives a pattern of light and dark areas. The pattern is produced by the way the light is deflected by the fibres of the cloth. The light is said to be **diffracted**. The pattern is a **diffraction pattern** (figure 3.19b).

Diffraction patterns can be produced by shining a beam of X-rays at a crystal (figure 3.19c).

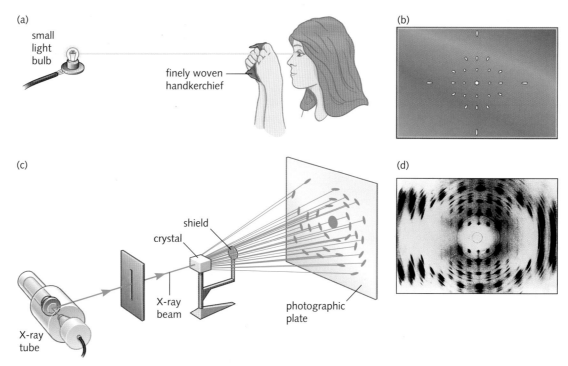

Figure 3.19 (a) A simple method for showing the diffraction of light by the fibres of cloth. (b) If you look at the light through the cloth, you should see a pattern of bright dots. (c) X-ray diffraction by a crystal produces a similar pattern. (d) The X-ray diffraction pattern produced by a crystal of DNA.

Photographs are taken of the pattern and computers used to analyse them. From the patterns, the positions of the particles in a crystal can be worked out. The X-ray diffraction pattern of DNA (figure 3.19d) helped Watson and Crick to work out its 'double helix' structure in 1953.

Given evidence of which particles are present, how they are bonded and, finally, how they are arranged, we can start to explain the measurable physical properties of various substances.

3.16 Metal crystals

The regular packing of metal ions into a lattice surrounded by a 'sea of mobile electrons' helps to explain many of the general properties of metals. In most metals the packing is as close as is physically possible. This explains why metals generally have a high density. For two metals where the packing arrangements and the atomic sizes are similar, for example lead and aluminium, the metal with the higher atomic mass will have the greater density. So lead is much more dense than aluminium. This means that the metals in the lower part of the Periodic Table have the highest densities. In some metals the ions are less closely packed. These metals, for example the alkali metals, have the lowest densities of all metals. So, lithium and sodium will float on water.

The layers of identical ions in a pure metal can be moved over one another without breaking the structure (see figure 3.21 on page 90). This flexibility in the layered structure means that metals can be beaten or rolled into sheets (they are **malleable**). Metals are more malleable when hot, and steel, for instance, is rolled when hot. They can also be stretched into wires (they are **ductile**). The strength of the metallic bonds means that the metal does not easily break under these forces. The bonds are strong but not rigid. This means that metals generally have a high tensile strength.

The mobility of the delocalised electrons in a metal means that metals conduct electricity very well. Copper is a particularly good conductor, and most electrical wires are made from it. For overhead power lines, a composite cable is made with an inner steel core surrounded by an outer sheath of aluminium.

The freedom of movement of the mobile free electrons in a metal means that they can easily transfer heat energy along the metal. Metals are very good conductors of heat.

Metals have a crystalline structure. This can show itself if we look at a metal surface under the microscope. Look, too, at the surface of a galvanised iron lamp-post or some railings or the inside of a dustbin or iron bucket. Irregular-shaped

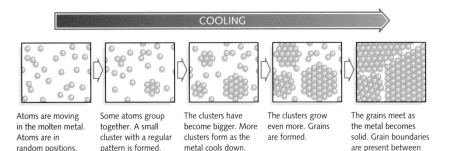

COOLING

| Atoms are moving in the molten metal. Atoms are in random positions. | Some atoms group together. A small cluster with a regular pattern is formed. | The clusters have become bigger. More clusters form as the metal cools down. | The clusters grow even more. Grains are formed. | The grains meet as the metal becomes solid. Grain boundaries are present between the grains. |

Figure 3.20 The process of formation of grains as a molten metal cools.

zinc crystals can be seen (zinc is coated on iron in the galvanisation process). These crystalline areas are called **grains**. The boundaries between them are the **grain boundaries**. Figure 3.20 describes their formation. In general, the smaller the grain size, the stronger and harder the metal.

Controlling the formation and re-formation of the grains in a metal can be achieved by melting and re-cooling the metal. Hot metal at high temperature can be allowed to cool slowly, producing a large grain size. This process is known as **annealing**, and it makes the metal softer and easier to shape. If the metal is heated strongly and then cooled rapidly by plunging it into water, the grain size is very small. This is known as **quenching**, and it produces a metal that is strong and hard, but brittle. The hardness of a metal can also be controlled by 'working' it, that is by beating or rolling it. The strength and hardness of a metal can be controlled in these ways to suit the purpose for which it is to be used.

3.17 Alloys

Making alloys with other metals is one of the most common ways of changing the properties of metals. Alloys are formed by mixing molten metals together and allowing them to cool. When liquid, the metals mix thoroughly; the alloys produced are a **solid solution.**

Alloying often results in a metal that is stronger than the original individual metals. Aluminium is a low-density metal that is not very strong. When mixed with 4% copper and smaller amounts of other elements, it gives a metal (duralumin) that combines strength and lightness and is ideal for aircraft building. Other example of alloys and their properties are given in table 3.8.

Figure 3.21 shows how the presence of the 'impurity' atoms reduces slip between the layers by 'keying' them together. The presence of the larger atoms also reduces the size of grains formed during cooling. This also increases the strength of the metal. As the strength increases, the metal becomes more brittle. In practice, the proportions of the metals being mixed to produce an alloy are chosen by experiment. The metal is designed to fit its eventual use.

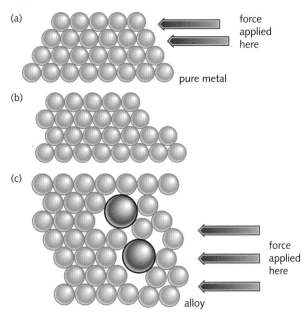

(a) force applied here

pure metal

(b)

(c) force applied here

alloy

Figure 3.21 (a) The positions of atoms in a pure metal crystal before a force is applied. (b) After the force is applied, slippage has taken place. The layers in a pure metal can slide over each other. (c) In an alloy, slippage is prevented because the atoms of different size cannot slide over each other.

Strength is not the only property to think about when designing an alloy. For example, solder is an alloy of tin and lead. It is useful for making electrical connections because its melting point is lower than that of either of the two separate metals. Also, steel, which rusts when in contact with oxygen and water, can be prevented from doing so when alloyed with chromium and nickel. This forms stainless steel (see table 3.8).

3.18 Ionic crystals

Ionic compounds form lattices consisting of positive and negative ions. In an ionic lattice, the nearest neighbours of an ion are always of the opposite

Table 3.8 Some important alloys

Alloy	Typical composition		Particular properties
Brass	copper	70%	harder than pure copper; 'gold' coloured
	zinc	30%	
Bronze	copper	90%	harder than pure copper
	tin	10%	
Mild steel	iron	99.7%	stronger and harder than pure iron
	carbon	0.3%	
Stainless steel	iron	70%	harder than pure iron; does not rust
	chromium	20%	
	nickel	10%	
Solder	tin	50%	lower melting point than either tin or lead
	lead	50%	

charge. Thus, in sodium chloride, each sodium (Na^+) ion is surrounded by six chloride (Cl^-) ions (figure 3.22), and each Cl^- ion is surrounded by six Na^+ ions. Overall there are equal numbers of Na^+ and Cl^- ions, so that the charges balance.

The actual arrangement of the ions in other compounds depends on the number of ions involved, and on their sizes. However, it is important to remember that all ionic compounds are electrically neutral.

Ionic crystals are hard but much more brittle than metallic crystals. This is a result of the structure of the layers. In a *metallic* crystal the ions are identical and held together by the mobile electrons. This remains true if one layer is slid against the next. However, pushing one layer against another in an *ionic* crystal brings ions of the same charge next to each other. The repulsions force the layers apart (figure 3.23).

Disruption of an ionic lattice is also brought about by water. Many ionic compounds dissolve in water. Water molecules are able to interact with both positive and negative ions. When an ionic crystal dissolves, each ion becomes surrounded by water molecules. This breaks up the lattice and keeps the ions apart. For those ionic compounds

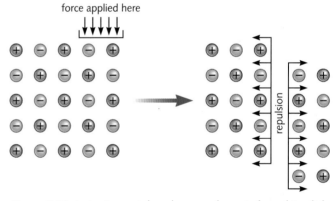

Figure 3.23 In ionic crystals, when one layer is forced to slide against another, repulsions cause the crystal to fracture.

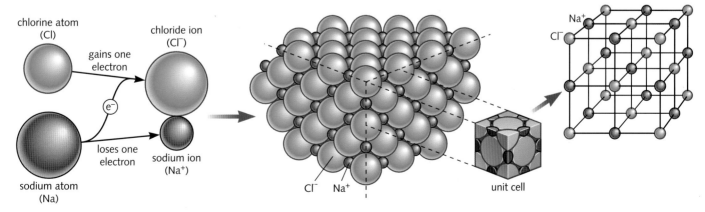

Figure 3.22 The arrangement of the positive and negative ions in a sodium chloride crystal.

91

that do not dissolve in water, the forces between the ions must be very strong.

Ions in solution are able to move. This means that the solution can carry an electric current. Ionic compounds can conduct electricity when dissolved in water. This is also true when they are melted because, here again, the ions are able to move through the liquid and carry the current.

3.19 Giant molecular crystals

Giant molecular crystals are held together by strong covalent bonds. This type of structure is shown by some elements (for example carbon in the form of diamond and graphite), and also by some compounds (for example silica, SiO_2). The structures of diamond (figure 3.24a) and silica are very similar. As a result, they show similar physical properties. They are both very hard and have high melting points.

The properties of diamond reflect the fact that the strong covalent bonds extend in all directions through the whole crystal. Each carbon atom is attached to four others – the atoms are arranged **tetrahedrally**. The bonds are rigid, however, and these structures are much more brittle than giant metallic lattices. All the outer electrons of the atoms in these structures are used to form covalent bonds. There are no electrons free to move. Diamond is therefore a typical non-metallic element in that it does not conduct electricity.

There is a form of carbon that is unusual in that it *does* conduct electricity; this is graphite. The carbon atoms adopt a very different giant molecular structure in graphite. They are arranged in flat layers of linked hexagons (figure 3.24b). Each graphite layer is a two-dimensional giant molecule. Within these layers, each carbon atom is bonded to three others by strong covalent bonds. Between the

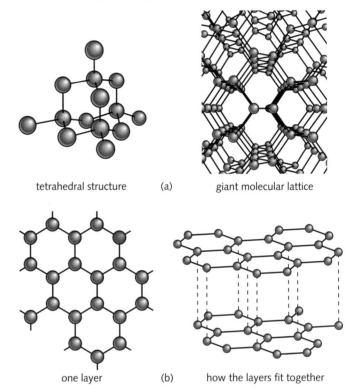

tetrahedral structure   (a)   giant molecular lattice

one layer   (b)   how the layers fit together

Figure 3.24 (a) The structure of diamond. (b) The layered structure of graphite.

Table 3.9 A comparison of the properties and uses of diamond and graphite

| | Diamond | | Graphite | |
	Property	Use	Property	Use
Appearance	colourless, transparent crystals that sparkle in light	in jewellery and ornamental objects	dark grey, shiny solid	
Hardness	the hardest natural substance	in drill bits, diamond saws and glass-cutters	soft – the layers can slide over each other – and solid has a slippery feel	in pencils, and as a lubricant
Density	more dense than graphite (3.51g/cm³)		less dense than diamond (2.25 g/cm³)	
Electrical conductivity	does not conduct electricity		conducts electricity	as electrodes and for the brushes in electric motors

layers there are weak forces of attraction (**van der Waals' forces**). The layers are able to slide over each other easily. This produces some of the characteristic properties of graphite (table 3.9). The most distinctive property, however, arises from the free electrons not used by the layered atoms in covalent bonding. These electrons can move between the layers carrying charge so that graphite can conduct electricity in a similar way to metals.

Summary of core material

You should know that:

- there is a link between the physical properties of a solid substance and the microscopic structure of its atoms, ions or molecules
- there are a wide range of physical properties to be considered, from hardness and density through to solubility
- the microscopic structure of regular solids can be investigated by X-ray crystallography
- these investigations can show us the characteristic features of metallic, ionic and giant covalent structures
- understanding the closely packed structure of metals can explain the characteristic properties of metals and how one metal can strengthen another when the two form an alloy
- the characteristic properties of metals can be adapted to suit a specific purpose by alloying
- alloys can be designed, for example, for strength (steel and duralumin), resistance to corrosion (stainless steel), or low melting point (solder)
- ionic substances are often soluble in water because water molecules can break down the structure of the ionic crystal
- ionic compounds are solid at room temperature and form crystals where the positive and negative ions are next to each other in a framework (lattice)
- some covalent substances consist of giant lattices
- giant molecular structures linked by covalent bonds can be formed by some elements and compounds
- diamond and graphite are two different forms of carbon, with different structures and distinctly different physical properties.

3.17 Aluminium is hard, conducts electricity and can be hammered into sheets. A simple model of the structure is shown.

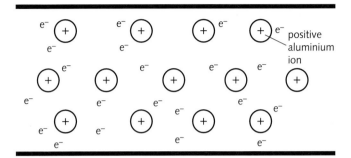

Explain the following.

(a) Why the metal is hard. [1]

(b) Why the metal conducts electricity. [1]

(c) Why the metal can be hammered into sheets. [1]

(NISEAC, 1995)

3.18 The diagrams below show three materials **A**, **B** and **C** before and after a heavy weight is applied.

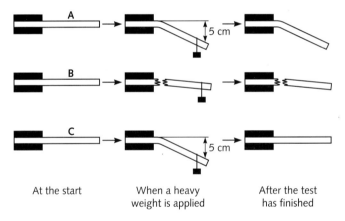

| At the start | When a heavy weight is applied | After the test has finished |

(a) Which material, **A**, **B** or **C**, is the most elastic? [1]

(b) Which material, **A**, **B** or **C**, is very brittle? [1]

(c) Write down the name of a material that **C** could be. [1]

(NISEAC, 1995)

3.19 Minerals and fossil fuels are obtained from the Earth's crust. To find out about the rocks below the surface, a borehole is drilled. The tip of a drill is coated with diamonds. The structure of diamond is drawn here.

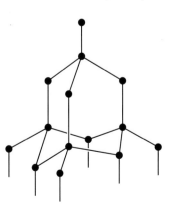

Graphite could be used to lubricate the drill and as a conductor in the motor that drives the drill.

(a) Describe the structure of graphite. [2]

(b) Why is diamond hard and graphite soft? [2]

(c) Why is graphite a good conductor of electricity? [1]

(IGCSE, 1993)

3.20 The Periodic Table may help you answer some parts of this question.

(a) The diagram below shows the structure of sodium chloride.

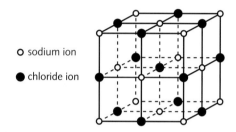

○ sodium ion

● chloride ion

   (i) How does the structure of a sodium ion differ from the structure of a sodium atom? [1]
   (ii) How does the structure of a chloride ion differ from the structure of a chlorine atom? [1]
   (iii) What type of chemical bond is present in sodium chloride? [1]

(b) Use the diagram of sodium chloride to help you to explain why:
   (i) sodium chloride crystals can be cube-shaped; [1]
   (ii) solid sodium chloride has a high melting point; [2]
   (iii) solid sodium chloride is an electrical insulator; [2]
   (iv) molten sodium chloride will undergo electrolysis. [2]

(SEG, 1995)

3.21

(a) Lead and tin are two metallic elements which can be mixed to form the alloys pewter and solder.
   (i) Copy and complete the boxes in the diagram, to show the arrangements of the particles.
     ○ is a lead particle, ● is a tin particle. [2]
   (ii) What is an element? [2]

(iii) Would pewter be a conductor of electricity? Explain your answer. [2]

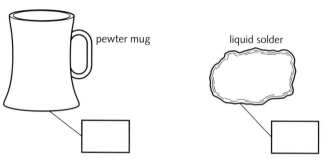

pewter mug

liquid solder

(b) The table below gives information about the melting points of various lead/tin alloys.

Percentage tin	Percentage lead	Melting point (°C)
0	100	327
20	80	280
40	60	230
60	40	185
80	20	209
100	0	237

   (i) Plot the information from the table on a graph. Draw two straight lines through the points. [4]
   (ii) What percentage of lead and tin should be mixed to obtain an alloy with the lowest possible melting point? [1]
   (iii) From your graph work out the percentage composition of the alloy having a melting point of 250°C. [2]
   (iv) Below what temperature would an alloy containing equal quantities of tin and lead be a solid? [1]
   (v) Why are alloys used rather than pure tin or pure lead? [2]
   (vi) Why do plumbers use lead-free solder? [1]

(SEG, 1993)

EXTENSION

Allotropy

Carbon is an element that can exist as a solid in more than one structural form. Diamond and graphite are allotropes of carbon. Although both diamond and graphite contain only carbon atoms, they have very different physical properties, and they can be used for different purposes (table 3.9 on page 92).

- When an element can exist in more than one structural form in the same physical state, this is called **allotropy**.
- The different forms of the same element are known as **allotropes**.

Carbon is not the only element to show allotropy. Sulphur, iron, tin and phosphorus all exhibit allotropy in the solid state; sulphur also does so in the liquid state; and oxygen exists as allotropes in the gas state in the Earth's atmosphere, as the diatomic molecule O_2 and as ozone, O_3.

Carbon itself has recently been shown to be far more versatile in the solid state than was thought. In 1985 it was found that the action of laser beams on graphite produced a spherical molecule made of 60 carbon atoms covalently bonded together (figure 3.25a). This perfect sphere is now called **buckminsterfullerene**. It is named after the American architect, Buckminster Fuller, who designed geodesic domes for large international exhibitions (for example Expo, Montreal). The atoms are bonded together in 20 hexagons and 12 pentagons, which are arranged like the panels on some soccer balls. Other cage and tubular structures of carbon have now been discovered (figure 3.25b). Together, these allotropes are known as **fullerenes** or '**bucky-balls**'. It is thought that they may prove of great use as semiconductors, superconductors, lubricants and catalysts.

In 1996, Kroto, Curl and Smalley won the Nobel Prize for Chemistry for their discovery of these new forms of carbon.

Simple molecular structures

A simple molecular structure contains small molecules. The atoms are held together *within* the molecules by strong covalent bonds (the **intra-molecular forces**). However, the forces *between* the molecules (the **inter-molecular forces**) are only weak. They include such weak interactions as van der Waals' forces, which increase as the size of the molecule increases. As a result, a great number of substances that have simple molecular structures are liquids or gases under normal conditions. Even those which are solids have relatively low melting points. The forces between the molecules in the solid and liquid states are sufficiently weak that very little energy is needed to break up the structure.

In many cases the temperature range over which the substance is liquid is quite low. In a few cases, the forces of attraction between the molecules are so weak that the solid **sublimes** (changes directly to a gas). Solid *carbon dioxide* ('dry ice') sublimes under normal conditions. If some solid CO_2 is put in a clear plastic bag and the bag is sealed, the solid sublimes and the bag 'blows up'. No liquid is seen in the bag. *Iodine* has a crystal structure in which the I_2 molecules are packed together. The forces between the molecules are only weak. So iodine is a flaky solid that sublimes if heated gently. Crystals of substances such as iodine are easily crushed. The solid or liquid forms of simple molecular substances vaporise easily, and often have characteristic smells. They also dissolve or mix most easily with organic solvents such as cyclohexane; and not in water. The solutions produced do not conduct electricity as there are no ions present to carry the current.

The noble gases are very difficult to solidify; they have the lowest melting points of all. Indeed, helium cannot be crystallised solely by lowering the temperature; the pressure must be increased too. The forces between the atoms are simply very weak van der Waals' forces.

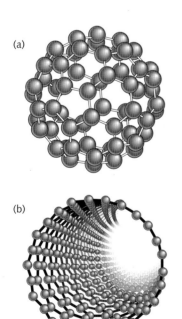

(a)

(b)

Figure 3.25 (a) A spherical C_{60} molecule of buckminsterfullerene, a 'bucky-ball'. (b) A 'bucky-tube' of carbon atoms.

Trends across the Periodic Table

We have seen earlier that there is a gradual shift in properties as we move across each horizontal row in the Periodic Table. For example, the general trend across Period 3 is

metal → metalloid → non-metal

Closer examination shows that this trend is linked to the type of structure adopted by each element.

The elements to the left of the period have few outer electrons. Atoms of these elements can readily lose these electrons and so they form metallic solids. The strength of the metallic bonding gets stronger as more electrons are released by the atoms to form ions. The three metals at the start of the period show increasing melting points, boiling points and densities (figure 3.26).

Of the non-metals, silicon has the highest value for each of these physical properties. This is a result of its giant molecular structure. The melting points and boiling points then decrease steadily to the end of the period. Chlorine and argon have low densities as they are gaseous simple molecular substances.

Glasses and ceramics

Glasses

Glass is one of the oldest manufactured materials. It was discovered some 5000 years ago in Egypt and Mesopotamia (present-day Iraq). There are several kinds of glass, but they all have one common ingredient – sand. The commonest glass is **soda-lime glass**. This is a general-purpose material made by heating a mixture of sand, limestone and sodium carbonate (together with recycled glass) to 1500 °C.

On cooling, a giant, but irregular, covalent structure of silicon and oxygen atoms is formed (figure 3.27). Some of the oxygen atoms in the structure are negatively charged. Trapped in this silicate lattice are Ca^{2+} and Na^+ ions. While soft, glass can be moulded and shaped, or cooled as sheets. X-ray analysis shows that glasses do not have the orderly packing of atoms found in other solids, that is they are **amorphous**.

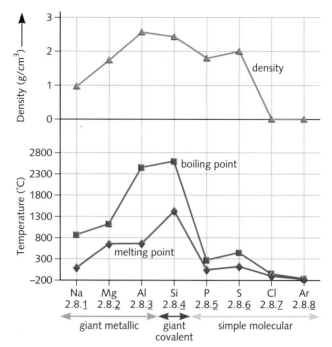

Figure 3.26 Trends in the structure and physical properties of the elements across Period 3.

They are neither liquids nor crystalline solids, but supercooled liquids – appearing solid but without a distinct melting point.

Different glasses can be made by adding other compounds to the starting mixture. Pyrex is a type of glass designed to withstand sudden changes in temperature without cracking. It is a **borosilicate glass** made by including some boron oxide (B_2O_3) in the original mixture.

Ceramics

Traditional ceramics, for example pottery and brick, are made from a mixture of clay and silica. Clay contains the mineral kaolinite, $Al_2Si_2O_5(OH)_4$, which has a structure consisting of several layers. When wet, clay can be

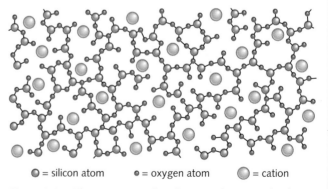

● = silicon atom   ● = oxygen atom   ◯ = cation

Figure 3.27 The structure of a glass is a framework of silicon and oxygen atoms, with metal cations (such as Na^+ and Ca^{2+}) trapped in it.

moulded because the sheets can slide over each other. However, when dry, the clay becomes rigid because the crystals stick together. When 'fired' at temperatures of 1000 °C, reactions occur that form other minerals and glass. The final ceramic material consists of many very small mineral crystals bonded together with glass.

Modern engineering ceramics have been devised to work in demanding situations, for example at high temperatures, as high-voltage electrical insulators, inside the human body, and at the heart of computers. They include such materials as aluminium oxide, magnesium oxide and zirconium oxide (table 3.10). They are made by taking very fine powders of these substances and heating them to high temperatures under pressure. These ceramic materials have very high melting temperatures and some specific uses (table 3.10).

Properties of glasses and ceramics

Since their structures share so many similarities, the properties of glasses and ceramics are very similar:

- they are both hard,
- both have high melting points, though those of glasses are lower than those of ceramics,
- both are electrical insulators,
- they both conduct heat, though not as well as metals,
- both are strong under compression and do not crumble under pressure,
- they are not ductile, so they cannot withstand stretching,
- they are brittle and shatter when dropped since their structure is rigid and irregular – some points in the structure are weaker than others,
- they can be broken by temperature shock.

The one major difference between the two is that glasses are transparent whereas ceramics are opaque.

Space-age ceramics

The most heat-resistant material ever made is probably the ceramic 'wool' used to make the tiles that cover the outside of the Space Shuttle. These tiles protect the Shuttle from high temperatures (about 1500 °C) and prevent it burning-up during re-entry into the Earth's atmosphere. The tiles are made of thin fibres of silica and air trapped between these fibres; 95% of the mass of the tiles is air. In fact, these tiles can be regarded as a composite material.

Composite materials

One way of designing a material to suit a given working situation is to combine the structures of two different materials to produce a **composite material** (figure 3.28). Bone, wood, ivory and teeth are natural composite materials. For example, bone is a composite consisting of protein and calcium phosphate. Several synthetic composites find widespread everyday use,

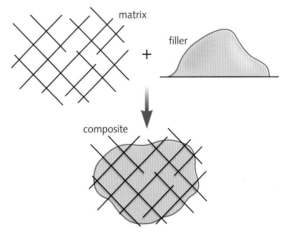

Figure 3.28 A composite material uses a matrix to provide the structure that holds the filler in place.

Table 3.10 Examples of modern engineering ceramics

Material	Formula	Melting point (°C)	Use
Aluminium oxide	Al_2O_3	2054	bio-ceramic implants for the human body
Magnesium oxide	MgO	2800	refractory bricks for furnaces, e.g. blast furnace
Zirconium oxide	ZrO_2	2770	ceramic coating on diesel engine cylinders end piston heads

for example concrete, glass-fibre reinforced plastic and safety glass.

- *Concrete*
  Concrete consists of aggregate (a mixture of stone chips and sand) bound together by cement. Cement is made by heating limestone with clay. To make concrete, cement is mixed with aggregate and then water is added. On 'setting', particles in the cement bond together to form a hard mass of crystals. Some of the water is trapped within the crystals as water of crystallisation. Concrete is strong under compression, but weak under tension. To improve its tensile strength, concrete is often reinforced by embedding steel rods or mesh in it before setting. This is reinforced concrete.

- *Glass-fibre reinforced plastic*
  This is based on a similar idea to reinforced concrete. Glass fibres or mesh are mixed with a liquid plastic resin. The resin then sets hard to make a strong material that does not shatter easily. It has many uses, for example making boats, canoes and surfboards.

- *Safety glass*
  This is another shatterproof material. It is an example of a laminated structure. A molten plastic film is layered between sheets of glass, where it sets. When the glass is hit, it does not break into dangerous fragments.

Table 3.11 summarises some of the basic properties of various types of material.

Table 3.11 The physical properties of some common materials

	Metal	Glass	Ceramic	Composite
Transparent	no	yes	no	no
Brittle	no	yes	yes	no
Conducts electricity	yes	no	no	sometimes
Conducts heat	yes	moderately	sometimes	not often
Dense	usually	moderately	moderately	not often
Ductile	yes	no	no	no
Strong	yes	yes	yes	yes
Tough	yes	no	no	yes
Flexible	yes	no	no	no

Summary of extension material

You should know that:

- some elements can exist in more than one physical form (allotropy), for example carbon as diamond, graphite and the fullerenes

- there are a range of complex structures, the glasses and ceramics, which have distinctive properties that make them useful for specific construction purposes

- composite materials can be constructed that combine the useful properties of different materials.

3.22 Golf club shafts need to be strong and reasonably stiff. They are made from wood, metal or composite materials such as carbon-fibre reinforced plastic.

(a) What do you understand by the term 'composite material'? [2]

Some properties of selected materials are given below.

Material	Density (g/cm³)	Relative strength	Relative stiffness
Wood	0.6	1	20
Steel	7.8	10	105
Aluminium	2.7	2	35
Glass-fibre reinforced plastic	1.9	15	10
Carbon-fibre reinforced plastic	1.6	18	100
Nylon	1.1	0.8	1.5

(b) Which material from the list above would be least suitable for the shafts of golf clubs? Give a reason for your choice. [2]

(c) Reinforced glass, a composite material, is often used in school windows. Give *one* advantage and *one* disadvantage if reinforced glass is used instead of ordinary glass. [2]

(NISEAC, 1995)

3.23 The table below shows some typical properties of different materials. Only some of the properties of ceramics are included.

Type of material	Typical properties
Metals	strong; hard; malleable; high density; conduct heat and electricity well; some react with air, water and acids
Ceramics	strong when compressed, weak when stretched
Plastic	flexible; easily melted and moulded; wide range of properties depending on the specific plastic; some burn when heated in air

(a) Give *two* other typical properties of ceramic materials. [2]

(b) Give *one* essential difference between a glass and a ceramic. [1]

(NISEAC, 1994)

3.24 Sand is silicon(IV) oxide. It has a structure similar to that of diamond. Part of its structure is shown in the diagram.

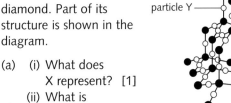

(a) (i) What does X represent? [1]
    (ii) What is particle Y? [2]
    (iii) What type of structure is shown by the diagram? Choose your answer from the following. [1]
    giant ionic solid   giant molecular solid
    simple ionic solid   simple molecular solid

(b) Predict *one* physical property of silicon(IV) oxide and explain how the property you have predicted is due to its structure. [2]

(SEG, part question 1994)

3.25 Copper is a dense, ductile (that is, can be drawn out into a wire) metal with a high resistance to corrosion. Aluminium bronze is an alloy of copper and aluminium. This alloy has the same resistance to corrosion as copper but has twice the strength. The greatest strength is obtained when the alloy contains 10% of aluminium by mass.

(a) Draw axes similar to those shown below. On your axes, sketch a graph to show how the strength of aluminium bronze changes with composition. [1]

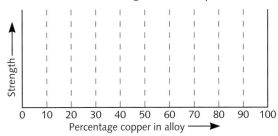

(b) The diagram shows the arrangement of atoms in pure copper metal. Use the diagram to help you to explain why copper metal:
    (i) is dense; [2]
    (ii) is ductile. [2]

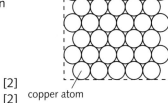

copper atom

(c) (i) Using the symbols shown, draw a labelled diagram to show the arrangement of atoms in aluminium bronze. [2]
    (ii) Use your completed diagram to help you to explain why aluminium bronze is much stronger than pure copper. [2]

○ copper atom

● aluminium atom

(SEG, part question, 1994)

4 Chemical change

Chemical reactions and equations

This section covers the following ideas:

- the differences between physical and chemical changes
- the different ways of writing an equation for a chemical reaction
  - word equations
  - balanced chemical equations
- a method for writing and balancing symbolic chemical equations
- some of the different types of chemical reaction
  - synthesis and decomposition
  - neutralisation and precipitation
  - displacement reactions
  - combustion, oxidation and reduction
- the use of state symbols to add information to an equation
- the writing of ionic equations
- the extension of the definition of oxidation and reduction to involve the transfer of electrons.

The Chinese character for 'chemistry' literally means 'change study'. Chemistry deals with how substances react with each other. Chemical reactions range from very simple reactions to the interconnecting reactions that keep our bodies alive. We need answers to questions like: What controls such reactions? How can we decide which changes are possible and which are not? What are the products of various changes? Under what circumstances do particular reactions happen? Can we predict chemical changes?

But first we must ask: What is a chemical reaction?

4.1 Physical and chemical change

Physical change

Ice, snow and water may look different, but they are all made of water molecules (H_2O). They are different *physical* forms of the same substance – water – existing under different conditions of temperature and pressure. One form can change into another by changing those conditions. In such changes, no new *chemical* substances are formed. Dissolving sugar in ethanol or water is another example of a physical change. It produces a solution, but the substances can easily be separated again by distillation.

This is what we know about **physical changes**.

- In a physical change, the substances present remain chemically the same: no new substances are formed.
- Physical changes are often easy to reverse. Any mixtures produced are usually easy to separate.

Physical changes do involve energy changes, but these are usually quite small. One unusual use of a heat change linked to a physical process is a 'Heat Solution' hand-warmer. This 'heat pack' contains a supersaturated solution of a salt called sodium ethanoate. When the solution is physically disturbed, the salt crystallises out, giving out heat.

Chemical change

When magnesium burns in oxygen (figure 4.1), the white ash produced is a new substance – the compound, magnesium oxide. Burning magnesium

Figure 4.1 Magnesium burns strongly in oxygen.

produces a brilliant white flame. Energy is *given out* in the form of heat and light. The reaction is **exothermic**. The combination of the two elements magnesium and oxygen to form the new compound is difficult to reverse. Some other chemical reactions, such as those in 'light-sticks', also give out energy in the form of light.

The reaction between nitrogen and oxygen to make nitrogen monoxide is an example of another type of reaction. During this reaction, heat energy is *taken in* from the surroundings. The reaction is **endothermic**. Such reactions are much less common.

Figure 4.2 *The decomposition of ammonium dichromate – the 'volcano experiment' – produces heat, light and an apparently large amount of powder.*

> This is what we know about **chemical changes**.
>
> - The major feature of a chemical change, or **reaction**, is that new substance(s) are made during the reaction.
> - Many reactions, but not all of them, are difficult to reverse.
> - During a chemical reaction energy can be given out or taken in:
>   – when energy is given out, the reaction is **exothermic**,
>   – when energy is taken in, the reaction is **endothermic**.
> - There are many more exothermic reactions than endothermic reactions.

4.2 Equations for chemical reactions

When some chemical reactions occur, it is obvious that 'something has happened'. But this is not the case for others. When a solid explosive reacts to produce large amounts of gas products, the rapid expansion may blast the surroundings apart. The 'volcano reaction', in which ammonium dichromate is **decomposed**, gives out a large amount of energy and produces nitrogen gas (figure 4.2). Other reactions produce gases much less violently. The neutralisation of an acid solution with an alkali produces no change that you can see. However, a reaction *has* happened. The temperature of the mixture increases, and the new substances have formed which can be separated and purified.

Word equations

We can write out descriptions of chemical reactions, but these would be quite long. To understand and group similar reactions together, it is useful to have a shorter way of describing them. The simplest way to do this is in the form of a **word equation**.

This type of equation links together the names of the substances that react (the **reactants**) with those of the new substances formed (the **products**). The word equation for burning magnesium in oxygen would be:

$$\underset{\text{reactants}}{\text{magnesium} + \text{oxygen}} \rightarrow \underset{\text{product}}{\text{magnesium oxide}}$$

The reaction between hydrogen and oxygen is another highly exothermic reaction. The take-off of the Space Shuttle depends on the energy given out in this reaction. Large tanks beneath the Shuttle contain liquid hydrogen and liquid oxygen as fuel. The word equation for this reaction is:

$$\text{hydrogen} + \text{oxygen} \rightarrow \text{water}$$

Note that, although a large amount of energy is produced in this reaction, it is *not* included in the equation. An equation includes only the chemical substances involved: energy is not a chemical substance.

This type of equation gives us *some* information. But equations can be made even more useful if we write them using chemical formulas.

The conservation of mass and the use of symbolic equations

From investigations of a large number of different chemical reactions, a very important point about all reactions has been discovered. It is summed up in a law, known as the law of the conservation of mass.

The law of conservation of mass

The total mass of all the products of a chemical reaction is equal to the total mass of all the reactants.

No matter how spectacular the reaction, this statement is always true – though it is easier to collect all the products in some cases than in others!

This important law becomes clear if we consider what is happening to the atoms and molecules involved in a reaction. During a chemical reaction, the atoms of one element are not changed into those of another element. Nor do atoms disappear from the mixture, or appear from nowhere. A reaction involves the breaking of some bonds between atoms, and then the making of new bonds between atoms to give the new products. During a chemical reaction, some of the atoms present 'change partners'.

Look more closely at the reaction between hydrogen and oxygen molecules:

hydrogen + oxygen → water

Each molecule of water (formula H_2O) contains only one oxygen atom (O). It follows that one molecule of oxygen (O_2) has enough oxygen atoms to produce two molecules of water (H_2O). Therefore, two molecules of hydrogen (H_2) will be needed to provide enough hydrogen atoms (H) to react with each oxygen molecule. The numbers of hydrogen and oxygen atoms are then the same on both sides of the equation.

The symbol equation for the reaction between hydrogen and oxygen is therefore written:

$$2H_2 + O_2 \rightarrow 2H_2O$$

This is a **balanced equation**. The numbers of each type of atom are the same on both the reactant side

and product side of the equation: four hydrogen atoms and two oxygen atoms on each side.

Writing balanced equations

A balanced equation gives us more information about a reaction than we can get from a simple word equation. Below is a step-by-step approach to working out the balanced equation for a reaction.

- *Step 1*   Make sure you know what the reactants and products are. For example, magnesium burns in air (oxygen) to form magnesium oxide.

- *Step 2*   From this you can write out the word equation:

magnesium + oxygen → magnesium oxide

- *Step 3*   Write out the equation using the formulas of the elements and compounds:

$$Mg + O_2 \rightarrow MgO$$

Remember that oxygen exists as diatomic molecules. This equation is not balanced: there are two oxygen atoms on the left, but only one on the right.

- *Step 4*   Balance the equation:

$$2Mg + O_2 \rightarrow 2MgO$$

Remember that we cannot alter the formulas of the substances involved in the reaction. These are fixed by the bonding in the substance itself. We can only put multiplying numbers in front of each formula where necessary.

Chemical reactions do not only involve *elements* reacting together. In most reactions, *compounds* are involved.

For example, sodium metal is very reactive and gives hydrogen gas when it comes into contact with water. Sodium reacts with water to produce sodium hydroxide and hydrogen. All the alkali metals do this (figure 4.3). So, if you know one of these reactions, you know them all. In fact, you could learn the general equation:

alkali metal + water
    → metal hydroxide + hydrogen

Therefore

sodium + water → sodium hydroxide + hydrogen

Figure 4.3 (a) Sodium and (b) potassium react strongly with water to produce hydrogen.

Then

$$Na + H_2O \rightarrow NaOH + H_2$$

This symbolic equation needs to be balanced. An even number of H atoms is needed on the product side, because on the reactant side the hydrogen occurs as H_2O. Therefore, the amount of NaOH must be doubled. Then the number of sodium atoms and water molecules must be doubled on the left:

$$2Na + 2H_2O \rightarrow 2NaOH + H_2$$

This equation is now balanced. Check for yourself that the numbers of the three types of atom are the same on both sides.

4.3 Types of chemical reaction

There are very many different chemical reactions. To make sense of them, it is useful to try to group certain types of reaction together (figure 4.4). These types do not cover all reactions; and some, such as redox reactions (see page 106), may fit into more than one category. Organic reactions such as polymerisation have been left until later chapters.

Synthesis and decomposition

It is possible to distinguish reactions in which complex compounds are built from simpler substances (synthesis), from those where the reverse happens (decomposition).

Synthesis (or direct combination) reactions occur where two or more substances react together to form just *one* product. The reaction between iron and sulphur would be an example of this (figure 4.5):

iron + sulphur → iron(II) sulphide

$$Fe + S \rightarrow FeS$$

Heat is required to start the reaction but, once started, it continues exothermically.

Various salts can be prepared by this method, for example aluminium iodide. The reaction between aluminium and iodine powders is quite spectacular. If the two powders are mixed well, then the reaction can be started by a few drops of water. No heating is needed:

aluminium + iodine → aluminium iodide

$$2Al + 3I_2 \rightarrow 2AlI_3$$

The synthesis reaction between aluminium foil and bromine liquid is similarly **spontaneous** (figure 4.6 on page 104).

Reactions such as the burning of magnesium and the explosive reaction of a hydrogen–oxygen mixture could also be included in this category. Synthesis reactions such as those above are usually *exothermic*, though they often require an input of heat energy to start them.

CHEMICAL REACTIONS

synthesis (including photosynthesis) — combustion (including respiration) — displacement — decomposition (thermal and photochemical)

single displacement — double displacement

redox reactions do not fall in a single category – they include combustion, single displacement, and some synthesis reactions; *and* some other reactions

acid–base neutralisation — ionic precipitation

Figure 4.4 A summary of some of the different types of chemical reaction.

Figure 4.5 The synthesis reaction between iron and sulphur.

Figure 4.6 *The reaction between aluminium and bromine is very vigorous – producing aluminium bromide. This experiment should not be attempted in the laboratory.*

However, there is one very important synthesis reaction which is *endothermic*: namely **photosynthesis**. This reaction is essential for life on Earth. It takes place in the green leaves of plants and requires energy from sunlight. It is a **photochemical reaction**. Small molecules of carbon dioxide and water are used to make glucose:

$$\text{carbon dioxide} + \text{water} \xrightarrow[\text{chlorophyll}]{\text{sunlight}} \text{glucose} + \text{oxygen}$$

$$6CO_2 + 6H_2O \rightarrow C_6H_{12}O_6 + 6O_2$$

The green pigment *chlorophyll* is essential for this reaction because it traps energy from the Sun.

Decomposition reactions have just one reactant, which breaks down to give two or more simpler products. Joseph Priestley (in 1774) first made oxygen by heating mercury(II) oxide:

$$\text{mercury(II) oxide} \xrightarrow{\text{heat}} \text{mercury} + \text{oxygen}$$

$$2HgO \xrightarrow{\text{heat}} 2Hg + O_2$$

Lime for agriculture and for making cement is manufactured industrially by the decomposition of limestone (calcium carbonate):

$$\underset{\text{limestone}}{\text{calcium carbonate}} \xrightarrow{\text{heat}} \underset{\text{lime}}{\text{calcium oxide}} + \underset{\text{dioxide}}{\text{carbon}}$$

$$CaCO_3 \xrightarrow{\text{heat}} CaO + CO_2$$

These reactions are endothermic. They require heat energy. Decomposition caused by heat energy is called **thermal decomposition.**

Decomposition can also be caused by light energy. For example, silver chloride, a white solid, turns grey in sunlight because silver metal is formed:

$$\text{silver chloride} \xrightarrow{\text{light}} \text{silver} + \text{chlorine}$$

$$2AgCl \xrightarrow{\text{light}} 2Ag + Cl_2$$

Silver bromide and silver iodide behave in the same way. These photochemical reactions are the basis of photography (see section 7.6 on page 195).

Neutralisation and precipitation

A few salts, mainly chlorides, bromides and iodides, can be made by synthesis (direct combination) as mentioned above. The majority, though, have to be made either by neutralisation or precipitation.

Neutralisation reactions involve acids. When acids react with bases or alkalis, their acidity is destroyed. They are **neutralised** and a **salt** is produced. Such reactions are known as **neutralisation reactions**. An example is

$$H_2SO_4 + CuO \rightarrow CuSO_4 + H_2O$$

$$\text{acid} \quad + \text{base} \rightarrow \text{salt} \quad + \text{water}$$

Precipitation reactions involve the formation of an insoluble product.

Precipitation is the sudden formation of a solid, either:

- when two solutions are mixed, or
- when a gas is bubbled into a solution.

This type of reaction can be used to prepare insoluble salts. For example, lead(II) iodide can be made by mixing solutions of lead(II) nitrate and potassium iodide. A yellow precipitate of lead(II) iodide is formed (figure 4.7a):

$$Pb(NO_3)_2 + 2KI \rightarrow PbI_2\downarrow + 2KNO_3$$

Potassium nitrate is soluble in water, so it stays in solution. The lead(II) iodide precipitates because it is insoluble; the downward arrow can be used to show this. Lead(II) nitrate solution can be used as an analytical test for iodides.

The **limewater** test for carbon dioxide also depends on precipitation. Here the insoluble product is calcium carbonate (figure 4.7b). A milky suspension of the insoluble calcium carbonate is formed:

$$CO_2 + Ca(OH)_2 \rightarrow CaCO_3\downarrow + H_2O$$

Figure 4.7 Precipitation reactions produce an insoluble product. (a) Yellow lead(II) iodide is precipitated from lead(II) nitrate solution by potassium iodide. (b) Calcium carbonate is precipitated from limewater by carbon dioxide.

Precipitation reactions are very useful in analysis and can also be used in the paint industry for making insoluble pigments.

Displacement reactions

Displacement reactions are useful in working out the patterns of reactivity of elements of the same type. A **displacement reaction** occurs because a more reactive element will displace a less reactive one from a solution of one of its compounds.

Zinc is a more reactive metal than copper. If a piece of zinc is placed in a copper(II) sulphate solution, a red-brown deposit of copper forms on the zinc. The blue colour of the copper(II) sulphate solution fades. Zinc displaces copper from copper(II) sulphate solution (figure 4.8a):

$$Zn + CuSO_4 \rightarrow ZnSO_4 + Cu$$

A similar reaction takes place when reactive metals are placed in acids. Hydrogen is displaced from the acid solution by the metal:

$$Mg + 2HCl \rightarrow MgCl_2 + H_2$$

Some metals are so reactive that they will displace hydrogen from water (see figure 4.3 on page 103), for example

$$2K + 2H_2O \rightarrow 2KOH + H_2$$

The halogens can be placed in order of reactivity using displacement reactions. Thus, chlorine gas will displace iodine from potassium iodide solution. The colourless solution turns yellow-brown as iodine appears (figure 4.8b):

$$Cl_2 + 2KI \rightarrow 2KCl + I_2$$

Figure 4.8 Displacement reactions. (a) Zinc will displace copper from copper sulphate solution, and the colour of the solution fades as the copper forms on the zinc surface. (b) Chlorine displaces iodine from a potassium iodide solution. The colourless solution turns yellow-brown.

Combustion, oxidation and reduction

Combustion reactions are of great importance and can be very useful or destructive.

- **Combustion** of a substance involves its reaction with oxygen and the release of energy.
- These reactions are exothermic and often involve a flame.
- Combustion in which a flame is produced is described as **burning**.

The combustion of natural gas is an important source of energy for homes and industry. Natural gas is mainly methane. Its complete combustion produces carbon dioxide and water vapour:

methane + oxygen → carbon dioxide + water

$$CH_4 + 2O_2 \rightarrow CO_2 + 2H_2O$$

Substances such as methane, which undergo combustion readily and give out a large amount of energy, are known as **fuels**.

Our bodies need energy to make possible the reactions that take place in our cells. These reactions allow us to carry out our everyday activities. We need energy to stay alive. We get this energy from food. During **digestion**, food is broken down into simpler substances. For example, the carbohydrates in rice, potatoes and bread are broken down to form glucose. The combustion of glucose with oxygen in the cells of our body provides energy:

glucose + oxygen → carbon dioxide + water

$$C_6H_{12}O_6 + 6O_2 \rightarrow 6CO_2 + 6H_2O$$

This reaction is exothermic and is known by a special name: **respiration**.

In combustion reactions, the substance involved is **oxidised**. Oxygen is added and oxides are formed. Not all reactions with oxygen produce a great amount of energy. For example, when air is passed over heated copper, the surface becomes coated with black copper(II) oxide. There is no flame, nor is the reaction very exothermic. But it is still an **oxidation** reaction (figure 4.9a):

copper + oxygen $\xrightarrow{\text{heat}}$ copper(II) oxide

$$2Cu + O_2 \xrightarrow{\text{heat}} 2CuO$$

This process can be reversed, and the copper surface regenerated, if hydrogen gas is passed over the heated material. The black coating on the surface turns pink as the reaction takes place (figure 4.9b):

copper(II) oxide + hydrogen $\xrightarrow{\text{heat}}$ copper + water

$$CuO + H_2 \xrightarrow{\text{heat}} Cu + H_2O$$

(with oxidation from CuO to H₂O, and reduction from CuO to Cu)

- If a substance *gains* oxygen during a reaction, it is **oxidised**.
- If a substance *loses* oxygen during a reaction, it is **reduced**.

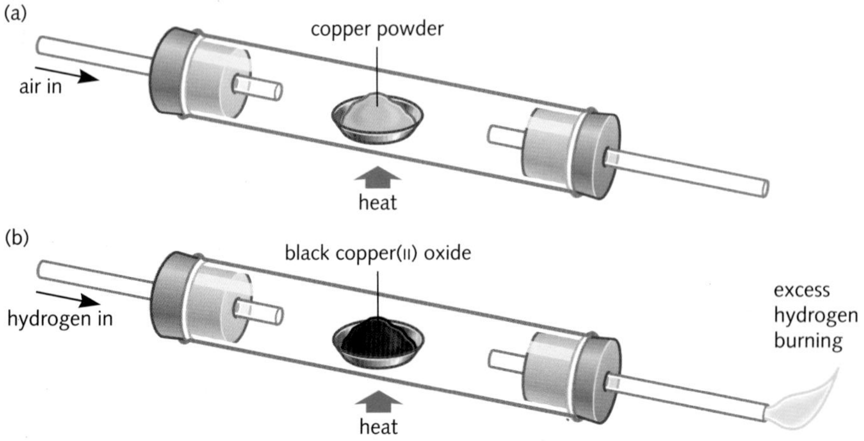

(a)

(b)

Figure 4.9 (a) The oxidation of copper to copper oxide. (b) The reduction of copper oxide back to copper using hydrogen.

During this reaction, the copper(II) oxide is losing oxygen. It is being **reduced**. The hydrogen is gaining oxygen. It is being **oxidised**.

Notice that the two processes of oxidation and reduction take place together during the same reaction. This is true for a whole range of similar reactions. Consider the following reaction:

zinc oxide + carbon → zinc + carbon monoxide

$$ZnO + C \rightarrow Zn + CO$$

(with oxidation from ZnO to CO, and reduction from ZnO to Zn)

Again, in this reaction, the two processes occur together. Since oxidation never takes place without reduction, it is better to call these reactions **oxidation–reduction reactions** or **redox reactions**.

In this last example, carbon removes oxygen from zinc oxide. Carbon is an example of a **reducing agent**.

- A **reducing agent** is an element or compound that will *remove* oxygen from other substances.
- The commonest reducing agents are hydrogen, carbon and carbon monoxide.

Reduction is very important in industry as it provides a way of extracting metals from the metal oxide ores that occur in the Earth's crust. A good example is the blast furnace for extracting iron from haematite (Fe_2O_3) (see section 10.2 on page 278).

Some substances are capable of giving oxygen to others. These substances are known as **oxidising agents**.

- An **oxidising agent** is a substance that will *add* oxygen to another substance.
- The commonest oxidising agents are oxygen (or air), hydrogen peroxide, potassium manganate(VII) and potassium dichromate(VI).

There are two common examples of oxidation reactions which we might meet in our everyday lives.

- *Corrosion*
  If a metal is reactive, its surface may be attacked by air, water, or other substances around it. The effect is called **corrosion**. When iron or steel slowly corrode in damp air, the product is a brown, flaky substance we call **rust**. Rust is a form of iron(III) oxide. Rusting weakens structures such as car bodies, iron railings, ships' hulls and bridges. Rust prevention is a major economic cost.

- *Rancidity*
  Oxidation also has damaging effects on food. When the fats and oils in butter and margarine are oxidised, they become **rancid**. Their taste and smell change and become very unpleasant. Manufacturers sometimes add anti-oxidants to fatty foods and oils to prevent oxidation. Keeping foods in a refrigerator can slow down the oxidation process. Storage in air-tight containers also helps. Crisps manufacturers fill crisps bags with nitrogen to prevent the crisps being oxidised.

Summary of core material

You should know that:

- chemical reactions differ from physical changes such as melting or dissolving because new chemical substance(s) are produced
- there is no loss or gain in total mass during a chemical reaction (the law of conservation of mass)
- reactions can be represented by word equations and balanced chemical equations
- balancing an equation involves making sure that there are the same numbers of each type of atom involved on the reactants side and products side of the equation
- reactions involve an energy change – with most reactions being exothermic and only a few being endothermic
- there are a variety of different types of chemical reaction
- synthesis and decomposition represent opposite processes

- neutralisation reactions involve the reaction of an acid with a base to produce a salt and water only
- insoluble salts can be produced by precipitation reactions
- reactive elements can displace other, less reactive, elements from their compounds in displacement reactions
- combustion reactions involve reaction with oxygen and include the biologically important reaction known as respiration, while combustion reactions that produce a flame are known as burning
- redox reactions involve the loss or gain of oxygen by substances – oxidation being the gain of oxygen and reduction being the loss of oxygen
- some substances are reducing agents (for example hydrogen, carbon), while others are oxidising agents (for example oxygen, potassium manganate(VII)).

4.1 In 1774, a British scientist called Joseph Priestley heated mercury oxide and produced a gas. Carl Scheele, a Swedish chemist, did similar experiments, but it was Antoine Lavoisier, a Frenchman, who managed to explain the facts. He worked out that the gas was the active part of air and gave it the name oxygen. The inactive part he called azote.

(a) What is the modern name for the major gas in the air which Lavoisier called azote? [1]

(b) Priestley used the apparatus below to make oxygen.

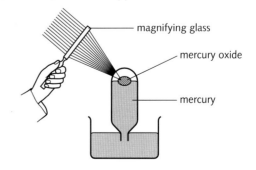

magnifying glass
mercury oxide
mercury

(i) Priestley used the heat of the Sun to decompose mercury oxide. What could you use in the laboratory today? [1]

(ii) Copy out and balance the following equation for the decomposition of mercury oxide.
...HgO → ...Hg + O$_2$ [1]

(iii) How would you know when the decomposition of the mercury oxide was complete? [1]

(IGCSE, part question, 1993)

4.2 Magnesium is a very reactive metal which will react vigorously with oxygen and even with nitrogen and carbon dioxide.

(a) The following diagram shows magnesium burning in oxygen.

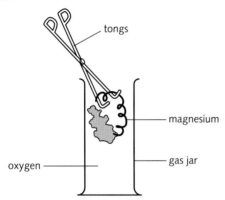

(i) Copy out and balance the following equation for the reaction.
...Mg + O$_2$ → ...MgO [2]

(ii) Describe what you see when the magnesium burns. [2]

(b) When burning magnesium is placed in a gas jar of carbon dioxide it continues to burn and a black solid is produced.

(i) How could you show that the gas jar contains carbon dioxide? [2]

(ii) Suggest what the black solid is. [1]

(iii) Suggest the name of the other product of the reaction. [1]

(IGCSE, part question, 1996)

4.3

(a) Write a word equation for the reaction between magnesium and carbon dioxide in Q4.2. [2]

(b) Copy out and complete the following balanced symbol equations for these reactions:
(i) ...Mg + CO$_2$ → ...MgO + ... [2]
(ii) ...Mg + N$_2$ → .... [2]
(iii) .... + 3H$_2$O → .... + ...NH$_3$ [2]

(c) The reaction between magnesium and carbon dioxide involves magnesium removing oxygen from carbon dioxide. What is the name given to this process? [1]

4.4 Some types of chemical reaction are listed below.

decomposition　　　neutralisation　　　combustion
oxidation–reduction (redox)

Which reaction type best describes the following changes?

(a) hexane + oxygen → carbon dioxide + water

(b) calcium carbonate → calcium oxide + carbon dioxide

(c) magnesium + copper oxide → magnesium oxide + copper

(d) hydrochloric acid + sodium hydroxide → sodium chloride + water [4]

4.5

(a) Copy out and balance the following equations:
(i) ...Cu + O$_2$ → ...CuO
(ii) N$_2$ + ...H$_2$ ⇌ ...NH$_3$
(iii) ...Na + O$_2$ → ...Na$_2$O
(iv) ...NaOH + H$_2$SO$_4$ → Na$_2$SO$_4$ + ...H$_2$O
(v) ...Al + ...Cl$_2$ → ...AlCl$_3$
(vi) ...Fe + ...H$_2$O → ...Fe$_3$O$_4$ + ...H$_2$ [6]

(b) Write word and balanced chemical equations for the reactions between:
(i) sodium and water,
(ii) magnesium and steam,
(iii) calcium and oxygen,
(iv) bromine and potassium iodide solution,
(v) zinc and copper sulphate solution. [15]

4.6 Copy out and complete the diagrams to show what is used and what is produced in (a) burning, (b) respiration and (c) rusting. [3]

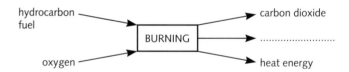

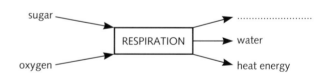

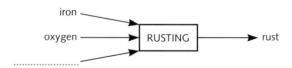

What type of chemical change is involved in all of the reactions (a), (b) and (c)? [1]

4.7 The reactivity of magnesium may be shown by the reaction of magnesium with copper(II) oxide. This reaction can be carried out using the apparatus below.

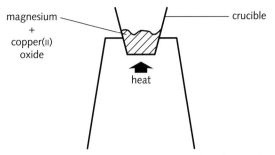

The reaction is very fast and may be said to be explosive. A flash occurs and a puff of smoke is seen.

The reaction may be represented by the equation:

$$Mg + CuO \rightarrow MgO + Cu$$

(a) Write the word equation for this reaction. [4]

(b) Describe the appearance of the reactants and the products. The description of magnesium is completed for you. [3]

Mg   a silvery shiny solid
CuO
MgO
Cu

(c) The reaction gives out a great deal of heat. What term describes this type of reaction? [1]

(IGCSE, 1995)

EXTENSION

A closer look at reactions, particularly redox reactions

State symbols

So far, our equations have told us nothing about the physical state of the reactants and products.

Table 4.1 The state symbols used in chemical equations

Symbol	Meaning
s	solid
l	liquid
g	gas
aq	aqueous solution, i.e. dissolved in water

Chemical equations can be made more useful by including symbols that give us this information. These are called **state symbols**. They show clearly whether a gas is given off or a solid precipitate is formed during a reaction. The four symbols used are shown in table 4.1.

The following examples show how they can be used (the points of particular interest are shown in **bold type**):

magnesium + nitric acid
→ magnesium nitrate + hydrogen

$$Mg(s) + 2HNO_3(aq)$$
$$\rightarrow Mg(NO_3)_2(aq) + \mathbf{H_2(g)}$$

hydrochloric acid + sodium hydroxide
→ sodium chloride + water

$$HCl(aq) + NaOH(aq) \rightarrow NaCl(aq) + \mathbf{H_2O(l)}$$

copper(II) sulphate + sodium hydroxide
→ copper(II) hydroxide + sodium sulphate

$$CuSO_4(aq) + 2NaOH(aq)$$
$$\rightarrow \mathbf{Cu(OH)_2(s)} + Na_2SO_4(aq)$$

Ionic equations

The last two examples above are useful for showing a further modification in writing equations. This modification identifies more clearly those particles which are actually taking part in a particular reaction. These reactions involve mixing solutions that contain ions. Only some of the ions present actually change their status – by changing either their bonding or their physical state. The other ions present are simply **spectator ions** to the change; they do not take part in the reaction.

The equation given above for neutralising hydrochloric acid with sodium hydroxide solution is:

$$HCl(aq) + NaOH(aq) \rightarrow NaCl(aq) + H_2O(l)$$

Writing out all the ions present, we get

$$[H^+(aq) + \cancel{Cl^-(aq)}] + [\cancel{Na^+(aq)} + OH^-(aq)]$$
$$\rightarrow [\cancel{Na^+(aq)} + \cancel{Cl^-(aq)}] + H_2O(l)$$

The use of state symbols clearly shows which ions have not changed during the reaction. They have been crossed out (~~like this~~) and can be left out of the equation. This leaves us with the essential ionic equation for all neutralisation reactions:

$$H^+(aq) + OH^-(aq) \rightarrow H_2O(l)$$

Applying the same principles to a precipitation reaction again gives us a clear picture of which ions are reacting (figure 4.10).

So the reaction

$$CuSO_4(aq) + 2NaOH(aq)$$
$$\rightarrow Cu(OH)_2(s) + Na_2SO_4(aq)$$

for the precipitation of copper(II) hydroxide, which was given above, becomes

$$Cu^{2+}(aq) + 2OH^-(aq) \rightarrow Cu(OH)_2(s)$$

This is the essential ionic equation for the precipitation of copper(II) hydroxide; the spectator ions (sulphate and sodium ions) have been left out.

Redox reactions

Chemists' ideas about oxidation and reduction have expanded as a wider range of reactions have been studied. Look again at the reaction between copper and oxygen:

$$copper + oxygen \xrightarrow{heat} copper(II)\ oxide$$

$$2Cu + O_2 \xrightarrow{heat} 2CuO$$

It is clear that copper has been oxidised; but what has been reduced? We can apply the ideas behind ionic equations to analyse the changes taking place during this reaction. It then becomes clear that:

- the copper atoms in the metal have become copper ions (Cu^{2+}) in copper(II) oxide,
- the oxygen molecules in the gas have split and become oxide ions (O^{2-}) in the black solid copper(II) oxide.

The copper atoms, which clearly were oxidised during the reaction, have in the process *lost* electrons. The oxygen atoms have *gained* electrons in the process.

(a)

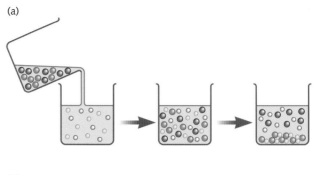

(b)

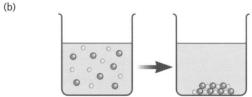

Figure 4.10 A precipitation reaction in which two solutions containing ions are mixed: (a) the overall reaction; (b) the net reaction with the spectator ions not shown.

A new, broader definition of oxidation and reduction can now be put forward.

- **Oxidation** is the *loss* of electrons.
- **Reduction** is the *gain* of electrons.

We can remember this by using the memory aid 'OILRIG' (*o*xidation *i*s *l*oss, *r*eduction *i*s *g*ain of electrons).

OILRIG

<u>o</u>xidation <u>i</u>s the <u>l</u>oss of electrons
<u>r</u>eduction <u>i</u>s the <u>g</u>ain of electrons

This new definition of redox changes increases the number of reactions that can be called redox reactions. For instance, displacement reactions where there is no transfer of oxygen are now included. This is best seen by looking at an ionic equation, for example:

$$Zn(s) + CuSO_4(aq) \rightarrow ZnSO_4(aq) + Cu(s)$$

As an ionic equation this becomes:

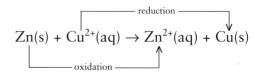

$$Zn(s) + Cu^{2+}(aq) \rightarrow Zn^{2+}(aq) + Cu(s)$$

Zinc has lost two electrons and copper has gained them. The loss or gain of electrons in the reaction means that changes in oxidation state have taken place:

$$\text{Zn(s)} + \text{Cu}^{2+}\text{(aq)} \rightarrow \text{Zn}^{2+}\text{(aq)} + \text{Cu(s)}$$

reduction

oxidation

0   +2   +2   0   Oxidation state

During the reaction, the oxidation state of zinc has increased by 2, from 0 to +2. Meanwhile the oxidation state of copper has decreased by 2, from +2 to 0.

Thus the definitions of oxidation and reduction may be adapted still further to apply to particular atoms or ions during a reaction.

- **Oxidation** is the *increase* in oxidation number of an atom or ion.
- **Reduction** is the *decrease* in oxidation number of an atom or ion.

Chlorine is a good oxidising agent. It displaces iodine from potassium iodide solution (see figure 4.8b on page 105). Is this reaction a redox reaction? Consider the changes in oxidation state during the reaction:

reduction

$$\text{Cl}_2\text{(g)} + 2\text{KI(aq)} \rightarrow 2\text{KCl(aq)} + \text{I}_2\text{(aq)}$$

0   +1   −1   +1   −1   0   Oxidation state

oxidation

- The oxidation state of I changes from −1 to 0. It has increased. Iodide ions are *oxidised* to iodine.
- The oxidation state of Cl changes from 0 to −1. It has decreased. Chlorine is *reduced* to chloride ions.

Tests for oxidising and reducing agents

Reactions involving potassium iodide can be very useful as a test for any oxidising agent, because there is a colour change produced. The iodide ion (I^-) is oxidised to iodine (I_2). The colour of the solution changes from colourless to yellow-brown. If starch indicator is added, then a dark blue colour is produced.

Reactions involving acidified potassium manganate(VII) are useful for detecting a reducing agent. The manganese is in a very high oxidation state (+7) in the manganate(VII) ion (MnO_4^-). A solution containing the manganate(VII) ion has a purple colour. When it is reduced, the manganate(VII) ion loses its purple colour and the solution becomes colourless. Acidified potassium dichromate solution could also be used. In this case the colour change seen is from orange to green.

Summary of extension material

You should know that:

- equations can be made more informative by including state symbols
- for reactions involving ions (for example neutralisation and precipitation reactions), an equation can be simplified to include only those ions taking part in the reaction – the 'spectator ions' are eliminated from the equation
- the definitions of oxidation and reduction can be extended to include reactions involving the transfer of electrons – oxidation is the loss of electrons and reduction is the gain of electrons.

4.8

(a) Explain the meaning of the symbols (s), (l), (aq) and (g) in the following equation, with reference to each reactant and product: [4]

$Na_2CO_3(s) + 2HCl(aq)$
$\rightarrow 2NaCl(aq) + H_2O(l) + CO_2(g)$

(b) Write an ionic equation, including state symbols, for each of the following reactions: [8]
   (i) silver nitrate solution + sodium chloride solution → silver chloride + silver nitrate solution
   (ii) sodium sulphate solution + barium nitrate solution → sodium nitrate solution + barium sulphate
   (iii) dilute hydrochloric acid + potassium hydroxide solution → potassium chloride solution + water
   (iv) dilute hydrochloric acid + copper carbonate → copper chloride solution + water + carbon dioxide

4.9 Certain photochemicals are used in photography. A film, which is coated with silver bromide particles, is exposed to light and the image 'captured' on the film. When this film is developed, the developer changes only those silver ions that were exposed to light into silver atoms. Finally, the unreacted silver ions are removed.

(a) Copy and complete the equation for the changing of silver ions into silver atoms. [1]

$Ag^+ + \ldots \rightarrow \ldots$

(b) What type of reagent is the developer? [1]

(c) Suggest a reason why the developed film should not be exposed to light until the unreacted silver ions have been removed. [1]

(d) The diagram shows the image on the film and the same film after developing.

bright area on image   same area dark when film developed

image   image on film after developing

Explain why some areas of the developed film are darker than others. [3]

(IGCSE, part question, 1993)

Electrolysis

This section covers the following ideas:

- electrical conductivity in metals and graphite
- the electrolysis of ionic compounds
  - electrolytes and non-electrolytes
- the movement of ions in an electric field
- industrial applications of electrolysis
  - the extraction of aluminium
  - the electrolysis of concentrated brine
  - electroplating
  - the refining of copper
- the electrolysis of solutions in water
- redox changes during electrolysis.

Electricity has had a great effect on our way of living. Large urban areas, such as Hong Kong, could not function without the electricity supply. The results of the large-scale supply of electricity can be seen in the pylons and power lines that mark our landscape. But electricity is also important on the very small scale. The silicon chip enables a vast range of products to work, and many people now have access to products containing electronic circuits – from personal stereos to washing machines.

4.4 Conductivity in solids

Conductors and insulators

The ability to conduct electricity is the major simple distinction between elements that are metals and non-metals. All metals conduct electricity, but carbon in the form of graphite is the only non-metallic element that conducts electricity. A simple circuit can be used to test whether any solid conducts or not (figure 4.11). The circuit is made up of a cell or a battery of cells (a source of direct current), some connecting copper wires fitted with clips, and a light bulb to show when a current is flowing. The material to be tested is clipped into the circuit. If the bulb lights up, then the material is an **electrical conductor**.

For a solid to conduct, it must have a structure that contains 'free' electrons that are able to flow through it. There is a flow of electrons in the completed circuit. The battery acts as an 'electron pump'. Electrons are repelled (pushed) into the circuit from the negative terminal of the battery. They are attracted to the positive terminal. Metals (and graphite) conduct electricity because they have mobile free electrons in their structure. The battery 'pumps' all the free electrons in one direction. Metallic alloys are held together by the same type of bonding as the metal elements, so they also can conduct electricity. Solid covalent non-metals do not conduct electricity. Whether they are giant molecular or simple molecular structures, there are no electrons that are not involved in bonding – there are no free electrons. Such substances are called **non-conductors** or **insulators** (table 4.2).

There is no chemical change when an electric current is passed through a metal or graphite. The copper wire is still copper when the current is switched off!

> A **conductor** is a substance that conducts electricity but is not chemically changed in the process.

Supplying electricity

Electricity is transmitted along power cables. Many of these cables are made of copper, because copper is a very good electrical conductor – it has a very high **electrical conductivity**. Overhead power cables have a core of steel, which conducts well. This core is surrounded by aluminium. Aluminium is less dense than steel, and is used to reduce the weight and so prevent the cable sagging too much. Aluminium is also very resistant to corrosion.

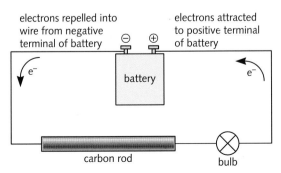

Figure 4.11 Testing a solid material to see if it conducts electricity by lighting a bulb.

Table 4.2 Solid electrical conductors and insulators

Conductors	Insulators (non-conductors)	
	Giant molecular	Simple molecular
copper	diamond	sulphur
silver	poly(ethene)	iodine
aluminium	poly(chloroethene), PVC	
steel	poly(tetrafluoroethene), PTFE	
brass		
graphite		

Domestic cables are covered (sheathed) in plastic, which is a non-conductor. This cover (or insulation) is needed for safety reasons. Leakage of power from overhead cables is prevented by using ceramic materials between the cable and the pylons. These plastic and ceramic materials are examples of **insulators**.

4.5 Conductivity in liquids

The conductivity of liquids can be tested in a similar way to solids, but the simple testing circuit is changed (figure 4.12 on page 114). Instead of clipping the solid material to be tested into the circuit, now graphite rods are dipped into the test liquid. Liquid compounds, solutions and molten materials can all be tested in this way. Molten metals, for example mercury, conduct electricity. Electrons are still able to move through the liquid metal to carry the charge. As in conductivity in solid metals, no chemical change takes place when liquid metals conduct electricity.

Electrolytes and non-electrolytes

Different results are obtained if the apparatus in figure 4.12 is used to test a range of liquid compounds or solutions. Liquids such as ethanol, paraffin, petrol and methylbenzene do not conduct electricity. The bonding in these compounds is covalent. There are no free electrons or other charged particles to flow through them. Distilled water contains very few ions indeed, and so is usually regarded as non-conducting. Solutions of covalent compounds, for example sugar solution, do not conduct.

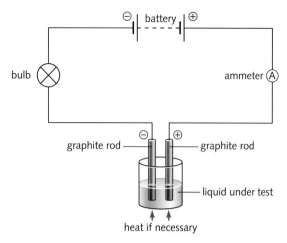

Figure 4.12 The apparatus for testing the conductivity of liquids.

Ionic compounds do contain charged particles (ions), but in the solid they are not free to move. An ionic *solid* does not conduct electricity. However, the ions present can become free to move if the solid is *melted* or *dissolved* in water. Then the ions can carry their charge through the liquid, the current flows and the bulb will light up. Examples of molten ionic compounds which conduct electricity are molten lead (II) bromide or zinc chloride.

There is an important difference that happens when passing a current through a metal salt compound compared to a liquid metal. In the case of a metal salt, the liquid does not remain chemically unchanged. In fact, the compound is decomposed by the passage of the current:

$$PbBr_2(l) \xrightarrow{\text{electrical energy}} Pb(l) + Br_2(g)$$

$$ZnCl_2(l) \xrightarrow{\text{electrical energy}} Zn(l) + Cl_2(g)$$

Decomposition of an ionic compound by electricity is called **electrolysis**, and the liquid that decomposes is called an **electrolyte**. Liquids which do not conduct electricity, such as distilled water, are called **non-electrolytes**. Some substances, for example ethanoic acid solution, light the bulb moderately in the circuit in figure 4.12. They are *weak* electrolytes. Others, such as a solution of potassium chromate, light the bulb strongly. They are *strong* electrolytes.

Solutions of ionic compounds in water are also electrolytes; and again a chemical change occurs.

Testing a solution of copper(II) chloride shows that it is split into copper and chlorine. Table 4.3 lists some electrolytes and non-electrolytes.

In summary, the following substances are **electrolytes**:

• molten salts,

• solutions of salts in water,

• solutions of acids,

• solutions of alkalis.

The two distinct types of **electrical conductivity** are called metallic and electrolytic conductivity. They differ from each other in important ways.

Metallic conductivity:
• electrons flow,
• a property of elements (metals and carbon, as graphite) and alloys,
• takes place in solids and liquids,
• no chemical change takes place.

Electrolytic conductivity:
• ions flow,
• a property of ionic compounds,
• takes place in liquids and solutions (not solids),
• chemical decomposition takes place.

Table 4.3 Some electrolytes and non-electrolytes

Electrolytes	Non-electrolytes
molten zinc chloride	distilled water
molten lead bromide	ethanol
sodium chloride solution	paraffin
hydrochloric acid	molten sulphur
copper(II) chloride solution	sugar solution
ethanoic acid	solid sodium chloride
sulphuric acid	
sodium hydroxide solution	

The movement of ions

The conductivity of ionic compounds is explained by the fact that ions move in a particular direction in an electric field. This can be shown in experiments with coloured salts. For example, copper(II) chromate(VI) (CuCrO$_4$) dissolves in water to give a green solution. This solution is placed in the lower part of a U-tube (it can be made denser by dissolving some gelatine in the solution). A colourless solution of dilute hydrochloric acid is then layered on top of the salt solution in each arm. Graphite rods are fitted as shown in figure 4.13. These rods carry the current into and out of the solution. They are known as **electrodes**. In electrolysis, the *negative* electrode is called the **cathode**; the *positive* electrode is the **anode**.

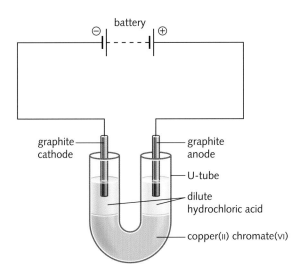

Figure 4.13 *An experiment to show ionic movement by using a salt solution containing coloured ions. The acid solution was colourless at the start of the experiment.*

After passing the current for a short time, the solution around the cathode becomes blue. Around the anode the solution becomes yellow. These colours are produced by the movement (migration) of the ions in the salt. The positive copper ions (Cu^{2+}) are blue in solution. They are attracted to the cathode (the negative electrode). The negative chromate ions (CrO$_4^{2-}$) are yellow in solution. They are attracted to the anode (the positive electrode). The use of coloured ions in solution has shown the direction that positive and negative ions move in an electric field.

During electrolysis:
- *positive ions* (metal ions or H$^+$ ions) move towards the *cathode*; they are known as **cations**,
- *negative ions* (non-metal ions) move towards the *anode*; they are known as **anions**.

The electrolytic cell

The apparatus in which electrolysis is carried out is known as an **electrolytic cell**. The direct current is supplied by a battery or power pack. Graphite electrodes carry the current into and out of the liquid electrolyte. Graphite is chosen because it is quite unreactive (inert). It will not react with the electrolyte or with the products of electrolysis. Electrons flow from the negative terminal of the battery around the circuit and back to the positive terminal. In the electrolyte it is the *ions* that move to carry the current.

4.6 Electrolysis of molten compounds

An electrolytic cell can be used to electrolyse molten compounds. Heat must be supplied to keep the salt molten. Figure 4.14 on page 116 shows the electrolysis of molten zinc chloride.

When the switch is closed the current flows and chlorine gas (which is pale green) begins to bubble off at the anode. After a little time a bead of molten zinc collects at the cathode. The electrical energy from the cell has caused a chemical change (decomposition). The cell decomposes the molten zinc chloride because the ions present move to opposite electrodes where they lose their charge (they are **discharged**). Figure 4.14 on page 116 shows this movement. The chloride ions (Cl$^-$) move to the anode. Each chloride ion gives up (donates) one electron to become a chlorine atom:

at the anode $Cl^- \rightarrow Cl + e^-$

Then two chlorine atoms bond together to make a chlorine molecule:

$Cl + Cl \rightarrow Cl_2$

The zinc ions (Zn^{2+}) move to the cathode. There each zinc ion picks up (accepts) two electrons and becomes a zinc atom:

at the cathode $Zn^{2+} + 2e^- \rightarrow Zn$

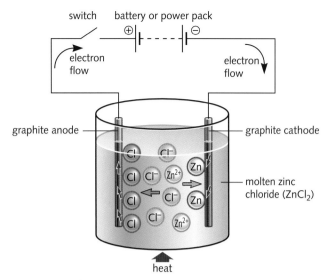

Figure 4.14 The movement of ions in the electrolysis of a molten salt, zinc chloride.

During electrolysis, the flow of electrons is kept going through the circuit. For every two electrons taken from the cathode by a zinc ion, two electrons are set free at the anode by two chloride ions. So overall the electrons released at the anode flow through the circuit towards the cathode. During the electrolysis of molten salts, the metal ions, which are always positive (cations), move to the cathode and are discharged. Non-metal ions (except hydrogen), however, are always negative. They are anions and move to the anode to be discharged.

When a molten ionic compound is electrolysed:

- the metal is always formed at the cathode,
- the non-metal is always formed at the anode.

Table 4.4 shows some further examples of this type of electrolysis. Electrolysis of molten salts is easier if the melting point of the salt is not too high.

Industrial electrolysis of molten compounds

Electrolysis is important industrially because it is the only method of extraction available for the most reactive metals. Metals in Groups I and II, and aluminium, are too reactive to be extracted by chemical reduction using carbon like other metals. Metals such as sodium and magnesium are obtained by electrolysis of their molten chlorides. The metal is produced at the cathode.

One of the most important discoveries in industrial electrolysis was finding suitable conditions for extracting aluminium from its mineral ore, bauxite. The bauxite ore is first treated to produce pure aluminium oxide. This is then dissolved in molten cryolite (sodium aluminium fluoride). The melting point of the mixture is much lower than that of pure aluminium oxide. The mixture is electrolysed between graphite electrodes (figure 4.15). Molten aluminium is attracted to the cathode and collects at the bottom of the cell:

at the cathode $\qquad Al^{3+} + 3e^- \rightarrow Al$

Oxygen is released at the anodes:

at the anode $\qquad 2O^{2-} \rightarrow O_2 + 4e^-$

At the operating temperature of about 1000 °C, the graphite anodes burn away in the oxygen to give carbon dioxide. So they have to be replaced regularly.

4.7 Electrolysis of solutions

Electrolysis of molten compounds and ionic solutions both produce chemical change. However, the products from electrolysis of a solution of a salt may be different from those obtained by electrolysis of the molten salt. This is because water itself produces ions.

Table 4.4 Some examples of the electrolysis of molten salts

Electrolyte	Decomposition products	Cathode reaction	Anode reaction*
Lead bromide, $PbBr_2$	lead (Pb) and bromine (Br_2)	$Pb^{2+} + 2e^- \rightarrow Pb$	$2Br^- \rightarrow Br_2 + 2e^-$
Sodium chloride, NaCl	sodium (Na) and chlorine (Cl_2)	$Na^+ + e^- \rightarrow Na$	$2Cl^- \rightarrow Cl_2 + 2e^-$
Potassium iodide, KI	potassium (K) and iodine (I_2)	$K^+ + e^- \rightarrow K$	$2I^- \rightarrow I_2 + 2e^-$
Copper(II) bromide, $CuBr_2$	copper (Cu) and bromine (Br_2)	$Cu^{2+} + 2e^- \rightarrow Cu$	$2Br^- \rightarrow Br_2 + 2e^-$

*These anode reactions are the sum of the two stages written in the text. The loss of an electron from a negative ion like Cl^- can also be written $2Cl^- - 2e^- \rightarrow Cl_2$.

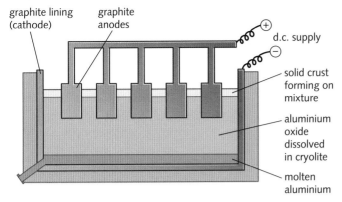

Figure 4.15 *The industrial electrolysis of molten aluminium oxide to produce aluminium.*

Although water is a simple molecular substance, a very small fraction of its molecules split into hydrogen ions (H^+) and hydroxide ions (OH^-):

$$H_2O \rightleftharpoons H^+ + OH^-$$

most molecules intact — only a very few molecules split into ions

Not enough ions are produced for water to conduct electricity very well on its own. During electrolysis, however, these hydrogen and hydroxide ions are also able to move to the electrodes. They compete with the ions from the salt to be discharged at the electrodes. But at each electrode just *one* type of ion gets discharged. Which of the competing ions produce the reaction products in these circumstances?

Table 4.5 summarises these ideas. They can be demonstrated by looking at some examples of electrolysis (table 4.6 on page 118).

Table 4.5 The ease of discharge of ions during electrolysis in solution

Positive ions* (cations)		Negative ions (anions)
K^+		SO_4^{2-}
Na^+	ease of	NO_3^-
Ca^{2+}	discharge	OH^-
Mg^{2+}	of ions	Cl^-
H^+	increases	Br^-
Cu^{2+}	downwards	I^-
Ag^+		

*For the metal ions this series (the electrochemical series) closely parallels the reactivity series.

At the **cathode**

- The more reactive a metal, the more it tends to stay as ions and not be discharged. The H^+ ions will accept electrons instead. Hydrogen molecules will be formed, leaving the ions of the reactive metal, for example Na^+ ions, in solution.

- In contrast, the ions of less reactive metals, for example Cu^{2+} ions, will accept electrons readily and form metal atoms. In this case, the metal will be discharged, leaving the H^+ ions in solution.

At the **anode**

- If the ions of a halogen (Cl^-, Br^-, or I^-) are present in a high enough concentration, they will give up electrons more readily than OH^- ions. Molecules of chlorine, bromine, or iodine are formed. The OH^- ions remain in solution.

- If no halogen ions are present, the OH^- ions will give up electrons more easily than any other non-metal anion. Sulphate and nitrate ions are not discharged in preference to OH^- ions. When OH^- ions are discharged, oxygen is formed.

Electrolysis of sodium chloride solution

A concentrated solution of sodium chloride can be electrolysed in the laboratory (figure 4.16 on page 118). There are four different ions present in the solution. The positive ions (cations), Na^+ and H^+, flow to the cathode, attracted by its negative charge. The negative ions (anions), Cl^- and OH^-, travel to the anode.

At the *cathode*, it is the H^+ ions that accept electrons as sodium is more reactive than hydrogen:

$$H^+ + e^- \rightarrow H$$

Then two hydrogen atoms combine to form a hydrogen molecule:

$$H + H \rightarrow H_2$$

So overall hydrogen gas bubbles off at the cathode:

$$2H^+ + 2e^- \rightarrow H_2$$

117

Table 4.6 Results of electrolysis of various salt solutions

	Salt solution	Product at cathode	Product at anode
metals increasingly reactive upwards	Potassium bromide, KBr(aq)	hydrogen $2H^+ + 2e^- \rightarrow H_2$	bromine $2Br^- \rightarrow Br_2 + 2e^-$
	Magnesium sulphate, MgSO$_4$(aq)	hydrogen $2H^+ + 2e^- \rightarrow H_2$	oxygen $4OH^- \rightarrow 2H_2O + O_2 + 4e^-$
	Copper sulphate, CuSO$_4$(aq)	copper $Cu^{2+} + 2e^- \rightarrow Cu$	oxygen $4OH^- \rightarrow 2H_2O + O_2 + 4e^-$
	Silver nitrate, AgNO$_3$(aq)	silver $Ag^+ + e^- \rightarrow Ag$	oxygen $4OH^- \rightarrow 2H_2O + O_2 + 4e^-$

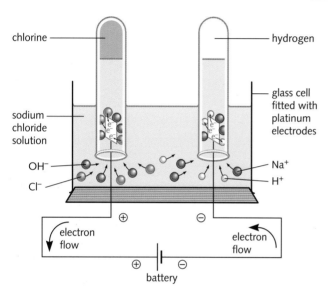

Figure 4.16 The movement and discharge of ions in the electrolysis of sodium chloride solution.

At the *anode*, the Cl$^-$ ions are discharged more readily than the OH$^-$ ions:

$$Cl^- \rightarrow Cl + e^-$$

Then two chlorine atoms combine to make a chlorine molecule:

$$Cl + Cl \rightarrow Cl_2$$

So overall pale green chlorine gas bubbles off at the anode:

$$2Cl^- \rightarrow Cl_2 + 2e^-$$

Left behind in solution are Na$^+$ and OH$^-$ ions; this is sodium hydroxide solution. The solution therefore becomes alkaline. This can be shown by adding indicator to the solution. These products – hydrogen, chlorine and sodium hydroxide – are very important industrially as the basis for the chlor-alkali industry. So, the electrolysis of concentrated brine (salt water) is a very important manufacturing process.

Several different types of electrolytic cell have been used for the electrolysis of brine. The modern membrane cell (figure 4.17) is the safest for the environment and uses the least electricity. Other types of cell use either a flowing mercury cathode, or a diaphragm (partition) made from asbestos.

The **membrane cell** has a titanium anode and a nickel cathode. Titanium is chosen for the anode as it is not attacked by chlorine. The anode and cathode compartments are separated by an ion-exchange membrane. This membrane is selective; it allows Na$^+$ ions and water to flow through, but no other ions. This means that, while Na$^+$ ions can move freely to the cathode, the products are kept separate and cannot react with each other. The Na$^+$ and OH$^-$ ions collect in the cathode

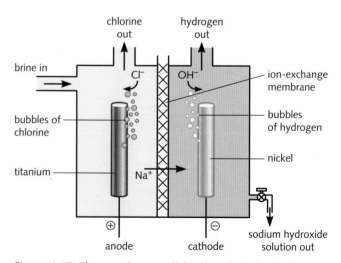

Figure 4.17 The membrane cell for the electrolysis of concentrated brine. The selective ion-exchange membrane only allows Na$^+$ ions to pass through it.

compartment. The sodium hydroxide solution is removed and purified.

Electrolysis of copper(II) chloride

Copper is a metal that is less reactive than hydrogen. As a result, electrolysing solutions of copper salts using graphite electrodes produces red-brown deposits of copper on the *cathode* – hydrogen ions are not discharged:

$$Cu^{2+} + 2e^- \rightarrow Cu$$

As in the electrolysis of sodium chloride solution, when copper(II) chloride is electrolysed, pale green chlorine gas bubbles off from the *anode* (figure 4.18):

$$2Cl^- \rightarrow Cl_2 + 2e^-$$

Other salt solutions

A whole range of soluble ionic salts can be electrolysed using inert graphite or platinum electrodes. The results fit the basic rules listed earlier (tables 4.5 and 4.6). However, one point must be emphasised from such experiments. In the electrolysis of sulphate or nitrate solutions, the SO_4^{2-} or NO_3^- ions are not discharged. Instead, the OH^- ions give up electrons to form oxygen, which is given off at the anode, and water.

Electroplating

The fact that an unreactive metal can be coated onto the surface of the cathode by electrolysis means that useful metal objects can be 'plated'

with a chosen metal. **Electroplating** can be used to coat one metal with another.

For electroplating, the electrolysis cell is adapted from the type normally used. The anode is not made from inert graphite or platinum, but from the metal present in the electrolyte solution. In these cases the anode is not inert; it slowly dissolves in the solution as the current is passed. This means that the concentration of metal ions in the solution stays the same.

The most commonly used metals for electroplating are copper, chromium, silver and tin. One purpose of electroplating is to give a protective coating to the metal underneath; an example is in tin-plating steel cans to prevent them rusting. This is also the idea behind chromium-plating articles such as car bumpers, kettles, bath taps, etc. Chromium does not corrode, it is a hard metal that resists scratching and wear, and can also be polished to give an attractive finish.

The attractive appearance of silver can be achieved by electroplating silver onto an article made from a cheaper metal such as nickel silver. The 'EPNS' seen on cutlery and other objects stands for 'electroplated nickel silver'. 'Nickel silver' is an alloy of copper, zinc and nickel – it contains no silver at all! It is often used as the base metal for silver-plated articles.

The electrolysis must be carried out under careful control to make sure that the metal layer sticks firmly to the article being plated. Steel objects often have to be coated first with layers of copper and nickel, before they can be chromium-plated. Chromium will not stick firmly to steel directly. Figure 4.19 shows in outline how an object is

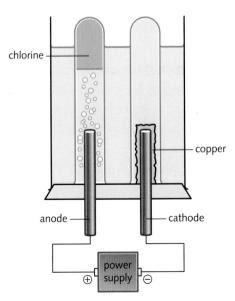

Figure 4.18 The electrolysis of copper(II) chloride solution.

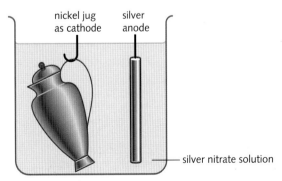

Figure 4.19 Electroplating – the basic requirements for silver-plating

silver-plated. The object must be very clean and free of grease. It must also be rotated so that the layer forms evenly on all sides. The current, the temperature and the concentration of the electrolyte must be controlled so that the layer does not form too fast, otherwise it will flake off.

The basic rules for **electroplating** an object with metal M are as follows:

- the object must be made the cathode,
- the electrolyte must be a solution of a salt of metal M,
- the anode is made of a strip of metal M.

Electrolysis of acid solutions

Pure water is a very poor conductor of electricity. However, it can be made to decompose if some dilute sulphuric acid is added. A Hofmann voltameter (figure 4.20) can be used to keep the gases produced separate. After a short time the volume of gas in each arm can be measured and tested. The gas collected above the cathode is hydrogen. Oxygen collects at the anode. The ratio of the volumes is approximately 2:1. Effectively this experiment is the electrolysis of water:

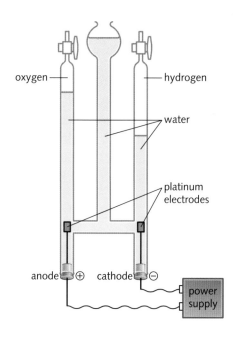

Figure 4.20 The Hofmann voltameter for the electrolysis of water.

at the cathode	$2H^+ + 2e^- \rightarrow H_2$
at the anode	$4OH^- \rightarrow 2H_2O + O_2 + 4e^-$

The electrolysis of concentrated hydrochloric acid can also be carried out in this apparatus. Again two gases are collected, this time hydrogen and chlorine:

at the cathode	$2H^+ + 2e^- \rightarrow H_2$
at the anode	$2Cl^- \rightarrow Cl_2 + 2e^-$

Summary of core material

You should know that:

- metals conduct electricity whereas non-metals (except graphite) do not
- in metallic conductivity, the current is produced by electrons moving through the solid or liquid metal
- there is a different type of conductivity, known as electrolytic conductivity, in which ionic compounds conduct when molten or dissolved in water
- electrolytic conductivity involves the movement of ions and results in a chemical change (electrolysis)
- liquids or solutions can be classified as electrolytes or non-electrolytes

- an electrolytic cell consists of positive (anode) and negative (cathode) electrodes and an electrolyte
- the products of electrolysis appear at the electrodes where ions are discharged
- there are various rules that help us to predict the products of electrolysis, but generally metals or hydrogen are always produced at the negative electrode (the cathode)
- electrolysis is industrially important for the extraction of very reactive metals (for example aluminium) and the production of sodium hydroxide and chlorine
- electroplating can be used to produce a protective and/or decorative layer of one metal on another.

4.10 A student was finding out about the effect of electricity on three compounds. The results of the experiments are shown in the table.

Compounds	Does the solid conduct electricity?	Does the solution in water conduct electricity?
Potassium chromate, K_2CrO_4	no	yes
Potassium sulphate, K_2SO_4	no	yes
Copper sulphate, $CuSO_4$	no	yes

(a) Explain why these compounds do not conduct electricity when solid but do conduct electricity in solution. [2]

(b) The student set up another experiment like this:

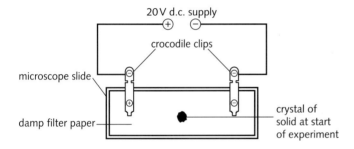

The results are shown in the table.

Substance	Colour of crystals	Changes seen on the filter paper
Potassium chromate, K_2CrO_4	yellow	yellow colour moves towards positive
Potassium sulphate, K_2SO_4	white	no colours seen
Copper sulphate, $CuSO_4$	blue	blue colour moves towards negative

(i) Select which of these ions is yellow. [1]
    chromate   copper   potassium   sulphate
(ii) Explain why the yellow colour moves towards the positive terminal in the potassium chromate experiment. [2]
(iii) Suggest and explain what will happen if this experiment is repeated with copper chromate. [2]

(MEG, 1995)

4.11 Below are the results of the electrolysis of a number of aqueous solutions using inert electrodes.

Solution (electrolyte)	Gas given off at the anode	Gas given off or metal deposited at the cathode	Substance left in solution at the end of electrolysis
Copper(II) sulphate	oxygen	copper	sulphuric acid
Sodium sulphate	oxygen	hydrogen	sodium sulphate
Silver nitrate	oxygen	silver	nitric acid
Concentrated sodium chloride	chlorine	hydrogen	sodium hydroxide
Copper(II) nitrate	oxygen	copper	nitric acid

Solution (electrolyte)	Gas given off at the anode	Gas given off or metal deposited at the cathode	Substance left in solution at the end of electrolysis
Silver sulphate	oxygen		
Sodium nitrate		hydrogen	sodium nitrate

(a) Use the information in the table above to complete the table on the left. You may assume that the solutions were electrolysed under exactly the same conditions as the ones above. [3]

(b) Explain what is meant by electrolysis. [1]

(c) The apparatus below was used to plate a strip of metal with copper. One electrode was made of copper and the other was the metal strip to be plated.

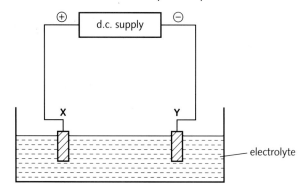

(i) Which electrode, **X** or **Y**, is the metal strip? [1]
(ii) Is the metal strip an anode or a cathode? [1]

(d) If graphite were used instead of the copper electrode in (c), what would the electrolyte be at the end of the experiment? [1]

(e) In industry some plastics are electroplated. Why must the plastic be coated with a thin film of graphite before plating? [1]

(MEG, 1993)

4.12 Which diagram shows how to electroplate a copper ring with a coating of nickel?

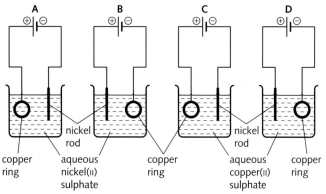

(IGCSE, 1991)

4.13 An experiment was carried out by a student to investigate the effect of electricity on molten lead(II) iodide (PbI₂). Below is an extract from the student's note book.

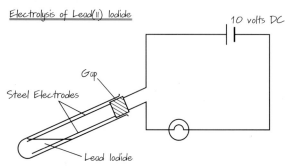

I set the experiment up as in the diagram. I observed purple fumes coming from the positive electrode which formed dark crystals at the top of the tube. Nothing happened at the negative electrode.

(a) (i) What happens to a compound during electrolysis? [2]
(ii) Why does solid lead(II) iodide not allow the passage of electricity? [2]
(iii) What piece of apparatus is missing from the diagram above, which is necessary to carry out electrolysis? [1]
(iv) Explain the reasons for the student's observations at the positive electrode. [3]
(v) Why was a gap left at the top of the test tube? [1]

(b) The reaction occurring at the negative electrode was:
$Pb^{2+} + 2e^- \rightarrow Pb$
(i) Explain the student's observation at the negative electrode. [2]
(ii) Why is this reaction a reduction process? [1]
(iii) Give *one* reason why this electrolysis should be carried out in a fume cupboard. [1]

(SEG, 1993)

4.14 Aluminium is the most abundant metallic element in the Earth's crust. The most important ore of aluminium is bauxite, an impure form of aluminium oxide (Al_2O_3). The aluminium oxide is purified and aluminium is then obtained by electrolysis as shown in the diagram below.

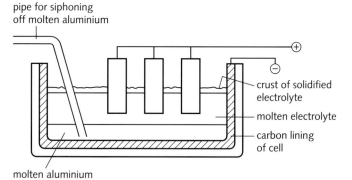

Both anode and cathode are made of carbon. The molten electrolyte is at a temperature of 900 °C and consists of a mixture of purified aluminium oxide and another ore of aluminium, cryolite (Na_3AlF_6). Cryolite is not electrolysed in the process.

(a) What is the purpose of adding cryolite and how does this help in the economics of the process? [2]

(b) Copy and complete the equations for the reactions occurring at the anode and cathode.
Anode $O^{2-} \rightarrow$ [1]
Cathode $Al^{3+} \rightarrow$ [1]

(c) The anodes have to be replaced from time to time. What is the reason for this? [1]

(d) Articles made of aluminium such as milk bottle tops and waste window frames are 'recycled' to obtain the aluminium, simply by melting. State *two* advantages of recycling aluminium. [2]

(WJEC, 1993)

4.15 Electrolysis of a solution of sodium chloride in water is used for the manufacture of sodium hydroxide.

(a) (i) Name the gas produced at each electrode. [2]
   (ii) Write a balanced equation to show the electron transfer involved in the formation of *one* of these gases. [2]
   (iii) In the electrolysis cell used to manufacture sodium hydroxide, the anodes are made of titanium. Titanium is a very expensive metal. Give *one* reason for using titanium rather than steel for the positive electrodes. [2]
   (iv) The solution of sodium chloride in water is an electrolyte. What is the meaning of the term electrolyte? [2]

(b) State why:
   (i) solid sodium chloride does not conduct electricity;
   (ii) pure water is a poor conductor of electricity;
   (iii) an aqueous solution of sodium chloride does conduct electricity. [3]

(c) A solution of sodium chloride containing universal (pH) indicator is electrolysed as shown below.

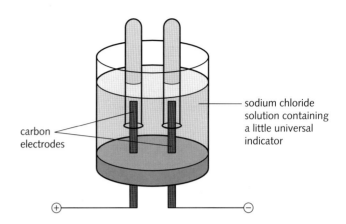

carbon electrodes

sodium chloride solution containing a little universal indicator

(+) (−)

State three changes that would be noticed during the electrolysis. Give a reason for each observation. [6]

(SEG, 1988)

EXTENSION

A closer look at electrode reactions

The electrolysis of hydrochloric acid demonstrates one factor that is important in electrolysis: the *concentration* of the ions present.

When the concentration of the acid is lowered, the gas given off at the anode changes. As the solution becomes very dilute, chloride ions are not discharged. At these low concentrations, oxygen is produced from the discharge of hydroxide ions. The different products of the electrolysis of hydrochloric acid are shown in table 4.7.

There is a similar change in the product at the anode for very dilute solutions of sodium chloride. Again, oxygen is given off rather than chlorine. These results suggest that the

discharge of Cl^- ions over OH^- ions (called **preferential discharge**) only applies if the concentration of Cl^- is sufficiently high.

Oxidation and reduction during electrolysis

The reactions that take place at the electrodes during electrolysis involve the loss and gain of electrons. Negative ions always travel to the anode, where they lose electrons. In contrast, positive ions always flow to the cathode, where they gain electrons. As we saw earlier (page 106), oxidation can be defined as the loss of electrons, and reduction as the gain of electrons. Therefore, electrolysis can be seen as a process in which oxidation and reduction are physically separated.

Table 4.7 Electrolysis of dilute and concentrated hydrochloric acid

Product at anode	Electrolyte	Product at cathode
chlorine $2Cl^- \rightarrow Cl_2 + 2e^-$	concentrated hydrochloric acid	hydrogen $2H^+ + 2e^- \rightarrow H_2$
oxygen $4OH^- \rightarrow 2H_2O + O_2 + 4e^-$	very dilute hydrochloric acid	hydrogen $2H^+ + 2e^- \rightarrow H_2$

During **electrolysis**:

- the oxidation of non-metal ions always takes place at the anode,
- the reduction of metal or hydrogen ions always occurs at the cathode.

Just as in normal redox reactions, where both oxidation and reduction occur at the same time, the two processes must take place together to produce electrolytic decomposition.

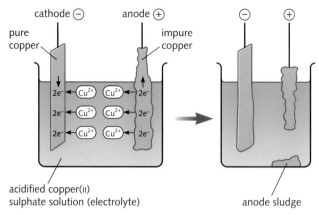

Figure 4.21 *The purification of copper by electrolysis. The movement of ions effectively transfers copper from one electrode to another.*

Electroplating and the purification of copper

Closer examination of an electroplating cell suggests an interesting method of purifying a metal. During electroplating the oxidation process at the anode involves the metal anode actually dissolving. Metal atoms lose electrons and pass into solution as positive metal ions. In turn, metal ions are discharged at the cathode as the object becomes plated.

A cell can be set up to electrolyse copper(II) sulphate solution using *copper* electrodes (not graphite). As electrolysis takes place, the cathode gains mass as copper is deposited on it (figure 4.21):

at the cathode $Cu^{2+}(aq) + 2e^- \rightarrow Cu(s)$

The anode, however, loses mass as copper dissolves from it:

at the anode $Cu(s) \rightarrow Cu^{2+}(aq) + 2e^-$

So, overall, there is a transfer of copper from the anode to the cathode. The colour of the copper(II) sulphate solution does not change because the concentration of the Cu^{2+} ions remains the same.

The copper used in electrical wiring must be very pure (99.99%). Copper made by roasting its sulphide ore in air is about 99.5% pure (so it

has an impurity level of 0.5%). This level of impurity cuts down its electrical conductivity significantly. Blocks of this impure metal are used as the anodes in a cell containing acidified copper(II) sulphate solution (figure 4.21). The cathodes are made of thin sheets of pure copper. During the refining process pure copper is removed from the impure anodes and deposited on the cathodes. Any impurities fall to the bottom of the cell. This material, or **anode sludge**, contains precious metals such as gold, silver and platinum. These can be purified from this sludge.

Although unusual, the anode reactions in copper refining and electroplating are still oxidation reactions (table 4.8). Electrons are being lost from the metal atoms as they pass into solution. These electrons are then 'pumped' round the circuit by the power source.

Table 4.8 **Reactions that occur during refining and plating**

	Electrolyte	Anode reaction (oxidation)	Cathode reaction (reduction)
Copper refining	copper sulphate solution	$Cu(s) \rightarrow Cu^{2+}(aq) + 2e^-$	$Cu^{2+}(aq) + 2e^- \rightarrow Cu(s)$
Silver-plating	silver nitrate solution	$Ag(s) \rightarrow Ag^+(aq) + e^-$	$Ag^+(aq) + e^- \rightarrow Ag(s)$
Chromium-plating	chromium(III) sulphate solution	$Cr(s) \rightarrow Cr^{3+}(aq) + 3e^-$	$Cr^{3+}(aq) + 3e^- \rightarrow Cr(s)$

Summary of extension material

You should know that:

- the reactions taking place at the electrodes during electrolysis can be regarded as oxidation or reduction reactions because the ions either lose or gain electrons when they are discharged
- oxidation takes place at the positive electrode (the anode), and reduction at the cathode

- the products of electrolysis can depend on the concentration of ions in the solution
- the method of electroplating can be adapted to provide a method of purifying (refining) copper – in these processes the electrodes are not inert and the anode actually dissolves.

4.16 In 1818, the Swedish scientist Berzelius discovered the element selenium. It has similar chemistry to that of sulphur, which is in the same group in the Periodic Table. Selenium is now obtained from the 'anode sludge' in the refining of copper by electrolysis.

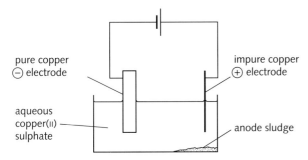

(a) Explain why the anode becomes smaller during this electrolysis. [1]

(b) Write an equation for the reaction at the negative electrode. [1]

(c) What technique could be used to separate the 'anode sludge' from the electrolyte? [1]

(IGCSE, part question, 1993)

4.17 The following diagram shows an experiment that can be carried out in a school laboratory.

(a) Dilute sulphuric acid contains the ions $H^+(aq)$, $OH^-(aq)$ and $SO_4^{2-}(aq)$. Name the gases formed at the positive and negative electrodes. [2]

(b) State the formula of aluminium oxide. [1]

(c) In a similar experiment, a piece of copper was used instead of the aluminium. No gas was formed at the positive electrode which became thinner. Explain these observations. [2]

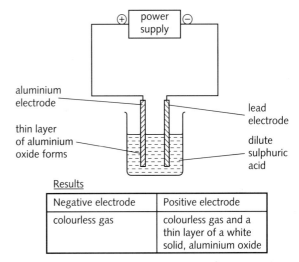

Results

Negative electrode	Positive electrode
colourless gas	colourless gas and a thin layer of a white solid, aluminium oxide

(IGCSE, part question, 1990)

4.18 Magnesium is obtained by the electrolysis of magnesium chloride in a cell similar to the one shown below.

(a) (i) What is the cathode made from? [1]
    (ii) What is the anode made from? [1]

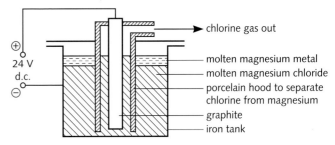

(iii) Why is the chlorine gas kept separate from the magnesium metal? [1]

(b) The magnesium chloride is made by the following reaction:
$$MgO + C + Cl_2 \rightarrow MgCl_2 + CO$$
Rewrite the equation in words. [2]

(c) Name *two* other metals that are obtained by electrolysis. [2]

(IGCSE, 1993)

5 Acids, bases and salts

An introduction to acids and alkalis

This section covers the following ideas:

- the acid–base properties of non-metal oxides and metal oxides
- common acids – where and how they occur
- organic acids and mineral acids
- the pH scale
- indicators – the colour changes of litmus and universal indicator
- the ions present in acid and alkali solutions
- the differences between acids and alkalis.

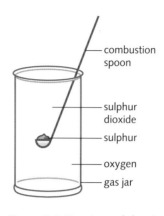

Figure 5.1 *Burning sulphur in a gas jar of oxygen.*

Venus, the Earth's nearest neighbour, is identical in size and density to the Earth. But Venus has yielded its secrets reluctantly, because it is veiled in clouds and has an atmosphere that destroys space probes. Magellan, the latest space probe to Venus, has looked from a distance. If it went into the atmosphere, it would meet with thick clouds of sulphuric acid and temperatures similar to those in a self-cleaning oven – acid rain with a vengeance! The probe would not last long!

The sulphuric acid clouds of Venus are the product of great volcanic activity. This has thrown out huge amounts of water vapour and the oxides of sulphur into the planet's atmosphere. Similar acidic clouds can be made in a gas jar by lowering burning sulphur into oxygen (figure 5.1):

$$S(s) + O_2(g) \rightarrow SO_2(g)$$

Other burning non-metals (carbon, for example) react in the same way to produce acidic gases:

$$C(s) + O_2(g) \rightarrow CO_2(g)$$

Water added to the gas jars dissolves the gases and gives solutions that *turn blue litmus paper red*. Metals burning in oxygen produce solid products. Some of these dissolve in water to give solutions that *turn red litmus paper blue*. You might be able to work out a pattern in the reactions of some elements with oxygen shown in table 5.1.

The characteristics of **oxides**:

- **non-metals** generally form oxides that dissolve in water to form *acidic* solutions,
- **metals** form oxides that are solids. If they dissolve in water, these oxides give *alkaline* solutions.

Turning litmus paper red shows that these solutions contain acids. But what is an acid? Indeed, what type of substance is litmus?

5.1 What is an acid?

Originally the word *acid* was applied to substances with a 'sour' taste. Vinegar, lemon juice, grapefruit juice and spoilt milk are all sour tasting because of the presence of acids. These acids are present in animal and plant material and are known as **organic acids** (table 5.2).

Carbonic acid from carbon dioxide dissolved in water is present in Coke, Pepsi and other fizzy drinks. The acids present in these circumstances are weak and dilute. But taste is not a test that should be tried – some acids would be dangerous, even deadly, to taste!

A number of acids are also **corrosive**. They can eat their way through clothing, are dangerous on the

Table 5.1 The reactions of certain elements with oxygen

Element	How it reacts	Product	Effect of adding water and testing with litmus
Sulphur	burns with bright blue flame	colourless gas (sulphur dioxide, SO_2)	dissolves, turns litmus *red*
Phosphorus	burns with yellow flame	white solid (phosphorus(v) oxide, P_2O_5)	dissolves, turns litmus *red*
Carbon	glows red	colourless gas (carbon dioxide, CO_2)	dissolves slightly, slowly turns litmus *red*
Sodium	burns with yellow flame	white solid (sodium oxide, Na_2O)	dissolves, turns litmus *blue*
Magnesium	burns with bright white flame	white solid (magnesium oxide, MgO)	dissolves slightly, turns litmus *blue*
Calcium	burns with red flame	white solid (calcium oxide, CaO)	dissolves, turns litmus *blue*
Iron	burns with yellow sparks	blue-black solid (iron oxide, FeO)	insoluble
Copper	does not burn, turns black	black solid (copper oxide, CuO)	insoluble

skin, and some are able to attack stonework and metals. These powerful acids are often called **mineral acids** (table 5.2). Table 5.2 also gives us some idea of how commonly acids occur.

5.2 What is litmus?

Certain coloured substances (many extracted from plants) have been found to change colour if added to an acid solution. This colour change is reversed if the acid is 'cancelled out' or neutralised. Substances that do this are known as **indicators**.

Coloured extracts can be made from red cabbage or blackberries, but probably the most used indicator is **litmus**. This is extracted from lichens.

Litmus is purple in neutral solution. When added to an acidic solution, it turns *red*. Changing this red colour of litmus needs a chemical reaction. The molecules of the indicator are actually changed in the presence of the acid. Substances with the opposite chemical effect to acids are needed to reverse the change, and these are called **alkalis**. They turn litmus solution *blue*. Litmus can also be

Table 5.2 Some common acids

Type	Name	Formula	Strong or weak?	Where found or used
Mineral acids	Carbonic acid	H_2CO_3	weak	in fizzy soft drinks
	Hydrochloric acid	HCl	strong	used in cleaning metal surfaces; found as the dilute acid in the stomach
	Nitric acid	HNO_3	strong	used in making fertilisers and explosives
	Sulphuric acid	H_2SO_4	strong	in car batteries; used in making fertilisers, paints and detergents
	Phosphoric acid	H_3PO_4	strong	in anti-rust paint; used in making fertilisers
Organic acids	Ethanoic acid	CH_3COOH	weak	in vinegar
	Methanoic acid	$HCOOH$	weak	in ant and nettle stings; used in kettle descaler
	Lactic acid	$CH_3CH(OH)$ | $COOH$	weak	in sour milk
	Citric acid	$C_6H_8O_7$	weak	in lemons, oranges and other citrus fruits

used in paper form. Here it comes in blue and red forms. The blue form of litmus paper changes colour to red when dipped into acid solutions. Red litmus paper turns blue in alkali solutions. Litmus is a single chemical compound. It gives a single colour change:

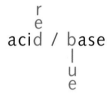

Litmus is not the only single indicator that chemists find useful. Others that are used frequently are **phenolphthalein** and **methyl orange**. They give different colour changes to litmus (table 5.3). These changes are sometimes easier to 'see' than that of litmus.

Another commonly used indicator, **universal indicator** (or full-range indicator), is a mixture of dyes. Such an indicator is useful because it gives a range of colours (a 'spectrum') depending on the strength of the acid or alkali added (figure 5.2). When you use universal indicator, you see that solutions of different acids produce different colours. Indeed, solutions of the same acid with different concentrations give different colours.

The more acidic solutions (for example battery acid) turn universal indicator bright red. A less acidic solution (for example vinegar) will only turn it orange-yellow. There are also colour differences

Table 5.3 Some common indicator colour changes

Indicator	Colour in acid	Neutral colour	Colour in alkali
Litmus	red	purple	blue
Phenolphthalein	colourless	colourless	pink
Methyl orange	red	orange	yellow

produced with different alkali solutions. The most alkaline solutions give a violet colour.

5.3 The pH scale

A much more useful measure of the strength of an acid solution was worked out by the Danish biochemist S. Sorensen. He worked in the laboratories of the Carlsberg breweries and was interested in checking the acidity of beer. The scale he introduced was the **pH scale**. The scale runs from 1 to 14, and the following general rules apply.

Rules for the **pH scale**:

- acids have a pH less than 7,
- the more acidic a solution, the lower the pH,
- neutral substances, such as pure water, have a pH of 7,
- alkalis have a pH greater than 7,
- the more alkaline a solution, the higher the pH.

The pH of a solution can be measured in several ways. Universal indicator papers that are sensitive over the full range of values can be used. Alternatively, if the approximate pH value is known, then we can use a more accurate test paper that is sensitive over a narrow range. The most accurate method is to use a **pH meter**, which uses an electrode to measure pH electrically. The pH values of some common solutions are shown in table 5.4.

5.4 The ionic nature of acid and alkali solutions

If we look again at the chemical formulas of some of the most well-known acids, we see that one element is common to them all. They all contain *hydrogen*. If solutions of these acids are checked to see if they conduct electricity, we find that they all

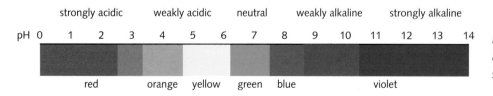

Figure 5.2 How the colour of universal indicator changes in solutions of different pH values.

Table 5.4 The pH values of some common solutions

	Substances	pH
Strongly acidic	Hydrochloric acid (HCl)	0.0
	Gastric juices	1.0
	Lemon juice	2.5
	Vinegar	3.0
	Wine	3.5
	Tomato juice	4.1
	Black coffee	5.0
	Acid rain	5.6
	Urine	6.0
Weakly acidic	Rain water	6.5
	Milk	6.5
Neutral	Pure water	7.0
Weakly alkaline	Blood	7.4
	Baking soda solution	8.5
	Toothpaste	9.0
	Borax solution	9.2
	Milk of Magnesia	10.5
	Limewater	11.0
Strongly alkaline	Household ammonia	12.0
	Sodium hydroxide (NaOH)	14.0

do. Also, they conduct much better than distilled water. This shows that the solutions contain *ions*. Water itself contains very few ions. In pure water the concentrations of hydrogen ions (H^+) and hydroxide ions (OH^-) are equal. All acids dissolve in water to produce hydrogen ions (H^+ ions). Therefore, all acid solutions contain an excess of H^+ ions.

Alkali solutions also conduct electricity better than distilled water. All alkalis dissolve in water to produce hydroxide ions (OH^- ions). Therefore, all alkali solutions contain an excess of OH^- ions.

An indicator, like litmus, is affected by the presence of H^+ or OH^- ions.

- The **hydrogen ions** (H^+) in acids make litmus go *red*.
- The **hydroxide ions** (OH^-) in alkalis make litmus go *blue*.

The ions present in some important acid and alkali solutions are given in table 5.5.

5.5 The importance of water

When is an acid not an acid, but simply an 'acid-in-waiting'? Hydrochloric acid is a good example to illustrate this problem. The gas hydrogen chloride is made up of covalently bonded molecules. If the gas is dissolved in an organic solvent, such as methylbenzene, it does not show any of the properties of an acid. For example, it does not conduct electricity or turn a piece of blue litmus paper red. However, when the gas is dissolved in water, a strongly acidic solution *is* produced. The **acidic oxides** of sulphur, phosphorus and carbon listed in table 5.1 on page 127 are similar. They are covalent molecules when pure, but show acidic properties when dissolved in water.

An **acid** is a substance that dissolves in water to produce hydrogen ions (H^+). This gives a solution which:

- contains an excess of H^+ ions,
- turns litmus red,
- has a pH lower than 7.

An **alkali** is a substance that dissolves in water to produce hydroxide ions (OH^-). This gives a solution which:

- contains an excess of OH^- ions,
- turns litmus blue,
- has a pH higher than 7

Table 5.5 The ions present in solutions of the main acids and alkalis

	Name	Ions present
Acids	Hydrochloric acid	$H^+(aq)$ and $Cl^-(aq)$
	Nitric acid	$H^+(aq)$ and $NO_3^-(aq)$
	Sulphuric acid	$H^+(aq)$, $HSO_4^-(aq)$ and $SO_4^{2-}(aq)$
Alkalis	Sodium hydroxide	$Na^+(aq)$ and $OH^-(aq)$
	Potassium hydroxide	$K^+(aq)$ and $OH^-(aq)$
	Calcium hydroxide	$Ca^{2+}(aq)$ and $OH^-(aq)$
	Ammonia solution	$NH_4^+(aq)$ and $OH^-(aq)$

Thus, in our most useful definition of an acid, the characteristic properties of an acid are shown when dissolved in water. Alkalis are also normally used in aqueous solution. Both acids and alkalis can be used in dilute or concentrated solutions. If a large volume of water is added to a small amount of acid or alkali, then the solution is **dilute**; using less water gives a more **concentrated** solution.

Summary of core material

You should know that:

- the oxides of non-metals mainly form acidic solutions, and the oxides of metals, if soluble, mainly form alkaline solutions
- all acids contain hydrogen and dissolve in water to give solutions with a pH below 7
- pH is a measure of the acidity or alkalinity of an aqueous solution of a substance
  - solutions with a pH less than 7 are acidic
  - solutions with a pH greater than 7 are alkaline
  - a pH of 7 shows that a solution is neutral
- acid and alkali solutions conduct electricity – they contain ions
- acid solutions contain an excess of hydrogen ions, and alkali solutions contain an excess of hydroxide ions
- acids turn litmus red, and alkalis turn litmus blue – other single indicators have their own specific colour change
- universal indicator shows a range of colours depending on the pH of the solution tested.

5.1 In table 5.2 on page 127, methanoic acid, ethanoic acid and lactic acid all have one group of atoms in common.

(a) What is the formula of that group? [1]

(b) The formulas of citric acid and ascorbic acid (vitamin C) can be written:

citric acid

ascorbic acid

Do citric acid and ascorbic acid contain the same group as found in ethanoic acid?
 (i) Citric acid? [1]
 (ii) Ascorbic acid? [1]

(c) Tartaric acid has the structure:

What would be its molecular formula? [1]

5.2 Read the following passage and answer the questions that follow.

A chemical factory needs to use four liquids in a new process. The Chemical Engineer tested five metals in order to find which would be the least corroded by the liquids so that the most suitable could be chosen to make the pipes to carry these liquids. The results of the tests are shown in the table below.

More ✓s = more corrosion

Results

Metal	Water	Dilute acid	Dilute alkali	Salt solution
A	✓	✓	✓✓	✓
B	✓✓	✓✓	✓✓✓	✓✓✓✓
C	✓	✓✓✓	✓✓	✓✓
D	✓✓	✓✓✓✓	✓	✓✓
E	✓	✓✓	✓✓	✓✓✓

(a) Which metal would be the best for the pipe to carry acid? [1]

(b) Which metal would be best for the pipe to carry alkali? [1]

(c) Which metal would be best for carrying most of the liquids? [1]

(d) Which is the least suitable metal to carry the salt solution? [1]

(WJEC, 1993)

5.3 Seven steel bars were placed in solutions of different pH for the same length of time. The amount of corrosion was estimated. The percentage corrosion is given in the table:

Solution pH	1	2	3	4	5	6	7
Corrosion (%)	60	55	50	45	15	10	5

(a) Using graph paper, plot the percentage corrosion against the pH of the solution. [3]

(b) From your graph make an estimate of the percentage corrosion at pH 4.5. [1]

5.4 A group of students measured the pH of some substances they found in their homes. Their results are given in the table below.

Substance	pH
Apples	3.0
Baking soda (sodium hydrogencarbonate)	8.5
Black coffee	5.0
Household ammonia	12.0
Lemon juice	2.5
Milk	6.5
Salt	7.0
Sugar	7.0
Toothpaste	9.0
Vinegar	3.0
Washing soda (sodium carbonate)	11.5

(a) What would the students have used to measure the pH? [1]

(b) Which solution is
(i) the most acidic? [1]
(ii) the most alkaline? [1]

(c) Which solutions are neutral? [2]

(d) A first aid manual suggests that vinegar should be used to treat wasp stings and baking soda for bee stings.
(i) What does this information tell you about the chemical nature of wasp stings? [1]
(ii) If there was no baking soda in the house what other household substance could you use to treat bee stings? [1]

(NISEAC, 1993)

5.5 The descriptions that follow are taken from 'HAZARD CARDS' for two mineral acids.

(a) Which of the hazard symbols (1–8) would you put on bottles of the following solutions:
(i) concentrated sulphuric acid, [1]
(ii) bench dilute sulphuric acid (1 mol/dm^3), [1]
(iii) bench dilute hydrochloric acid (2 mol/dm^3)? [1]

(b) What safety equipment should you always wear when using either of these acids? [2]

SULPHURIC ACID

VERY CORROSIVE

Causes severe burns.

Solutions of concentration 1.5 mol/dm^3 or greater should be labelled CORROSIVE.

Solutions of concentration between 0.5 and 1.5 mol/dm^3 should be labelled IRRITANT.

Fuming sulphuric acid (oleum) is more hazardous and is not recommended for use in schools.

DANGEROUS WITH:

Water. Vigorous reaction when the concentrated acid is diluted.

Hydrochloric Acid, Chlorides. Hydrogen chloride given off.

Sodium, Potassium and many other metals. Dangerous reactions can take place.

ALWAYS ADD THE CONCENTRATED ACID SLOWLY TO COLD WATER WHEN DILUTING, NEVER THE REVERSE.

STIR FREQUENTLY TO ENSURE THOROUGH MIXING.

HYDROCHLORIC ACID

CORROSIVE

May cause burns.

The vapour is very irritating to the respiratory system.

Solutions of concentration 6.5 mol/dm^3 or greater are CORROSIVE.

Solutions of concentration 2 mol/dm^3 or greater are IRRITANT.

It may be sensible to label 1 mol/dm^3 solutions as irritant as well.

(c) Comparing solutions of the two acids with the same concentration, which of the two acids do you think is the more dangerous? Explain your reasons. [3]

5.6 Below is a safety label of the kind that would be on a road tanker in Britain.

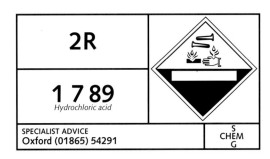

(a) What chemical is this road tanker carrying? [1]

(b) What is the missing word under the picture on the label? [1]

(c) A newspaper carried the following report after a road accident involving the tanker.

> A road tanker carrying acid was involved in an accident and its contents spilled onto the road. At the side of the road iron drain covers began melting and fizzing as the acid ran over them. A specialist has been called to see if the acid has leaked into the nearby river.

Explain how the specialist could carry out a simple test to see if the nearby river contains any acid. [2]

(d) If the specialist finds that a lot of acid has leaked into the river, suggest what chemical advice the specialist might give to overcome this problem. [2]

(e) The word *melting* is incorrectly used in the report. Explain what is the correct meaning of melting and suggest a word that should have been used instead of melting in the report. [3]

(f) Explain why the drain covers began fizzing as the acid ran over them. [3]

(SEG, 1990)

The chemical reactions of acids and bases

This section covers the following ideas:

- some common examples of the importance of acids and pH, including soil pH and plant growth
- alkalis and bases
- uses of common alkalis and bases
- antacids
- characteristic reactions of acids
  - with metals
  - with alkalis and bases, called neutralisation
  - with metal carbonates
- acids and alkalis in the analysis of salts.

5.6 Acid reactions in everyday life

Indigestion, headaches and neutralisation

The dilute hydrochloric acid in our stomach is there to help digest our food. However, excess acid causes indigestion, which can be painful. To ease this, we can take an antacid treatment. **Antacids** (or 'anti-acids') are a broad group of compounds with no toxic effects on the body. They are used to neutralise the effects of acid indigestion.

Some of these antacids, such as 'Milk of Magnesia', contain insoluble material to counteract the acid. 'Milk of Magnesia' contains insoluble magnesium hydroxide.

Other **effervescent** or 'fizzy' antacids, such as 'Alka-Seltzer', contain soluble material, including sodium hydrogencarbonate. These tablets also contain some citric acid – a solid acid. On adding water, the acid and some of the sodium hydrogencarbonate react, producing carbon dioxide gas – the 'fizz' in the glass. This helps to spread and dissolve the other less soluble material. When drunk, more sodium hydrogencarbonate neutralises the excess hydrochloric acid in the stomach, easing the indigestion.

Some antacid tablets also contain a painkiller to relieve headaches. 'Soluble aspirin' tablets dissolve and work in a similar way to 'Alka-Seltzer' tablets. Vitamin C (ascorbic acid – another soluble acid) can also be added to the tablet. Note the importance of adding water to start the action of the acid. The tablets do not react in the packet!

Descaling kettles

Limescale collects inside kettles and water heaters in hard water areas. Hard water contains more dissolved calcium ions than normal water (see page 231). Calcium carbonate forms when the water is boiled. This limescale can be removed by treatment with an acid that is strong enough to react with calcium carbonate, but not strong enough to damage the metal. Vinegar can be used to descale kettles. Commercial 'descalers' use other acid solutions such as methanoic acid.

Toothpaste and tooth decay

Acid forms in the mouth after sugary food has been eaten. The pH of a sugar solution is about 7. However, bacteria in your mouth break down the sugar to form acids, for example lactic acid. These acids lower the pH. Tooth decay begins when the pH falls below 5.8. This happens about 2–3 minutes after eating sweet things. The tooth enamel can be attacked by the acid.

To help take away this acidity, many toothpastes contain substances to neutralise the acid. Their pH is alkaline (higher than 7) (see table 5.4 on page 129). The pH of saliva is slightly alkaline (pH 7.4), so it can also help to counteract the acid, particularly after a meal. After eating a sweet, for example, it takes about 15 minutes for saliva to raise the pH above 5.8, and stop further decay.

Soil pH and plant growth

Plant growth is affected by the acidity or alkalinity of the soil. Soils with a high peat content, or with minerals such as iron compounds, or with rotting vegetation and lack of oxygen, tend to be acidic. Their **soil pH** can reach as low as pH 4. Soils in limestone or chalky areas are alkaline – up to pH 8.3. The soil pH is also affected by the use of fertilisers and the acidity of rainfall. Different plants prefer different pH conditions (table 5.6). Farmers and gardeners can test the soil pH to see whether it suits the needs of particular plants.

Table 5.6 Preferred soil pH conditions for different vegetables

Vegetables	Preferred pH range
Potatoes	4.5–6.0
Chicory, parsley	5.0–6.5
Carrot, sweet potato	5.5–6.5
Cauliflower, garlic, tomato	5.5–7.5
Broad bean, onion, cabbage and many others	6.0–7.5

If the soil is too *acidic*, it is usually treated by 'liming'. 'Lime' here is a loose term meaning either calcium oxide, calcium hydroxide, or powdered chalk or limestone (calcium carbonate). These compounds all have the effect of neutralising the acidity of the soil. If the soil is too *alkaline*, it helps to dig in some peat or decaying organic matter (compost or manure).

Some flowering plants carry their own 'built-in' pH indicator. The flowers of a hydrangea bush are blue when grown on acid soil and pink when the soil pH is alkaline.

5.7 Alkalis and bases

What type of substances are alkalis and bases?

In section 5.6 we saw that the effects of acids could be neutralised by alkalis. Alkalis are substances that dissolve in water to give solutions with a pH greater than 7 and turn litmus blue. The solutions contain an excess of hydroxide, OH^-, ions.

However, among the antacids we use to relieve indigestion is *insoluble* magnesium hydroxide, which also neutralises acids. As we investigate further, it is found that *all* metal oxides and hydroxides will neutralise acids, whether they dissolve in water or not. Therefore the soluble **alkalis** are just a small part of a group of substances – the oxides and hydroxides of metals – that neutralise acids. These substances are known as **bases** (figure 5.3).

Figure 5.3 This Venn diagram shows the relationship between bases and alkalis. All alkalis are bases, but not all bases are alkalis.

These bases all react in the same way with acids. A base will neutralise an acid, and in the process a **salt** is formed. This type of reaction is known as a **neutralisation reaction**. It can be summed up in a general equation:

acid + base → salt + water

Therefore a base can be defined in the following way.

A **base** is a substance that reacts with an acid to form a salt and water only.

Most bases are insoluble in water. This makes the few bases that *do* dissolve in water more significant. They are given a special name – **alkalis**.

An **alkali** is a base that is soluble in water.

The common alkalis are:

- sodium hydroxide,
- potassium hydroxide,
- calcium hydroxide (often known as limewater),
- ammonia solution (also known as ammonium hydroxide).

These solutions contain OH^- ions, turn litmus blue and have a pH higher than 7. The first two are stronger alkalis than the others.

Properties and uses of alkalis and bases

Alkalis feel soapy to the skin. They convert the oils in your skin into soap. They are used as degreasing agents because they convert oil and grease into soluble soaps, which can be washed away easily. The common uses of some alkalis and bases are shown in table 5.7.

The properties of bases, alkalis and antacids can be summarised as follows.

Bases:

- neutralise acids to give a salt and water only,
- are the oxides and hydroxides of metals,
- are mainly insoluble in water.

Alkalis are bases that dissolve in water and:

- feel soapy to the skin,
- turn litmus blue,
- give solutions with a pH greater than 7,
- give solutions that contain OH^- ions.

Antacids are compounds that are used to neutralise acid indigestion and include:

- magnesium oxide and magnesium hydroxide,
- sodium carbonate and sodium hydrogencarbonate,
- calcium carbonate and magnesium carbonate.

5.8 Characteristic reactions of acids

All acids can take part in neutralisation reactions. But are there any other reactions that are characteristic of all acids? The answer is 'Yes'. There are three major chemical reactions in which all acids will take part. These reactions are best seen using dilute acid solutions. In these reactions, the acid reacts with:

- a reactive metal (for example magnesium or zinc),
- a base (or alkali) – a neutralisation reaction,
- a metal carbonate (or metal hydrogencarbonate).

Table 5.7 Some common alkalis and bases

Type	Name	Formula	Strong or weak?	Where found or used
Alkalis	Sodium hydroxide (caustic soda)	NaOH	strong	in oven cleaners (degreasing agent); in making soap and paper; other industrial uses
	Calcium hydroxide (limewater)	$Ca(OH)_2$	strong	to neutralise soil acidity; to neutralise acid gases produced by power stations
	Ammonia solution (ammonium hydroxide)	$NH_3(aq)$ or (NH_4OH)	weak	in cleaning fluids in the home (degreasing agent); making fertilisers
Bases	Calcium oxide	CaO	strong	neutralising soil acidity and industrial waste; making cement and concrete
	Magnesium oxide	MgO	strong	in antacid indigestion tablets

One type of product is common to all these reactions. They all produce a metal compound called a **salt**. In all of them, the hydrogen present in the acid is replaced by a metal to give the salt. The acid from which the salt is made is often called the **parent acid** of the salt.

Normally we use the word *salt* to mean 'common salt', which is sodium chloride. This is the salt we put on our food, the main salt found in sea water, and the salt used over centuries to preserve food. However, in chemistry, the word has a more general meaning.

A **salt** is a compound made from an acid when a metal takes the place of the hydrogen in the acid.

The reaction of acids with metals

Metals that are *quite* reactive (not the *very* reactive ones, see page 269) can displace the hydrogen from an acid safely. Hydrogen gas is given off. The salt made depends on the combination of metal and acid used:

metal + acid → salt + hydrogen

It is unsafe to try this reaction with *very* reactive metals such as sodium or calcium. The reaction is too violent. No reaction occurs with metals such as copper, which are less reactive than lead. Even with lead, it is difficult to see any reaction in a short time.

The **salt** made depends on the acid:
- hydrochloric acid always gives a chloride,
- nitric acid always gives a nitrate,
- sulphuric acid always gives a sulphate,
- ethanoic acid always gives an ethanoate.

For example

magnesium + nitric acid
    → magnesium nitrate + hydrogen

$Mg(s) + 2HNO_3(aq)$
    $→ Mg(NO_3)_2(aq) + H_2(g)$

zinc + hydrochloric acid
    → zinc chloride + hydrogen

$Zn(s) + 2HCl(aq) → ZnCl_2(aq) + H_2(g)$

The reaction of acids with bases and alkalis

This is the neutralisation reaction that we saw on page 133:

acid + base → salt + water

The salt produced by this reaction will again depend on the combination of reactants used. To make a particular salt, you choose a suitable acid and base to give a neutral solution of the salt you want. For example

sodium hydroxide + hydrochloric acid
    → sodium chloride + water

$NaOH(aq) + HCl(aq) → NaCl(aq) + H_2O(l)$

Other examples of salts made by different combinations of acid and base are shown in table 5.8.

Table 5.8 Some examples of making salts

Base	Acid		
	Hydrochloric acid (HCl)	Nitric acid (HNO$_3$)	Sulphuric acid (H$_2$SO$_4$)
Sodium hydroxide (NaOH)	sodium chloride, NaCl	sodium nitrate, NaNO$_3$	sodium sulphate, Na$_2$SO$_4$
Potassium hydroxide (KOH)	potassium chloride, KCl	potassium nitrate, KNO$_3$	potassium sulphate, K$_2$SO$_4$
Magnesium oxide (MgO)	magnesium chloride, MgCl$_2$	magnesium nitrate, Mg(NO$_3$)$_2$	magnesium sulphate, MgSO$_4$
Copper oxide (CuO)	copper chloride, CuCl$_2$	copper nitrate, Cu(NO$_3$)$_2$	copper sulphate, CuSO$_4$

The reaction of acids with carbonates

All carbonates give off carbon dioxide when they react with acids. We have seen that this reaction occurs with effervescent antacid tablets. The result is to neutralise the acid and produce a salt solution:

> acid + metal carbonate
> → salt + water + carbon dioxide

The normal method of preparing carbon dioxide in the laboratory is based on this reaction. Dilute hydrochloric acid is reacted with marble chips (calcium carbonate):

hydrochloric acid + calcium carbonate
→ calcium chloride + water + carbon dioxide

$2HCl(aq) + CaCO_3(s)$
$→ CaCl_2(aq) + H_2O(l) + CO_2(g)$

5.9 Acids and bases in chemical analysis

The test for carbonates using acid

All carbonates will react with acids to give off carbon dioxide. We can use this as a test to find out if an unknown substance is a carbonate or not. A piece of rock that we think is limestone can be checked by dropping a few drops of vinegar on it. If it 'fizzes', then it could be limestone. A more usual test would be to add dilute hydrochloric acid to the powdered substance. Any gas given off would be passed into **limewater** (calcium hydroxide solution) to see if it went cloudy. If the limewater *does* turn cloudy, the gas is carbon dioxide, and the substance is a carbonate. Figure 5.4 shows how an antacid tablet can be tested to see if it contains a carbonate.

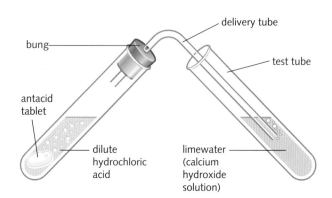

Figure 5.4 Testing an antacid tablet.

Table 5.9 The ions making up certain important salts

Salt	Positive ions	Negative ions
Sodium chloride	Na^+ ions	Cl^- ions
Potassium nitrate	K^+ ions	NO_3^- ions
Copper(II) sulphate	Cu^{2+} ions	SO_4^{2-} ions
Calcium carbonate	Ca^{2+} ions	CO_3^{2-} ions
Sodium ethanoate	Na^+ ions	CH_3COO^- ions

Tests for metal ions in salts using alkalis

All salts are ionic compounds. They are made up of a positive metal ion, combined with a negative non-metal ion. Thus common salt, sodium chloride, is made up of sodium metal ions (Na^+ ions) and chloride non-metal ions (Cl^- ions). Table 5.9 shows the ions that form certain important salts.

In analysis it would be useful to have tests for the metal ions in salts. We have seen that most metal hydroxides are insoluble. Some of them are also coloured. As a result, a solution of a salt can be tested by adding an alkali to it and checking the colour of the precipitate (figure 5.5):

- copper(II) salts give a light blue precipitate of copper(II) hydroxide.
- iron(II) salts give a light green precipitate of iron(II) hydroxide.
- iron(III) salts give a red-brown precipitate of iron(III) hydroxide.

For example

iron(II) sulphate + sodium hydroxide
→ iron(II) hydroxide + sodium sulphate

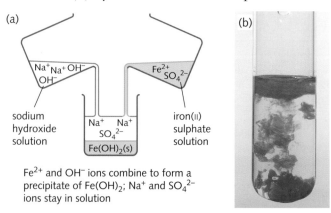

(a)

sodium hydroxide solution

iron(II) sulphate solution

$Fe(OH)_2(s)$

Fe^{2+} and OH^- ions combine to form a precipitate of $Fe(OH)_2$; Na^+ and SO_4^{2-} ions stay in solution

(b)

Figure 5.5 (a) The precipitation of iron(II) hydroxide. (b) The precipitation of iron(III) hydroxide. Note the different colour of the precipitates.

$FeSO_4(aq) + 2NaOH(aq)$
$\rightarrow Fe(OH)_2(s) + Na_2SO_4(aq)$

The test for ammonium salts using alkali

Ammonium salts are important as fertilisers, for example ammonium nitrate and ammonium sulphate (see section 10.11 on page 293). These are industrially important chemicals made by reacting ammonia with nitric acid or sulphuric acid, respectively. They are salts containing ammonium ions, NH_4^+ ions. These salts react with alkali solutions to produce ammonia gas, which can be detected because it turns damp red litmus paper blue:

ammonium nitrate + sodium hydroxide
$\rightarrow$ sodium nitrate + water + ammonia

$NH_4NO_3(s) + NaOH(aq)$
$\rightarrow NaNO_3(aq) + H_2O(l) + NH_3(g)$

This reaction can be used to test an unknown substance for ammonium ions. It can also be used to prepare ammonia in the laboratory.

Summary of core material

You should know that:

- bases are the 'chemical opposites' of acids and neutralise the effects of acids

- some bases are soluble in water – these bases are called alkalis

- acids react with bases to produce a salt and water only – this is a neutralisation reaction

- acids also show characteristic reactions with
  – some metals, to give a salt and hydrogen gas
  – metal carbonates, to give a salt, water and carbon dioxide gas.

5.7 A garden centre sells a simple soil testing kit. It consists of a tube containing a small amount of an off-white solid and an instruction card. The instructions follow.

(a) How was the colour produced in the tube? [3]

(b) What scale do scientists use to measure acidity and alkalinity? [1]

(c) Give the name of *one* substance that a gardener would use to remove acidity from the soil. [1]

(d) Gardeners sometimes treat an alkaline soil by adding peat. What does this tell you about the chemical nature of peat? [1]

(1) Take a sample of soil from 10 cm below the surface of the soil.
(2) Quarter fill the tube with the soil sample.
(3) Three quarters fill the tube with water.
(4) Shake the tube for half a minute and then allow to settle.
(5) Compare the colour of the liquid with the card (on the instruction card):

Chart colour	Soil
bright orange	very acid
pale orange	acid
pale green	neutral
dark green	alkaline

(NISEAC, 1992)

5.8 A seed catalogue states the preferred soil pH ranges for plants.

Type of plant	Preferred pH range
Heather	4.5–6.0
Violet	5.0–7.5
Primrose	5.5–6.5
Daffodil	6.0–6.5

(a) Which plant will grow over the largest pH range? [1]
   A heather **B** violet **C** primrose **D** daffodil

(b) At which soil pH will a gardener be able to grow all of these plants? [1]
   A 4.5 **B** 5.0 **C** 5.5 **D** 6.0

(c) Which plant can be grown in alkaline soil? [1]
   A heather **B** violet **C** primrose **D** daffodil

(d) The soil in a garden has a pH of 4.5. Which substance needs to be added to the soil in order to grow daffodils? [1]
   A salt **B** lime **C** sand **D** peat

(MEG, 1993)

5.9 Copy and complete the following word equations:

(a) zinc + sulphuric acid $\rightarrow$ .... + ... [2]

(b) sodium hydroxide + nitric acid $\rightarrow$ .... + ... [2]

(c) magnesium carbonate + hydrochloric acid $\rightarrow$ .... + ... + water [2]

(NEAB, 1992)

5.10 Bases have the following properties in common.
1 Bases react with acids to make salts.
2 Soluble bases can change the colour of indicators.
3 Soluble bases react with fats and oils to make soaps.

(a) What name is given to the chemical reaction which occurs when a base reacts with an acid? [1]

(b) What name is used to describe soluble bases? [1]

137

(c) What colour would universal (full range) indicator be turned by a soluble base? [1]

(d) Sodium hydroxide is used in oven cleaner. On which of the above properties, **1**, **2**, or **3**, does this use depend? [1]

(NEAB, 1991)

5.11 The diagram on the right shows some reactions of dilute sulphuric acid. Use it to answer the questions which follow.

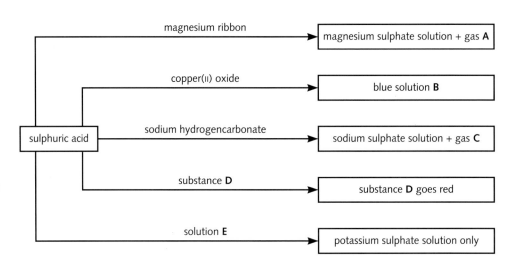

Name or give the formula of each of the following:

(a) gas **A**; [1]

(b) solution **B**; [1]

(c) gas **C**; [1]

(d) substance **D**; [1]

(e) solution **E**. [1]

(NEAB, 1991)

5.12 Reactions that give off carbon dioxide are used to raise dough when baking bread. On cooking, the bubbles of carbon dioxide become trapped in the dough and give the bread a pleasing texture.

The ingredients are made into a dough which is left in a warm place for about 30 minutes. The volume of the dough increases as carbon dioxide is produced from the sugar by the yeast.

(a) There are two ionic compounds in the recipe. Name *one* of them. [1]

The dough is then placed in a hot oven and the baking powder produces more carbon dioxide as the naan bread cooks.

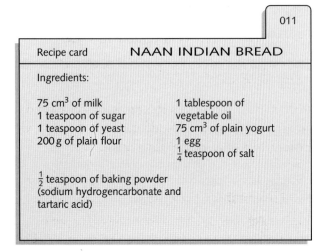

Sodium hydrogencarbonate decomposes when heated:

$$2NaHCO_3 \rightarrow Na_2CO_3 + CO_2 + H_2O$$

Sodium carbonate has an unpleasant taste. It reacts with the tartaric acid to form sodium tartrate which has a pleasant flavour.

(b) What type of compound is sodium tartrate? [1]

(c) Suggest *two* reasons why *baking powder* is a mixture of tartaric acid and sodium hydrogencarbonate, and not just sodium hydrogencarbonate. [2]

(IGCSE, part question, 1990)

Salts and their preparation

This section covers the following ideas:

- salts and some of their uses
- the importance of 'common salt' (sodium chloride)
- the solubility of salts in water
- the preparation of soluble salts by various methods, including titration
- preparing insoluble salts by precipitation
- making salts by direct combination
- efflorescence and deliquescence.

5.10 The importance of salts

A **salt** is a compound formed from an acid by the replacement of the hydrogen in the acid by a metal. They are ionic compounds. There are a wide range of types of salt. A great number of them play an important part in our everyday life (table 5.10).

Table 5.10 Salts in common use

Salt	Parent acid	Colour and other characteristics	Uses
Ammonium chloride	hydrochloric acid	white crystals	fertilisers; dry cells (batteries)
Ammonium nitrate	nitric acid	white crystals	fertilisers; explosives
Ammonium sulphate	sulphuric acid	white crystals	fertilisers
Calcium carbonate (marble, limestone, chalk)	carbonic acid	white	decorative stones; making lime, cement and iron
Calcium sulphate (gypsum, plaster of Paris)	sulphuric acid	white crystals	wall plaster; plaster casts
Sodium carbonate (washing soda)	carbonic acid	white crystals or powder	in cleaning; water-softening; making glass
Magnesium sulphate (Epsom salts)	sulphuric acid	white crystals	health salts (laxative)
Copper(II) sulphate	sulphuric acid	blue crystals	fungicides
Calcium phosphate	phosphoric acid	white	making fertilisers

Many important minerals are single salts, for example fluorite (calcium fluoride) and gypsum (calcium sulphate). Common salt (sodium chloride) is mined from underground in Britain and other parts of the world. These salt deposits were formed by the evaporation of ancient seas millions of years ago. Solid 'rock salt' is mined in only one British mine, the Winsford mine in Cheshire. In other mines, the salt is dissolved underground and the solution, known as 'brine', is pumped up to the surface.

In hotter regions where the land is flat, for example the west coast of France and the coast near Adelaide in Australia, the sea can be fed into shallow inland pools. Here the water slowly evaporates in the sun and crystals of 'sea salt' form. These crystals are then scraped up from the surface. 'Sea salt' is not just sodium chloride; it also contains magnesium chloride, calcium sulphate, potassium bromide and other salts. Where vast inland saltwater lakes have evaporated naturally, such as in Utah, USA, huge salt 'flats' have been formed. The Bonneville Salt Flats have been used as a place to set world land speed records.

Sodium chloride is essential for life and is an important raw material for industries. Biologically, it has a number of functions: it is involved in muscle contraction; it enables the conduction of nerve impulses in the nervous system; it regulates osmosis (the passage of solvent molecules through membranes); and it is converted into the hydrochloric acid that aids digestion in the stomach. When we sweat, we lose both water and sodium chloride. Loss of too much salt during sport and exercise can give us muscle cramp. Isotonic drinks, such as 'Isostar', are designed to replace this loss of water and to restore energy and the balance of mineral ions in our body. Figure 5.6 on page 140 shows some industrial uses of sodium chloride.

While a number of salts can be obtained by mining, others must be made by industry. Therefore, it is worth considering the methods available to make salts. Some of these can be investigated in the laboratory. Two things are important in working out a method of preparation.

- Is the salt soluble or insoluble in water?
- Do crystals of the salt contain water of crystallisation?

The first point influences the preparation method chosen. The second point affects how the crystals are handled at the end of the experiment.

5.11 The solubility of salts

Soluble salts are made by neutralising an acid. Insoluble salts are made by other methods. Table

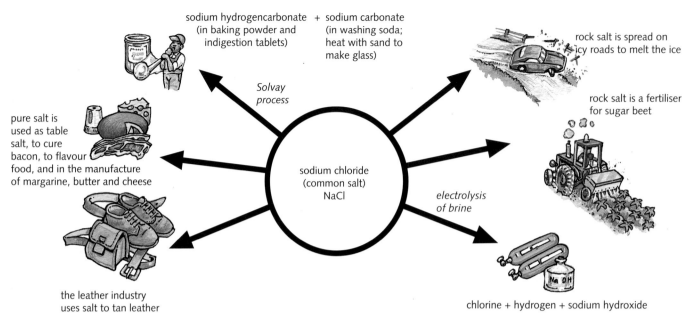

sodium hydrogencarbonate + sodium carbonate
(in baking powder and (in washing soda;
indigestion tablets) heat with sand to
make glass)

rock salt is spread on icy roads to melt the ice

rock salt is a fertiliser for sugar beet

pure salt is used as table salt, to cure bacon, to flavour food, and in the manufacture of margarine, butter and cheese

Solvay process

sodium chloride
(common salt)
NaCl

electrolysis
of brine

the leather industry uses salt to tan leather

chlorine + hydrogen + sodium hydroxide

Figure 5.6 Some uses of sodium chloride in industry.

5.11 outlines the general patterns of solubility for the more usual salts. We shall look at the preparation of both soluble salts and insoluble salts. But first we consider the second point mentioned above.

5.12 Water of crystallisation

The crystals of some salts contain **water of crystallisation**. This water gives the crystals their shape. In some cases it also gives them their colour. Such salts are known as **hydrated salts** (table 5.12). When these hydrated salts are heated, their water of crystallisation is driven off as steam. The crystals lose their shape and become a powder. Copper(II) sulphate crystals are blue, but when heated they are **dehydrated** to form a white powder:

copper(II) sulphate crystals
$\rightarrow$ anhydrous copper(II) sulphate + water vapour

$$CuSO_4 \cdot 5H_2O(s) \rightarrow CuSO_4(s) + 5H_2O(g)$$

Crystals that have lost their water of crystallisation are called **anhydrous**. If water is added back to the white anhydrous copper(II) sulphate powder, the

Table 5.11 The patterns of solubility for various types of salts

Salts	Soluble	Insoluble
Sodium salts	all are soluble	none
Potassium salts	all are soluble	none
Ammonium salts	all are soluble	none
Chlorides	most are soluble	silver chloride, lead(II) chloride
Nitrates	all are soluble	none
Sulphates	most are soluble	barium sulphate, lead(II) sulphate, calcium sulphate
Ethanoates	all are soluble	none
Carbonates	sodium, potassium and ammonium carbonates	most are insoluble

Table 5.12 Some hydrated salts

Hydrated salt	Formula	Colour
Copper(II) sulphate	$CuSO_4 \cdot 5H_2O$	blue
Cobalt(II) chloride	$CoCl_2 \cdot 6H_2O$	pink
Iron(II) sulphate	$FeSO_4 \cdot 6H_2O$	green
Magnesium sulphate	$MgSO_4 \cdot 7H_2O$	white
Sodium carbonate	$Na_2CO_3 \cdot 10H_2O$	white
Calcium sulphate	$CaSO_4 \cdot 2H_2O$	white

powder turns blue again and heat is given out. This can be used as a test for the presence of water.

When preparing crystals of a hydrated salt, we must be careful not to heat them too strongly when drying them.

5.13 Preparing soluble salts

Soluble salts can be made from their parent acid using any of the three characteristic reactions of acids we outlined earlier (section 5.8). The reaction method chosen depends on the following.

- Is the metal reactive enough to displace the hydrogen in the acid? If it is, is it too reactive and therefore unsafe?
- Is the base or carbonate soluble or insoluble?

Figure 5.7 shows a flow chart listing the choices available for making a soluble salt.

Method A (figure 5.8 on page 142)

Method A is essentially the same whether starting with a solid metal, a solid base, or a solid carbonate. The method can be divided into four stages.

- *Stage 1* An *excess* (more than enough) of the solid is added to the acid and allowed to react. Using an excess of the solid makes sure that all the acid is used up. If it is not used up at this stage, the acid would become more concentrated when the water is evaporated later (stage 3).

- *Stage 2* The excess solid is filtered out.
- *Stage 3* The filtrate is gently evaporated to concentrate the salt solution. This can be done on a heated water bath. Do not heat too strongly or 'spitting' might take place.
- *Stage 4* The concentrated solution is cooled to let the crystals form. Filter off the crystals. Wash them with a little distilled water. Dry the crystals carefully between filter papers.

Method B (figure 5.9 on page 142)

Method B (the **titration** method) involves the neutralisation of an acid with an alkali (for example sodium hydroxide) or a soluble carbonate (for example sodium carbonate). Since both the reactants and the products are colourless, an indicator is used to find the neutralisation point or **end point** (when all the acid has *just* been neutralised). The method is divided into three stages.

- *Stage 1* The acid solution is poured into a burette. The **burette** is used to measure the volume of solution added accurately. A known volume of alkali solution is placed in a conical flask using a pipette. The **pipette** delivers a fixed volume accurately. A few drops of an indicator (for example phenolphthalein or methyl orange) are added to the flask.
- *Stage 2* The acid solution is run into the flask from the burette until the indicator *just* changes colour. Having found the end point for the

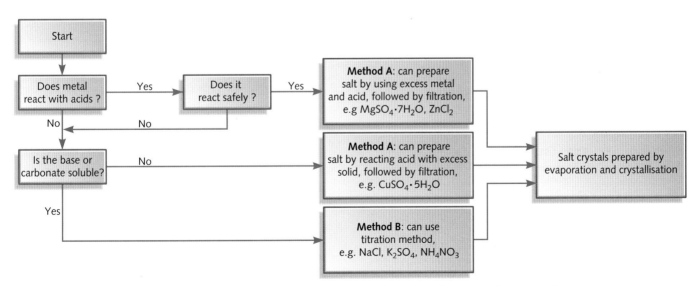

Figure 5.7 Flow chart showing which method to use for preparing soluble salts. The two methods A and B are described in the text and figures 5.8 and 5.9.

(a)
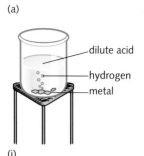
(i)
Warm the acid. Switch off the Bunsen burner.
Add an excess of the metal to the acid.
Wait until no more hydrogen is given off.

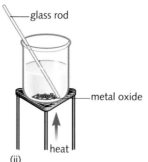
(ii)
Add an excess of the metal oxide
to the acid. Wait until the solution
no longer turns blue litmus paper red.

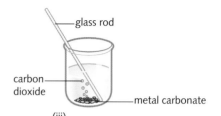
(iii)
Add an excess of the metal carbonate
to the acid. Wait until no more carbon
dioxide is given off.

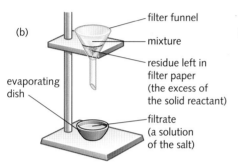
(b)

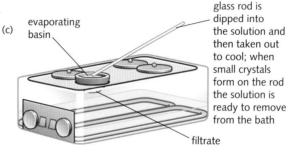
(c)

glass rod is
dipped into
the solution and
then taken out
to cool; when
small crystals
form on the rod
the solution is
ready to remove
from the bath

(d)

crystals form as solution cools;
filter, wash and then dry them

*Figure 5.8 Method A for preparing a soluble salt. (a) Stage 1:
the acid is reacted with either (i) a metal, (ii) a base or
(iii) a carbonate. (b) Stage 2: the excess solid is filtered out.
(c) Stage 3: the solution is carefully evaporated.
(d) Stage 4: the crystals are allowed to form.*

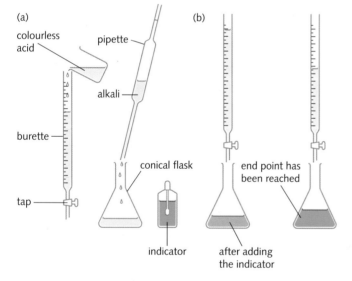
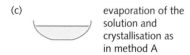

*Figure 5.9 Method B (the titration method) for preparing a
soluble salt. (a) Stage 1: the burette is filled with acid and a
known volume of alkali is added to the conical flask.
(b) Stage 2: the acid is added to the alkali until the end point
is reached. (c) Stage 3: the solution is evaporated and
crystallised as for method A.*

reaction, the volume of acid run into the flask is
noted. The experiment is then repeated without
using the indicator. The same known volume of
alkali is used in the flask. The same volume of
acid as noted in the first part is then run into the
flask. Alternatively, activated charcoal can be
added to remove the coloured indicator. The
charcoal can then be filtered off.

- *Stage 3*   The salt solution is evaporated and
  cooled to form crystals as described in method A.

Summary of core material

You should know that:

- salts are substances produced from acids by
  reactions in which the hydrogen in the acid is
  replaced by a metal
- salts are widely used in the home and industry
- salts are ionic compounds and many are soluble
  in water
- soluble salts can be made by reaction between
  – an acid and an alkali
  – an acid and (an excess of) a metal
  – an acid and (an excess of) a metal oxide
  – an acid and (an excess of) a metal carbonate.

5.13 The label shows the ingredients in a packet of 'Lo Salt'.

INGREDIENTS:
Potassium Chloride, Sodium Chloride, anti-caking agent (Magnesium Carbonate)

It is suggested that persons having diabetes, heart or kidney disease should consult their family doctor who will advise on how to use this salt alternative.

(a) Why do some people put salt on their food? [1]

(b) Suggest why some people use 'Lo Salt' instead of ordinary salt. [1]

(c) Describe how you could obtain pure magnesium carbonate from a sample of 'Lo Salt'. [3]

(SEG, 1992)

5.14 Common salt (sodium chloride) has been an important chemical for thousands of years. The Romans set up salt mines during their occupation of Britain and elsewhere.

More recently a technique called 'solution mining' has been introduced to collect the salt. This involves drilling into a salt deposit and passing hot water down a pipe into the hole. A strong solution of salt, called brine, is forced up a second pipe. When all the salt is removed the cavity is left full of water and the surface hole is closed up.

(a) Suggest an advantage and a disadvantage of solution mining over traditional methods of mining. [2]

Some tribes in East Africa extract salt from papyrus leaves. They first burn the leaves, then mix the ash with water. Salt solution is obtained using the apparatus shown below.

ash and water

bowl with holes in bottom

banana leaves

jug

salt solution

(b) (i) Name the technique shown in the diagram. [1]
(ii) What difference in properties between ash and salt do the tribes make use of in extracting the salt? [1]

(c) Salt can also be obtained by the evaporation of sea water by the Sun. In which pool (A, B, or C) will the salt crystals form fastest? [1]

pools containing sea water

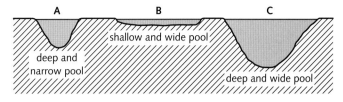

A   B   C
deep and narrow pool   shallow and wide pool   deep and wide pool

(d) The diagram shows some of the substances produced industrially from sodium chloride. By which process are both chlorine and hydrogen produced from sodium chloride? [1]

A anodising   **B** distillation
C electrolysis   **D** electroplating
E neutralisation

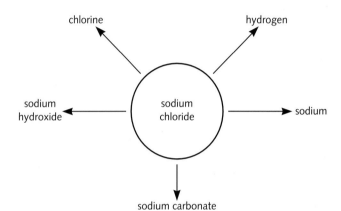

chlorine

hydrogen

sodium hydroxide

sodium chloride

sodium

sodium carbonate

(MEG 1992, 1993 and SEG, 1988)

5.15 Small pieces of limestone react with hydrochloric acid producing effervescence (bubbling).

(a) Copy out and balance the equation for the reaction: [1]

...$CaCO_3(s)$ + ...$HCl(aq)$
→ ...$CaCl_2(aq)$ + ...$H_2O(l)$ + ...$CO_2(g)$

(b) If small pieces of limestone are added to sulphuric acid of the same concentration as the hydrochloric acid, some effervescence is seen but the reaction soon stops. The equation for the reaction, with its state symbols, is:
$CaCO_3(s)$ + $H_2SO_4(aq)$
→ $CaSO_4(s)$ + $H_2O(l)$ + $CO_2(g)$

Explain why the reaction stops. [3]

(SEG, 1995)

5.16 A drug company makes zinc sulphate tablets. They are given to people whose normal diet does not contain enough zinc ions. The starting materials are the ore calamine (zinc carbonate) and dilute sulphuric acid. On the next page is a flow diagram for one process.

(a) How would the manufacturer know that the reaction between the calamine and the acid was complete? [1]

(b) Explain why the solution was concentrated by heating and then allowed to cool. [2]

143

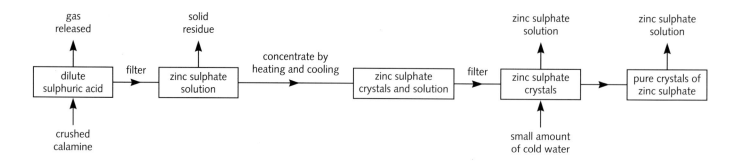

(c) Why are the zinc sulphate crystals washed with a *small* amount of *cold* water? [1]

(d) Write the word equation and the balanced symbol equation for the reaction between zinc carbonate and dilute sulphuric acid. [3]

(NISEAC, 1991)

EXTENSION

More about salts

5.14 The preparation of insoluble salts

Some salts are insoluble in water (for example silver chloride, barium sulphate – see table 5.11 on page 140). Such salts are generally made by ionic precipitation.

Precipitation is the sudden formation of a solid either:

- when two solutions are mixed, or
- when a gas is bubbled into a solution.

For example, barium sulphate can be made by taking a solution of a soluble sulphate (for example sodium sulphate). This is added to a solution of a soluble barium salt (for example barium chloride). The insoluble barium sulphate is formed immediately. This solid 'falls' to the bottom of the tube or beaker as a **precipitate** (figure 5.10). The precipitate can be filtered off. It is then washed with distilled water and dried in a warm oven. The equation for this reaction is:

barium chloride + sodium sulphate
→ barium sulphate + sodium chloride

$$BaCl_2(aq) + Na_2SO_4(aq) \rightarrow BaSO_4(s) + 2NaCl(aq)$$

This shows how important state symbols can be – it is the only way we can tell that this equation shows a precipitation.

The equation can be simplified to show *only* those ions which take part in the reaction and their products:

$$Ba^{2+}(aq) + SO_4^{2-}(aq) \rightarrow BaSO_4(s)$$

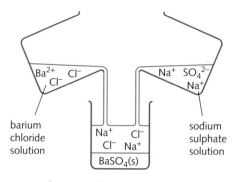

Ba^{2+} and SO_4^{2-} ions combine to form a precipitate of $BaSO_4$; Na^+ and Cl^- ions stay in solution

Figure 5.10 The precipitation of barium sulphate. The solid can be collected by filtration or centrifugation.

This type of equation is known as an **ionic equation**. The ions that remain in solution are left out of the equation. They are known as **spectator ions**.

Precipitation reactions are often used in analysis to identify salts such as chlorides, iodides and sulphates (see section 13.1 on page 348).

5.15 Making salts by direct combination

Some salts can be made by directly reacting two elements together. This is called direct combination (or synthesis).

> In **direct combination** (or synthesis) reactions, two substances (either elements or compounds) react to produce *one* substance.

This type of reaction is mainly possible for metal chlorides, bromides and iodides. For instance, if a piece of burning sodium is lowered into a gas jar of chlorine (a violent reaction!), a white powder of sodium chloride is made:

$$2Na(s) + Cl_2(g) \rightarrow 2NaCl(s)$$

Other chlorides can also be prepared by this method. It is often used to make samples of *anhydrous* aluminium chloride or iron(III) chloride (figure 5.11):

$$2Al(s) + 3Cl_2(g) \rightarrow 2AlCl_3(s)$$

$$2Fe(s) + 3Cl_2(g) \rightarrow 2FeCl_3(s)$$

Direct combination reactions do *not* produce crystals of the salt, only a powder.

The reaction between ammonia gas and hydrogen chloride gas is also a synthesis reaction:

$$NH_3(g) + HCl(g) \rightarrow NH_4Cl(s)$$

5.16 Efflorescence and deliquescence

Some salt crystals need storing carefully because they *give out* some or all of their water of crystallisation to the atmosphere. These salts are said to be **efflorescent**. Thus transparent crystals of hydrated sodium carbonate become white and powdery on the surface when they are left open to the air:

$$Na_2CO_3 \cdot 10H_2O(s) \rightarrow Na_2CO_3 \cdot H_2O(s) + 9H_2O(g)$$

Other crystals show the opposite effect. In this case they *absorb* water from the air and turn into a solution. These salts are **deliquescent**. Copper(II) nitrate and zinc chloride are both deliquescent salts. They can be stored in a desiccator to keep them dry. Sodium hydroxide is another deliquescent substance.

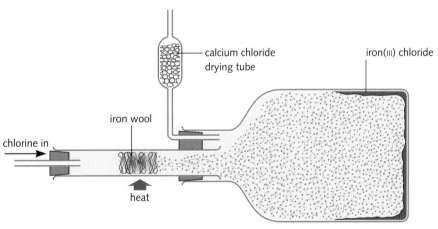

Figure 5.11 The preparation of anhydrous iron(III) chloride.

EXTENSION

The ionic nature of acids, bases and salts

This section covers the following ideas:

- strong acids and strong alkalis are completely ionised in water
- weak acids and weak alkalis are partially dissociated into ions in water
- dynamic equilibria in solutions of weak acids and weak alkalis
- pH and the balance of hydrogen ions and hydroxide ions in water
- the ionic reactions in acid–base neutralisation and in acid–antacid reactions
- acids as proton donors and bases as proton acceptors
- the 'basicity' of acids
- the pH of salt solutions
- titration curves using indicators, temperature changes and conductivity
- neutral and amphoteric oxides
- amphoteric metal hydroxides and analysis.

5.17 Strong and weak acids

Not all acids are equally strong. The vinegar used in salad dressing and to pickle vegetables is significantly less acidic than a hydrochloric acid solution of the same concentration. If differences in concentration are not the reason for this, then what does cause the difference? After all, we can eat fruit, and drink wine and carbonated drinks without damage. Yet our bodies are not as resistant to all acids.

The difference lies in the ionic nature of acid solutions; more precisely in the concentration of hydrogen ions (H^+ ions) in a solution. In section 5.5 on page 129 we stressed the importance of water as the necessary solvent for acid solutions. If hydrogen chloride (HCl) gas is dissolved in an organic solvent such as methylbenzene, it does *not* show acidic properties (table 5.13). There is a relationship between H^+ ion concentration, acidity and

pH: the higher the H^+ ion concentration, the higher the acidity and the lower the pH. We saw in section 5.3 on page 128 that the pH scale goes from 1 to 14. Each pH unit means a ten-fold difference in H^+ ion concentration. An acid of pH 1.0 has ten times the H^+ ion concentration of an acid of pH 2.0.

When hydrochloric acid is formed in water, the hydrogen chloride molecules completely separate into ions:

$$HCl(g) \xrightarrow{H_2O} H^+(aq) + Cl^-(aq)$$

In a similar way, sulphuric acid and nitric acid molecules completely separate into ions when dissolved in water:

$$H_2SO_4(l) \xrightarrow{H_2O} H^+(aq) + HSO_4^-(aq)$$

$$HNO_3(l) \xrightarrow{H_2O} H^+(aq) + NO_3^-(aq)$$

(In general, two equivalent terms are used instead of 'separate into ions': we say that the acids 'ionise' or 'dissociate into ions'. Also, for various substances the separation into ions may or may not be complete. In this book, if the separation *is* complete, we say the substance is '**completely ionised**'. If the separation is *not* complete, we say the substance is '**partially dissociated into ions**'.)

Table 5.13 Properties of hydrogen chloride in different solvents

	HCl dissolved in water	HCl dissolved in methylbenzene
Conducts electricity	yes	no
Temperature change on dissolving	exothermic	very little change
Colour change with indicators	turns litmus red, etc.	no change
Reaction with metals	hydrogen given off	no reaction
Reaction with carbonates	carbon dioxide given off	no reaction

Complete separation into ions (complete ionisation) produces the maximum possible concentration of H^+ ions, and so the lowest possible pH for that solution.

When pure ethanoic acid is dissolved in water, only a small fraction of the covalently bonded molecules are dissociated into hydrogen ions and ethanoate ions:

$$CH_3COOH(l) \xrightarrow{H_2O} H^+(aq) + CH_3COO^-(aq)$$

most molecules intact — only a small number of molecules are dissociated into ions at any one time

Thus an ethanoic acid solution will have far fewer hydrogen ions present in it than a hydrochloric acid solution of the same concentration, and its pH will be higher. In school laboratory ethanoic acid solution, only one molecule in 250 is dissociated into ions.

The other organic acids, such as methanoic acid, citric acid, etc. (see table 5.2 on page 127), also only partially dissociate into ions when dissolved in water.

Carbonic acid (H_2CO_3) is an example of a weak mineral acid.

- **Strong acids** are *completely ionised* in solution in water.
- **Weak acids** are *partially dissociated into ions* in solution in water.

5.18 Strong and weak alkalis

Alkalis can also differ in the way that they are ionised when dissolved in water. Sodium hydroxide and potassium hydroxide are ionic solids. When they dissolve in water, the crystal lattice is broken down and the ions are spread throughout the solution. These alkalis are completely ionised in water:

$$Na^+OH^-(s) \xrightarrow{H_2O} Na^+(aq) + OH^-(aq)$$

ionic crystals — ions spread through the solution

This means that a solution contains the maximum possible concentration of OH^- ions, and therefore has the maximum possible pH. The pH of calcium hydroxide as an alkali is limited by its poor solubility.

Ammonia solution, on the other hand, is a weak alkali because it is only partially dissociated into ions:

$$NH_3(g) + H_2O(l) \rightarrow NH_4^+(aq) + OH^-(aq)$$

most remain as molecules — only a few ions present

Such a solution only contains a low concentration of ammonium (NH_4^+) ions and hydroxide (OH^-) ions. Solutions of ammonia only have a moderately high pH value.

- **Strong alkalis** are *completely ionised* in solution in water.
- **Weak alkalis** are *partially dissociated into ions* in solution in water.

Because of their high concentration of ions, solutions of strong acids and strong alkalis conduct electricity well. Compounds such as nitric acid, sulphuric acid and sodium hydroxide are **strong electrolytes** in solution. Ethanoic acid and ammonia solution are only **weak electrolytes**.

5.19 Dynamic equilibria in solutions of weak acids and weak alkalis

In solutions of weak acids and weak alkalis, only a small number of molecules are dissociated into ions at any given time. For weak acids and weak alkalis, the process of dissociation is **reversible**. In an ethanoic acid solution, molecules are constantly dissociating into ions. At the same time, ethanoate ions and hydrogen ions are also re-combining. These two processes are happening at the same rate. Therefore, the concentrations of the molecules and ions do not change. This is known as a **dynamic equilibrium** (see page 199) and the equation can be written:

$$CH_3COOH(aq) \rightleftharpoons H^+(aq) + CH_3COO^-(aq)$$

In this case we say that the position of the equilibrium lies well over to the left-hand side, because the concentration of molecules is much greater than the concentration of ions.

The partial dissociation of ammonia solution is also an equilibrium. Again the position of the equilibrium lies over to the left-hand side:

$$NH_3(g) + H_2O(l) \rightleftharpoons NH_4^+(aq) + OH^-(aq)$$

All the dissociation reactions of weak acids and weak alkalis are equilibria.

5.20 pH and the ionic balance in water

Water is a liquid consisting mainly of covalent H_2O molecules. However, pure, freshly distilled water does conduct electricity to a very small extent. This shows the presence of a small proportion of ions (figure 5.12):

$$H_2O(l) \rightleftharpoons H^+(aq) + OH^-(aq)$$

most molecules   only a very few molecules
intact   dissociate into ions

This partial dissociation of water into ions is another example of a dynamic equilibrium. The position of the equilibrium lies very much to the left-hand side. But each water molecule that does dissociate produces *one* hydrogen ion (H^+) and *one* hydroxide ion (OH^-). Therefore, in pure water, the number of H^+ and OH^- ions must be equal, and the pH of water is 7.

Acids or alkalis disturb this balance when dissolved in water. Adding an acid to water creates an excess of H^+ ions in the solution. This gives the solution a pH below 7 and turns litmus red (figure 5.13). Adding a weak acid will not imbalance the system so much as adding a strong acid of the same concentration. The weak acid contains fewer H^+ ions and its pH will not be as low as that of the strong acid.

Adding an alkali to water creates an excess of OH^- ions, tilting the balance in the opposite direction. This solution has a pH higher than 7 and turns litmus blue (figure 5.13). A weak alkali will not have as high a pH as a strong alkali.

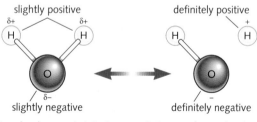

slightly positive   definitely positive

Most molecules remain intact. They have a slightly negative oxygen atom and slightly positive hydrogen atoms, because the oxygen atom pulls the electrons in each O–H bond towards it.

But a very few molecules split into ions. The pull of the oxygen atom is enough to break one of the O–H bonds. A negative OH^- ion and a positive H^+ ion are formed.

Figure 5.12 Water is partially ionised into H^+ and OH^- ions.

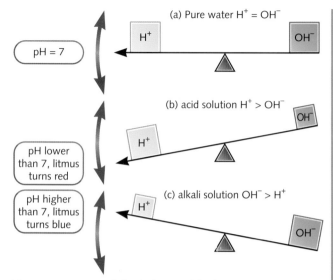

(a) Pure water $H^+ = OH^-$

pH = 7

(b) acid solution $H^+ > OH^-$

pH lower than 7, litmus turns red

(c) alkali solution $OH^- > H^+$

pH higher than 7, litmus turns blue

Figure 5.13 pH and the balance of hydrogen ions and hydroxide ions in solution.

5.21 What happens to the ions in neutralisation?

The reactions of acids with bases and alkalis

An acid can be neutralised by an alkali to produce a salt and water only, according to the general equation:

acid + alkali → salt + water

For example,

hydrochloric acid + sodium hydroxide
→ sodium chloride + water

$$HCl(aq) + NaOH(aq) \rightarrow NaCl(aq) + H_2O(l)$$

All these compounds are completely ionised, except for the water produced. The hydrogen ions from the acid and the hydroxide ions from the alkali have combined to form water molecules:

$$H^+(aq) + OH^-(aq) \rightarrow H_2O(l)$$

This is the **ionic equation** for this neutralisation reaction. The spectator ions (chloride and sodium ions) remain in solution – which becomes a solution of sodium chloride (figure 5.14). By evaporating some of the water, the salt can be crystallised out. In fact, the *same* ionic equation can be used for *any* reaction between an acid and an alkali.

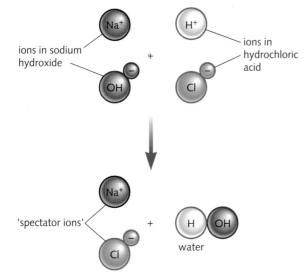

Figure 5.14 The reactions of the ions when hydrochloric acid is mixed with sodium hydroxide.

If the acid is neutralised by an insoluble base instead of an alkali, water is again formed:

acid + base → salt + water

For example,

sulphuric acid + zinc oxide
  → zinc sulphate + water

$H_2SO_4(aq) + ZnO(s) → ZnSO_4(aq) + H_2O(l)$

In this case the **ionic equation** is:

$2H^+(aq) + O^{2-}(s) → H_2O(l)$

The hydrogen ions have been neutralised by the oxide ions from the base. The zinc ions and sulphate ions remain in solution – which becomes a solution of zinc sulphate. Zinc sulphate can be crystallised from the solution.

It is possible to summarise a neutralisation reaction in terms of the ionic reaction taking place.

Neutralisation is the combination of hydrogen ions from an acid with either

• hydroxide ions from an alkali, or
• oxide ions from a base,

to form water molecules. In the process a salt is formed.

In these reactions the acid is providing hydrogen ions to react with the base. In turn, the base is supplying hydroxide ions or oxide ions to accept the H^+ ions and react with them. This leads to a further definition of an acid and a base in terms of hydrogen ion (proton) transfer.

• An **acid** is a molecule or ion that is able to *donate a proton* (H^+ ion) to a base.
• A **base** is a molecule or ion that is able to *accept a proton.*

The reaction of antacids with acids

When 'antacids' containing carbonate or hydrogencarbonate ions react with an acid, they also produce a salt and water. But, in addition, carbon dioxide is given off:

acid + carbonate
  → salt + water + carbon dioxide

For example

hydrochloric acid + magnesium carbonate
  → magnesium chloride + water
    + carbon dioxide

$2HCl(aq) + MgCO_3(s)$
  $→ MgCl_2(s) + H_2O(l) + CO_2(g)$

The **ionic equation** for this reaction shows clearly the hydrogen ions reacting with the carbonate ions to form water and release carbon dioxide:

$2H^+(aq) + CO_3^{2-}(s) → H_2O(l) + CO_2(g)$

A very similar reaction takes place between hydrochloric acid and sodium hydrogencarbonate.

Although they are the negative ions present in salts, in these reactions the carbonate and hydrogencarbonate ions are accepting hydrogen ions. By the above ionic definition, these ions can be classified as *bases*. Indeed, the idea of a base as a proton (H^+ ion) acceptor means that other negative ions normally thought of as being present in salts, for example sulphate and phosphate ions, can be classified as bases.

5.22 The 'basicity' of acids

Sodium carbonate and sodium hydrogencarbonate are both salts of carbonic acid (H_2CO_3). Two different salts of this acid exist because there are two hydrogen atoms present that can be replaced by a metal. Carbonic acid is said to be a **dibasic acid** because it has *two* replaceable hydrogen atoms per molecule.

Sulphuric acid is the most important dibasic acid in the laboratory. It too forms two different salts, depending on the amount of alkali used to react with the acid:

$H_2SO_4(aq) + NaOH(aq)$
$\rightarrow NaHSO_4(aq) + H_2O(l)$
sodium hydrogensulphate

$H_2SO_4(aq) + 2NaOH(aq)$
$\rightarrow Na_2SO_4(aq) + 2H_2O(l)$
sodium sulphate

Hydrochloric acid, nitric acid and ethanoic acid are all **monobasic acids**. They have *one* replaceable hydrogen atom per molecule and they each produce only one salt. Phosphoric acid (H_3PO_4) is a **tribasic acid**, producing three salts (table 5.14). Since the acidity of a solution depends on the number of hydrogen ions (protons) released by each acid molecule, a dibasic acid can also be known as a **diprotic acid** (see table 5.14).

The salts formed from dibasic or tribasic acids in which not all the hydrogens have been replaced by a metal are known as **acid salts**. They still have hydrogen atom(s) that can be replaced. The salt formed when all the hydrogens have been replaced in such an acid is called the **normal salt**. The pH of a solution of an acid salt is lower than that of the normal salt of the same acid at the same concentration (table 5.15).

For the same reason, the pH of a solution of 'washing soda' (hydrated sodium carbonate, pH 11.5) is higher than that of a 'baking soda' solution (sodium hydrogencarbonate, pH 8.5).

5.23 The pH of salt solutions

Table 5.15 shows us that not all salt solutions have a pH of 7. Certainly sodium chloride, like sodium sulphate, produces neutral solutions. They are the salts of *strong acids* and *strong alkalis*. However, salts made from a *weak acid* and a *strong alkali* give solutions with an alkaline pH; for example aqueous sodium ethanoate has a pH of 9.

Ammonium salts are particularly important because they are used as fertilisers (see section 10.11 on page 293). They are salts of a *weak alkali* with *strong acids*. They give solutions with an acidic pH (lower than 7). If fields are

Table 5.14 The basicity of some common acids

Acid type	Name	Formula	Normal salts	Acid salts
Monobasic (monoprotic) acids	Hydrochloric acid	HCl	chlorides, e.g. NaCl	
	Nitric acid	HNO_3	nitrates, e.g. $NaNO_3$	
	Ethanoic acid	CH_3COOH	ethanoates, e.g. CH_3COONa	
Dibasic (diprotic) acids	Carbonic acid	H_2CO_3	carbonates, e.g. Na_2CO_3	hydrogencarbonates, e.g. $NaHCO_3$
	Sulphuric acid	H_2SO_4	sulphates, e.g. Na_2SO_4	hydrogensulphates, e.g. $NaHSO_4$
Tribasic (triprotic) acids	Phosphoric acid	H_3PO_4	phosphates, e.g. Na_3PO_4	dihydrogenphosphates, e.g. NaH_2PO_4, and hydrogenphosphates, e.g. Na_2HPO_4

frequently treated with ammonium fertilisers, the soil becomes acidic (sometimes known as 'sour soil'). Such soil can be neutralised using 'lime'.

Table 5.15 The pH of comparable solutions of the salts of sulphuric acid

Solution	Na_2SO_4	$NaHSO_4$	H_2SO_4
pH	7	3	1

5.24 Following neutralisation: the end point

Titration pH curves and indicators

Neutralisation in solution can be 'tracked' by following the change in pH during the reaction using a pH meter. The pH change is most clear and noticeable if a strong acid (for example hydrochloric acid) is titrated against a strong alkali (for example sodium hydroxide). Figure 5.15 shows the pH curve obtained when $25\,cm^3$ of $0.10\,mol/dm^3$ hydrochloric acid is titrated by adding small volumes of $0.10\,mol/dm^3$ sodium hydroxide (say $5\,cm^3$ at a time), measuring the pH after each addition. The volumes added can be made smaller near the **end point**.

Figure 5.15 shows that the change in pH around the end point takes place over a small change in volume. This is the reason an end point can be found accurately using the right indicator; the colour change takes place sharply. A number of indicators can be used for the above titration. The colour change needs to be clearly seen, and phenolphthalein is often chosen for that reason. Its colour changes from colourless to pink, as shown.

However, for other experiments the choice of indicator may be more important. This is because different indicators change colour at different pH values (table 5.16). Care must be taken to choose the right indicator for the combination of acid and alkali being studied.

Other methods

Neutralisation reactions are exothermic (they produce heat). Therefore, the end point of such a reaction can be found by following the **temperature change** as the acid and alkali are mixed. The alkali is placed in an insulated

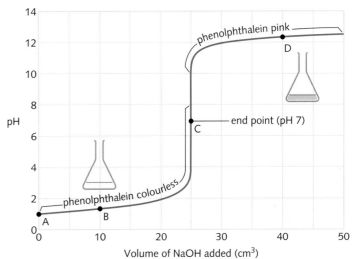

Figure 5.15 The titration pH curve for $25\,cm^3$ of $0.10\,mol/dm^3$ hydrochloric acid against $0.10\,mol/dm^3$ sodium hydroxide. At A, the pH is low because hydrochloric acid is a strong acid. At B, adding sodium hydroxide has little effect. At C, there is a sudden jump in pH near the end point. At D, the final pH is high because sodium hydroxide is a strong alkali.

container and acid is added in small volumes. The temperature rises with each addition of acid until neutralisation is complete. The volume of acid added when the temperature reaches a maximum is the amount just needed to neutralise the alkali.

Strong acids and alkalis are strong electrolytes, but water is a very poor electrolyte. The acid–alkali reaction produces a salt and water. Therefore, if the solution delivered from the burette is relatively concentrated (so as not to add too much water), the reaction can be followed by **electrical conductivity** measurement. The conductivity falls to a minimum value at the

Table 5.16 The pH values at which different indicators change colour

Indicator	Colour change acid → alkali	pH of change
Methyl orange	red → yellow	3.5
Bromocresol green	yellow → blue	4.5
Litmus	red → blue	6.0
Bromothymol blue	yellow → blue	7.0
Phenolphthalein	colourless → pink	9.5

151

end point. The fall in conductivity is greater if the salt produced is insoluble. The ions involved in forming the salt will disappear from the solution.

5.25 Neutral and amphoteric oxides

Water has a pH of 7 and is therefore a **neutral oxide**. It is an exception to the broad 'rule' that the oxides of non-metals are acidic oxides. There are a few other exceptions to this 'rule' (see figure 5.16). In all but water the non-metal shows a lower-than-usual oxidation state. The most important is carbon monoxide (CO), noted for being poisonous. The 'rule' that most non-metal oxides are acidic remains useful and important.

The classification of water itself becomes more of a problem if we consider the general definition of an acid as a proton (hydrogen ion) donor. When hydrogen chloride gas dissolves in water, it completely ionises (it is a strong acid) to produce hydrogen ions and chloride ions in solution. So far, we have represented this ionisation by the equation:

$$HCl(g) \xrightarrow{H_2O} H^+(aq) + Cl^-(aq)$$

However, closer study suggests that a **hydrated proton** or **oxonium ion** (H_3O^+) is formed during this ionisation. The detailed equation is:

$$HCl(g) + H_2O(l) \rightarrow H_3O^+(aq) + Cl^-(aq)$$

The equation can be shown as a diagram:

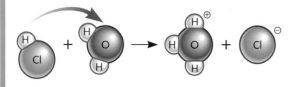

The hydrated proton (oxonium ion) is thought to be the form that the hydrogen ion takes in all acid solutions. Importantly, in forming this ion, a water molecule is acting as an acid – it is accepting a proton.

Water can also give up a proton. When ammonia dissolves in water, ammonium and hydroxide ions are formed. The solution becomes alkaline:

$$NH_3(g) + H_2O(l) \rightarrow NH_4^+(aq) + OH^-(aq)$$

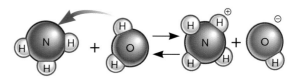

Here, water is acting as a proton donor; it is acting as a base.

> A molecule or ion that can react either as an acid or as a base is said to be **amphoteric**.

The term 'amphoteric compound' is useful even in simpler definitions of acids and bases. There are metal oxides and hydroxides that not only can react with acids to give a salt and water, but also can do the same with alkalis.

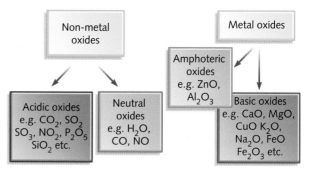

Figure 5.16 The classification of non-metal and metal oxides.

> An **amphoteric metal oxide or hydroxide** is one that reacts with both an acid and an alkali to give a salt and water.

The most important examples of metals with compounds that are amphoteric are zinc and aluminium. The fact that zinc hydroxide and aluminium hydroxide are amphoteric helps in the identification of salts of these metals using sodium hydroxide. If sodium hydroxide solution is added to a solution of a salt of either of these metals, a white precipitate of the metal hydroxide is formed. For example

$$ZnCl_2(aq) + 2NaOH(aq)$$
$$\rightarrow Zn(OH)_2(s) + 2NaCl(aq)$$

$$Zn^{2+}(aq) + 2OH^-(aq) \rightarrow Zn(OH)_2(s)$$

However, this precipitate will re-dissolve if excess sodium hydroxide is added, because zinc hydroxide is amphoteric:

zinc hydroxide + sodium hydroxide
→ sodium zincate + water

$$Zn(OH)_2(s) + 2NaOH(aq)$$
$$\rightarrow Na_2ZnO_2(aq) + 2H_2O(l)$$

Aluminium salts will give a similar set of reactions. This test distinguishes zinc and aluminium salts from others, but not from each other. We can tell zinc and aluminium salts apart by repeating the test using ammonia solution (a weak alkali). The precipitate of zinc hydroxide re-dissolves in ammonia solution, but the aluminium hydroxide does not.

Summary of extension material

You should know that:

- acids and alkalis can be either strong or weak
- strong acids and strong alkalis are completely ionised in water
- weak acids and weak alkalis are only partially dissociated into ions in water
- the dissociations of weak acids and weak alkalis into ions are examples of dynamic equilibria
- water itself is partially dissociated into ions, the concentrations of hydrogen ions and hydroxide ions in water being equal
- the pH of a solution depends on the balance of hydrogen ions and hydroxide ions in the solution
- the neutralisation of any acid with any alkali can be represented by the ionic equation $H^+(aq) + OH^-(aq) \rightarrow H_2O(l)$
- acids can be defined as molecules or ions that can donate a proton (H^+ ion)
- bases can be defined as molecules or ions that can accept a proton

- acids may be monobasic, dibasic, or tribasic depending on how many hydrogen ions can be released by each acid molecule
- salts can be either normal salts or acid salts
- not all salt solutions have a pH of 7
- neutralisation can be followed by measuring pH, temperature, or conductivity
- a common way of measuring pH is to use an indicator
- not all indicators change colour at the same pH
- a few non-metal oxides are neutral, but most are acidic
- some metal oxides and hydroxides are amphoteric – they react with both acids and alkalis
- a water molecule can lose a proton to become a hydroxide ion (OH^-), and can accept a proton to become an oxonium ion (H_3O^+).

5.17 Copy and complete the table on the right, which describes the preparation of some salts. The first line has been done for you.

(MEG, 1986)

5.18

	Reactants	Products
(i)	calcium hydroxide + hydrochloric acid	calcium chloride + water
(ii)	.... + ...	zinc chloride + water
(iii)	sulphuric acid + ...	lead(II) sulphate + nitric acid

(a) The experiments on page 154 were carried out on aqueous solutions of acid **X** and acid **Y**, each solution having a concentration of 1.0 mol/dm³.
   (i) Explain the term *acid*. [2]

(ii) What type of reaction has taken place in experiment **2**? [1]
(iii) Suggest an explanation why the acids give different results in these experiments. [2]

Experiment	Acid X	Acid Y
1 Measure the electrical conductivity of the solutions of these acids, i.e. the current which flows under identical conditions	0.3 A	0.020 A
2 Measure the temperature increase when the same volume of aqueous sodium hydroxide is added to equal volumes of these acids	3 °C	2 °C
3 Measure the time for equal volumes of the solutions of these acids to react with identical pieces of magnesium	2 minutes	20 minutes

(iv) Which would have the higher pH value, a solution of acid **X** or a solution of acid **Y**, each of the same concentration? Explain your answer. [2]

(v) Describe *two* ways of reducing the time for a solution of acid **Y** to react with magnesium. [2]

(b) Methods of preparing salts are:

Method A – add an excess of a chemical to a dilute acid and then filter.
Method B – use a burette and indicator.
Method C – mix two solutions and obtain the salt by precipitation.

For each of the following salt preparations, choose *one* of the methods A, B, or C and name any additional reagent needed. Equations are not required.

(i) Preparation of the soluble salt, nickel sulphate, from the insoluble compound nickel carbonate. [2]

(ii) Preparation of lithium chloride from lithium hydroxide: both compounds are soluble in water. [2]

(c) The formula of a compound can be determined by knowing the formulas of the ions that are present in the compound or by experiment.

(i) State the formula of the compound which contains Ca^{2+} and PO_4^{3-} ions. [1]

(ii) A $3\,cm^3$ sample of a solution of the nitrate of metal **Q**, concentration $1.0\,mol/dm^3$, was added to $2\,cm^3$ of potassium fluoride, concentration $1.0\,mol/dm^3$. When the precipitate had settled, its height was measured. The experiment was then repeated using different volumes of potassium fluoride solution. The results are shown in the diagram below.

volume of potassium fluoride solution added (cm^3)

What is the formula of the fluoride of metal **Q**? [2]

(IGCSE, 1990)

5.19

(a) Ammonia reacts with phosphoric acid to produce ammonium phosphate. Copy and complete the following word equations to show the production of other ammonium salts. [3]

ammonia + ... → ammonium nitrate

ammonia + carbonic acid → ....

ammonia + ... → ammonium chloride

(b) Ammonium phosphate is acidic. How would you use the fertiliser on soil but keep the pH neutral? [1]

(IGCSE, 1990)

5.20 Table 5.16 on page 151 shows the pH at which some indicators change colour.

(a) What colour is a solution of pH 10 when a few drops of bromocresol green are added? [1]

(b) Which indicator would you use to distinguish between of ammonia (pH 8) and dilute sodium hydroxide (pH 12)? [1]

(c) A solution turns yellow when either methyl orange or bromothymol blue is added. Suggest the approximate pH of the solution. [1]

(d) A mixture of all five indicators is added to a strong acid. Suggest the colour of the solution. [1]

5.21 A student carried out an experiment to measure the temperature changes during the neutralisation of sodium hydroxide solution with dilute hydrochloric acid. The instructions were as follows.

Step 1. Allow the acid and alkali to stand in the laboratory for about 15 minutes.
Step 2. Pour $25\,cm^3$ of the alkali into a polystyrene beaker and record its temperature.
Step 3. Add $10\,cm^3$ of acid to the alkali, stirring all the time. Record the highest temperature reached.
Step 4. Repeat the experiment, using $25\,cm^3$ of alkali with different volumes of acid.

The results of all the experiments are shown in the table.

Volume of alkali (cm^3)	25	25	25	25	25	25
Volume of acid added (cm^3)	0	10	20	30	40	50
Highest temperature recorded (°C)	28	32	36	37	35	33

(a) Why were the solutions left standing in the laboratory for about 15 minutes before the experiment? [1]

(b) Why were the reactions carried out in a polystyrene beaker rather than a glass beaker? [1]

(c) (i) Plot the results on graph paper. Plot the highest temperature recorded against the volume of acid added. Draw two straight lines through the points and extend them until they cross. [3]
(ii) What was the temperature in the laboratory? [1]
(iii) Circle on the graph where the mixture becomes neutral. [1]
(iv) What volume of acid was needed to neutralise $25\,cm^3$ of the alkali? [1]

(d) Name the salt solution formed in this reaction. [1]

(e) Why can this reaction be described as 'exothermic'? [1]

(f) Write a symbol equation for the reaction. [1]

(NEAB, 1991)

5.22

(a) Copy out and complete the passage: [2]

The neutralisation of an acid involves the transfer of protons. Compounds that can accept protons from acids are called .... To make ammonium sulphate, sulphuric acid would need to react with the chemical, ...

(b) Rock phosphate is mined in North Africa. It is insoluble in water and must be changed into a more soluble phosphate for use in fertilisers. Sulphuric acid changes rock phosphate into superphosphate:

$Ca_3(PO_4)_2 + 2H_2SO_4 \rightarrow Ca(H_2PO_4)_2 + 2CaSO_4$

(i) Use the above equation to deduce the charge on the phosphate ion. [1]
(ii) Why must the chemicals in fertilisers be soluble in water? [1]
(iii) The phosphate ion is behaving as a base in this reaction. What is a base? [2]
(iv) What other fertiliser is made using sulphuric acid? [1]

(IGCSE, 1994, 1995)

5.23

(a) (i) Oxides can be classified as acidic, amphoteric or basic. Copy out and classify the following. [3]
Magnesium oxide is ....
Aluminium oxide is ....
Silicon(IV) oxide (silicon dioxide) is ....
(ii) Name a reagent that reacts with an amphoteric oxide but not with a basic one. [1]
(iii) Name a reagent that reacts with a basic oxide and with an amphoteric oxide. [1]

(b) Beryllium hydroxide is amphoteric.
(i) Describe what would be observed when an excess of aqueous sodium hydroxide is gradually added to aqueous beryllium sulphate. [2]
(ii) Name another metal, other than beryllium or aluminium, which has an amphoteric hydroxide. [1]
(iii) Copy out and complete the ionic equation: [1]
$Be^{2+} + ... \rightarrow Be(OH)_2$

(c) Arsenic(III) oxide is amphoteric. State how it would react, if at all, with sodium hydroxide and with hydrochloric acid.
(i) With sodium hydroxide. [1]
(ii) With hydrochloric acid. [1]

(IGCSE, 1993, 1994)

5.24 The reaction between solutions of hydrochloric acid and potassium hydroxide was studied by conductivity (conductance) measurement. $15\,cm^3$ of $0.1\,mol/dm^3$ hydrochloric acid solution was used. The conductivity was measured as the potassium hydroxide was added. The results are shown in the graph.

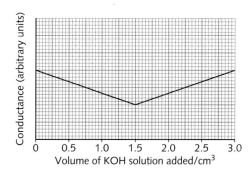

(a) What volume of potassium hydroxide solution neutralised the acid? [1]

(b) Why does the conductivity (conductance) rise in the later part of the experiment? [2]

(c) What was the concentration of the potassium hydroxide solution? [2]

6 Quantitative chemistry

Chemical analysis and formulas

This section covers the following ideas:

- the relative atomic mass of elements
- the relative formula mass of compounds
- calculating the percentage by mass of an element in a compound
- that substances react in fixed proportions by mass.

The fertiliser bags found around a farm often carry three numbers. They are arranged beneath the symbolic letters N:P:K. The numbers tell the farmer the amounts of the three key elements present in the fertiliser: that is, the percentages of nitrogen (N), phosphorus (P) and potassium (K). It is important to know not only *what* is in a chemical product, but also *how much* of each substance is there. The same idea lies behind the rules controlling the food industry. For instance, European Union regulations mean that all breakfast cereal packets must show the amounts of the various chemical substances (such as protein, fat and vitamins) present in the cereal.

In many areas of chemistry, it is very important to know the amounts of substances used and produced in reactions. An environmental chemist needs to check levels of pollutants in the air caused by burning a particular fuel. A polymer chemist needs an estimate of how much material a new and different reaction method will yield. He or she needs to check on losses through the purification process. A medical researcher must find out a safe dose for an experimental drug. He or she must consider its possible side-effects by measuring the amounts of its metabolic products in cells. A chemical formula or equation not only tells us what happens but puts 'numbers' to it. This is vital to modern chemistry.

6.1 Chemical 'accountancy'

We need to be able to predict the amounts of substances involved in chemical reactions. To do

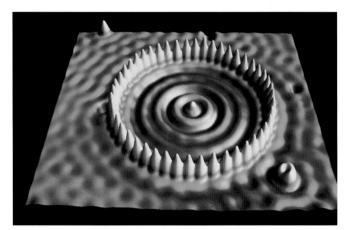

Figure 6.1 An image of 40 iron atoms in a circle on a copper surface. This photo was produced by a scanning tunnelling microscope. The diameter of the ring is about 20 000 times smaller than the diameter of a human hair.

this, we must have a good understanding of the atom. Exciting new types of microscope have now made it possible for us to 'see' individual atoms (figure 6.1). However, for some time, the **mass spectrometer** (see figure 2.26 on page 56) has given us a way of weighing atoms.

Relative atomic mass

The **mass** of a single hydrogen atom is incredibly small when measured in grams (g):

mass of one hydrogen atom
$$= 1.7 \times 10^{-24} \text{g}$$

$$= 0.000\,000\,000\,000\,000\,000\,000\,0017\,\text{g}$$

It is much more useful and convenient to measure the masses of atoms relative to each other (table 6.1). To do this, a standard atom has been chosen, against which all others are then compared. This **standard atom** is an atom of the carbon-12

Table 6.1 The relative masses of some atoms

Atom	Mass in grams	Whole-number ratio
Hydrogen (protium)	1.7×10^{-24}	1
Carbon-12	2.0×10^{-23}	12
Fluorine	3.2×10^{-23}	19

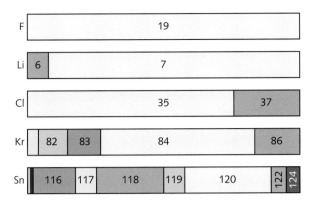

Figure 6.2 Many different elements have more than one isotope. These bars show the proportions of different isotopes for some elements. Fluorine is rare in having just one.

isotope, the 'mass' of which is given the value of exactly 12.

The use of the mass spectrometer first showed the existence of **isotopes**. These are atoms of the same element that have different masses because they have different numbers of neutrons in the nucleus (see page 53). The majority of elements have several isotopes (figure 6.2). This must be taken into account. The **relative atomic mass** (A_r) of an element is the average mass of an atom of the element taking into account the different natural isotopes of that element (table 6.2). So most relative atomic masses are not whole numbers. But, in this book, with the exception of chlorine, they are rounded to the nearest whole number to make our calculations easier.

Table 6.2 The relative atomic masses of some elements*

Element	Symbol	Relative atomic mass, A_r
Hydrogen	H	1
Carbon	C	12
Nitrogen	N	14
Oxygen	O	16
Fluorine	F	19
Sodium	Na	23
Magnesium	Mg	24
Aluminium	Al	27
Sulphur	S	32
Chlorine	Cl	35.5
Copper	Cu	64

* Except for Chlorine, all values have been rounded to the nearest whole number.

The **relative atomic mass** (A_r) of an element is the average mass of the naturally occurring atoms of the element, using a scale where an atom of carbon-12 has a mass of exactly 12.

It is important to note that the mass of an ion will be the same as that of the parent atom. The mass of the electron(s) gained or lost in forming the ion can be ignored in comparison to the total mass of the atom.

Relative formula mass

Atoms combine to form molecules or groups of ions. The total masses of these molecules or groups of ions provide useful information on the way the elements have combined with each other. The **formula** of an element or compound is taken as the basic unit (the **formula unit**). The masses of the atoms or ions in the formula are added together. The mass of a substance found in this way is called the **relative formula mass** (M_r). We shall illustrate the method by calculating the relative formula masses of three simple substances.

- *Hydrogen*
  Hydrogen gas is made up of H_2 molecules (H—H). Each molecule contains two hydrogen atoms. So its relative formula mass is twice the relative atomic mass of hydrogen:
  $M_r(H_2) = 2 \times 1 = 2$

- *Water*
  Water is a liquid made up of H_2O molecules (H—O—H). Each molecule contains two hydrogen atoms and one oxygen atom. So its relative formula mass is twice the relative atomic mass of hydrogen plus the relative atomic mass of oxygen:
  $M_r(H_2O) = (2 \times 1) + 16 = 18$

- *Sodium chloride*
  Sodium chloride is an ionic solid. It contains one chloride ion for each sodium ion present. The formula unit of sodium chloride is therefore Na^+Cl^-. So its relative formula mass is the relative atomic mass of sodium plus the relative atomic mass of chlorine:
  $M_r(NaCl) = 23 + 35.5 = 58.5$

157

- The **relative formula mass** (M_r) of a substance is the sum of the relative atomic masses of the elements present in a formula unit.
- If the substance is made of simple molecules, this mass may also be called the **relative molecular mass** (M_r).

The practical result of these definitions can be seen by looking at further examples (table 6.3).

The *percentage by mass of a particular element* in a compound can be found from calculations of relative formula mass. This is useful, for instance, in estimating the efficiency of one fertiliser compared with another. Ammonium nitrate is a commonly used fertiliser. It is an important source of nitrogen. What percentage of the mass of the compound is nitrogen?

The formula of ammonium nitrate is NH_4NO_3 (it contains the ions NH_4^+ and NO_3^-). Using the A_r values for N, H and O we get

$$M_r = (2 \times 14) + (4 \times 1) + (3 \times 16)$$
$$= 28 + 4 + 48 = 80$$

Then

mass of nitrogen in the formula = 28

mass of nitrogen as a fraction of the total $= \dfrac{28}{80}$

mass of nitrogen as percentage of total mass $= \dfrac{28}{80} \times 100 = 35\%$

Similar calculations can be used to work out the *percentage by mass of water of crystallisation* in crystals of a hydrated salt, for example magnesium sulphate (Epsom salts).

The formula of magnesium sulphate is $MgSO_4 \cdot 7H_2O$. Using the A_r values for Mg, S, O and H we get

$$M_r = 24 + 32 + (4 \times 16) + (7 \times 18) = 246$$

Then

mass of water in formula = 126

mass of water as a fraction of the total $= \dfrac{126}{246}$

percentage mass of water in the crystals $= \dfrac{126}{246} \times 100 = 51.2\%$

Table 6.3 The relative formula masses of some compounds

Substance	Formula	Atoms in formula	Relative atomic masses	Relative formula mass, M_r
Hydrogen	H_2	2H	H = 1	2×1 = 2
Carbon dioxide	CO_2	1C 2O	C = 12 O = 16	1×12 = 12 2×16 = 32 —— 44
Calcium carbonate	$CaCO_3$ (one Ca^{2+} ion, one CO_3^{2-} ion)	1Ca 1C 3O	Ca = 40 C = 12 O = 16	1×40 = 40 1×12 = 12 3×16 = 48 —— 100
Ammonium sulphate*	$(NH_4)_2SO_4$ (two NH_4^+ ions, one SO_4^{2-} ion)	2N 8H 1S 4O	N = 14 H = 1 S = 32 O = 16	2×14 = 28 8×1 = 8 1×32 = 32 4×16 = 64 —— 132
Hydrated magnesium sulphate†	$MgSO_4 \cdot 7H_2O$ (one Mg^{2+} ion, one SO_4^{2-} ion, seven H_2O molecules)	1Mg 1S 4O 14H 7O	Mg = 24 S = 32 O = 16 H = 1	1×24 = 24 1×32 = 32 4×16 = 64 14×1 = 14 7×16 = 112 —— 246

* The figure 2 outside the brackets multiplies everything in the brackets; there are two ammonium ions in this formula.
† The 7 means there are seven H_2O molecules per $MgSO_4$ formula unit.

6.2 Compound formation and chemical formulas

The idea that **compounds** are made up of elements combined in fixed amounts can be shown experimentally. Samples of the *same compound* made in different ways always contain the *same elements*. Also, the masses of the elements present are always in the *same ratio*.

Several different groups in a class can prepare magnesium oxide by heating a coil of magnesium in a crucible (figure 6.3). The crucible must first be weighed empty, and then re-weighed with the magnesium in it. The crucible is then heated strongly. Air is allowed in by occasionally lifting the lid very carefully. Solid must not be allowed to escape as a white smoke. After a while the lid may be taken off and the open crucible heated strongly. The crucible and products are then allowed to cool before re-weighing.

The increase in mass is due to the oxygen that has now combined with the magnesium. The mass of magnesium used and the mass of magnesium oxide produced can be found from the results. Here are some results obtained from this experiment:

(a) mass of empty crucible + lid   = 8.52 g
(b) mass of crucible + lid + magnesium = 8.88 g
(c) mass of crucible + lid +
     magnesium oxide   = 9.12 g
     mass of magnesium (b − a)   = 0.36 g
     mass of magnesium oxide (c − a)   = 0.60 g

The results of the various experiments in the class can be plotted on a graph. The mass of oxygen combined with the magnesium (y axis) is plotted

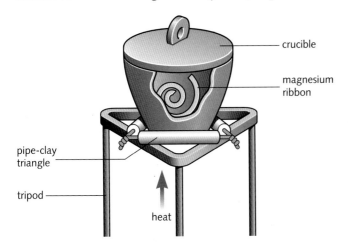

Figure 6.3 Heating magnesium in a crucible.

against the mass of magnesium used (*x* axis). Figure 6.4 shows some results obtained for this experiment.

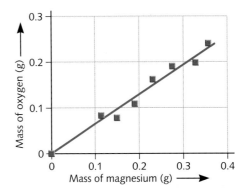

Figure 6.4 A graph of the results obtained from heating magnesium in air. The graph shows the mass of oxygen (from the air) that reacts with various masses of magnesium.

The experiment shows that:
(i) the more magnesium used, the more oxygen combines with it from the air and the more magnesium oxide is produced,
(ii) the curve is a straight line, showing that the ratio of magnesium to oxygen in magnesium oxide is fixed. A definite compound is formed by a chemical reaction.

- A particular **compound** always contains the same elements.

- These elements are always present in the same proportions by mass.

- It does not matter where the compound is found or how it is made.

- These proportions cannot be changed.

For example, magnesium oxide always contains 60% magnesium and 40% oxygen by mass; and ammonium nitrate always contains 35% nitrogen, 60% oxygen and 5% hydrogen by mass.

Similar experiments can be done to show that the water of crystallisation present in a particular hydrated salt, for example hydrated copper(II) sulphate ($CuSO_4 \cdot 5H_2O$), is always the same fraction of the total mass of the salt.

6.3 Reacting amounts of substance

Relative formula masses can also be used to calculate the amounts of compounds reacted together or produced in reactions. Here is an example.

If 0.24 g of magnesium react with 0.16 g of oxygen to produce 0.40 g of magnesium oxide (figure 6.4 on page 159), how much magnesium oxide (MgO) will be produced by burning 12 g of magnesium?

We have

0.24 g Mg producing 0.40 g MgO

so 1 g Mg produces $\dfrac{0.40}{0.24}$ g MgO

= 1.67 g MgO

so 12 g Mg produces 12 × 1.67 g MgO

= 20 g MgO

Calculations of quantities like these are a very important part of chemistry. These calculations show how there is a great deal of information 'stored' in chemical formulas and equations.

Summary of core material

You should know that:

- the mass of an atom can be found using a mass spectrometer

- many elements are made up of different isotopes – atoms of the same element with different mass numbers

- the masses of atoms are measured relative to a standard – a carbon-12 atom is fixed as having a mass of 12 exactly

- calculation of the average mass of an atom of an element must take into account the different isotopes present

- this average mass is known as the relative atomic mass

- the relative formula mass of a compound can be calculated by adding up the masses of the atoms or ions in the formula

- relative formula masses are useful for calculating the percentage by mass of an element in a compound

- experiments show that compounds are made from elements combining in fixed ratios by mass.

6.1 Calculate the relative formula masses (M_r) of the following substances: [8]

(a) oxygen, O_2

(b) ammonia, NH_3

(c) sulphur dioxide, SO_2

(d) octane, C_8H_{18}

(e) sulphuric acid, H_2SO_4

(f) potassium bromide, KBr

(g) copper nitrate, $Cu(NO_3)_2$

(h) aluminium chloride, $AlCl_3$

(Relative atomic masses: H = 1, C = 12, N = 14, O = 16, Al = 27, S = 32, Cl = 35.5, K = 39, Cu = 64, Br = 80)

6.2 Calculate the percentage by mass of nitrogen in the following fertilisers and nitrogen-containing compounds: [10]

(a) ammonium sulphate, $(NH_4)_2SO_4$

(b) ammonium phosphate, $(NH_4)_3PO_4$

(c) urea, $CO(NH_2)_2$

(d) calcium cyanamide, $CaCN_2$

(e) glycine, $CH_2(NH_2)COOH$ (an amino acid)

(Relative atomic masses: H = 1, C = 12, N = 14, O = 16, P = 31, S = 32, Ca = 40)

6.3 A student investigates the effect of heating magnesium in air.

(a) First he weighs an empty crucible and its lid. From the diagram, what is the mass of the crucible and its lid? [1]

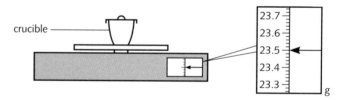

(b) Then he re-weighs the crucible, its lid and some magnesium.

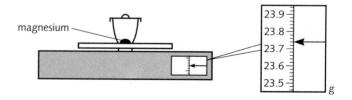

(i) From the diagram, what is the mass of the crucible, its lid and the magnesium? [1]

(ii) What mass of magnesium is in the crucible? [1]

(c) Next he heats the crucible containing the magnesium. The lid is placed slightly open to allow air to react with the magnesium.

(i) Explain why it is important not to let any white smoke escape from the crucible. [2]

(ii) After five minutes of heating the crucible is allowed to cool and then re-weighed. This part of the procedure is repeated three more times. Copy out the first and last lines of the diagram. Record the mass of the crucible and its contents for each weighing. [4]

Time in minutes	5	10	15	20
Mass displayed	23.9⊣ 23.8⊣ ← 23.7⊣ 23.6⊣ 23.5⊣	23.9⊣ 23.8⊣ ← 23.7⊣ 23.6⊣ 23.5⊣	23.9⊣ ← 23.8⊣ 23.7⊣ 23.6⊣ 23.5⊣	23.9⊣ ← 23.8⊣ 23.7⊣ 23.6⊣ 23.5⊣
Mass in grams				

(iii) Explain why these weighings are taken after each reheating of the crucible and its contents. [2]

(d) The table below shows the results of the experiments from the class of students.

Experiment	Mass in grams of		
	Magnesium	Magnesium oxide	Oxygen
1	0.06	0.10	0.04
2	0.15	0.25	0.10
3	0.22	0.36	0.14
4	0.24	0.40	0.16
5	0.30	0.50	
6	0.28	0.46	
7	0.10	0.16	
8	0.20	0.32	

(i) Write down the correct mass of oxygen that reacts with the magnesium in the last four experiments. [4]

(ii) Plot a graph of the mass of oxygen reacted against the mass of magnesium used. Draw in the best line for these points. [3]

(iii) Comment on what this graph line shows about the composition of magnesium oxide. [2]

(SEG, 1991)

6.4

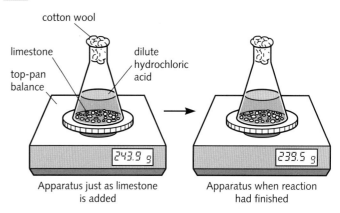

cotton wool
limestone
top-pan balance
dilute hydrochloric acid

243.9 g — Apparatus just as limestone is added

239.5 g — Apparatus when reaction had finished

(a) The shells of some sea-animals form limestone. The amount of calcium carbonate in limestone can be found from the loss of mass when it reacts with an excess of acid.

The chemical equation for this reaction is:

$$CaCO_3(s) + 2HCl(aq) \rightarrow CaCl_2(aq) + CO_2(g) + H_2O(l)$$

(i) When the acid reacts with the calcium carbonate a fine spray of solution is formed. In this experiment how is the spray of solution stopped from leaving the flask? [1]

(ii) How would you be able to tell when the reaction had finished? [1]

(iii) From the diagrams work out the loss of mass of the flask and its contents. [1]

(iv) What causes the loss of mass that you have worked out? [2]

(b) The percentage of calcium carbonate present in the limestone can be found by following the steps below.

Step 1
The formula mass of carbon dioxide (CO_2) is 44. Work out the formula mass of calcium carbonate, given that the relative atomic masses are Ca = 40, C = 12, O = 16. [1]

Step 2
Mass of calcium carbonate

$$= \frac{\text{loss of mass of flask and its contents}}{} \times \frac{\text{formula mass } CaCO_3}{\text{formula mass } CO_2}$$

Using the equation above, the loss of mass from (a)(iii) and the formula masses from step 1 work out the mass of calcium carbonate in the limestone. [2]

Step 3
The mass of limestone used was 20 g. Use your answer from step 2 to work out the percentage of calcium carbonate in this limestone. [2]

(SEG, 1988)

EXTENSION

The mole and chemical reactions

This section covers the following ideas:

- the mole as the 'accounting unit' in chemistry
- simple calculations on the mole
- using the idea of the mole to work out chemical formulas
- the difference between the empirical formula and molecular formula of some covalent compounds
- the mole and reacting masses – calculations based on chemical equations
- percentage yield and percentage purity
- calculations involving gases.

A particular compound always contains the same elements. They are always present in a fixed ratio by mass (figure 6.5). These two experimental results were of great historical importance in developing the ideas of chemical formulas and the bonding of atoms. How can we make the link between mass ratios and the chemical formula of a compound? To do this, we need to use the idea of the *mole*.

6.4 The mole – the chemical counting unit

When carrying out an experiment, a chemist cannot weigh out a single atom or molecule, and then react it with another one. Atoms and molecules are simply too small. A 'counting unit' must be found that is useful in practical chemistry. This idea is not unusual when dealing with large numbers of small objects. For example, banks weigh coins rather than count them – they know that a fixed number of a particular coin will always have the same mass. The number of sweets in a jar can be estimated from their mass. Assuming that you know the mass of one sweet, you could calculate how many sweets were in the jar from their total mass. How can we estimate the number of iron atoms in an iron block? Again, we can try to link mass to the number of items present.

Chemists count atoms and molecules by weighing them. The standard 'unit' of the 'amount' of a substance is taken as the relative formula mass of the substance in grams. This 'unit' is called one **mole** (1 mol) of the substance (mol is the symbol or shortened form of mole or moles). The unit 'moles' is used to measure amounts of elements and compounds. The idea becomes clearer if we consider some examples (table 6.4).

One mole of each of these different substances contains the *same* number of atoms, molecules, or formula units. That number per mole has been worked out by several different experimental methods. It is named after the nineteenth-century Italian chemist, Amedeo Avogadro, and is 6.02×10^{23} per mole (this is called the **Avogadro constant**, and is given the symbol L). The vast size of this constant shows just how small atoms are! For instance, it has been estimated that 6.02×10^{23} soft-drink cans stacked together would cover the surface of the Earth to a height of 200 miles.

- **One mole** of a substance has a mass equal to its relative formula mass in grams.
- **One mole** of a substance contains 6.02×10^{23} per mole (**Avogadro constant**) of atoms, molecules, or formula units, depending on the substance considered.

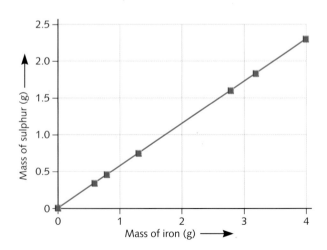

Figure 6.5 Experiments on heating iron with sulphur show that the two elements react in a fixed ratio by mass to produce iron sulphide.

Table 6.4 Calculating the mass of one mole of various substances

Substance	Formula	Relative formula mass, M_r	Mass of one mole (molar mass)	This mass (1 mol) contains
Carbon	C	12	12 g	6.02×10^{23} carbon atoms
Iron	Fe	56	56 g	6.02×10^{23} iron atoms
Hydrogen	H_2	$2 \times 1 = 2$	2 g	6.02×10^{23} molecules
Oxygen	O_2	$2 \times 16 = 32$	32 g	6.02×10^{23} molecules
Water	H_2O	$(2 \times 1) + 16 = 18$	18 g	6.02×10^{23} molecules
Magnesium oxide	MgO	$24 + 16 = 40$	40 g	6.02×10^{23} 'formula units'
Calcium carbonate	$CaCO_3$	$40 + 12 + (3 \times 16) = 100$	100 g	6.02×10^{23} 'formula units'
Silicon(IV) oxide	SiO_2	$28 + (2 \times 16) = 60$	60 g	6.02×10^{23} 'formula units'

6.5 Calculations on the mole

You can find the **molar mass** (mass of one mole) of any substance by following these steps.

1 Write down the formula of the substance; for example ethanol is C_2H_5OH.
2 Work out its relative formula mass; for example ethanol contains two carbon atoms ($A_r = 12$), six hydrogen atoms ($A_r = 1$) and one oxygen atom ($A_r = 16$). So for ethanol $M_r = (2 \times 12) + (6 \times 1) + 16 = 46$.
3 Express this in grams per mole; for example the molar mass of ethanol = 46 g/mol.

In experimental work, chemists work with varying masses. They cannot always use one mole of a substance. The equation that links the mass of a substance to the number of moles present is:

$$\text{number of moles} = \frac{\text{mass}}{\text{molar mass}}$$

where the mass is in grams and the molar mass is in grams per mole. The triangle shown can be a useful aid to memory: cover the item to be found and you are left with how to work this item out.

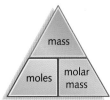

This shows that if we need to calculate the mass of one mole of some substance, the straightforward way is to work out the relative

formula mass of the substance and write the word 'grams' after it.

Using the above equation it is possible to convert any mass of a particular substance into moles, or vice versa. We shall look at two examples.

(i) How many moles are there in 60 g of sodium hydroxide?

We have: the relative formula mass of sodium hydroxide is

$$M_r(\text{NaOH}) = 23 + 16 + 1 = 40$$

molar mass of NaOH = 40 g/mol

$$\text{number of moles} = \frac{\text{mass}}{\text{molar mass}}$$

$$= \frac{60\,\text{g}}{40\,\text{g/mol}}$$

$$= 1.5\,\text{mol}$$

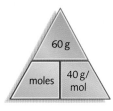

(ii) What is the mass of 0.5 mol of copper(II) sulphate crystals?

We have: the relative formula mass of hydrated copper(II) sulphate is

$$M_r(\text{CuSO}_4 \cdot 5H_2O)$$
$$= 64 + 32 + (4 \times 16) + (5 \times 18) = 250$$

molar mass of $CuSO_4 \cdot 5H_2O$ = 250 g/mol

number of moles = $\dfrac{\text{mass}}{\text{molar mass}}$

Therefore,

$0.5\,\text{mol} = \dfrac{\text{mass}}{250\,\text{g/mol}}$

mass = $0.5 \times 250 = 125\,\text{g}$

Working out chemical formulas

The idea of the mole means that we can now work out chemical formulas from experimental data on combining masses. It provides the link between the mass of an element in a compound and the number of its atoms present.

In the experiment to make magnesium oxide (see section 6.2 on page 159), a constant ratio was found between the reacting amounts of magnesium and oxygen. If 0.24 g of magnesium is burnt, then 0.40 g of magnesium oxide is formed. This means that 0.24 g of magnesium combines with 0.16 g of oxygen (0.40 – 0.24 = 0.16 g). We can now use these results to find the formula of magnesium oxide (figure 6.6).

The formula of magnesium oxide tells us that 1 mol of magnesium atoms combine with 1 mol of

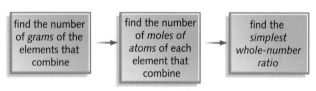

	Mg	O
Mass combined	0.24 g	0.16 g
Molar mass	24 g/mol	16 g/mol
Number of moles	0.01 mol	0.01 mol
Simplest ratio	1	1
Formula		MgO

Figure 6.6 *Calculating the empirical formula of magnesium oxide from experimental data on the masses of magnesium and oxygen that react together.*

oxygen atoms. The atoms react in a 1:1 ratio to form a giant ionic lattice of Mg^{2+} and O^{2-} ions. For giant structures, the formula of the compound is the simplest whole-number formula – in this example, MgO. A formula found by this method is also known as the **empirical formula**.

Silicon(IV) oxide is a giant covalent structure. A sample of silicon oxide is found to contain 47% by mass of silicon. How can we find its empirical formula? This is done in figure 6.7. The empirical formula of silicon(IV) oxide is SiO_2. It consists of a giant molecular lattice of covalently bonded silicon and oxygen atoms in a ratio 1:2. Since it is a giant structure, the formula we use for this compound is SiO_2.

Empirical formulas and molecular formulas

Not all compounds are giant structures – some are made up of simple molecules. Here we sometimes have to make a distinction between the empirical formula and the actual formula of the molecule, the **molecular formula**.

Phosphorus burns in air to produce white clouds of phosphorus oxide. From experiments it is

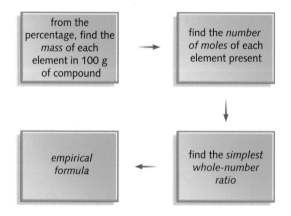

	Si	O
Percentage by mass	47%	100 – 47 = 53%
Mass in 100 g	47 g	53 g
Molar mass	28 g/mol	16 g/mol
Number of moles	1.68 mol	3.31 mol
Simplest ratio	1	2
Formula		SiO_2

Figure 6.7 *Finding the empirical formula of silicon(IV) oxide from percentage mass data.*

found that the oxide contains 44% phosphorus. The empirical formula of phosphorus oxide is P_2O_5 (table 6.5). However, it is found experimentally that its relative molecular mass (M_r) is 284. The sum of the relative atomic masses in the empirical formula (P_2O_5) is $(2 \times 31) + (5 \times 16) = 142$. The actual relative molecular mass is twice this value. Therefore the molecular formula of phosphorus oxide is $(P_2O_5)_2$ or P_4O_{10}. The empirical formula is *not* the actual molecular formula of phosphorus oxide. A molecule of phosphorus oxide contains four P atoms and ten O atoms.

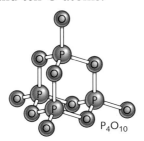

P_4O_{10}

- The **empirical formula** of a compound is the simplest whole-number formula.

- For simple molecular compounds, the empirical formula may not be the actual molecular formula. The **molecular formula** must be calculated using the relative molecular mass (M_r) of the compound found by experiment.

Hydrated salts

The mass of water present in crystals of hydrated salts is always a fixed proportion of the total mass. The formula of such a salt can be worked out by a method similar to that used to calculate the empirical formula of a compound.

If 5.0 g of hydrated copper(II) sulphate crystals are heated to drive off the water of crystallisation, the remaining solid has a mass of 3.2 g. The ratio of the salt and water in the crystal can be calculated. This gives the formula of the crystals (table 6.6).

6.6 The mole and chemical equations

We can now see that the chemical equation for a reaction is more than simply a record of what is produced. In addition to telling us *what* the

Table 6.5 Calculating the empirical formula of phosphorus oxide

	P	O
Percentage by mass	44%	100 − 44 = 56%
Mass in 100 g	44 g	56 g
Molar mass	31 g/mol	16 g/mol
Number of moles	1.4 mol	3.5 mol
Simplest ratio	1	2.5
or	2	5
Formula	P_2O_5	

reactants and products are, it tells us *how much* product we can expect from particular amounts of reactants. When iron reacts with sulphur, the equation is:

$$Fe + S \rightarrow FeS$$

This indicates that we need equal numbers of atoms of iron and sulphur to react. We know that 1 mol of iron (56 g) and 1 mol of sulphur (32 g) contain the same numbers of atoms. Reacting these amounts should give us 1 mol of iron(II) sulphide (88 g). The equation is showing us that

Fe	+	S	→	FeS
1 mol		1 mol		1 mol
56 g		32 g		88 g

The mass of the product is equal to the total mass of the reactants. This is the **law of conservation of mass**, which we met earlier. Although the atoms have rearranged themselves, their total mass remains the same. A chemical equation must be balanced. In practice, we may not want to react such large amounts. We could **scale down** the quantities (that is use *smaller*

Table 6.6 Calculating the formula of hydrated copper(II) sulphate

	$CuSO_4$	H_2O
Mass	3.2 g	5.0 − 3.2 = 1.8 g
Molar mass	160 g/mol	18 g/mol
Number of moles	0.02 mol	0.10 mol
Simplest ratio	1	5
Formula	$CuSO_4 \cdot 5H_2O$	

amounts). However, the mass of iron and the mass of sulphur must always be in the ratio 56:32. Thus

Fe   +   S $\rightarrow$ FeS
5.6 g   3.2 g   8.8 g

If we tried to react 5 g of sulphur with 5.6 g of iron, the excess sulphur would remain unreacted. Only 3.2 g of sulphur could react with the 5.6 g of iron: 1.8 g of sulphur (5.0 − 3.2 = 1.8 g) would remain unreacted.

> When we write a **chemical equation**, we are indicating the *number of moles* of reactants and products involved in the reaction.

The reacting amounts given by an equation can also be **scaled up** (that is use *larger* amounts). In industry, tonnes of chemical reactants may be used, but the ratios given by the equation still apply. The manufacture of lime is important for the cement industry and agriculture. Lime is made by heating limestone in lime kilns. The reaction is an example of thermal decomposition:

calcium carbonate	$\rightarrow$	calcium oxide	+	carbon dioxide
$CaCO_3$	$\rightarrow$	CaO	+	CO_2
1 mol		1 mol		1 mol
40 + 12 + (3 × 16)		40 + 16		12 + (2 × 16)
= 100 g		= 56 g		= 44 g

This can be scaled up to work in tonnes:

100 tonnes   56 tonnes   44 tonnes

Therefore, if 10 tonnes of calcium carbonate were heated, we should expect to produce 5.6 tonnes of lime (calcium oxide).

A chemical 'footbridge'

We can use the idea of the mole to find reactant or product masses from the equation for a reaction. There are various ways of doing these calculations. The balanced equation itself can be used as a numerical 'footbridge' between the two sides of the reaction (figure 6.8).

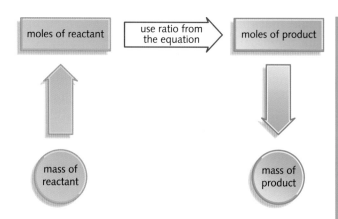

Figure 6.8 A chemical 'footbridge'. Following the sequence 'up–across–down' helps to relate the amount of product made to the mass of reactant used. The 'bridge' can, of course, be used in the reverse direction.

We shall consider an example. What mass of aluminium oxide is produced from 9.2 g of aluminium metal reacting completely with oxygen gas?

To answer this question, we first work out the balanced equation:

4Al   +   3O$_2$ $\rightarrow$ 2Al$_2$O$_3$

$\uparrow$ ratio = 4 mol : 2 mol $\downarrow$
9.2 g   mass = ?

Then we work through the steps of the 'footbridge'.

- *Step 1* (the 'up' stage)   Convert 9.2 g of Al into moles:

$$\text{number of moles} = \frac{9.2\,g}{27\,g/mol} = 0.34\,mol$$

- *Step 2* (the 'across' stage)   Use the ratio from the equation to work out how many moles of Al_2O_3 are produced:

4 mol of Al produce 2 mol of Al_2O_3

so

0.34 mol of Al produce 0.17 mol of Al_2O_3

- *Step 3* (the 'down' stage)   Work out the mass of this amount of aluminium oxide (the relative formula mass of Al_2O_3 is 102):

$$0.17\,mol = \frac{mass}{102\,g/mol}$$

so

mass of Al_2O_3 produced = 0.17 × 102 g

= 17.3 g

Percentage yield and percentage purity of product

A reaction may not always yield the total amount of product predicted by the equation. The loss may be due to several factors.

- The reaction may not be totally complete.
- Errors may be made in weighing the reactants or the products.
- Material may be lost in carrying out the reaction, or in transferring and separating the product.

The equation gives us an ideal figure for the yield of a reaction; reality often produces less. This can be expressed as the **percentage yield** for a particular experiment.

Consider an example. Heating 12.4 g of copper(II) carbonate in a crucible produced only 7.0 g of copper(II) oxide. What was the percentage yield of copper(II) oxide?

$CuCO_3$	$\rightarrow$	CuO	+	CO_2
1 mol		1 mol		1 mol
64 + 12 + 48		64 + 16		
= 124 g		= 80 g		

Therefore heating 12.4 g of copper(II) carbonate should have produced 8.0 g of copper(II) oxide. So

expected yield = 8.0 g

actual yield = 7.0 g

and

percentage yield = $\frac{7.0}{8.0}$ × 100 = 87.5%

In other, more complex, reactions, a particular product may be **contaminated** by other products or unreacted material. The 'crude' product may prove to contain less than 100% of the required substance. The **percentage purity** of the crude product can be calculated in a similar way to the percentage yield.

6.7 Calculations involving gases

The volume of one mole of a gas

Many reactions, including some of those we have just considered, involve gases. Weighing solids or liquids is relatively straightforward. In contrast, weighing a gas is quite difficult. It is much easier to measure the **volume** of a gas. But how does gas volume relate to the number of atoms or molecules present?

In a gas, the particles are relatively far apart. Indeed, any gas can be regarded as largely empty space. Equal volumes of gases are found to contain the same number of particles (this is **Avogadro's law**). This leads to a simple rule about the volume of one mole of a gas (see table 6.7).

- **One mole of any gas** occupies a volume of approximately 24 dm^3 (24 litres) at room temperature and pressure (r.t.p.).
- The **molar volume** of any gas therefore has the value 24 dm^3/mol at r.t.p.
- Remember that 1 dm^3 (1 litre) = 1000 cm^3.

Table 6.7 The molar mass and molar volume of various gases

Substance	Molar mass (g/mol)	Molar volume (dm^3/mol)	Number of particles
Hydrogen (H_2)	2	24	6.02×10^{23} hydrogen molecules
Oxygen (O_2)	32	24	6.02×10^{23} oxygen molecules
Carbon dioxide (CO_2)	44	24	6.02×10^{23} carbon dioxide molecules
Ethane (C_2H_6)	30	24	6.02×10^{23} ethane molecules

This rule applies to all gases. This makes it easy to convert the volume of any gas into moles, or moles into volume:

$$\text{number of moles} = \frac{\text{volume}}{\text{molar volume}}$$

where the volume is in cubic decimetres (dm^3) and the molar volume is $24\,dm^3/mol$.

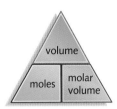

Reactions involving gases

For reactions in which gases are produced, the calculation of product volume is similar to those we have seen already.

For example, consider the reaction of sulphur burning in oxygen:

sulphur	+	oxygen	→	sulphur dioxide
S(s)	+	O_2(g)	→	SO_2(g)
1 mol		1 mol		1 mol
= 32 g		= 24 dm^3		= 24 dm^3

If 8 g of sulphur are burnt, what volume of SO_2 is produced?

We have

$$\text{number of moles of sulphur burnt} = \frac{8\,g}{32\,g/mol}$$

$$= 0.25\,mol$$

From the equation

1 mol of sulphur → 1 mol of SO_2

Therefore

0.25 mol of sulphur → 0.25 mol of SO_2

So from the above rule that

$$\text{number of moles} = \frac{\text{volume}}{\text{molar volume}}$$

$$0.25\,mol = \frac{\text{volume}}{24\,dm^3/mol}$$

volume of sulphur dioxide = $0.25 \times 24\,dm^3$
= $6\,dm^3$ at r.t.p.

The approach used is an adaptation of the 'bridge' method used earlier for calculations involving solids. It is shown in figure 6.9.

Some important reactions involve only gases. For such reactions, the calculations of expected yield are simplified by the fact that the value for molar volume applies to any gas. For example

hydrogen	+	chlorine	→	hydrogen chloride
H_2(g)	+	Cl_2(g)	→	2HCl(g)
1 mol		1 mol		2 mol
= 24 dm^3		= 24 dm^3		= 48 dm^3

The volumes of the gases involved are in the same ratio as the number of moles given by the equation:

H_2(g)	+	Cl_2(g)	→	2HCl(g)
1 volume		1 volume		2 volumes

If we react $20\,cm^3$ of hydrogen with sufficient chlorine, it will produce $40\,cm^3$ of hydrogen chloride gas.

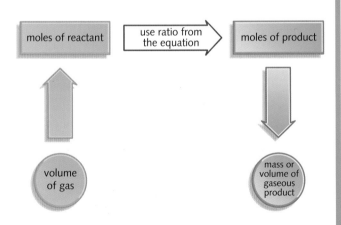

Figure 6.9 An outline of the 'footbridge' method for calculations involving gases.

Summary of extension material

You should know that:

- the mole is the unit used in chemistry to express the amount of a substance taking part in a reaction

- one mole of any substance contains the same number of constituent particles per mole (the Avogadro constant) whether they are atoms, molecules or formula units

- the idea of the mole can be used to calculate empirical formulas and molecular formulas from data on the masses of elements in a compound

- the formulas of hydrated salts can be worked out in a similar way

- the balanced chemical equation can be used to calculate the reacting masses of substances and the amount of product formed

- one mole of any gas has a volume of approximately $24\,dm^3$ at room temperature and pressure

- for reactions involving only gases, the ratio of the reactant volume and product volume is the same as the ratio of the number of moles in the balanced equation.

6.5 Natural copper consists of two types of atoms.

Type of atom	Relative percentage present	Number of particles in each atom		
		Protons	Electrons	Neutrons
$^{63}_{29}Cu$	69.10	29	29	34
$^{65}_{29}Cu$	30.90			

(a) Copy and complete the table above. [2]

(b) What name is given to these two types of atom? [1]

(c) Show by calculation why the relative atomic mass of copper is 63.62. [3]

(d) Which, if either, of these two types of copper atom would be most reactive? [2]

(SEG, 1992)

6.6 Rock salt is used to treat ice on roads. The salt is analysed to see if it is suitable for spreading by machines. The following procedure is used to find the mass of sodium chloride in a sample of rock salt.

Procedure
Step 1. Weigh the rock salt and crush in a pestle and mortar.
Step 2. Add $100\,cm^3$ of water to the rock salt.
Step 3. Filter and collect the salt solution in an evaporating dish.
Step 4. Gently heat the dish to evaporate the water.
Step 5. Allow the evaporating dish to cool and weigh the dish containing the pure salt.
Step 6. Wash out the evaporating dish, dry it and weigh it.

(a) Draw a labelled diagram to show how step 3 is carried out. [3]

(b) State the purpose of crushing the rock salt in step 1. [2]

(c) The following results were obtained.

Mass of dish	+	rock salt	=	36.75 g
Mass of dish	+	pure salt	=	36.25 g
Mass of dish			=	35.25 g
Mass of pure salt			=	g
Mass of rock salt			=	g

(i) Copy and complete the table. [2]
(ii) Calculate the percentage by mass of pure salt in rock salt using the following equation: [2]

$$\text{percentage by mass of salt} = \frac{\text{mass of pure salt}}{\text{mass of rock salt}} \times 100$$

(IGCSE, 1996)

6.7

(a) Copper is a pink coloured metal with excellent thermal and electrical conductivities. It is mostly found in sulphide ores as the mineral chalcopyrite. These ores are low-grade and typically contain about 3% by mass of chalcopyrite, the rest being waste material.

Laboratory analysis shows that 15.15g of chalcopyrite has the following composition by mass: copper 5.27 g and iron 4.61g. Sulphur is the only other element present. Use these figures to find the empirical formula of chalcopyrite. [3]

(b) Bromine is used to make 1,2-dibromoethane. This is an additive in leaded petrol. 1,2-Dibromoethane reacts with sodium hydroxide to form a compound that has the composition by mass: carbon, 38.7%; hydrogen, 9.7%; oxygen, 51.6%.

(i) Calculate its empirical formula. [2]

(ii) The relative molecular mass of the compound is 62. What is its molecular formula? [1]

(MEG, 1993 and IGCSE, 1994)

6.8 Copper(ɪɪ) oxide can be reduced to copper metal by heating it in a stream of hydrogen gas. Dry copper(ɪɪ) oxide was placed in a weighed tube and the tube re-weighed. The apparatus was then set up as in the diagram below.

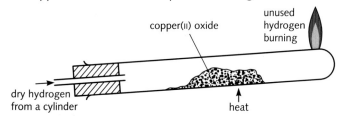

copper(ɪɪ) oxide

unused hydrogen burning

dry hydrogen from a cylinder

heat

Hydrogen was passed through the tube for 15 seconds before the escaping gas was lit.

The tube was heated for a few minutes.

The apparatus was then allowed to cool with hydrogen still passing through.

The tube was re-weighed.

The process was repeated until there was no further change in mass.

(a) (i) Where is the most suitable place to clamp the tube? [1]

(ii) Copy and complete the word equation for the reaction: [1]
copper(ɪɪ) oxide + hydrogen → ....

(iii) Why was the hydrogen passed through for 15 seconds before the gas was lit? [1]

(iv) Why was it necessary to repeat the process until there was no further change in mass? [1]

(b) The results for the experiment are given below.
A   Mass of empty tube   = 46.12 g
B   Mass of tube + copper(ɪɪ) oxide   = 47.72 g
C   Mass of copper(ɪɪ) oxide (B − A)   = ...g
D   Mass of tube + copper   = 47.40 g
E   Mass of copper produced (D − A)   = ...g
F   Mass of oxygen in the copper(ɪɪ) oxide = ...g

(i) Copy out and complete the results table above. [3]

(ii) How many moles of copper atoms are involved in the reaction? (Relative atomic mass: Cu = 64) [1]

(iii) How many moles of oxygen atoms are involved in the reaction? (Relative atomic mass: O = 16) [1]

(iv) From the results of the experiment how many moles of oxygen atoms will combine with one mole of copper atoms? [1]

(v) From the results of the experiment what is the formula of copper(ɪɪ) oxide? [1]

(vi) Using your formula for copper(ɪɪ) oxide write a full balanced equation for the reaction with hydrogen. [2]

(ULEAC, 1992)

6.9 Joseph Gay-Lussac was Professor of Chemistry at the University of Paris. In 1810, he carried out a series of experiments to measure the volumes of reacting gases. A modern version of one of his experiments is described below.

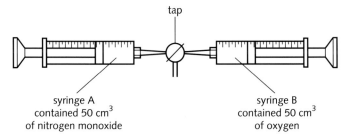

tap

syringe A
contained 50 cm^3
of nitrogen monoxide

syringe B
contained 50 cm^3
of oxygen

Nitrogen monoxide reacts with oxygen to form one product. This is a brown gas. In the experiment, 5.0 cm^3 portions of oxygen were pushed from syringe B into syringe A. After each addition, the tap was closed and, after waiting for the gases to cool, the total volume of gases remaining was measured. The results are shown as a graph.

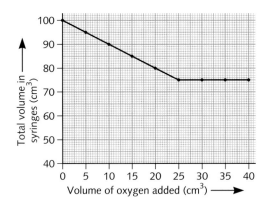

Total volume in syringes (cm^3)

Volume of oxygen added (cm^3)

(a) What is the total volume of gases when the reaction is complete? [1]

(b) What volume of oxygen reacts with 50 cm^3 of nitrogen monoxide? [1]

(c) What is the volume of the brown gas formed? [1]

(d) Copy and complete the following to work out the formula of the brown gas: [2]

...NO   +   O$_2$ →   ....
50 cm^3 ...cm^3 ...cm^3

(IGCSE, part question, 1991)

EXTENSION

Moles and solution chemistry

This section covers the following ideas:

- the concentration of solutions
- the titration of acid and alkali solutions
- solubility curves
- the calculations involved in electrolysis – the Faraday constant as the quantity of electric charge equivalent to the transfer of one mole of electrons.

Colourful tricks can be played with chemical substances. A simple reaction can produce a 'water into wine' colour change – when two colourless solutions mixed together produce a wine-coloured mixture. Far more complex reactions in solution can produce oscillating colour changes. For example, in the Belousov–Zhabotinskii reaction, the reaction mixture goes red–blue–red–blue–red over about 80 seconds. These reactions all take place in solution, as do many others. The usual solvent is water. When setting up such reactions, we normally measure out the solutions by volume. To know how much of the reactants we are actually mixing, we need to know the *concentrations* of the solutions.

6.8 The concentration of solutions

When a chemical substance (the **solute**) is dissolved in a volume of **solvent**, we can measure the 'quantity' of solute in two ways. We can measure either its *mass* (in grams) or its *amount* (in moles). The final volume of the *solution* is normally measured in cubic decimetres, dm^3 ($1\,dm^3$ = 1 litre or $1000\,cm^3$). When we measure the *mass* of the solute in *grams*, it is the **mass concentration** that we obtain, in grams per cubic decimetre of solution (g/dm^3). But it is more useful to measure the *amount* in *moles*, in which case we get the **concentration** in moles per cubic decimetre of solution (mol/dm^3):

$$\text{concentration} = \frac{\text{amount of solute}}{\text{volume of solution}}$$

- The **mass concentration** of a solution is measured in grams per cubic decimetre (g/dm^3).
- The **concentration** of a solution is measured in moles per cubic decimetre (mol/dm^3).
- When 1 mol of a substance is dissolved in water and the solution is made up to $1\,dm^3$ ($1000\,cm^3$), a solution with a concentration of **$1\,mol/dm^3$** is produced.

For example, a $1\,mol/dm^3$ solution of sodium chloride contains $58.5\,g$ of NaCl (1 mol) dissolved in water and made up to a final volume of $1000\,cm^3$. Figure 6.10 shows how the units are expressed for solutions of differing concentrations. It also shows how solutions of the same final concentration can be made up in different ways.

Calculations using solution concentrations

The following equation is useful when working out the number of moles of a substance present in a particular solution:

$$\begin{array}{l}\text{number of} \\ \text{moles in} \\ \text{solution}\end{array} = \frac{\text{concentration}}{1000} \times \begin{array}{l}\text{volume of} \\ \text{solution} \\ \text{(in } cm^3)\end{array}$$

where concentration is in moles per cubic decimetre, but volume of solution is in cubic centimetres.

For example, how many moles of sugar are there in $500\,cm^3$ of a $3.0\,mol/dm^3$ sugar solution?

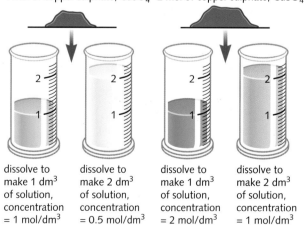

1 mol of copper sulphate, $CuSO_4$ 2 mol of copper sulphate, $CuSO_4$

dissolve to make $1\,dm^3$ of solution, concentration = $1\,mol/dm^3$

dissolve to make $2\,dm^3$ of solution, concentration = $0.5\,mol/dm^3$

dissolve to make $1\,dm^3$ of solution, concentration = $2\,mol/dm^3$

dissolve to make $2\,dm^3$ of solution, concentration = $1\,mol/dm^3$

Figure 6.10 Making copper(ii) sulphate solutions of different concentrations.

We get

$$\text{number of moles} = \frac{3.0}{1000} \times 500 = 1.5 \, \text{mol}$$

In practice, a chemist still has to weigh out a substance in grams. So questions and experiments may also involve converting between moles and grams. We shall look at an example.

Calculate the concentration of a solution of sodium hydroxide, NaOH, that contains 10 g of NaOH in a final volume of 250 cm³.

• *Step 1* Find out how many moles of NaOH are present:

relative formula mass of NaOH
= 23 + 16 + 1 = 40

$$\text{number of moles of NaOH} = \frac{10}{40} = 0.25 \, \text{mol}$$

• *Step 2* Find the concentration:

$$\text{number of moles} = \frac{\text{concentration}}{1000} \times \text{volume (in cm}^3)$$

$$0.25 = \frac{\text{concentration}}{1000} \times 250$$

$$\text{concentration} = \frac{0.25 \times 1000}{250}$$

$$= 1 \, \text{mol/dm}^3$$

6.9 Acid–base titrations

The concentration of an unknown acid solution can be found if it is reacted with a standard solution of an alkali. A **standard solution** is one that has been carefully made up so that its concentration is known precisely. The reaction is carried out in a carefully controlled way. The volumes are measured accurately using a pipette and a burette. Just sufficient acid is added to the alkali to neutralise the alkali. This end point is found using an indicator. The method is known as **titration**, and can be adapted to prepare a soluble salt. The method is summarised in figure 6.11.

We shall now look at an example of the type of calculation that can be carried out. A solution of hydrochloric acid is titrated against a standard sodium hydroxide solution. It is found that 20.0 cm³ of acid neutralise 25.0 cm³ of 0.10 mol/dm³ NaOH solution. What is the concentration of the hydrochloric acid solution?

The calculation goes like this.

• *Step 1* Use information on the standard solution. *How many moles of alkali are in the flask?*

We have

$$\text{number of moles of NaOH} = \frac{\text{concentration}}{1000} \times \text{volume (in cm}^3)$$

$$= \frac{0.10}{1000} \times 25$$

$$= 2.5 \times 10^{-3} \, \text{mol}$$

• *Step 2* Use the chemical equation. *How many moles of acid are used?*

The equation is

HCl   +   NaOH   →   NaCl   +   H₂O
1 mol   1 mol

So 1 mol of NaOH neutralises 1 mol of HCl and so:

2.5 × 10⁻³ mol of NaOH neutralise
2.5 × 10⁻³ mol of HCl

• *Step 3* Use the titration value. *What is the concentration of the acid?*

The acid solution contains 2.5×10^{-3} mol in 20.0 cm³.

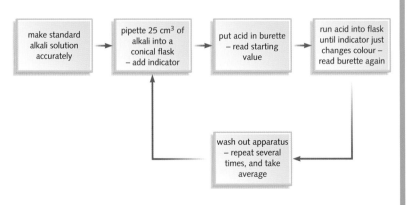

Figure 6.11 Summary of the titration method.

So

$$\text{number of moles} = \frac{\text{concentration}}{1000} \times \text{volume (in cm}^3\text{)}$$

$$2.5 \times 10^{-3} = \frac{\text{concentration}}{1000} \times 20.0$$

$$\text{concentration of acid} = \frac{2.5 \times 10^{-3} \times 1000}{20}$$

$$= 0.125 \, \text{mol/dm}^3$$

The method uses a further variation of the 'bridge' approach to link the reactants and products (figure 6.12).

6.10 Solubility curves

In general, water-soluble solids dissolve more with increasing temperature. The **solubility** of a particular solid in water can be measured over a range of temperatures up to 100°C. The *maximum* mass of solid that will dissolve in 100g of water is found at each temperature. Such a solution is said to be **saturated** at that temperature. The values at each temperature can then be plotted to give a **solubility curve**.

Figure 6.13 shows the solubility curves for potassium nitrate and potassium chloride. The curves show that:

- at room temperature (20°C), the solubility of the two salts is equal,
- the solubility of both salts increases with temperature,
- the solubility of potassium nitrate increases much more than that of potassium chloride with increasing temperature.

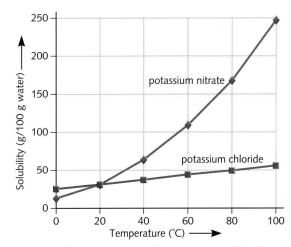

Figure 6.13 *Solubility curves for potassium chloride and potassium nitrate. The solubility is measured in grams of solute per 100g of solvent. The solute is potassium chloride or nitrate and the solvent is water.*

Using solubility curves

There are various ways in which data can be obtained from solubility curves. For example, look at the following.

(i) What mass of potassium nitrate dissolves in 100g of water at (a) 90°C and (b) 30°C? From the graph:
  (a) at 90°C, 205g of KNO_3 dissolve in 100g of water
  (b) at 30°C, 45g of KNO_3 dissolve in 100g of water

(ii) What mass of potassium nitrate will crystallise out when a saturated solution in 100g of water is cooled from 90°C to 30°C? From the graph:

  mass of KNO_3 crystallising
  = 205 − 45
  = 160g

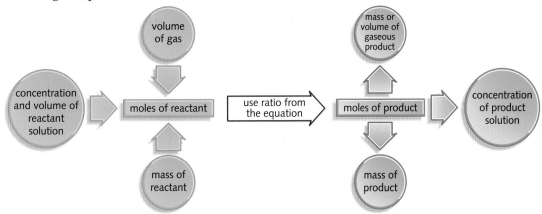

Figure 6.12 *A summary of the different ways in which a balanced equation acts as a 'bridge' in calculations.*

6.11 Calculations in electrolysis

The idea of the mole provides a means of predicting how much product will be obtained at the electrodes during electrolysis. This is particularly applicable to electroplating methods, where it is useful to know how much metal will be deposited on the cathode. However, the calculations apply to all electrolytic cells, whether the electrolyte is molten or in solution. The amount of substance produced in an electrode reaction depends firstly on the quantity of electricity passed.

Measuring the amount of electricity used

The quantity of electricity or **charge** (Q) flowing through an electrolysis cell is measured in coulombs (C). One **coulomb** (1 C) is equivalent to a current of one ampere (1 A) flowing for one second (1 s):

quantity of charge = current × time
for which current flows

$$Q = It$$

The current (I) is measured in amperes (A) and the time (t) in seconds (s). If a current of 2 A is passed for 5 minutes, then $t = 5 \times 60 = 300\,s$ and

$$Q = It = 2 \times 300 = 600\,C$$

Calculating the mass of the electrode product

For a given quantity of electricity (charge) passed, the amount of substance produced at an electrode depends on the charge on the ion being discharged.

During silver-plating, silver ions are discharged at the cathode. The electrode equation is:

$$Ag^+(aq) + e^- \rightarrow Ag(s)$$
1 mol   1 mol   1 mol

So to deposit 1 mol of silver (108 g) would require the transfer of 1 mol of electrons.

However, if copper(II) sulphate solution is electrolysed, copper is deposited at the cathode:

$$Cu^{2+}(aq) + 2e^- \rightarrow Cu(s)$$
1 mol   2 mol   1 mol

So to obtain a deposit of 1 mol of copper (64 g) would require the transfer of 2 mol of electrons.

Experiments have shown that the quantity of electricity (charge) transferred by 1 mol of electrons is equal to 96 500 coulombs per mole (96 500 C/mol). This is known as the **Faraday constant**. Thus, 96 500 C of charge will deposit 1 mol (108 g) of silver; and $2 \times 96\,500\,C = 193\,000\,C$ of charge will deposit 1 mol (64 g) of copper during electrolysis. If we consider other electrode reactions, we arrive at the 'ladder' shown in figure 6.14.

- The charge on one mole of electrons is 96 500 coulombs.
- The **Faraday constant** = 96 500 C/mol.

A useful equation that links the quantity of charge passed to the number of moles of electrons passed is:

$$\frac{\text{number of moles of}}{\text{electrons passed}} = \frac{\text{charge passed}}{\text{Faraday constant}}$$

Worked example 1

In an experiment on electroplating, a current of 0.1 A was passed through a solution of silver ions for 1 hour. How much silver was deposited?

- *Step 1*   Find the number of moles of electrons:

charge passed $Q = It = 0.1 \times 1 \times 60 \times 60$
$$= 360\,C$$

$$\frac{\text{number of moles of}}{\text{electrons passed}} = \frac{360\,C}{96\,500\,C/mol}$$

$$= 0.0037\,mol$$

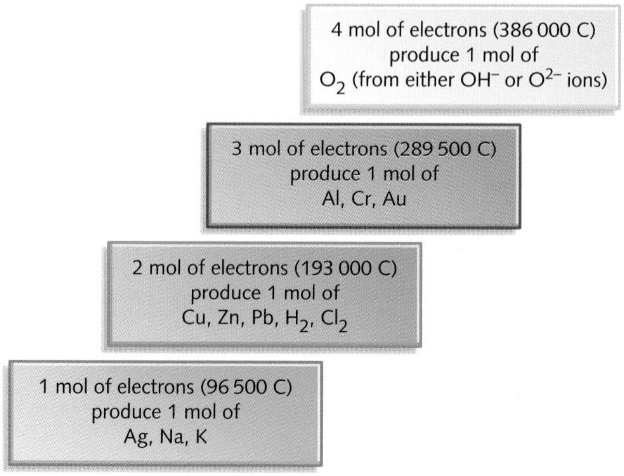

4 mol of electrons (386 000 C) produce 1 mol of O_2 (from either OH^- or O^{2-} ions)

3 mol of electrons (289 500 C) produce 1 mol of Al, Cr, Au

2 mol of electrons (193 000 C) produce 1 mol of Cu, Zn, Pb, H_2, Cl_2

1 mol of electrons (96 500 C) produce 1 mol of Ag, Na, K

Figure 6.14 The amounts of charge required to deposit 1 mol of various substances, in 'ladder' form.

- *Step 2* Find the mass of silver:

  the equation is

  $Ag^+(aq)$ + e^- → $Ag(s)$
  1 mol   1 mol   1 mol

  So

  1 mol of electrons deposit 1 mol (108 g) of silver

  0.0037 mol of electrons deposit 0.0037 mol of silver

  0.0037 mol of electrons deposit
  $0.0037 \times 108 = 0.40$ g of silver

Worked example 2

Calculate the volume of oxygen gas, measured at r.t.p., liberated at the anode in the electrolysis of acidified water by 289 500 C of electricity.

- *Step 1* Find the number of moles of electrons:

  number of moles of electrons passed $= \dfrac{289\,500\,C}{96\,500\,C/mol}$

  $= 3$ mol

- *Step 2* Find the volume of oxygen:

  the equation is

  $4OH^-(aq)$ → $2H_2O(l)$ + $O_2(g)$ + $4e^-$
                                    1 mol   4 mol

  So we have

  4 mol of electrons gives 1 mol of O_2

  1 mol of electrons gives 0.25 mol of O_2

  3 mol of electrons gives $0.25 \times 3 = 0.75$ mol of O_2

  But using the equation from section 6.7 on page 168:

  $$\text{number of moles} = \frac{\text{volume}}{\text{molar volume}}$$

  and remembering that the molar volume of any gas is 24 dm³/mol at r.t.p.

  $$0.75\,\text{mol} = \frac{\text{volume}}{24\,\text{dm}^3/\text{mol}}$$

  volume of O_2 = 0.75 mol × 24 dm³/mol
                         = 18 dm³ at r.t.p.

Summary of extension material

You should know that:

- the 'concentration' of a solution can be expressed in terms of the mass of solute dissolved (in grams) – this gives the *mass concentration* in grams per cubic decimetre (g/dm³)
- the 'concentration' of a solution can be more usefully expressed in terms of the amount of solute dissolved (in moles) – this gives the *concentration* in moles per cubic decimetre (mol/dm³)
- the concentration values (mol/dm³) are important in calculating the results of titration experiments

- calculations using solubilities can be used to predict the mass of crystals formed by cooling a solution
- the idea of the mole can be applied to the electrode reactions occurring during electrolysis, with the charge passed through the circuit being related to the number of moles of electrons flowing
- the charge equivalent to the transfer of one mole of electrons (the Faraday constant = 96 500 C/mol) is known and therefore the quantities of the elements released at the electrodes can be calculated.

6.10 Calculate the concentration (in mol/dm³) of the following solutions. [5]

(a) 1.0 mol of sodium hydroxide is dissolved in distilled water to make 500 cm³ of solution.

(b) 0.2 mol of sodium chloride is dissolved in distilled water to make 1000 cm³ of solution.

(c) 0.1 mol of sodium nitrate is dissolved in distilled water to make 100 cm³ of solution.

(d) 0.8 g of solid sodium hydroxide are dissolved in distilled water to a final volume of 1 dm³.

(Relative atomic masses: H = 1, O = 16, Na = 23)

6.11 A packet of washing soda crystals has been left open to the atmosphere for some time. The crystals have formed a white powder which may be represented by the formula $Na_2CO_3 \cdot xH_2O$. The value of x may be found by dissolving a known quantity of the powder in water and titrating the solution with acid of known concentration.

In one experiment a student weighed out 1.59 g of the powder and dissolved it in water. The volume of the solution was made up to exactly 250 cm³. 25 cm³ of this solution was titrated with hydrochloric acid of concentration 0.10 mol/dm³ (mol per litre). 25.6 cm³ of the acid was required for complete reaction. The equation for this reaction is:

$$Na_2CO_3 + 2HCl \rightarrow 2NaCl + H_2O + CO_2$$

(a) Calculate the number of moles of hydrochloric acid used in the titration. [2]

(b) Calculate the number of moles of sodium carbonate in the 25 cm³ sample of solution which reacted with the hydrochloric acid. [2]

(c) How many moles of sodium carbonate were in the 250 cm³ of solution? [1]

(d) Calculate the mass of sodium carbonate in the 250 cm³ of solution. (Relative atomic masses: C = 12, O = 16, Na = 23) [2]

(e) Using your answer to part (d), what mass of water was in the original powder? [1]

(f) How many moles of water were present in the original powder? (Relative atomic masses: H = 1, O = 16) [2]

(g) Using your answers to parts (c) and (f), calculate the value of x. [2]

(NISEAC, 1995)

6.12 In this question you must select from the graph a letter that represents the solid described in the questions. (Each letter may be used once, more than once or not at all.)

The solubility curves for potassium nitrate and five solids, **A**, **B**, **C**, **D** and **E**, are shown for the temperature range

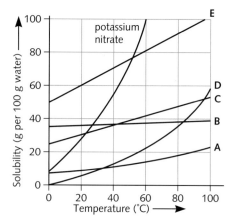

0°C to 100°C. The solubility is given in grams of the solid that will dissolve in 100 grams of water.

Which solid:

(a) has the lowest solubility at 60°C? [1]

(b) has the same solubility as potassium nitrate at 52°C? [1]

(c) has a solubility that changes least with temperature? [1]

(d) would give a deposit of 20 g if a saturated solution in 100 grams of water at 60°C is cooled to 20°C? [2]

(e) would be deposited in the greatest mass if a saturated solution in 100 grams of water at 100°C is cooled to 80°C? [2]

6.13 Three important chemicals, sodium hydroxide, chlorine and hydrogen, are obtained from the electrolysis of brine (sodium chloride solution) in a diaphragm cell. These chemicals are used to make other useful chemicals such as hydrochloric acid, HCl, and bleach, NaClO.

(a) In a diaphragm cell a current of 10 A passes through brine for 6 hours. Calculate how much charge flows during the 6 hours. [3]

(b) (i) In another diaphragm cell 288 500 coulombs of charge flows in 6 hours. Calculate the number of moles of chlorine molecules produced in the cell. (The charge on one mole of electrons is 96 500 coulombs.) [2]

(ii) What mass and volume of chlorine is produced in (b)(i)? (Assume all measurements are made at room temperature and atmospheric pressure.) [3]

(MEG, 1995)

6.14 The diagram on page 177 shows three electrolysis cells in series.

Cell 1 contains silver electrodes dipping into aqueous silver nitrate solution.

Cell 2 contains copper electrodes dipping into aqueous copper(II) sulphate solution.

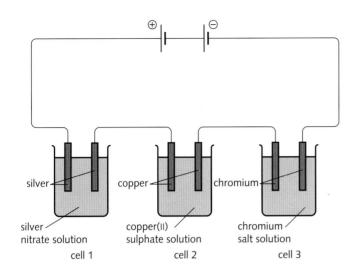

silver

copper

chromium

silver
nitrate solution
cell 1

copper(II)
sulphate solution
cell 2

chromium
salt solution
cell 3

Cell 3 contains chromium electrodes dipping into an aqueous chromium salt solution.

(a) Aqueous copper(II) sulphate solution contains Cu^{2+}, SO_4^{2-}, H^+ and OH^- ions. Which ions are present in aqueous silver nitrate? [1]

(b) One product formed in cell 2 is copper. Write ionic equations for the reactions which take place at the electrodes in cell 2. [2]

(c) A current was passed through the circuit. If 0.540 g of silver was deposited at the cathode in cell 1 and 0.130 g of chromium at the cathode in cell 3:
   (i) calculate the mass of copper deposited at the cathode in cell 2; [2]
   (ii) calculate the charge on the chromium ion in cell 3. [3]

(MEG, 1995)

177

Energy changes in chemical reactions

This section covers the following ideas:

- breaking bonds in a reaction as an endothermic process
- making bonds as an exothermic process
- heat of reaction
- experiments on heat of reaction
- activation energy.

Some chemical reactions are capable of releasing vast amounts of energy. For example, at the end of the Gulf War, oil and gas fires in the oil-fields were left burning out of control. The heat given out was sufficient to turn the sand around the burning wells into glass. Forest fires can rage impressively, producing overpowering waves of heat. Bringing such fires under control requires great expertise, and a great deal of courage!

Yet we use similar reactions, under control, to provide heat for the home and for industry. Natural gas, which is mainly methane, is burnt under controlled conditions to produce heat for cooking in millions of homes.

7.1 The reaction between methane and oxygen

Hydrocarbon molecules contain only the elements carbon and hydrogen (see page 306). Methane is the simplest hydrocarbon molecule. When it burns, it reacts with oxygen. The products are carbon dioxide and water vapour:

methane + oxygen
$\rightarrow$ carbon dioxide + water

$CH_4(g) + 2O_2(g)$
$\rightarrow CO_2(g) + 2H_2O(g)$

During this reaction, as with all others, bonds are first broken and then new bonds are made (figure 7.1). In methane molecules, carbon

atoms are covalently bonded to hydrogen atoms. In oxygen gas, the atoms are held together in diatomic molecules. During the reaction, all these bonds must be broken. Chemical **bonds** are forces of attraction between atoms or ions. To break these bonds requires energy; energy must be taken in to pull the atoms apart.

Breaking chemical bonds takes in energy from the surroundings. This is an **endothermic** process.

New bonds are then formed: between carbon and oxygen to make carbon dioxide, and between hydrogen and oxygen to form water. Forming these bonds gives out energy.

Making chemical bonds gives out energy to the surroundings. This is an **exothermic** process.

When methane reacts with oxygen, the total energy given out is greater than the total energy taken in. So, overall, this reaction gives out energy – it is an exothermic reaction. The energy is released as heat.

The overall change in energy for this exothermic reaction can be shown in an **energy level diagram** (or energy profile) (figure 7.2). In this reaction,

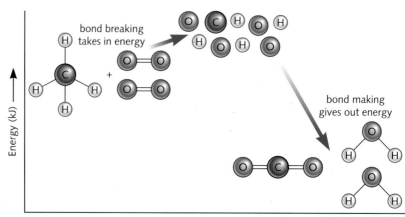

Figure 7.1 The burning of methane first involves the breaking of bonds in the reactants. This is followed by the formation of the new bonds of the products.

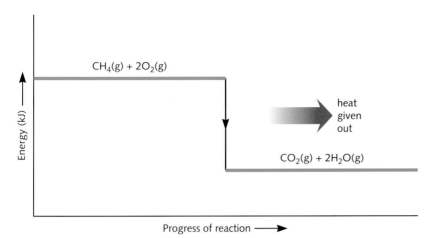

Figure 7.2 An energy profile for the burning of methane. The products are more stable than the reactants. Energy is given out to the surroundings. This is an exothermic reaction.

energy is given out because the bonds in the products (CO_2 and H_2O) are stronger than those in the reactants (CH_4 and O_2). This means that the products are more **stable** than the reactants.

> Some bonds are stronger than others. They require more energy to break them, but they give out more energy when they are formed.

Generally, the combustion reactions of fossil fuels (see page 327) such as oil and gas are exothermic. Indeed, the major characteristics that make these fuels so useful are that:

• they are easy to ignite and burn

• they are capable of releasing large amounts of energy as heat.

Other reactions are less obviously exothermic, but may have new and unusual uses. For example the rusting reaction of iron generates heat for several hours and is used in pocket hand-warmers for expeditions to cold regions.

7.2 The reaction between nitrogen and oxygen

Endothermic reactions are far less common than exothermic ones. Here, energy is absorbed from the surroundings. The reaction between nitrogen and oxygen is endothermic. It is one of the reactions that take place when fuel is burnt in car engines. The equation for this reaction is:

nitrogen + oxygen → nitrogen monoxide

$$N_2(g) + O_2(g) \rightarrow 2NO(g)$$

Here the bonding in the products is weaker than in the reactants. Overall, energy is taken in by the reaction (figure 7.3).

Photosynthesis in green plants and the thermal decomposition of limestone are other important examples of endothermic reactions. They will be studied later in this chapter on pages 195 and 202.

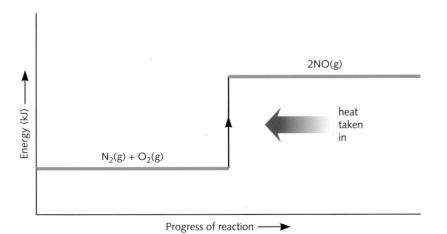

Figure 7.3 An energy profile for the reaction between nitrogen and oxygen. The products are less stable than the reactants. Energy is taken in from the surroundings. This is an endothermic reaction.

Summary of core material

You should know that:

• chemical reactions involve changes in energy

• most reactions release energy to their surroundings and this is usually in the form of heat – these are exothermic reactions

• some reactions take in energy from the surroundings – these are endothermic reactions.

EXTENSION

Heat of reaction

The energy change in going from reactants to products in a chemical reaction is known as the **heat of reaction** (figures 7.2 and 7.3 on page 179). It is given the symbol ΔH (pronounced 'delta aitch' – the symbol Δ means 'change in'). The energy given out or taken in is measured in **kilojoules** (kJ); 1 kilojoule (1 kJ) = 1000 joules (1000 J). It is usually calculated per mole of a specific reactant or product (kJ/mol).

The starting point for the calculation is the reacting mixture. If a reaction gives out heat to the surroundings, the mixture has lost energy. It is an exothermic reaction. In an *EX*othermic reaction, heat *EX*its the reaction mixture. An exothermic reaction has a negative value of ΔH.

If a reaction takes in heat from the surroundings, the mixture has gained energy. It is an endothermic reaction. In an *EN*dothermic reaction, heat *EN*ters the reaction mixture. An endothermic reaction has a positive value of ΔH.

This is what we know about **heat of reaction**:

- for **exothermic** reactions, heat energy is given out (exits) and ΔH is *negative*,
- for **endothermic** reactions, heat energy is taken in (enters) and ΔH is *positive*.

These ideas fit with the direction of the arrows shown in the energy diagrams (figures 7.2 and 7.3 on page 179). The heat of reaction for the burning of methane is high. This makes it a useful fuel:

$$CH_4(g) + 2O_2(g) \rightarrow CO_2(g) + 2H_2O(g)$$

$$\Delta H = -728 \text{ kJ/mol}$$

Making and breaking bonds

Experiments have been carried out to find out how much energy is needed to break various covalent bonds in compounds. The average value obtained for a particular bond is known as the **bond energy** (table 7.1). It is a measure of the strength of the bond.

Table 7.1 The bond energies for some covalent bonds

Bond	Bond energy (kJ/mol)	Comment
H—H	436	in hydrogen
C—H	435	average of four bonds in methane
O—H	464	in water
C—C	347	average of many compounds
O=O	497	in oxygen
C=O	803	in carbon dioxide
N≡N	945	in nitrogen

We can use these values to find the heat of reaction for the burning of methane. The equation is

$$CH_4(g) + 2O_2(g) \rightarrow CO_2(g) + 2H_2O(g)$$

- The left-hand side involves *bond breaking* and needs energy:

four C—H bonds	4×435	= 1740 kJ/mol
two O=O bonds	2×497	= 994 kJ/mol
total energy needed		= 2734 kJ/mol

- The right-hand side involves *bond making* and gives out energy:

two C=O bonds	2×803	= 1606 kJ/mol
four O—H bonds	4×464	= 1856 kJ/mol
total energy given out		= 3462 kJ/mol

- The heat of reaction, ΔH, is the energy change on going from reactants to products. So for the burning of methane,

heat of reaction = energy difference

ΔH = (energy needed to break bonds) – (energy given out when bonds form)
$\Delta H = 2734 - 3462$
$\Delta H = -728$ kJ/mol

7.3 Experimental thermochemistry

Heat of combustion

The **heat of combustion** is the energy change of a reaction when a substance is burnt. For liquid fuels such as ethanol, it can be found using a metal **calorimeter** and a spirit burner (figure

7.4). The experiment involves heating a known volume of water with the flame from burning ethanol. The temperature rise of the water is measured. From this, the heat energy given to the water is calculated using

heat energy (in J) = mass of water (in kg) × 4200 × temperature rise (in K)

Here 4200 J/kg K is the **specific heat capacity** of water, the energy needed to raise the temperature of 1 kg of water by 1 K (or 1°C).

The spirit burner containing ethanol is weighed before and after the experiment. This gives the mass of ethanol burnt. From this, the number of moles of ethanol burnt to produce the heat can be calculated. These values can then be used to find the heat of combustion of ethanol.

For example, suppose we obtained the following results in the experiment:

volume of water in calorimeter   = 200 cm³

temperature rise of water   = 12°C

mass of ethanol + burner at start = 66.87 g

mass of ethanol + burner at end   = 66.41 g

Since the density of water = 1 g/cm³, the mass of water in the calorimeter is 200 g or 0.2 kg. So the above equation becomes

heat energy (J) = mass of water (kg) × 4200
$$\times \text{ temperature rise (K)}$$

$$= 0.2 \times 4200 \times 12$$

$$= 10\,080\,\text{J} = 10.08\,\text{kJ}$$

We can work out that

mass of ethanol burnt = 66.87 − 66.41 = 0.46 g

The relative molecular mass of ethanol is

$M_r(C_2H_5OH) = (2 \times 12) + (6 \times 1) + 16 = 46$

Therefore

number of moles of ethanol burnt = $\dfrac{0.46}{46}$

$$= 0.01\,\text{mol}$$

This amount of ethanol gave us the heat energy we obtained above. That is

0.01 mol ethanol gives out 10.08 kJ heat energy

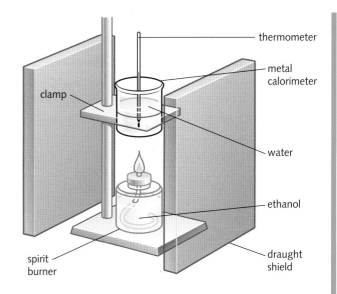

Figure 7.4 Apparatus for finding the heat of combustion of ethanol.

So

1 mol ethanol would give out 1008 kJ heat energy

Finally we can write this as

heat of combustion of ethanol = −1008 kJ/mol

Heat of neutralisation

Styrofoam is a good heat insulator and is used to make disposable cups for warm drinks. These cups can be used as simple calorimeters to measure the temperature rise of exothermic reactions between solutions. The solutions are mixed in a styrofoam cup and the initial temperature is measured quickly. The mixture is then stirred well with the thermometer. The temperature is checked frequently during the reaction and the maximum temperature is recorded.

This equipment can be used to measure the heat energy given out during the neutralisation reactions between acids and alkalis. This energy change is known as the **heat of neutralisation**. By using solutions whose concentration is known, it can be calculated in a similar way to the heat of combustion shown above. For a strong acid reacting with a strong alkali this value is −57 kilojoules per mole of water produced, that is −57 kJ/mol.

Activation energy

Although the vast majority of reactions are exothermic, only a few are totally **spontaneous** and begin without help at normal temperatures; for example sodium or potassium reacting with water. More usually energy is required to start the reaction. When fuels are burnt, for example, energy is needed to ignite them (figure 7.5). This energy may come from a spark, a match, or sunlight.

This energy is called the **activation energy** (given the symbol E_A). It is required because initially

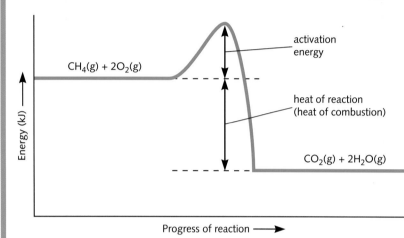

some bonds must be broken before any reaction can take place. Sufficient atoms or **fragments** of molecules must be freed for the new bonds to begin forming. Once started, the energy released as new bonds are formed causes the reaction to continue.

All reactions require some activation energy. For the reaction of sodium or potassium with water the activation energy is low, and there is enough energy available from the surroundings at room temperature for the reaction to begin spontaneously. Other exothermic reactions have a higher activation energy, for example the burning of magnesium can be started with heat from a Bunsen burner.

Reactions can be thought of as the result of collisions between atoms, molecules, or ions. In many of these collisions, the colliding particles do not have enough energy to react, and just bounce apart, rather like 'dodgem cars'. A chemical reaction will only happen if the total energy of the colliding particles is greater than the required activation energy of the reaction.

Figure 7.5 An energy profile for the burning of methane, showing the need for activation energy to start the reaction.

Summary of extension material

You should know that:

- chemical bonds must first be broken during a reaction so that new, different, bonds can be formed

- the breaking of bonds is an endothermic process requiring energy, while the making of bonds is an exothermic process with energy being released

- the heat change taking place during a reaction can be measured using a simple calorimeter

- very few reactions are spontaneous, and even strongly exothermic reactions require an initial input of energy to start them

- the 'energy barrier' that must be overcome at the start of a reaction is known as the activation energy of a particular reaction

- the activation energy is needed because bonds must first be broken before new 'attachments' can be made

- the energy released by the forming of new bonds causes the reaction to continue.

7.1 Hydrogen and bromine react to form hydrogen bromide:

$$H_2 + Br_2 \rightarrow 2HBr$$

When a reaction takes place, chemical bonds are broken and new chemical bonds are formed.

To break a chemical bond, energy has to be supplied; this is represented by +.

When a chemical bond forms, energy is given out; this is represented by −.

(a) Copy out and insert the missing signs and the missing value in the table below. [3]

Energy to break H—H = +436 kJ
Energy to break Br—Br = ...190 kJ
Energy to make H—Br = ...366 kJ
Energy to make H—Br = ...kJ

(b) Calculate the overall energy change for this reaction. [1]

(c) Is the overall reaction exothermic or endothermic? [1]

(IGCSE, 1994)

7.2 Hexane is a liquid hydrocarbon. An experiment is used to measure the amount of heat energy released by burning hexane.

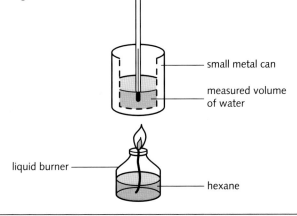

Mass of water	100 g
Initial temperature of water	18 °C
Final temperature of water	58 °C
Mass of hexane burnt	0.43 g

Heat given out in kJ = mass of water (g)
  × temperature rise (°C)
  × $\dfrac{4.2}{1000}$

(a) Use the equation above to work out the heat given out (in kJ) when 0.43 g of hexane burns in air. [2]

(b) Work out the formula mass (one mole) of hexane (C_6H_{14}). The relative atomic masses are C = 12, H = 1. [1]

(c) How many moles are in 0.43 g of hexane? [2]

(d) Calculate the amount of heat that would be given out if one mole of hexane burns in air (in kJ/mol). [2]

(e) The accurate value of the heat given out by burning one mole of hexane is 4194.7 kJ/mol. Give *three* reasons why the value you calculated is less than this value. [3]

(SEG, 1988)

7.3 A student carried out a series of experiments to investigate the reaction between hydrochloric acid and two different alkalis, aqueous sodium hydroxide and aqueous ammonia.

Experiment 1
A 25.0 cm³ sample of aqueous sodium hydroxide and a few drops of indicator were placed in a flask. Hydrochloric acid was placed in a burette and run into the flask until the indicator changed colour.

(a) Record the burette readings from the diagrams below. [1]

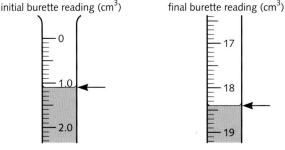

Experiment 2
Experiment 1 was repeated using aqueous ammonia instead of aqueous sodium hydroxide.

(b) Record the burette readings from the diagrams below. [1]

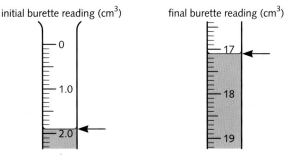

Experiment 3
A 100 cm³ sample of the hydrochloric acid was placed in a polystyrene cup and the temperature of the acid measured. Then, 100 cm³ of the aqueous sodium hydroxide were added to the cup and the mixture was stirred. The maximum temperature reached was measured.

(c) Record the temperatures from the thermometer diagrams on page 184. [2]

initial temperature of acid (°C)   maximum temperature of mixture (°C)

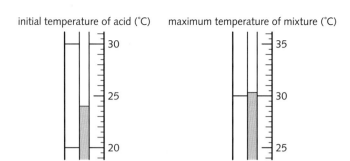

Experiment 4
Experiment 3 was repeated using aqueous ammonia instead of aqueous sodium hydroxide.

(d) Record the temperatures from these diagrams. [2]

initial temperature of acid (°C)   maximum temperature of mixture (°C)

(e) (i) Name a suitable indicator that you could use in experiment 1.
    (ii) What colour change would you expect if this indicator were used? [3]

(f) What volume of hydrochloric acid was required to react with
    (i) 25.0 cm³ of aqueous sodium hydroxide,
    (ii) 25.0 cm³ of aqueous ammonia? [2]

(g) Explain why the volumes of hydrochloric acid in (f) are not the same. [2]

(h) What is the change in temperature in
    (i) experiment 3,   (ii) experiment 4? [3]

(i) (i) What type of reaction occurs between hydrochloric acid and the two alkalis? [1]
    (ii) Suggest why a polystyrene cup was used instead of a metal container. [2]

(j) Predict the change in temperature if experiment 4 were repeated using solutions which were twice as concentrated. [2]

(IGCSE, 1992)

7.4 Walkers and climbers can buy 'warm packs'. In use, these packs become hot and remain at a temperature of about 40 °C for several hours. They can be used as hand or body warmers.

A 'warm pack' contains several chemicals evenly mixed together in a porous bag. The whole pack is contained in a polythene bag. The label from one 'warm pack' is printed below.

> **This pack contains**
> Finely powdered iron
> Water and sodium chloride absorbed on an inert powder
> Carbon catalyst

When the polythene bag is opened, air enters the pack. The iron in the pack rusts, forming iron oxide, Fe_2O_3.

The rusting process produces heat and the pack becomes warm. The rate at which the heat energy is produced depends on the rate of rusting.

(a) Give a balanced chemical equation for the rusting of iron to produce iron oxide. [2]
(b) (i) Is the rusting process exothermic or endothermic?
    (ii) Sketch an energy level diagram for the rusting of iron. [3]

A student investigated the reaction occurring in the pack by placing the opened pack on a top-pan balance. The change in mass of the opened pack was recorded at intervals over a period of several hours. The results are shown below.

Time in hours	Mass of pack in grams	Mass increase in grams
0	52.20	0.00
4	53.50	
8	54.80	2.60
12	56.00	3.80
16	56.70	
20	56.90	4.70
24	56.95	4.75
28	57.00	4.80
32	57.00	4.80
36	57.00	4.80
40	57.00	4.80

(c) (i) Copy out and complete the results table by filling in the two blanks.
    (ii) Plot a graph of the results of the investigation.
    (iii) Why does the pack increase in mass?
    (iv) How long would the pack have been effective as a hand warmer? [8]

(d) The results indicate that 4.8 g of oxygen is used in the reaction.

    (i) Calculate the number of moles of oxygen atoms used in the reaction.
    (Relative atomic mass: O = 16)

(ii) Given that the formula of the iron oxide produced is Fe_2O_3, how many moles of iron atoms were used in the reaction?

(iii) What mass of iron is contained in the pack?
(Relative atomic mass: Fe = 56) [4]

(e) How might the working of the pack be affected by
(i) very cold conditions?
(ii) use at very high altitudes? [3]

(f) How are rusting and respiration similar chemical processes? [1]

(ULEAC, part question, 1991)

Rates of reaction

This section covers the following ideas:

- factors affecting the rate of reaction
  - surface area of reactants
  - reactant concentration
  - temperature
- the role of catalysts in a reaction
- catalytic converters
- enzymes in biological systems
- collision theory and activation energy
- photochemical reactions
- photography using silver salts.

On 7 May 1915, the British liner *Lusitania* was sunk off the south-west coast of Ireland. The liner was torpedoed by a German submarine and 1153 passengers lost their lives. The sinking was accompanied by a second explosion. This explosion gave possible support to the idea that the ship was carrying explosives to Britain for use in the war. The wreck of the *Lusitania* has now been investigated by divers. Evidence suggests that the second explosion was caused by coal dust exploding in the hold. If so, this is a dramatic example of explosive combustion.

This type of explosion can also occur with fine powders in flour mills, in mines when dangerous gases collect, and with dust. Dust particles have a large surface area in contact with the air. A simple spark can set off an explosive reaction. For example, *Lycopodium* powder piled in a dish does not burn easily – but if it is sprayed across a Bunsen flame, it produces a spectacular reaction.

The same idea does have a more positive use. In some modern coal-fired power stations, powdered coal is burnt instead of the usual lumps of coal because it burns very efficiently.

7.4 Factors affecting the rate of reaction

Explosive reactions represent one end of the 'spectrum' of reaction rates. Other reactions, such as rusting, take place over much longer time periods. What factors influence the speed of a reaction? Experiments have studied a wide range of reactions, and there seem to be five major influences on reaction rate:

- the **surface area** of any solid reactants
- the **concentration** of the reactants
- the **temperature** at which the reaction is carried out
- the use of a **catalyst**
- the influence of **light** on some reactions.

These investigations have also built up a picture of how reactions occur based on the collision theory. This is dealt with later in this chapter on page 193.

The surface area of solid reactants

Where one or more of the reactants is a solid, the more finely powdered (or finely divided) the solid(s), the greater is the rate of reaction. This is because reactions involving solids take place on the surface of the solids. A solid has a much larger surface area when it is powdered than when it is in larger pieces.

For reactions involving two solids, grinding the reactants means that they can be better mixed. The mixed powders are then in greater contact with each other and are more likely to react.

If a solid is being reacted with a liquid (or solution), the greater the surface area, the more the solid is exposed to the liquid. A good demonstration of this is the reaction between limestone or marble chips (two forms of calcium carbonate) and dilute hydrochloric acid:

calcium carbonate + hydrochloric acid
→ calcium chloride + water + carbon dioxide

$CaCO_3(s) + 2HCl(aq)$
$→ CaCl_2(aq) + H_2O(l) + CO_2(g)$

The experiment can be done as shown in figure 7.6. Using this arrangement, we can compare two samples of marble chips, one sample (B) being more powdered than the other (A). The experiment is carried out twice, once with sample A and once with sample B. In each experiment the mass of sample used is the same and the same volume and concentration of hydrochloric acid is used. The flask sits on the balance during the reaction. A loose cotton wool plug prevents liquid spraying out of the flask but allows the carbon dioxide gas to escape into the air. This means that the flask will lose mass during the reaction. Balance readings are taken at regular time intervals and the loss in mass can be worked out. When the loss in mass is plotted against time, curves such as those in figure 7.7 are obtained.

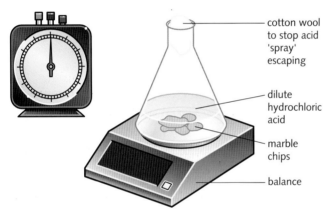

Figure 7.6 Experiments A and B: the reaction of marble chips with dilute hydrochloric acid. The loss of carbon dioxide from the flask produces a loss in mass. This is detected by the balance.

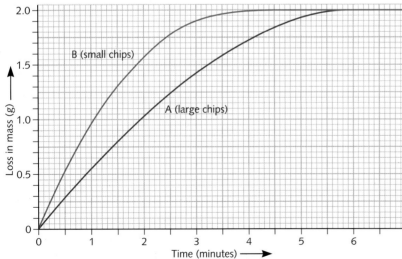

Figure 7.7 The graph shows the loss in mass against time for experiments A and B. The reaction is faster if the marble chips are broken into smaller pieces (curve B).

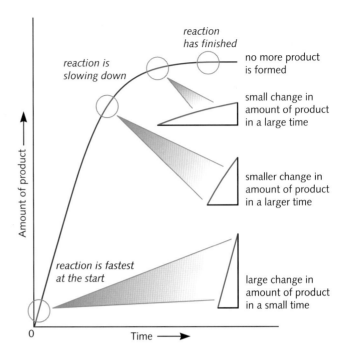

Figure 7.8 A chemical reaction is fastest at the start. It slows down as the reactants are used up.

There are several important points about the graph.

1 The reaction is fastest at the start. This is shown by the steepness of the curves over the first few minutes. Curve B is steeper than curve A. This means that gas (CO_2) is being produced faster with sample B. The finely powdered sample, with a greater surface area, reacts faster. Beyond this early period, both reactions slow down as the reactants are used up (figure 7.8).

2 The total volume of gas released is the same in both experiments. The mass of $CaCO_3$ and the amount of acid are the same in both cases. Both curves flatten out at the same final volume. Sample B reaches the horizontal part of the curve (the plateau) first.

These results show that:

the **rate of a reaction** increases when the *surface area* of a solid reactant is *increased*.

The concentration of reactants

Reactions that produce gases are also very useful in studying the effect of solution concentration on the reaction rate. The reaction between marble chips and acid could be adapted for this. Another reaction which can be used to study this is the reaction between magnesium and excess dilute hydrochloric acid:

magnesium + hydrochloric acid
→ magnesium chloride + hydrogen

$$Mg(s) + 2HCl(aq) \rightarrow MgCl_2(aq) + H_2(g)$$

The apparatus is shown in figure 7.9. As in the previous experiment, we will compare two different cases, which we will call C and D. The acid in experiment C is twice as concentrated as in experiment D. Apart from changing the concentration of the acid, everything else must stay the same. So the volume of acid, the temperature and the mass of magnesium used must be the same in both experiments. The gas produced in this reaction is hydrogen and is collected in a gas syringe. The volume of gas produced is measured at frequent time intervals. We can then plot a graph of volume of gas collected against time, like that in figure 7.10.

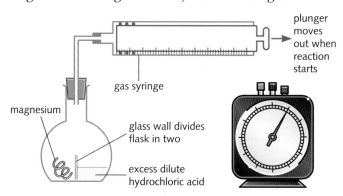

Figure 7.9 Experiments C and D: the reaction of magnesium with dilute hydrochloric acid. The hydrogen given off can be collected and measured in a gas syringe.

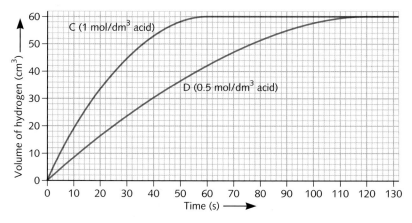

Figure 7.10 The graph shows the volume of hydrogen against time for experiments C and D. The reaction is faster if the acid solution is more concentrated (curve C).

Again the graph shows some important points.

1 The curve for C is steeper than for D. This shows clearly that reaction C, using more concentrated acid, is faster than reaction D.

2 The curve for experiment C starts off twice as steeply as for D. This means that the reaction in C is twice as fast as in experiment D initially. So doubling the concentration of the acid doubles the rate of reaction.

3 The total volume of hydrogen produced is the same in both experiments. Both reactions produce the same volume of hydrogen, though experiment C produces it faster.

These results show that:

the **rate of a reaction** increases when the *concentration* of a reactant in solution is *increased*.

We most often use the term 'concentration' in chemistry when talking about solutions. But we can also change the concentration of a gas mixture by compressing it into a smaller volume. A gas at high pressure is more concentrated than at low pressure.

This is used in the petrol engine. During the compression stroke in the engine, the piston moves up and compresses the mixture of petrol vapour and air. The concentrated mixture reacts explosively when ignited by the sparking plug. The piston is forced downwards by the explosion. This movement of the piston turns the crankshaft, which then turns the road wheels of the car.

Temperature

A reaction can be made to go faster or slower by changing the temperature of the reactants. Some food is stored in a refrigerator, because the food 'keeps better'. The rate of decay and oxidation is slower at lower temperatures.

The previous experiments (A/B or C/D) could be altered to study the effect of temperature on the production of gas. A different approach is possible by using the reaction between sodium thiosulphate and hydrochloric acid. In this case (which we shall call experiment E), the formation of a **precipitate** is used to measure the rate of reaction.

sodium thiosulphate + hydrochloric acid
   → sodium chloride + sulphur + sulphur dioxide
   + water

$$Na_2S_2O_3(aq) + 2HCl(aq)$$
$$\rightarrow 2NaCl(aq) + S(s) + SO_2(g) + H_2O(l)$$

The experiment is shown in figure 7.11. A cross is marked on a piece of paper. A flask containing sodium thiosulphate solution is placed on top of the paper. Hydrochloric acid is added quickly. The yellow precipitate of sulphur produced is very fine and stays **suspended** in the liquid. With time, as more and more sulphur is formed, the liquid becomes more cloudy and difficult to see through. The time taken for the cross to 'disappear' is measured. The faster the reaction, the shorter the length of time during which the cross is visible. The experiment is carried out several times with solutions pre-warmed to different temperatures. The solutions and conditions of the experiment must remain the same, only the temperature is altered. A graph can then be plotted of the time taken for the cross to disappear against temperature, like that shown in figure 7.12.

The graph shows two important points:

1 the cross disappears quicker at higher temperatures. The shorter the time needed for the cross to disappear, the faster the reaction.

2 the curve is not a straight line.

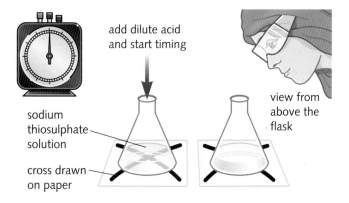

Figure 7.11 Experiment E: the reaction between hydrochloric acid and sodium thiosulphate. This can be studied by following the appearance of the precipitate. The cross drawn on the paper grows fainter with time. Time how long it takes for the cross to disappear.

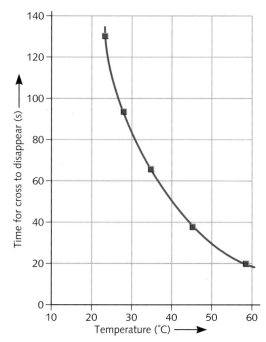

Figure 7.12 The graph for experiment E. As the temperature is increased, the time taken for the cross to disappear is shortened. The reaction speeds up at higher temperature.

These results show that:

the **rate of a reaction** increases when the *temperature* of the reaction mixture is *increased*.

To be more precise, the speed of the reaction is *inversely proportional* to the time taken for the reaction to finish:

$$\text{rate of reaction} \propto \frac{1}{\text{time}}$$

A graph of 1/time against temperature would show how the rate increases with a rise in temperature. If we plotted such a graph, the curve obtained would be a straight line. From its slope we could work out that:

the rate of the reaction doubles with every 10 °C rise in temperature. (This is true of many reactions but is only an approximation and should not be taken too precisely.)

7.5 Catalysts

The decomposition of hydrogen peroxide

Hydrogen peroxide is a colourless liquid with the formula H_2O_2. It is a very reactive oxidising agent.

Hydrogen peroxide decomposes to form water and oxygen:

hydrogen peroxide → water + oxygen

$$2H_2O_2(l) \rightarrow 2H_2O(l) + O_2(g)$$

We can follow the rate of this reaction by collecting the oxygen in a gas syringe. The formation of oxygen is very slow at room temperature. However, the addition of 0.5 g of powdered manganese(IV) oxide (MnO_2) makes the reaction go much faster (we shall call this experiment F). The black powder does not disappear during the reaction (figure 7.13). Indeed, if the solid is filtered and dried at the end of the reaction, the same mass of powder remains. If the amount of MnO_2 powder added is doubled (experiment G), the rate of reaction increases (figure 7.14). If the powder is more finely divided (powdered), the reaction also speeds up. Both these results suggest that it is the surface of the manganese(IV) oxide powder that is important here. By increasing the surface area, the rate of reaction is increased. We say that manganese(IV) oxide is a **catalyst** for this reaction.

> A **catalyst** is a substance that *increases* the rate of a chemical reaction. The catalyst remains *chemically unchanged* at the end of the reaction.

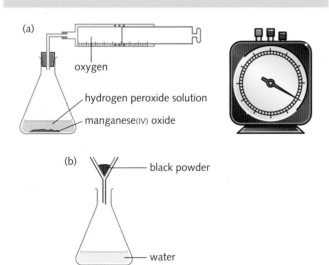

Figure 7.13 Experiments F and G: the decomposition of hydrogen peroxide to water and oxygen. The decomposition is very slow at room temperature. (a) It can be speeded up by adding a catalyst, manganese(IV) oxide. (b) The catalyst is unchanged at the end, and can be separated from the water by filtration.

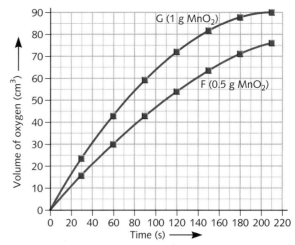

Figure 7.14 Increasing the amount of catalyst increases the rate of reaction. Here the amount of manganese(IV) oxide has been doubled in experiment G compared to F.

Many catalysts work by providing a surface on which other molecules or atoms can react. However, others work in more complex ways. Thus it is wrong to say that catalysts do not take part in the reaction; some do. But at the end of the reaction, there is the same amount of catalyst as at the beginning and it is chemically unchanged.

Other examples of catalysts

Catalysts have been found for a wide range of reactions. They are useful because a *small* amount of catalyst can produce a *large* change in the rate of a reaction. Also, since they are unchanged at the end of a reaction, they can be re-used. Industrially, they are very important. Industrial chemists use catalysts to make everything from polythene and painkillers, to fertilisers and fabrics. If catalysts did not exist, many chemical processes would go very slowly and some reactions would need much higher temperatures and pressures to proceed at a reasonable rate. All these factors would make these processes more expensive so that the product would cost much more. If it cost more than people wanted to pay for it, it would be **uneconomic**.

Table 7.2 on page 190 shows some examples of industrial catalysts. You should notice that transition elements (see page 262) or their compounds make particularly good catalysts.

Catalytic converters

One way to reduce the polluting effects of car exhaust fumes is to fit the car with a catalytic

Table 7.2 Some examples of industrial catalysts

Industrial process	Catalyst
Ammonia manufacture (Haber process)	iron
Sulphuric acid manufacture (contact process)	vanadium(v) oxide
Margarine production (hydrogenation of fats)	nickel
Nitric acid manufacture (oxidation of ammonia)	platinum–rhodium
Fermentation of sugars (alcoholic drinks industry)	enzymes (in yeast)
Conversion of methanol to hydrocarbons	zeolite ZSM-5

converter. In some countries these converters are already a legal requirement. Car exhaust fumes contain gases such as carbon monoxide (CO), nitrogen monoxide (nitrogen(II) oxide, NO) and unburnt hydrocarbons (HC) from the fuel which cause pollution in the air. The catalytic converter converts these to less harmful products such as carbon dioxide (CO_2), nitrogen (N_2) and water (H_2O). Some of the reactions that occur are the following:

carbon monoxide + oxygen → carbon dioxide

$2CO(g) + O_2(g) \rightarrow 2CO_2(g)$

nitrogen monoxide + carbon monoxide
 → nitrogen + carbon dioxide

$2NO(g) + 2CO(g) \rightarrow N_2(g) + 2CO_2(g)$

nitrogen monoxide → nitrogen + oxygen

$2NO(g) \rightarrow N_2(g) + O_2(g)$

hydrocarbons + oxygen
 → carbon dioxide + water

The catalytic converter therefore 'removes' polluting oxides and completes the oxidation of unburnt hydrocarbon fuel. It speeds up these reactions considerably by providing a 'honeycombed' surface on which the gases can react. The converter contains a thin coating of rhodium and platinum catalysts on a solid honeycomb surface. These catalysts have many tiny pores which provide a large surface area for the reactions.

Catalytic converters can only be used with unleaded petrol. The presence of lead would 'poison' the catalyst and stop it working. Other impurities do get deposited on the catalyst surface,

so the converter eventually needs replacing after a number of years.

Biological catalysts (enzymes)

Living cells also produce catalysts. They are protein molecules called **enzymes**. Many thousands of biochemical reactions happen in every kind of organism. Enzymes are used to speed up these reactions. Each enzyme works only for a particular reaction. We say that it is **specific** for that reaction. The reaction may be one step in a sequence of reactions making up an important biological process.

Hydrogen peroxide (H_2O_2) is a natural metabolic waste-product in our bodies. However, it is extremely damaging and must be decomposed rapidly. **Catalase** is an enzyme in our blood and liver that converts hydrogen peroxide into harmless water and oxygen:

$2H_2O_2 \rightarrow 2H_2O + O_2$

You will remember that in the laboratory this reaction can be speeded up by adding powdered manganese(IV) oxide as a catalyst. Catalase is more efficient than manganese(IV) oxide at decomposing hydrogen peroxide.

The general features of **enzymes** are:

- enzymes are *proteins*,
- they are very *specific* – each enzyme controls one reaction,
- they are generally *temperature-sensitive* – they are inactivated by heat (most stop working above 45 °C),
- They are *sensitive to pH* – most enzymes work best in neutral conditions around pH 7.

Enzymes are being used increasingly in industry (see page 342). Biological washing powders use enzymes to remove biological stains such as sweat, blood and food. The enzymes in these powders are those which break down proteins and fats. Because the enzymes are temperature-sensitive, these powders are used at a wash temperature of around 40 °C.

Summary of core material

You should know that:

- chemical reactions can occur at vastly different rates, from the explosively rapid to those taking place over a timescale of years

- the rate of a particular reaction can be changed by altering several factors concerning the reactants, including
  - the surface area of any solids present
  - the concentration of any solutions involved
  - the temperature at which the reaction is carried out

- some reactions can be speeded up by the presence of a catalyst

- catalysts increase the rate of a reaction but remain chemically unchanged at the end of the reaction

- transition elements or their compounds are particularly useful as catalysts

- catalysts are important for a wide range of industrial processes

- enzymes are biological catalysts

- these enzyme proteins are highly specific and sensitive to conditions of temperature and pH.

7.5

(a) This label has been taken from a packet of Andrews Antacid.
   (i) How does the pH change when the tablets 'neutralise excess acid' in the stomach? [1]
   (ii) Write the simplest ionic equation which represents a neutralisation reaction. [1]
   (iii) Chewing the tablet cures indigestion faster than swallowing the tablet whole. Explain why. [1]
   (iv) Write the formula of the magnesium compound present in Andrews Antacid. [1]

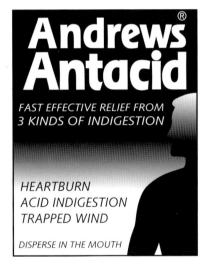

Andrews® Antacid

FAST EFFECTIVE RELIEF FROM 3 KINDS OF INDIGESTION

HEARTBURN
ACID INDIGESTION
TRAPPED WIND

DISPERSE IN THE MOUTH

When your stomach produces more acid than it can cope with, symptoms can strike in different ways.
Andrews Antacid tablets neutralise excess acid and give fast and effective relief from all 3 kinds of indigestion – heartburn, acid indigestion and trapped wind.
DOSAGE: Adults – suck or chew 1 to 2 tablets as required.
Not recommended for children.

Do not exceed 12 tablets in 24 hours. If symptoms persist consult your doctor. Store below 25 °C in a dry place.

Active ingredients:	
Calcium Carbonate	600mg.
Magnesium Carbonate	125mg.

STERLING HEALTH

GUILDFORD. SURREY
PL 0071 0321

(b) The active ingredients in the antacid react with hydrochloric acid in the stomach to give salts, water and carbon dioxide.

A student investigated how quickly the tablets react with excess hydrochloric acid. 40 cm³ of dilute hydrochloric acid were placed in a conical flask. The flask was placed on a direct reading balance. Two antacid tablets were quickly added to the flask. The apparatus was weighed immediately. At the same time, a stop clock was started. The mass was recorded every half minute for 5 minutes. The results are shown in the table.

The main active ingredient in Andrews Antacid is calcium carbonate.
   (i) Balance the equation which represents the reaction between calcium carbonate and hydrochloric acid:

$CaCO_3(s) + ...HCl(aq)$
$\rightarrow CaCl_2(aq) + H_2O(l) + CO_2(g)$ [1]
   (ii) Why does the mass of the flask and contents decrease? [2]

(c) Plot the results on graph paper, and draw a smooth curve to show how the mass of the flask and its contents changes with time. Label this curve 'A'. [2]

(d) The student did a second experiment. The only change was that the acid was twice as concentrated. On the graph, sketch a second curve to show a possible result for this experiment. Label this curve 'B'. [2]

(e) Suggest *two* other ways by which the rate of reaction could be changed. [2]

(NEAB, 1995)

Mass of flask + contents (g)	92.0	90.0	89.0	88.3	87.8	87.5	87.3	87.1	87.0	87.0	87.0
Time (minutes)	0	0.5	1.0	1.5	2.0	2.5	3.0	3.5	4.0	4.5	5.0

Time (s)	0	10	20	30	40	50	60	70	80	90
Volume (cm³)	0	60	90	105	112	116	118	120	120	120

7.6 Hydrogen peroxide decomposes according to the equation

$$2H_2O_2 \rightarrow 2H_2O + O_2$$

The addition of solid manganese(IV) oxide to the hydrogen peroxide causes the decomposition to take place rapidly. 1.00 g of manganese(IV) oxide was added to 100 cm³ of hydrogen peroxide solution at 25°C. The volume of oxygen released was measured at 10 second intervals and recorded in the table above.

(a) (i) Plot the volume of oxygen against the time on graph paper and use your graph to answer parts (ii) and (iii) below. [5]

    (ii) What volume of oxygen was collected in the first 8 seconds? [1]

    (iii) How long did it take to collect 100 cm³ of oxygen? [1]

    (iv) Why did the volume not increase beyond 120 cm³? [1]

(b) A second experiment was performed. It was identical to the first except that the hydrogen peroxide solution was cooled to 5°C before starting the experiment.

    (i) How would you cool the solution of hydrogen peroxide in preparation for the experiment? [1]

    (ii) Sketch a curve on the same grid as your graph in part (a) which would represent the results of the second experiment. Label this curve 'second experiment'. [3]

(c) In order to establish that no manganese(IV) oxide was used up during the experiment pupils were asked to separate the manganese(IV) oxide after the first experiment, dry it and then weigh it.

    (i) Draw and label a diagram of the apparatus which you would use to separate the insoluble manganese(IV) oxide. [3]

    (ii) How would you dry the manganese(IV) oxide? [1]

    (iii) All pupils who carried out the experiment carefully found that 1.00 g of manganese(IV) oxide remained. This is the correct result. What is the name given to the manganese(IV) oxide to describe the part which it plays in this reaction? [1]

(NISEAC, 1991)

7.7 If sodium thiosulphate solution is mixed with dilute acid a reaction occurs and the mixture goes cloudy:

$$Na_2S_2O_3(aq) + 2HCl(aq)$$
$$\rightarrow 2NaCl(aq) + S(s) + SO_2(g) + H_2O(l)$$

Some experiments were carried out to investigate the speed of this reaction. 50 cm³ of sodium thiosulphate solution was poured into a 100 cm³ conical flask. 10 cm³ of hydrochloric acid was then added. The time was taken for the mixture to become so cloudy that the cross could not be seen (see diagram below). This was called experiment 1. The experiment was repeated 4 times using different volumes of sodium thiosulphate as shown in the table below. All the results were recorded in the table. All experiments were carried out at room temperature (20°C).

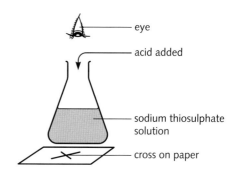

Experiment	Volume of sodium thiosulphate in cm³	Volume of water in cm³	Time for cross to disappear in seconds
1	50	0	43
2	40	10	55
3	30	20	75
4	20	30	124
5	10	40	255

(a) (i) Why is the total volume of solution kept constant? [2]

    (ii) What conclusions can you make from these results? [2]

(b) (i) Plot the results on graph paper to show how the volume of sodium thiosulphate solution affects the time of the reaction. Draw a smooth line graph and label this curve 20°C. [4]

    (ii) Sketch on the same grid the graph line you would expect to obtain if the experiments were repeated at 40°C. Label this curve, 40°C. [2]

(c) The experiments were repeated using a 250 cm³ conical flask instead of a 100 cm³ conical flask.

    Suggest how the results to the experiment would change if a 250 cm³ conical flask were used instead of a 100 cm³ flask. [2]

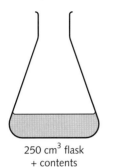

250 cm³ flask
+ contents

100 cm³ flask
+ contents

(d) (i) Explain why the reaction mixture goes cloudy. [2]
(ii) A student suggested that the reaction should be carried out in a fume cupboard. Explain why the student made this suggestion. [2]

(SEG, part question, 1992)

7.8 Experiments were carried out to investigate the action of two enzymes at different pH values. The enzymes were amylase and pepsin (a protease). All experiments were carried out at 37 °C for 20 minutes. The results are shown on the graph.

(a) (i) Name the enzyme which works best in acid conditions. [1]
(ii) How much substance (in mg) was produced in the pepsin-controlled reaction at pH 3? [1]

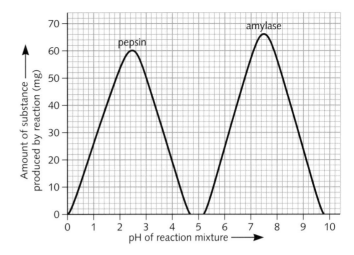

(b) At which pH values were 60 mg of substance produced by:
(i) pepsin;
(ii) amylase? [3]

(ULEAC, part question, 1994)

EXTENSION

Surface catalysts and collision theory

Solid catalysts

Different chemical reactions need different catalysts. One broad group of catalysts works by adsorbing molecules onto a solid surface. This process of **adsorption** brings the molecules of reactants closer together. Some of the most important examples of industrial catalysts work in this way, for example iron in the Haber process (page 199), vanadium(V) oxide in the contact process (page 221), and finely divided nickel where hydrogen is added to unsaturated hydrocarbons (figure 7.15).

Collision theory

The importance of surface catalysts to many reactions gives clues about how reactions happen. The **collision theory** builds on the **kinetic theory** (section 2.10 on page 46) by emphasising that reactions happen when particles collide with each other. This is supported by the results of experiments on the effect of temperature and concentration on reaction rates.

The reacting molecules attach to the surface

The bonds in the molecules are weakened, so that they break more easily

New bonds can then form which are more stable, and the products are formed

The products then detach from the surface

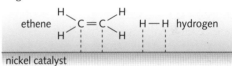

Figure 7.15 The reaction between ethene (C_2H_4) and hydrogen (H_2) on the surface of a nickel catalyst. The catalyst speeds up the reaction.

193

When solutions are more concentrated, the speed of a reaction is faster. A more concentrated solution means that there are more reactant particles in a given volume. Collisions will occur more often. The more often they collide, the more chance the particles have of reacting. This means that the rate of a chemical reaction will increase if the concentration of the reactants is increased (figure 7.16).

When the temperature is raised, a reaction takes place faster. At higher temperatures, the particles are moving faster. Again, this means that collisions will occur more often, giving more chance of reaction. Also, the particles have more energy at the higher temperature. This increases the chances that a collision will result in bonds in the reactants breaking and new bonds forming to make the products (figure 7.16).

A closer look at activation energy

Not every collision between particles in a reaction mixture produces a reaction. We have seen earlier that a certain amount of energy is needed to begin to break bonds. This minimum amount of energy is known as the **activation energy** of the reaction. Each reaction has its own different value of activation energy.

When particles collide, they must have a combined energy greater than this activation energy otherwise they will not react.

Chemical reactions occur when the reactant particles collide with each other.

A catalyst increases the rate of reaction by reducing the amount of energy that is needed to break the bonds. This reduces the activation energy of the reaction and makes sure that more collisions are likely to give products. The rate of the reaction is therefore increased.

We can think of an 'analogy' for this (figure 7.17). Suppose we are hiking in the Alps. We start on one side of a mountain and want to get to the other side. We *could* go right over the summit of the mountain. This would require us to be very energetic. What we might prefer to do would be to find an alternative route along a pass through the mountains. This would be less energetic. In our analogy, the starting point corresponds to the reactants and the finishing point to the products. The route over the top of the mountain would be the uncatalysed path. The easier route through the pass would be a catalysed path.

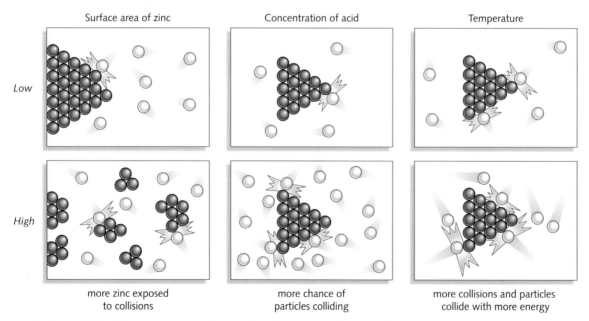

Figure 7.16 *The collision theory can be used to explain how various factors affect the rate of the reaction. Here we use the reaction between zinc and hydrochloric acid as an example.*

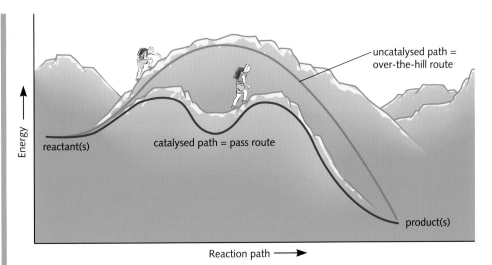

Table 7.3 Some of the end-products of photosynthesis

Biomass	Fossil fuels
food	coal
biogas	oil
peat	natural gas
wood	
vegetable oils	
alcohols	

Figure 7.17 The barrier between reactant(s) and product(s) may be so high that it defeats all but the most energetic. The catalyst's route is an easy pass through the mountains.

7.6 Photochemical reactions

Photosynthesis

Heat is not the only form of energy that can break bonds and start chemical reactions. Some chemical reactions are affected by light energy. Life on this planet would be impossible without photochemical reactions. **Photosynthesis** traps energy when sunlight falls on leaves containing the green pigment **chlorophyll** (figure 7.18). The reaction converts water and carbon dioxide into glucose and oxygen:

$$\text{carbon dioxide} + \text{water} \xrightarrow[\text{chlorophyll}]{\text{sunlight}} \text{glucose} + \text{oxygen}$$

$$6CO_2 + 6H_2O \rightarrow C_6H_{12}O_6 + 6O_2$$

The glucose produced is used to make other sugars and starch. These are **carbohydrates**. It is estimated that the mass of carbon 'fixed' as carbohydrate is 2×10^{11} tonnes per year. Algae, some bacteria and marine micro-organisms can also get their energy directly from sunlight by photosynthesis.

Photosynthesis is part of a global cycle of carbon atoms (figure 8.25 on page 225). It has been estimated that, on average, all the carbon dioxide on Earth passes through the process of **photosynthesis** once every 300 years and all the oxygen once every 2000 years. Every carbon atom in your body has been through the photosynthetic cycle many times. The energy stored directly by plant life through photosynthesis is called **biomass** energy and it provides us with important sources of food and warmth. As a result of heat and pressure over millions of years, biomass can be changed into fossil fuels (figure 8.25 on page 225). The energy stored in biomass and fossil fuels can be used to generate electricity, to manufacture clothing, to run cars and to pursue many other activities (table 7.3).

Photography

People were aware that silver salts darken on exposure to light as long ago as the sixteenth century. The darkening is caused by the

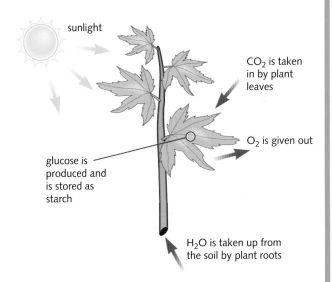

Figure 7.18 Green plants contain chlorophyll and take part in photosynthesis. This is a process that is crucial to the existence of life on Earth.

production of specks of silver metal. Precipitates of silver chloride (white) or silver bromide (cream) will darken if left to stand in sunlight for a few hours. For example,

$$2AgBr \xrightarrow{\text{sunlight}} 2Ag + Br_2$$

The reaction is a **redox reaction** (page 110); bromide ions lose electrons (they are oxidised), and silver ions gain electrons (they are reduced):

$$2Br^- \rightarrow Br_2 + 2e^-$$

$$Ag^+ + e^- \rightarrow Ag$$

This photochemical reaction, in which silver ions are converted to silver atoms, is used as the basis of both black-and-white and colour photography. The photographic film itself is simply a flexible plastic support for the light-sensitive 'emulsion'. An 'emulsion' in photography is not a true emulsion (see section 2.4 on page 32) but a layer of gelatine with millions of microcrystals of silver bromide spread through it. Black-and-white film has a single layer of 'emulsion'. Colour film has three layers, each layer containing a different dye.

The basis of producing a photographic print is as follows.

1 Light falls on the silver halide crystals in the photographic film. The silver ions in the exposed part of the film are converted to silver atoms. The more light that falls on a part of the film, the more silver atoms are deposited.

2 The film is immersed in a developer. The partly exposed crystals are completely converted to silver.

3 The film is immersed in a fixer. Unchanged (that is unexposed) silver halide crystals dissolve. This leaves black metallic silver where the film was exposed to light. This is the 'negative'.

4 To produce a photographic print, the negative image is then transferred to photographic paper using an enlarger.

Print-paper 'emulsion' usually contains silver chloride. This reacts more slowly than silver bromide, giving the photographer greater control of the image. High-speed films use silver iodide, the most light-sensitive of the three salts.

Other important photochemical reactions, such as the chlorination of methane (page 310) and the reactions involved in ozone depletion and 'photochemical smog' (page 23), are discussed in other chapters.

Summary of extension material

You should know that:

- the factors controlling the rate of a reaction can be explained on the basis of collision theory

- changes that increase the frequency of collision between reactant particles (for example an increase in temperature) will increase the rate of a reaction

- not all collisions produce reactions – the colliding particles must possess a certain minimum energy to react

- this minimum energy is the activation energy of the reaction

- certain reactions respond to light energy – these reactions are known as photochemical reactions.

7.9 The table contains information about the complete combustion of two fuels.

Fuel	Graphical formula	Energy released per mole burned (kJ)
Methane	H H—C—H H	890
Propane	H H H H—C—C—C—H H H H	2219

If methane is mixed with oxygen at room temperature, no reaction occurs. If a lighted match is applied to the mixture, an explosive reaction takes place producing carbon dioxide and water.

The bonds in carbon dioxide are very strong.

Use your knowledge of the bonds between atoms to explain the following statements.

(a) Methane does not burn until a lighted match is applied. [2]

(b) Energy is released in this reaction. [2]

(c) More energy is released from a mole of propane than from a mole of methane. [2]

(d) Write a balanced equation for the complete combustion of propane. [2]

(MEG, 1995)

7.10 An investigation into the reaction of lithium with water is tried by two students both using the apparatus shown below. Lithium is stored in a similar way to sodium and potassium.

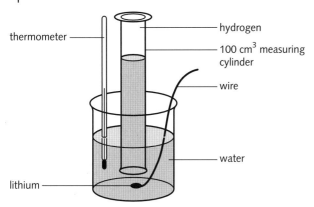

The volume of hydrogen collected at 10-second intervals is noted. Their results are given in the table below.

(a) (i) The results of the first student (A) have been plotted. Copy the graph and draw in the graph line for these results. [1]

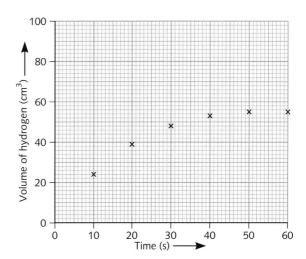

(ii) On the same grid plot the results of the second student (B) and draw in the graph line. This student was unable to record the volume of hydrogen at 60 seconds. [3]

(b) (i) From the information give *one* reason why student B was unable to record the volume of hydrogen at 60 seconds. [1]

(ii) Suggest possible reasons why there are differences in the shape of the graph lines recorded by student A and student B. [3]

(c) Both students found that the temperature of the water increased during the experiment.
(i) What does this result show about the reaction of lithium with water? [1]
(ii) Describe an investigation, using similar apparatus, by which the students could measure more accurately the temperature rise of this reaction. Note that the volume of hydrogen collected does not need to be recorded. [4]

(SEG, 1989)

Time in seconds	0	10	20	30	40	50	60
Volume of hydrogen in cm^3							
first student (A)	0	24	39	48	53	55	55
second student (B)	0	9	35	62	81	95	–

Reversible reactions and chemical equilibria

This section covers the following ideas:

- some reactions are reversible
- dynamic equilibria
- the Haber process as an industrially important reversible reaction – the effect of changing conditions

- Le Chatelier's principle
- the contact process
- the manufacture of lime
- weak acids and alkalis.

The physical and biological world is the product of a complex set of chemical interactions and reactions. Some reactions can even be **reversed** if we change the conditions.

Our life depends on the reversible attachment of oxygen to a protein called **haemoglobin**. This protein is found in our red blood cells. Oxygen is picked up as these cells pass through the blood vessels of the lungs. It is then carried to tissues in other parts of the body. As the conditions change in other regions of our body, for example the muscles and brain, the oxygen is detached and used by the cells of these organs.

Simpler reactions that can be reversed by changing the conditions include the re-formation of hydrated salts by adding back the water to the dehydrated powder.

However, there are reactions that are more complex than this. In these reactions, under the same conditions in a **closed system**, the products can interact to reverse the reaction. No sooner are the products formed than some molecules of the product react to give back the original reactants. One industrially important example of this is the reaction between nitrogen and hydrogen to produce ammonia:

$$N_2(g) + 3H_2(g) \rightleftharpoons 2NH_3(g)$$

A German chemist, Fritz Haber, was the first to show how this reaction could be controlled to make useful amounts of ammonia. The first industrial plant making ammonia by the Haber process opened in Germany in 1913. Now, over 100 million tonnes of ammonia are produced each year by this process.

7.7 The reversible hydration of salts

Thermal decomposition of salts such as hydrated copper(II) sulphate ($CuSO_4 \cdot 5H_2O$) results in the dehydration of the salt:

$$\underset{\text{light blue crystals}}{CuSO_4 \cdot 5H_2O(s)} \xrightarrow{\text{heat}} \underset{\text{white powder}}{CuSO_4(s)} + 5H_2O(g)$$

In this case, the reaction results in a colour change from blue to white. The physical structure of the crystals is also destroyed.

The water driven off can be condensed separately (figure 7.19). The white anhydrous copper(II) sulphate and the water are cooled down. Then the dehydration reaction can be reversed by slowly adding the water back to the powder. This reaction is strongly exothermic and the colour of the powder returns to blue:

$$CuSO_4 \cdot 5H_2O(s) \underset{\text{mix reactants}}{\overset{\text{heat}}{\rightleftharpoons}} CuSO_4(s) + 5H_2O(l)$$

Some reactions, for example the dehydration of hydrated salts, can be reversed if the conditions are changed.

The decomposition of ammonium chloride is a further example of this type of change. When warmed in a test tube, the white solid decomposes to ammonia and hydrogen chloride:

$$NH_4Cl(s) \rightarrow NH_3(g) + HCl(g)$$

However, on the cooler surface of the upper part of the tube, the white solid is re-formed:

$$NH_3(g) + HCl(g) \rightarrow NH_4Cl(s)$$

Here we have an **open system**. We are heating the solid in an *open* test tube. If a sample of ammonium chloride were heated in a *closed* container, both the forward and reverse reactions would be set up at the same time. In this case, an **equilibrium** would be set up.

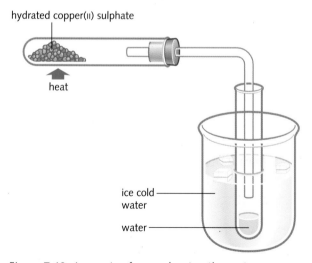

Figure 7.19 Apparatus for condensing the water vapour driven off from blue crystals of hydrated copper(II) sulphate by heating. The change can be reversed by adding the liquid water back to the white anhydrous copper(II) sulphate.

Summary of core material

You should know that:

- certain reactions can be reversed if the conditions are changed

- some of these reactions can be vital to life, for example the transport of oxygen by haemoglobin.

EXTENSION

Reversible reactions and chemical equilibria

Imagine a hotel swimming pool on a hot, sunny day. Some people are by the pool sunbathing; others are swimming in the pool. Over the most popular part of the day the number of people swimming remains approximately the same. However, it is not the same people all the time. Some stop swimming to sunbathe, while other sunbathers take a swim. The balance between the number of people entering and leaving the pool keeps the overall number swimming the same. This is a **dynamic equilibrium**. The pool and the sunbathing area are the system, and the system is in equilibrium. This example will help you to understand dynamic equilibria in chemical reactions.

The Haber process – making ammonia

The reaction to produce ammonia from nitrogen and hydrogen is a **reversible reaction**. That is why the symbol $\rightleftharpoons$ is used in the equation

$$N_2(g) + 3H_2(g) \rightleftharpoons 2NH_3(g)$$

When nitrogen and hydrogen are mixed, they react to form ammonia – this is the **forward reaction**:

$$N_2(g) + 3H_2(g) \rightarrow 2NH_3(g)$$

However, this reaction never goes to completion – the reactants are not all used up. This is because ammonia molecules collide and break down under the same conditions – this is the **reverse reaction**:

$$2NH_3(g) \rightarrow N_2(g) + 3H_2(g)$$

In the reaction mixture, these two competing reactions are going on at the same time.

As the reactions proceed, a **dynamic equilibrium** is reached. Ammonia molecules are breaking down as fast as they are being formed. The rate of the forward reaction is the same as the rate of the reverse reaction. The concentrations of N_2, H_2 and NH_3 do not change even though molecules are reacting.

This reaction is a difficult one to get to work at a reasonable rate. A catalyst can be added. Chemists have tried more than 2500 different combinations of metals and metal oxides as catalysts for this reaction. Finely divided iron has been found to be the best. However, the presence of a catalyst does not alter the equilibrium concentrations of N_2, H_2 and NH_3. The catalyst shortens the time taken to reach equilibrium by increasing the rates of both the forward and reverse reactions.

- A **reversible reaction** is in equilibrium when the rates of the forward and reverse reactions are equal.

- At **equilibrium**, the concentrations of reactants and products do not change.

- The **equilibrium concentrations** (the equilibrium position) for a particular reaction depend on the conditions used. Changing the temperature alters the equilibrium position. Changing the working pressure can also alter the equilibrium position for some reactions involving gases.

- For a reversible reaction, a **catalyst** does not alter the equilibrium concentrations of reactants and products. It does increase the rate at which equilibrium is reached.

Because of its importance, the Haber process for making ammonia has been studied under a wide range of conditions of temperature and pressure (figure 7.20 on page 200). The percentage amount of ammonia in the equilibrium mixture depends on both the temperature and the pressure. Under the conditions Haber first used, only 8% of the equilibrium mixture was ammonia. Modern plants now use a temperature of about 450°C, a pressure of 200 atmospheres and an iron catalyst (see page 292).

How could conditions be changed to improve this yield? The French chemist Le Chatelier put forward a generalisation that gives chemists clues as to how this can be done.

> **Le Chatelier's principle** states that:
>
> when a change is made to the conditions of a system in dynamic equilibrium, the system moves so as to *oppose* that change.

So how can this reaction system be changed to produce more ammonia at equilibrium – to shift the equilibrium to the right (figure 7.21)?

- *Changing the pressure*
  How will increasing the pressure affect the amount of ammonia made? The pressure of a gas is caused by collisions of the gas particles with the walls of the container – the fewer molecules present, the lower the pressure. If we apply more pressure to the equilibrium, the system will shift to favour the side of the equation that has fewer molecules:

  $$N_2(g) + 3H_2(g) \rightleftharpoons 2NH_3(g)$$
  four molecules   two molecules

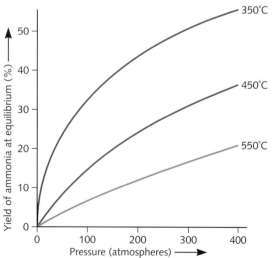

Figure 7.20 A wide range of conditions of temperature and pressure have been tried for the Haber process. The curves show the yields that would be obtained for some of them.

So there will be a shift to the right. More ammonia will form to reduce the number of molecules in the mixture. High pressures will increase the yield of ammonia (figure 7.21). Modern industrial plants use a pressure of 200 atmospheres. Higher pressures could be used, but high-pressure reaction vessels are expensive to build.

- *Changing the temperature*
  The forward reaction producing ammonia is exothermic, and the reverse reaction is therefore endothermic:

  $$N_2(g) + 3H_2(g) \rightarrow 2NH_3(g)$$
  exothermic – heat given out

  $$2NH_3(g) \rightarrow N_2(g) + 3H_2(g)$$
  endothermic – heat taken in

  If we raise the temperature of the system, more ammonia will break down to take in the heat supplied. Less ammonia will be produced at high temperatures. Lowering the temperature will favour ammonia production (figure 7.21). However, the rate at which the ammonia is produced will be so slow as to be uneconomic. In practice, a compromise or **optimum temperature** is used to produce enough ammonia at an acceptable rate. Modern plants use temperatures of about 450°C.

- *Reducing the concentration of ammonia*
  If the system was at equilibrium and then some of the ammonia was removed, more

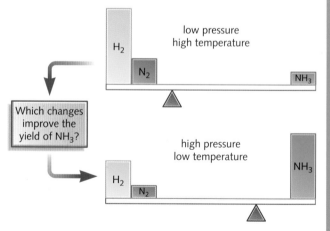

Figure 7.21 What shifts in the conditions will favour ammonia production in the Haber process? Increasing the pressure and lowering the temperature both move the equilibrium to the right to give more ammonia in the mixture.

Table 7.4 The boiling points of nitrogen, hydrogen and ammonia

Compound	Boiling point (°C)
Nitrogen (N_2)	−196
Hydrogen (H_2)	−253
Ammonia (NH_3)	−33

ammonia would be produced to replace that removed. Industrially, it is easy to remove ammonia. It has a much higher boiling point than nitrogen or hydrogen (table 7.4) and condenses easily, leaving the others still as gases. In modern plants, the gas mixture is removed from the reaction chamber when the percentage of ammonia is about 15%. The ammonia is condensed by cooling, and the remaining nitrogen and hydrogen are recycled.

The conditions used in the **Haber process** are as follows.

- N_2 and H_2 are mixed in a ratio of 3:1.
- An optimum temperature of 450°C is chosen.
- A pressure of 200 atmospheres is applied.
- A catalyst of finely divided iron is used.
- The ammonia is condensed out of the reaction mixture and the remaining N_2 and H_2 recycled.

Conditions affecting a chemical equilibrium

The general ideas resulting from our discussion of the effects of changing the conditions of a reaction in equilibrium are summarised in table 7.5. The effects are consistent with Le Chatelier's principle.

The contact process – making sulphuric acid

In the manufacture of sulphuric acid, the main reaction that converts sulphur dioxide (SO_2) to sulphur trioxide (SO_3) is reversible:

$$2SO_2(g) + O_2(g) \rightleftharpoons 2SO_3(g)$$
$$\Delta H = -197\,kJ/mol$$

The ideas of Le Chatelier can be applied to this equilibrium too. The reaction to produce sulphur trioxide is exothermic. This means that sulphur trioxide production would be favoured by low temperatures. The reaction would be too slow to be economic if the temperature were too low. An optimum temperature of 450°C is used. This gives sufficient sulphur trioxide at an economical rate. A catalyst of vanadium(V) oxide is also used to increase the rate. There are fewer gas molecules on the right of the equation. Therefore, increasing the pressure would favour the production of sulphur trioxide. In fact the process is run at atmospheric pressure because the conversion of sulphur dioxide to sulphur trioxide is about 96% complete under these conditions.

Table 7.5 The effect of changing conditions on a chemical equilibrium

Condition	Effect on equilibrium position
Catalyst	Using a catalyst does *not* affect the position of equilibrium, but the reaction reaches equilibrium faster
Temperature*	*Increasing* the temperature makes the reaction move in the direction that takes in heat (the endothermic direction)
Concentration*	*Increasing* the concentration of one substance in the mixture makes the equilibrium move in the direction that produces less of that substance
Pressure*	This *only* affects reactions involving gases – *increasing* the pressure shifts the equilibrium in the direction that produces fewer gas molecules

* The reverse of these statements is true when these factors are decreased.

The conditions used in the **contact process** are as follows.

- An optimum temperature of about 450 °C is chosen.
- A catalyst of vanadium(V) oxide is used.
- An operating pressure of 1 atmosphere is applied.

The manufacture of lime

Limestone (calcium carbonate) can be decomposed by heat in a lime kiln to produce lime (calcium oxide):

$$CaCO_3(s) \rightarrow CaO(s) + CO_2(g)$$

If this reaction is carried out in a *closed* container, it is actually a reversible reaction:

$$CaCO_3(s) \rightleftharpoons CaO(s) + CO_2(g)$$

Not all the calcium carbonate decomposes. An equilibrium is set up with a limiting pressure of carbon dioxide in the container.

However, a lime kiln is *open* and the carbon dioxide can escape from the furnace (figure 7.22). This means that the reaction never reaches equilibrium. More and more calcium carbonate decomposes in an attempt to reach an equilibrium that can never be achieved. Eventually, all the calcium carbonate decomposes.

Weak acids and alkalis

Dynamic equilibria are set up in solutions of weak acids such as ethanoic acid:

$$CH_3COOH(aq) \rightleftharpoons CH_3COO^-(aq) + H^+(aq)$$

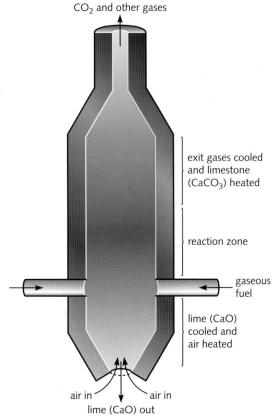

Figure 7.22 *In the industrial manufacture of lime, limestone (calcium carbonate) is decomposed in a lime kiln. This is an open system where the carbon dioxide can escape. No equilibrium is possible, and all the limestone decomposes.*

and in solutions of weak alkalis such as ammonia solution:

$$NH_3(g) + H_2O(l) \rightleftharpoons NH_4^+(aq) + OH^-(aq)$$

Because these molecules are only partially dissociated into ions in water, their pH values are not as low as those of solutions of strong acids or as high as those of strong alkalis of the same concentration (section 5.19 on page 147).

Summary of extension material

You should know that:

- reversible reactions in a closed system reach a position of dynamic equilibrium
- at equilibrium, the rate of the reverse reaction equals that of the forward reaction
- at equilibrium, the overall concentrations of the reactants and products do not change
- the position of an equilibrium can be altered by

changing the temperature of the system

- for reversible reactions involving gases, the position of equilibrium can be altered by changing the pressure
- several important industrial reactions, for example the Haber process, are based on reversible reactions

- the conditions used industrially for these reactions are optimised to produce enough product at an economic rate

- a catalyst is often involved in these processes, but its presence does not alter the equilibrium position

- solutions of weak acids, for example ethanoic acid, which are only partially dissociated into ions, are also examples of dynamic equilibria.

7.11 When sulphur dioxide reacts with oxygen to form sulphur trioxide, the reaction eventually reaches equilibrium:

$$2SO_2(g) + O_2(g) \rightleftharpoons 2SO_3(g)$$

At this equilibrium point:
A either sulphur dioxide or oxygen has all been used up
B sulphur dioxide and oxygen no longer react to form sulphur trioxide
C sulphur trioxide no longer decomposes to form sulphur dioxide and oxygen
D the amount of sulphur trioxide remains unchanged

(SEG, 1993)

7.12 The reaction between calcium oxide and carbon dioxide is shown by the following equation:

$$CaO + CO_2 \rightleftharpoons CaCO_3$$

Which of these statements are correct?
1 The reaction is reversible.
2 Calcium carbonate breaks down to form calcium oxide and carbon dioxide.
3 Calcium oxide and carbon dioxide do not react together.

A 1 and 2   B 1 and 3   C 2 and 3   D 1, 2 and 3

(SEG, 1993)

7.13 This equation represents a reaction between substance W and substance X to manufacture substances Y and Z:

$$\underset{\text{endothermic}}{\overset{\text{exothermic}}{W(g) + X(g) \rightleftharpoons Y(s) + Z(g)}}$$

(The letters used are *not* the symbols for the elements.)

	Sets of conditions	
	Temperature	Pressure
A	high	high
B	high	low
C	low	high
D	low	low

Which set of conditions will produce the greatest amount of substances Y and Z at equilibrium?

(SEG, 1993)

7.14 The world's largest plant to extract bromine from sea water is in Britain. Chlorine is bubbled through acidified sea water. Bromine is formed.

(a) How is chlorine manufactured from concentrated aqueous sodium chloride? [2]

(b) Combine the following equations to write the overall ionic equation for the reaction between chlorine molecules and bromide ions. [2]

$$Cl_2 + 2e^- \rightarrow 2Cl^-$$

$$2Br^- - 2e^- \rightarrow Br_2$$

(c) Bromine reacts with water:

$$Br_2 + H_2O \rightleftharpoons Br^- + BrO^- + 2H^+$$

To increase the yield of bromine, the pH of the sea water is adjusted to 3.5 by the addition of sulphuric acid. Explain why a low pH increases the yield of bromine. [3]

(IGCSE, 1994)

7.15 Large quantities of ammonia are manufactured by the Haber process:

$$N_2(g) + 3H_2(g) \rightleftharpoons 2NH_3(g)$$

The hydrogen required is made from methane by this reaction:

$$CH_4(g) + H_2O(g) \rightleftharpoons 3H_2(g) + CO(g)$$

Nitrogen is obtained from the air.

The graph on page 204 shows the yield of ammonia at different temperatures and pressures.

(a) (i) Deduce from the graph the best conditions to obtain a good yield of ammonia. [2]
    (ii) Suggest why these conditions are not those necessarily used in the Haber process. [2]

(b) What do you understand by the term *non-renewable resource*? Give an example that is mentioned earlier in this question. [2]

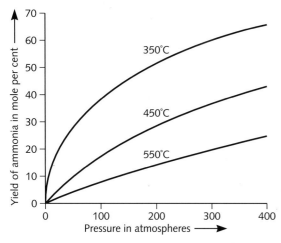

(c) The molar volume of a gas is 24 dm³ at room temperature and pressure. If 24 dm³ of nitrogen completely reacted with 72 dm³ of hydrogen, what volume of ammonia would be formed? (All volumes measured under same conditions.)　　　[2]

(SEG, 1992)

7.16

(a) The Haber process is a reversible reaction. What does 'reversible reaction' mean?　　　[1]

(b) The graphs show the amount of ammonia produced at different temperatures and pressures.

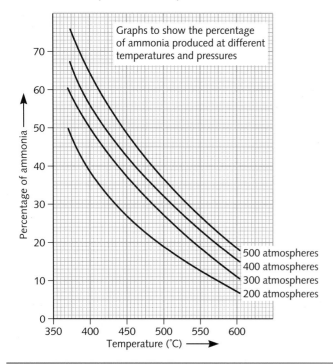

(i) What conditions favour the production of ammonia?　　　[2]

(ii) In industry the reaction is carried out at 450 °C and 200 atmospheres pressure. Use the graph to explain why these conditions are used.　　　[4]

(c) (i) Some energy has to be put into the chemicals to start the reaction. Explain how this energy helps the reaction to start.　　　[2]

(ii) Here is an energy level diagram for this reaction. Is this reaction exothermic or endothermic? Explain your answer in detail.　　　[3]

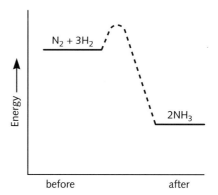

(NEAB, 1995)

Patterns and properties of non-metals

Hydrogen and water

This section covers the following ideas:

- the chemistry of hydrogen
- the manufacture of hydrogen
- hydrogen as a fuel (the 'hydrogen economy')
- water and the oceans
- the water cycle
- domestic and industrial water supplies
- sewage treatment
- chemical and physical tests for water.

The **properties** of hydrogen:

- colourless gas, without smell
- very low density
- flammable
- almost insoluble in water

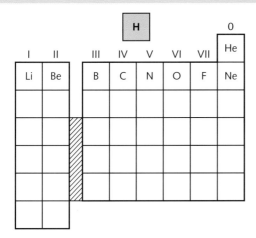

8.1 Hydrogen

Hydrogen is the simplest element of all. An atom of its commonest isotope (**protium**) contains just one proton and one electron. Hydrogen gas is made up of diatomic molecules (H_2) and has the lowest density of any substance. It is the commonest element in the Universe, and is the main element present in the Sun. Solar energy powers life on Earth. Heat and light energy from the Sun are produced by nuclear reactions in which hydrogen is converted to helium.

There is very little hydrogen in the Earth's atmosphere. Its molecules are so light that they are not held by the Earth's gravity and diffuse into space. However, hydrogen occurs in many compounds on Earth, including some of the most important such as water and methane.

Hydrogen has a very low density and it was once thought that this property would be a great advantage in air transport. Early in the twentieth century hydrogen was used to fill airships, and trans-Atlantic flights flew between Europe and New York between 1928 and 1937. Unfortunately the flammability of hydrogen was responsible for some terrible disasters. The British airship R101 crashed in France on its way to India in 1930. After this, the British stopped building airships. The Germans continued their flights until the Hindenburg disaster of May 1937. The hydrogen in the 'balloon' of this airship burst into flames as it was docking at its mooring mast at Lakehurst, New Jersey, USA. As it crashed to the ground, the whole airship was engulfed in fire. This tragic demonstration that hydrogen is a **flammable** gas ended the commercial use of passenger airships. Modern airships use helium gas, which is non-flammable.

The reaction between hydrogen and oxygen also offers promise as a source of pollution-free energy. There is much research going on into the possibility of using hydrogen in this way. However, the Space Shuttle *Challenger* disaster of 1986 showed us the dangers to be guarded against. During take-off on 28 January, a sealing ring on one of the booster rockets failed. The flame produced caused the main hydrogen fuel tank to break. The *Challenger* exploded 73 seconds into its flight, and the crew of seven died.

8.2 The chemistry of hydrogen

Hydrogen in the laboratory

Hydrogen can be produced by a number of reactions in which it is **displaced** from water or acids by various metals. The most reactive metals will react with *cold water* to produce hydrogen. Metals such as potassium, sodium and calcium (figure 8.1a) react strongly, releasing hydrogen:

metal + water → metal hydroxide + hydrogen

$$2Na(s) + 2H_2O(l) \rightarrow 2NaOH(aq) + H_2(g)$$

$$Ca(s) + 2H_2O(l) \rightarrow Ca(OH)_2(aq) + H_2(g)$$

The less reactive metals, for example magnesium, zinc and iron, react with *steam* in a similar way:

metal + water → metal oxide + hydrogen

$$Zn(s) + H_2O(g) \rightarrow ZnO(s) + H_2(g)$$

The more usual laboratory preparation is to react zinc with dilute hydrochloric acid (figure 8.1b):

metal + acid
→ salt + hydrogen

$$Zn(s) + 2HCl(aq) \rightarrow ZnCl_2(aq) + H_2(g)$$

A dilute solution of many electrolytes, including dilute acids, will also give hydrogen gas at the cathode during electrolysis (page 117).

The production of hydrogen by any of these methods can be tested easily. The gas burns with a 'squeaky pop' when a lighted splint is held in a test tube of hydrogen.

The reaction with oxygen or air takes other forms. A jet of hydrogen burns with a light blue flame. A mixture of hydrogen and oxygen in approximately 2:1 proportions explodes violently when lit. The reaction in all these cases produces water:

$$2H_2(g) + O_2(g) \rightarrow 2H_2O(g)$$

The reaction is so exothermic that it is used to power some rockets used in the NASA space programme.

Hydrogen's ability to combine with oxygen makes it a strong **reducing agent**. It will remove oxygen from many metal oxides on heating. For example, it will reduce black copper(II) oxide to metallic copper:

$$CuO(s) + H_2(g) \rightarrow Cu(s) + H_2O(g)$$

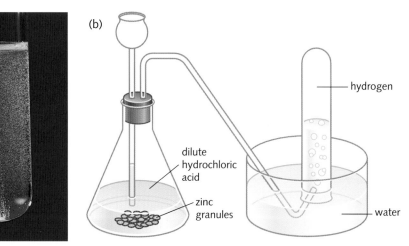

Figure 8.1 (a) The most reactive metals, like calcium, will react readily with cold water to produce hydrogen. (b) In the usual laboratory preparation of hydrogen, zinc is reacted with dilute hydrochloric acid.

EXTENSION

The industrial manufacture of hydrogen

The production of hydrogen is centred on two processes at the moment.

One is the **electrolysis** of brine, the main process of the chlor–alkali industry. Here hydrogen is given off at the cathode during electrolysis.

$$2NaCl(aq) + 2H_2O(l) \rightarrow H_2(g) + Cl_2(g) + 2NaOH(aq)$$

The major alternative to this is to obtain hydrogen by the **steam re-forming** of natural gas. The methane in natural gas is reacted with steam in a reversible reaction:

$$CH_4(g) + H_2O(g) \rightleftharpoons 3H_2(g) + CO(g)$$

Conditions are chosen to make sure that the equilibrium position is well to the right. The process is carried out at 750°C and 30 atmospheres pressure, using a nickel catalyst. The carbon monoxide is then allowed to reduce some of the unreacted steam to produce more hydrogen gas:

$$CO(g) + H_2O(g) \rightarrow H_2(g) + CO_2(g)$$

This method is the main source of hydrogen for the production of ammonia by the **Haber process** (page 199).

The search for better and cheaper sources of hydrogen continues. This is stimulated by the prospect of hydrogen being a very useful fuel for the future.

8.3 The 'hydrogen economy'

Hydrogen gas has attractions as a **fuel**. All it produces on burning is water. When hydrogen burns, it produces more energy per gram than any other fuel (figure 8.2).

A future 'hydrogen economy' has been talked of, but there are problems of storage and transport. The gas itself is difficult to store and transport because of its low density. At the moment, the only vehicles that run on hydrogen are the rockets of the American space programme. Here the gas is condensed to a liquid at $-253\,°C$. NASA is serviced by road and rail tankers carrying 5 tonnes at a time. Keeping hydrogen in liquid form requires very low temperatures and high costs. An alternative is to store hydrogen in a solid form as a transition-element hydride. The hydrogen is stored within the metal's crystal lattice (a gas–solid solution), and can be released

when needed. Lanthanum–nickel and iron–titanium alloys have been tested for storing hydrogen in experimental cars. Hydrogen is produced on a large scale for the chemical industry and some of it is piped to industrial sites. This would have to be extended if hydrogen is to become widely used as a fuel. Cheaper sources of hydrogen are always being looked for.

The electrolysis of water is not very economic. Attempts to split water photochemically have not been successful enough to support a hydrogen economy. It may be that cheap surplus electricity from nuclear power may make electrolysis more economic. Others have suggested the use of electricity from solar power.

Despite these difficulties, experimental hydrogen-powered cars are being tried. Nissan and Mazda in Japan, and Daimler-Benz in Germany, have built and tested cars. The Japanese burn the hydrogen in the engine, while the

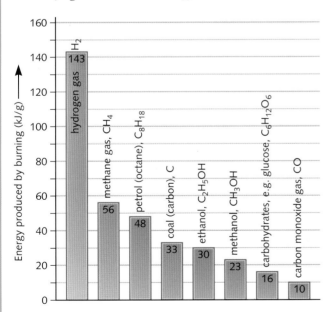

Figure 8.2 The energy produced on burning one gram of various fuels, to produce water and carbon dioxide. Hydrogen produces more energy per gram than any other fuel.

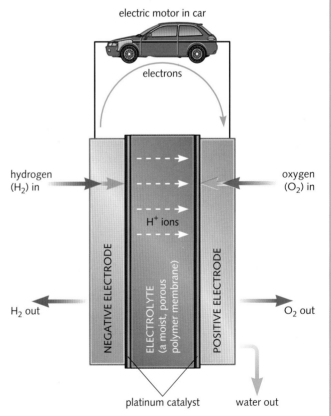

Figure 8.3 How a car runs on a hydrogen fuel cell. The car is powered by electrons released at the negative electrode. In the fuel cell itself, hydrogen ions move to the positive electrode to replace those used up in the reaction with oxygen. (For equations and more details, see page 275.)

German–Swiss–British venture uses the hydrogen in a **fuel cell**. Electricity from this cell then powers an electric motor (figure 8.3 on page 207). Using a fuel cell operating an electric motor, hydrogen has an **efficiency** of 60% compared with 35% for a petrol engine. The 'hydrogen economy' may have life in it yet! The advantages and disadvantages are summarised in table 8.1.

Table 8.1 The advantages and disadvantages of hydrogen as a fuel for motor vehicles

Advantages	Disadvantages
renewable if produced using solar energy	non-renewable if generated by nuclear energy or energy from fossil fuels
lower flammability	large fuel tank required
virtually emission-free	no distribution system in place (unless an 'in car' method of producing H_2 from petrol is developed)
zero emissions of CO_2	engine redesign needed or a fuel cell system
non-toxic	currently expensive

8.4 Water

Water first appeared on Earth thousands of millions of years ago as water vapour, in the gases that burst out of volcanoes. As the planet cooled, the water vapour condensed and formed the oceans. Water now covers over 71% of the Earth's surface. Some 97% of this water is in the oceans. The Pacific Ocean alone covers almost half the surface of the Earth, as can be seen from satellite pictures.

The oceans

> Water, water, everywhere, nor any drop to drink.
>
> *Samuel Taylor Coleridge*

The 'Ancient Mariner' in Coleridge's poem is surrounded by sea water, but is unable to drink any of it. This is more than poetic fantasy, it is a physiological reality.

The oceans are not simply just pure water. They contain some of every element found in the Earth's crust, dissolved in one vast **solution**. For millions of years, rain, streams, rivers and the ocean itself have been wearing away at the Earth's crust. The winds also carry sand and dust far out to sea. The gases of the air dissolve in water. Thermal vents deep on the ocean floor erupt and thrust hot fluids rich in dissolved **minerals** into the surrounding water (figure 8.4). Figure 8.5 shows some of the major ions found in sea water.

Figure 8.4 A deep-sea thermal vent. Super-heated water gushes from these vents, carrying minerals rich in iron, zinc and copper.

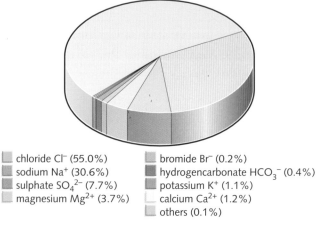

- chloride Cl⁻ (55.0%)
- sodium Na⁺ (30.6%)
- sulphate SO₄²⁻ (7.7%)
- magnesium Mg²⁺ (3.7%)
- bromide Br⁻ (0.2%)
- hydrogencarbonate HCO₃⁻ (0.4%)
- potassium K⁺ (1.1%)
- calcium Ca²⁺ (1.2%)
- others (0.1%)

Figure 8.5 The percentages by mass of various ions in sea water.

But for some countries, the sea *is* a major source of drinking water. The world's largest desalination plant is located at Jubail, Saudi Arabia. It provides 50% of that country's drinking water. The plant was very much in the news during the Gulf War in 1991 because it was threatened by a large oil slick released from pipelines passing through Kuwait.

Distillation, ion exchange and **reverse osmosis** are the methods used to produce fresh drinking water from sea water.

Such plants are increasing throughout the world – Florida, for example, has 109 reverse osmosis plants – but they are expensive to run. Possible climate change and increasing demand for water have led to water companies in Britain proposing to build reverse osmosis plants to help with supply in the UK.

As a result of the level of dissolved ions, the seas are a chemical resource. Sodium chloride (NaCl) is the most abundant resource in sea water. It is extracted in several parts of the world by evaporation, for example in France, Saudi Arabia and Australia. Sodium chloride is the basic resource for a major branch of industrial chemical production, the **chlor–alkali industry** (page 295).

EXTENSION

A large proportion (80%) of the world's supply of bromine is extracted from sea water. The sea water is first concentrated by evaporating some of the water. Bromine is then displaced from this concentrated solution. Bromine is present in sea water as bromide ions (Br^-). Chlorine, being more reactive, converts these ions into bromine (Br_2):

$$Cl_2 + 2Br^- \rightarrow 2Cl^- + Br_2$$

The bromine produced is then purified.

Magnesium is also extracted from sea water. The magnesium ions present are precipitated as magnesium hydroxide. This is then converted into magnesium chloride using hydrochloric acid. Electrolysis of molten magnesium chloride is then carried out to produce magnesium. This metal is used in various alloys that are important in the space and aviation industries.

Interestingly, **nodules** (small rounded lumps) of manganese have been found on the deep ocean floor in various regions. The nodules contain iron as well as manganese. There are also traces of nickel, cobalt and copper in them. These nodules could provide a valuable source of these metals in the future.

The oceans provide an important means of spreading the heat energy of the Sun over the whole of the Earth's surface. This is achieved not just by the currents in the ocean itself, but by the processes of evaporation and condensation involved in the water cycle (see below).

8.5 The water cycle

The processes of **evaporation** and **condensation** of water affect the temperature of different parts of the Earth in two ways.

- Although there is heavy rainfall in parts of the tropics, the balance there is in favour of evaporation. Evaporation takes in energy. The tropics are cooled by evaporation. The water vapour in the air is driven by winds to the colder, non-tropical areas. Condensation gives out heat. The non-tropical regions are warmed by condensation.

- More water vapour is evaporated from the oceans than falls back into them directly. Water vapour is transferred to the land where it condenses as rainfall. The land is warmed through condensation.

These features are part of the global **water cycle** (figure 8.6 on page 210) in which the flow of rivers and streams completes the cycle. The properties of water make it an ideal liquid for transferring the Sun's energy around the world.

The living world fits into the cycle in various ways. Rainfall over the land causes both **run-off** over the

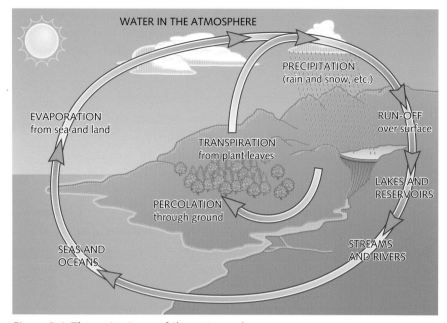

Figure 8.6 *The main stages of the water cycle.*

surface into streams or rivers and **percolation** through the ground. Plants and trees soak up ground water through their roots. They use it for photosynthesis and in their cells and fluids. They give out water vapour back to the atmosphere by **transpiration**. Rain water is also returned to the atmosphere by **evaporation** from the ground and plant surfaces.

All living forms on Earth depend on water for their survival. Life began in the oceans. Even the simplest of bacteria contain a little water. The human body is an aqueous environment – approximately 60% water by mass. Most of it is

in our cells; the rest is in our blood, saliva and other body fluids. Every day we lose about 7% of this water (about 4% of our body mass) in sweat and urine, and as water vapour. If necessary, humans can survive for a few weeks without food; but without water, we would die in a matter of days.

We replace water by eating and drinking. We have also set up water supply systems over the land to cover our needs for agriculture and irrigation (figure 8.7), for industrial use and for domestic purposes. In many countries waste water from houses and factories is filtered and cleaned up at sewage works, and then pumped back into the rivers and seas.

8.6 Domestic and industrial water supplies

The water cycle provides a natural recycling and purification process for fresh water. However, differences in rainfall mean that some regions have sufficient water, while others do not. The use of water in a country or region varies greatly with how developed the area is (figure 8.8). As the population of an area increases and more industries are built, the demand for water will increase. Water shortages will occur in areas where there is already a problem with supply. Some people see the water supply problem in certain regions becoming a potential flash-point for war.

Figure 8.7 *The landscape is changed to provide irrigation for agriculture.*

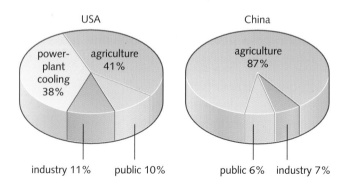

Figure 8.8 *A comparison of the use of water in a developed country (the USA) and a developing country (China).*

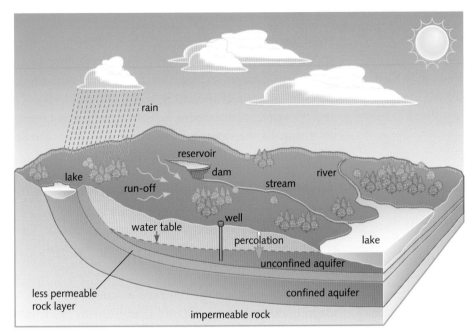

Figure 8.9 Water supplies can be drawn from several sources, both above and below ground.

Global warming might also cause changes in rainfall patterns and disrupt water supplies in ways that we cannot predict.

We draw our water supply from **surface water** (for example rivers, lakes and reservoirs) and from

ground water (underground aquifers and lakes) (figure 8.9). Water from these sources is never completely pure, particularly if it is drawn from a river. The water may contain:

- bacteria,
- dissolved substances – salts from the soil and rocks, and gases from the air,
- solid substances and debris – mud, sand, twigs, refuse and litter.

Before water is safe to drink, the bacteria and solid substances must be removed.

Concern over the levels of pesticides in river water has led to an improved form of advanced water treatment (AWT) plant (figure 8.10). This system uses ozone to disinfect the water and for efficient removal of trace chemicals (like pesticides) from the water. This is an extra stage compared to earlier methods. The ozone is converted to harmless oxygen. AWT also has the advantage that

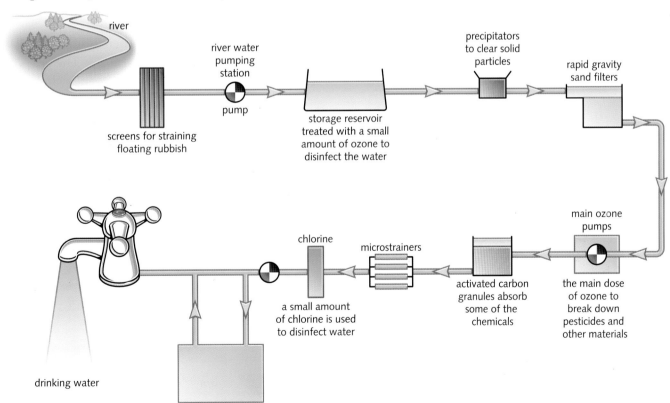

Figure 8.10 Purifying water for the domestic and industrial supply.

less chlorine is used in later stages of treatment. The process involves **filtration, sedimentation, ozone treatment** and **chlorination**. In some countries and regions, sodium fluoride is added to the water supply to help prevent tooth decay. The water is pumped to storage tanks, and then to homes and factories.

Waste water and sewage treatment

In Western Europe each person uses about $180\,dm^3$ of water per day. Figure 8.11 shows how this is used. After use, the water becomes **sewage**. It contains a wide variety of materials: soap, detergent, grease, food, body waste and factory waste. Before this water can be returned into circulation, it must be purified. Sewage treatment involves **filtration, sedimentation** and **bacterial digestion** of the waste material (figure 8.12).

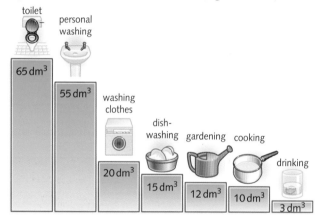

Figure 8.11 The main uses of water in a British home. The numbers show how much water is used per person for each activity every day.

8.7 Water as a solvent

The Dead Sea is the lowest point on Earth, almost 400 m below normal sea level. The River Jordan flows into it in the north, but there is no outflow. It is like a giant evaporating basin (figure 8.13) and its salt concentration is over eight times larger than that of the open oceans. Water is an excellent **solvent** for many ionic substances. The water molecule itself does not have an even spread of charge (see figure 3.17 on page 84). This means that the water molecules can break down ionic crystals and separate the ions from each other. The water molecules form a 'shell' around the ions, keeping them apart (figure 8.14).

Substances that are made up of covalent molecules, including organic compounds, are not very soluble in water. They are covalently bonded and do not contain ions. Generally, they do not interact with water and do not mix or dissolve well. Iodine (I_2), for instance, is only slightly soluble in water. However, it dissolves about ten times as well in cyclohexane (an organic solvent) to give a purple solution (figure 8.15). Cyclohexane is much better than water at separating the iodine molecules in the solid from each other.

Gases also dissolve in water. Their solubility, however, *decreases* with temperature. The gases from the air dissolve in water: oxygen is slightly

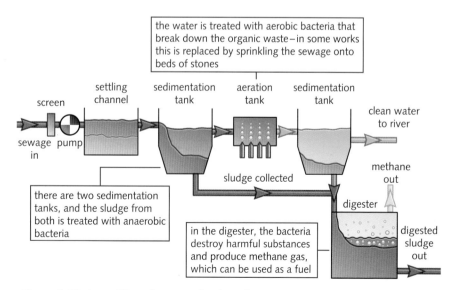

Figure 8.12 An outline of sewage treatment.

Figure 8.13 Columns of salt arise in the Dead Sea by evaporation.

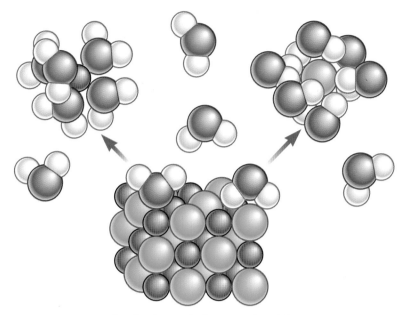

Figure 8.14 Water molecules form 'shells' around metal (grey) and non-metal (green) ions. This helps ionic substances (like sodium chloride, NaCl) to dissolve in water.

more soluble than nitrogen. This is particularly important for fish and other aquatic life which take in oxygen from the water not from air. Power stations can use river or sea water as a coolant. As it cools down the power station equipment or nuclear reactor, the water itself is warmed up. If this warmer water is discharged straight back into the river or sea, it can cause **thermal pollution**. This is because oxygen is less soluble in the warmer water. For example, salmon need the river temperature to stay below about 19 °C. Above this temperature not enough oxygen remains dissolved in the water for them to be able to absorb what they need to live.

Nitrogen and oxygen do not react with water when they dissolve. However, gases such as carbon dioxide, sulphur dioxide and hydrogen chloride are more soluble than others because they *do* react with water to give acidic solutions.

Mineral waters

In some locations the water has naturally high concentrations of dissolved gases such as carbon dioxide (CO_2) and hydrogen sulphide (H_2S). For centuries, some of these 'waters' were thought to have health-giving properties. Spa towns and resorts grew up in these places: for example, Bath (England), Baden-Baden (Germany) and White Sulfur Springs (USA). People would flock to these spas to bathe in and drink the water. Those who could not afford to 'take the waters' at these resorts were able to buy the bottled 'mineral water'. Many different bottled waters are now available, each with their different origin: 'Evian', 'Volvic' and 'Malvern', for example. The Perrier spring near Marseilles in southern France is the source for 'Perrier' water. Over 1000 million bottles of this water are sold every year. It is described as a naturally carbonated mineral water – the fizz comes from carbon dioxide produced naturally underground rather than from adding manufactured gas from a cylinder.

8.8 Chemical and physical tests for water

How can we test if an unknown colourless liquid contains water or if it is pure water? The *presence* of water in the liquid will do the following.

Figure 8.15 Iodine is ten times more soluble in cyclohexane (a) than in water (b). Cyclohexane is an organic solvent and does not mix with water (c).

- Water will turn anhydrous copper(II) sulphate from white to blue.
- Water will turn anhydrous cobalt(II) chloride from blue to pink.

The equations for these two reactions are:

$$CuSO_4(s) + 5H_2O(l) \rightarrow CuSO_4 \cdot 5H_2O(s)$$
whiteblue

$$CoCl_2(s) + 6H_2O(l) \rightarrow CoCl_2 \cdot 6H_2O(s)$$
bluepink

To find out if a liquid is *pure* water, its boiling point or its freezing point must be measured.

Pure water boils at exactly 100 °C and freezes at exactly 0 °C at one atmosphere pressure.

Summary of core material

You should know that:

- hydrogen is a low-density, colourless, flammable gas
- it can be prepared by the reaction of some metals with water or dilute acids
- water plays an important role in the Earth's environment as part of the global water cycle

- water must be treated before being supplied for domestic and industrial use
- waste water and sewage must be treated in a sewage plant before it can be returned safely to rivers and oceans
- in the laboratory, water is an important solvent, particularly for ionic compounds.

Summary of extension material

You should know that:

- hydrogen is made industrially for use in the Haber process, and in the manufacture of margarine

- it could become increasingly important as a 'clean' fuel for the future.

8.1 Deuterium and tritium are isotopes of hydrogen. Tritium is radioactive but hydrogen and deuterium are not.

Isotope	Symbol	Structure
hydrogen	H	
deuterium	D	
tritium	T	

Key
X is an electron
⊕ is a proton
○ is a neutron

(a) Copy and complete the following statement: [3]

Isotopes of hydrogen always contain the same numbers of .... and .... but different numbers of ....

(b) Copy the table. Calculate the nucleon numbers (mass numbers) of hydrogen, deuterium and tritium. [2]

	Nucleon number
Hydrogen	
Deuterium	
Tritium	

(c) Draw the structures of H_2 and D^+ showing the nucleons and electrons (if present). [2]

(d) Water has the formula H_2O and 'heavy water' has the formula D_2O. Small pieces of calcium were added separately to samples of water and heavy water. In each case the gas given off was collected.
  (i) Draw a labelled diagram of the apparatus you would use to carry out the experiment and collect the gas given off. [3]
  (ii) Name the gas given off in each case: [2]
    (A) with water,
    (B) with heavy water.

(e) (i) State *one* medical use of radioactive isotopes. [1]
  (ii) State *one* industrial use of radioactive isotopes. [1]

(IGCSE, 1991)

8.2 *'Hydrogen – Fuel of the Future'*

It has been suggested that hydrogen could be used as a fuel instead of the fossil fuels that are used at present. The equation below shows how hydrogen burns in air:

$$2H_2 + O_2 \rightarrow 2H_2O \qquad \text{heat given out}$$

The hydrogen would be made from water using energy obtained from renewable sources such as wind or solar power. The water splitting reaction requires a lot of energy.

(a) Hydrogen was successfully used as a fuel for a Soviet airliner in 1988. Why would hydrogen be a good fuel for use in an aeroplane? [2]

(b) The water splitting reaction is shown in the equation below:

$$2H_2O \rightarrow 2H_2 + O_2$$

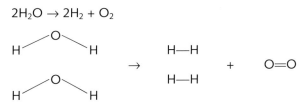

  (i) Calculate the energy needed to split the water molecules in the equation into H and O atoms (see page 180 for bond energy values):
    $2H_2O \rightarrow 4H + 2O$ [3]
  (ii) Calculate the energy change when the H and O atoms join to form H_2 and O_2 molecules:
    $4H + 2O \rightarrow 2H_2 + O_2$ [2]
  (iii) Is the overall reaction:
    $2H_2O \rightarrow 2H_2 + O_2$
    exothermic or endothermic? Use your answers to (i) and (ii) to explain your choice. [4]

(c) In the Periodic Table, hydrogen is placed on its own at the top and in the middle. It is difficult to position because it has properties of metals and non-metals.
  (i) Where would you expect hydrogen to be placed in the Periodic Table on the basis of the arrangement of electrons in hydrogen atoms? Explain your answer. [2]
  (ii) Give *one* way in which hydrogen behaves like a metal. [1]
  (iii) Give *one* way in which hydrogen behaves like a non-metal. [1]

(NEAB, 1994)

8.3 The element hydrogen was first isolated in 1766 by the English scientist Cavendish.

(a) Cavendish reacted zinc with dilute acid. Because the zinc was impure, the hydrogen contained other gases, such as hydrogen arsenide.
  (i) Copy and complete the ionic equation: [1]
    $Zn + 2H^+ \rightarrow \ldots\ldots + \ldots\ldots$
  (ii) What type of reaction is this? [1]

(b) Uses of hydrogen include the manufacture of ammonia and of margarine. It was formerly used to fill balloons.
  (i) Explain why helium, which has a higher density, is now used for filling balloons instead of hydrogen. [1]
  (ii) Calculate the mass of one dm^3 of hydrogen at r.t.p. [2]

(IGCSE, part question, 1993)

8.4 The label shows the ions present in Buxton mineral water. (Remember that 1 litre = $1\,dm^3$. Also 'bicarbonate' is the old name for 'hydrogencarbonate'.)

OFFICIAL ANALYSIS		
		mg/l
Calcium	Ca^{2+}	55
Magnesium	Mg^{2+}	19
Sodium	Na^+	24
Potassium	K^+	1
Bicarbonates	HCO_3^-	248
Chloride	Cl^-	42
Sulphates	SO_4^{2-}	23
Nitrates	NO_3^-	<0.1
Iron		0
Aluminium		0
Total dissolved solids at 180°C		280
pH at source		7.4

SPARKLING

2 litre e
BOTTLED AT SOURCE

DERBYSHIRE PEAK DISTRICT

BUXTON

Carbonated Natural Mineral Water

FROM THE ST ANN'S SRPING BUXTON

(a) What is an ion? [1]

(b) Which ion is present in the greatest concentration? [1]

(c) Use the information on the label to write formulas for *two* compounds, containing each of the following ions:
  (i) a potassium ion, [1]
  (ii) a sulphate ion. [1]

(d) How would you measure the 'total dissolved solids'? [2]

(MEG, 1993)

8.5 The diagram below shows some of the activities and industries based on a large river.

Samples of water were collected at sites W, X, Y and Z. The results of the tests carried out on these samples are shown below.

(a) Suggest a reason why the town's water supply is taken from the river at W and not closer to the town. [1]

(b) What is the most likely reason for the big temperature difference between X and Y? [1]

(c) The river at Z is becoming choked with water plants. Suggest *two* reasons why plants are growing very quickly in this section of the river. [2]

(d) The plants would provide a food supply for fish. Suggest a reason why there are no fish in this section of the river. [1]

(e) The small stream from the peat bog has a low pH. This could be caused by rain water draining through the bog and dissolving acids in the peat. Another possible reason is 'acid rain' caused by the nearby power station. Describe an experiment which could be used to decide whether acids in the peat or 'acid rain' is the reason for the high acidity of this stream. [2]

Test	Sample from W	Sample from X	Sample from Y	Sample from Z
Temperature, in °C	5	6	13	10
Dissolved oxygen, in parts per million	15	13	9	3
pH	7	8.5	6	6

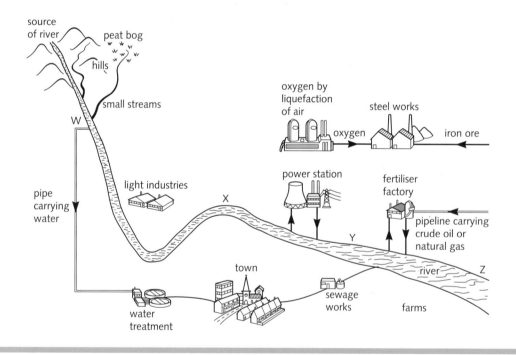

(IGCSE, part question, 1990)

Oxygen and sulphur

This section covers the following ideas:

- the air as a resource
- fractional distillation of liquid air
- oxygen and the fire triangle
- combustion and respiration
- the extraction of sulphur
- the solid and liquid allotropes of sulphur
- the oxides of sulphur
- sulphuric acid and its properties.

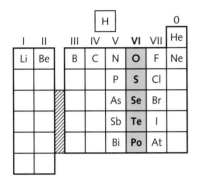

8.9 The air as a resource

The air we breathe is necessary to keep us alive, but it is also a chemical resource. Oxygen is used in steel-making (see page 279), and nitrogen is used in making fertilisers (see page 293). To use them in these ways, the gases from the atmosphere must first be separated. The method used is the **fractional distillation** of liquid air. The gases present in the mixture have different boiling points (table 8.2).

More details are given in figure 8.16. The gases collected as the different **fractions** from this distillation have important uses, which are discussed in later sections (pages 236 and 247).

The process of **fractional distillation** involves essentially two stages.

- First the air must be cooled until it turns into a liquid.
- Then the liquid air is allowed to warm up again. The various gases boil off at different temperatures.

Table 8.2 The boiling points of the gases in air

Gas	Boiling point (°C)	Proportion in mixture (%)
Carbon dioxide (sublimes)	−32	0.03
Xenon	−108	−*
Krypton	−153	−*
Oxygen	−183	20.99
Argon	−186	0.93
Nitrogen	−196	78.03
Neon	−246	−*
Helium	−249	−*

*All the other gases in the air make up 0.02% of the total.

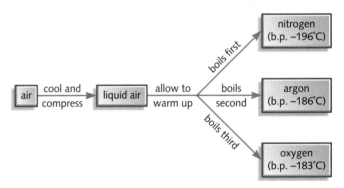

Figure 8.16 The fractional distillation of liquid air.

8.10 Oxygen

Oxygen occurs in the atmosphere all around us as *diatomic* molecules, O_2. Our life on Earth depends on it. But *three* oxygen atoms can also bond together to form **ozone**, O_3. This gas is found in the upper atmosphere, and prevents harmful ultra-violet radiation from reaching Earth.

One major use of oxygen is as a breathing aid in various situations. Oxygen is carried by astronauts and deep-sea divers. Aeroplanes also have their own oxygen supply for emergency use. In hospitals, oxygen is given to patients who have breathing difficulties, including young babies and severe asthmatics.

Oxygen also has uses in industry and in the workplace. It is blown into molten iron to purify it. Other metals and carbon are then added to make steel (see page 280). A mixture of oxygen and ethyne (acetylene) burns very exothermically. The

217

mixture is used in oxyacetylene welding torches because it gives a very hot flame that melts metals.

> The **properties** of **oxygen**:
> - colourless gas, without smell
> - most reactive gas in the Earth's atmosphere
> - supports combustion
> - important for life on the planet.

Many elements burn in oxygen to produce oxides. Those other elements which do not burn become coated with an oxide layer when heated in the gas. These oxides show different properties depending on the type of elements involved.

- Most **metal oxides** are basic oxides – they react with acids to neutralise them. Some oxides of metals are amphoteric (for example Al_2O_3, ZnO) – which means that they react with both acids and alkalis.
- Most **non-metal oxides** are acidic oxides. A few are neutral, for example water (H_2O) and carbon monoxide (CO).

8.11 The fire triangle

The proportion of oxygen in the air seems to have stayed at its present level for several hundred million years. Evidence for this comes from geological charcoal records. Oxygen levels below 15% do not support fires. In contrast, levels above 25% would make forest fires and other types of fire impossible to put out.

The importance of oxygen in supporting a fire is emphasised in the fire triangle (figure 8.17). Any

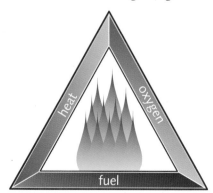

Figure 8.17 The fire triangle. Any fire needs fuel, oxygen and heat. Fire extinguishers remove different parts of the triangle.

fire needs a **fuel**, **oxygen** and **heat** to be present. Remove any one of them and the fire will go out. Methods of extinguishing fires are based on understanding the fire triangle. To stop a fire, we must remove one of the parts of the 'triangle'.

- *Cut off the fuel*
  Where possible, turn off gas or electricity, and remove any material that might burn. A fire-break through a forest is an attempt to stop a fire in advance.

- *Remove the heat*
  When water is used to put out a fire, the idea is to cool down the burning material. The evaporation of water takes in heat. However, there are certain situations where using water makes things *more* dangerous. Water should *not* be used on burning oil or petrol – they do not mix with water and the burning mixture is spread further. Water should not be used on electrical fires either, as water can conduct electricity and give an electric shock. Fires that involve burning metals must also be extinguished by different methods, as the burning metal can react with water to give hydrogen.

- *Cut off the air supply*
  Many fires can be put out by covering them to cut off the air supply. A cooking-oil fire in the kitchen can be extinguished by covering the pan with a fire blanket or a damp cloth. Foam, dry powder and carbon dioxide fire extinguishers also work by cutting off the air supply to the fire.

8.12 Combustion and respiration

There are some reactions where fuels and other substances burn to produce a flame. These are **combustion reactions**. But there are also other combustion reactions: exothermic reactions where no flame is evident. The most important of these is the crucial biochemical reaction that releases energy in cells: **respiration**. We breathe air containing oxygen into our lungs, where it passes into thousands of small air-sacs (alveoli). These air-sacs provide a very large surface area of membranes. Oxygen diffuses through the membranes into the blood. It bonds to haemoglobin in red blood cells and is carried by the blood to the millions of cells of the body. Respiration takes place in each cell, with glucose and oxygen reacting to produce carbon dioxide and water. The reaction is exothermic and gives out energy. This energy supports many other cell reactions and keeps our heart and muscles working. It also keeps us warm. The carbon dioxide and water pass back into the blood, and eventually we breathe them out (table 8.3). Respiration takes place in the cells of all living things. Fish use the oxygen dissolved in water, which they take in through their gills. Plants also respire, taking in air through small pores in their leaves.

Table 8.3 The composition of inhaled and exhaled air

| Gas | Proportion (%) | |
	In inhaled air	In exhaled air
Nitrogen	78	75
Oxygen	21	16
Argon	0.9	0.9
Carbon dioxide	0.03	4
Water vapour	0–4	4

8.13 Sulphur

Sulphur is one of the few elements found **native** in the Earth's crust (that is, not combined with any other elements). The presence of sulphur is strongly associated with volcanoes (figure 8.18). There are three major sources of sulphur.

- *Volcanic regions*
  Native sulphur is found in volcanic regions, past and present. Large underground sulphur beds are found in Poland, Mexico and the USA. Sulphur is extracted from these in the following way (the **Frasch process**). Super-heated water (at 170°C) and hot compressed air are forced underground through pipes into the sulphur bed. A mixture of molten sulphur and water is forced to the surface (figure 8.19). Sulphur does not mix with water, so it is very easily separated. The elemental sulphur obtained is 99.5% pure. The method depends on the relatively low melting point of sulphur (about 112°C). This low melting point is also an advantage when transporting sulphur. It is often shipped and transported as a liquid. The advantages are that a liquid can be pumped from one container to another, and that the container tanks can be filled completely.

- *Oil and gas*
  Natural gas and crude oil are contaminated with sulphur. This is now removed, as it causes environmental problems when these fossil fuels are burnt. The 'desulphurisation' of fossil fuels is now an important source of sulphur. Sulphur obtained in this way is known as recovered sulphur.

Figure 8.18 Sulphur is present in volcanic areas. Here it is deposited on the rim of a steam vent.

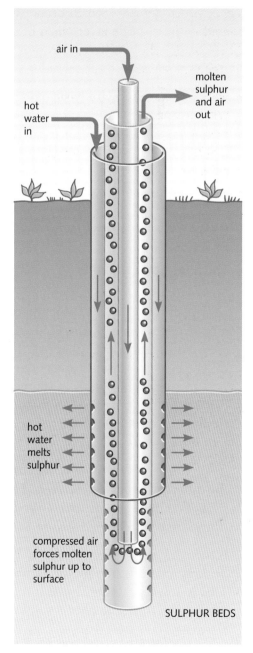

Figure 8.19 Sulphur is mined from underground deposits using super-heated water and compressed air.

• *Minerals*

Some important metal ores contain sulphur. Zinc-blende (ZnS), galena (PbS) and copper pyrites (CuFeS$_2$) are all important ores. In the process of extracting the metal, the ores are roasted in air (see page 284). This produces sulphur dioxide, which is used directly to make sulphuric acid.

The properties of sulphur:

• non-metallic yellow solid at room temperature

• brittle

• insoluble in water

• soluble in organic solvents, for example methylbenzene

• non-conductor of electricity whether solid, molten or dissolved

• relatively low melting point and boiling point.

8.14 The chemistry of sulphur and its oxides

Sulphur burns in air with a blue flame, forming **sulphur dioxide**:

$$S(s) + O_2(g) \rightarrow SO_2(g)$$

This is an acidic gas with a choking smell.

• Sulphur dioxide is poisonous to all organisms, particularly bacteria. It is used as a **food preservative** (E220) in the preparation of fruit juices and soft drinks, and to kill bacteria during wine-making. It is a reducing agent and bleaches certain coloured substances by reduction. It is used as a bleaching agent in paper-making.

• Sulphur dioxide is a typical non-metal oxide in that it dissolves in water to form **sulphurous acid**:

$$SO_2(g) + H_2O(l) \rightarrow H_2SO_3(l)$$

This acid is one of those present in **acid rain**. The sulphur dioxide formed from the burning of fuels containing sulphur dissolves in rain

---

EXTENSION

The allotropy of sulphur

Solid sulphur has two crystalline solid forms or **allotropes**: these are rhombic sulphur and monoclinic sulphur (figure 8.20). These names are used because of the shape of the crystals. The difference comes from the way the molecules are packed together. Crystals of **rhombic sulphur** are denser and more stable than those of **monoclinic sulphur** at room temperature.

Sulphur also shows allotropy in the liquid state. If sulphur is heated slowly, the changes between the different forms can be seen. The changes show themselves in the colour and **viscosity** (thickness) of the liquid (figure 8.21).

If the dark brown liquid sulphur is poured into a beaker of cold water, **plastic sulphur** is formed. This is an elastic, rubber-like form of sulphur. After some time, the plastic sulphur loses its elasticity.

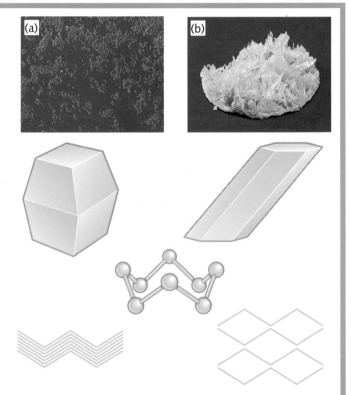

Figure 8.20 There are two crystal forms of solid sulphur: (a) rhombic sulphur and (b) monoclinic sulphur. Both allotropes of solid sulphur are made of S$_8$ rings, but the molecules are stacked in different ways. Rhombic sulphur is the denser of the two.

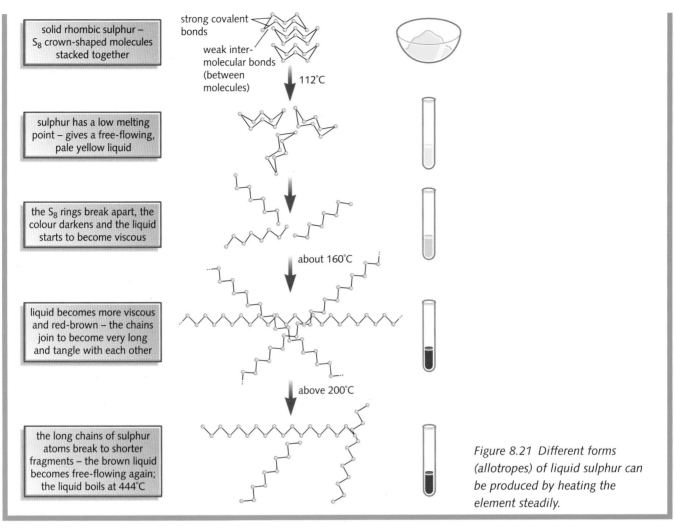

solid rhombic sulphur – S₈ crown-shaped molecules stacked together

strong covalent bonds

weak inter-molecular bonds (between molecules)

112°C

sulphur has a low melting point – gives a free-flowing, pale yellow liquid

the S₈ rings break apart, the colour darkens and the liquid starts to become viscous

about 160°C

liquid becomes more viscous and red-brown – the chains join to become very long and tangle with each other

above 200°C

the long chains of sulphur atoms break to shorter fragments – the brown liquid becomes free-flowing again; the liquid boils at 444°C

Figure 8.21 Different forms (allotropes) of liquid sulphur can be produced by heating the element steadily.

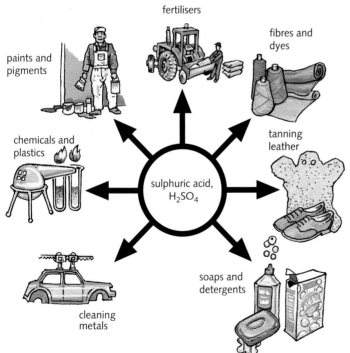

fertilisers

fibres and dyes

paints and pigments

tanning leather

chemicals and plastics

sulphuric acid, H₂SO₄

cleaning metals

soaps and detergents

Figure 8.22 The uses of sulphuric acid.

water to produce sulphurous acid. Then it further reacts with oxygen to produce sulphuric acid.

There is a second oxide of sulphur, **sulphur trioxide** (SO_3). This is a white crystalline solid at room temperature. It is important because it dissolves in water to form **sulphuric acid**.

8.15 Sulphuric acid and sulphates

Sulphuric acid (H_2SO_4) is perhaps the most important industrially produced chemical. Historically, the level of sulphuric acid production in a country has been linked to the amount of industry and prosperity in that country. But the connection is less true in modern economies. It is used as a raw material for the manufacture of a very wide range of other substances (figure 8.22). Some of the most important are fertilisers such as ammonium sulphate and calcium

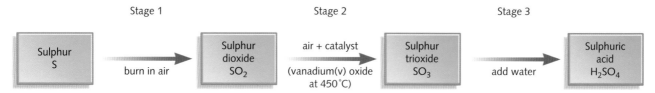

Figure 8.23 *A summary of the three stages in the contact process for making sulphuric acid.*

superphosphate. The process used all over the world to make sulphuric acid is known as the **contact process**. Figure 8.23 outlines the three major stages of the process.

In the laboratory, sulphuric acid is used in two different forms: dilute and concentrated sulphuric acid.

Concentrated sulphuric acid is 98% H_2SO_4 and 2% water. It is particularly dangerous to handle because it is a powerful **dehydrating agent**. It will remove water from other substances.

Dehydration is the removal of water, or the elements of water, from a substance.

This can be demonstrated in the laboratory by its reaction with sugar (sucrose) as shown in figure 8.24. Sugar is a **carbohydrate** – it contains carbon, hydrogen and oxygen. The concentrated acid removes the hydrogen and oxygen as water, leaving carbon behind:

$$\text{sugar (sucrose)} \xrightarrow[\text{(--water)}]{\text{conc. } H_2SO_4} \text{carbon}$$

$$C_{12}H_{22}O_{11} \xrightarrow[\text{(--11}H_2O)]{\text{conc. } H_2SO_4} 12C$$

The acid will dehydrate other carbohydrate materials, for example paper, clothing and wood, in a similar way. It is a very corrosive substance and will also remove water from flesh!

The **properties** of **concentrated sulphuric acid**:

- powerful dehydrating agent
- very corrosive.

The water of crystallisation in blue copper(II) sulphate crystals can also be removed with concentrated H_2SO_4. The colour of the solid changes from blue to white in the process:

$$\text{hydrated} \xrightarrow[\text{(--water)}]{\text{conc. } H_2SO_4} \text{anhydrous}$$
$$\text{copper(II) sulphate} \quad\quad \text{copper(II) sulphate}$$

$$\underset{\text{blue}}{CuSO_4 \cdot 5H_2O} \xrightarrow[\text{(--5}H_2O)]{\text{conc. } H_2SO_4} \underset{\text{white}}{CuSO_4}$$

Dilute sulphuric acid is about 10% H_2SO_4 and 90% water. It is much safer to handle, but must still be treated with care. The dilute acid must *always* be made by carefully adding the concentrated acid to the water. (*Never* the other way round: the addition is strongly exothermic and the acid could spit out and cause burns.)

Dilute sulphuric acid (H_2SO_4) is a strong, **dibasic** acid (page 150). It can be reacted with alkali to produce both **acid salts** (for example sodium

Figure 8.24 *Concentrated sulphuric acid will dehydrate sugar.*
(a) shows the start of the reaction, (b) is when it is completed

The **properties** of **dilute sulphuric acid** are typical of an acid:

- turns blue litmus red
- reacts with metals to give hydrogen, and salts called sulphates
- reacts with bases (metal oxides and hydroxides) to form sulphates and water
- reacts with metal carbonates to give sulphates, water and carbon dioxide
- a strong acid, completely ionised in water
- a good electrolyte and is used in car batteries.

hydrogensulphate, $NaHSO_4$) and **normal salts** (for example sodium sulphate). Sulphates are the salts of sulphuric acid. Some of them have important uses (table 8.4).

A solution containing a sulphate can be identified by a simple test tube reaction. The solution is acidified with a few drops of dilute hydrochloric acid and then barium chloride solution is added. If a sulphate is present, a white precipitate of barium

Table 8.4 Some useful sulphates

Salt	Formula	Use
Calcium sulphate	$CaSO_4 \bullet 2H_2O$	gypsum for cement and concrete
	$2CaSO_4 \bullet H_2O$	'plaster of Paris' for plaster casts
Ammonium sulphate	$(NH_4)_2SO_4$	fertiliser
Magnesium sulphate	$MgSO_4 \bullet 7H_2O$	a laxative
Barium sulphate	$BaSO_4$	barium meal, taken before an X-ray

sulphate is formed. For example

barium chloride + sodium sulphate
→ barium sulphate + sodium chloride

$BaCl_2(aq) + Na_2SO_4(aq)$
→ $\underset{\text{white precipitate}}{BaSO_4(s)} + 2NaCl(aq)$

The ionic equation for this reaction is:

$Ba^{2+}(aq) + SO_4^{2-}(aq) \rightarrow BaSO_4(s)$

Summary of core material

You should know that:

- the air is a resource from which we obtain gases such as oxygen by fractional distillation
- oxygen is a colourless gas that supports the important reactions of combustion and respiration
- oxygen is one of the components of the 'fire triangle'
- sulphur is in the same group as oxygen and is a yellow, non-metallic solid
- sulphur can form two acidic oxides – sulphur dioxide (SO_2) and sulphur trioxide (SO_3)

- these oxides form two acids when dissolved in water – these acids contribute to 'acid rain'
- the most important of these acids is sulphuric acid (H_2SO_4), which is manufactured industrially by the contact process
- sulphuric acid is a strong acid and is used as either a dilute or concentrated solution
- concentrated sulphuric acid is a powerful dehydrating agent.

Summary of extension material

You should know that:

- sulphur exists in two allotropic forms in the solid state – rhombic sulphur and monoclinic sulphur

- sulphur also shows allotropy in the liquid state.

8.6

(a) Name the gas used in this fire extinguisher to force the water out. [1]

(b) How does this type of extinguisher put out a fire? [1]

(c) Why would this extinguisher not be used on electrical fires? [1]

(d) Would this extinguisher be suitable for putting out a chip pan fire? [1]

(e) Explain your answer to (d). [1]

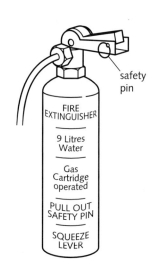

safety pin

FIRE EXTINGUISHER

9 Litres Water

Gas Cartridge operated

PULL OUT SAFETY PIN

SQUEEZE LEVER

(WJEC, 1991)

8.7

(a) When coal is burnt in power stations, sulphur dioxide is formed. The amount of sulphur dioxide released into the atmosphere can be reduced by flue gas desulphurisation (FGD). The diagram below shows how FGD works.

  (i) Explain why it is important to try to reduce the amount of sulphur dioxide released into the atmosphere. [3]

  (ii) Sulphur dioxide can be formed from burning coal, containing sulphur impurities. Write a balanced chemical equation for this reaction. [2]

  (iii) Why is the amount of carbon dioxide in the cleaned gas greater than in the gases from the burning coal? [1]

  (iv) Using the information in the diagram below, what is the formula of gypsum? [1]

(b) Some of the sulphur dioxide is used to make sulphuric acid by the contact process.

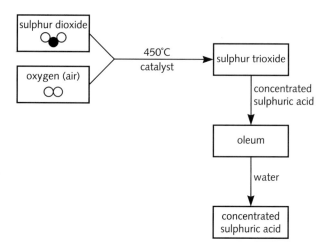

sulphur dioxide

oxygen (air)

450°C catalyst

sulphur trioxide

concentrated sulphuric acid

oleum

water

concentrated sulphuric acid

  (i) Draw a molecule of sulphur trioxide. Let ○ be oxygen and ● be sulphur. [1]

  (ii) What is a catalyst? [2]

  (iii) Name the catalyst used in the contact process. [1]

  (iv) Why is sulphur trioxide not added directly to water to form sulphuric acid? [1]

  (v) Which of the signs below would be found on a tanker of oleum? [1]

  (vi) Name *one* substance used in everyday life which uses sulphuric acid in its manufacture. [1]

(SEG, 1993)

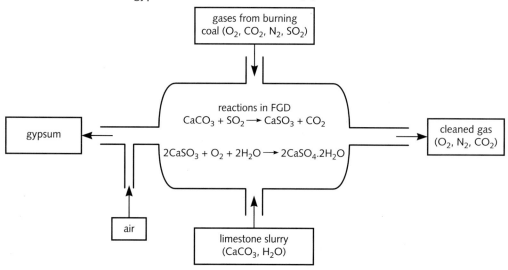

gases from burning coal (O_2, CO_2, N_2, SO_2)

gypsum

reactions in FGD
$CaCO_3 + SO_2 \rightarrow CaSO_3 + CO_2$

$2CaSO_3 + O_2 + 2H_2O \rightarrow 2CaSO_4.2H_2O$

cleaned gas (O_2, N_2, CO_2)

air

limestone slurry ($CaCO_3$, H_2O)

Carbon and silicon

This section covers the following ideas:

- the carbon cycle
- the oxides of carbon
- carbonates and hydrogencarbonates
- hard water
  - causes
  - water softening
- silicon as a semiconductor.

			H				0
I	II	III	IV	V	VI	VII	He
Li	Be	B	C	N	O	F	Ne
		Al	Si	P			
		Ga	Ge	As			
		In	Sn	Sb			
		Tl	Pb	Bi			

the Earth's crust. It occurs there in two forms, **diamond** and **graphite**. However, this is misleading. There are more compounds of carbon than of *all* the other elements taken together. This wide variety is crucial to the existence of the complex molecules of life (for example carbohydrates, proteins, fats and nucleic acids). The transfer of carbon atoms from living to non-living forms is extremely important. It is linked to the transfer of energy and the basic processes by which life survives on this planet. The exchange of carbon centres around two processes, **respiration** (combustion) and **photosynthesis**, and one compound, **carbon dioxide** (CO_2).

The global cycle involving these processes is known as the **carbon cycle** (figure 8.25). The cycle centres on the apparently insignificant amount (0.03%) of CO_2 in the atmosphere.

> The gas which constitutes the raw material of life … is not one of the principal components of air but rather a ridiculous remnant, an 'impurity' thirty times less abundant than argon, which nobody even notices …
>
> *Primo Levi, The Periodic Table*

8.16 Carbon molecules in space

Deep in space, interstellar clouds containing a wide range of molecules have been detected. Attempts to understand the formation of these molecules led to the discovery of a third form of carbon. Between diamond (the hardest material known) and graphite (one of the softest) lie the **fullerenes** (page 95). The discovery of fullerenes has opened up whole new areas of chemistry and physics with many potential applications in industry. Carbon has now replaced sulphur as the element with the largest number of different forms (allotropes).

8.17 The carbon cycle

Only a small amount of carbon occurs as the **native** element in

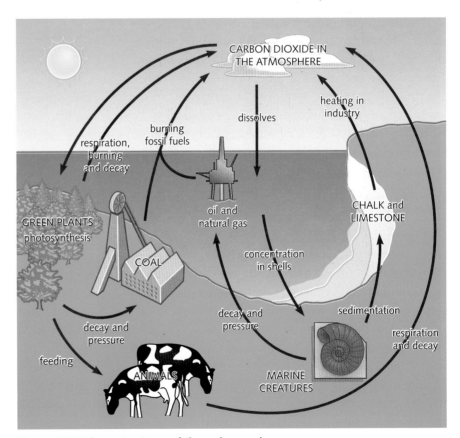

Figure 8.25 The main stages of the carbon cycle.

The levels of the minor constituents in the air can be measured as a percentage (that is, parts per hundred). But the 'numbers' are small and can have many zeros after the decimal point, as shown in a question in chapter 1 (question 1.11 on page 25). Often, such small amounts are quoted as 'parts per million' (ppm) or 'parts per billion' (ppb). (A billion is a thousand million.) So, a CO_2 level of 0.03% is the same as 300 ppm, and a dinitrogen oxide level of 0.000 03% is the same as 300 ppb. Even changes at these very low concentrations can have environmental effects (question 8.9).

Let us consider how the small, but important, level of carbon dioxide is maintained in the atmosphere.

Removal of atmospheric CO_2

Carbon dioxide is removed from the atmosphere by **photosynthesis**. Plants take in CO_2 from the air, and water from the soil, to make glucose. Photosynthesis takes place in chloroplasts in the green leaves of plants. This process uses light energy from the Sun 'trapped' by **chlorophyll**, the green pigment in leaves:

$$6CO_2 + 6H_2O \xrightarrow[\text{chlorophyll}]{\text{sunlight}} C_6H_{12}O_6 + 6O_2$$

Within the plant, glucose is first converted into starch. Then the carbon atoms are used to build proteins and the other complex compounds needed for structure and life. The plants provide food for the animals on Earth, including humans, and so the cycle extends to all living forms. In geological history, plants that died, in some areas, built up into thick layers of **peat**. Over a longer time, these layers were submerged by movements of the Earth's crust. The layers were crushed and heated to form various types of **coal** (see page 331). Coal is one of the major fossil fuels that we use as an energy source.

Vegetation is involved in the land-based removal of CO_2 from the air. But the oceans also remove CO_2. Carbon dioxide dissolves in water better than other gases of the air. However, this is not the only means of CO_2 removal. Tiny marine plants (phytoplankton) are able to remove CO_2 from the atmosphere into the oceans for photosynthesis. Included among these microscopic marine creatures are the coccolithophorids. These single-cell **algae** are covered with tiny scales. They use the dissolved CO_2 to make their scales from calcium carbonate.

They are also able to use the dissolved salts present in the oceans. Some of these salts come from the erosion and weathering of cliffs and landforms by the ceaseless pounding of the tidal seas. When these marine organisms die, they sink to the ocean depths and are buried in the sediments. Over geological time and under immense pressure, earlier sediments have been converted into limestone and chalk. The 'white cliffs of Dover' are made of chalk built from the shells of dead prehistoric sea creatures. Under different geological conditions, the dead bodies of these marine creatures also form **crude oil** and **natural gas** – the other two major fossil fuels (see page 327).

Production of atmospheric CO_2

We have considered the various ways in which CO_2 is removed from the atmosphere – but how is it replaced? Animals and plants give out CO_2 during (aerobic) **respiration**:

glucose + oxygen $\rightarrow$ carbon dioxide + water

$$C_6H_{12}O_6 + 6O_2 \rightarrow 6CO_2 + 6H_2O$$

Respiration releases energy for use by living cells and returns CO_2 to the atmosphere. Dead animals and plants decay, providing a source of nutrients for bacteria to live on. This provides a further route for carbon atoms to re-enter the cycle.

Carbon dioxide and a few other gases in the atmosphere, such as methane and water vapour, are known as 'greenhouse' gases. They help to trap some of the energy from the Sun which strikes the Earth and prevent it from being radiated back into space. This is known as the **greenhouse effect** and it is essential for life on Earth. If this effect did not happen, the Earth's surface would be cooler and would not be able to support living things.

The burning of carbon-containing fuels such as wood, peat and fossil fuels returns carbon dioxide to the air. The roasting of limestone also releases CO_2. The increasing use of fossil fuels in the developed world and the deforestation of large areas of tropical rainforest have led to an increase in the levels of CO_2 in the air which may be causing an imbalance in the carbon cycle. Increased atmospheric CO_2 is thought to be one factor contributing to an **increased greenhouse effect** which may be causing **global warming**.

8.18 The oxides of carbon

Carbon forms two oxides – carbon monoxide (CO) and carbon dioxide (CO_2). Both can be produced when organic materials and fossil fuels burn. Carbon dioxide is the product when there is a sufficient supply of air (oxygen), for example burning natural gas in a domestic gas fire:

$$CH_4(g) + 2O_2(g) \rightarrow CO_2(g) + 2H_2O(g)$$

However, carbon monoxide can be produced when the oxygen supply is limited:

$$CH_4(g) + 1\tfrac{1}{2}O_2(g) \rightarrow CO(g) + 2H_2O(g)$$

an equation that is more usually presented doubled to remove the fraction:

$$2CH_4(g) + 3O_2(g) \rightarrow 2CO(g) + 4H_2O(g)$$

Carbon monoxide

Carbon monoxide is a dangerous gas to produce in such a situation at home (figure 8.26). It is colourless and has no smell, but is very poisonous. It interferes with the transport of oxygen around the body by the **haemoglobin** in red blood cells.

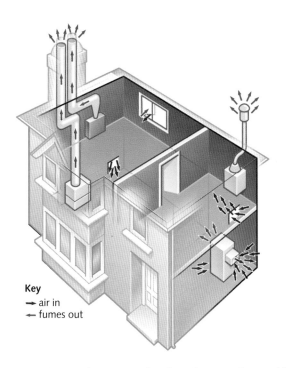

Key
→ air in
← fumes out

Figure 8.26 Gas appliances need to breathe in and out – like you! The production of carbon monoxide in the home by burning natural gas without proper ventilation is dangerous. The oxygen needed may come in from outside the house or from a well-ventilated room. The fumes need to be taken straight out of the house.

Instead of oxygen, it is carbon monoxide that bonds chemically to haemoglobin, and the binding is **irreversible**. Carbon monoxide is also present in the exhaust fumes of cars due to the incomplete combustion of petrol (gasoline). Catalytic converters are designed to reduce the levels of these carbon monoxide emissions. The use of oxygenated fuels such as 'gasohol' also lowers the amount of CO in car exhaust fumes.

Carbon monoxide is a colourless gas that burns with a blue flame:

$$2CO(g) + O_2(g) \rightarrow 2CO_2(g)$$

The **properties** of **carbon monoxide**:

- colourless gas, without smell
- burns with blue flame
- strong reducing agent
- very poisonous
- interferes with oxygen transport around the body.

Its affinity for oxygen – that is its ability to bond rapidly and easily with oxygen – makes it a strong **reducing agent**. It is the effective reducing agent in the blast furnace extraction of iron from iron ore (see page 278):

$$Fe_2O_3(s) + 3CO(g) \rightarrow 2Fe(s) + 3CO_2(g)$$

Carbon dioxide

Carbon dioxide is a globally important gas. It can be prepared in the laboratory by reacting marble chips (a form of calcium carbonate, $CaCO_3$) with dilute hydrochloric acid:

calcium carbonate + hydrochloric acid
→ calcium chloride + water + carbon dioxide

$$CaCO_3(s) + 2HCl(aq)$$
$$\rightarrow CaCl_2(aq) + H_2O(l) + CO_2(g)$$

Carbon dioxide is denser than air and can be collected by downward delivery (see page 350). Since it is only slightly soluble, it can also be collected over water (figure 8.27 on page 228). The loss of some carbon dioxide by dissolving can be reduced by using warm water in which it is less soluble.

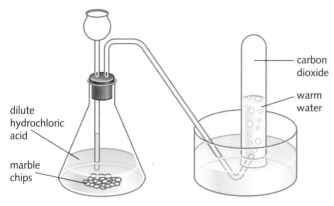

Figure 8.27 Preparing carbon dioxide in the laboratory.

Carbon dioxide is a colourless gas. When it dissolves in water, some of the gas reacts to produce a weak acid, **carbonic acid** (H_2CO_3). The solution has a pH between 4 and 6:

$$CO_2(g) + H_2O(l) \rightarrow H_2CO_3(aq)$$

Unpolluted rain water, and distilled water that has stood in the laboratory, have a pH below 7 because of dissolved CO_2 from the air. Carbonated soft drinks, some beers and champagne have more CO_2 in solution because the gas is dissolved under pressure.

Carbon dioxide is useful as a fire extinguisher because it does not support the combustion of most materials. The fact that it is denser than air means that a layer of carbon dioxide covers the fire and starves it of oxygen. The suffocating effect of carbon dioxide was tragically shown in West Africa during 1986. Lake Nyos in Cameroon is a volcanic lake. On the 21 August, the volcano released a vast amount of carbon dioxide during the night. The gas burst out through the lake and hung like a cloud over a nearby village. All 1200 villagers were suffocated in their sleep.

Some very strongly burning substances, for example magnesium, will continue to burn in carbon dioxide:

magnesium + carbon dioxide
→ magnesium oxide + carbon

$$2Mg(s) + CO_2(g) \rightarrow 2MgO(s) + C(s)$$

The burning reactive metal decomposes the carbon dioxide. The reaction is an example of a **redox reaction** – the reactive metal acts as a reducing agent and is itself oxidised.

The chemical test for carbon dioxide is to bubble the gas through **limewater** (calcium hydroxide solution). A white precipitate of calcium carbonate is formed:

$$CO_2(g) + Ca(OH)_2(aq) \rightarrow CaCO_3(s) + H_2O(l)$$

The precipitate causes the solution to appear *milky*. If more carbon dioxide is bubbled through this suspension, then the precipitate re-dissolves. This is because soluble calcium hydrogencarbonate is formed:

$$CaCO_3(s) + H_2O(l) + CO_2(g) \rightarrow$$
$$Ca(HCO_3)_2(aq)$$

This reaction has consequences for the mineral content of the water supply in certain regions (see 'Hard and soft water' on page 232). Limestone and chalk are important geological forms of calcium carbonate.

The **properties** of **carbon dioxide**:

- colourless gas
- denser than air
- slightly soluble in water
- puts out fires
- turns limewater milky.

8.19 Carbonates and hydrogencarbonates

Metal carbonates

Carbonates are an important range of compounds. They are all **normal salts** of carbonic acid (H_2CO_3) and contain the carbonate ion (CO_3^{2-}). Several of them occur naturally in rock formations. Limestone, chalk and marble are different mineral forms of calcium carbonate; malachite is copper(II) carbonate; and dolomite, which occurs notably in northern Italy, contains magnesium carbonate.

Because carbonates are the salts of carbonic acid, they are sources of carbon dioxide. The carbon dioxide can be released in two ways: by reaction with acids or by thermal decomposition.

All carbonates react with acids to form salts, carbon dioxide and water. For example

copper(II) carbonate + hydrochloric acid
→ copper(II) chloride + carbon dioxide + water

$$CuCO_3(s) + 2HCl(aq)$$
$$\rightarrow CuCl_2(aq) + CO_2(g) + H_2O(l)$$

The reaction between dilute hydrochloric acid and marble chips (calcium carbonate) is the usual way to prepare carbon dioxide in the laboratory. Because all carbonates react in this way, this reaction is used as the test for carbonate ions in an unknown substance. The carbon dioxide produced causes an **effervescence** (a rapid production of gas bubbles). When the gas is bubbled through limewater, a chalky white precipitate is formed.

Most metal carbonates decompose when heated to form the metal oxide and carbon dioxide. For example

$$copper(\text{II}) \ carbonate \xrightarrow{\text{heat}} copper(\text{II}) \ oxide$$
$$+ carbon \ dioxide$$

$$\underset{\text{green powder}}{CaCO_3(s)} \xrightarrow{\text{heat}} \underset{\text{black powder}}{CuO(s)} + CO_2(g)$$

The decomposition of limestone to form lime (calcium oxide, CaO) is an industrially important process (see page 202).

It is only the carbonates of the most reactive metals that do *not* decompose with heating. Lithium carbonate does decompose, but the carbonates of the other Group I metals, including sodium carbonate and potassium carbonate, do not decompose when heated. All carbonates are insoluble in water except for sodium, potassium and ammonium carbonates. The insolubility of calcium carbonate is of natural importance. The protective shells of certain animals and organisms are produced from calcium carbonate. The hardness of water in certain regions is due to acidic rain water passing down through rocks containing calcium carbonate (see 'Hard and soft water' on page 231).

Summary of core material

You should know that:

- carbon is important as the basis of the complex molecules involved in living organisms
- carbon atoms are recycled between living and non-living forms through the carbon cycle
- two important chemical reactions in this cycle are photosynthesis and respiration
- carbon forms two oxides – carbon monoxide (CO) and carbon dioxide (CO_2)
- carbon monoxide is a poisonous gas and is a strong reducing agent

- carbon dioxide is a crucial link in the carbon cycle and is a 'greenhouse gas'
- carbon dioxide can be made by reacting a metal carbonate with an acid and does not support the combustion of most substances
- carbon dioxide dissolves in water to form a weak acid, carbonic acid, and the normal salts of this acid, the carbonates, are important minerals.

8.8 The diagram shows part of the carbon cycle.

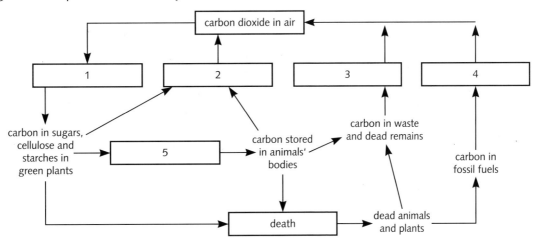

Using the best words from the following list, write down the words that go in boxes 1, 2, 3, 4 and 5 in the diagram: [5]

combustion   decomposition   feeding
photosynthesis ·   respiration   transpiration

(MEG, 1995)

8.9

(a) The graphs below show the changes in the levels of three 'greenhouse effect' gases in the atmosphere since 1975.

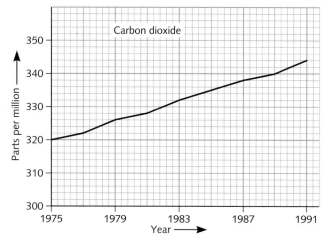

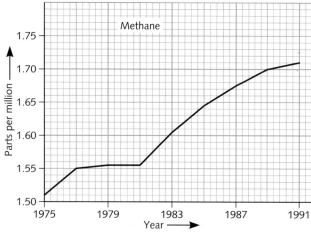

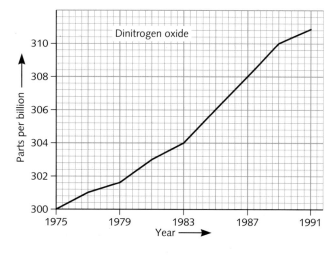

(i) What is meant by the term 'greenhouse effect' gas? [2]
(ii) Which of these 'greenhouse effect' gases has shown the greatest percentage increase since 1975? [1]

(b) Choose *one* of the gases shown in the graphs and explain why its concentration has risen. [2]

(c) It is believed that a continued rise in the levels of 'greenhouse effect' gases would affect the Earth's climate and the amount of land available for cultivation. Suggest reasons for this. [3]

(ULEAC, 1994)

8.10 This question is mainly concerned with air pollution.

(a) Increased amounts of carbon dioxide in the atmosphere are thought to be causing an increase in the 'greenhouse effect', which will cause global warming. In a class discussion a student suggested that carbon dioxide from power stations could be removed from the gases produced when coal or fuel oil burns. The gases would be passed up towers down which a mixture of calcium hydroxide and water falls:

$$Ca(OH)_2(aq) + CO_2(g) \rightarrow CaCO_3(s) + H_2O(l)$$

Calcium hydroxide is made by roasting limestone:

$$CaCO_3(s) \rightarrow CaO(s) + CO_2(g)$$

and then adding water to the residue:

$$CaO(s) + H_2O(l) \rightarrow Ca(OH)_2(s)$$

(i) How are large amounts of carbon dioxide produced by power stations?
(ii) Does the suggested method of absorbing carbon dioxide seem promising? Explain your answer.
(iii) The first of the three equations represents a reaction commonly used in school laboratories. For what is the reaction used? [5]

(b) Car exhausts contain additional pollutant gases including carbon monoxide, CO, and nitrogen monoxide, NO.
(i) How is carbon monoxide formed in the engine?
(ii) What is the source of the nitrogen in the nitrogen monoxide?
(iii) Which of the gases coming from the exhaust contributes to 'acid rain'?
(iv) What is particularly dangerous about carbon monoxide? [5]

(c) Some vehicles are fitted with a catalytic converter, which changes the exhaust gases into a more acceptable form of emission.

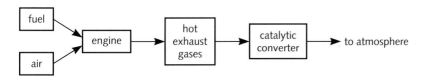

One design of catalytic converter is shown below.

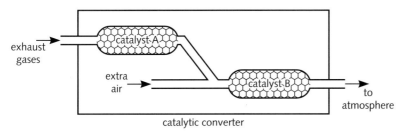

catalytic converter

Each of the catalysts, which only work at a fairly high temperature, brings about one of the following reactions:

$$2CO(g) + O_2(g) \rightarrow 2CO_2(g)$$

$$2NO(g) \rightarrow N_2(g) + O_2(g)$$

(i) What is a catalyst?
(ii) Which of the gases is removed (converted) by catalyst B? Give a reason for your answer.
(iii) If the volume of the nitrogen monoxide, NO, was much greater than the volume of carbon monoxide, CO, one feature of the design could be removed. Which part of the converter could be removed? Explain why.
(iv) One catalyst is platinum, which is coated on aluminium beads. State *two* reasons for coating beads rather than using platinum on its own.
(v) If a large excess of air were drawn into the engine with the fuel, any carbon monoxide which was formed in the hot engine would burn away. This would avoid the problem of carbon monoxide. Suggest why this is not done. (*Hint*: Many engine parts in contact with the very hot gases are made of iron.) [10]

(ULEAC, 1993)

EXTENSION

Metal hydrogencarbonates

Hydrogencarbonates are all **acid salts** of carbonic acid (H_2CO_3) and contain the hydrogencarbonate ion (HCO_3^-). Most hydrogencarbonates are unstable and are only found in solution (in water). Sodium hydrogencarbonate ($NaHCO_3$) is the most common solid hydrogencarbonate. It is used in indigestion tablets because it reacts with the excess stomach acid (HCl) that is a cause of indigestion:

$$NaHCO_3(s) + HCl(aq) \rightarrow NaCl(aq) + H_2O(l) + CO_2(g)$$

Sodium hydrogencarbonate is used as 'baking soda'. It is added to 'plain' flour to make 'self-raising' flour. When heated, the sodium hydrogencarbonate in the flour decomposes. This produces carbon dioxide gas, causing the bread or cakes to rise:

sodium hydrogencarbonate $\xrightarrow{\text{heat}}$ sodium carbonate + water + carbon dioxide

$$2NaHCO_3(s) \xrightarrow{\text{heat}} Na_2CO_3(s) + H_2O(l) + CO_2(g)$$

Calcium and magnesium hydrogencarbonates are two of the hydrogencarbonates that are only stable in solution. They are the chemical compounds responsible for the hardness of water.

8.20 Hard and soft water

In many supermarkets, it is possible to buy limescale remover. This is often a solution of methanoic acid (formic acid). This weak acid is strong enough to react with the limescale but not with metal. But what is limescale? It is produced inside water pipes and kettles in areas where the water is hard. Another effect of hard water is that it makes soap difficult to lather. Instead, the water becomes cloudy. This cloudiness is caused by the formation of a solid precipitate or 'scum'. Hardness of water is caused by the presence of higher-than-usual levels of calcium (Ca^{2+}) and/or magnesium (Mg^{2+}) ions in the water. Hard water can cause inconvenience in the home and can be a major problem in industry. A look at a map of hard and soft water areas in England and Wales gives a clue as to why the problem arises (figure 8.28).

Rain water dissolves carbon dioxide as it falls through the atmosphere. This produces a weakly acidic solution of carbonic acid. As this solution passes over and through rocks containing chalk, limestone or dolomite, the rain water very slowly dissolves them:

calcium carbonate + water + carbon dioxide
→ calcium hydrogencarbonate

$$CaCO_3(s) + H_2O(l) + CO_2(g) \rightarrow Ca(HCO_3)_2(aq)$$
limestone rocks   acidic rain water   causes hard water

This reaction is one we have met before: it is the reaction that causes the precipitate to re-dissolve when the limewater test for carbon dioxide is carried on for a long time. Some of the rocks may contain gypsum ($CaSO_4 \cdot 2H_2O$), anhydrite ($CaSO_4$) or kieserite ($MgSO_4 \cdot H_2O$), which can dissolve to a limited extent in water. The presence of these dissolved substances also causes the water to be hard.

Temporary and permanent hardness

The hard water in some areas can be softened simply by boiling the water, but this is not true in all cases. This means that the hardness in water can be divided into two types – temporary and permanent hardness.

Temporary hardness can be removed by boiling the water. It is caused by the presence of calcium hydrogencarbonate or magnesium hydrogencarbonate in the water. When the water is boiled, these hydrogencarbonates decompose:

calcium hydrogencarbonate $\xrightarrow{\text{heat}}$
calcium carbonate + water + carbon dioxide

$$Ca(HCO_3)_2(aq) \xrightarrow{\text{heat}} CaCO_3(s) + H_2O(l) + CO_2(g)$$

This decomposition causes the 'furring' of kettles, hot water pipes (figure 8.29) and shower-heads. The **limescale** that forms is calcium carbonate.

A very impressive demonstration of this reaction is the formation of **stalactites** and **stalagmites** in limestone caves. These spectacular formations are caused by the slow decomposition of hard water to form pillars of calcium carbonate. Evaporation of water, dripping over thousands of years, produces these imposing structures.

Permanent hardness cannot be removed by boiling. It is caused by the presence of calcium sulphate and magnesium sulphate. These sulphates do not decompose when heated.

The water supply in an area may be affected by both temporary and permanent hardness. The total hardness of the water supply depends on the total concentration of Ca^{2+} and Mg^{2+} ions.

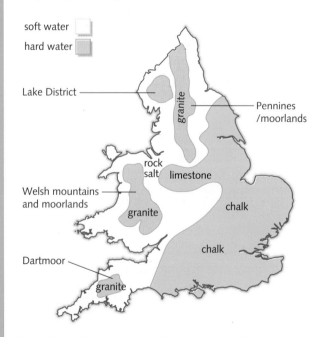

Figure 8.28 The hard and soft water areas of England and Wales.

Figure 8.29 Hard water causes the blocking of hot water pipes with limescale (calcium carbonate).

- **Hard water** is caused by the presence of high levels of calcium and magnesium ions. Hardness of water can be divided into two types, temporary and permanent.
- **Temporary hardness** is caused by $Ca(HCO_3)_2$ and/or $Mg(HCO_3)_2$ and *can* be removed by boiling.
- **Permanent hardness** is caused by $CaSO_4$ and/or $MgSO_4$ and *cannot* be removed by boiling.

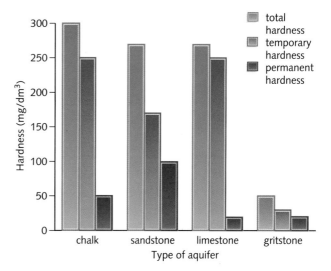

Figure 8.30 The hardness of water from various types of aquifer.

A concentration over 150 milligrams per cubic decimetre (mg/dm^3) is considered hard. The upper limit allowed is $300\,mg/dm^3$. Figure 8.30 gives information on water obtained from different types of aquifer. Various mineral waters are often hard waters, showing that some of the effects of hardness are healthy.

When **soap** is used with hard water, a 'scum' forms on the surface. This is the result of a precipitation reaction. Soaps are the sodium or potassium salts of long-chain organic acids (see page 321). These are made from animal fats by treatment with alkali. A common soap is sodium stearate (Na^+St^-, where $St^- = C_{17}H_{35}COO^-$). Sodium stearate is soluble in water, but calcium stearate is not. When soap is mixed with hard water, a white precipitate of calcium stearate is formed:

sodium stearate + calcium hydrogencarbonate

soap   in hard water

$\rightarrow$ calcium stearate + sodium hydrogencarbonate

scum

$$2NaSt(aq) + Ca(HCO_3)_2(aq)$$
$$\rightarrow CaSt_2(s) + 2NaHCO_3(aq)$$

The ionic equation for this reaction is:

$$Ca^{2+}(aq) + 2St^-(aq) \rightarrow CaSt_2(s)$$

This means that some soap is wasted when washing and more must be used for an efficient wash. The amount of soap needed to just produce a froth can be used to estimate the hardness of water. The problems of scum formation only occur with soaps. Soapless detergents do not produce a scum.

Advantages and disadvantages of hard water

There are disadvantages to having a water supply that is hard, particularly for industry. This is why water softening methods are available commercially. However, there are some advantages to hard water too. Table 8.5 gives a summary of these disadvantages and advantages.

Table 8.5 **The disadvantages and advantages of hard water supplies**

Disadvantages	Advantages
wastes soap	improves the taste of water
causes limescale in kettles and water boilers	calcium ions in hard water used by body for bones and teeth
causes hot water pipes to become blocked	coats lead water pipes* with a precipitate of lead sulphate or carbonate; cuts down on lead poisoning
spoils the finish of some fabrics	good for brewing beer

* Many cities in Europe and the USA still have extensive lead piping in their water supply systems.

Removal of hardness

- *Boiling*

  Temporary hardness can easily be removed by boiling. However, this does not offer an easy solution for the treatment of a large-scale water supply, nor does it remove permanent hardness.

- *Distillation*

  Distillation removes all impurities from water. Distilled water can be bought in supermarkets for use in steam irons. However, this method is too expensive to be used on a large scale.

- *Precipitation*

  'Washing soda' (hydrated sodium carbonate crystals, $Na_2CO_3 \cdot 10H_2O$) can be used to precipitate calcium and magnesium ions from the water before washing with soap:

  $$Ca^{2+}(aq) + CO_3^{2-}(aq) \rightarrow CaCO_3(s)$$

  calcium ions   carbonate ions   calcium carbonate

  Washing soda was often used in the days when all washing was done with soap.

- *Softeners*

  Many modern washing powders now have softeners added to them. They are often phosphates. The phosphate ions react with calcium ions to form calcium phosphate and remove the hardness. However, phosphates can cause a pollution problem in rivers and streams. The problem is similar to that caused by fertilisers when they run off into rivers. The increased use of soapless detergents removes the problems of scum formation with hard water.

- *Ion exchange*

  The most convenient way to soften water is to use an ion exchange column. The water entering a house or factory is run through a column containing an ion exchange resin (figure 8.31). The resin beads are porous and contain sodium ions. When the hard water runs through the resin, the calcium and magnesium ions in the water are exchanged for the sodium ions on the column. This removes calcium ions from the water. They are replaced by sodium ions, which do not make the water hard. When all the sodium ions have been removed from the resin, it is regenerated by pouring a strong solution of salt through it.

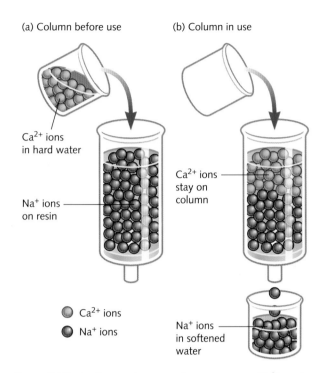

(a) Column before use   (b) Column in use

Ca^{2+} ions in hard water

Na^+ ions on resin

Ca^{2+} ions stay on column

Ca^{2+} ions

Na^+ ions

Na^+ ions in softened water

Figure 8.31 *An ion exchange column removes Ca^{2+} and Mg^{2+} ions from water. It replaces them with Na^+ ions.*

8.21 Silicon and silica

Silicon is an element that is usually classified as a non-metal. It has a tetrahedral giant covalent structure very similar to diamond. It combines with oxygen to form silicon(IV) oxide (silica, SiO_2), which also has a giant covalent structure.

Silicon has become a vital element in the modern electronics industry. It is an unusual element in being a **semiconductor**: its behaviour is between that of a conductor and that of an insulator. More accurately, silicon is categorised as a **semi-metal** or **metalloid**.

The electronics industry demands very pure large crystals of the element for making silicon chips. These are produced by a technique called **zone refining**. This method depends on the fact that, when a dilute solution is cooled, only the pure solvent crystallises. It is a technique used widely to produce very pure crystals of metalloids such as silicon and germanium. When a single crystal of silicon is 'pulled' from molten silicon, it contains less than one atom of impurity per billion silicon atoms.

Summary of extension material

You should know that:

- carbonic acid also forms acid salts known as hydrogencarbonates
- the formation of soluble calcium and magnesium hydrogencarbonates by the action of rain water on rocks such as limestone is a major cause of the hardness of water in some areas
- hardness of water is caused by higher-than-normal levels of calcium (Ca^{2+}) and/or magnesium (Mg^{2+}) ions in the water

- there are two types of hardness of water – temporary hardness and permanent hardness
- the most effective way of softening water is by ion exchange
- silicon is another important element in Group IV and is purified by zone refining for use in the electronics industry.

8.11 A report from the public analyst on the drinking water of a city gave the following information: 'On average in 1000 kg of water there are 250 g of dissolved substances.' The table shows some of these substances.

Substance	Number of grams of substance in 1000 kg of water
Permanent hardness due to calcium compounds	112
Temporary hardness due to calcium compounds	74
Chloride in compounds	15.5
Chlorine gas	0.023
Fluoride in compounds	0.013
Nitrogen in compounds	0.12
Oxygen gas	0.95

(a) When rain water soaks through some types of rock it becomes hard.
   (i) Name *three* naturally occurring rocks which cause hardness in water. [3]
   (ii) Name *two* compounds which, when dissolved, make water hard. [2]

(b) (i) What is the total amount of hardness in 1000 kg of water? [1]
   (ii) How may temporary hardness be removed from water? [1]

(c) Give *one* advantage and *one* disadvantage of hard water. [2]

(d) Describe how the following behave when shaken in hard water:
   (i) soap, [1]
   (ii) soapless detergent. [1]

(e) Give the name of a nitrogen-containing compound which could be dissolved in the water. [1]

(f) (i) In the drinking water, where does the dissolved oxygen come from? [1]
   (ii) What happens to the dissolved oxygen when the water is boiled? [1]

(ULEAC, 1995)

8.12 Germanium (Ge) is an element in Group IV which has similar properties and structure to diamond and silicon.

(a) Germanium is obtained by heating germanium(IV) oxide in hydrogen. The main use of the element is in semiconductors and it is needed in a high state of purity. Slight traces of impurities change its electrical properties, e.g. resistance.

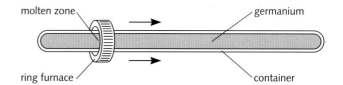

molten zone   germanium

ring furnace   container

Germanium is purified by zone refining. A ring furnace is moved along the rod in the direction shown. The high temperature inside the ring melts the impure germanium. A solution of the impurities in molten germanium is formed. As the ring furnace moves along the rod, the molten zone travels with it to the end of the rod.

The principle of zone refining is that when a dilute solution is cooled only the pure solvent crystallises.

   (i) Write an equation for the reduction of germanium(IV) oxide to germanium by hydrogen. [1]
   (ii) What is the usual laboratory method for showing that a solid is pure? [1]

235

(iii) Suggest a better method than the one given in part (ii) for testing the purity of germanium. [1]

(iv) The furnace has passed along the rod once. Where does the germanium have the highest purity? Also where is the greatest concentration of impurities? [2]

(v) Suggest how the principle of zone refining could be used to provide pure water from sea water. [2]

(b) (i) By considering the position of the element in the Periodic Table, predict *two* physical properties of germanium. [1]

(ii) Germanium(IV) oxide is a white crystalline solid which has a high melting point. Describe its structure.

(iii) Draw a diagram which shows the arrangement of the valency (outer) electrons in a compound of germanium and chlorine. [2]

(iv) A compound of germanium and hydrogen contains 96.05% of germanium. Calculate its *empirical* formula. If the relative molecular mass of this compound is 152, what is its *molecular* formula? Draw its *structural* formula. [4]
(Relative atomic mass for germanium = 73)

(IGCSE, 1988)

Nitrogen and ammonia

This section covers the following ideas:

- the nitrogen cycle
- manufacture of ammonia and nitric acid
- laboratory preparation of ammonia and its properties
- nitric acid and its properties.

8.22 Nitrogen

Nitrogen is all around us. It makes up about 78% of the air we breathe. At any moment we are breathing the gas in and then out again without any chemical change. Nitrogen is a colourless gas, without any smell, and is very unreactive. It has a very low boiling point of −196°C. The element has the formula N_2. The molecules in the gas consist of two nitrogen atoms covalently bonded together by a triple bond (see figure 3.8 on page 74). The triple bond is very strong and requires a large amount of energy to break it, so a nitrogen molecule is very **stable**. Only very high temperatures, or an electric

spark, will cause it to react with oxygen. This occurs during lightning flashes in the atmosphere, and in the internal combustion engine of a car. Oxides of nitrogen (NO_x) are formed, for example nitrogen monoxide (nitrogen(II) oxide, NO) and nitrogen dioxide (nitrogen(IV) oxide, NO_2). These gases dissolve in rain and make it acidic. Catalytic converters are designed to change these oxides back to nitrogen and oxygen.

Nitrogen is obtained industrially by the **fractional distillation** of liquid air (see section 8.9 on page 217). It has a large number of uses. Its major use is in the production of ammonia and nitric acid. It is used as a refrigerant for freezing food. Liquid nitrogen is also used to store living cells and biologically important tissues. A wide range of animal cells, from skin cells to sperm, can be stored intact at the low temperature of this liquid. The cells can be revived and they function properly. A whole range of methods, from skin grafting for burns victims to in vitro fertilisation (test tube babies), rely on the use of liquid nitrogen. Because of its stability, nitrogen gas is used as an unreactive atmosphere for various potentially dangerous industrial processes. It is also used in food packaging to keep food fresh, for example in crisp packets.

The **properties** of **nitrogen**:

- colourless gas, without smell
- very unreactive
- very low boiling point
- needed in usable form by plants for growth.

8.23 The nitrogen cycle

Nitrogen is essential for all life. It is present in proteins and nucleic acids, and so is essential for growth and good health. As with carbon, another essential element, there is a global cycle known as the **nitrogen cycle**. Nitrogen atoms are cycled between various forms of life, and between the soil and the atmosphere, by a series of connected chemical changes (figure 8.32). Animals obtain the nitrogen they need for making proteins by feeding on plants and other animals. Most plants obtain the nitrogen they require from the soil, where it is found as **nitrates**. Nitrates are the soluble salts of nitric acid. The solubility of nitrates is important, as they are absorbed in solution by plants through their root systems. Nitrates occur in the soil through the effect of lightning on atmospheric nitrogen and oxygen, and through the decay of dead plants and animals. There are also bacteria in the soil that can convert ('fix') nitrogen in the air directly into nitrates. These are called **nitrogen-fixing bacteria**. Some plants are also able to 'fix' atmospheric nitrogen because their roots have nodules that contain nitrogen-fixing bacteria. These plants are known as leguminous plants or **legumes**. They include beans and clover.

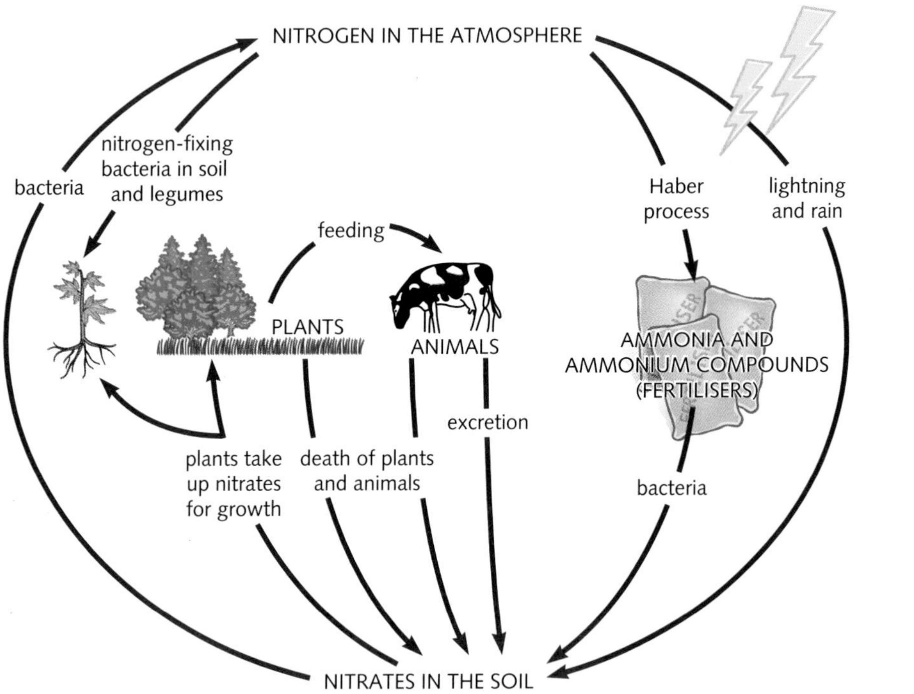

When soils are heavily cultivated, eventually they do not have enough nitrogen for good plant growth (they become **nitrogen-deficient**). Crops are harvested and removed rather than left to decay. Nitrates are used up or washed out of the soil by rain. Without decay, the replacement of nitrates in the soil is insufficient and the soil becomes infertile. Farmers need to add substances containing nitrates to the soil. Such substances are known as **fertilisers**. Organic fertilisers, such as farmyard manure or compost, can be used, but intensive agriculture has led to the production of artificial fertilisers on a very large scale. One of the most commonly used fertilisers is **ammonium nitrate**, which is made from ammonia gas and nitric acid.

8.24 Ammonia

The Haber process

The problem of artificially fixing nitrogen was solved by Fritz Haber in 1908. He discovered a way to make nitrogen react with hydrogen directly:

nitrogen + hydrogen $\rightarrow$ ammonia

$$N_2(g) + 3H_2(g) \rightarrow 2NH_3(g)$$

Carl Bosch, a chemical engineer, adapted Haber's conditions to an industrial scale and the first plant was in production in 1913. The process is summarised in figure 8.33 on page 238. The raw materials used for the process are:

- air – which supplies the nitrogen

- natural gas (methane) – which is reacted with steam to produce hydrogen and is also used as the heating fuel for the system

- iron – which is used in a finely divided form as the catalyst.

Figure 8.32 The main stages of the nitrogen cycle.

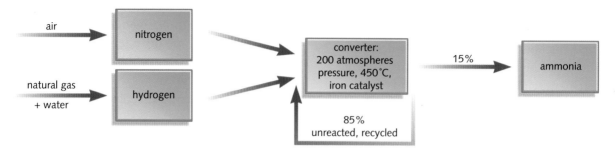

Figure 8.33 A flow chart for the Haber process for ammonia production.

Making ammonia in the laboratory

Small amounts of ammonia gas are produced when any ammonium salt is heated with an alkali. In the normal laboratory preparation (figure 8.34), a solid mixture of calcium hydroxide and ammonium chloride is heated:

    calcium hydroxide + ammonium chloride
    → calcium chloride + water + ammonia

$$Ca(OH)_2(s) + 2NH_4Cl(s)$$
$$\rightarrow CaCl_2(s) + 2H_2O(g) + 2NH_3(g)$$

The water vapour is removed by passing the gas through a drying tube containing calcium oxide. In general, this reaction between ammonium salts and alkali is used as the chemical test for ammonium ions. Sodium hydroxide solution is used as the alkali. The ammonia produced is detected because it turns moist red litmus paper blue.

The properties and uses of ammonia

Ammonia is a colourless gas with a distinctive sharp smell. It has the formula NH_3. It is less dense than air and is very soluble in water. The solution produced is a weak alkali. The high solubility of ammonia in water can be shown using the 'fountain experiment' (figure 8.35). As the first drop of water reaches the top of the tube, some of the ammonia dissolves in it. This reduces the pressure in the upper flask and water rises up the tube, creating a fountain. The presence of an indicator shows that the ammonia solution is alkaline. A similar experiment can be done with hydrogen chloride or sulphur dioxide – but these gases produce acidic solutions.

The **properties** of **ammonia**:

- colourless gas
- distinctive smell
- less dense than air
- very soluble in water to give an alkaline solution.

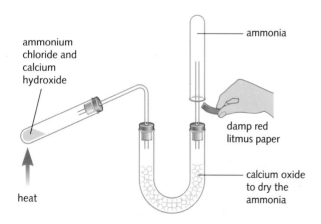

Figure 8.34 Making ammonia in the laboratory.

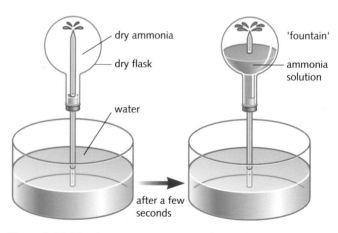

Figure 8.35 The fountain experiment shows that ammonia is very soluble.

Ammonia is distinctive in producing an alkaline solution. It dissolves so well in water because it reacts. The solution is partially dissociated into ions, so ammonia is only a weak alkali:

$$NH_3(g) + H_2O(aq) \rightleftharpoons NH_4^+(aq) + OH^-(aq)$$

Ammonia solution or gas will react with an acid to produce an ammonium salt, for example

ammonia + sulphuric acid → ammonium sulphate

$$2NH_3(g) + H_2SO_4(aq) \rightarrow (NH_4)_2SO_4(aq)$$

ammonia + hydrochloric acid
   → ammonium chloride

$$NH_3(aq) + HCl(aq) \rightarrow NH_4Cl(aq)$$

The white smoke formed when NH_3 and HCl fumes meet can be used as a simple test for ammonia.

Ammonium salts are ionic compounds containing the ammonium (NH_4^+) ion. The salts are all soluble in water.

The uses of ammonia are summarised in figure 8.36. The majority of ammonia production is used in making fertilisers. It can also be oxidised to form nitrogen dioxide (NO_2). This is then reacted with water to produce nitric acid (HNO_3).

8.25 Nitric acid

Nitric acid production

In the first stage, ammonia is mixed with air and compressed. The gas mixture is then passed over a heated catalyst of platinum–rhodium. The catalyst is in the form of a fine gauze. This catalyses the reaction:

$$\text{ammonia} + \text{oxygen} \xrightarrow{900\,°C} \text{nitrogen dioxide} + \text{water}$$

$$4NH_3(g) + 7O_2(g) \xrightarrow{900\,°C} 4NO_2(g) + 6H_2O(g)$$

The nitrogen dioxide produced is cooled, mixed with more air and reacted with water:

$$4NO_2(g) + O_2(g) + 2H_2O(l) \rightarrow 4HNO_3(aq)$$

The nitric acid itself is important in the fertiliser industry. It is also used to make explosives (for example trinitrotoluene, TNT), in the manufacture

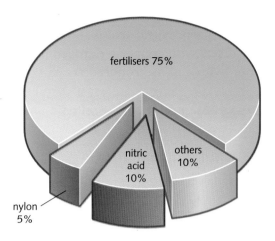

Figure 8.36 The manufacturing uses of ammonia.

of various polymers (for example nylon and terylene), and in making some dyes and drugs.

The properties of nitric acid

Nitric acid is a strong acid. The concentrated acid is a powerful oxidising agent. In dilute solution it shows most of the characteristic properties of an acid. It is completely ionised in solution.

It reacts with bases such as sodium hydroxide and zinc oxide to give nitrates and water:

sodium hydroxide + nitric acid
   → sodium nitrate + water

$$NaOH(aq) + HNO_3(aq) \rightarrow NaNO_3(aq) + H_2O(l)$$

zinc oxide + nitric acid → zinc nitrate + water

$$ZnO(s) + 2HNO_3(aq) \rightarrow Zn(NO_3)_2(aq) + H_2O(l)$$

It reacts with all carbonates to give a nitrate, water and carbon dioxide gas:

magnesium carbonate + nitric acid
   → magnesium nitrate + water + carbon dioxide

$$MgCO_3(s) + 2HNO_3(aq) \rightarrow Mg(NO_3)_2(aq) + H_2O(l) + CO_2(g)$$

The reaction with metals is complicated by the fact that nitric acid is a strong oxidising agent. The more reactive metals *do* give hydrogen, for example

magnesium + nitric acid
   → magnesium nitrate + hydrogen

$$Mg(s) + 2HNO_3(aq) \rightarrow Mg(NO_3)_2(aq) + H_2(g)$$

However, other metals such as iron do not react to produce hydrogen. Nitric acid is the only dilute acid that reacts with copper – nitrogen monoxide (NO), not hydrogen, is produced.

The **properties** of **dilute nitric acid** are typical of an acid:

- turns blue litmus red
- a strong acid, completely ionised in water
- reacts with bases to form salts (nitrates) and water
- reacts with carbonates to give nitrates, water and carbon dioxide.

EXTENSION

The oxidising properties of nitric acid become most obvious when the acid is concentrated. It is a powerful oxidising agent, reacting with both metals and non-metals.

It will oxidise carbon to carbon dioxide:

$$C(s) + 4HNO_3(aq) \rightarrow CO_2(g) + 4NO_2(g) + 2H_2O(l)$$

It will oxidise copper to copper(II) nitrate, in a rapid and 'colourful' reaction, producing brown fumes of nitrogen dioxide (NO_2):

$$Cu(s) + 4HNO_3(aq) \rightarrow Cu(NO_3)_2(aq) + 2NO_2(g) + 2H_2O(l)$$

The copper content of most coins, including 'silver' coins, can be shown by placing a few drops of concentrated nitric acid on the coin.

Summary of core material

You should know that:

- nitrogen is the major gas in the Earth's atmosphere
- nitrogen is an unreactive gas but is essential for all forms of life
- nitrogen atoms are recycled in the global nitrogen cycle
- the conversion of nitrogen into compounds such as nitrates, which plants can use for making proteins, is known as 'nitrogen fixing'

- nitrogen can be 'fixed' artificially on a large scale by the Haber process – nitrogen is converted to ammonia by reaction with hydrogen
- ammonia (NH_3) is a strong-smelling alkaline gas that reacts with acids to make an important series of salts known as ammonium salts
- ammonia can also be oxidised to form nitric acid – one of the three major strong acids.

8.13 The diagram on page 241 shows the nitrogen cycle but some parts are missing.

(a) Copy the diagram and complete the nitrogen cycle by writing the correct letter in each of the boxes. You may use each letter once, more than once or not at all. Choose the letters from the table below. The first one has been done for you. [5]

(b) Suggest what might happen to a plant if it could not absorb nitrates. [1]

(c) (i) Why is it important that nitrogen is cycled?
    (ii) Carbon is also cycled. Name *two* processes which release carbon dioxide into the atmosphere. [2]

Letter	A	B	C	D	E
Part of nitrogen cycle	urine and faeces	nitrogen fixation in root nodules, e.g. of pea plants	denitrifying bacteria	death	decay

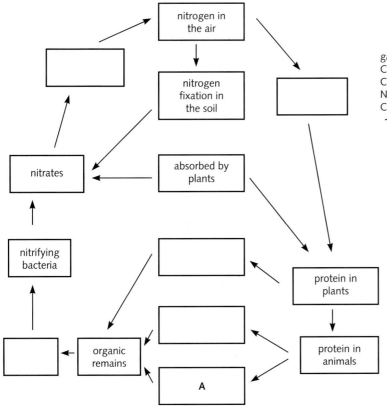

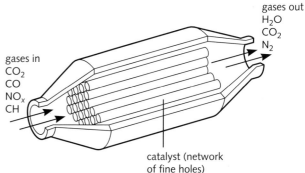

catalyst (network
of fine holes)

(iv) Nitrogen oxides are represented by the formula NO_x. How are nitrogen oxides produced in a car exhaust? [2]

(v) Why are nitrogen oxides regarded as pollutants on the surface of the Earth? [2]

(c) (i) What type of substance is represented by the formula CH? [1]

(ii) Is CH a correct molecular formula? Explain your answer. [2]

(d) Suggest why lead-free fuel must be used by cars fitted with a catalytic converter. [1]

(e) Does a catalytic converter stop all air pollution from cars? Explain your answer. [2]

(IGCSE, 1991 and SEG, 1992)

8.15 The formation of ammonia from hydrogen and nitrogen using an iron catalyst was discovered by the German chemist Fritz Haber. It is now known as the Haber process:

$$N_2 + 3H_2 \rightleftharpoons 2NH_3$$

The process can be demonstrated in the laboratory using the apparatus below.

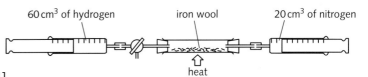

60 cm³ of hydrogen   iron wool   20 cm³ of nitrogen

heat

The mixture of hydrogen and nitrogen is passed backwards and forwards over the iron.

(a) The Haber process gives out heat. What name is given to a reaction that gives out heat? [1]

(b) The iron wool acts as a catalyst.

(i) What is a catalyst? [2]

(ii) Why is the iron in the form of wool rather than solid lumps? [2]

(iii) Why is it necessary to make sure that no air is present before the iron is heated? [1]

(c) At the end of the experiment, a small amount of ammonia is present in the syringes. Describe how you

(ULEAC, 1994)

8.14 Nitrogen oxides are thought to pollute the upper and lower atmosphere.

(a) In the upper atmosphere there is the worry that supersonic aircraft such as Concorde produce nitrogen oxides, which remove ozone:

$$NO + O_3 \longrightarrow NO_2 + O_2$$
$$\text{ozone}$$

Nitrogen monoxide, NO, gains an oxygen atom and ozone loses an oxygen atom.

(i) What is the name given to the loss of oxygen? [1]

(ii) What is the name given to the gain of oxygen? [1]

(b) On the Earth's surface, catalytic converters are used in car exhausts to reduce pollution, including that from nitrogen oxides. The diagram shows the main features of a converter. Use the diagram to answer the questions.

(i) Which substance in car exhausts is not affected by the catalyst? [1]

(ii) Explain what is meant by a catalyst. [2]

(iii) Suggest why the catalyst is a network of fine holes. [2]

would show by a chemical test that ammonia is present. [3]

(d) Ammonia from the Haber process is used to make fertilisers and explosives.
   (i) Why is ammonia used in making fertiliser? [1]
   (ii) Solid ammonium nitrate decomposes explosively to produce a mixture of gases:
$$NH_4NO_3(s) \rightarrow N_2O(g) + 2H_2O(g)$$
Suggest why an explosion results. [2]

(e) Ammonia can be used as a source of hydrogen. When decomposed, 75% (by volume) of the resulting gas mixture is hydrogen:

$$2NH_3 \rightarrow N_2 + 3H_2$$

There is no need to remove the nitrogen as the mixture acts as though it were almost pure hydrogen.
   (i) Suggest what would happen if a lighted splint was applied to the gas mixture. [2]
   (ii) Suggest what purpose the gas mixture could be used for in industry. [2]

(IGCSE, 1994)

8.16 Ammonia may be prepared in the laboratory using the apparatus below:

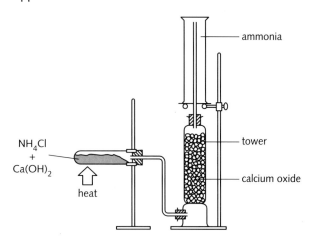

(a) (i) The equation for the reaction is:
$$2NH_4Cl + Ca(OH)_2 \rightarrow CaCl_2 + 2NH_3 + 2H_2O$$
Give the word equation for this reaction. [2]

(ii) Suggest the purpose of the calcium oxide labelled in the diagram. [1]
(iii) Suggest why the ammonia is collected as shown. [1]
(iv) How would you test to see if ammonia was being collected in the gas jar? [2]

(b) In contact with heated platinum, ammonia is oxidised by air to nitrogen monoxide. This is shown below:

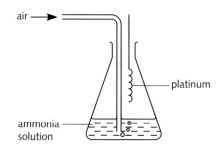

(i) Complete the symbol equation below: [2]
$$4NH_3 + ...O_2 \rightarrow ...NO + 6H_2O$$
(ii) Nitrogen oxides are found in the air. Where do they come from? [1]
(iii) Why does the presence of nitrogen oxides in the air cause problems? [1]

(c) Ammonia reacts with hot copper(II) oxide:
$$3CuO + 2NH_3 \rightarrow 3Cu + N_2 + 3H_2O$$

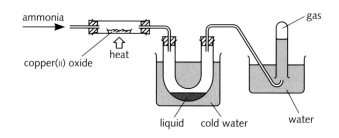

(i) How can you tell when copper has been formed in the tube? [1]
(ii) Describe how you could test the liquid collected to show that it is water. [2]
(iii) Name the gas collected in the test tube. [1]

(IGCSE, part question, 1992)

Chlorine and the halogens

This section covers the following ideas:

- the chemical reactivity of the halogens
- displacement reactions
- the uses of the halogens.

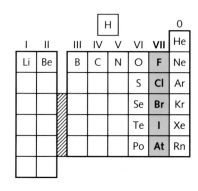

Gas! GAS! Quick, boys! – An ecstasy of
  fumbling,
Fitting the clumsy helmets just in time,
But someone still was yelling out and stumbling
And floundering like a man in fire or lime –
Dim through the misty panes and thick green
  light,
As under a green sea, I saw him drowning.

In all my dreams before my helpless sight
He plunges at me, guttering, choking,
  drowning.
(from 'Dulce et Decorum Est' by Wilfred Owen)

This is part of one of the finest and most telling poems of the First World War. It was written by Wilfred Owen during the last year of his life – he was killed in action on 4 November 1914. In it, he describes the death of a soldier from chlorine poisoning.

The **halogens**, Group VII elements, are the most reactive of the non-metals, and chlorine is the element with which we are most familiar. Many of us know its smell from swimming pools. Chlorine, in very small quantities, is put into the water of swimming pools to kill bacteria and stop infection. It is also used in the treatment of water for domestic supply. Iodine is another halogen that we use at home. A brown solution of iodine in alcohol is often kept in medicine cabinets for disinfecting cuts.

Household bleaches also smell of chlorine. These bleaches contain chlorine and chlorine compounds, which are important bleaching agents. These reactive substances oxidise the coloured dyes in cloth, turning them into colourless compounds.

8.26 The family likeness

The halogen family found in Group VII of the Periodic Table shows clearly the similarities of elements in the group. They are all non-metals and exist as **diatomic molecules**. The atoms in each molecule are linked by a single covalent bond. The properties of the elements change gradually as you go down the group (figure 8.37). The first halogen, fluorine, is the most reactive non-metallic element and is very dangerous to handle. The last halogen, astatine, is highly radioactive and has never been prepared in large amounts.

The **halogens** have the following **common properties**.

- They are all poisonous and have a similar strong smell.
- They are all non-metals.
- They all form diatomic molecules (for example Cl_2, Br_2, I_2).
- They all have a **valency** of 1 and form compounds with similar formulas, for example hydrogen chloride (HCl), hydrogen bromide (HBr), hydrogen iodide (HI).
- Their compounds with hydrogen are usually strong acids when dissolved in water, for example hydrochloric acid (HCl), hydrobromic acid (HBr), hydroiodic acid (HI).
- They each produce a series of salts: chlorides, bromides and iodides. Together these are known as **halides**.
- The halogens themselves can react directly with metals to form salts.
- They all form negative ions carrying a single charge, for example chloride ions (Cl^-), bromide ions (Br^-), iodide ions (I^-).

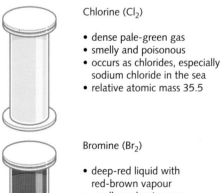

Chlorine (Cl_2)

- dense pale-green gas
- smelly and poisonous
- occurs as chlorides, especially sodium chloride in the sea
- relative atomic mass 35.5

Bromine (Br_2)

- deep-red liquid with red-brown vapour
- smelly and poisonous
- occurs as bromides, especially magnesium bromide in the sea
- relative atomic mass 80

Iodine (I_2)

- grey solid with purple vapour
- smelly and poisonous
- occurs as iodides and iodates in some rocks and in seaweed
- relative atomic mass 127

Figure 8.37 The properties of the halogens change systematically going down the group.

There are gradual changes in properties between the halogens (figure 8.37). As you go down the group, the boiling points increase. Also there is a change from gas to liquid to solid. The intensity of the colour of the element also increases, from pale to dark. Following these trends, it should not surprise you to know that fluorine is a pale yellow gas at room temperature.

8.27 The chemical reactivity of the halogens

Fluorine and chlorine are very reactive. They combine strongly with both metals and non-metals. A piece of Dutch metal foil – an alloy of copper and zinc – will burst into flames when placed in a gas jar of chlorine. When chlorine is passed over heated aluminium, the metal glows white and turns to aluminium chloride:

$$2Al(s) + 3Cl_2(g) \overset{heat}{\rightarrow} 2AlCl_3(s)$$

Aluminium also reacts strongly with bromine and iodine. The reaction between a dry mixture of powdered aluminium and iodine can be triggered by adding just a few drops of water. The reaction is highly exothermic and some of the iodine is given off as purple fumes before it has a chance to react.

Hydrogen will burn in chlorine to form hydrogen chloride. Carried out a different way the reaction can be explosive:

$$H_2(g) + Cl_2(g) \rightarrow 2HCl(g)$$

Chlorine dissolves in water to give an acidic solution. This mixture is called **chlorine water** and contains two acids:

$$Cl_2(g) + H_2O(l) \rightarrow HCl + HClO$$
hydrochloric hypochlorous
acid   acid

Chlorine water acts as an oxidising agent – hypochlorous acid can give up its oxygen to other substances. It also acts as a bleach because some coloured substances lose their colour when they are oxidised. This reaction is used as the chemical test for chlorine gas. Damp litmus or universal indicator paper is bleached when held in the gas.

The halogens become steadily less reactive as you go down the group. This is typical of a group of non-metals; and is the opposite of the trend in a group of metals (page 67). With non-metals, the most reactive element is at the top of the group. With metals, the most reactive element is at the bottom of the group. Table 8.6 gives some examples of the reactivity of the halogens.

The displacement reactions shown in table 8.6 demonstrate the order of reactivity of the three major halogens. For example, if you add chlorine to a solution of potassium bromide, the chlorine displaces bromine (figure 8.38). Chlorine is more reactive than bromine, so it replaces it and potassium chloride is formed. Potassium bromide solution is colourless. It turns orange when chlorine is bubbled through it:

$$Cl_2(g) + 2KBr(aq) \rightarrow 2KCl(aq) + Br_2(aq)$$
colourless   orange

Chlorine will also displace iodine from potassium iodide:

$$Cl_2(g) + 2KI(aq) \rightarrow 2KCl(aq) + I_2(aq)$$
colourless   yellow-brown

Table 8.6 Some reactions of the halogens

Reaction with	Chlorine	Bromine	Iodine
Coloured dyes	bleaches easily	bleaches slowly	bleaches very slowly
Iron wool	iron wool reacts strongly to form iron(III) chloride; needs heat to start	iron reacts steadily to form iron(III) bromide; needs continuous heating	iron reacts slowly even with continuous heating to form iron(III) iodide
Chlorides	–	no reaction	no reaction
Bromides	displaces bromine, e.g. $Cl_2 + 2KBr \rightarrow 2KCl + Br_2$	–	no reaction
Iodides	displaces iodine, e.g. $Cl_2 + 2KI \rightarrow 2KCl + I_2$	displaces iodine, e.g. $Br_2 + 2KI \rightarrow 2KBr + I_2$	–

Figure 8.38 Bromine is displaced from a colourless solution of potassium bromide by bubbling chlorine through it.

8.28 The uses of the halogens

The halogens are a very important group of elements. Because of their reactivity, they form a wide range of useful compounds, including polymers (PVC, PTFE, page 336), solvents, bleaches and disinfectants. Their uses are summed up in table 8.7. Some of these compounds have become notorious in recent years for their damaging effect on the environment. CFCs and the pesticide, methyl bromide, are involved in damaging the protective ozone layer. However, many other halogen compounds have become important and extremely useful. Indeed, the

Table 8.7 The halogens are involved in the making of a wide range of useful products

Halogen	Product and/or use
Fluorine	fluoride in toothpaste and drinking water PTFE – non-stick coating for pans, etc. aerosol propellants and refrigerants
Chlorine	water treatment bleach PVC – plastic pipes, windows, clothing fabric, etc. aerosol propellants and refrigerants solvents for dry-cleaning and degreasing disinfectants and antiseptics pesticides
Bromine	flame retardants pesticides petrol additives photographic film
Iodine	antiseptics photographic film and paper

replacements for CFCs include HFCs (hydrofluorocarbons), which appear to have no effect on the ozone layer.

The industrial source of chlorine is the electrolysis of concentrated **brine**. This is a solution of sodium chloride, the best known of all salts. Sodium chloride (NaCl) is often known as common salt. It occurs naturally as rock salt and in sea water. Sodium chloride is the starting point for the manufacture of a wide range of chemicals (the chlor–alkali industry). Metal bromides and iodides also provide the starting points for important processes such as photography (page 195).

The light-sensitive nature of silver chloride and silver bromide has been exploited not only in photography but also in making photochromic sunglasses. The salts are incorporated into the glasses of the lenses. When exposed to sunlight, the silver ions are converted to silver atoms, and the lenses darken. The reverse happens when the light decreases.

Silver chloride is insoluble in water and therefore its production can be used as a test for chloride ions. Any solution containing chloride ions will react with acidified silver nitrate solution to produce a white precipitate of silver chloride:

sodium chloride + silver nitrate
→ silver chloride + sodium nitrate

$NaCl(aq) + AgNO_3(aq)$
$→ AgCl(s) + NaNO_3(aq)$

The ionic equation for this reaction is:

$Ag^+(aq) + Cl^-(aq) → AgCl(s)$

Summary of core material

You should know that:

- the halogens are a group of reactive non-metals – Group VII in the Periodic Table
- they all exist as diatomic molecules (Cl_2, for example)
- their physical properties change as you go down the group – their melting points and boiling points increase, and the intensity of their colour deepens

- their chemical reactivity decreases down the group – the more reactive halogens will displace the lower halogens from salts

- the halogens and their compounds are used in a wide range of situations – from plastics, antiseptics and pesticides, to photographic films.

8.17

(a) Iodine is a member of Group VII of the Periodic Table.
(i) Copy and complete the following table which lists some of the properties of the halogens. [3]

Halogen	Symbol	State	Appearance
Chlorine	Cl	gas	green-yellow
Bromine	Br	liquid	red-brown
Iodine			

(ii) An iodine molecule is *diatomic*. Explain this term. [2]

(b) Iodine is less reactive than both bromine and chlorine. Write a word equation for the reaction of sodium iodide with chlorine. [2]

(c) Iodine reacts with most metals. It reacts with iron to form iron(II) iodide, FeI_2, and with sodium to form sodium iodide.
(i) Describe how you could show that iron(II) ions are present in iron(II) iodide. [3]
(ii) Describe how you could show that iodide ions are present in sodium iodide. [3]
(iii) Describe the formation of an ionic bond in sodium iodide. [3]

(d) Iodine also reacts with non-metals. It forms hydrogen iodide, HI, which is similar to hydrogen chloride. Describe the formation of a covalent bond in hydrogen iodide. [3]

(e) Radioactive iodine is used in the medical treatment of the thyroid gland. State another medical use of a radioactive isotope.

(IGCSE, 1996)

8.18 Ozone, O_3, is a form of oxygen found naturally in the ozone layer of the upper atmosphere. It is formed as part of a natural cycle similar to the nitrogen and carbon cycles. The ozone in the upper atmosphere is essential because it absorbs some of the dangerous ultra-violet radiation from the Sun that would be harmful to life on Earth. The first step in the formation of ozone is the decomposition of oxygen molecules into atoms by low-energy ultra-violet (u.v.) light:

Step 1
O_2 + low-energy u.v. light → O + O

This is followed by the reaction between oxygen molecules and oxygen atoms, which forms ozone molecules:

Step 2
O_2 + O → O_3

Ozone molecules, however, absorb u.v. light of higher energy and are decomposed in the process:

Step 3
O_3 + high-energy u.v. light → O_2 + O

(a) Use the information above to copy and complete the diagram below showing the 'ozone cycle' by filling in the boxes. [3]

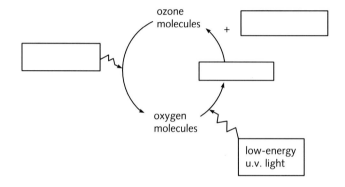

Chlorofluorocarbons, CFCs, destroy ozone in the upper atmosphere. One example of a CFC is the compound CFC-113 with the formula $C_2F_3Cl_3$. CFC-113 is an inert, synthetic compound used in the electronics industry.

(b) Copy the table below and fill in the spaces. [2]

Compound	M.p. (°C)	B.p. (°C)	Physical state at room temperature	Electrical conductivity at room temperature
$C_2F_3Cl_3$	−35	48		

(c) What characteristic of this CFC allows its vapour to reach the upper atmosphere chemically unchanged? [1]

Once the CFC vapour reaches the upper atmosphere the following reactions occur in order:

CFC + u.v. light → CFC fragment + Cl   reaction 1

Cl + O_3 → ClO + O_2 reaction 2

ClO + O → Cl + O_2 reaction 3

(d) Describe and explain what has happened in reaction 2 in terms of the processes of oxidation and reduction. [2]

(e) It has been suggested that one chlorine atom destroys many ozone molecules. Suggest, by reference to reactions 2 and 3, how this could happen.

Some data about CFC-113 are given below:

Bond	Energy needed to break the bond (kJ/mol)
C—Cl	+330
C—C	+346
C—F	+450

The structure of the CFC-113 molecule is

$$\begin{array}{ccc} Cl & & F \\ | & & | \\ F-C-&C-&Cl \\ | & & | \\ Cl & & F \end{array}$$

The energy of u.v. light is equivalent to 400 kJ/mol.

Use these data in your answers to the following.

(f) (i) Suggest reasons why the CFC is decomposed by u.v. light to form chlorine atoms rather than fluorine atoms.
     (ii) Suggest a further bond change you would expect to occur in the CFC molecule. [3]

(g) The formation of ozone in the upper atmosphere can be represented by a single equation:

$$3O_2(g) \rightarrow 2O_3(g) \qquad \Delta H = +286 \text{ kJ/mol}$$

Draw an energy level diagram for this reaction. [3]

(ULEAC, 1991)

The noble gases

This section covers the following ideas:

• the properties and uses of the noble gases.

The noble gases are the most unreactive group of elements in the Periodic Table. Their atoms have the most stable arrangement of electrons possible for each period. The elements at the top of the group do not form any compounds. For this reason the group was often referred to as the *inert gases*. However, some compounds of xenon and krypton *have* now been made, so that description

is incorrect. We probably know these gases best for their lighting effects. An electric discharge excites atoms of these gases to produce light of particular colours (figure 8.39). Since their discovery, these gases are now obtained by the fractional distillation of liquid air.

8.29 Helium

Helium is the most abundant element in the Universe after hydrogen. It is rare on Earth because its atoms are so light that they can escape from the atmosphere into space. It does not accumulate in the atmosphere even though it is continuously produced by radioactive decay deep in the Earth. Some helium is trapped in uranium-containing rock formations and it is found in natural gas. Helium has the lowest boiling point of any element and cannot be solidified without an increased pressure being applied. It is a useful substance for the study of matter at low temperatures (**cryogenics**). At very low temperatures (below −271 °C), a super-fluid allotrope of liquid helium exists that can 'climb' out of its container.

Figure 8.39 The colours of this 'neon' lighting art by Dan Flavin are produced by excited noble gas atoms.

Helium is twice as dense as hydrogen but has the advantage of being non-flammable. For this reason, it is used in modern airships and weather balloons. Other uses of helium include:

- the inflation of the tyres of large aircraft
- helium–neon lasers for medical use (figure 8.40),
- as a coolant in nuclear reactors
- the helium–oxygen mixtures used by deep-sea divers.

8.30 The other noble gases

Neon, which emits a red glow when an electric current flows through it, is widely used in advertising signs.

Argon is the most abundant of these elements in the atmosphere (0.9% of the total volume). It is used to provide an inert atmosphere for welding and to fill various types of light bulb, to prevent the metal filament burning away.

Krypton gives an intense white light when a current is passed through it. It is used in airport runway lighting and lighthouse lamps.

Xenon also gives an intense white light and is used in photographic flash units and stroboscopic disco lights.

Radon is a radioactive gas that leaks out of rocks as a product of the radioactive decay of uranium. There is some concern about the gas collecting in homes and buildings in certain areas, particularly in granite regions. This could pose a health problem by increasing the levels of radiation to which people are exposed.

Figure 8.40 Helium–neon lasers are used for micro-surgery on the eye.

Summary of core material

You should know that:

- the noble gases are the most unreactive group of elements in the Periodic Table
- their atoms have the most stable arrangement of electrons possible for each period
- they are obtained from the fractions produced by the fractional distillation of liquid air
- partly because of their unreactivity, each of the noble gases has some industrial use.

8.19 Argon is a gas which was discovered by William Ramsay in 1895. He found that if he removed all the known gases from the air he was left with a small volume of an unreactive gas. When all the elements are arranged in order of atomic number, elements with similar properties to argon appear in a periodic pattern. This group of similar elements includes helium and neon.

(a) Explain what is meant by the terms:
  (i) atomic number, [1]
  (ii) periodic pattern. [1]

(b) (i) State *one* physical property and *one* chemical property shared by helium, argon and neon. [2]
  (ii) What name is given to this group of elements? [1]

(c) The metal filaments of electric light bulbs work at very high temperatures. Most of these bulbs are filled with argon gas.
  (i) Suggest what might happen to the metal filament if the bulb was filled with air. [1]
  (ii) Why will this not happen when the bulb is filled with argon? [1]

(MEG, 1995)

8.20

(a) Over millions of years and, to a smaller extent, more recently the composition of the Earth's atmosphere has changed. Before the evolution of plants, the major gases in the atmosphere included ammonia, methane and carbon dioxide: there was no oxygen. Suggest how plants changed the composition of this atmosphere. [3]

(b) In 1894, the scientist, W. Ramsay, carried out the following experiments starting with 100 cm³ of air.

The 100 cm³ of air were passed through solution X to remove traces of acidic gases. Then the air was bubbled through concentrated sulphuric acid to remove water vapour. The remaining gases were

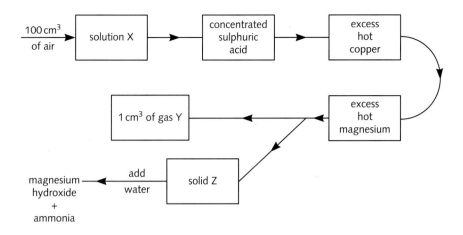

heated with an excess of copper and the volume decreased from almost 100 cm³ to 80 cm³.

The gases that did not react with hot copper were heated with magnesium. 1 cm³ of gas Y remained and a white solid Z was formed. Solid Z reacted with water to form only magnesium hydroxide and ammonia.

  (i) Suggest a value for the pH of solution X.   [1]

 (ii) Name the ion, in solution X, which reacts with the acidic gases.   [1]

(iii) What is the formula of solid Z?   [2]

(iv) Describe the test for ammonia.   [2]

 (v) Gas Y has a density of 1.66 g/dm³ at r.t.p. Calculate the mass of 1 mol of gas Y and so identify the gas.   [3]

(vi) Most gases are identified by a chemical test. Why must gas Y be identified using a physical property?   [1]

(IGCSE, part question, 1989)

Patterns and properties of metals

The alkali metals

This section covers the following ideas:

- the alkali metals
- their reaction with water
- flame tests.

				H				0
I	II	III	IV	V	VI	VII		He
Li	Be	B	C	N	O	F		Ne
Na	Mg							
K	Ca							
Rb	Sr							
Cs	Ba							
Fr	Ra							

The distinctive metals of Group I are called the **alkali metals** (figure 9.1). The most memorable thing about them is their spectacular reaction with cold water. These metals do not have many uses because they are so reactive and tarnish easily. They have to be stored under oil. The one familiar use of sodium is in sodium vapour lamps. These are the yellow street and motorway lights seen throughout towns and cities. The melting points of the alkali metals decrease gradually as you go down the group. There is a similar trend in the hardness of the metals. They are all soft, low-density metals. Lithium is the hardest, but it can

still be cut with a knife. The metals get easier to cut going down the group.

There are many ways in which the different elements of Group I show similar properties. Some of these common characteristics are given below.

The **common properties** of the **alkali metals** are as follows.

- They are all reactive metals. They have to be stored under oil to stop them reacting with the oxygen and water vapour in the air (table 9.1 on page 252).
- They are soft and can be cut with a knife.
- They have low densities. Lithium, sodium and potassium all float on water (they have a density of less than $1.0\,g/cm^3$).
- Like all metals they form positive ions. The metals of Group I form ions with a single positive charge (for example Li^+, Na^+, K^+).
- As a result they form compounds that have similar formulas; for example their carbonates are lithium carbonate (Li_2CO_3), sodium carbonate (Na_2CO_3) and potassium carbonate (K_2CO_3).
- They all react strongly and directly with non-metals to form salts. These salts are all white, crystalline, ionic solids that dissolve in water.

  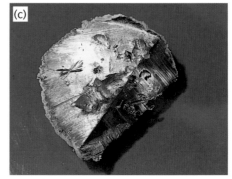

Figure 9.1 The alkali metals: (a) lithium, (b) sodium and (c) potassium.

Table 9.1 Reactions of lithium, sodium and potassium with air and water

Element	Reaction with water	Reaction with air	
Lithium	reacts steadily $2Li + 2H_2O \rightarrow 2LiOH + H_2$	tarnishes slowly to give a layer of oxide	
Sodium	reacts strongly $2Na + 2H_2O \rightarrow 2NaOH + H_2$	tarnishes quickly to give a layer of oxide	increasing reactivity
Potassium	reacts violently $2K + 2H_2O \rightarrow 2KOH + H_2$	tarnishes very quickly to give a layer of oxide	

9.1 The reaction of the alkali metals with water

All the alkali metals react spontaneously with water to produce hydrogen gas and the metal hydroxide (table 9.1). The reactions are **exothermic**. The heat produced is sufficient to melt sodium and potassium as they skid over the surface of the water. Lithium does not melt as it reacts. This begins to show the gradual differences in reactivity between the metals as you go down the group. Lithium (at the top) is the least reactive and caesium (at the bottom) is the most reactive.

The reaction with water is the same in each case:

metal + water → metal hydroxide + hydrogen

For example,

sodium + water → sodium hydroxide + hydrogen

$$2Na(s) + 2H_2O(l) \rightarrow 2NaOH(aq) + H_2(g)$$

The reaction gets more vigorous as you move down the group. The reaction of **lithium** with water is quite steady: the metal does not melt and the hydrogen does not ignite. **Sodium** reacts more strongly: the metal melts but, if the sodium is free to move, the hydrogen does not usually ignite. Restricting the movement of the sodium by placing it on a piece of filter paper on the water surface results in the hydrogen gas igniting. The flame is coloured yellow by the sodium. **Potassium** reacts so strongly with water that the hydrogen gas ignites spontaneously. The potassium may even explode dangerously. The flame is coloured lilac. **Rubidium** and **caesium** explode as soon as they are put into water. The metal hydroxide produced in each case makes the water become alkaline.

9.2 Flame tests for the metals

Compounds of the alkali metals can be detected by a **flame test**. All alkali-metal ions give characteristic colours in a Bunsen flame (figure 9.2). Table 9.2 lists the colours obtained.

Table 9.2 Flame colours of Group I metal ions

Metal ion		Flame colour
Lithium	Li^+	scarlet
Sodium	Na^+	yellow
Potassium	K^+	lilac

Figure 9.2 (a) Lithium, (b) sodium and (c) potassium give characteristic colours in the flame test.

251

The intensity (brightness) of the flame colour can be measured using a **flame photometer**. This instrument is used in hospitals to measure the levels of sodium ions and potassium ions in body fluids. Sodium and potassium are essential to good health. The cells in our body are surrounded by a solution which usually contains more sodium ions, while the fluid inside the cells contains more potassium ions. The balance between the two ions is very important. The nerve impulses in our bodies are controlled by the movement of these two ions.

Our bodies can store excess sodium ions but not potassium ions. This means that the body levels of potassium ions, which come from fresh fruit and vegetables, may fall in some people. An imbalance between sodium and potassium is set up, which can lead to high blood pressure. A low-sodium alternative to ordinary table salt can be purchased that contains two-thirds potassium chloride and only one-third sodium chloride. This can be used instead of common table salt in cooking and for flavouring food. This salt alternative must be used carefully by people who have other medical conditions.

9.3 Compounds of the alkali metals

The alkali metals themselves do not have many general uses. But the compounds of the alkali metals are very important. Sodium chloride (common salt) has a very wide range of uses, both domestic and industrial. Its importance stretches back in history. Salt is a major food preservative, which was even more significant before the development of refrigeration. The word 'salary' dates from workers being paid with salt. In 1930, when Britain still ruled over India, Mahatma Gandhi led a protest march to the sea to collect salt. This was to demonstrate the Indians' wish to be free of the British monopoly of salt and the taxes they imposed on it.

Sodium nitrate and potassium nitrate deposits in South America, particularly in Chile, were of great importance as fertilisers and explosives. These salts were so important that masses of 'guano', droppings deposited by sea birds, were transported from South America to Europe. Potassium nitrate is used as the oxidiser in black gunpowder – a

mixture of nitrate, charcoal and sulphur. When ignited, the reactions produce large quantities of gases. This causes a sudden expansion in volume. In the home, sodium carbonate (washing soda), sodium hydrogencarbonate (bicarbonate of soda, baking soda) and sodium hydroxide (oven cleaner) all have their use. Sodium hydroxide is important in the laboratory in testing for metal and ammonium ions.

Summary of core material

You should know that:

- the alkali metals (Group I) are soft metals with low densities
- they are very reactive – they displace hydrogen from cold water and must be stored under oil
- their reactivity increases as you move down the group
- their compounds give characteristic flame test colours.

9.1 Lithium was allowed to react with water as shown in the diagram.
What were the products of this reaction?

A lithium hydride and hydrogen
B lithium hydride and oxygen
C lithium hydroxide and hydrogen
D lithium hydroxide and oxygen

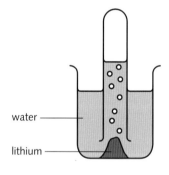

(IGCSE, 1993)

9.2 The Group I metals, lithium, potassium and sodium, may be reacted with chlorine in the apparatus shown below.

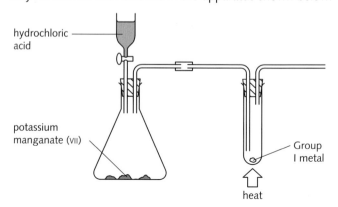

(a) Name *two* other Group I metals. [2]

(b) Why is it necessary to carry out the experiment in a fume cupboard? [1]

(c) Suggest why the apparatus is filled with chlorine before the metal is heated. [1]

(d) Describe a chemical test which would show when chlorine starts to leave the apparatus. [2]

(e) Complete the following equation for the reaction of sodium with chlorine: [1]

...Na + Cl$_2$ → ...NaCl

(f) Place lithium, potassium and sodium in order of their reactivity with chlorine (putting the most reactive element first). [2]

(g) The product from the reaction of sodium with chlorine was dissolved in water. Dilute nitric acid was then added followed by aqueous silver nitrate.
   (i) Describe what you would see. [2]
   (ii) Write a word equation for the reaction taking place. [1]

(h) The reaction of sodium with chlorine may be reversed. The electrolysis of molten sodium chloride gives sodium and chlorine.
   (i) Why is it necessary for the sodium chloride to be molten? [1]
   (ii) Predict the products from the electrolysis of molten lithium bromide. [2]
       Product at anode (positive electrode)
       Product at cathode (negative electrode)

(IGCSE, 1991)

9.3 Potassium was first obtained by Humphrey Davy in 1807 by the electrolysis of potassium hydroxide.

(a) Potassium hydroxide may be electrolysed in the laboratory using the apparatus shown in the diagram.
   (i) Why is it necessary for the potassium hydroxide to be molten? [1]

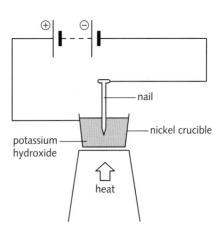

   (ii) At which electrode will the potassium be obtained? [1]
   (iii) Suggest why a solution of potassium hydroxide is not used. [1]

(b) Potassium salts occur frequently in nature. Potassium carbonate was known as potash or pot-ashes. The residue from the ashes of wood contains 15% by mass of potassium carbonate.
   (i) Potassium carbonate is soluble in water. Explain how you could obtain a pure, dry sample of potassium carbonate from wood ashes. [3]
   (ii) How could you test your sample to show it contained a carbonate? [2]
   (iii) Why might potassium carbonate be useful as a fertiliser? [1]

(c) The Group I metals are sometimes known as the *alkali metals*. Suggest why they have this name. [2]

(d) All potassium compounds are weakly radioactive because they contain some atoms of potassium-40:

$^{40}_{19}$K

State the number of protons, neutrons and electrons in this isotope. [3]

(IGCSE, 1996)

Calcium, magnesium and other Group II metals

This section covers the following ideas:

- the alkaline earth metals
- their reactivity
- the limestone cycle.

			H				0
I	II	III	IV	V	VI	VII	He
Li	Be	B	C	N	O	F	Ne
Na	Mg	Al					
K	Ca	Ga					
Rb	Sr	In					
Cs	Ba	Tl					
Fr	Ra						

The Group II metals are called the **alkaline earth metals** (figure 9.3). They are less reactive than the

Figure 9.3 The alkaline earth metals: (a) magnesium, (b) calcium and (c) strontium.

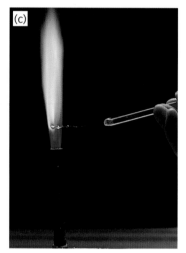

Figure 9.4 Some Group II metals give characteristic colours in the flame test: (a) calcium, (b) strontium and (c) barium.

metals in Group I, but still take part in a wide range of reactions. Like the alkali metals, compounds of these metals produce characteristic flame colours (figure 9.4). The colours obtained are listed in table 9.3. Compounds of the Group II metals are often used in fireworks, because of these colours.

Magnesium ions do not give a characteristic flame colour. Magnesium metal burns fiercely with a brilliant (very bright) white light. For this reason it is used in distress flares, in flashbulbs and in fireworks that give a white light.

Table 9.3 Flame colours of Group II metal ions

Metal ion		Flame colour
Calcium	Ca^{2+}	brick red
Strontium	Sr^{2+}	crimson
Barium	Ba^{2+}	apple green

The **common properties** of **Group II metals**:

- they are reactive and tarnish easily in air
- they have low density compared with most metals, but they do not float on water
- they form ions with two positive charges (for example Mg^{2+}, Ca^{2+}, Ba^{2+})
- they form compounds with similar formulas because they all have a valency of 2; for example magnesium chloride ($MgCl_2$), calcium chloride ($CaCl_2$) and barium chloride ($BaCl_2$)
- they react with non-metals to form ionic salts that are white.

9.4 Trends in reactivity

As in Group I, the **reactivity** of the alkaline earth metals increases going down the group. Beryllium (at the top) is the least reactive and barium (at the bottom) is the most reactive. Again the change in reactivity is best shown by using their reactions with water.

Magnesium reacts *very slowly* when placed in *cold* water. If left for some time, then hydrogen can be collected and the solution becomes slightly alkaline:

magnesium + water
  → magnesium hydroxide + hydrogen

$$Mg(s) + 2H_2O(l) \rightarrow Mg(OH)_2(s) + H_2(g)$$

Magnesium hydroxide is not very soluble in water. The reaction is speeded up if *warm* water is used.

A much *more vigorous* reaction is obtained if *steam* is passed over heated magnesium. The magnesium glows brightly to form hydrogen and magnesium oxide:

magnesium + steam
  → magnesium oxide + hydrogen

$$Mg(s) + H_2O(g) \rightarrow MgO(s) + H_2(g)$$

Calcium, however, *reacts strongly* with *cold* water, giving off hydrogen rapidly:

calcium + water → calcium hydroxide + hydrogen

$$Ca(s) + 2H_2O(l) \rightarrow Ca(OH)_2(aq) + H_2(g)$$

Calcium hydroxide is more soluble than magnesium hydroxide, so an alkaline solution is produced (**limewater**). As the reaction proceeds, a white suspension is obtained, because not all the calcium hydroxide dissolves.

9.5 The reactions of burning magnesium

Magnesium burns readily in air with a brilliant white flame. It burns even brighter in pure oxygen, producing a white ash, magnesium oxide:

magnesium + oxygen → magnesium oxide

$$2Mg(s) + O_2(g) \rightarrow 2MgO(s)$$

9.6 Uses and importance of magnesium and calcium

These metals have a relatively low density, but they are not particularly strong. Magnesium is often combined with other metals to produce **alloys** with more useful properties. These magnesium alloys

---

EXTENSION

When magnesium burns in air, the white ash produced is not just magnesium oxide. Magnesium is sufficiently reactive to form a compound with nitrogen. This compound, magnesium nitride, is also present in the white ash:

magnesium + nitrogen
  → magnesium nitride

$$3Mg(s) + N_2(g) \rightarrow Mg_3N_2(s)$$

The powerful reactivity of magnesium is also shown by the fact that magnesium continues to burn when placed in carbon dioxide:

magnesium + carbon dioxide
  → magnesium oxide + carbon

$$2Mg(s) + CO_2(g) \rightarrow 2MgO(s) + C(s)$$

---

combine lightness with strength and are used in the aircraft, car and bicycle industries.

Biologically, these metal ions are very important. Plants need magnesium for healthy growth. Magnesium is one of the elements needed to make **chlorophyll**, the green pigment involved in photosynthesis. In animal cells, magnesium ions are necessary for the activity of certain key **enzymes** involved in cell growth. Magnesium deficiency results in lack of growth and in learning disabilities.

Calcium is an essential part of the diet of animals. A deficiency of calcium prevents bones and teeth developing properly. Lack of calcium results in rickets, a condition in which bones soften and become deformed, and osteoporosis in older people, where the bones become brittle.

Calcium and magnesium compounds are present in the Earth's crust in various mineral forms. Calcium carbonate is particularly important since it occurs in three different forms: **limestone, chalk** and **marble**. The effect of rain water on these rocks results in hard water in certain geographical regions (page 231).

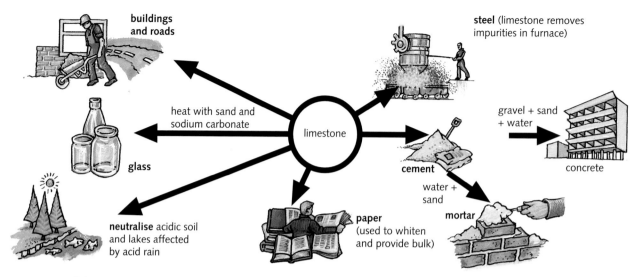

Figure 9.5 *Some of the uses of limestone (calcium carbonate).*

9.7 The limestone cycle

Limestone is an important resource from which a useful range of compounds can be made. Figure 9.5 shows some of the important uses of limestone and the related compounds quicklime and slaked lime.

The reactions involved in producing these compounds can be imitated in the laboratory. We can complete what is sometimes referred to as the **limestone cycle** (figure 9.6). A piece of calcium carbonate can be heated strongly for some time to produce lime (quicklime, calcium oxide). The piece of lime is allowed to cool and then a few drops of water are added. The solid flakes and expands, crumbling into 'slaked lime'. This reaction is strongly exothermic. If more water is added, an alkaline solution of limewater is obtained. The cycle can be completed by bubbling carbon

dioxide into the solution. A white precipitate of calcium carbonate is formed.

9.8 Reactivity in groups of metals

In both Groups I and II we have seen that reactivity increases down the group. The reason for this lies in the nature of chemical bonding. Metals react to form ionic compounds. In forming ionic bonds, the metal atoms lose their outer electrons. Atomic size increases down a group. The larger the atom, the further the outer electrons are from the nucleus. This means that the outer electrons in the larger atoms of a group are less strongly held and so are lost more easily. A larger atom, such as calcium, loses electrons more easily than a smaller atom, such as magnesium. This means that calcium is more reactive than magnesium.

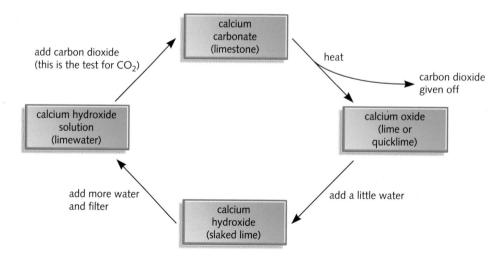

Figure 9.6 *The limestone cycle.*

Summary of core material

You should know that:

- as with the Group I metals, the reactivity of the alkaline earth metals (Group II) increases down the group
- therefore calcium is more reactive than magnesium – calcium reacts strongly with cold water, displacing hydrogen

- magnesium burns in air with a characteristic brilliant white light
- limestone, a mineral form of calcium carbonate, is an important resource – the range of compounds made from limestone forms the limestone cycle.

9.4 The diagram shows an experiment to test the oxide produced by burning magnesium.

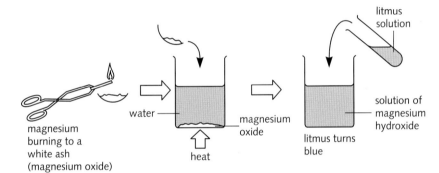

magnesium burning to a white ash (magnesium oxide)

water — magnesium oxide

heat

litmus turns blue

litmus solution

solution of magnesium hydroxide

This experiment shows that magnesium oxide is:
A acidic   B basic
C insoluble   D neutral

(IGCSE, 1991)

9.5 Rubidium has similar properties to sodium and potassium. Rubidium is used in photocells.

(a) Rubidium was first isolated by R. Bunsen in 1861 by heating rubidium chloride with calcium. Copy and label on the equation below: [3]
  the change which is *oxidation*
  the change which is *reduction*
  the chemical which is the *oxidising agent*

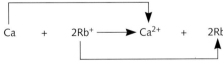

$$Ca + 2Rb^+ \longrightarrow Ca^{2+} + 2Rb$$

(b) Photocells change light energy into electrical energy.
  (i) Name a process that changes light energy into chemical energy. [1]
  (ii) Name a device that changes chemical energy into electrical energy. [1]

(c) Aqueous rubidium chloride can be electrolysed using carbon electrodes. Name the products of this electrolysis. [2]
  (i) Product at negative electrode
  (ii) Product at positive electrode

(d) The next element to rubidium in the Periodic Table is strontium. Strontium is similar to calcium. The rubidium ion is Rb^+ and the strontium ion is Sr^{2+}. Because these ions have different charges, ionic compounds of rubidium and strontium behave differently when heated. Explain why rubidium and strontium form ions that have different charges. [2]

(IGCSE, part question, 1996)

9.6 The manufacture of lime can be traced back to the Romans, Greeks and Egyptians. Calcium carbonate was heated as shown in the diagram on page 258.

The calcium carbonate decomposes as shown in reaction I below:
Reaction I
$$CaCO_3 \rightarrow CaO + CO_2$$

257

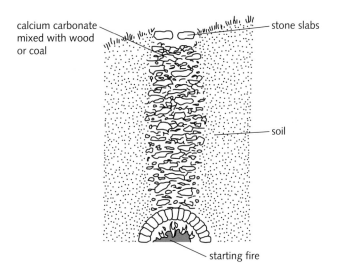

calcium carbonate mixed with wood or coal — stone slabs

soil

starting fire

Water is then added to the lime, calcium oxide, CaO, to produce slaked lime, calcium hydroxide, Ca(OH)$_2$ – reaction II:

Reaction II
$$CaO + H_2O \rightarrow Ca(OH)_2$$

(a) Suggest the purpose of the layers of wood or coal. [2]

(b) Reaction I absorbs heat and reaction II gives out heat.
    (i) What is the name given to a reaction that gives out heat? [1]
    (ii) What is the name given to a reaction that absorbs heat? [1]

(c) Slaked lime dissolves in water to produce limewater.

    Describe and explain what happens to limewater when you blow through it for a few seconds, using a straw. [2]

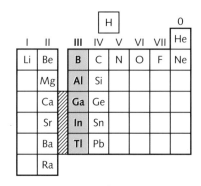

blow
straw
limewater

(d) Name *two* uses of lime or slaked lime, apart from making other calcium compounds. [2]

(e) Calcium may be prepared by the electrolysis of molten calcium chloride.

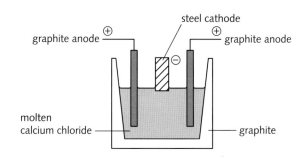

steel cathode
graphite anode ⊕   ⊕ graphite anode
⊖
molten calcium chloride   graphite

    (i) How would you convert lime (calcium oxide) into anhydrous calcium chloride? [2]
    (ii) What element are the anodes made from? [1]
    (iii) Why is it very important that the calcium chloride is dry? [1]
    (iv) At which electrode is the calcium produced? [1]
    (v) Name the other substance produced during this electrolysis. [1]

(IGCSE, 1991)

Aluminium

This section covers the following ideas:

• aluminium
• the protective oxide layer
• the thermit reaction.

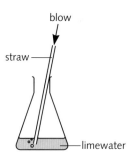

Aluminium was, for a long time, an expensive and little used metal. In France, around the 1860s, at the Court of Napoleon III (the nephew of the better-known Napoleon Bonaparte), honoured guests used cutlery made of aluminium rather than gold. At that time the metal was expensively extracted from aluminium chloride using sodium:

    aluminium chloride + sodium
      → sodium chloride + aluminium

$$AlCl_3(s) + 3Na(s) \rightarrow 3NaCl(s) + Al(s)$$

The breakthrough came in 1886 when Charles Hall and Paul Heroult independently found a way to obtain the metal by electrolysis (see section 10.7).

Aluminium is the most **abundant** metal in the Earth's crust. The percentages of the metals in the crust are 32% aluminium, 21% iron, 15% calcium, 12% sodium, 11% potassium and 9% magnesium. The one major ore of aluminium is **bauxite**, and aluminium oxide is purified from this. Electrolysis of molten aluminium oxide produces aluminium at the cathode.

9.9 Aluminium's protective oxide layer

Aluminium is a light, strong metal and has good electrical conductivity. Increasingly it is being used for construction purposes. The Lunar Rover 'moon-buggy' was built out of aluminium, and so too are some cars, like the Audi A8. For use in aeroplanes, it is usually alloyed with other metals such as copper. Its low density and good conductivity have led to its use in overhead power lines. Figure 9.7 shows the uses made of aluminium produced in the USA. Its use is helped by the fact that it is effectively protected from corrosion by the stable layer of aluminium oxide that forms on its surface. This protective film masks the true reactivity of the aluminium. Indeed the oxide layer can be artificially thickened by electrolysis. The product is known as **anodised aluminium**.

9.10 The thermit reaction

The high reactivity of aluminium is used to extract some metals from their oxides in small quantities.

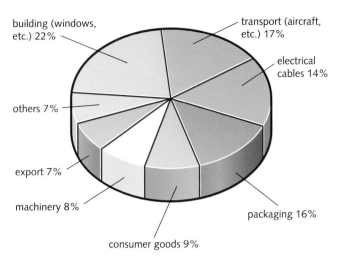

Figure 9.7 *The widespread and increasing uses of the aluminium produced in the USA.*

Thus aluminium can be used to produce iron from iron(III) oxide:

iron(III) oxide + aluminium
→ aluminium oxide + iron

$$Fe_2O_3(s) + 2Al(s) \rightarrow Al_2O_3(s) + 2Fe(l)$$

The aluminium and iron(III) oxide are powdered and well mixed to help them react (figure 9.8a on page 260). The reaction is powerful, exothermic and produces iron in the molten state. Because of this the reaction is used to weld together damaged railway lines (figure 9.8b on page 260). The reaction is an example of reduction–oxidation (**redox**) and is known as the **thermit reaction**. Other metals such as chromium and titanium are

---

EXTENSION

The presence of the oxide layer on the surface of aluminium often prevents any further reaction and disguises the metal's true reactivity. If the metal surface is rubbed with a tissue that has been dipped in mercury(II) chloride, the oxide layer is removed. The metal will then react very strongly with dilute acid. Hydrogen gas is given off. For example

aluminium + hydrochloric acid
→ aluminium chloride + hydrogen

$$2Al(s) + 6HCl(aq) \rightarrow 2AlCl_3(aq) + 3H_2(g)$$

The 'hidden' reactivity of aluminium sometimes leads to problems. Warship designers have favoured using aluminium in building modern, fast destroyers and frigates. This is because it is so much lighter than steel, about one-third the density. However, aluminium burns in air if heated enough, and it will even continue burning under water. The water simply supplies more oxygen, setting hydrogen free, which is itself flammable. During the Falklands War of 1982, the aluminium-hulled British destroyer HMS *Sheffield* burned furiously after being hit by a single Exocet missile. The intense heat caused the aluminium superstructure to collapse. This catastrophic event has led naval designers to re-think the use of aluminium in warships.

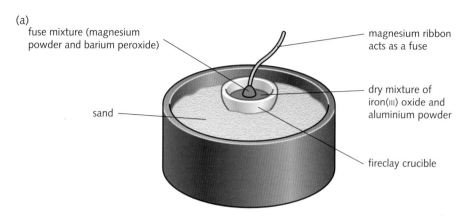

Figure 9.8 (a) The thermit reaction. (b) Using the thermit reaction to weld fractured railway lines.

also prepared from their oxides by such redox reactions. For example

chromium(III) oxide + aluminium
→ aluminium oxide + chromium

$$Cr_2O_3(s) + 2Al(s) \rightarrow Al_2O_3(s) + 2Cr(s)$$

9.11 The analytical test for aluminium ions

Aluminium ions do not give a characteristic colour in the flame test. The presence of aluminium ions (Al^{3+}) in a compound must be detected by some other method. If an aluminium salt is dissolved in water and sodium hydroxide solution is added, a white precipitate is formed. For example

aluminium chloride + sodium hydroxide
→ aluminium hydroxide + sodium chloride

$$AlCl_3(aq) + 3NaOH(aq)$$
$$\rightarrow Al(OH)_3(s) + 3NaCl(aq)$$
white precipitate

Other metal ions such as calcium and magnesium also give a white precipitate in this test, so this may not seem to help very much. However, the aluminium hydroxide precipitate will re-dissolve if **excess** sodium hydroxide is added. The precipitates of calcium hydroxide or magnesium hydroxide will not do this; they are **basic** hydroxides, whereas aluminium hydroxide is **amphoteric** (page 152). Aluminium hydroxide reacts with sodium hydroxide to produce the soluble salt, sodium aluminate:

aluminium hydroxide + sodium hydroxide
→ sodium aluminate

$$Al(OH)_3(s) + 3NaOH(aq) \rightarrow Na_3Al(OH)_6(aq)$$
white precipitate   colourless solution

A strong alkali such as sodium hydroxide is needed to produce this reaction. Ammonia solution, which is only a weak alkali, will not re-dissolve the aluminium hydroxide precipitate.

Summary of core material

You should know that:

- aluminium is a reactive metal, but its reactivity is masked by a protective oxide layer

- aluminium is used to extract small quantities of some metals from their oxides (for example, iron from iron(III) oxide)

- its properties as a strong metal with low density combined with its resistance to corrosion make it a useful construction metal.

9.7 The most important export from Jamaica is aluminium oxide, which is obtained from an ore called bauxite. Bauxite is hydrated aluminium oxide and contains iron(III) oxide as the main impurity.

Aqueous sodium hydroxide is added to the ore to dissolve the aluminium oxide. The iron(III) oxide does not dissolve in aqueous sodium hydroxide. The impurities, together with the waste sodium hydroxide, are known as red mud.

(a) Suggest *two* ways by which you could speed up the dissolving of aluminium oxide in aqueous sodium hydroxide. [2]

(b) The red mud, which has a pH of 12 to 13, is stored in large ponds which cause pollution. Chemists are trying to devise ways of using the chemicals in the red mud.
  (i) Why is the pH of the red mud so high? [1]
  (ii) What is *pollution*? [2]
  (iii) Name the substance that causes the mud to be red. [1]

(c) There is a danger of sodium hydroxide from the red mud ponds leaking into the water supply of Jamaica.
  (i) If water from the ponds leaked into the water supply, how should it be treated to change its pH to 7? [2]
  (ii) State *two* other ways in which water is treated to make it fit to drink. [2]

(d) Aluminium is made from aluminium oxide by electrolysis.
  (i) Solid aluminium oxide does not conduct electricity. In industry, how is it made to conduct? [1]
  (ii) Name the element used to make the electrodes in the manufacture of aluminium. [1]
  (iii) At which electrode is aluminium obtained? [1]

(IGCSE, part question, 1992)

9.8 Pure aluminium was first obtained by the French scientist Deville in 1854. He reduced aluminium chloride to the metal by heating it with sodium in a platinum crucible. The very reactive metal, sodium, had been isolated thirty years earlier. Its use in the extraction made aluminium more expensive than silver.

(a) (i) Name a metal, other than silver, which is expensive because it is rare. [1]
  (ii) Suggest another metal which is expensive because of difficulty in extracting it from its compounds. [1]
  (iii) Aluminium is used to make food containers. Give the most important reason why it is used for this purpose. [1]
  (iv) Suggest a reason why a crucible made out of platinum was used. [1]
  (v) The reduction of an aluminium compound by sodium can be described by two ionic equations. Complete the second equation: [1]
  $$Na \rightarrow Na^+ + e^-$$
  $$Al^{3+} + \ldots\ldots \rightarrow Al$$

(b) Sodium had been isolated by the electrolysis of its molten chloride. This chloride melts at about 800°C and when molten it is a good conductor of electricity. Molten aluminium chloride is a poor conductor of electricity and aluminium oxide has a very high melting point, 2000°C. The modern method of extracting aluminium was discovered by C. Hall in the USA. Aluminium oxide was dissolved in molten cryolite and the mixture electrolysed.
  (i) Suggest an explanation why molten sodium chloride is a good conductor but molten aluminium chloride is a poor conductor of electricity. [2]
  (ii) Explain why the cryolite was needed in the molten mixture. [1]
  (iii) Sketch and complete the labelling of the diagram below which shows the electrolysis of aluminium oxide in cryolite. [3]

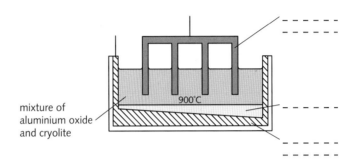

mixture of aluminium oxide and cryolite

900°C

  (iv) Explain why aluminium cans should be collected and recycled. [1]

(c) To find out if a metal can was made of aluminium, the following experiment was performed.

  A small piece of the metal was added to an excess of dilute hydrochloric acid: then aqueous sodium hydroxide was added dropwise until it was in excess.

  Describe what would be observed if the metal was aluminium. [3]

(IGCSE, 1992)

The transition elements

This section covers the following ideas:

- the transition elements
- the distinctive properties of these metals
  - coloured compounds
  - multiple valencies
  - use as catalysts
  - the magnetism of iron, cobalt and nickel
- some particular reactions of iron, copper and zinc.

II												III
Be												B
Mg												Al
Ca	Sc	Ti	V	Cr	Mn	Fe	Co	Ni	Cu	Zn		Ga
Sr	Y	Zr	Nb	Mo	Tc	Ru	Rh	Pd	Ag	Cd		In
Ba		Hf	Ta	W	Re	Os	Ir	Pt	Au	Hg		Tl
Ra												

The famous bridge at Ironbridge in Shropshire, England (figure 9.9), marks a historic industrial revolution in Europe. Made from cast iron and opened in 1781, it was the first iron bridge in the world. The metal iron is a transition element. We use about nine times more iron than all the other metals put together. Modern bridges (such as the Forth road bridge, in Scotland) are now made of steel, where iron is alloyed with other transition elements and carbon to make it stronger.

The general features of **transition elements** (also called transition metals) make them the most useful metallic elements available to us. They are much less reactive than the metals in Groups I and II. Many have excellent corrosion resistance, for example chromium. The very high melting point of tungsten (3410 °C) has led to its use in the filaments of light bulbs.

The **transition elements** have the following **general features:**

- they are hard
- they have high tensile strength
- they have high density
- they have high melting and boiling points
- they are good conductors of heat and electricity
- they are malleable and ductile.

These *general* properties mean that the transition elements are useful in a number of different ways. In addition there are *particular* properties that make these metals distinctive and useful for more specific purposes.

The **distinctive properties** of the **transition elements:**

- many of their compounds are coloured
- these metals often show more than one valency – they form more than one type of ion
- the metals or their compounds often make useful catalysts
- a few of the metals are strongly magnetic (iron, cobalt and nickel).

Figure 9.9 *The bridge at Ironbridge was the first ever built of iron.*

9.12 Coloured compounds

The salts of the metals in Groups I, II and III are generally white solids. They give colourless solutions if they dissolve in water. In contrast, the salts of the transition elements are often coloured and produce coloured solutions when dissolved. For example, vanadium compounds in solution can be yellow, blue, green or purple. Some other examples of the colours produced by transition-element ions are given in table 9.4. The presence of such metals in negative ions also gives rise to colour (table 9.4).

The transition elements are one of the major contributors to colour in our lives. The impressive colours of stained glass windows are produced by the presence of these metal ions in the glass (figure 9.10 on page 263). Similar **trace amounts** (very

Table 9.4 **The colours of some transition-element ions in solution***

Metal ion in solution		Colour
Copper(II)	Cu^{2+}	blue
Iron(II)	Fe^{2+}	green
Iron(III)	Fe^{3+}	red-brown
Chromium(III)	Cr^{3+}	green
Cobalt(II)	Co^{2+}	blue
Manganate(VII)	MnO_4^-	purple
Chromate(VI)	CrO_4^{2-}	yellow
Dichromate(VI)	$Cr_2O_7^{2-}$	orange

* Including some negative ions that contain these metals.

small amounts) of metals produce the colours of gemstones such as sapphire and ruby. These stones are **corundum**, the naturally occurring, colourless, crystalline form of aluminium oxide (Al_2O_3). Trace amounts of titanium and iron ions together produce the blue colour of sapphires, while chromium ions (Cr^{3+}) produce the red colour of rubies.

Some of the pigments used in paints also involve transition-element compounds, though many others are organic compounds. The yellow lines that restrict parking at the roadside are produced using paint that contains chrome yellow (lead(II) chromate). This was a pigment put to much more artistic use by Van Gogh in his painting 'A Wheatfield, with Cypresses'. Very detailed analysis has shown that he used chrome yellow mixed with zinc white and other pigments to produce the different shades of yellow in the wheatfield. Other examples of transition-element pigments include red ochre and yellow ochre, which are different forms of iron(III) oxide. In oil painting, these pigments are mixed with oil to spread them on the canvas. As the oil dries, it hardens into a film, which protects the pigment.

The colours associated with transition elements also help in chemical analysis. When testing a salt solution by adding sodium hydroxide, the transition elements give hydroxide precipitates with a characteristic colour. For example, iron(II) hydroxide is grey-green whereas iron(III) hydroxide is red-brown.

Figure 9.10 The Rose Window at York Minster. The colours of the stained glass are due to the presence of transition metal ions in the glass.

9.13 Variable valency

The metals in Group I always show a **valency** of 1. When reacting to form ionic compounds, their atoms *lose* their one outer electron to form ions with a single positive charge (Na^+, K^+, etc.). The metals in Group II all show a valency of 2; they form ions with two positive charges (Mg^{2+}, Ca^{2+}, etc.). Aluminium in Group III has a valency of 3 and always forms the Al^{3+} ion.

Transition-element atoms, however, are not so straightforward. For example, iron atoms can lose either two electrons, to form the Fe^{2+} ion, or three electrons, to give Fe^{3+}. Compounds containing these ions have different colours and different properties. A distinction is made in their name: iron(II) oxide has the formula FeO, iron(III) oxide the formula Fe_2O_3. Other transition elements also have more than one valency.

9.14 Catalytic properties

Catalysts are substances that speed up a chemical reaction without themselves being used up or changed at the end of the reaction. Many of the important industrial catalysts are either transition elements or their compounds, for example iron in the Haber process, and nickel in the hydrogenation of fats to make margarine. An example is shown in figure 9.11.

9.15 Magnetic properties

Three of the first row of transition elements are strongly **magnetic** (or **ferromagnetic**). These are iron, cobalt and nickel. The liquid iron and nickel of the Earth's outer core produce the planet's magnetic field, while the solid inner core may anchor the field.

Figure 9.11 A surface catalyst used in the cracking of oil.

EXTENSION

The reactions of certain transition elements

Iron

Iron is only a moderately reactive metal, but it will still react with steam or acids to displace hydrogen gas. For example

iron + hydrochloric acid
→ iron(II) chloride + hydrogen

$Fe(s) + 2HCl(aq) \rightarrow FeCl_2(aq) + H_2(g)$

The fact that iron can form two different positive ions means that an **analytical test** is needed to distinguish between the two. The salt being tested is dissolved in water and then alkali is added.

With solutions of **iron(II) salts**, a grey-green **gelatinous** (jelly-like) precipitate of iron(II) hydroxide is formed on adding the alkali:

iron(II) chloride + sodium hydroxide
→ iron(II) hydroxide + sodium chloride

$FeCl_2(aq) + 2NaOH(aq)$
$\rightarrow Fe(OH)_2(s) + 2NaCl(aq)$
grey-green precipitate

The precipitate is not affected by adding excess alkali. Also, the same precipitate is formed if ammonia solution is used instead of sodium hydroxide. If the precipitate is allowed to stand, it slowly turns brown at the surface. It is oxidised by the air to iron(III) hydroxide.

With solutions of **iron(III) salts**, a red-brown gelatinous precipitate of iron(III) hydroxide is formed when alkali is added:

iron(III) chloride + sodium hydroxide
→ iron(III) hydroxide + sodium chloride

$FeCl_3(aq) + 3NaOH(aq)$
$\rightarrow Fe(OH)_3(s) + 3NaCl(aq)$
red-brown precipitate

Copper

Copper has a distinctive colour. It is one of the least reactive metals in common use. It does *not* react with dilute acids to produce hydrogen. If the metal is heated in air, then a black layer of copper(II) oxide is formed on the metal:

copper + oxygen $\xrightarrow{\text{heat}}$ copper(II) oxide

$2Cu(s) + O_2(g) \rightarrow 2CuO(s)$

Copper statues become coated in a green layer of basic copper(II) carbonate (figure 9.12) when exposed to the atmosphere for a long time.

Figure 9.12 *The Statue of Liberty is made of copper sheets and has become coated in a layer of green copper carbonate.*

Copper(II) carbonate is also found in the Earth's crust as the mineral malachite. Like most other carbonates, copper(II) carbonate will decompose on heating to release carbon dioxide:

copper(II) carbonate $\xrightarrow{\text{heat}}$
copper(II) oxide + carbon dioxide

$CuCO_3(s) \xrightarrow{\text{heat}} CuO(s) + CO_2(g)$
green   black

The presence of copper ions in compounds can be detected using the **flame test**. It gives a characteristic blue-green colour. Solutions of copper salts also give a blue gelatinous precipitate of copper(II) hydroxide if sodium hydroxide is added:

copper(II) sulphate + sodium hydroxide
→ copper(II) hydroxide + sodium sulphate

$CuSO_4(aq) + 2NaOH(aq)$
$\rightarrow Cu(OH)_2(s) + Na_2SO_4(aq)$
blue precipitate

If the precipitate formed is heated carefully, it will turn black. Copper(II) hydroxide is unstable when heated and is converted to copper(II) oxide.

Ammonia solution will also produce the same blue precipitate of copper(II) hydroxide when added to copper(II) sulphate solution. However, if excess ammonia is added, the precipitate re-dissolves to give a deep-blue solution.

Zinc

Zinc is a moderately reactive metal that will displace hydrogen from steam or dilute acids:

zinc + steam $\xrightarrow{\text{heat}}$ zinc oxide + hydrogen

$Zn(s) + H_2O(g) \xrightarrow{\text{heat}} ZnO(s) + H_2(g)$

zinc + hydrochloric acid
→ zinc chloride + hydrogen

$Zn(s) + 2HCl(aq) \rightarrow ZnCl_2(aq) + H_2(g)$

Zinc carbonate decomposes on heating to give off carbon dioxide:

zinc carbonate $\xrightarrow{\text{heat}}$ zinc oxide + carbon dioxide

$\underset{\text{white}}{ZnCO_3(s)} \xrightarrow{\text{heat}} \underset{\text{white}}{ZnO(s)} + CO_2(g)$

Interestingly, when hot, the zinc oxide produced is yellow. However, when it cools down it turns white again. This is simply a **physical change** that occurs on heating, not a chemical reaction.

Solutions of zinc salts produce a white precipitate of zinc hydroxide when sodium hydroxide solution is added:

zinc sulphate + sodium hydroxide
→ zinc hydroxide + sodium sulphate

$ZnSO_4(aq) + 2NaOH(aq)$
$\rightarrow \underset{\text{white precipitate}}{Zn(OH)_2(s)} + Na_2SO_4(aq)$

Zinc hydroxide, like aluminium hydroxide, is an **amphoteric** hydroxide and it re-dissolves if excess sodium hydroxide is added. Zinc hydroxide reacts with excess sodium hydroxide to form sodium zincate:

zinc hydroxide + sodium hydroxide
→ sodium zincate

$\underset{\text{white precipitate}}{Zn(OH)_2(s)} + 2NaOH(aq) \rightarrow \underset{\text{colourless solution}}{Na_2Zn(OH)_4(aq)}$

These reactions with sodium hydroxide do not help us to distinguish between zinc salts and aluminium salts. Both give white precipitates that re-dissolve in excess alkali. The two *can* be distinguished, however, if ammonia solution is used, not sodium hydroxide. In both cases, the hydroxide precipitate forms; but zinc hydroxide re-dissolves in excess ammonia solution, whereas aluminium hydroxide does not.

Summary of core material

You should know that:

- the transition elements are less reactive than the metals in Groups I and II
- they have certain distinctive properties, which include
  - their variable valency
  - the formation of coloured compounds
  - the metals or their compounds often make good catalysts.

Summary of extension material

You should know that:

- the salts of iron, copper and zinc have characteristic reactions with sodium hydroxide and ammonia solutions that help to distinguish them in analysis.

9.9 A student collected samples of two minerals, **A** and **B**, whilst on a field course. Both minerals were colourless and crystalline, though **B** was obviously mixed with small amounts of a red-brown solid.

(a) Fragments of each sample were moistened with concentrated hydrochloric acid and held in a Bunsen flame. The results were as shown. Copy and complete the table. [2]

Sample	Flame test colour	Ion present
A	dull red	
B	yellow	

(b) **A** was insoluble in water. It dissolved in dilute hydrochloric acid with the evolution of a gas which turned limewater cloudy (milky).
   (i) What was the gas? [1]
   (ii) Write the name or formula of **A**. [1]
   (iii) Write a balanced equation for the action of acid on **A**. [2]

(c) **B** was found to be almost completely soluble in water. When dilute nitric acid was added to the solution followed by aqueous silver nitrate, a white precipitate was obtained.
   (i) Write the name or formula for **B**. [1]
   (ii) Write a balanced equation to show what happened in this test. [2]

(d) The only part of **B** which did not dissolve in water was the red-brown solid. This was filtered off and washed well. It dissolved in hot dilute hydrochloric acid but did not effervesce. The resulting pale yellow solution gave a brown gelatinous precipitate with aqueous sodium hydroxide.
   (i) Give the formula of the cation in the red-brown solid and the pale yellow solution. [1]
   (ii) Suggest a possible identity for the red-brown solid impurity in **B**. [1]

(ULEAC, 1995)

9.10 The word cobalt is derived from the German word *kobald*, an evil spirit. The name was used for ores which did not give metals when treated. The word was used for minerals which coloured glass blue. Brandt isolated the metal cobalt in 1742.

(a) Cobalt ores are roasted to give cobalt oxide, CoO, which may be reduced to cobalt using hydrogen. Water is formed as the other product.
   (i) Write a word equation for this reaction. [2]
   (ii) Name another substance which you would expect to reduce cobalt oxide. [1]

(b) Cobalt is a transition metal. State *three* properties of cobalt which are typical only of a transition metal. [3]

(c) Cobalt has been used in electroplating in a similar way to copper. Draw a fully labelled diagram to show how you could electroplate a spoon with copper. [4]

(d) Cobalt-60 is an isotope of cobalt. It is a powerful emitter of gamma-rays.
   (i) Explain what is meant by the term *isotope*. [2]
   (ii) Suggest a use of a radioactive isotope such as cobalt-60. [1]

(e) The chemical properties of cobalt are similar to those of iron.
   (i) Write a word equation for the reaction of cobalt with dilute hydrochloric acid. [1]
   (ii) Write a word equation for the reaction of cobalt with chlorine. [1]
   (iii) What are the *two* common oxidation states of cobalt? [2]
   (iv) Describe a simple experiment to find out which metal, iron or cobalt, is the more reactive. [2]

(f) Cobalt hydroxides are amphoteric. What would be seen when an excess of aqueous sodium hydroxide is added gradually to aqueous cobalt sulphate? (It is *not* necessary to mention colours.) [2]

(g) Describe, giving essential practical details, the preparation of cobalt sulphate crystals from the insoluble compound cobalt carbonate. [4]

(IGCSE, 1991 and 1996)

9.11 Nickel is a transition element in the fourth period of the Periodic Table.

(a) Potassium and nickel are both metals.
   (i) Give *one* property possessed by both metals.
   (ii) Describe *two* differences in the properties of these metals.

(b) Nickel was first isolated in 1751 in Sweden. Large amounts of nickel are now extracted in Canada. Nickel ore is heated in air to give nickel oxide. This is reduced to impure nickel by heating with carbon.
   (i) Complete the equation
   $...NiO + C \rightarrow$ .... + ... [1]
   (ii) Carbon is the reducing agent. Suggest *two* other chemicals that could reduce nickel oxide to nickel. [2]

(c) One way of refining nickel is to react the impure metal with carbon monoxide. Only nickel reacts with the carbon monoxide and forms a volatile compound, nickel carbonyl. This can be decomposed to give pure nickel and carbon monoxide.
   (i) Suggest how nickel carbonyl might be decomposed. [1]
   (ii) What type is the reaction between nickel and carbon monoxide? [1]
   (iii) What is meant by *volatile*? [1]

(iv) Explain how this method separates nickel from the impurities. [2]

(d) Like copper, nickel can be refined by electrolysis. Copy and label the diagram to show the purification of nickel in the laboratory. [3]

(e) Nickel carbonyl has a formula of the type Ni(CO)$_n$. Its relative molecular mass is 171. Calculate the value of n. [2]

(IGCSE, 1995)

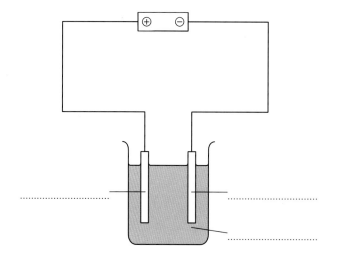

The reactivity of metals

This section covers the following ideas:

- the reactivity series
- methods of extraction in relation to reactivity
- metal displacement reactions.

Most of the elements in the Periodic Table are metals. Many of them are useful for a wide variety of purposes; some, such as iron, have an enormous number of uses. The early history of human life is marked by the metals used in making jewellery, ornaments and tools. Early civilisations used metals that could be found native (for example gold) for decorative items, and then alloys such as bronze. Later, iron was used for tools. Even after the Bronze and Iron Ages, only a few metals continued to be used widely. Other more reactive metals could not be obtained until the nineteenth century. Even among the metals that were available, there were obvious differences in resistance to corrosion. The Viking sword in figure 9.13 emphasises the different reactivities of gold and silver from that of iron.

We have seen how **reactivity** changes in a particular group. But the more important metals we use come from more than one group. Is there a broader picture in which we can compare these?

9.16 An overview of reactivity

We can get information on reactivity by investigating the following aspects of metal chemistry:

- ease of extraction
- reactions with air or oxygen
- reactions with water
- reactions with dilute acids
- metal displacement reactions and redox reactions
- heat stability of metal compounds.

The overall picture that emerges is summarised in figure 9.14 on page 268. This is known as the **reactivity series** of metals.

Figure 9.13 This Viking sword had a handle made from gold and silver and an iron blade. The blade has corroded badly but the handle is untouched.

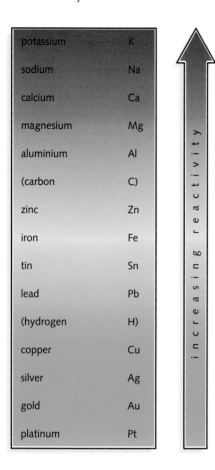

Figure 9.14 The reactivity series for metals.

9.17 The extraction of metals

A few metals are so *unreactive* that they occur in an uncombined (**native**) state. These **unreactive metals** include copper, gold and silver. The metals that occur native form the first broad group of metals.

However, most metals are *too reactive* to exist on their own in the ground. They exist combined with other elements as compounds called **ores** (table 9.5). These are the raw materials for making metals. The metals that must be mined as ores can be subdivided into two other broad groups.

The **moderately reactive metals** such as iron, zinc, tin and lead occur either as oxide or as sulphide ores. The sulphide ores can easily be converted to the oxide by heating in air. For example

zinc sulphide + oxygen
→ zinc oxide + sulphur dioxide

$$2ZnS(s) + 3O_2(g) \rightarrow 2ZnO(s) + 2SO_2(g)$$

To obtain the metal then requires **reduction** of the oxide. Carbon, in the form of coke, is used for this. Coke can be made cheaply from coal. At high temperatures, carbon has a strong tendency to react with oxygen. It is a good reducing agent and will remove oxygen from these metal ores:

zinc oxide + carbon → zinc + carbon dioxide

$$2ZnO(s) + C(s) \rightarrow 2Zn(s) + CO_2(g)$$

So this group of moderately reactive metals can be extracted by reduction with carbon using essentially the blast furnace method (page 284).

However, some metals are too reactive to be extracted by this method. The **very reactive metals** such as aluminium, magnesium and sodium have to be extracted by **electrolysis** of their molten ores. The three broad groups are summarised in table 9.6.

Table 9.5 Some metals and their ores

Metal	Name of ore	Compound present
Aluminium	bauxite	aluminium oxide, Al_2O_3
Copper	copper pyrites	copper iron sulphide, $CuFeS_2$
Iron	haematite	iron(III) oxide, Fe_2O_3
Sodium	rock salt	sodium chloride, NaCl
Tin	cassiterite	tin(IV) oxide, SnO_2
Zinc	zinc-blende	zinc sulphide, ZnS
Lead	galena	lead(II) sulphide, PbS

Table 9.6 Methods of extraction in relation to the reactivity series

	Metal	Method of extraction
decreasing reactivity	Potassium Sodium Calcium Magnesium Aluminium	*electrolysis* of molten ores
	Zinc Iron Tin Lead	*reduction* of oxides with carbon (sulphide ores heated to give oxide)
	Copper Silver Gold	*occur native* in the ground

9.18 Reactions of metals with air, water and dilute acids

Considering the methods of extraction of the metals gives a broad pattern of reactivity. More detail can be found by looking at certain basic reactions of metals. The results are summarised in table 9.7 below.

9.19 Metal displacement reactions

This type of reaction can help us to place particular metals more precisely in the reactivity series. We can use it to compare directly the reactivity of two metals. In a **displacement reaction**, a more reactive metal displaces a less reactive metal from solutions of salts of the less reactive metal.

In this type of reaction, the two metals are in direct 'competition'. If a piece of zinc is left to stand in a solution of copper(II) sulphate, a reaction occurs:

zinc + copper(II) sulphate
→ zinc sulphate + copper

$$Zn(s) + CuSO_4(aq) \rightarrow ZnSO_4(aq) + Cu(s)$$
grey   blue   colourless   red-brown

The observed effect of the reaction is that the zinc metal becomes coated with a red-brown layer of copper. The blue colour of the solution fades. The solution will eventually become colourless zinc sulphate.

> Zinc displaces copper from solution, so zinc is more reactive than copper.

The reverse reaction does not happen. A piece of copper does not react with zinc sulphate solution.

It is possible to confirm the reactivity series using displacement reactions of this type. For example, if copper metal is put into colourless silver nitrate solution, the copper will become coated with silver, and the solution becomes blue, owing to the formation of copper nitrate solution:

$$2AgNO_3(aq) + Cu(s) \rightarrow Cu(NO_3)_2(aq) + 2Ag(s)$$

> Copper displaces silver from solution, so copper is more reactive than silver.

9.20 Other redox competition reactions

Reactive metals are good **reducing agents**. The thermit reaction on page 259 is an example of a competition reaction in the solid state. Aluminium, the more reactive metal, removes oxygen from the less reactive iron in iron(III) oxide:

iron(III) oxide + aluminium $\xrightarrow{\text{heat}}$
aluminium oxide + iron

$$Fe_2O_3(s) + 2Al(s) \xrightarrow{\text{heat}} Al_2O_3(s) + 2Fe(s)$$

This is a **redox reaction** (page 106).

Table 9.7 The reaction of metals with air, water and dilute hydrochloric acid

Reactivity series	Reaction with		
	Air	Water	Dilute HCl
Sodium Calcium Magnesium	burn very strongly in air to form oxide	react with cold water to give hydrogen	react very strongly to give hydrogen
Aluminium* Zinc Iron	burn less strongly in air to form oxide	react with steam, when heated, to give hydrogen	react less strongly to give hydrogen
Lead Copper	react slowly to form oxide layer when heated	do not react	do not react
Silver Gold	do not react	do not react	do not react

*The reactivity of aluminium is masked by a layer of aluminium oxide. This position is established with the layer removed.

EXTENSION

The nature of the reaction taking place between zinc and copper sulphate can be explored in more detail by looking at the ionic equation:

zinc + copper(II) ions → zinc ions + copper

$$Zn(s) + Cu^{2+}(aq) \rightarrow Zn^{2+}(aq) + Cu(s)$$

This shows that the reaction is a **redox reaction** involving the transfer of two electrons from zinc atoms to copper(II) ions. Zinc atoms are oxidised to zinc ions, while copper(II) ions are reduced (figure 9.15). In general, the atoms of the more reactive metal lose electrons to become positive ions. A consideration of the **oxidation numbers** of the atoms and ions involved also shows that this is a redox reaction.

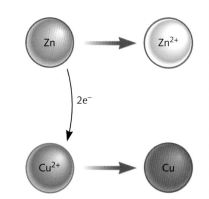

REDUCING AGENT
- Zn loses electrons
- Zn is oxidised
- Oxidation number increases

$2e^-$

OXIDISING AGENT
- Cu^{2+} gains electrons
- Cu^{2+} is reduced
- Oxidation number decreases

Figure 9.15 The displacement reaction between zinc and copper(II) sulphate is a redox reaction. A summary of the redox change in terms of oxidation number and electron exchange is shown.

Similar redox reactions can be used to extract metals other than iron. As we noted on page 258, before the electrolytic method for extracting aluminium was devised, the metal was prepared from aluminium chloride using sodium as a reducing agent:

aluminium chloride + sodium $\xrightarrow{\text{heat}}$
sodium chloride + aluminium

$$AlCl_3(s) + 3Na(s) \xrightarrow{\text{heat}} 3NaCl(s) + Al(s)$$

Like displacement reactions in solution, this type of reaction helps us to compare directly the reactivity of two metals and to establish the order of the reactivity series.

9.21 Thermal decomposition of metal compounds

The **stability** of certain metal compounds is related to the reactivity of the metal. For instance, most metal carbonates are decomposed on heating:

magnesium carbonate $\xrightarrow{\text{heat}}$
magnesium oxide + carbon dioxide

$$MgCO_3(s) \xrightarrow{\text{heat}} MgO(s) + CO_2(g)$$

However, sodium carbonate is stable to heat. So also are the carbonates of metals below sodium in Group I as they are more reactive than sodium.

Metal hydroxides and nitrates are also unstable to heat. Most decompose to give the metal oxide:

magnesium hydroxide $\xrightarrow{\text{heat}}$
magnesium oxide + water

$$Mg(OH)_2(s) \xrightarrow{\text{heat}} MgO(s) + H_2O(g)$$

lead(II) nitrate $\xrightarrow{\text{heat}}$ lead(II) oxide +
nitrogen dioxide + oxygen

$$2Pb(NO_3)_2(s) \xrightarrow{\text{heat}} 2PbO(s) + 4NO_2(g) + O_2(g)$$

However, sodium and potassium hydroxides are stable to heat: they do not decompose. The nitrates of sodium and potassium do not decompose as far as those of less reactive metals. They lose oxygen to form sodium or potassium nitrite:

potassium nitrate $\xrightarrow{\text{heat}}$ potassium nitrite + oxygen

$$2KNO_3(s) \xrightarrow{\text{heat}} 2KNO_2(s) + O_2(g)$$

Summary of core material

You should know that:

- the metals can be arranged into a series based on their ease of extraction and reactivity in a number of different situations

- the most reactive metals lie to the left of the Periodic Table, while the least reactive are found among the transition elements

- within a particular group of metals in the Periodic Table, reactivity increases down the group.

9.12

(a) When magnesium is heated in steam it reacts rapidly, forming a white solid and hydrogen gas.

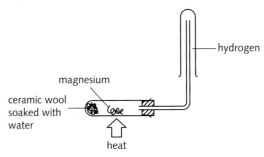

- (i) Why can hydrogen be collected as shown in the diagram above? [1]
- (ii) How would you show that the gas collected in the test tube is hydrogen? [2]
- (iii) Write word and balanced chemical equations for the reaction of magnesium with steam. [3]

(b) (i) Choose *one* metal, from the reactivity series, that will not react with steam. [1]
- (ii) Choose *one* metal, from the reactivity series, that will safely react with dilute sulphuric acid. [1]
- (iii) Name the salt formed when your chosen metal in (ii) reacts with sulphuric acid. [1]

(c) In each of the experiments below a piece of metal is placed in a metal salt solution. In the table of observations below the diagrams, what are (i)–(vi)? [6]

		zinc	zinc	tin	silver	copper
		tin(II) chloride solution	copper(II) sulphate solution	copper(II) sulphate solution	copper(II) sulphate solution	silver nitrate solution
At start	Colour of metal	grey	(i)	silver-coloured	silver-coloured	(v)
	Colour of solution	colourless	(ii)	blue	blue	colourless
At end	Colour of metal	coated with silver-coloured crystals	(iii)	coated with a brown solid	silver-coloured	coated with silver-coloured crystals
	Colour of solution	colourless	(iv)	colourless	blue	(vi)

(d) Use these results to place the metals copper, silver, tin and zinc in order of reactivity (put the most reactive metal first). [3]

(SEG, 1990)

9.13 Chromium (Cr) is a useful, dense, silvery metal obtained from chromium oxide. The oxide is reacted with aluminium metal to give chromium metal. The equation for this reaction, which is strongly exothermic, is shown below:

chromium oxide + aluminium
$\rightarrow$ aluminium oxide + chromium

$Cr_2O_3 + 2Al \rightarrow Al_2O_3 + 2Cr$

(a) (i) In what period of the Periodic Table is chromium? [1]

(ii) Name *one* element that will have properties similar to those of chromium. [1]

(iii) How many neutrons are there in an atom of chromium with a mass number of 52? [1]

(iv) Chromium forms ions for which the symbol is Cr^{3+}. What is the total number of electrons in one of these ions? [1]

(v) What type of reaction is shown by the equation at the start of the question? Chose the correct answer from the following: [1]

displacement   double decomposition
neutralisation   synthesis

(vi) What information, given in the question, shows that aluminium is higher in the reactivity series than chromium? [1]

(vii) Chromium is, in fact, fairly low in the reactivity series. Suggest *one* reason why being low in the reactivity series makes chromium useful. [1]

(viii) One of the major costs in the extraction of aluminium is the provision of energy. Why is the provision of energy not a major cost to the manufacturers of chromium? [1]

(b) Metals are good conductors of electricity even in the solid state. Explain how the bonding of atoms in a metal enables it to conduct electricity in this solid state. [2]

(SEG, 1995)

9.14

(a) A group of students looked at the reactions of metal sulphate solutions with different metals. They used the same concentration and always added an excess of the metal. Their observations are given in the table below.

Metal sulphate	Colour of sulphate solution	Metals			
		Chromium	Cobalt	Copper	Magnesium
Chromium	green	–	no reaction	no reaction	colourless solution, grey solid
Cobalt	pink	green solution, grey solid	–	no reaction	colourless solution, grey solid
Copper	blue	green solution, grey solid	pink solution, grey solid	–	colourless solution, grey solid
Magnesium	colourless	no reaction	no reaction	no reaction	–

(i) Which metal reacted with all the other metal sulphate solutions? [1]

(ii) Which metal did not react with any of the other metal sulphate solutions? [1]

(iii) Put the metals in their order of reactivity, with the most reactive first. [2]

(iv) Iron is slightly more reactive than cobalt. With which other metal sulphate solution will it react? [1]

(b) One method of joining railway lines is the 'thermit' reaction. Iron(III) oxide and powdered aluminium are mixed together, and heated until the reaction starts. After the reaction has started it becomes red hot. The melted iron runs into the gap between the railway lines.

(i) From this reaction what can you conclude about the reactivity of aluminium compared to iron? [1]

(ii) Is the reaction exothermic or endothermic? Give a reason for your answer. [2]

(iii) Write a word equation for the reaction. [1]

(NISEAC, 1991)

9.15

(a) There are two main methods of extracting metals from their compounds – reduction with carbon and electrolysis.

(i) Why does the method chosen depend upon the position of the metal in the reactivity series of metals? [2]

(ii) Use the Periodic Table to suggest why gallium is more likely to be manufactured by electrolysis. [2]

(b) Gallium can be obtained by the electrolysis of gallium chloride.

(i) Using the Periodic Table, state the charge that will be present on a gallium ion, and the reason for this. [2]

(ii) If the current flowing is 200 A, calculate the number of hours required to deposit one kilogram of gallium. [3]
(4114 coulombs are required to deposit 1 g of gallium.)

(c) Gallium, like most metals, has a high density.

(i) Draw a diagram to show the arrangement of atoms in a pure metal. [1]

(ii) Explain why metals such as gallium have a high density. [2]

(d) State the formula of any *one* compound of gallium. Predict, with a reason, *one* chemical property of it. [3]

(ULEAC, 1995)

This section covers the following ideas:
- electrochemical cells
- fuel cells.

9.22 Electrochemical cells

The reactivity series of metals is based on the fact that some metals are more ready to form ions than others. Such metals are more reactive than others. A piece of zinc is more likely to form ions than a piece of copper when placed in an electrolyte solution. This difference is the basis of **electrochemical cells** and **batteries**. It also helps us to confirm the order of the metals in the reactivity series.

An unusual way to power a simple digital clock is with an electrical cell made using a potato. The current is produced by pushing two different metals (for example copper and zinc) into the potato. The metals make contact with the solution that moistens the flesh of the potato. Connecting up these electrodes to the clock results in a small current. You could even use the apple you were going to have for lunch or a water melon to power the clock!

A simple **cell** works best if the metals used as the electrodes are far apart in the reactivity series. The voltage of a cell made using zinc and copper

electrodes is about 1.1 V. If a magnesium strip is used instead of zinc, then the voltage increases to about 2.7 V because magnesium is more reactive than zinc (figure 9.16). The further apart the metals are in the reactivity series, the greater the cell voltage becomes. This explains the use of lithium, the very reactive metal at the top of Group I, as one of the electrodes in modern lithium batteries. The aim is to make the difference in reactivity as large as is safely possible.

9.23 Portable power

The first cells made were not very portable because they contained liquids. Modern 'dry' cells use a damp electrolyte paste between the electrodes (figure 9.17). Alkaline cells are longer-

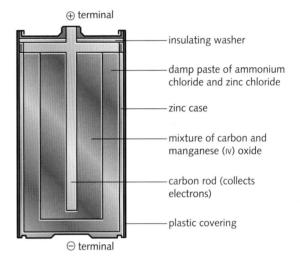

Figure 9.17 A zinc–carbon 'dry' cell.

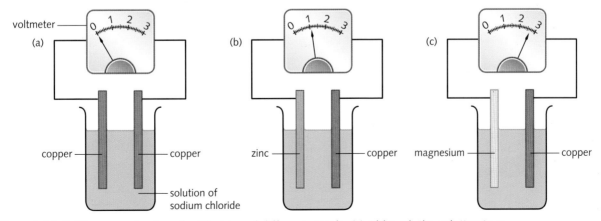

Figure 9.16 Setting up a simple cell with strips of different metals. (a) Although the solution is an electrolyte, with two copper strips nothing happens. (b) With one zinc and one copper electrode, there is a voltage. (c) With magnesium and copper electrodes, the voltage is even bigger.

273

lasting and use a mixture of MnO_2 and KOH in the paste. Small 'button' cells use either mercury(II) oxide or silver oxide as the cathode (figure 9.18). They are small and useful for watches, hearing aids, etc.

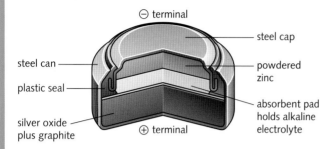

Figure 9.18 A button cell.

A **battery** consists of several cells arranged in series to produce a higher voltage. A **primary** battery or cell cannot be recharged. A **secondary** battery or cell such as the lead–acid car battery is rechargeable. The 12 V car battery contains six 2 V lead–acid cells in series (figure 9.19). The chemical reaction that takes place in these cells is **reversible**. When the battery is in use, the following reaction occurs:

lead + lead(IV) oxide + sulphuric acid
→ lead(II) sulphate + water

When it is recharged, current is supplied to reverse the chemical reaction, restoring the

chemicals to their original state:

$$lead(II)\ sulphate + water \xrightarrow[\text{energy}]{\text{electrical}} lead +$$
lead(IV) oxide + sulphuric acid

9.24 Oxidation and reduction in power cells

In electrical power cells, the electrode made from the more reactive metal is the one at which electrons are released. The first electrochemical cell, for example, consisted of zinc and copper electrodes in a copper(II) sulphate solution. Zinc is more reactive than copper. At this electrode, zinc atoms become zinc ions:

$$Zn(s) \rightarrow Zn^{2+}(aq) + 2e^- \qquad \text{oxidation}$$

while at the other terminal, copper ions become copper atoms:

$$Cu^{2+}(aq) + 2e^- \rightarrow Cu(s) \qquad \text{reduction}$$

The zinc electrode becomes the negative terminal as electrons are released (oxidation takes place). The copper electrode becomes the positive terminal where electrons are removed, and gained by the copper(II) ions (reduction takes place). The overall reaction of the cell is the same as the ionic equation for the displacement reaction that can be done in a test tube:

$$Zn(s) + Cu^{2+}(aq) \rightarrow Zn^{2+}(aq) + Cu(s)$$

These ideas make it important that we know how to name the electrodes in both this type of power cell and in electrolytic cells (see page 115). The same rule applies to both types of cell.

In *all* types of cell:
- the **anode** is the electrode at which electrons are released (oxidation occurs)
- the **cathode** is the electrode at which electrons are gained (reduction occurs).

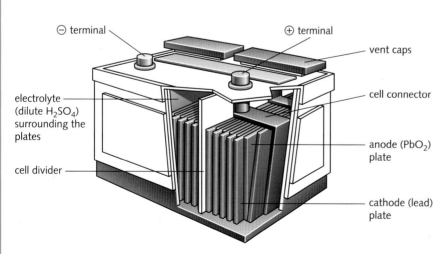

Figure 9.19 Car batteries are made up of six cells connected together – they are rechargeable.

This means that the anode has the opposite sign in the two types of cell, as table 9.8 makes clear.

Table 9.8 Signs of electrodes in two types of cell

Cell type	Anode	Cathode
Power cells	negative electrode (−)	positive electrode (+)
Electrolytic cells	positive electrode (+)	negative electrode (−)

9.25 Fuel cells

Research has found a much more efficient way of changing chemical energy into electrical energy by using a **fuel cell**. A typical fuel cell was shown in the previous chapter (figure 8.3 on page 207), where it was used to power an electric car. Such a cell operates continuously, with no need for recharging. The cell supplies energy as long as the reactants are fed in to the electrodes. The overall reaction of the hydrogen–oxygen fuel cell (figure 9.20) is that of the combustion of hydrogen.

The reaction at the anode (−) is:

$$H_2(g) \rightarrow 2H^+(aq) + 2e^-$$
oxidation

The reaction at the cathode (+) is:

$$4H^+(aq) + O_2(g) + 4e^- \rightarrow 2H_2O(g)$$
reduction

Thus, overall:

hydrogen + oxygen → water

$$2H_2(g) + O_2(g) \rightarrow 2H_2O(g)$$

Such a cell was used in the NASA space programme to supply power and to produce water for the astronauts. The failure of one of these cells led to the *Columbia* mission of 1997 being recalled early. Other fuel cells are based on different combustion reactions, for example the methane–oxygen fuel cell.

Intriguingly, electric eels are mobile, natural fuel cells. The eel's head is the cathode (positive terminal) and its tail is the anode (negative terminal). A 1 m long eel has a potential difference of about 350 V. By a quirk of nature, an electric catfish has the opposite polarity.

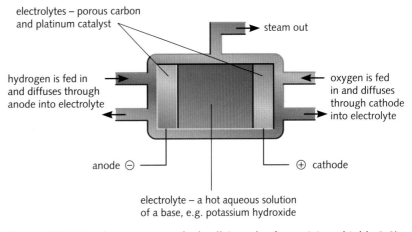

Figure 9.20 A hydrogen–oxygen fuel cell (see also figure 8.3 and table 9.8).

Summary of extension material

You should know that:

- differences in reactivity between metals can be used to generate electrical energy in cells and batteries
- the further apart the metals are in the reactivity series, the greater the voltage of the cell
- a primary cell cannot be recharged, whereas the reaction in a secondary cell is reversible and such a cell can be recharged
- the reactions taking place in cells are redox reactions
- the anode is the electrode at which oxidation takes place (electrons are released)
- the cathode is the electrode where reduction occurs (electrons are gained)
- fuel cells are continuously operating cells that do not require recharging – they may offer some solutions to energy problems in the future.

9.16 A cell is set up as shown in the diagram.

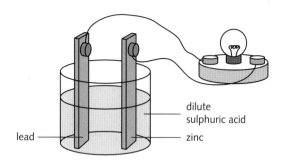

The bulb lights up. Bubbles of gas form on the zinc. The zinc metal starts to dissolve.

(a) How can you tell that a chemical reaction is taking place? [1]

(b) The cell is left connected to the light bulb. Suggest why the bulb slowly goes out. [1]

(c) A car battery is made of lead plates dipping into sulphuric acid. A car battery can be recharged.

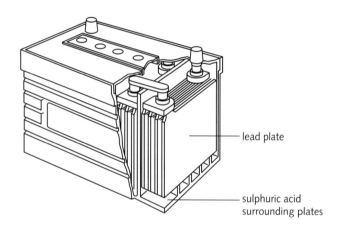

(i) What is meant by *recharged*? [1]
(ii) When the car battery is used, a chemical reaction takes place. What happens to this reaction when the battery is recharged? [1]

(d) When the car battery is used, lead atoms on the negative electrode lose electrons to form ions. Complete the equation to show what happens at this electrode: [1]

$$Pb(s) \rightarrow \ldots\ldots(aq) + 2e^-$$

(MEG, 1995)

9.17 A student set up four electrochemical cells using various metals. An example of the apparatus is shown in the diagram.

(a) (i) Name the piece of apparatus labelled V. [1]
(ii) Explain the meaning of the word 'electrolyte'. [1]
(iii) Name a substance which could be used in solution as an electrolyte. [1]

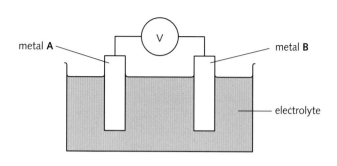

(b) The student measured the voltage produced by the four cells. Two of the results are shown in the table below.

Cell number	Metal A	Metal B	Voltage (volts)
1	iron	copper	0.8
2	magnesium	copper	2.7
3	copper	copper	
4	zinc	copper	

(i) Copy and complete the last two lines of the table of voltages by selecting from the following list: [2]
3.4 volts   1.1 volts   0.3 volts   0.0 volts
(ii) State *two* factors which must remain the same in all the experiments if the comparison of the voltages is to be fair. [2]
(iii) Name *two* metals which could safely be used to give a value bigger than 2.7 volts if they were connected together in a similar cell. [1]

(NEAB, 1991)

9.18 The batteries in watches and calculators must be small. They are often called button cells. The diagram below shows the structure of such a button cell.

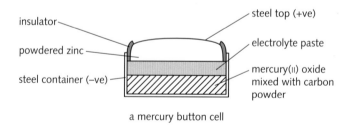

a mercury button cell

(a) The insulator separates the steel top from the bottom part of the cell.
(i) What is an *insulator*? [1]
(ii) Why is the insulator placed between the top and the bottom of the cell? [1]
(iii) Suggest a material from which the insulator for the battery might be made. [1]

(b) The electricity is produced in the cell by the reaction of zinc with mercury(II) ions in mercury(II) oxide. Zinc atoms lose electrons and mercury(II) ions accept them.

(i) What is an *ion*? [2]

(ii) Copy and complete the following equations by using e⁻, the symbol for an electron: [2]

$$Zn \rightarrow Zn^{2+} + \ldots\ldots$$
$$Hg^{2+} + \ldots\ldots \rightarrow Hg$$

(iii) The zinc is oxidised at the same time that the mercury(II) oxide is reduced. What name is used for oxidation and reduction taking place at the same time? [1]

(iv) Suggest why the chemicals in the battery are powdered rather than solid lumps. [1]

(IGCSE, part question, 1990)

9.19 The diagram below shows a Daniell cell which produces one volt.

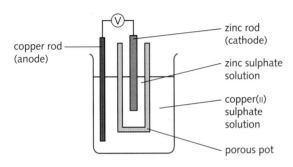

copper rod (anode)

zinc rod (cathode)

zinc sulphate solution

copper(II) sulphate solution

porous pot

(a) Sketch the diagram and mark on it the direction in which the electrons would flow. [1]

(b) (i) If magnesium was used in place of the zinc would you expect it to produce a greater or smaller voltage? Explain your answer. [1]

(ii) What will cause the cell to eventually stop working? [1]

(MEG, part question, 1993)

9.20 Redox reactions, whether they occur in a test tube, during electrolysis or in a cell, involve the transfer of electrons.

(a) To find the order of reactivity of the metals cobalt, manganese, mercury and tin, the following experiments were carried out.

Experiment	Result
Tin and mercury(II) nitrate solution	silvery layer on the tin
Tin and cobalt(II) nitrate solution	no reaction
Manganese and tin(II) nitrate solution	grey deposit formed on the surface of manganese

(i) Give as far as possible the order of reactivity of these metals. Write the least reactive first. [2]

(ii) What additional experiment needs to be done to put all four metals in order of reactivity? [1]

(iii) For which of the above four metals is it most difficult to lose electrons to form a positive ion? [1]

(iv) Write an ionic equation for the reaction between atoms of tin and mercury(II) ions to form tin(II) ions and mercury atoms. Indicate on this equation which change is oxidation and which is reduction. (Tin has atomic number 50, mercury has atomic number 80.) [2]

(b) A cell consists of two metals in a solution of an electrolyte. Three possible constructions for such a cell are shown below.

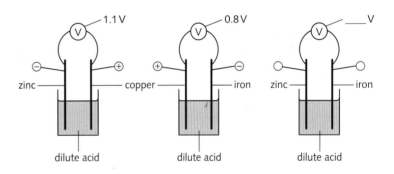

(i) Work out the voltage produced by the zinc/iron cell, and say which is the positive and negative electrode. [2]

(ii) A battery for a hearing aid needs a much larger voltage than those above. Suggest *two* metals which could be used for this battery. [1]

(IGCSE, part question, 1988)

10 Industrial inorganic chemistry

Chemical extraction of metals

This section covers the following ideas:

- the chemical extraction of metals
- the blast furnace extraction of iron
- steel-making
- rusting and rust prevention
- the extraction of zinc, lead and copper.

10.1 Iron and steel

In our modern world, we have invented and shaped many machines and clever devices. These are often made of **steel**. It is the most widely used of all metals. The durability, tensile strength (see page 87) and low cost of steel make it the basis of countless industries, from ship-building to watch-making.

Steel is made by hardening iron by adding small amounts of carbon and other elements (see page 279). Careful adjustment of the levels of **trace elements** (elements required in small amounts), which are often other transition elements, gives rise to a large number of carbon steels and alloy steels (see tables 10.1 and 10.2 on page 280). These have distinctive properties that suit them for particular applications. The **magnetic** properties of iron make it easy to separate steel products from other waste. This means that the metal can be efficiently recycled (see page 302).

10.2 The production of iron in the blast furnace

The main ore of iron is haematite (Fe_2O_3). The iron is obtained by reduction (see page 106) in a **blast furnace** (figure 10.1). The furnace is a steel tower about 30 metres high. It is lined with **refractory** (heat-resistant) bricks of magnesium oxide which are cooled by water. The furnace is loaded with the 'charge' consisting of iron ore, coke (a form of carbon made from coal) and limestone (calcium carbonate). The charge is **sintered** (heated to the melting point of the lowest-melting solid) to make sure the solids mix well.

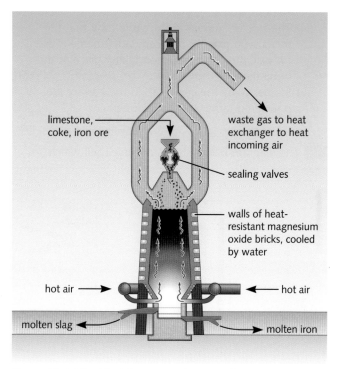

Figure 10.1 The blast furnace reduction of iron ore to iron.

Blasts of hot air are sent in through holes near the bottom of the furnace. The carbon burns in the air blast and the furnace gets very hot.

A series of chemical reactions takes place to produce molten iron (figure 10.2). The most important reaction that occurs is the reduction of the ore by carbon monoxide:

$$Fe_2O_3(s) + 3CO(g) \rightarrow 2Fe(s) + 3CO_2(g)$$

The iron produced flows to the bottom of the furnace where it can be 'tapped off' because the temperature at the bottom of the furnace is higher than the melting point of iron.

One of the major impurities in iron ore is sand (silica, SiO_2). The limestone added to the furnace helps to remove this impurity. The limestone decomposes to lime in the furnace. This then reacts with the silica:

$$limestone \xrightarrow{heat} lime + carbon\ dioxide$$

$$CaCO_3(s) \xrightarrow{heat} CaO(s) + CO_2(g)$$

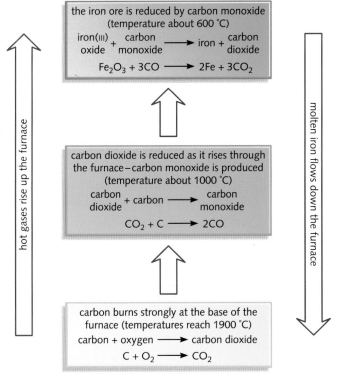

Figure 10.2 Iron is produced in the blast furnace by a series of reactions. Carbon monoxide is thought to be the main reducing agent.

lime + silica → calcium silicate

$$CaO(s) + SiO_2(s) \rightarrow CaSiO_3(l)$$

The calcium silicate formed is also molten. It flows down the furnace and forms a molten layer of **slag** on top of the iron. It does not mix with the iron, and is less dense. The molten slag is 'tapped off' separately. When solidified, the slag is used by builders and road-makers for foundations. The hot waste gases escape from the top of the furnace. They are used in heat exchangers to heat the incoming air. This helps to reduce the energy costs of the process. The extraction of iron is a continuous process. It is much cheaper than the electrolytic processes used to extract other metals (see pages 286–290).

The **blast furnace** extraction of iron:

- uses iron ore, coke, limestone and hot air
- involves the reduction of iron(III) oxide by carbon monoxide
- uses limestone to remove the main impurity (sand) as slag (calcium silicate).

10.3 Steel-making

The iron produced by the blast furnace is known as 'pig iron' or 'cast iron' and is not pure. It contains about 4% carbon, and other impurities. This amount of carbon makes the iron **brittle**. This limits the usefulness of the iron, though it can be cast (moulded) into large objects that are not likely to be subjected to deforming forces.

Most of the pig iron produced is taken to make steel. The carbon content is reduced by burning it off as carbon monoxide and carbon dioxide. Any sulphur contamination is oxidised to sulphur dioxide. This **basic oxygen process** is carried out in a tilting furnace (figure 10.3). The method is fast: 350 tonnes of molten iron can be converted in 40 minutes. Scrap steel is added to the molten pig iron for recycling. A high-speed jet of oxygen is blown into the vessel through a water-cooled lance. Some impurities, for example silicon and phosphorus, do not produce gaseous oxides, so lime (CaO) is added to the furnace. The impurities form a 'slag', which floats on top of the molten iron. The molten iron is poured off by tilting the furnace. Controlled amounts of carbon and other elements are added to make different types of steel (see tables 10.1 and 10.2 on page 280).

Figure 10.3 The different stages of the steel-making process (the basic oxygen process). (a) The furnace is charged with scrap steel and molten iron. (b) Oxygen is blown in through an 'oxygen lance'. (c) The molten steel, and then the slag, are poured from the furnace by tilting it in different directions.

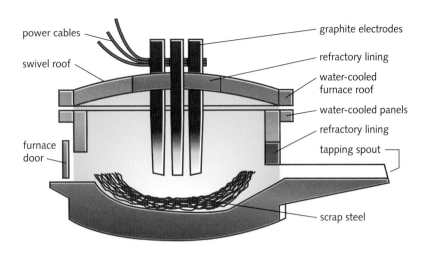

Figure 10.4 *The electric arc furnace for recycling scrap steel.*

An alternative process, known as the **electric arc furnace**, is used to make steel from scrap metal (figure 10.4). As more and more steel is recycled world-wide, it is predicted that this method will increase in use. Currently about 25% of the world's steel is produced by this method.

Carbon steels and alloy steels

Metallurgists have designed a wide variety of steels to suit particular applications. Some steels are alloys of iron and carbon only; the amount of carbon added varies up to 1.5% of the total composition. These **carbon steels**, which include the mild steel used for car bodies, are listed in table 10.1.

But carbon steels tend to rust unless protected. So other metals, for example chromium, are added to prevent corrosion and to make the steel harder. Some of these **alloy steels** are listed in table 10.2.

10.4 The rusting of iron

When a metal is attacked by air, water or other surrounding substances, it is said to **corrode**. In the case of iron and steel, the corrosion process is also known as **rusting**. Rusting is a serious economic problem. Large sums of money are spent each year replacing damaged iron and steel structures, or protecting structures from such damage. Rust is a red-brown powder consisting mainly of hydrated iron(III) oxide ($Fe_2O_3 \cdot xH_2O$). Water and oxygen are essential for iron to rust (figure 10.5). The

Table 10.1 Cast iron and carbon steels

Metal	Carbon content (%)	Properties	Uses
Mild steel	< 0.25	easily worked; not brittle	car bodies, chains, pylons
Medium steel	0.25–0.45	tougher than mild steel	car springs, axles, bridges
High-carbon steel	0.45–1.5	hard and brittle	chisels, cutting tools, razor blades
Cast iron	2.5–4.5	cheaper than steel; easily moulded	gear boxes, engine blocks, brake discs

Table 10.2 Some typical alloy steels

Steel*	Typical composition		Properties	Uses
Stainless steel	iron	74%	tough; does not corrode	cutlery, surgical instruments, kitchen sinks
	chromium	18%		
	nickel	8%		
Tungsten steel	iron	95%	tough; hard, even at high temperatures	edges of high-speed cutting tools
	tungsten	5%		
Manganese steel	iron	87%	tough; springy	drill bits, springs
	manganese	13%		

* All these alloys contain a low content of carbon (< 0.45%).

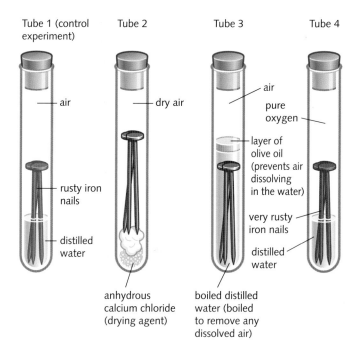

Tube 1 (control experiment) — air — rusty iron nails — distilled water

Tube 2 — dry air — anhydrous calcium chloride (drying agent)

Tube 3 — air — pure oxygen — layer of olive oil (prevents air dissolving in the water) — very rusty iron nails — distilled water — boiled distilled water (boiled to remove any dissolved air)

Tube 4

Figure 10.5 Investigating the factors that are involved in rusting. In tube 2, the air is dry, so the nails do not rust. In tube 3, there is no oxygen in the water, so the nails do not rust. In tube 4, pure oxygen and water are present, so the nails are very rusty.

problem is made worse by the presence of salt; sea water increases the rate of corrosion. Pictures from the sea-bed of the wreck of the *Titanic* show that it has a huge amount of rust. Acid rain also increases the rate at which iron objects rust.

Aluminium is *more* reactive than iron, but it does not corrode in the damaging way that iron does. Both metals react with air. In the case of aluminium, a very thin *single layer* of aluminium oxide forms, which sticks strongly to the surface of the metal. This **micro-layer** seals the metal surface and protects it from further attack. Aluminium is a useful construction material because it is protected by this layer. The protective layer can be made thicker by electrolysis (**anodising**, see page 290). In contrast, when iron corrodes, the rust forms in *flakes*. It does *not* form a single layer. The attack on the metal can continue over time as the rust flakes come off. Indeed, a sheet of iron can be eaten right through by the rusting process.

Chromium is another metal, similar to aluminium, that is protected by an oxide layer. If chromium is

alloyed with iron, a '**stainless**' steel is produced. However, it would be too expensive to use stainless steel for all the objects built out of iron. Electroplating a layer of chromium on steel is used to protect some objects from rusting, for example car bumpers, bicycle handlebars.

Rust prevention

There is a saying that: 'Necessity is the mother of invention!'. The need to protect iron and steel from rusting has led to many methods being devised. Some of these are outlined here.

- *Painting*
  This method is widespread for objects ranging in size from ships and bridges to garden gates. Some paints react with the iron to form a stronger protective layer. However, generally painting only protects the metal as long as the paint layer is unscratched. Regular re-painting is often necessary to keep this protection intact.

- *Oiling and greasing*
  The oiling and/or greasing of the moving parts of machinery forms a protective film, preventing rusting. Again the treatment must be repeated to continue the protection.

- *Plastic coatings*
  These are used to form a protective layer on items such as refrigerators, garden chairs, etc. The plastic PVC (see page 336) is often used for this purpose.

- *Electroplating*
  An iron or steel object can be electroplated (see page 290) with a layer of chromium or tin to protect against rusting. A 'tin can' is made of steel coated on both sides with a fine layer of tin. Tin is used because it is unreactive and non-toxic. However, this does raise a problem. With both these metals, if the protective layer is broken, then the steel beneath will begin to rust.

- *Galvanising*
  An object may be coated with a layer of the more reactive metal, zinc. This is called galvanising. It has the advantage over other plating methods in that the protection still works even if the zinc layer is badly scratched. The zinc layer can be applied by several different methods. These include electroplating

or dipping the object into molten zinc. The bodies of cars are dipped into a bath of molten zinc to form a protective layer.

- *Sacrificial protection*

   This is a method of rust prevention in which blocks of a reactive metal are attached to the iron surface. Zinc or magnesium blocks are attached to oil-rigs and to the hulls of ships (figure 10.6). These metals are more reactive than iron and will be corroded in preference to it. Underground gas and water pipes are connected by wire to blocks of magnesium to obtain the same protection. In all cases the metal blocks lose electrons in preference to the iron, and so prevent the iron forming iron(III) oxide.

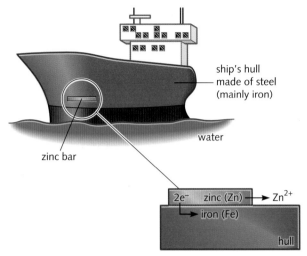

Figure 10.6 Blocks of zinc (or magnesium) are used for the sacrificial protection of the hulls of ships.

Summary of core material

You should know that:

- the extraction of iron in the blast furnace is the most important example of chemical reduction

- the iron produced can be converted into various forms of steel designed to suit a particular purpose

- iron and steel, although the major construction metals, suffer from problems of corrosion

- various methods exist to protect iron objects from corrosion (rusting).

10.1

(a) Copy out and balance the equation below for the reduction of iron(III) oxide with carbon monoxide: [2]

$$Fe_2O_3 + \ldots CO \rightarrow \ldots Fe + \ldots CO_2$$

(b) Although iron and sodium are obtained from compounds which are quite cheap, sodium is much more expensive than iron. Why is this so? [3]

(IGCSE, part question, 1991)

10.2

(a) Three tubes are set up as shown to find out what causes iron to rust.

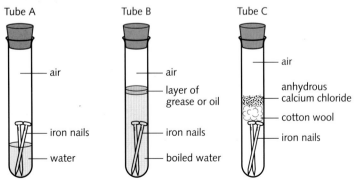

(i) Air dissolves in water. Why is the water boiled before use in tube B? [1]
(ii) Why is a layer of grease or oil put onto the water in tube B? [1]
(iii) Why are the following used in tube C? [3]
   Anhydrous calcium chloride
   Cotton wool
   The stopper
(iv) Copy the table. Give a reason for the observations made after a few days. [3]

Observation	Reason
Nails in tube A rust	
Nails in tube B do not rust	
Nails in tube C do not rust	

(v) What would happen if a lighted spill is put just into the open mouth of tube A at the end of the experiment? [1]
(vi) Give a reason for your answer to (v). [1]

(b) Zinc blocks are attached to the steel legs of oil platforms.

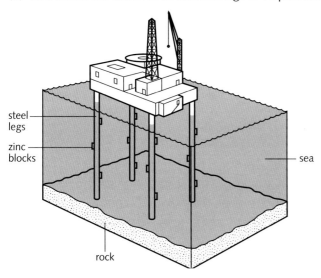

steel legs

zinc blocks

sea

rock

(i) Explain why the zinc blocks protect the steel legs from rusting. [2]

(ii) From the reactivity series name another metal that could be used for the blocks in place of zinc. [1]

(iii) Give another method that is also used to protect the steel legs from rusting. [1]

(iv) State how the method given in (iii) works. [1]

(v) Steel is an alloy. What is an *alloy*? [1]

(SEG, part question, 1988)

10.3 The main ore of iron, haematite, contains the compound iron(III) oxide, Fe_2O_3. The iron(III) oxide is reduced in a blast furnace to form iron.

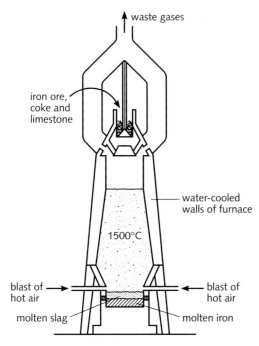

waste gases

iron ore, coke and limestone

water-cooled walls of furnace

1500°C

blast of hot air

blast of hot air

molten slag

molten iron

(a) Explain how the furnace is heated to the high temperatures needed for the reduction of the iron(III) oxide. [2]

(b) Give *two* ways by which carbon dioxide can be formed in the blast furnace. [2]

(c) Carbon dioxide reacts with carbon to form carbon monoxide. Write a balanced chemical equation for this reaction. [2]

(d) A molten slag forms in the furnace from the impurities present. The slag is formed by the reaction of silicon dioxide and calcium oxide. Explain why these two oxides react with each other. [2]

(e) The relative atomic masses are Fe 56, O 16.
(i) Work out the formula mass of iron(III) oxide, Fe_2O_3. [1]
(ii) Work out the percentage of iron in iron(III) oxide. [1]

(f) A blast furnace produces molten iron which contains impurities such as carbon and sulphur. To make steel, oxygen is blown onto the surface of the molten iron, as shown in the diagram. Other elements are then added to give the type of steel required.

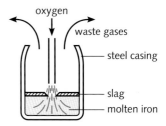

oxygen

waste gases

steel casing

slag

molten iron

(i) What is *slag*? [1]
(ii) Name the *two* waste gases formed when the oxygen reacts with the impurities. [2]
(iii) Give *one* reason why these waste gases could be harmful. [1]
(iv) Name *one* element which is added to iron to make steel. [1]

(SEG, part question, 1990 and 1993)

10.4
(a) Rusting involves the oxidation of iron to iron(III) oxide.
(i) Explain the meaning of *oxidation*. [1]
(ii) Copy and complete the equation for the oxidation of iron: [2]
$$...Fe + ...O_2 \rightarrow ...Fe_2O_3$$

(b) The rust on an iron surface may be removed by using dilute acid. Both iron and iron(III) oxide react with dilute sulphuric acid.
Copy and complete the following word equations: [2]

iron + sulphuric acid → iron(II) sulphate +
iron(III) oxide + sulphuric acid → iron(III) sulphate +

(c) Iron may be converted to mild steel and stainless steel.
(i) Name *one* use of mild steel.
(ii) Name *one* use of stainless steel. [2]

(IGCSE, part question, 1991)

EXTENSION

The extraction of zinc, lead and copper

Metals can be extracted from their ores by methods that depend on the reactivity of the metal concerned. Moderately reactive metals such as iron, zinc and lead may be extracted by chemical reduction using carbon.

10.5 The extraction of zinc and lead

The principal ores of both these metals are their sulphides: zinc-blende (ZnS) and galena (PbS). The extraction method used is similar for both. Both the ores first need purification, and this is achieved by **froth flotation**. The crushed ore is fed into tanks of water containing an oil–detergent mixture. Air is blown through the mixture, which is also stirred. The heavier contaminating silicate material sinks. The oil-coated, lighter mineral particles rise in an oily froth to the surface. The mineral particles are skimmed off with the froth, and then cleaned and dried.

In both cases the enriched sulphide ore is then heated very strongly in a current of air. This converts the sulphide to the metal oxide:

$$\text{metal sulphide} + \text{oxygen} \xrightarrow{\text{heat}} \text{metal oxide} + \text{sulphur dioxide}$$

$$2ZnS(s) + 3O_2(g) \xrightarrow{\text{heat}} 2ZnO(s) + 2SO_2(g)$$

$$2PbS(s) + 3O_2(g) \xrightarrow{\text{heat}} 2PbO(s) + 2SO_2(g)$$

The sulphur dioxide produced can be used to make sulphuric acid. The metal oxide is heated in a blast furnace with coke. Carbon monoxide reduces the oxides to the metal:

$$\text{zinc oxide} + \text{carbon monoxide} \xrightarrow{\text{heat}} \text{zinc} + \text{carbon dioxide}$$

$$ZnO(s) + CO(g) \xrightarrow{\text{heat}} Zn(g) + CO_2(g)$$

$$\text{lead(II) oxide} + \text{carbon monoxide} \xrightarrow{\text{heat}} \text{lead} + \text{carbon dioxide}$$

$$PbO(s) + CO(g) \xrightarrow{\text{heat}} Pb(l) + CO_2(g)$$

Zinc vapour passes out of the furnace and is cooled and condensed. Molten lead is collected from the bottom of the furnace.

Zinc is used in alloys such as brass and for galvanising iron. Lead is used in making batteries.

10.6 The extraction of copper

Copper is less reactive than the other metals we have considered so far. It can be found **native** in the USA, but most copper is extracted from copper pyrites, $CuFeS_2$. The crushed ore is again concentrated by froth flotation. The mineral particles are roasted in a limited supply of air to produce copper(I) sulphide:

$$\text{copper pyrites} + \text{oxygen} \xrightarrow{\text{heat}} \text{copper(I) sulphide} + \text{sulphur dioxide} + \text{iron(II) oxide}$$

$$2CuFeS_2(s) + 4O_2(g) \xrightarrow{\text{heat}} Cu_2S(s) + 3SO_2(g) + 2FeO(s)$$

Silica is added and the mixture heated to remove the iron(II) oxide as iron(II) silicate. The copper(I) sulphide can then be reduced to copper by heating in air:

$$\text{copper(I) sulphide} + \text{oxygen} \xrightarrow{\text{heat}} \text{copper} + \text{sulphur dioxide}$$

$$Cu_2S(s) + O_2(g) \xrightarrow{\text{heat}} 2Cu(s) + SO_2(g)$$

The copper produced by this method is suitable for piping and boilers. When it is to be used for electrical wiring, it must be **refined** (purified) by electrolysis (see page 124).

Figure 10.7 summarises the overall approach to extracting these metals from the middle to lower range of the reactivity series chemically.

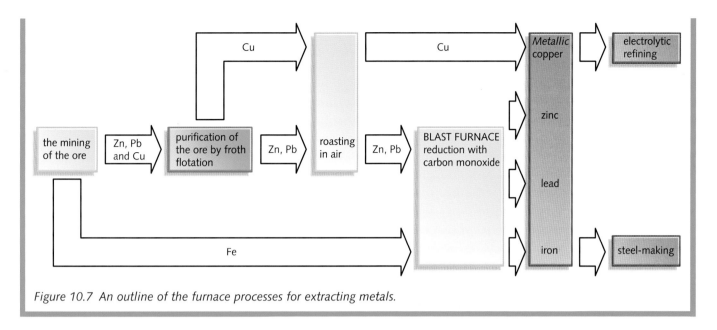

Figure 10.7 An outline of the furnace processes for extracting metals.

Summary of extension material

You should know that:

- moderately reactive metals may be extracted by chemical reduction using carbon

- metals such as zinc, lead and copper can be extracted by methods similar to the blast furnace process for iron.

10.5 Lead is obtained from its ore, which is an impure form of lead(II) sulphide. The ore is heated in air in order to convert the lead(II) sulphide into lead(II) oxide. Lead is extracted from its oxide by heating with limestone and coke, in a blast furnace. This is a similar process to the extraction of iron. Lead is a very dense metal.

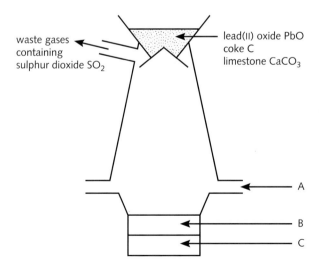

(a) (i) The lead(II) ion has the formula Pb^{2+} and the sulphide ion S^{2-}. What is the formula of lead(II) sulphide? [1]

(ii) Write the word equation for the reaction when the lead(II) sulphide is heated in air. [1]

(iii) Write the symbol equation for the same reaction. [2]

(iv) Suggest a use for the waste sulphur dioxide. [1]

(b) Complete the labelling of the diagram by naming the substance which goes into the furnace at A, and the products B and C. [3]

(c) What is the reason for adding:
(i) the coke? [1]
(ii) the limestone? [1]

(NEAB, part question, 1992)

10.6

Aluminium alloys are used in spacecraft. They can be reinforced with silicon carbide (SiC). These reinforced alloys are both strong and resistant to corrosion.

(a) What property, other than those given, makes an aluminium alloy suitable for use in spacecraft? [1]

(b) Why are aluminium alloys resistant to corrosion? [2]

(c) Silicon carbide has a macromolecular structure. Each atom in the structure is strongly bonded to four other atoms. Predict *three* properties of silicon carbide. [3]

(IGCSE, part question, 1996)

285

10.7

(a) The USA is a major producer of copper but its richer ores have been exhausted. The material mined is low grade, containing only 1% of copper pyrites, $CuFeS_2$. About 80% of the world's annual consumption of copper is obtained from ores and 20% by refining scrap copper.
   (i) If the price of copper is £1200 per tonne, what is the value of the copper in 1000 tonnes of the mined material? [3]
   (ii) Name the technique used to refine pure copper and explain why an increasing proportion of copper is being recycled. [2]
   (iii) 60% of the annual consumption of copper is used in electrical wiring and equipment. Describe the structure of copper and explain why it is suited to this use. [3]

(b) At Rio Tinto in Spain, large piles of copper pyrites, $CuFeS_2$, were left in the open air for several weeks. Copper(II) sulphate and traces of iron(II) sulphate were extracted from the pile by washing with water. Scrap iron was added to this solution to obtain copper.
   (i) Which substance reacts with copper pyrites to form copper(II) sulphate? [1]
   (ii) Both iron and zinc precipitate copper from a solution containing copper(II) sulphate and iron(II) sulphate. Give an economic reason and a chemical reason for using iron in preference to zinc. [3]
   (iii) Write an equation for the reaction between iron and copper(II) sulphate solution. [1]

(IGCSE, part question, 1989)

Electrolytic extraction of metals

This section covers the following ideas:

- the electrolytic extraction of metals
- the extraction of aluminium
- the extraction of sodium and magnesium
- the extraction of zinc
- anodising aluminium
- electroplating and copper refining.

Chemical reduction is not an economic method for extracting the most reactive metals in the amounts required to meet demand. The chloride and oxide ores of the metals above zinc in the reactivity series are held together by strong ionic bonds. Disrupting these forces and achieving reduction must be done using electrical energy. Electrolysis of the molten purified ore is carried out in a **smelter** to produce the pure metal. So to get pure metal in this way is a three-stage process:

1 mining the ore

2 purification of the ore

3 electrolysis of the molten ore (**smelting** – during which the metal is produced at the cathode).

The extraction of a metal by electrolysis is expensive. Energy costs to keep the ore molten and to separate the ions can be very high. To counteract this, many metal smelters are situated in regions where hydro-electric power is available. Aluminium smelters are the most important examples of this type of plant. They produce sufficient aluminium to make it the second most widely used metal after iron.

10.7 The extraction of aluminium

Bauxite, the major ore of aluminium, takes its name from the mediaeval village of Les Baux in France, where it was first mined. Napoleon III saw its possibilities for military purposes and ordered studies on its commercial production. A method of extraction using sodium to displace aluminium from aluminium chloride existed at that time. So, indirectly, interest was also developed into the commercial extraction of sodium. However, in 1886, the Hall–Heroult electrolytic method for extracting aluminium was devised.

Figure 10.8 The mineral, bauxite.

EXTENSION

The Hall–Heroult process

Bauxite (figure 10.8) is an impure form of aluminium oxide. It usually occurs in shallow surface deposits and is mined by open-cast methods in places such as Jamaica, Brazil and Australia. Up to 25% of bauxite consists of the impurities iron(III) oxide and sand. The iron(III) oxide gives it a red-brown colour.

The **Hall–Heroult process** involves the following stages.

- The bauxite is treated with sodium hydroxide to obtain pure aluminium oxide (alumina). The waste produced is an alkaline suspension of iron(III) oxide ('**red mud**'). It is pumped into vast red mud ponds. This waste poses environmental problems, as even when dried out it is not stable enough to build on. There is also concern about the seeping of alkali into the water supply. The alumina produced is shipped to the smelting plant. Much of the Jamaican alumina is shipped to Canada or the USA.

- The purified aluminium oxide (Al_2O_3) is then dissolved in molten cryolite (sodium aluminium fluoride, Na_3AlF_6). Cryolite is a mineral found naturally in Greenland. It is no longer mined commercially there, and all the cryolite now used is made synthetically. Cryolite is used to lower the working temperature of the electrolytic cell. The melting

point of aluminium oxide is 2030 °C. This is reduced to 900–1000 °C by dissolving it in cryolite. The cryolite thus provides a considerable saving in energy costs.

- The molten mixture of aluminium oxide and cryolite is electrolysed in a cell fitted with graphite electrodes (figure 10.9). There are complicated reactions that take place. The overall effect is the reduction of the oxide. Molten aluminium is produced at the cathode and sinks to the bottom of the cell. Oxygen is formed at the anode. At the working temperature of the cell, the oxygen reacts with the graphite anodes to form carbon dioxide:

$$carbon + oxygen \xrightarrow{heat} carbon\ dioxide$$

$$C(s) + O_2(g) \xrightarrow{heat} CO_2(g)$$

The anodes burn away and have to be replaced regularly.

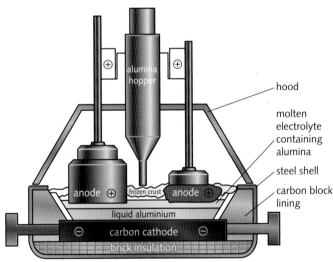

Figure 10.9 A cross-section of the electrolytic cell for extracting aluminium. At the cathode: $Al^{3+} + 3e^- \rightarrow Al$. At the anode: $2O^{2-} \rightarrow O_2 + 4e^-$.

The Hall–Heroult process is very energy-intensive. Aluminium production by itself accounts for 5% of the total use of electricity in the USA. It has been calculated that a current of 1 A must flow for 80 h to produce enough aluminium for one soft-drink can!

In fact, modern cells operate at 150 000–300 000 A and 4–4.5 V. Each produces between 1 and 2 tonnes per day. A typical smelter plant will

contain nearly 400 cells and produce 200 000 tonnes of aluminium per year. The cost of electricity is the most important thing to consider when locating a smelting plant. Aluminium smelters are located where hydro-electric power is available, or near reserves of coal or natural gas. The high energy demand also emphasises the need for recycling. It is *much* cheaper to recycle the metal than to manufacture it. The energy requirement for recycling is about 5% of that needed to manufacture the same amount of 'new' metal (see page 302).

Environmental aspects of aluminium production

There are environmental problems associated with the extraction of aluminium. Those of most concern are the following.

• The red mud waste (see page 287) from purifying the bauxite is a major problem. People

are worried about alkali getting into the water supply. Even when dry, the waste is not stable enough to build on. So **reclamation** and re-vegetation of the land is required.

• There are fluoride emissions produced in the complicated reactions during electrolysis. More modern dry scrubbing equipment has dramatically reduced the level of these fluoride emissions. Earlier, such emissions had been known to pollute agricultural land, killing grass and causing lameness in cattle.

Summary of core material

You should know that:

• metals can be extracted from their ores by methods that depend on the reactivity of the metal concerned

• the most reactive metals must be extracted from their molten ores by electrolysis

• aluminium is the major example of a metal extracted from its ore (bauxite) by electrolysis

• aluminium is a useful construction metal because it is protected from corrosion by an oxide layer

• the production of aluminium by electrolysis is expensive

• methods of recycling aluminium and steel are becoming increasingly important.

10.8 A common way of packaging food and drink is to use steel cans or aluminium cans. In Britain, over 10 billion cans are thrown away every year.

(a) Some soft drinks are weakly acidic and are sold in aluminium cans which are not corroded by weak acids.
  (i) Suggest a further advantage in using aluminium. [1]
  (ii) How could you show that lemonade is acidic? [2]

(b) A disadvantage of using steel cans is that they may rust.
  (i) State *two* conditions that would encourage a steel can to rust. [2]
  (ii) What is the appearance of rust? [2]
  (iii) How should the can be stored to prevent it rusting? [1]
  (iv) What does steel contain in addition to iron? [1]

(c) The cans may be recycled.
  (i) What is meant by the term *recycled*? [1]
  (ii) Explain *one* advantage in recycling cans. [2]
  (iii) Suggest how steel cans might be separated from aluminium cans. [1]

(IGCSE, part question, 1994)

EXTENSION

Further industrially important processes

10.8 The extraction of sodium and magnesium

Sodium

Sodium is a very reactive metal. It is extracted by the electrolysis of molten sodium chloride. Sodium chloride may be obtained by the

evaporation of sea water or mined as rock salt. The electrolyte used is a mixture of sodium chloride and calcium chloride. The calcium chloride is present to lower the working temperature from 801°C (the melting point of NaCl) to 600°C (the melting point of the mixture). This saves electricity and makes the process more economic. Electrolysis is carried out in a cell fitted with a steel cathode and graphite anode (figure 10.10). The cathode is a circle of steel around the graphite anode. Sodium is produced at the cathode and chlorine at the anode. At 600 °C the sodium and chlorine produced would react violently if allowed to come into contact. To prevent this, the cell has a steel gauze 'hood' around the anode to keep them apart.

The molten sodium floats on the electrolyte and is run off for storage. When it is formed at the cathode, the sodium contains some calcium (from the calcium chloride). However, the calcium crystallises out when the mixture cools and relatively pure sodium metal remains.

Magnesium

Magnesium metal is extracted from molten magnesium chloride. One major source of

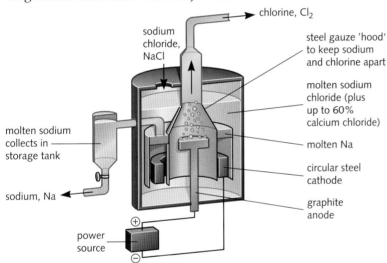

Figure 10.10 The extraction of sodium by electrolysis of molten sodium chloride (the Downs cell). Reduction occurs at the cathode: $2Na^+ + 2e^- \rightarrow 2Na$. Oxidation occurs at the anode: $2Cl^- \rightarrow Cl_2 + 2e^-$.

magnesium chloride is sea water. The electrolytic cell used is very similar in design to that used to extract sodium. Molten magnesium metal is produced at the cathode, and chlorine is generated at the anode:

at the cathode

$$Mg^{2+}(l) + 2e^- \rightarrow Mg(l)$$

at the anode

$$2Cl^-(l) \rightarrow Cl_2(g) + 2e^-$$

Norway is the major producer of magnesium in Europe, as it has access to cheap hydro-electric power.

10.9 Other industrial electrolytic processes

The extraction of zinc

As we have seen earlier (page 284), zinc can be extracted from its sulphide ore by roasting it in the air and then reducing the oxide with carbon monoxide. However, less than 20% of zinc is produced this way (figure 10.11). The vast majority of commercial zinc production involves the electrolysis of zinc sulphate solution.

Zinc oxide is prepared by roasting zinc sulphide in air. The oxide is then converted to zinc sulphate by reacting it with sulphuric acid. Then the zinc sulphate is dissolved in

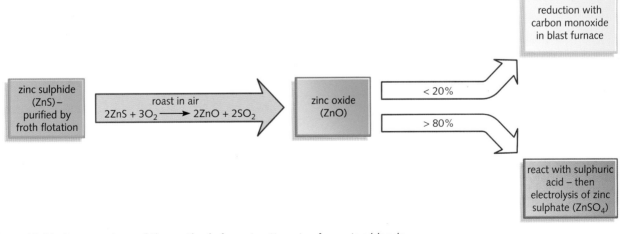

Figure 10.11 A comparison of the methods for extracting zinc from zinc-blende.

water and the solution is electrolysed. Zinc is formed at the cathode and oxygen at the anode:

at the cathode

$$Zn^{2+}(aq) + 2e^- \rightarrow Zn(s)$$

at the anode

$$4OH^-(aq) \rightarrow 2H_2O(l) + O_2(g) + 4e^-$$

The production of zinc at the cathode is unexpected – if the electrode was made of graphite hydrogen would be produced. Here the cathode is made of lead, and zinc is discharged preferentially instead of hydrogen. This illustrates the fact that the basic reactivity series (see page 117) worked out with inert graphite electrodes can be changed if different materials are used (another example is the mercury cathode used in one method of making sodium hydroxide industrially, see page 295). The anode is made of aluminium sheet.

Anodising aluminium

The protective layer of oxide that covers the surface of aluminium can be artificially thickened by **anodising**. The aluminium is used as the anode in an electrolytic cell which contains dilute sulphuric acid and has a carbon cathode. The oxygen produced at the anode reacts with the aluminium, thickening the oxide film. A coloured dye can be included during electrolysis; the oxide layer formed traps the dye to give a coloured surface to the metal.

Electroplating and copper refining

When electrolytic cells are set up with appropriate metal electrodes, metal can be effectively transferred from the anode to the cathode. Such methods can be used to plate objects with metals such as chromium or tin, or to refine copper to a very high degree of purity (see page 124).

Summary of extension material

You should know that:

* reactive metals such as sodium and magnesium are produced by very similar methods in which their molten chlorides are electrolysed

* zinc can be extracted by an electrolytic process and highly purified copper can be produced by electrolytic refining.

10.9 Norway is the main producer of magnesium in Europe. First of all, magnesium oxide is obtained from sea water by the following scheme.

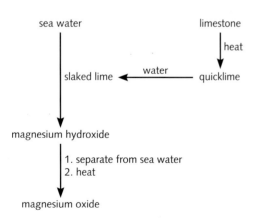

(a) What are the chemical names for limestone, quicklime and slaked lime? [3]

(b) Suggest how the precipitate of magnesium hydroxide would be removed from sea water. [1]

(c) How many tonnes of magnesium could be obtained from 1000 tonnes of sea water, given that sea water contains 0.13 % of magnesium, by mass? [2]

(d) When magnesium hydroxide is heated, it decomposes to form magnesium oxide and water. How would you show in the laboratory that water is produced when dry magnesium hydroxide is heated? [2]

(e) The magnesium oxide obtained in the process is sold to various industries. One of the products made from it is Milk of Magnesia, which reacts with hydrochloric acid in the stomach and cures acid indigestion.
  (i) Name the *two* products formed from the reaction of hydrochloric acid with magnesium oxide. [2]
  (ii) What is the name given to the reaction of an acid with a base? [1]

(f) The magnesium oxide to be used for magnesium manufacture is made to react with chlorine to form magnesium chloride which is then electrolysed.
  (i) Why is molten magnesium chloride used in the electrolysis? [1]
  (ii) At which electrode is the magnesium formed? [1]
  (iii) Suggest why Norway is one of the few countries that is able to use electrolysis to produce magnesium cheaply. [1]

(IGCSE, 1993)

10.10 Calcium is obtained by the electrolysis of molten calcium chloride. Calcium chloride is mixed with about one-sixth of its mass of calcium fluoride to lower the melting point. The calcium collects around a water-cooled steel tube.

(a) Explain why the calcium chloride needs to be melted for electrolysis to take place. [2]

(b) (i) What is the positive electrode (anode) made from? [1]
  (ii) At which electrode will calcium be obtained? [1]
  (iii) Name the *two* products obtained at the positive electrode (anode) during the electrolysis. [2]

(c) The calcium from the electrolysis is melted in an atmosphere of argon to separate it from the electrolyte, and then distilled in a vacuum to give a purer product.

(i) Why is the calcium heated in argon rather than in air? [2]
(ii) If the calcium is impure how will its boiling point be affected? [1]

(d) Calcium is found in Group II of the Periodic Table. Name *two* other elements in Group II. [2]

(e) Calcium is a reactive metal. Name the *two* products obtained when calcium reacts with hydrochloric acid. [2]

(IGCSE, 1995)

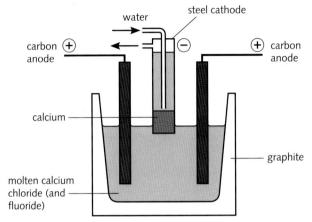

© Holderness, *Advanced level Inorganic Chemistry*, 1979, adapted by permission of William Heinemann.

Manufacturing economically important compounds

This section covers the following ideas:

- the manufacture of ammonia by the Haber process
- making nitric acid
- NPK fertilisers
- the contact process for making sulphuric acid
- the chlor–alkali industry
- chemicals from limestone.

10.10 Ammonia and nitric acid

The Haber–Bosch process for the synthesis of **ammonia** was one of the most significant new ideas of the twentieth century. It was developed in 1913 following Haber's earlier experiment (figure 10.12), and it allowed industrial chemists to make ammonia cheaply and on a huge scale. As a raw material for both fertilisers and explosives, ammonia played a large part in moulding human history. It helped to feed a growing population in peace-time, and it fuelled the destruction of war.

The largest ammonia and fertiliser plant in Britain is at Billingham in the north-east of England (see figure 10.22 on page 301). The purpose of the plant (and of the whole industry) is to manufacture ammonia for agriculture because the majority of plants cannot directly use (**fix**) nitrogen from the air. In the Haber process (figure 10.13 on page 292),

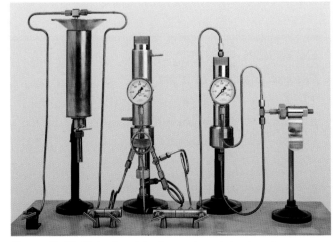

Figure 10.12 Haber's original experimental apparatus.

nitrogen and hydrogen are directly combined to form ammonia:

nitrogen + hydrogen $\rightleftharpoons$ ammonia

$$N_2(g) + 3H_2(g) \rightleftharpoons 2NH_3(g)$$

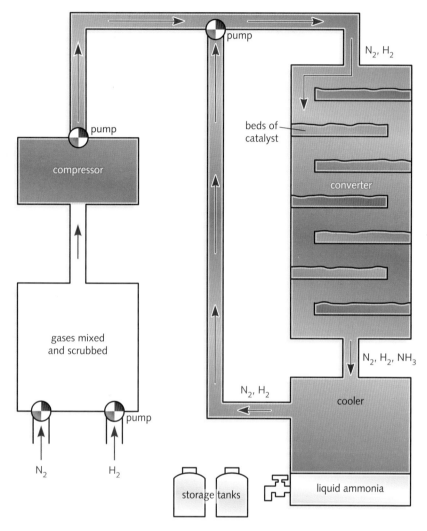

Figure 10.13 *A schematic drawing of the different stages of the Haber process. Nitrogen and hydrogen are mixed in a ratio of 1:3 at the start of the process.*

Nitrogen is obtained from air, and hydrogen from natural gas (see page 237) by reaction with steam. The two gases are mixed in a 1:3 ratio and compressed to 200 atmospheres. They are then passed over a series of **catalyst** (see page 189) beds containing finely divided iron. The temperature of the converter is about 450 °C. The reaction is reversible and does not go to completion. A mixture of nitrogen, hydrogen and ammonia leaves the converter. The proportion of ammonia in the mixture is about 15%. This is separated from the other gases by cooling the mixture. Ammonia has a much higher boiling point than nitrogen or hydrogen, so it condenses easily. The unchanged nitrogen and hydrogen gases are recirculated over the catalyst. By recycling in this way, an eventual **yield** of 98% can be achieved. The ammonia produced is stored as a liquid under pressure.

The majority of the ammonia produced is used to manufacture **fertilisers**. Liquid ammonia itself can in fact be used directly as a fertiliser, but it is an unpleasant liquid to handle and to transport. The majority is converted into a variety of *solid* fertilisers (see page 294). A substantial amount of ammonia is converted into nitric acid by oxidation.

EXTENSION

The manufacture of nitric acid

The manufacture of **nitric acid** (the Ostwald process) involves a complex group of reactions, but it takes place essentially in two stages (figure 10.14):

- catalytic oxidation of ammonia,
- absorption in water of the nitrogen dioxide produced.

Ammonia is first oxidised to form nitrogen monoxide (NO) and then nitrogen dioxide (NO$_2$). This is done in the following way. The ammonia gas is mixed with air and compressed. The mixture is passed through a series of platinum–rhodium gauzes (figure 10.15) at a temperature around 900 °C. At least 96% conversion of the ammonia takes place:

$$\text{ammonia} + \text{oxygen} \xrightarrow{900\,°C} \text{nitrogen monoxide} + \text{water}$$

$$4NH_3(g) + 5O_2(g) \xrightarrow{900\,°C} 4NO(g)$$
$$+ 6H_2O(g)$$

The gases leaving the converter are cooled and more air is added. The end-product is nitrogen dioxide:

nitrogen monoxide + oxygen
→ nitrogen dioxide

$$2NO(g) + O_2(g) \rightarrow 2NO_2(g)$$

The nitrogen dioxide produced is mixed with more air and reacted with water:

nitrogen dioxide + oxygen + water
→ nitric acid

$$4NO_2(g) + O_2(g) + 2H_2O(l)$$
$$\rightarrow 4HNO_3(aq)$$

The vast majority (about 80%) of nitric acid produced is used to make ammonium nitrate (NH_4NO_3). The rest is used to make organic nitrogen-containing compounds and in the manufacture of nylon (see page 337).

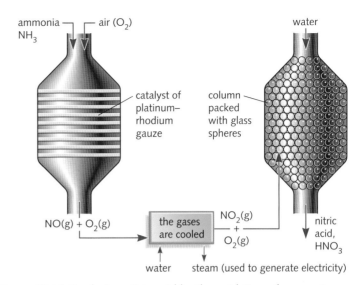

Figure 10.14 Producing nitric acid by the oxidation of ammonia.

Figure 10.15 The catalyst for the manufacture of nitric acid takes the form of a fine gauze of platinum and rhodium, seen here being fitted into a reaction vessel.

Summary of extension material

You should know that:

- nitric acid can be manufactured from ammonia by oxidation.

10.11 Ammonium nitrate and other fertilisers

Ammonium nitrate ('Nitram') is the most important of the **nitrogenous fertilisers**. It is produced when ammonia solution reacts with nitric acid:

ammonia + nitric acid → ammonium nitrate

$$NH_3(aq) + HNO_3(aq) \rightarrow NH_4NO_3(aq)$$

The ammonium nitrate can be crystallised into pellet form suitable for spreading on the land (figure 10.16).

Ammonium nitrate is soluble in water, as are all other ammonium salts, for example ammonium

Figure 10.16 Granules of ammonium nitrate fertiliser (a drying agent is added to prevent 'caking').

sulphate, $(NH_4)_2SO_4$. This solubility is important because plants need soluble nitrogen compounds that they can take up through their roots. There are two types of nitrogen compounds that plants can use – **ammonium** compounds (which contain the NH_4^+ ion) and **nitrates** (which contain the NO_3^- ion). Ammonium nitrate provides both these ions.

Ammonium salts tend to make the soil slightly acidic. To overcome this, they can be mixed with chalk (calcium carbonate), which will neutralise this effect. 'Nitro-chalk' is an example of a **compound fertiliser**.

A modern fertiliser factory will produce two main types of product:

- **straight N fertilisers** are solid nitrogen-containing fertilisers sold in pellet form, for example ammonium nitrate (NH_4NO_3), ammonium sulphate (($NH_4)_2SO_4$) and urea ($CO(NH_2)_2$)

- **NPK compound fertilisers** are mixtures that supply the three most essential elements lost from the soil by extensive use, namely nitrogen (N), phosphorus (P) and potassium (K). They are usually a mixture of ammonium nitrate, ammonium phosphate and potassium chloride, in different proportions to suit different conditions.

The production process for an NPK fertiliser is complex. It involves the production not only of ammonia, but also of sulphuric acid and phosphoric acid. A fertiliser factory is not just a single unit but six separate plants built close together on the same site (figure 10.17).

Environmental aspects of fertiliser use

Ammonium nitrate is a particularly good fertiliser. It contains 35% by mass of nitrogen, all of which is available to plants because the compound dissolves easily. However, this solubility poses problems. Some nitrate ions will be washed from the soil into nearby streams and rivers. This 'run-off' from the soil encourages rapid growth in the number of **algae**. The algae multiply swiftly to produce what is called an **algal bloom**. When the algae die, they are decomposed by bacteria. The increased bacterial activity uses up the oxygen dissolved in the water. Eventually there is little or no oxygen left, and fish die from lack of oxygen. This process is known as **eutrophication**.

A further problem directly affects the human population. Large quantities of water are taken from rivers and underground aquifers for drinking water. Dissolved nitrate ions are not removed by the normal purification methods. There are suggestions that high levels of nitrates in drinking water may cause problems for small babies. Their **haemoglobin** may be affected, so that it cannot

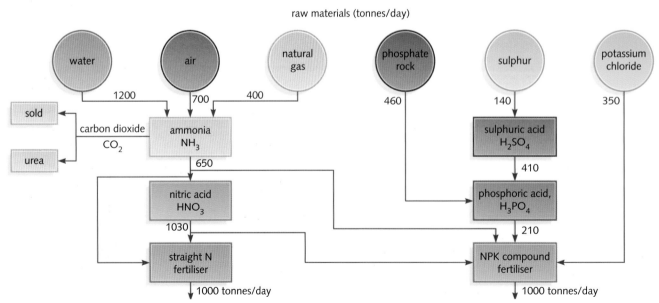

Figure 10.17 *The production of fertiliser requires the coordination of various industrial plants. The figures (in tonnes per day) show the raw materials needed to produce 1000 tonnes of straight and compound fertiliser per day.*

carry oxygen well. At its extreme, this may give rise to 'blue-baby syndrome'. Others suggest that nitrate ions may be converted into cancer-causing **nitrosamines** in the body. The European Union has set a maximum level of nitrates in drinking water at 50 mg/dm^3.

10.12 Explosives

Nitric acid is the major starting material for many explosives. **Gunpowder**, the first explosive used for warfare and in mining and quarrying, is now rarely used except in fireworks. **Ammonium nitrate** is used in 90% of the explosives and blasting agents used in mines and quarries. It is an oxidising agent and is mixed with fuel oil (which is readily oxidised). The reaction causes the release of large amounts of gaseous products. The rapid expansion caused by gas production forces the rocks apart.

Nitroglycerine and **trinitrotoluene** (TNT) are organic explosives that also require nitric acid for their manufacture. Nitroglycerine is a very unpredictable explosive. Alfred Nobel, the founder of the Nobel Prizes, made his fortune by discovering that it could be made safer by absorbing it in a type of clay (known as kieselguhr). In this form it is known as **dynamite**.

10.13 Sulphuric acid production

Sulphuric acid is a major product of the chemical industry. It is made by the **contact process**. The main reaction in the contact process is the one in which sulphur dioxide and oxygen combine to form sulphur trioxide. This reaction is **reversible**. The conditions needed to give the best equilibrium position are carefully considered. A temperature of 450°C and 1–2 atmospheres pressure are used. The gases are passed over a catalyst of vanadium(V) oxide. A yield of 98% sulphur trioxide is achieved. The overall process is summarised in the flow chart shown in figure 10.18.

The sulphur trioxide produced is dissolved in 98% sulphuric acid, and not water, in order to prevent environmental problems of acid mist. It also means that the acid is transported in concentrated form (98.5% acid, sometimes known as **oleum**) and then diluted on-site.

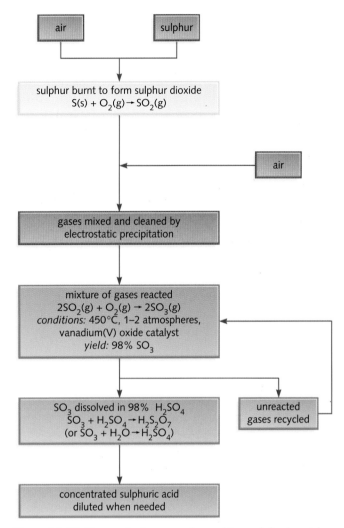

Figure 10.18 The contact process for making sulphuric acid.

Sulphuric acid is important for the fertiliser industry because it is needed to make ammonium sulphate and phosphoric acid.

10.14 The chlor–alkali industry

The chlor–alkali industry is a major branch of the chemical industry that has been built up around a single electrolysis reaction. The industry is centred around the electrolysis of concentrated sodium chloride solution (**brine**). Three different types of electrolytic cell have been used for this process.

- *Mercury cathode cell* In this, sodium (Na) is produced at, and dissolves in, the flowing mercury (Hg) cathode. Sodium hydroxide is produced by treating the Na–Hg cathode material with water.

- *Diaphragm cell* Here the products of electrolysis are kept separate by an asbestos diaphragm.

- *Membrane cell* This is the most modern system, and it uses a selective ion-exchange membrane (see page 118) to keep the products apart.

All three systems are currently in use, but the membrane cell is likely to replace the others.

The products and their uses are summarised in figure 10.19. The importance of the various products has changed recently. For many years there was not very much demand for chlorine. It held back the development of the industry. However, many new uses of chlorine have been found. The balance of importance has shifted. Concern over the environmental effects of some chlorine compounds (for example CFCs) may change the balance again. In Britain, the industry has developed around the Cheshire salt deposits (see page 300). In this region, salt is brought to the surface by both underground mining and solution mining.

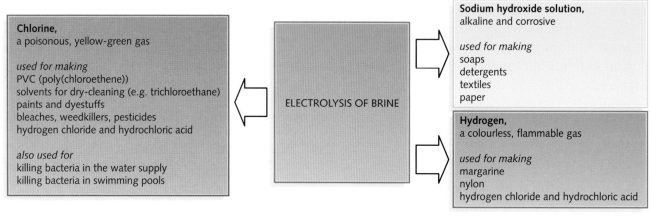

Figure 10.19 The chlor–alkali industry.

10.15 Limestone

Limestone is one form of calcium carbonate ($CaCO_3$). However, calcium carbonate is also found as chalk and marble. It is the second most abundant mineral in the Earth's crust, after the various different types of silicates. The different forms of calcium carbonate arise from the effect of different geological conditions. Deposits of **chalk** were formed from the shells of dead sea creatures. In some regions the chalk was covered with other rock and put under great pressure. The chalk changed from a relatively soft material into the harder material, **limestone**. In other regions **marble** was formed where chalk was subjected to conditions of high pressure and high temperature.

Limestone is quarried in large amounts world-wide. It has a wide range of uses (see figure 9.5 on page 256). In some of these, the limestone is used directly; in others, it acts as a raw material for making other compounds.

10.16 Direct uses

Powdered **limestone** is often used to neutralise acid soils and lakes acidified by acid rain. It is cheaper than using lime (calcium oxide), which has to be produced by heating limestone. In the blast furnace (see page 278), limestone is used to remove impurities found in the iron ore as slag (calcium silicate).

EXTENSION

Further uses of limestone

Cement is made by heating powdered limestone with clay in a rotary kiln. This material is then powdered and mixed with gypsum (calcium sulphate, $CaSO_4 \cdot 2H_2O$). When water is added to this mixture, complex chemical changes take place, giving a hard interlocked mass of crystals of hydrated calcium aluminate ($Ca(AlO_2)_2$) and calcium silicate ($CaSiO_3$).

Concrete is a mixture of cement and aggregate (stone chippings and gravel), which give it body. The mixture is mixed with water and can be poured into wooden moulds. It is then allowed to harden. Reinforced concrete is made by allowing the concrete to set around steel rods or mesh. This **composite material** has the greater tensile strength needed for constructing large bridges and tall buildings.

Sodium carbonate (Na_2CO_3) is an important industrial chemical. It is used in the manufacture of glass, soaps, detergents, paper, dyes and other chemicals. Sodium carbonate is manufactured in a continuous process that uses carbon dioxide (produced by heating calcium carbonate as limestone) and ammonia dissolved in brine (concentrated sodium chloride solution) as its starting materials. This is known as the **Solvay process**; a typical Solvay tower is shown in figure 10.20.

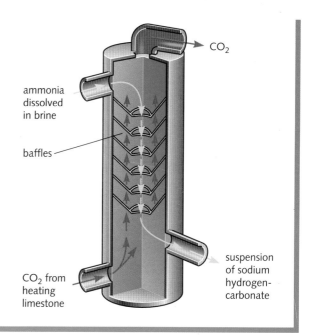

Figure 10.20 A Solvay tower. Sodium carbonate is produced by heating the sodium hydrogencarbonate suspension: $2NaHCO_3 \rightarrow Na_2CO_3 + H_2O + CO_2$.

The manufacture of lime (calcium oxide)

Lime (quicklime) is calcium oxide and is produced by roasting limestone in a lime kiln. The limestone is decomposed by heat:

calcium carbonate $\overset{heat}{\rightarrow}$ calcium oxide
$\qquad\qquad\qquad$ + carbon dioxide

$$CaCO_3(s) \overset{heat}{\rightarrow} CaO(s) + CO_2(g)$$

Lime is used in agriculture to neutralise acid soils and to improve drainage in soils containing a large amount of clay. It is used with sodium carbonate and sand in making glass. Large amounts of lime are converted into slaked lime (hydrated lime), which is calcium hydroxide ($Ca(OH)_2$). Equal amounts of lime and water are mixed to produce this material. It is used to make bleaching powder, in making glass and for water purification. It is mixed with sand to give mortar. When mixed with water and then allowed to dry, mortar sets into a strongly bonded material to hold bricks together: the calcium hydroxide reacts with carbon dioxide in the air to form calcium carbonate.

Summary of core material

You should know that:

- important chemical products such as ammonia and sulphuric acid can be manufactured using conditions which mean that reversible reactions still give economic amounts of the product
- ammonia is manufactured by the Haber process from nitrogen and hydrogen
- sulphuric acid is manufactured by the contact process from sulphur dioxide
- ammonia and sulphuric acid are important as the basis of the fertiliser and other industries

- nitric acid can react with ammonia to produce ammonium nitrate, which is used extensively as a fertiliser and explosive
- there are a range of fertilisers based on ammonia, but the most important elements added to the soil by these fertilisers are nitrogen, phosphorus and potassium (NPK)
- limestone is a very important raw material from which lime and cement, as well as other important materials, are made.

10.11 The modern method of manufacturing ammonia was developed by two German scientists, Haber and Bosch. In 1908, Haber discovered that nitrogen and hydrogen reacted under pressure and in the presence of platinum to give ammonia.

In 1913, Bosch designed a plant to produce 10 000 tonnes of ammonia per year. By 1915, production had risen to 180 000 tonnes per year.

Bosch used iron instead of platinum. To withstand the high pressures in the plant, high carbon steel was used. The carbon in the steel reacted with the hydrogen and made the steel brittle. Bosch lined the reaction vessel with low carbon steel and used an outer casing of high carbon steel to provide the strength. Bosch solved the problem of hydrogen diffusing through the lining of low carbon steel.

(a) (i) Write an equation for the reversible reaction between nitrogen and hydrogen to give ammonia. [2]

(ii) What was the purpose of the platinum? Suggest a reason why Bosch used iron instead. [1]

(b) The table below shows how the percentage of ammonia in the mixture leaving the reaction vessel varies under different conditions.

Pressure, in atmospheres	100	200	300	400
% of ammonia at 300°C	45	65	72	78
% of ammonia at 500°C	9	18	25	31

(i) Copy the grid and graph. Draw on your grid a graph of percentage of ammonia against pressure at 500°C. [2]

(ii) What is the percentage of ammonia formed at 250 atmospheres and 300°C? [1]

(iii) Use the graphs to estimate the percentage of ammonia formed at 400°C and 250 atmospheres. [1]

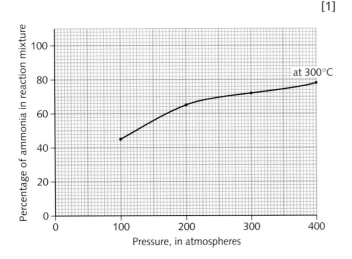

(iv) The advantage of using a low temperature is the large percentage of ammonia formed. What is the disadvantage of using a low temperature? [1]

(v) Suggest *two* advantages of using high pressure in the manufacture of ammonia. [2]

(IGCSE, part question, 1990)

10.12

(a) Nitric acid, HNO₃, is made from ammonia by the Ostwald process. There are three stages in the process (see page 292). The equation for the first stage is:

$$4NH_3 + 5O_2 \rightarrow 4NO + 6H_2O$$

(i) Name the catalyst used in this stage. [1]

(ii) Complete and balance the equations for the reactions taking place in stages 2 and 3. [2]
Stage 2:
$$2NO + O_2 \rightarrow \ldots\ldots\ldots$$
Stage 3:
$$\ldots NO_2 + \ldots H_2O + O_2 \rightarrow \ldots HNO_3$$

(b) Ammonium nitrate is an important fertiliser. It is made by reacting nitric acid with ammonia.

(i) State the type of reaction taking place. [1]

(ii) The equation for this reaction is

$$NH_3 + HNO_3 \rightarrow NH_4NO_3$$

Calculate the number of tonnes of ammonium nitrate that can be made from 68 tonnes of ammonia. (Relative atomic masses: H = 1, N = 14, O = 16) [3]

(NEAB, part question, 1995)

10.13 Ammonium nitrate, NH₄NO₃, is used around the world as a fertiliser and as an explosive.

(a) Ammonium nitrate may be made by the reaction of ammonia with nitric acid. Write a word equation for the reaction. [2]

(b) The percentage, by mass, of nitrogen in ammonium nitrate is 35. Calculate the mass of nitrogen in a 50 kg bag of ammonium nitrate fertiliser. [2]

(c) Ammonium nitrate is often mixed with potassium chloride and ammonium phosphate in fertilisers. Why is it mixed with these compounds? [2]

(IGCSE, part question, 1992)

10.14 As with many industrial processes the manufacture of sulphuric acid involves a series of stages.

Stage 1: The formation of sulphur dioxide from sulphur

(a) (i) Give *two* reasons why large quantities of sulphur are usually transported as a molten liquid rather than as a solid. [2]

(ii) Give a balanced chemical equation for the burning of sulphur to form sulphur dioxide. [2]

(iii) Give *two* reasons why small amounts of sulphur dioxide are collected in the laboratory by the method shown. [2]

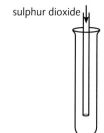

sulphur dioxide

(iv) Apart from the manufacture of sulphuric acid, give another use of sulphur dioxide. [1]

Stage 2: The formation of sulphur trioxide from sulphur dioxide

The diagram shows a converter used to convert sulphur dioxide into sulphur trioxide:

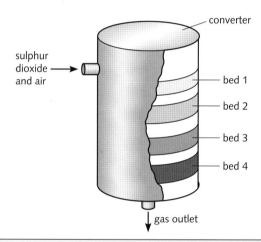

Vanadium(V) oxide bed	Temperature of gas before reaction in °C	Temperature of gas after reaction in °C	Percentage of SO$_2$ converted to SO$_3$
1	435	600	66
2	445	518	85
3	445	475	93
4	420	442	99.5

(b) (i) Write a balanced chemical equation to show the reversible reaction in which sulphur dioxide is converted into sulphur trioxide. [3]
(ii) What part does the vanadium(V) oxide play in this reaction? [1]
(iii) What do the differences in temperatures before and after the reaction show about this conversion? [1]
(iv) What happens to the gases each time before they move on to the next bed of vanadium(V) oxide? [1]
(v) What probably happens to the 0.5% unconverted sulphur dioxide that leaves the converter? [1]
(vi) Name the gas that is present in the greatest percentage in the mixture of gases that leaves the converter. [1]

Stage 3: The formation of sulphuric acid from sulphur trioxide

Sulphur trioxide is absorbed in 98% sulphuric acid and water is added to keep the concentration of the acid constant:

$$SO_3(g) + H_2O(l) \rightarrow H_2SO_4(aq)$$

(c) What is the maximum amount of sulphuric acid that can be made from 16 tonnes of sulphur? The relative atomic masses are S 32, H 1, O 16. [2]

(SEG, part question, 1988)

10.15 Quicklime (CaO) is produced from limestone (CaCO$_3$), in a lime kiln. In order to decompose limestone, heat has to be supplied continuously. Methane is passed into the kiln and burns in the air which flows through the kiln.

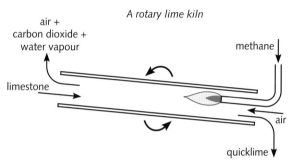

A rotary lime kiln

(a) The chemical equation for the decomposition of limestone is:

$$CaCO_3 \rightarrow CaO + CO_2$$

calcium   calcium   carbon
carbonate   oxide   dioxide

(i) State whether this reaction is exothermic or endothermic. [1]
(ii) What is the mass of one mole of calcium carbonate? (Relative atomic masses: C = 12, O = 16, Ca = 40) [1]
(iii) What mass of quicklime can be produced from one mole of calcium carbonate? [1]
(iv) Give *one* use of quicklime. [1]

(b) Suggest why carbon dioxide might be considered to pollute the atmosphere. [1]

(c) In order to protect the environment, the company operating the kiln wishes to separate the carbon dioxide from the waste gases. The first stage in this process involves cooling the gases.
(i) How could the company use heat energy from the waste gases? [1]
(ii) Suggest a use for the carbon dioxide. [1]

(NEAB, part question, 1991)

Resources, industry and recycling

This section covers the following ideas:

- the nature of minerals and ores
- siting a chemical plant
- recycling
  - paper
  - glass
  - steel
  - aluminium.

10.17 Minerals and ores

The solid raw materials in the Earth are often referred to as **mineral resources**. Rocks are made from crystals (or grains) of minerals. They contain one or more minerals and are often mixtures. A **mineral** is a single substance that occurs naturally. It has a definite chemical **formula**. However, more often than not they are dirty and contain impurities when first mined.

An **ore** is a mineral resource that:

- is a metallic compound found in the Earth's crust, and
- can be used as a commercial source of the metal.

Before starting to mine an ore, the mining company must consider many aspects of the situation. Some of these considerations are geological. How much ore is present? How pure is the ore? How physically accessible is it? But there are other questions that must be answered as well. These relate to the costs of access roads and buildings, and the availability of materials and a workforce. Under modern regulations the mining company would also need to bear in mind the cost of landscaping and the eventual clearing and restoration of the land. All these costs would have to be considered, together with the market value of the metal, in weighing up whether it was worthwhile to mine a particular mineral deposit.

Many of these considerations would apply more generally to the siting of *any* chemical plant.

10.18 Siting a chemical plant

The largest deposits of rock salt in the UK are located under the Cheshire plain. Figure 10.21 shows a map of the region and illustrates how local industries have built up around the exploitation of this mineral resource. Even 150 years ago, before the first factory electrolysing brine was set up, factories around Widnes were making sodium carbonate from salt. This was then used by other local factories to make soap and glass, and for treating textiles. When brine electrolysis was introduced in 1897, this increased the importance of the area as the centre for the chlor–alkali industry.

Figure 10.22 shows the location of the large ammonia and fertiliser plant at Billingham in the north-east of England. To avoid transporting the ammonia too far, all the chemical processes for making NPK fertilisers are carried out on the same site. The map shows that the plant is well placed for all the necessary raw materials (see figure 10.17 on page 294). Some of them are close at hand; for example potassium chloride is mined nearby, and natural gas is available from beneath

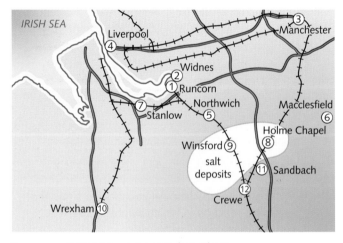

Key ▬ motorway ┼┼┼ main-line railway

① chlorine
sodium hydroxide
solvents
monomers

② inorganic chemicals
herbicides
organic chemicals
detergents

③ dyestuffs
plastics
pharmaceuticals
polymers
plasticisers

④ pharmaceuticals

⑤ alkali products

⑥ pharmaceuticals
agrichemicals
dyestuffs

⑦ petrochemicals
dyestuffs

⑧ pharmaceuticals

⑨ salt

⑩ rubber chemicals
pharmaceuticals

⑪ salt
inorganic chemicals

⑫ pharmaceuticals

Figure 10.21 The location of the chlor–alkali industry in Cheshire, England.

the North Sea. Sulphur and phosphate rock need to be imported, but the port of Teesside is nearby. Road and rail links are good, so the products can be easily transported to other parts of the country.

10.19 The environmental costs of industry

The original method of making sodium carbonate used the infamous Leblanc process. This process poured acidic fumes into the atmosphere, and piled up waste heaps of calcium sulphide. These heaps gave off hydrogen sulphide gas (the gas that smells of bad eggs!) as they sat in the rain. The effects must have been awful! They led to one of the first ever environmental laws being passed by the UK Parliament – the 'Alkali Act' of 1861.

All chemical industries must now consider the effects of building and using a plant in a particular area. Strict controls apply to the emission of gases that may be **toxic** or may cause environmental damage. Safety regulations and practices must be maintained to avoid the risk of accidental release of harmful materials. Such practices protect those working in the factory as well as those living nearby. In many cases regulation has led to the more efficient use of materials, with unused gases being recycled rather than simply emitted into the air. Control of **effluent** (waste) from power stations by the introduction of 'flue gas desulphurisers' (or 'scrubbers') needs to be continued to reduce the levels of acid rain.

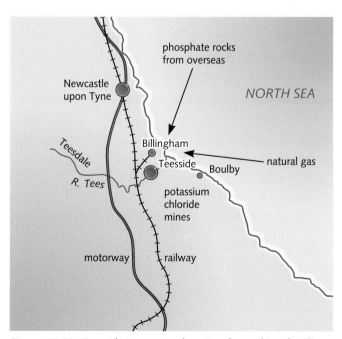

Figure 10.22 Teesside is a major location for making fertilisers.

Extracting large quantities of mineral resources from mines creates several problems. If the mines are underground, then subsidence is one problem. If, however, they are open-cast mines or quarries, then they can be unsightly or wasteful of land. Quarries and open-cast workings can be **reclaimed** by a process of 'landfill'. Mining companies are required to restore land to a very high standard. Two further problems associated with mines are noise and dust. They are caused by blasting and crushing processes, and also by the passage of heavy traffic.

All these considerations are environmental costs, which must be borne in mind by a company and local community when considering the location of a mine, quarry or plant. They are to be considered alongside the positive economic benefits to a community of increased local jobs, increased business for the local economy and improved infrastructure such as road and rail links.

10.20 Recycling

Each year, every man, woman and child in the USA produces around 20 times their own weight in garbage – a total of more than 300 million tonnes per annum. A small proportion of this waste is **recycled**, but the bulk of it is disposed of by **incineration** (burning) or by burial in large excavations (holes). This is called **landfill**. One of the largest of these is the Fresh Kills landfill on Staten Island, New York. With an estimated mass of 90 million tonnes, Fresh Kills is one of the largest artifical structures in North America.

Municipal waste – household and commercial refuse – is only a fraction of the total solid waste produced by a modern society. However, it is the fraction that attracts most attention, as we have most control over how we dispose of it. There are three main methods of dealing with it – **recycling, burial** or **burning**.

The best alternative is usually **recycling**:

- it reduces the volume of waste by up to 50%,
- it reduces the level of pollutants released into the air,
- it lessens the demand on raw materials and energy.

As an example of this last point, making aluminium from scrap rather than from bauxite (see page 286) gives an energy saving of about 95%. Recycling is not simply re-use; it is collecting and reprocessing the material so it can be made into new objects. Various materials can be recycled; here are some points about some of them.

- *Paper*
  About one-third of our domestic waste is paper and board. When compacted in a landfill, it does not necessarily degrade away, even though we might think that it is very **biodegradable**. In the UK, recycled paper has replaced much of the imported new material. To be recycled, paper must be clean and kept separate from other waste. Waxed paper and cartons are, by their nature, unpulpable.

- *Glass*
  In 1991, the UK reclaimed 21% of the glass bottles and jars that it produced (figure 10.23). The average across Europe that year was 46%, meaning that at least two out of every five glass containers in Europe were recycled. There is still room for improvement, especially in the UK. The fragility of glass becomes an advantage in recycling because it can easily be broken into small pieces for remelting. It is important to separate the different coloured glasses because they have different chemical compositions.

- *Steel*
  Steel is the most recycled metal in the world. Every year, 300 million tonnes are recycled, which represents 40% of world-wide production. Magnetic separation means that steel can be effectively sorted from other metals. Three-quarters of the cans we use for food, drinks, pet-food, etc., are made of steel.

- *Aluminium*
  This has a uniquely high scrap value because of the high expense of aluminium smelting. In the UK, demand for recycled aluminium outstrips production. In 1991, about 500 million aluminium cans were recycled in the UK, about 10% of consumption.

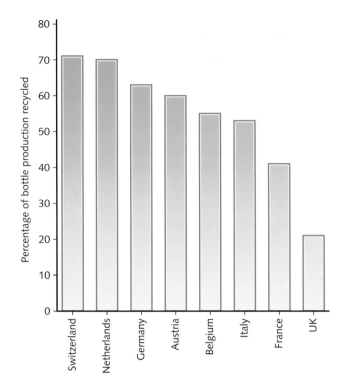

Figure 10.23 Glass recycling in Europe in 1991.

Summary of core material

You should know that:

- the siting of a modern chemical plant involves a wide range of considerations including important aspects of environmental planning

- recycling is an important aspect of managing the Earth's finite resources

- recycling is particularly important for aluminium, as the extraction process is expensive because of the high energy demand of the process.

10.16 An extract from a magazine highlights how much energy can be saved by recycling.

(a) Very large savings of energy can be made by recycling aluminium.
  (i) How much energy is needed to produce one tonne of aluminium by recycling? [2]
  (ii) Describe how aluminium is extracted from pure aluminium oxide. [4]
  (iii) Use the answer to (a)(ii) to explain why recycling saves so much energy. [1]
  (iv) Most metals need some surface coating (for example, paint) to prevent corrosion. Explain why aluminium does not need this protection. [1]

ENERGY SAVED BY RECYCLING

BOTTLE BANK

GREEN GLASS ONLY

ENVIRONMENTAL SERVICES

Material	Energy needed for original production (in GJ/tonne)	Energy saved by recycling (percentage %)
aluminium	250	95
plastics	100	88
paper	30	35
glass	16	5

1 GJ = 1000 million joules

To produce one tonne of paper from wood pulp requires 30 GJ of energy. To make one tonne of paper recycling saves $30 \times 35/100 = 10.5$ GJ.

(b) Glass is made from sodium carbonate, calcium carbonate and sand. Energy is supplied and the chemicals react to form a mixture of metal silicates. This is glass.
  (i) What type of reaction takes place when glass is made? [1]
  (ii) Copy and complete the equation: [1]
    $CaCO_3 + SiO_2 \rightarrow CaSiO_3 + \ldots\ldots$

(IGCSE, 1994)

10.17 The extraction and use of a metal, such as iron, involves these stages.

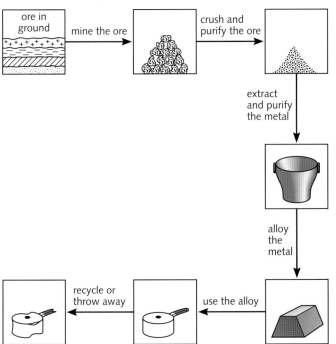

(a) (i) Give *two* ways in which the extraction of metals can affect the environment. [2]
  (ii) Apart from environmental costs, give *two* factors that contribute to the price of a metal. [2]
  (iii) Materials other than metals are used to make pan handles. Explain why. [2]

(b) Old metal pans should be recycled. Explain why. [3]

(c) An ore of iron contains 80% pure iron oxide, Fe_2O_3. Iron is extracted by reduction with carbon monoxide:

$$Fe_2O_3 + 3CO \rightarrow 2Fe + 3CO_2$$

  (i) What mass of iron can be extracted from 1000 kilograms (kg) of this iron ore? (The relative atomic masses are C 12; Fe 56; O 16.) [4]
  (ii) What mass of carbon dioxide will be released into the atmosphere by the extraction of iron from 1000 kg of this ore? [2]

(SEG, 1995)

10.18

(a) The major elements needed for plant growth are nitrogen, N, phosphorus, P, and potassium, K. The table below shows some of the different types of fertiliser.
  (i) Copy and complete the table, showing which elements needed for plant growth are present in each fertiliser. [2]

Type of fertiliser	Substances present in the fertiliser		Main elements needed for plant growth present in fertiliser
Nitram	ammonium nitrate	NH_4NO_3	N
Nitro-chalk	ammonium nitrate chalk	NH_4NO_3 $CaCO_3$	
Compound fertiliser	ammonium nitrate	NH_4NO_3	
	ammonium dihydrogen-phosphate	$NH_4H_2PO_4$	
	potassium chloride	KCl	

  (ii) Which one of the above type of fertilisers should be used on acidic soil? [1]

(b) The raw materials used to make fertilisers, together with their sources, are shown in the table below. Copy and complete the table. [3]

Name of raw material	Source	Used to make
Air	the atmosphere	ammonia and sulphuric acid
Water	reservoirs in Teesdale	ammonia and sulphuric acid
Natural gas		ammonia
Potassium chloride	mines in North Yorkshire	compound fertilisers
Phosphate rock	imported from overseas	
	imported from overseas	sulphuric acid

(c) Large quantities of fertilisers are made on a single site at Billingham. The map shows the location of Billingham.

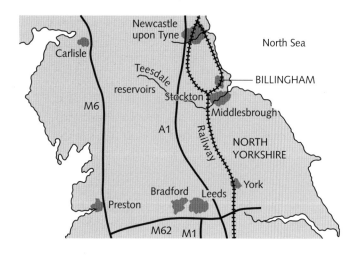

Use the information above and also the map to help you to answer the questions which follow.
(i) Give *one* reason why it is useful to have all the factories on one site. [1]
(ii) Give *three* reasons why Billingham is well situated for making fertilisers. [3]

(NEAB, part question, 1994)

10.19 The pie chart shows the composition of a common form of glass called soda glass. Cullet is the name given to old glass which is being recycled. The names of two other ingredients have been missed off the chart. The mixture is heated to 1500°C in a furnace.

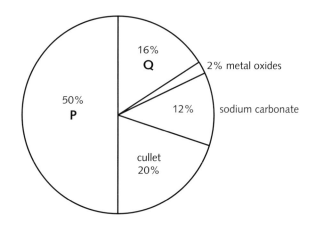

(a) Name the ingredients **P** and **Q**. [2]

(b) If 550 tonnes of soda glass are to be made, what mass of sodium carbonate will be required? [2]

(c) (i) Suggest *two* reasons why the use of cullet in the manufacture of glass should be encouraged. [2]
(ii) Give *two* reasons why glass recycling is not carried out on a larger scale than at present. [2]

The use of cullet is one way in which glass is recycled. Another form of recycling is the production of reusable bottles. In this country these are commonly used for milk and in Germany for doorstep beer deliveries. Using bottles appears to be more expensive than putting the milk in cardboard cartons.

Milk bottles cost the dairy 8.5 pence each.
Cardboard cartons cost only 3 pence each.
Milk bottles also cost 1.7 pence each to wash and re-fill.
On average a milk bottle can be used 24 times.

(d) Calculate how many times a milk bottle would need to be used before it became more economical than using cartons. [5]

(e) Name *two* other materials which are recycled on a large scale. [2]

(MEG, part question, 1992)

11 Organic chemistry

Hydrocarbons

This section covers the following ideas:

- the unique properties of carbon
- hydrocarbons as compounds of carbon and hydrogen only
- the alkanes and their properties
- isomerism
- the alkenes
- the halogen compounds of the alkanes
- the reactivity of the C=C double bond in alkenes
- addition reactions.

11.1 Molecular ancestors

Is there a 'Restaurant at the End of the Universe', as in Douglas Adams' books in *The Hitch Hiker's Guide to the Galaxy* series? Perhaps not, but the soup at the start of life's menu may have had some interesting ingredients. In the early 1950s Miller and Urey did experiments to imitate the reactions that may have occurred on the primitive Earth. They used a mixture of the gases that may have been found in the Earth's early atmosphere (namely methane CH_4, ammonia NH_3, water vapour H_2O and hydrogen H_2, see page 16). In their apparatus, this mixture was sparked by an electrical discharge ('artificial lightning'). After some time, amino acids such as glycine (NH_2CH_2COOH) were found in the condensed mixture (the **primordial soup**). Strikingly, many of the same compounds have been found in meteorites. In 1995, glycine hit the headlines when it was detected in the interstellar dust clouds where stars are born.

Titan, Saturn's giant moon, has conditions similar to those on the early Earth. Titan, which is as large as the planet Mercury, has an atmosphere ten times as massive as the Earth's. This atmosphere is about 90% nitrogen, with up to 10% methane also present. Simulation experiments with such atmospheric conditions have produced mixtures containing **amino acids** and **nucleotides** (the building blocks of nucleic acids). Such molecules are starting points for the molecules of life. But there is an enormous gap to bridge from these primordial molecules to the fossils of 11 different micro-organisms which have been found in the 3.5-billion-year-old rocks of Western Australia.

11.2 The unique properties of carbon

All living things on Earth, from micro-organisms such as bacteria to the largest plants and animals, reproduce and grow using systems based on **nucleic acids** and **proteins**. These are **macromolecules** – molecules on a very large scale. Proteins are made by assembling amino acids into long chains. These chains then fold and organise themselves into complex structures. For example, a molecule of haemoglobin contains four protein chains. Each chain is made up of more than 100 amino acids. The molecules of life are based on the distinctive properties of one element – **carbon**. Carbon is unique in the variety of molecules it can form. The chemistry of these molecules forms a separate branch of the subject known as **organic chemistry**.

Carbon is a non-metal in Group IV of the Periodic Table. It forms covalent compounds. The uniqueness of carbon lies in the versatility of that bonding.

There are three special features of **covalent bonding involving carbon.**

- Carbon atoms can join to each other to form long chains. Atoms of other elements can then attach to the chain.
- The carbon atoms in a chain can be linked by single, double or triple covalent bonds.
- Carbon atoms can also arrange themselves in rings.

Atoms of other elements (for example sulphur) can imitate parts of this versatility. But only carbon can achieve all these different bonding arrangements. Figure 11.1 gives some idea of how these bonding arrangements can produce different types of molecules.

11.3 Alkanes

Around *six million* compounds of carbon are already known! Because there are so many, it is helpful to pick out those compounds which have similar structures. One of the simplest types of organic compound is the **hydrocarbons**.

A **hydrocarbon** is a compound that contains carbon and hydrogen only.

(a) Carbon can form four bonds, and carbon atoms can join to one another to form long chains.

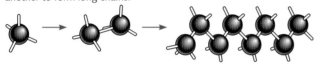

(b) In alkanes, only hydrogen atoms are joined to the side positions on the chains. Other atoms can be attached, forming various families of organic compounds.

(c) Double bonds can occur in simple molecules and in the long chains.

(d) Carbon atoms can also join to form ring molecules, for example glucose, as shown here.

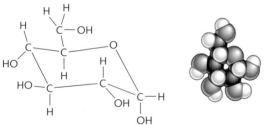

(e) Long-chain fat molecules can be formed, as well as numerous other molecules.

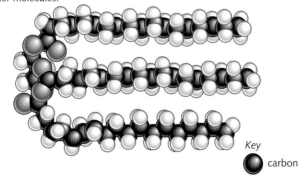

Figure 11.1 Carbon is very versatile.

Key

 carbon

 hydrogen

oxygen

The hydrocarbons that we study at this level can be subdivided into two **families**. Some hydrocarbons are **saturated**. These molecules contain *only* single covalent bonds between carbon atoms. Since carbon has a valency of 4, the bonds not used in making the chain are linked to hydrogen atoms (see figure 11.1). No further atoms can be added to molecules of these compounds. This family of saturated hydrocarbons is known as the **alkanes**.

- The **alkanes** are *saturated* hydrocarbons.
- Molecules of these compounds contain only *single bonds* between the carbon atoms in the chain.

Table 11.1 gives the names and formulas of the first six members of the series of alkanes. The simplest alkane contains one carbon atom and is called **methane**. Note that the names of this series of hydrocarbons all end in *...ane*. The first part of the name (the **prefix**) tells you the number of carbon atoms in the chain. These prefixes are used consistently in naming organic compounds. The formulas given in table 11.1 are the molecular formulas of the compounds. Each molecule increases by a $— CH_2—$ group as the chain gets longer (see figure 11.2). Indeed, the formulas of long-chain alkanes can be written showing the number of $— CH_2—$ groups in the chain. For example, octane (C_8H_{18}) can be written as $CH_3—(CH_2)_6—CH_3$. The formulas of these molecules all fit the general formula C_nH_{2n+2} (where n is the number of carbon atoms present).

In organic chemistry, the *structure* of a molecule is also very important. Figure 11.2 shows the structural formulas of the first six alkanes in the series. A **structural formula** shows the bonds between the atoms. As the length of the hydrocarbon chain increases, the opportunity for weak interactions between the molecules (**van der Waals' forces**, see page 95) is increased. This shows itself practically in the increasing boiling points of the members of the series (table 11.1). The melting points and boiling points of the alkanes increase gradually. Under normal conditions, the first four members of the family are gases, and those between C_5H_{12} and $C_{16}H_{34}$ (which

Table 11.1 Some details of the early members of the alkane series

Alkane	Molecular formula C_nH_{2n+2}	Number of carbon atoms	Boiling point (°C)		Physical state at room temperature
Methane	CH_4	1	−164		gas
Ethane	C_2H_6	2	−87		gas
Propane	C_3H_8	3	−42	b.p.	gas
Butane	C_4H_{10}	4	0	increasing	gas
Pentane	C_5H_{12}	5	+36		liquid
Hexane	C_6H_{14}	6	+69		liquid

in short are called C_5 to C_{16} alkanes) are liquids. The compounds in the alkane family with 17 or more carbon atoms are waxy solids.

One chemical property that all these alkanes have in common is that they burn very exothermically. They make good fuels. Controlling their availability and cost can have great political consequences. When they burn in a good supply of air, the products are carbon dioxide and water vapour:

methane + oxygen → carbon dioxide + water

$$CH_4(g) + 2O_2(g) \rightarrow CO_2(g) + 2H_2O(g)$$

ethane + oxygen → carbon dioxide + water

$$2C_2H_6(g) + 7O_2(g) \rightarrow 4CO_2(g) + 6H_2O(g)$$

Methane forms the major part of natural gas. Propane and butane burn with very hot flames and are sold as liquefied petroleum gas (LPG). They are kept as liquids under pressure, but they vaporise easily when that pressure is released. In areas where there is no mains supply of natural gas, you may have seen propane tanks in gardens, which supply the fuel for heating systems. Cylinders of butane (Calor gas) are used in portable gas fires in

methane

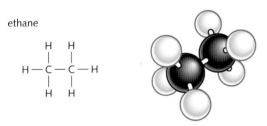

ethane

butane

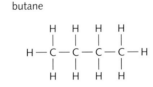

pentane

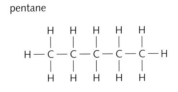

propane

hexane

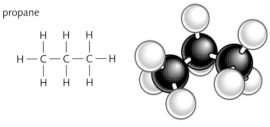

Figure 11.2 The structures of the first six alkanes.

the home. Butane is also used in portable blow-torches and gas-lighters.

The family of alkanes has similar chemical properties. Together they are an example of a **homologous series** of compounds.

> A **homologous series** is a family of organic compounds that:
>
> - have the same general formula,
> - have similar chemical properties, and
> - show a gradual increase in physical properties such as melting point and boiling point.

11.4 Alkenes

The ability of carbon atoms to form double bonds gives rise to the **alkenes**. The alkenes are another family of hydrocarbons or homologous series.

> - The **alkenes** are *unsaturated* hydrocarbons.
> - Molecules of these compounds contain at least one C=C *double bond* somewhere in the chain.

Alkenes that have just one C=C double bond have the general formula C_nH_{2n} (where *n* is the number of carbon atoms). Such molecules are unsaturated because it is possible to break this double bond and add extra atoms to the molecule.

The simplest alkene must contain *two* carbon atoms (needed for one C=C double bond) and is called **ethene** (figure 11.3). Table 11.2 shows the molecular formulas of the first alkenes. The boiling points of these compounds again show a gradual increase as the molecules get larger. Figure 11.3 shows the structures of the first three alkenes.

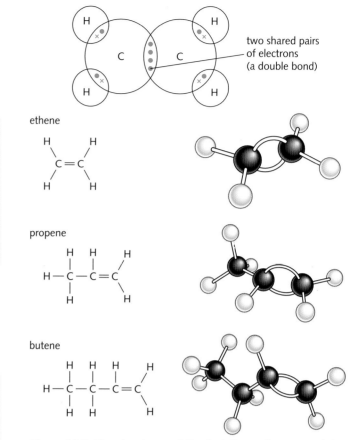

two shared pairs of electrons (a double bond)

Figure 11.3 *The structures of the first three alkenes, and the bonding in ethene.*

Alkenes are similar to other hydrocarbons when burnt. They give carbon dioxide and water vapour as long as the air supply is sufficient:

ethene + oxygen → carbon dioxide + water

$$C_2H_4(g) + 3O_2(g) \rightarrow 2CO_2(g) + 2H_2O(g)$$

The presence of the C=C double bond in an alkene molecule makes them much more **reactive** than alkanes (alkanes contain only C—C single bonds). Other atoms can add on to alkene molecules across the double bond. This difference produces a simple test for unsaturation.

Table 11.2 Details of the first four alkenes

Alkene	Molecular formula C_nH_{2n}	Number of carbon atoms	Boiling point (°C)		Physical state at room temperature
Ethene	C_2H_4	2	−104		gas
Propene	C_3H_6	3	−47	b.p.	gas
Butene	C_4H_8	4	−6	increasing	gas
Pentene	C_5H_{10}	5	+30		liquid

Chemical tests for unsaturation

If an alkene, such as ethene, is shaken with a solution of bromine in water, the bromine loses its colour. Bromine has reacted with ethene, producing a colourless compound:

ethene + bromine → 1,2-dibromoethane

$$C_2H_4(g) + Br_2(aq) \rightarrow C_2H_4Br_2(l)$$

orange-brown   colourless
solution

The double bond in ethene breaks open and forms new bonds to the bromine atoms (figure 11.4). This type of reaction, where a double bond breaks and adds two new atoms, is known as an **addition reaction**. An alkane would give no reaction with bromine water; the solution would stay orange-brown.

A similar colour reaction occurs between alkenes and an acidified dilute solution of potassium manganate(VII). This solution is purple, and it turns colourless when shaken with an unsaturated compound. Again, an alkane would produce no change.

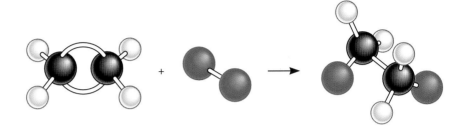

Figure 11.4 The addition of bromine to ethene.

EXTENSION

The importance of structure

11.5 Isomerism

The product formed when ethene reacts with bromine in solution illustrates the system of naming organic compounds.

- The product has *two* carbon atoms joined by a *single* bond. It is named after *ethane*.
- The molecule contains *two bromine* atoms. It is called *dibromoethane*.
- The bromine atoms are *not* both attached to the *same* carbon atom. One bromine atom is bonded to each carbon atom. The carbon atoms are numbered 1 and 2. The full name of the compound is *1,2-dibromoethane*.

The system of naming compounds emphasises the importance of structure. Molecules with the same molecular formula can have different structures. The same number of atoms can be connected together in different ways. This is known as **isomerism**.

There are two *different* compounds with the molecular formula C_4H_{10}:

- Butane

H   H   H   H
| | | |
H — C — C — C — C — H
| | | |
H   H   H   H
butane

colourless gas
burns in air to form CO_2 and H_2O
liquefies at $0\,°C$

- 2-Methylpropane

H
|
H — C — H   methyl group

H   H
| |
H — C — C — C — H
| | |
H   H   H
2-methylpropane

colourless gas
burns in air to form CO_2 and H_2O
liquefies at $-12\,°C$

In butane, all four carbon atoms are arranged in one 'straight' main chain. However, the atoms do not have to be arranged in this way. The fourth carbon atom can go off from the main chain to give the 'Y-shaped' or branched structure of

2-methylpropane. Compounds such as these are known as **isomers**. The properties of these particular isomers are quite similar; the difference shows itself mainly in their melting points and boiling points. Hydrocarbons containing branched chains have lower melting points and lower boiling points than straight-chain compounds with the same number of carbon atoms.

All the *alkane* molecules with four or more carbon atoms possess isomers. For example, there are three isomers with the formula C_5H_{12}.

The *alkenes* with four or more carbon atoms can show a different kind of isomerism. In this, the *position* of the $C=C$ double bond is moved along the chain. There are two molecules with a 'straight' chain of four carbon atoms and the molecular formula C_4H_8:

- But-1-ene

but-1-ene

- But-2-ene

but-2-ene

The structures are different. Again, the carbon atoms are numbered. The number added to the formula indicates the position of the double bond. In but-1-ene the double bond is between carbon atoms 1 and 2; in but-2-ene it is between carbon atoms 2 and 3.

> **Isomers** are compounds that have the same molecular formula but different structural formulas.

11.6 Alkynes

A third family of hydrocarbons exists in which the molecule contains a $C\equiv C$ triple bond. These are the **alkynes**. The simplest member is ethyne (C_2H_2). This highly reactive gas used to be known as acetylene. It is used in oxy-acetylene welding torches. We do not study the alkynes any further at this level.

11.7 Chemical reactions of the alkanes

The alkanes are rather unreactive compounds. They are saturated, so they cannot take part in addition reactions. They are unaffected by acids or alkalis. However, they can take part in substitution reactions, particularly with the halogens.

Substitution

The **substitution reaction** with chlorine is interesting because it is a **photochemical reaction**:

$$\text{methane} + \text{chlorine} \xrightarrow{\text{sunlight}} \text{chloromethane} + \text{hydrogen chloride}$$

$$CH_4(g) + Cl_2(g) \xrightarrow{\text{sunlight}} CH_3Cl(g) + HCl(g)$$

Methane and chlorine react in the presence of sunlight. Ultra-violet light splits chlorine molecules into separate energised atoms (**free radicals**). These

free radicals then react with methane. So the overall result is that a chlorine atom replaces (substitutes for) a hydrogen atom in a methane molecule to give chloromethane (CH_3Cl). The reaction can continue further as more hydrogen atoms are substituted. Compounds such as dichloromethane (CH_2Cl_2), trichloromethane ($CHCl_3$) and tetrachloromethane (CCl_4) are formed in this way.

Trichloromethane ($CHCl_3$), or chloroform, was an early **anaesthetic**. However, the dose which would kill a patient is not much higher than the amount needed to anaesthetise a patient! So it was very easy to make mistakes. Something else was needed. Investigations were carried out on the anaesthetic effect of other substituted alkanes. In 1956, halothane was discovered. It is a more useful anaesthetic. Its formula is $CF_3CHBrCl$, and its structure is:

$$H - \overset{\overset{\displaystyle Br}{|}}{\underset{\underset{\displaystyle Cl}{|}}{C}} - \overset{\overset{\displaystyle F}{|}}{\underset{\underset{\displaystyle F}{|}}{C}} - F$$

halothane

Substituted alkanes are also good organic solvents. 1,1,1-Trichloroethane is one solvent that is used a lot; in dry cleaning, for example.

Chlorofluorocarbons

Chlorofluorocarbons (CFCs) are a group of chemically unreactive compounds that have been widely used as solvents that vaporise easily. They have other uses, as shown in figure 11.5. During manufacture, in use and after disposal, these volatile compounds escape into the atmosphere.

The uses of CFCs:

- propellants in aerosol cans,
- solvents for cleaning electronic circuit-boards,
- refrigerants in fridges and air-conditioning units,
- blowing agents for making foam packaging and insulation.

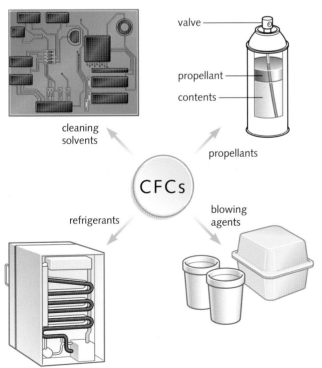

Figure 11.5 The uses of chlorofluorocarbons. Eventually, much of the CFCs will end up in the atmosphere.

One of the most-used CFCs was CFC-12, or dichlorodifluoromethane (CF_2Cl_2). Research into the effects of these compounds on the ozone layer in the upper atmosphere won Molina and Rowland the Nobel Prize in 1996. Their research showed the damage that these molecules can cause. The combination of CFCs and certain climatic conditions produces a much-reduced amount of ozone in the ozone layer, over various regions of the Earth, known as a 'hole'. The hole allows a greater amount of harmful ultra-violet radiation to reach the Earth's surface. In the stratosphere (see figure 1.18 on page 17), high-energy ultra-violet radiation splits chlorine atoms from the CFC molecules. These energised atoms (free radicals) then react with ozone to form oxygen:

$$O_3(g) + Cl(g) \rightarrow \underset{\substack{\text{another} \\ \text{free radical}}}{OCl(g)} + O_2(g)$$

Research is now aiming to find alternatives to CFCs. Hydrochlorofluorocarbons (HCFCs) have proved less harmful to the ozone layer (they destroy only a third as much ozone as CFCs). Hydrofluorocarbons (HFCs) appear to cause no damage to the ozone layer. HFC compounds should take over in various applications. There is agreement to end the use of HCFCs and CFCs world-wide between 2020 and 2040 (amendment to the 'Montreal Protocol', Vienna 1995). If nations keep to such international agreements, then the concentration of ozone in the stratosphere will return to pre-industrial levels in 50 years. The battle to save the ozone layer is not just an environmental issue. It now involves the complex politics of development. Plans on paper will come to nothing if rich countries do not provide the promised funds to help developing nations to switch to safer refrigerants.

11.8 Chemical reactions of the alkenes

Alkenes are much more reactive than alkanes. Under suitable conditions, molecules such as bromine, hydrogen and water (steam) will add across the C=C double bond.

Bromination

This reaction is used as the chemical test for an unsaturated hydrocarbon (see page 308). Bromine water is decolourised when shaken with an alkene. The reaction will also work with the bromine dissolved in an organic solvent such as 1,1,1-trichloroethane.

Hydrogenation

The addition of hydrogen across a C=C double bond is known as **hydrogenation**. Ethene reacts with hydrogen if the heated gases are passed together over a catalyst (see page 189). The unsaturated ethane is the product:

$$\text{ethene} + \text{hydrogen} \xrightarrow[\text{nickel}]{150-300\,°C} \text{ethane}$$

$$C_2H_4(g) + H_2(g) \xrightarrow[\text{nickel}]{150-300\,°C} C_2H_6(g)$$

Hydrogenation reactions similar to the reaction with ethene are used in the manufacture of margarine from vegetable oils. The vegetable oils of interest include corn oil and sunflower oil. They are edible oils and contain long-chain organic acids (**fatty acids**). The hydrocarbon chains of these acids contain one or more C=C double bonds; they are unsaturated molecules (figure 11.6). Oils such as sunflower oil are rich in **poly-unsaturated** molecules. This means that the melting point is relatively low and the oil remains liquid at normal temperatures (and even with refrigeration). By hydrogenating some, but not all, of the C=C double bonds, the liquid vegetable oil can be made into a solid but spreadable fat (margarine).

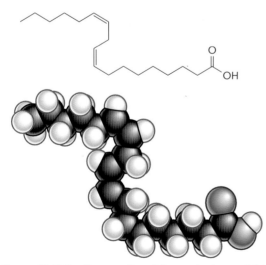

Figure 11.6 Sunflower oil and its products are rich in fats containing unsaturated molecules (note the C=C double bonds in the chain).

Animal fats tend to be more saturated than vegetable oils and fats. The animal fats in cream can be made into butter. Many doctors now believe that unsaturated fats are more healthy than saturated ones. This is why margarines are left partially unsaturated; not all the C=C double bonds are hydrogenated (figure 11.6). Olive oil is distinctive in having a high content of oleic acid, which is a **mono-unsaturated** fatty acid. Margarine can be made from olive oil without any hydrogenation.

Hydration

Another important addition reaction is the one used in the manufacture of ethanol. Ethanol is an important industrial chemical and solvent. It is formed when a mixture of steam and ethene is passed over a catalyst of **immobilised** phosphoric(V) acid (the acid is absorbed on silica pellets) at a temperature of 300°C and a pressure of 60 atmospheres:

$$\text{ethene} + \text{steam} \xrightarrow[\text{phosphoric acid}]{300\,°C,\ 60\ \text{atmospheres}} \text{ethanol}$$

$$C_2H_4(g) + H_2O(g) \longrightarrow C_2H_5OH(g)$$

This reaction produces the ethanol of high purity needed in industrial organic chemistry.

Summary of core material

You should know that:

* there is a vast range of carbon compounds, and the study of their properties is known as organic chemistry

* the simplest organic compounds are the hydrocarbons

* because of the versatility of carbon atoms in their bonding, there are whole 'families' (homologous series) of hydrocarbons

* the alkanes are a series of unsaturated hydrocarbons, the simplest member of which is methane, the main component of natural gas

* the alkanes are important as fuels but are fairly unreactive, though they can take part in substitution reactions, particularly with the halogens, whereas the alkenes are considerably more reactive because they contain a C=C double bond

• chlorofluorocarbons (CFCs) are a group of chemically unreactive compounds that have been widely used as solvents that vaporise easily.

11.1

(a) **A** to **H** are the structural formulae of some organic compounds.

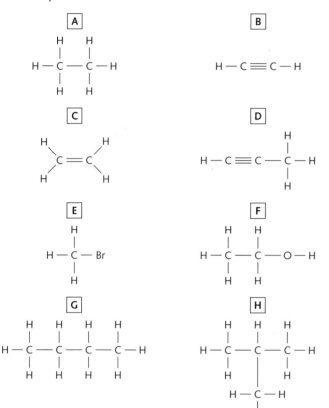

Give the letters which represent:
(i) *two* alkanes, [2]
(ii) *two* compounds which are not hydrocarbons. [2]
(iii) **B** and **D** are members of a homologous series. Give a reason why this statement is correct. [1]
(iv) How could **C** be converted into **A**? [1]

(b) Bromine is used to produce dibromoethane which is used as an additive in petrol. It is made by adding bromine to ethene.

dibromoethane

(i) What is the molecular formula of ethene? [1]
(ii) What is the formula of a bromine molecule? [1]
(iii) What is the molecular formula of dibromoethane?
[1]

(iv) Copy and complete the following equation by drawing the structures of the molecules: [2]

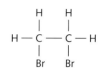

ethene + bromine ⟶ dibromoethane

(MEG, part question, 1993 and IGCSE, part question, 1995)

11.2

(a) Copy and complete the following table. [5]

(Relative atomic masses required: H = 1; C = 12)

Name of hydrocarbon	Ethane	Ethene
Molecular formula of hydrocarbon	C_2H_6	
Relative molecular mass of hydrocarbon		
Structural formula of hydrocarbon	H—C—C—H (ethane structure)	
Colour of bromine water after being shaken with the hydrocarbon		colourless

(b) The hydrocarbon, propane, is an important constituent of the fuel, liquid petroleum gas (LPG). For the burning of propane in an excess of air, give:
(i) a word equation, [1]
(ii) a balanced symbol equation. [2]
(iii) Use your answer to part (ii) to give the number of moles of water formed when one mole of propane is burned in an excess of air. [1]

(c) Bromine reacts with alkanes in a similar way to chlorine. Hydrogen bromide is made in the substitution reaction between propane and bromine:

propane + bromine → bromopropane + hydrogen bromide

(i) Draw the structure of propane. [1]
(ii) Draw the structure of a bromopropane. [1]
(iii) The reaction between propane and bromine is *photochemical*. Suggest what is meant by *photochemical*. [2]
(iv) Give the formula and name of the alkane which contains four carbon atoms in each molecule. [2]

(d) Unsaturated hydrocarbons take part in addition reactions.
(i) Write a word equation for the reaction between propene and hydrogen. [1]

(ii) Write a symbol equation for the reaction between propene and steam. [2]

(NISEAC, part question, 1991 and IGCSE, part question, 1994)

11.3 Aerosols are in use around the world. For example, a deodorant spray contains the deodorant dissolved in ethanol. This solution mixes completely with a liquid propellant.

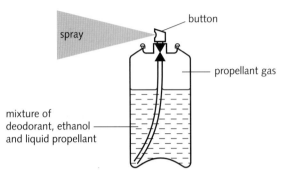

The diagram shows the inside of a can of deodorant spray. When the button is pressed, the liquid propellant boils and pushes out the deodorant as a spray.

(a) Use the kinetic theory to describe what happens to the liquids in the aerosol when they change into gases. [3]

(b) One propellant used is freon-12 which has the formula CF_2Cl_2.
    (i) In which group of the Periodic Table are fluorine and chlorine found? [1]
    (ii) Calculate the relative molecular mass, M_r, of freon-12. [3]
    (iii) Explain whether freon-12 is lighter or heavier than air. Regard air as a mixture of nitrogen and oxygen (M_r for nitrogen = 28; M_r for oxygen = 32). [2]

(c) A problem in using aerosols is that the gas freon-12 reacts with the ozone layer when it reaches the outer atmosphere. The removal of ozone is harmful because more of the dangerous ultra-violet rays from the Sun can then reach the surface of the Earth.
    (i) Name *two* elements which exist as gases in the atmosphere and are also very unreactive. [2]
    (ii) Explain whether it is possible to recycle freon-12. [1]
    (iii) Suggest how the problem in using aerosols, described above, might be solved. [2]

(IGCSE, part question, 1990)

11.4

(a) Calor gas mainly consists of the fourth member of the alkanes called butane. Methane (CH_4) is the first member of the alkanes and butane is the fourth member.
    (i) Give the formula of the third member of the alkanes. [1]
    (ii) Draw the structural formula of butane, and of an isomer of butane. [3]

(b) When butane is burned the following reaction takes place:

$$2C_4H_{10} + 13O_2 \rightarrow 8CO_2 + 10H_2O$$

(i) How many moles of butane have to be burned to produce 4 moles of carbon dioxide? [1]
(ii) Calculate the mass of one mole of butane (C_4H_{10}). [1]
(iii) Calculate the mass of one mole of carbon dioxide. [1]
(iv) How many grams of carbon dioxide would be produced if 5.8 g of butane were burned? [3]

(MEG, part question, 1992)

11.5 In 1916 Thomas Midgley discovered that a lead compound would improve the combustion of fuel in petrol engines. This was the beginning of leaded petrol.

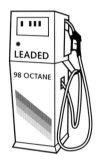

(a) Heptane is a constituent of petrol. Write the balanced equation for the complete combustion of heptane:

$$C_7H_{16} + O_2 \rightarrow \ldots\ldots + \ldots\ldots \qquad [2]$$

(b) The lead compound is made from chloroethane and an alloy of sodium and lead. Chloroethane is one of the chemicals manufactured from ethene.
    (i) Name the compound that reacts with ethene in an addition reaction to give chloroethane. [1]
    (ii) Draw the structural formula of chloroethane. [1]

(c) Chloroethane can also be made by a substitution reaction. What are the reagents and reaction conditions for this reaction? [3]

(d) The lead compound used by Midgley can be represented by the formula $Pb(C_2H_5)_n$. It contains 64% by mass of lead.
    (i) Calculate the composition by mass of 100 g of $Pb(C_2H_5)_n$ by the following steps (copy out and complete)
    Mass of lead in 100 g of the compound = 64 g
    Mass of $(C_2H_5)_n$ in 100 g of the compound = ___ g

    Now copy and complete the following.
    (ii) The number of moles of Pb in 100 g of $Pb(C_2H_5)_n$ =
    (iii) The mass of one mole of C_2H_5 =
    (iv) The number of moles of C_2H_5 in 100 g of the compound =
    (v) The mole ratio Pb:C_2H_5 is
    (vi) The value of n is [5]

(IGCSE, part question, 1996)

Alcohols

This section covers the following ideas:

- the alcohols as a homologous series
- fermentation as a source of ethanol
- the reactions of ethanol
- ethanol and health.

Ethanol is one of the best-known organic compounds. It is just one of a whole family of compounds – the alcohols. The alcohols are a **homologous series** of compounds that contain —OH as the functional group (figure 11.7). A **functional group** is a group of atoms in a structure that determines the characteristic reactions of a compound.

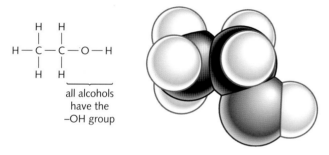

Figure 11.7 The structure of ethanol.

Table 11.3 shows the molecular formulas of the early members of the series. The simplest alcohol contains one carbon atom and is called **methanol**. Note that the names all have the same ending (...*ol*). The general formula of the alcohols is $C_nH_{2n+1}OH$, and they can be referred to as the *alkanols*. The structural formulas of the first three alcohols are as shown in figure 11.8. The early

Table 11.3 Some alcohols

Alcohol	Molecular formula $C_nH_{2n+1}OH$	Boiling point (°C)
Methanol	CH_3OH	65
Ethanol	C_2H_5OH	78
Propan-1-ol	C_3H_7OH	97
Butan-1-ol	C_4H_9OH	117
Pentan-1-ol	$C_5H_{11}OH$	137

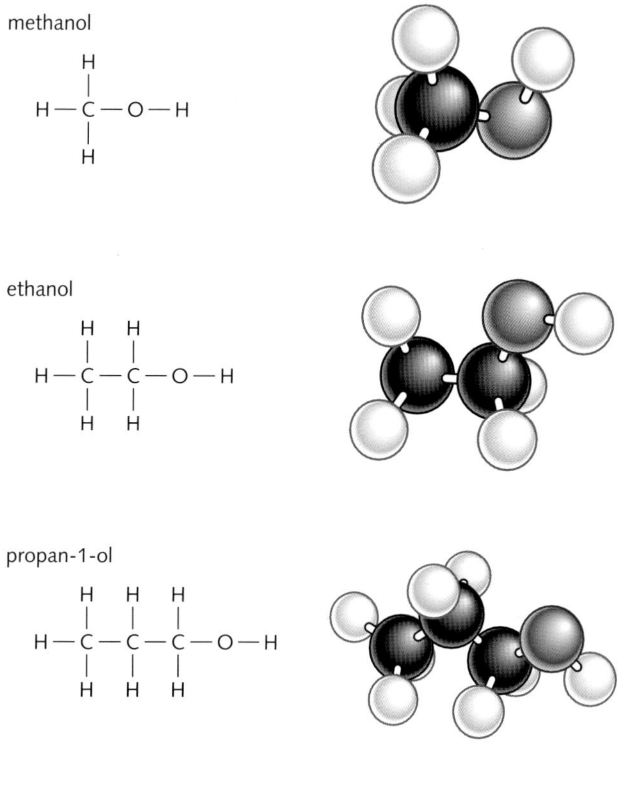

b.p. increasing

Figure 11.8 Alcohols are a homologous series – these are the structures of the first three members.

alcohols are all neutral, colourless liquids that do not conduct electricity.

11.9 Making ethanol

Hydration of ethene

The industrial method of making ethanol involves the addition reaction that we saw at the end of section 11.8 on page 312. In this, ethene and steam are compressed to 60 atmospheres and passed over a catalyst (immobilised phosphoric(V) acid) at 300 °C:

$$\text{ethene} + \text{steam} \xrightarrow[\text{phosphoric acid}]{\text{300 °C, 60 atmospheres}} \text{ethanol}$$

$$C_2H_4(g) + H_2O(g) \longrightarrow C_2H_5OH(g)$$

Ethanol is an important solvent and raw material for making other organic chemicals. Many everyday items use ethanol as a solvent. These include paints, glues, perfumes, aftershave, etc.

Fermentation

Ethanol and carbon dioxide are the natural waste products of **yeasts** when they ferment sugar. Sugar is present in all fruit and grains, and in the sap and nectar of all plants. Yeasts are found everywhere. The Babylonians and Egyptians found that, if they crushed grapes or germinated grain, the paste would bubble and produce a drink with a kick! Pasteur discovered that yeast are single-cell, living **fungi**. They ferment sugar to gain energy – by **anaerobic respiration**. As ethanol is toxic to yeast, fermentation is self-limiting. Once the ethanol concentration has reached about 14%, or the sugar runs out, the multiplying yeast die and fermentation ends. The best temperature for carrying out the process is 37°C. The reaction is catalysed by **enzymes** in the yeast:

$$glucose \xrightarrow{yeast} ethanol + carbon\ dioxide$$

$$C_6H_{12}O_6(aq) \xrightarrow{enzymes} 2C_2H_5OH(aq) + 2CO_2(g)$$

Alcoholic drinks such as beer and wine are made on a large scale in vast quantities in copper or steel fermentation vats. Beer is made from barley, with hops and other ingredients added to produce distinctive flavours. Wine is made by fermenting grape juice. Beer contains about 4% by volume of ethanol, whereas wine contains between 8 and 14%. Stronger, more alcoholic, drinks are made in one of two ways. Fortified wines, such as sherry and port, have pure ethanol added to them. Spirits, such as whisky, brandy and vodka, are made by **distillation** (see page 36).

Fermentation can be carried out in the laboratory using the apparatus in figure 11.9. The air-lock allows gas to escape from the vessel but prevents

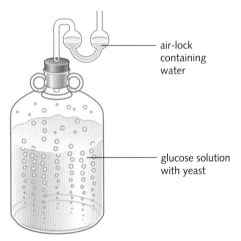

air-lock containing water

glucose solution with yeast

Figure 11.9 A laboratory fermentation vessel.

airborne bacteria entering. A small amount of sulphur dioxide is dissolved in the fermentation mixture to prevent bacterial growth.

11.10 The reactions of ethanol

Ethanol as a fuel

Ethanol burns with a clear flame, giving out quite a lot of heat:

$$ethanol + oxygen \rightarrow carbon\ dioxide + water$$

$$C_2H_5OH(l) + 3O_2(g) \rightarrow 2CO_2(g) + 3H_2O(g)$$

On a small scale, ethanol can be used as methylated spirit (ethanol mixed with methanol or other compounds) in spirit lamps and stoves. However, ethanol is such a useful fuel that some countries have developed it as a fuel for cars. Brazil has a climate suitable for growing sugar-cane. Ethanol produced by fermentation of sugar from sugar-cane has been used as an alternative fuel to gasoline (petrol), or mixed with gasoline to produce 'gasohol'. It is a **renewable resource** and has the potential to reduce petroleum imports. Currently about half of Brazil's cars run on ethanol or 'gasohol'. 'Gasohol' now accounts for 10% of the gasoline sales in the USA. 'Gasohol' and other 'oxygenated fuels' have the advantage of *reducing* the emissions of carbon monoxide from cars. But the emissions of the oxides of nitrogen are *increased* using such fuels. Also the concentrations of ozone in photochemical smog are greater. These findings cast doubt on claims that these fuels are a clean alternative for vehicles.

11.11 Alcohol and health

Ethanol is the only alcohol that is safe to drink. It must only be drunk in moderation. Methanol is very toxic and even in small amounts can cause blindness and death.

Ethanol mixes totally with water, which takes it everywhere in the body that water goes. The amount of alcohol that a person may drink varies with age, sex, weight and drinking history. The route taken by alcohol through the human body is as follows (figure 11.10). First, it goes into the mouth and throat ①, and then on to the stomach ②. Some alcohol is absorbed in the

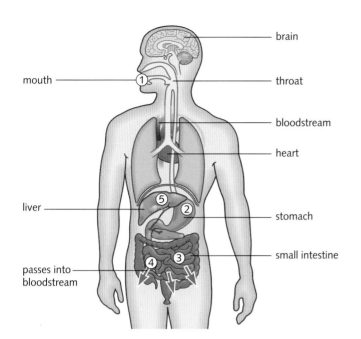

mouth

brain

throat

bloodstream

heart

liver

stomach

small intestine

passes into bloodstream

stomach, but most moves into the small intestine ③. From here it passes rapidly into the bloodstream ④. The presence of food can delay absorption – for up to six hours for one drink on a full stomach. Alcohol is spread throughout the body by the blood. It is broken down mainly in the liver ⑤, where it is converted into carbon dioxide and water.

Moderate amounts of alcohol seem to reduce coronary heart disease. Heavy drinking, however, eventually damages the muscle tissue of the heart. Heavy drinking can cause a healthy liver to become fatty and enlarged. Eventually scarring (**cirrhosis**) can cause liver failure and death. There may well

Figure 11.10 *The normal route of metabolism for ethanol in the human body.*

EXTENSION

Further reactions of alcohols

Oxidation

Vinegar is a weak solution of ethanoic acid (previously called acetic acid). It is produced commercially from wine by biochemical oxidation using bacteria (*Acetobacter*). Wine can also become 'vinegary' if it is left open to the air. The same oxidation can be achieved quickly by powerful oxidising agents (see page 106) such as warm acidified potassium dichromate(VI):

ethanol + oxygen → ethanoic acid + water
_(from oxidising agent)

$$C_2H_5OH + 2[O] \rightarrow CH_3COOH + H_2O$$

The colour of the potassium dichromate solution turns from orange to green.

The original 'Breathalyser' worked on the basis of this reaction. You had to breathe out through a tube containing orange crystals of potassium dichromate(VI). If the crystals turned green, this showed that you had too much alcohol in your breath.

Figure 11.11 *The dehydration of ethanol in the laboratory.*

Dehydration

Ethanol can be **dehydrated** to produce ethene. This is one way of preparing ethene in the laboratory. Ethanol vapour is passed over a heated catalyst. The catalyst can be aluminium oxide or broken pieces of porous pot. Ethene is not soluble in water, so it can be collected as shown in figure 11.11.

Esterification

Alcohols react with organic acids (see page 320) to form sweet-smelling oily liquids known as **esters**. For example

ethanoic acid + ethanol
→ ethyl ethanoate + water

$$CH_3COOH(l) + C_2H_5OH(l)$$
$$\rightarrow CH_3COOC_2H_5(l) + H_2O(l)$$

Concentrated sulphuric acid is added as a catalyst for this esterification reaction.

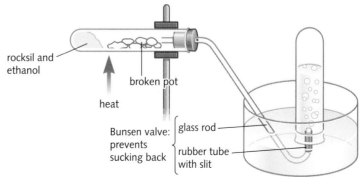

rocksil and ethanol

broken pot

heat

Bunsen valve: prevents sucking back

glass rod

rubber tube with slit

317

be some long-term damage to the brain with prolonged heavy drinking. Alcohol is a depressive drug and can be addictive. Drinking heavily on a

particular occasion produces drunkenness, during which speech becomes slurred, vision is blurred and reaction times are slowed.

Summary of core material

You should know that:

* series of organic compounds exist with different functional groups attached to the hydrocarbon 'backbone'

* one important homologous series is the alcohols, the most significant of which is ethanol

* ethanol can be manufactured chemically and also obtained by fermentation

* ethanol (alcohol) can have some potentially dangerous effects on the human body if drunk in excess.

11.6 Sugar-cane grows quickly in tropical areas. Sugar can be fermented to make ethanol. Either ethanol or mixtures of petrol and ethanol (gasohol) can be used as the fuel for cars.

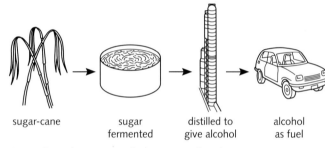

| sugar-cane | sugar fermented | distilled to give alcohol | alcohol as fuel |

(a) Ethanol consists of organic molecules.
   (i) What type of compound is ethanol? [1]
   (ii) Ethanol has the formula C_2H_5OH. Draw its structure. [2]

(b) Gasohol boils over a temperature range of 40°C–150°C in the laboratory. Ethanol has a boiling point of 78°C. Draw a labelled diagram to show how a sample of ethanol may be obtained from gasohol. [4]

(c) In Sao Paulo, the capital city of Brazil, atmospheric pollution has fallen by more than 18% since using gasohol. Gasohol does not need additives to improve it as petrol does.
   (i) Name *three* common pollutants that may be found in the atmosphere. [3]
   (ii) Suggest how pollution from cars may have been reduced by using gasohol. [1]

(IGCSE, 1990)

11.7 Alkenes are an important series of hydrocarbons.

(a) What do the structures of all alkenes have in common? [2]

(b) Give a simple test that could be used to show the presence of an alkene in a mixture with alkanes present. Describe the test and the expected result. [2]

(c) Ethanol can be made by the addition of water to ethene. Ethanol can also be made by fermentation of sugars.

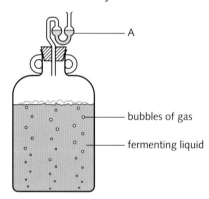

A
bubbles of gas
fermenting liquid

   (i) Name the gas produced during the fermentation shown above. [1]
   (ii) This gas escapes through the piece of apparatus labelled A. What is the main purpose of this piece of apparatus? [1]
   (iii) What must be added to a sugar solution to make it ferment? [1]
   (iv) At about what temperature does fermentation take place at its fastest rate? [1]
   (v) Explain your choice of temperature given in (iv). [2]
   (vi) Why can drinking ethanol be a possible danger to humans? [2]
   (vii) Ethanol can be used as a fuel. Write a balanced chemical equation for the combustion of ethanol in air. [2]

(SEG, part question, 1988)

11.8 In 1986, several people died in Italy as a result of drinking wine which contained methanol. The methanol had been added to the wine to increase its alcohol content.

Samples of the wine were reported to contain as much as 3% methanol, by volume. A level of 0.03% is the maximum allowed by law.

(a) (i) What name is given to the process by which grape juice is turned into wine? [1]
     (ii) At what temperature is this process best carried out? [1]
     (iii) What is added to grape juice for the process to occur? [1]

(b) Calculate how much methanol would be legally allowed in a litre bottle of wine. [2]

(c) The chemicals present in the wine, and some of their properties, are listed below:

Substance	Melting point (°C)	Boiling point (°C)	Solubility in water
Methanol	–94	65	mixes with water
Ethanol	–117	79	mixes with water
Water	0	100	mixes with water

   (i) Draw a labelled diagram of the apparatus you would use, in the laboratory, to obtain pure methanol from the wine. [4]
   (ii) How would you know whether the methanol obtained was pure? [2]

(d) Methanol and ethanol are members of a homologous series.
   (i) Draw the molecular structures of methanol and ethanol. [2]
   (ii) Explain what the term *homologous series* means. [2]

(e) Both methanol and ethanol burn in an excess of air to form the same products.
   (i) Name these products. [2]
   (ii) Suggest why it is not possible to set fire to the contents of a bottle of wine. [1]

(IGCSE, 1993)

11.9 In the USA, ethene is converted to ethanol.

   Equation I: ethene + steam → ethanol

In Europe, ethanol is often converted to ethene.

   Equation II: ethanol → ethene + steam

(a) Using a reversible sign (⇌), combine Equation I and Equation II into one equation. [1]

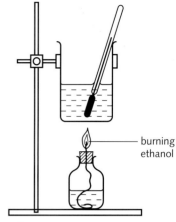

(b) Ethanol is a fuel. In laboratories that do not have a gas supply, it may be used in a spirit burner. The diagram shows a spirit burner being used to heat a beaker of water. A black solid is formed on the bottom of the beaker. The amount of ethanol needed to boil the water may be found by weighing the spirit burner.

burning ethanol

   (i) Name the black substance formed on the beaker. [1]
   (ii) Suggest why the black substance is formed when the ethanol is burned. [2]
   (iii) Calculate the mass of ethanol burnt from the following data: [2]
      mass of spirit burner + ethanol before burning = 25.26 g
      mass of spirit burner + ethanol after burning = 21.34 g

(c) Name *two* other fuels used in industry. [2]

(d) Ethene is unsaturated. Ethanol is saturated.
   (i) Explain what is meant by *unsaturated*. [1]
   (ii) Describe a simple chemical test that would show that ethene is unsaturated. [2]
   (iii) One use of ethene is to make ethanol. Name another important use of ethene. [1]

(IGCSE, part question, 1991)

11.10 This question is about alcohols.

(a) The alcohols are members of a homologous series.
   (i) Write down the general formula for this homologous series. [1]
   (ii) Write down the names and draw the structures of the two monohydric alcohols (alcohols that have only one —OH group) containing three carbon atoms per molecule. [4]

(b) On analysis, a 10.00 g sample of an alcohol was found to contain 3.75 g of carbon, 1.25 g of hydrogen, and 5.00 g of oxygen. Use this data to find the empirical formula of this alcohol. Suggest its molecular formula. [4]

(c) The dissociation energy of ethanol is shown below.

$C_2H_5OH(g) \rightarrow 2C(g) + 6H(g) + O(g)$
$\Delta H = +3234$ kJ/mol of ethanol

Using bond energy values given on page 180, calculate the bond energy of C—O per mole.

(MEG, 1995)

EXTENSION

Organic acids and esters

This section covers the following ideas:

- carboxylic acids as a homologous series
- ethanoic acid as a weak acid
- esterification
- soap-making (saponification) and synthetic detergents.

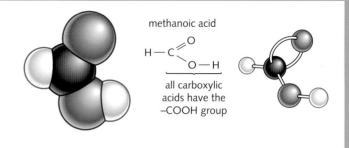

methanoic acid

all carboxylic acids have the —COOH group

ethanoic acid

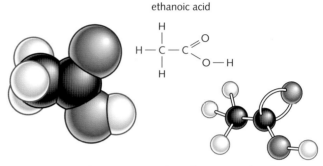

Figure 11.12 The structures of methanoic acid and ethanoic acid.

11.12 Carboxylic acids

The carboxylic acids are another **homologous series** of organic compounds. All these acids have the functional group —COOH attached to a hydrocarbon chain. Table 11.4 shows the molecular formulas of the first two members of the series. The compounds have the general formula $C_nH_{2n+1}COOH$ (or $C_nH_{2n+1}CO_2H$). Figure 11.12 shows the structural formulas of the first two acids in the series.

The first two acids in the series are liquids at room temperature, though ethanoic acid will solidify if the temperature falls only slightly. The acids dissolve in water to produce solutions that are weakly acidic. Methanoic acid is present in nettle stings and ant stings, while ethanoic acid (once called acetic acid) is well known as the acid in vinegar.

11.13 Ethanoic acid as a weak acid

Whereas a strong acid such as hydrochloric acid is completely split into ions, ethanoic acid only partially dissociates into ions in water. A **dynamic equilibrium** is set up in the solution. The solution does contain an excess of hydrogen ions (H^+) over hydroxide ions (OH^-), so the solution is

weakly acidic (see section 5.5 on page 129):

ethanoic acid $\rightleftharpoons$ ethanoate ions
+ hydrogen ions

$$CH_3COOH(aq) \rightleftharpoons CH_3COO^-(aq) + H^+(aq)$$

A solution of the acid will show the characteristic reactions of an acid. For example, it will react with bases to form salts:

ethanoic acid + sodium hydroxide
$\rightarrow$ sodium ethanoate + water

$$CH_3COOH(aq) + NaOH(aq)$$
$$\rightarrow CH_3COONa(aq) + H_2O(l)$$

Vinegar can be used as a 'descaler' in hard water areas. The ethanoic acid in vinegar reacts with limescale (calcium carbonate), producing carbon dioxide and dissolving the scale:

calcium carbonate + ethanoic acid
$\rightarrow$ calcium ethanoate + water
+ carbon dioxide

Table 11.4 The first two carboxylic acids

Carboxylic acid	Molecular formula $C_nH_{2n+1}COOH$	Melting point (°C)	Boiling point (°C)	
Methanoic acid	HCOOH	9	101	m.p. and b.p.
Ethanoic acid	CH_3COOH	17	118	increasing

$$CaCO_3(s) + 2CH_3COOH(aq)$$
$$\rightarrow (CH_3COO)_2Ca(aq) + H_2O(l) + CO_2(g)$$

Commercial descalers use methanoic acid, or other types of weak acid such as sulphamic acid.

11.14 Esterification

Ethanoic acid will react with ethanol, in the presence of a few drops of concentrated sulphuric acid, to produce ethyl ethanoate. The concentrated sulphuric acid is a catalyst for the reaction:

ethanoic acid + ethanol $\xrightarrow{\text{conc. } H_2SO_4}$
ethyl ethanoate + water

$$CH_3COOH(l) + C_2H_5OH(l)$$
$$\rightarrow CH_3COOC_2H_5(l) + H_2O(l)$$

This type of reaction is known as **esterification**. The structure of ethyl ethanoate is shown below:

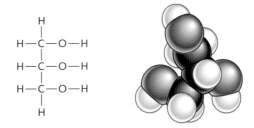

ethyl   ethanoate

Ethyl ethanoate is just one example of an **ester**. This family of compounds have strong and pleasant smells. Many of these compounds occur naturally. They are responsible for the flavours in fruits and for the scents of flowers (table 11.5). We use them as food flavourings and in perfumes. Fats and oils are naturally occurring esters used for energy storage in plants and animals.

Table 11.5 The smells of esters

Ester	Smell or flavour
ethyl 2-methylbutanoate	apple
3-methylbutyl ethanoate	pear
1-methylbutyl ethanoate	banana
butyl butanoate	pineapple
octyl ethanoate	orange
methylpropyl methanoate	raspberry
pentyl butanoate	strawberry

11.15 Soaps and detergents

Fats and oils as esters

Animal fats and vegetable oils are esters. They are liquids or solids depending on the size and shape of the molecules present. They are all esters of **glycerol**, an alcohol with three hydroxyl (—OH) groups (figure 11.13). Each —OH group forms an ester with a molecule of a carboxylic acid. These acids tend to have long chains (they are sometimes called **fatty acids**).

Stearic acid ($C_{17}H_{35}COOH$) (figure 11.14) is one such acid that occurs in animal fats. A complex molecule can be formed from glycerol and three molecules of stearic acid (figure 11.15 on page 322). This is the type of molecule present in fats and oils. Vegetable oils tend to have more unsaturated long-chain acids than animal fats.

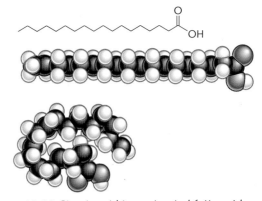

Figure 11.13 Glycerol is an alcohol with three —OH groups.

Figure 11.14 Stearic acid is a saturated fatty acid.

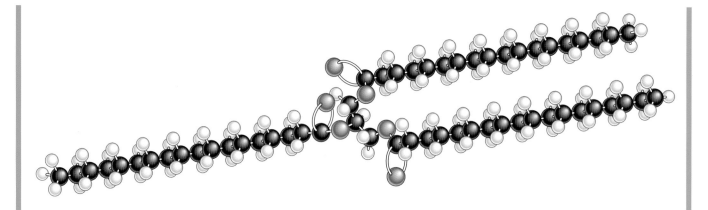

Figure 11.15 Glycerol and three molecules of stearic acid join together to form an ester present in animal fats.

Making soap and detergent

Water has a high **surface tension** and therefore does not necessarily wet things very well! In addition, it does not dissolve grease. To clean clothes with water, we need to add compounds to the water that will:

- wet and soak in between the fibres of the cloth,
- separate the grease, dirt and dust from the fibres, and
- suspend the grease in the water so that it can be washed away.

Similar needs apply when cleaning food from dishes. Anything that will do these things is known as a **detergent**.

There are two types of detergent:

- **soap detergents** (generally called 'soaps') are made from animal fats or vegetable oils,
- **soapless detergents** (usually just called 'detergents') are made using chemicals from oil.

Many millions of tonnes of soaps and detergents are made world-wide each year. Soap is made by heating animal fats or vegetable oils with sodium hydroxide solution. The esters present are broken down to glycerol and the sodium salts of the acids:

fat + sodium hydroxide → soap + glycerol

(sodium salts
of long-chain
fatty acids)

This process is known as **saponification**.

The action of soap and detergent

The cleaning properties of soap depend on its structure. Sodium stearate, for instance, consists of a long hydrocarbon chain, which is **hydrophobic** ('water-hating'), attached to an ionic head, which is **hydrophilic** ('water-loving') (figure 11.16). These molecules dissolve in water because of the ionic end to the molecule.

When added to water, the soap molecules lower the surface tension of the water, making it wet objects more easily. The molecules also interact with the grease present (figure 11.17). The hydrophobic hydrocarbon chain is attracted to the grease and becomes embedded in it. The hydrophilic ionic head of the molecule sits outside the grease in contact with water. When the water is agitated, the grease is released from the cloth fibre or dish and is completely surrounded by soap molecules. Rinsing with fresh water removes these grease–detergent droplets.

The use of soap gives problems in hard water areas because an insoluble scum is formed. Synthetic soapless detergents are now available that do not form a scum with hard water. Sodium alkylbenzenesulphonates (figure 11.18) were developed in the 1970s. They have a similar long hydrocarbon chain to soap molecules, but the ionic group at the hydrophilic head has been changed. The calcium and magnesium salts of these molecules are water-soluble.

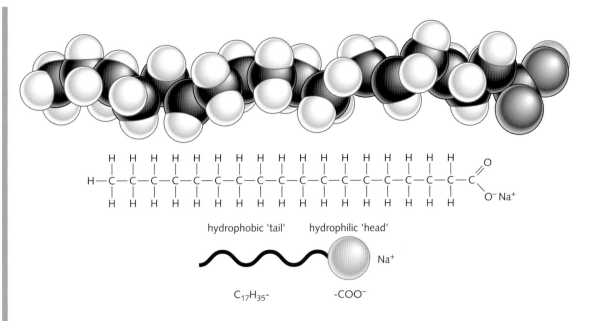

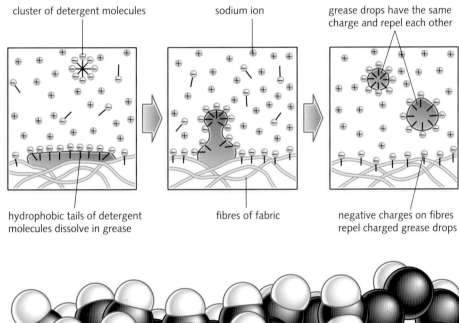

Figure 11.16 Sodium stearate in soap is a molecule with 'water-loving' (hydrophilic) and 'water-hating' (hydrophobic) regions.

cluster of detergent molecules

sodium ion

grease drops have the same charge and repel each other

hydrophobic tails of detergent molecules dissolve in grease

fibres of fabric

negative charges on fibres repel charged grease drops

Figure 11.17 Soap molecules arrange themselves in such a way that grease droplets are lifted from fabrics.

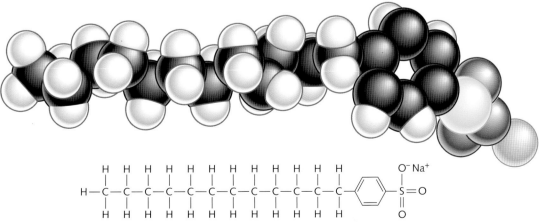

Figure 11.18 Synthetic detergents have a similar two-part structure to soaps.

The early synthetic detergent molecules were not **biodegradable**, and they caused pollution problems in rivers and streams. By changing the structure of the hydrophobic chain, modern soapless detergents are now biodegradable.

Some modern washing powders now contain enzymes (see page 190) to break down biological stains more effectively. These powders must be used at mild temperatures (40 °C) so as not to destroy the enzymes. A biological washing powder may contain a number of different ingredients:

- *synthetic detergents and soap* increase 'wetting power', loosen the bond between the fabric and the dirt, and keep the dirt in suspension,
- *builder* (complex chemicals) helps the cleaning process, softens water and suspends the dirt,

- *oxygen bleach* removes stains such as black tea and coffee; it gives added whiteness only at high temperatures and during long periods of soaking (so that at lower temperatures and short washes, 'coloureds' are not bleached),
- *metal protector* protects aluminium parts of washing machines
- *brightening agents* make 'whites' and 'coloureds' brighter,
- *blueing ingredient* gives a 'blue-white' hue to white fabrics,
- *enzymes* break down protein stains (e.g. blood, gravy),
- *perfume* gives clothes a fresh, clean fragrance.

Summary of extension material

You should know that:

- alcohols can be oxidised to produce another series of organic compounds that are acidic
- these organic acids (carboxylic acids) are weak acids, and ethanoic acid is the one most commonly used in the laboratory
- these compounds show all the characteristic reactions of acids but also react with alcohols to produce esters

- esters are important naturally occurring substances, being present in animal fats and vegetable oils
- as such, esters are important in our diet
- treatment of the esters of long-chain acids with sodium hydroxide produces soap.

11.11 Unsaturated compounds are manufactured from crude oil. (See chapter 12 for details of method.) They are also made in plants and animals.

(a) A difference in properties between fats and vegetable oils is their melting points. They are both esters of long-chain organic acids.
  (i) Explain the meaning of *melting point*. [2]
  (ii) How can the melting point of a substance show if it is a pure compound? [1]
  (iii) Name a chemical which reacts with these esters to form soaps. [1]

(b) Fats and vegetable oils can be saturated or unsaturated.

  A simple experiment can be carried out to measure the degree of unsaturation in these compounds.

  Five drops of a liquid or a similar volume of a solid is dissolved in 4 cm³ of ethanol. Dilute bromine water is

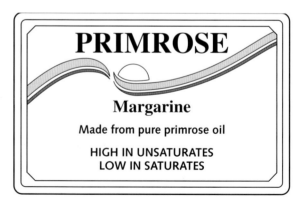

added a drop at a time. At first, the brown colour disappears. When enough bromine has been added to react with all the double bonds in the sample, the brown colour remains. The number of drops of bromine water needed to produce a permanent brown colour is recorded.

This test was carried out on a variety of cooking products. The results are shown below.

Cooking product	Mass of saturated fat in 100 g of cooking product (g)	Mass of unsaturated fat in 100 g of cooking product (g)	Number of drops of bromine water
Olive oil	11	84	14
Peanut oil	20	72	12
Butter	45	30	5
Soft margarine	35	40	7
Poly-unsaturated margarine	11	66	

(i) Why was ethanol, not water, used as a solvent in this experiment? [1]

(ii) One medical theory is that using unsaturated fats in the diet, instead of saturated fats, will reduce the number of cases of heart disease. Which of the cooking products in the table is the least likely to cause heart disease? [1]

(c) A more accurate method of measuring the degree of unsaturation of an oil is to find its iodine number. This is the mass of iodine that reacts with the double bonds in 100 g of the oil.

A solution of iodine in ethanol is added to a known mass of the oil. The volume of iodine solution needed to react with the double bonds is measured accurately.

(i) Suggest how you would know when all the double bonds in the oil have reacted with the iodine. [1]

(ii) The iodine number of a sample of linseed oil is 170 g of iodine/100 g of oil. The mass of one mole of linseed oil is approximately 900 g.
Copy and complete the following calculation to determine the number of double bonds in one molecule of linseed oil: [4]
100 g of oil react with 170 g of iodine;
900 g of oil react with ......g of iodine;
The mass of one mole of I_2 is ......g;
900 g of oil react with ......moles of I_2;
One mole of oil (900 g) reacts with ......moles of I_2;
The number of double bonds in one molecule of the oil is ......

(IGCSE, part question, 1991)

11.12 Alcohol (ethanol) is a product of many fermentation reactions. The molecular formula of ethanol is C_2H_5OH.

(a) Draw the graphical (structural) formula for ethanol. [1]

(b) When ethanol is heated with an excess of acidified potassium dichromate, it is converted to ethanoic acid:

$$C_2H_5OH \rightarrow CH_3COOH$$
ethanol   ethanoic acid

What type of chemical reaction is this? [1]

(c) Some synthetic flavourings are made by reacting an alcohol with a carboxylic acid:

alcohol + carboxylic acid → ester + water

What other substance and conditions are needed to carry out this reaction? [2]

(d) The structure of the ester propyl butanoate is shown here.

Draw the graphical (structural) formula of the carboxylic acid from which this ester is made. [1]

(MEG, part question, 1995)

11.13 French Dressing is put on salads and other foods. Two of its major constituents are olive oil and wine vinegar. Vinegar can be made from the alcohol ethanol.

FRENCH DRESSING

INGREDIENTS
vegetable oil, white wine vinegar, dijon mustard, salt, pepper, herbs

270 ml   shake well

(a) Alcohols form a homologous series. The second member of this series is ethanol.
(i) What is a homologous series? [2]
(ii) Name the third member of this series. [1]
(iii) Draw the structural formulae of *two* isomers which have the molecular formula C_4H_9OH. [2]
(iv) Ethanol is used in alcoholic drinks. State another use of ethanol. [1]

(b) The diagram below shows a method used in France to change wine into vinegar.

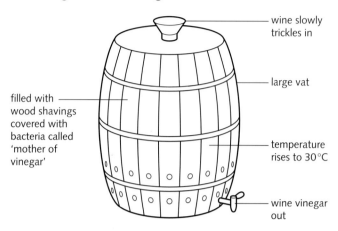

filled with wood shavings covered with bacteria called 'mother of vinegar'

wine slowly trickles in

large vat

temperature rises to 30°C

wine vinegar out

Living organisms bringing about a chemical change and producing a marketable product is an example of biotechnology.

(i) What type of reaction has occurred in the vat? [1]
(ii) Name a reagent, other than oxygen, that can change ethanol into ethanoic acid. [1]
(iii) Name a technique that could be used to separate ethanoic acid from the other liquids in vinegar. [1]
(iv) Describe a chemical test that would distinguish between wine and vinegar. [2]

(c) The flavour and smell of foods are partly due to esters. An ester can be made from ethanol and ethanoic acid.
(i) Name this ester. [1]
(ii) Write a word equation for the reaction between ethanol and ethanoic acid. [1]

(d) Olive oil and fats are esters.
(i) What type of compound is produced by the alkaline hydrolysis of olive oil? [1]
(ii) What other class of compound contains the ester linkage? [1]

(IGCSE, part question, 1992)

11.14 Soap is made by reacting sodium hydroxide with substances extracted from a natural source.

(a) Name a natural substance which may be used to make soap. [1]

(b) The diagram shows two types of detergent. Which one of these detergents is a soap? Give a reason for your choice. [2]

fat-loving tail   water-loving head   fat-loving tail   water-loving head

detergent **A**   detergent **B**

(c) Here is a simplified diagram of a detergent molecule.

fat-loving tail   water-loving head

Copy the diagram below and draw four of these molecules on it to show how they line up on the surface of the grease. [2]

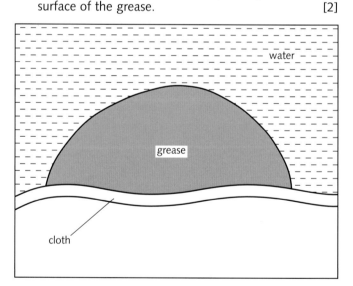

water

grease

cloth

(MEG, 1995)

12 Petrochemicals and polymers

Crude oil and other fossil fuels

This section covers the following ideas:

- fossil fuels
- the formation and fractional distillation of crude oil
- catalytic cracking
- alternative transport fuels
- coal
- biogas.

There are three major fossil fuels:

- coal,
- crude oil,
- natural gas.

Fossil fuels were formed in the Earth's crust from material that was once living. Coal comes from fossil plant material. Crude oil and natural gas are formed from the bodies of marine micro-organisms. The formation of these fuels took place over geological periods of time (many millions of years). These fuels are therefore a **non-renewable** and **finite resource**.

12.1 Crude oil

The formation of crude oil

Crude oil is one of the Earth's major natural resources. The oil is the result of a process that began up to 400 million years ago. Prehistoric marine creatures died and sank to the sea-bed and were covered and surrounded by mud. The change into crude oil and natural gas was brought about by high pressure, high temperature and bacteria acting over millions of years. The original organic material broke down into hydrocarbons. Compression of the mud above the hydrocarbon mixture transformed it into shale. Then geological movements and pressure changed this shale into harder rocks, squeezing out the oil and gas. The oil and gas moved upwards through the **porous** rocks, moving from high-pressure to low-pressure conditions. Sometimes they reached the surface, but often they became trapped by a layer of non-porous rock. Reservoirs of oil and gas were created. These occur where the rock layers form an anticline or at the junction of a fault (figure 12.1). These reservoirs are *not* lakes of oil or pockets of gas. Instead, the oil or gas is spread throughout the **pores** in coarse rocks such as sandstone or limestone, rather as water is held in a sponge.

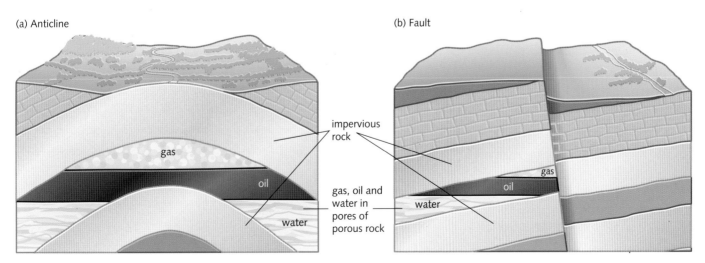

(a) Anticline

(b) Fault

impervious rock

gas

oil

water

gas, oil and water in pores of porous rock

water

gas

oil

Figure 12.1 Certain rock formations favour the accumulation of oil and natural gas.

Oil-fields and gas-fields are detected by a series of geological searches. Surveys from aeroplanes and satellites can provide detailed pictures of surface features. These give clues about the underlying rocks. Variations in gravity and magnetic field can also give clues. Finally, a **seismic** survey is carried out. These can be carried out both at sea and on land. Shock waves in the ground are produced by setting off small explosions. At sea, compressed air guns are used. Detailed information on the rock formations in an area can be found by tracking and timing the shock waves. Promising areas are then drilled. These drillings can simply be to gain more geological information. But if oil or gas is found, they can be used to see how extensive the oil-field or gas-field is. Once a field is established, then production oil-rigs can be set up.

Fractional distillation

Crude oil is a mixture of many different **hydrocarbon** molecules. Most of the crude oil that is extracted from the ground is used to make fuel, but around 10% is used as a **feedstock**, or raw material, in the chemical industry. Before it can be used, the various hydrocarbon molecules are separated by **refining**.

At a refinery, crude oil is separated into different **fractions** – groups of hydrocarbons that have different boiling points. These different boiling points are roughly related to the number of carbon atoms in the hydrocarbons (table 12.1).

Separation of the hydrocarbons takes place in a **fractional distillation column**, or fractionating tower. At the start of the refining process, crude oil is preheated to a temperature of 350–400 °C and pumped in at the base of the tower. As it boils, the vapour passes up the tower. It passes through a series of bubble caps and cools as it rises further up the column. The different fractions cool and condense at different temperatures, and therefore at different heights in the column. The fractions condensing at the different levels are collected on trays. Fractions from the top of the tower are called 'light' and those from the bottom 'heavy'. Each fraction contains a number of different hydrocarbons. The individual single hydrocarbons can then be obtained by further **distillation**. Figure 12.2 shows the separation into different fractions and some of their uses.

Catalytic cracking

The demand for the various fractions from the refinery does not necessarily match with their supply from the oil. For lighter fractions such as gasoline (petrol), the demand is greater than the supply. The opposite is true for heavier fractions such as kerosine (paraffin) and diesel. Larger molecules from these heavier fractions can be broken into smaller, more valuable, molecules. This process is called **catalytic cracking** ('cat cracking'). Cracking takes place in a huge reactor. In this reactor, particles of catalyst (made of powdered minerals such as silica, alumina and zeolites) are mixed with the hydrocarbon fraction

Table 12.1 Various crude oil* fractions

Fraction	Approximate number of carbon atoms in hydrocarbons		Approximate boiling range (°C)	
Refinery gas	1–4	(C_1-C_4)	below 25	
Petrol*	4–12	(C_4-C_{12})	40–100	
Naphtha	7–14	(C_7-C_{14})	90–150	b.p. and viscosity increasing
Paraffin*	9–16	(C_9-C_{16})	150–240	
Diesel oil	15–25	$(C_{15}-C_{25})$	220–250	
Lubricating oil	20–70	$(C_{20}-C_{70})$	255–350	
Bitumen residue	over 70	$(>C_{70})$	above 350	

* Different terms are used in the UK and the USA. Note that 'crude oil' (UK) is the same as 'petroleum' (USA); 'petrol' (UK) is the same as 'gasoline' (USA); and 'paraffin' (UK) is the same as 'kerosene' (USA).

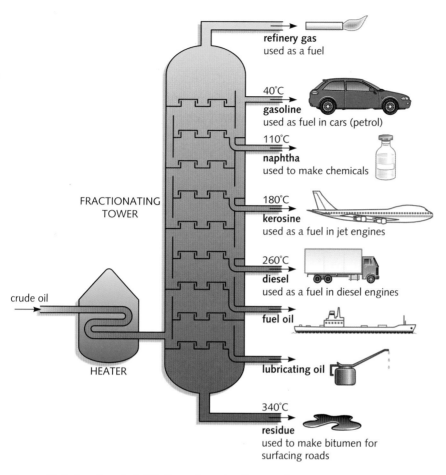

Figure 12.2 Fractional distillation of crude oil in a refinery.

This is just one possible reaction when decane is cracked. The molecules may not all break in the same place. The alkene fragment is not always ethene; propene and but-1-ene may also be produced.

All **cracking reactions** give two types of product:

- an *alkane* with a shorter chain than the original, and
- a short-chain *alkene* molecule.

Both these products are useful. The shortened alkanes can be blended with the gasoline fraction to enrich the petrol. The alkenes are useful as raw materials for making several important products. Figure 12.3 shows the various uses for the ethene produced. Propene polymerises to poly(propene) (trade-name 'polypropylene'), while butene polymerises to produce synthetic rubber.

The cracking reaction can be carried out in the laboratory using paraffin oil (figure 12.4 on page 330).

at a temperature around 500°C. The cracked vapours containing smaller molecules are separated by distillation.

The shortened hydrocarbon molecules are produced by the following type of reaction:

$$\text{decane} \xrightarrow[\text{catalyst}]{\text{heat}} \text{octane} + \text{ethene}$$

$$C_{10}H_{22} \rightarrow C_8H_{18} + C_2H_4$$

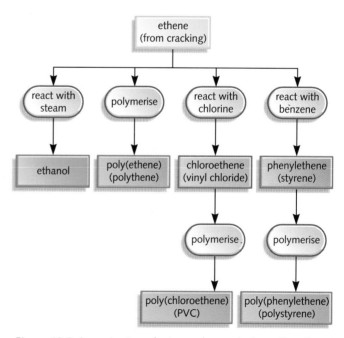

Figure 12.3 Important products can be made from the ethene produced by catalytic cracking.

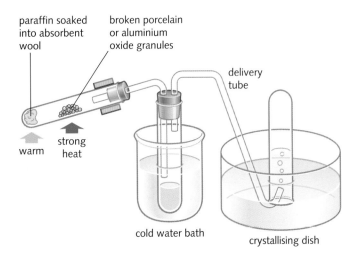

paraffin soaked into absorbent wool

broken porcelain or aluminium oxide granules

delivery tube

warm

strong heat

cold water bath

crystallising dish

Figure 12.4 The cracking of a long-chain alkane in the laboratory.

Blending gasoline

Some of the products from cracking are added to the gasoline fraction to improve the quality of the petrol. As many as 12 different components (containing over 300 different hydrocarbons and additives) may be used in a blend of petrol for the motorist. Different blends are made for winter and summer use. An important consideration is how easily the fuel vapour **ignites**. If the fuel ignites too easily, then the engine will not run smoothly – 'knocking' will occur. However, if the fuel is too difficult to ignite, then the engine will be difficult to start, especially on cold mornings. High-quality petrol contains many branched-chain hydrocarbons, made in a process known as **re-forming**, so that the fuel does not ignite too soon.

'Lead' (actually tetraethyl-lead) was added to gasoline to prevent 'knocking'. But this caused high levels of lead in the air, particularly in large cities. This led to concern over the link with brain damage in young children. Unleaded fuel is now widely available and *has* to be used in modern cars fitted with catalytic converters (the lead would poison the catalyst and so prevent it working).

The removal of sulphur from gasoline fractions is now very efficient. Car exhaust emissions contain very little sulphur dioxide. The carbon monoxide (CO), unburnt hydrocarbons (HC) and oxides of nitrogen (NO_x) in exhaust fumes do continue to

cause concern. The levels of emission of these compounds are reduced by fitting a catalytic converter to the exhaust.

Gasoline vapour also escapes into the air at petrol stations. Modern pumps now have hoods on the nozzles to cut down the escape of fumes. When handling liquid fuels generally, you need to consider the flash-point and ignition temperature of the fuel. These are not the same. The **flash-point** is the temperature at which the vapour will ignite in air in the presence of a flame. This temperature is usually low for a fuel (table 12.2). The **ignition temperature** is the temperature at which a fuel:air mixture ignites without a flame – for petrol it is 550 °C.

12.2 Alternative transport fuels

- *Gasoline from methanol*
  New Zealand has large reserves of natural gas (mainly methane) but very little crude oil. The problem of producing petrol has been transformed by a catalyst known as zeolite ZSM-5. (A zeolite is one of a large group of alumino-silicates of sodium, potassium, calcium and barium.) Methane is first converted into methanol. The methanol produced is then turned into hydrocarbons using the ZSM-5 catalyst:

$$\text{methanol} \xrightarrow{\text{ZSM-5}} \text{hydrocarbons} + \text{water}$$

$$n\text{CH}_3\text{OH} \rightarrow (\text{CH}_2)_n + n\text{H}_2\text{O}$$

ZSM-5 is an artificial zeolite composed of aluminium, silicon and oxygen. It was first made by two chemists working for the US Mobil Oil company.

- *Diesel*
  High-speed diesel engines in cars, buses and trucks use fuel (DERV – diesel engine road

Table 12.2 Flash-points of some common flammable liquids

Liquid	Flash-point (°C)
Methanol	+11
Ethanol	+13
Hexane	−21
Octane	+13

vehicle) containing hydrocarbon molecules consisting of between six and 20 carbon atoms (in short this is written as C_6–C_{20} molecules). Slower-speed diesel engines for ships, etc., use a slightly heavier fuel. Diesel engines are compression ignition engines (the fuel ignites spontaneously *without* a spark). Diesel engines are more efficient than petrol engines and produce much less carbon monoxide. However, because their working temperature is higher, they produce more oxides of nitrogen. The major problems are smoke and odour.

- *LPG and CNG*
  Liquid petroleum gas (LPG) is composed of propane and butane. Compressed natural gas (CNG) is 90% methane. These products already have a significant market in some countries. For example, all the taxis in Japan use LPG. Their use requires pressurised tanks for on-board storage.

- *Rapeseed oil*
  The potential for adding plant oils to diesel fuel is being investigated world-wide. Such fuel is widely used in China. The future use of these fuels will depend on economic factors. Some countries grow oil-producing crops but do not have their own reserves of crude oil.

- *Others*
  We discussed the use of ethanol- and hydrogen-powered cars on pages 316 and 207. Electric and solar-powered cars are also being investigated as alternatives to gasoline.

12.3 Coal and biogas

Coal

Coal is our most abundant fossil fuel. Many of the organic chemicals we now make from oil can also be made from coal. It may well be that coal will again become an important source of chemical raw materials.

Coal is not a single substance. It is a complex mixture of compounds that occur naturally in varying grades. It has the approximate composition formula $C_{135}H_{96}O_9NS$. There are several different types of coal depending on the geological processing of the deposit (table 12.3 on page 332). Peat is the first step in the coal-forming

These **chemicals** can be obtained from **coal**:

- **ammonia** (often turned into ammonium sulphate) – for fertilisers,
- **coal gas** (mainly hydrogen and carbon monoxide) – for industrial heating,
- **coal tar** (separated into various fractions like crude oil) – for paints, dyes, creosote and pitch,
- **coke** – for iron- and steel-making and for home and industrial heating.

process, but it is not itself a coal. With heat and pressure over a long timescale, it first forms 'lignite' (or 'brown coal'), and then the harder types of coal. Anthracite is the hardest coal, with the highest carbon content. Figure 12.5 shows how the balance of energy consumption changed world-wide between 1937 and 1994. The future use of coal will need to be cleaner. It must be visibly cleaner (less dust and soot), and must also produce lower amounts of acidic gases (SO_2 and NO_x).

Biogas

Methane gas is formed naturally under a number of different circumstances. **Anaerobic bacteria**

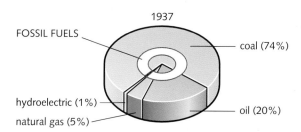

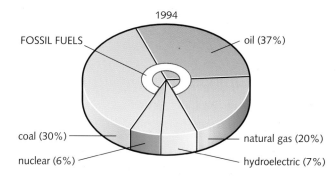

Figure 12.5 The shift in the balance of coal and oil consumption in the modern world.

Table 12.3 The different types of coal

Type		Description		Heat content	Sulphur content
Peat (not a coal) heat ↓ pressure		partially decayed plant matter in bogs and swamps		low	–
Lignite (brown coal) heat ↓ pressure	increasing moisture	limited supplies in most areas	increasing heat and	low	low
Bituminous coal (soft coal) heat ↓ pressure	content	heavily used because of high heat content and wide availability	carbon content	high	high
Anthracite (hard coal)		very desirable because of high heat content and low sulphur content, but limited supplies in most areas		high	low

helped decompose organic matter under geological conditions to produce natural gas. Methane accumulates in coal-mines, where it can cause explosions. Marsh gas, which bubbles up through the stagnant water of marshes, swamps and rice paddy-fields, is also methane. Methane produced in this way contributes to the 'greenhouse effect'.

Methane is produced from organic waste (**biomass**) when it decays in the absence of air. This can be exploited as a source of energy. In developing countries such as India and China, biomass digesters are important sources of fuel for villages. The methane is useful for heating and cooking, and the solid residue is used as a fertiliser.

Industrialised countries produce large amounts of waste, which is deposited in landfill sites. Biogas forms as the rubbish decays. This gas can be used as a fuel for local industry. On Merseyside in the UK, biogas is used to heat the ovens in a Cadbury's biscuit factory.

Summary of core material

You should know that:

- there are three major fossil fuels – coal, crude oil and natural gas
- these fuels were created by the action of heat and pressure on buried organic material acting over geological periods of time
- these resources are a source of energy and also of a wide variety of chemicals

- the fractional distillation of crude oil produces a series of different hydrocarbon fractions, each with its own uses
- these hydrocarbons can be further changed by processes such as catalytic cracking – producing shorter-chain alkane molecules and alkenes from the original longer chains.

12.1 Petroleum (crude oil) is a mixture of several compounds which are separated in a refinery by means of an apparatus as shown below.

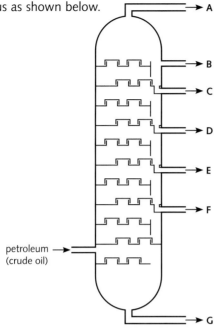

(a) What is the name of the apparatus? [1]

(b) What is the name of the process which is used in separating crude oil? [1]

(c) On what physical property of the compounds in the mixture does the separation depend? [1]

(d) Use the letters **A** to **G** to describe where the following could be found. [3]
  (i) The fraction that represents gases.
  (ii) The fraction with the largest molecules.
  (iii) The fraction that represents liquids with the lowest boiling point.

(WJEC, 1993)

12.2

(a) The apparatus below can be used to distil crude oil in the laboratory.

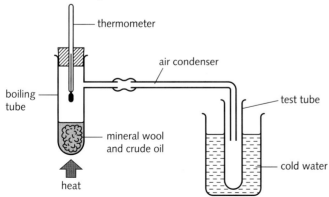

  (i) Explain how the air condenser works. [1]
  (ii) Name *three* fractions that will be obtained and the order in which they will be collected. Fraction 1 is collected first. [4]

(iii) Each of the fractions collected is a mixture of hydrocarbons. Explain what a 'hydrocarbon' is. [2]
(iv) Name the residue left at the end of the experiment. [1]

(b) Petroleum is a source of fuels. Name *two* fuels which are not obtained from petroleum. [2]

(c) Some of the hydrocarbons obtained in the distillation of petroleum are of limited use. To make them more useful, they are 'cracked' to make smaller alkanes and alkenes.
  (i) Determine x and y in the following balanced equation which describes a reaction that occurs during cracking: [2]
    $C_{20}H_{42} \rightarrow C_xH_y + 2C_2H_4$
  (ii) What is the difference in the molecular structures of an alkane and an alkene? [2]
  (iii) Describe, using as simple chemical test, how you would show the difference between an alkane and an alkene in the laboratory. [2]

(IGCSE, part question, 1993)

12.3 Deposits of crude oil are found trapped in some rock structures. Crude oil is a mixture of many different hydrocarbons.

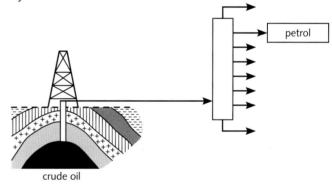

(a) Describe how petrol is obtained from crude oil. [2]

(b) Petrol (octane) can be made into ethene:

$C_8H_{18} \rightarrow 4C_2H_4 + H_2$
octane   ethene   hydrogen

  (i) State what happens to the octane in this reaction. [2]
  (ii) Give *two* conditions needed for this reaction. [2]

(c) Petrol is the main fuel used for cars. Every day large amounts of petrol and other fossil fuels are burned. This produces large amounts of carbon dioxide. Explain how the amount of oxygen and carbon dioxide in the atmosphere remain almost constant. You will be awarded up to *three* marks if you write your ideas clearly. [6]

(d) (i) Give a balanced symbolic equation for the complete combustion of petrol (octane) (C_8H_{18}). [1]
  (ii) What is the mass of one mole of octane (C_8H_{18})? [2]

(iii) The combustion of one mole of octane produces 5500 kJ. The density of octane is 0.7 g/cm³. Calculate the energy produced by one litre (1000 cm³) of octane. Show clearly how you obtain your answer. [4]

(SEG, part question, 1994)

12.4 Many villages in China use waste from plants and animals to produce methane gas for cooking. This happens inside a special digester.

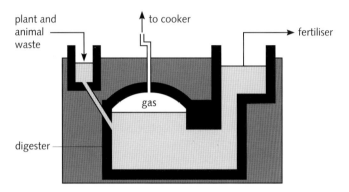

plant and animal waste — to cooker — fertiliser — gas — digester

- <u>Methane</u> bacteria produce methane gas from <u>organic acids</u>.
- Animal and plant wastes contain insoluble cellulose, <u>protein</u> and <u>fat</u>. Micro-organisms convert them into soluble <u>compounds</u>.
- <u>Acid</u> bacteria change these soluble compounds into organic acids.
- The liquid which comes out from the digester is a very good <u>fertiliser</u>.
- The digester also produces a gas called <u>carbon dioxide</u>.

Copy the diagram below. Choose underlined words from the sentences above to complete your diagram. [8]

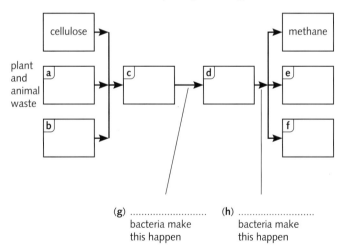

cellulose — methane

plant and animal waste

a **c** **d** **e**

b **f**

(g) .... bacteria make this happen

(h) .... bacteria make this happen

(NEAB, 1992)

12.5 Coal is an important fuel. It may also be used to produce a wide range of chemicals.

(a) Name *three* other fuels which contain carbon. [3]

(b) When heated in the apparatus shown below coal breaks down into a solid, a liquid and a gas.

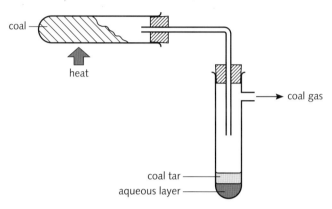

coal — heat — coal gas — coal tar — aqueous layer

(i) Why does the coal in the test tube not burn when heated? [1]
(ii) The solid left behind is coke. Explain how coke is used in the manufacture of iron. [3]
(iii) Coal gas is very dangerous because it contains carbon monoxide. Explain why carbon monoxide is dangerous. [1]

(c) The liquid collected is a mixture of an aqueous layer and coal tar. The tar is a source of hydrocarbons such as naphthalene.

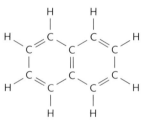

naphthalene, $C_{10}H_8$

(i) Define a *hydrocarbon*. [2]
(ii) Name the products if naphthalene is completely burnt. [2]
(iii) What is the relative molecular mass of naphthalene? [2]

(d) The aqueous layer contains ammonia. If it is treated with sulphuric acid, ammonium sulphate is formed.
(i) How could you demonstrate that the aqueous layer contains ammonia? [3]
(ii) What element in ammonium sulphate is responsible for its use as a fertiliser? [1]

(e) Sulphur dioxide is a common pollutant from burning coal. State *two* effects caused by this pollution. [2]

(IGCSE, 1996)

Polymerisation

This section covers the following ideas:

• addition polymerisation
• condensation polymerisation
• thermoplastic and thermosetting polymers
• the disposal and recycling of plastic waste.

All living things contain **polymers**. Proteins, carbohydrates, wood and natural rubber are all polymers. What nature first invented, chemists have learnt to copy, alter and use successfully. Synthetic polymers, often called **plastics**, are to be found everywhere in modern technological societies, made into bulky objects, films and fibres. They have properties to suit particular needs, ranging from car and aircraft components, to packaging and clothing.

Polymers are large organic **macromolecules**. They are made up of small repeating units known as **monomers**. These units are repeated any number of times from about a hundred to more than a million. Some are **homopolymers**, containing just one monomer. Poly(ethene), poly(propene) and poly(chloroethene) are three examples of homopolymers. Other macromolecules are **copolymers** made of two or more different types of monomer. For example, nylon is made from two monomers, and biological proteins are made from 20 different monomers, the amino acids.

The alkene fragments from the catalytic cracking of crude oil fractions produced the starting monomers for the first plastics.

12.4 Addition polymerisation

Alkenes such as ethene contain a C=C double bond. These molecules can take part in **addition reactions** (see page 309) where the double bond is broken and other atoms attach to the carbons. The double bond in ethene enables many molecules of ethene to join to each other to form a large molecule, poly(ethene) (figure 12.6). This is an **addition polymer**. When first made by ICI, it was a revolutionary new material called 'Alkathene'. It is now commonly called by the trade-name 'polythene'.

Various conditions can be used to produce different types of poly(ethene). Generally a high pressure, a temperature at or above room temperature and a catalyst are needed. The reaction can be summarised by the equation:

$$ethene \xrightarrow[\text{heat, catalyst}]{\text{high pressure}} poly(ethene)$$

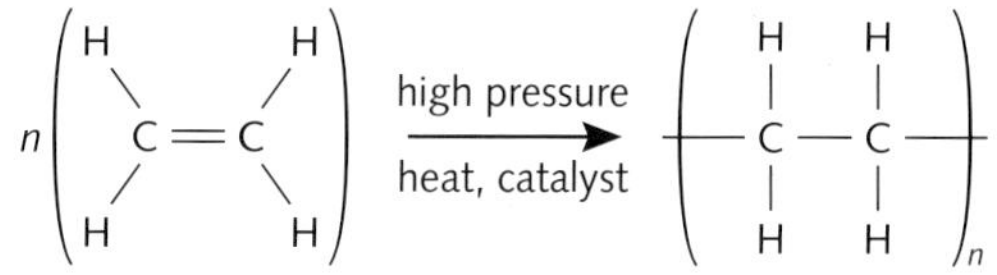

where n is a very large number.

Poly(ethene) was found to be a chemically resistant material that was very tough and durable, and a very good electrical insulator.

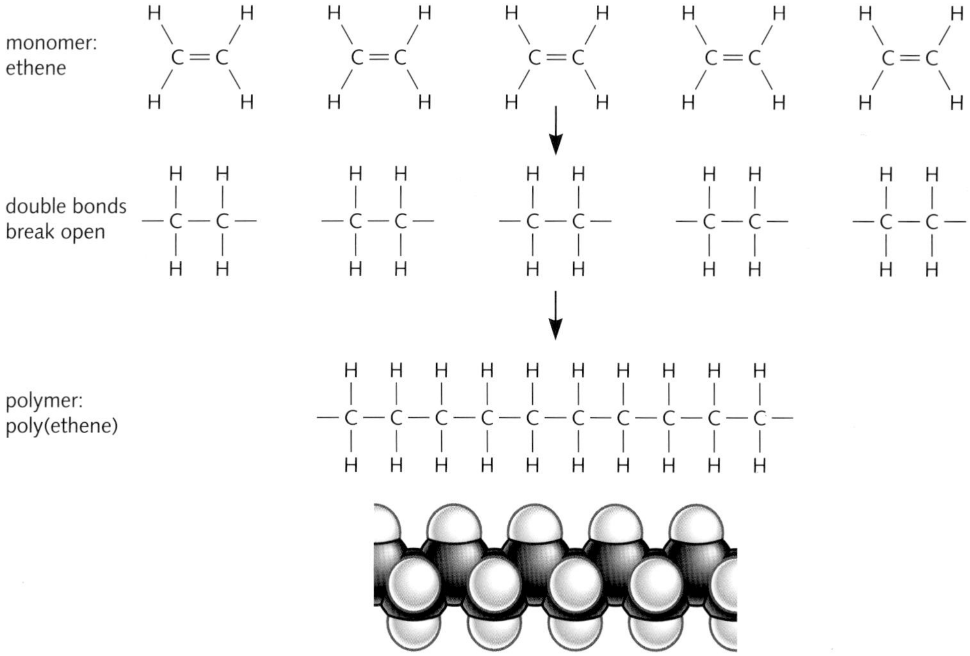

Figure 12.6 *The polymerisation of ethene produces poly(ethene), whose structure is shown.*

Other alkene molecules can also produce addition polymers. Propene will polymerise to produce poly(propene):

propene → poly(propene)

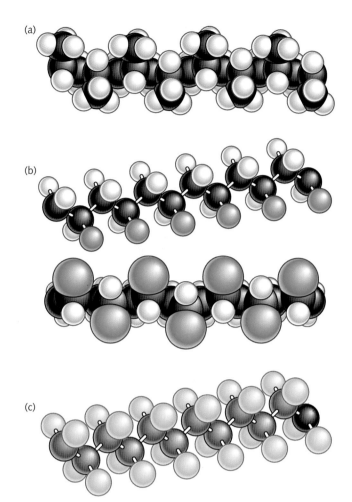

(a)

(b)

(c)

This long-chain molecule is similar in structure to poly(ethene) but with a methyl (—CH$_3$) group attached to every other carbon atom in the chain (figure 12.7a). It is commonly referred to by its trade-name 'polypropylene'.

Chemists also experimented with other substituted alkenes to produce plastics with particular properties in mind. Poly(chloroethene) (known by the trade-name of polyvinyl chloride or PVC) and poly(tetrafluoroethene) (known by the trade-name of polytetrafluoroethylene, 'teflon' or PTFE) are two such polymers:

chloroethene → poly(chloroethene)
(vinyl chloride)   (PVC)

tetrafluoroethene → poly(tetrafluoroethene)
(PTFE)

Their structures are shown in figures 12.7b and c.

Poly(chloroethene) (PVC) was found to be stronger and harder than poly(ethene) and therefore good for making pipes for plumbing. PTFE proved to have some unusual properties. It was very stable at high temperatures and formed a very slippery surface. The properties of some addition polymers

Figure 12.7 The structures of: (a) poly(propene), PP; (b) poly(chloroethene), PVC; and (c) poly(tetrafluoroethene), PTFE.

are given in table 12.4. Such synthetic polymers have proved to be very versatile. Many, for example poly(propene), are easy to shape by melting and moulding. Thus poly(propene) is used to make sturdy plastic objects such as crates. However, it can also be drawn out into long fibres for making ropes.

Some of the properties of **addition polymers**.

- All polymers are long-chain molecules made by joining together a large number of monomer molecules.
- Addition polymerisation involves monomer molecules that contain a C=C double bond.
- Addition polymers are homopolymers, made from a single monomer.
- During addition, the double bonds open up and the molecules join to themselves to make a molecule with a very long chain.

Table 12.4 Examples of some widely used addition polymers

Polymer (and trade-name(s))	Monomer	Properties	Examples of use
Poly(ethene) (polyethylene, polythene, PE)	ethene $CH_2 = CH_2$	tough, durable	plastic bags, bowls, bottles, packaging
Poly(propene) (polypropylene, PP)	propene $CH_3CH = CH_2$	tough, durable	crates and boxes, plastic rope
Poly(chloroethene) (polyvinyl chloride, PVC)	chloroethene $CH_2 = CHCl$	strong, hard (not as flexible as polythene)	insulation, pipes and guttering
Poly(tetrafluoroethene) (polytetrafluoroethylene, teflon, PTFE)	tetrafluoroethene $CF_2 = CF_2$	non-stick surface, withstands high temperatures	non-stick frying pans, non-stick taps and joints
Poly(phenylethene) (polystyrene, PS)	phenylethene (styrene) $C_6H_5CH = CH_2$	light, poor conductor of heat	insulation, packaging (foam)

Summary of core material

You should know that:

- alkene molecules (containing a $C = C$ double bond) can be polymerised into very useful products

- other unsaturated molecules can be polymerised to extend the range of useful addition polymers.

EXTENSION

Condensation polymers and plastics

12.5 Condensation polymerisation

Nylon

In the early 1930s, Dupont were interested in research into artificial fibres. Knowledge of silk and wool gave clues as to how protein molecules are built. Carothers imitated the linkage in proteins and produced the first **synthetic** fibre, 'nylon'.

Nylon is a solid when first formed, but it can then be melted and forced through small holes. The long filaments cool, and the fibres produced are stretched to align the polymer molecules and dried. The fibres can be woven into fabric to make shirts, ties, sheets, etc., or turned into ropes or racquet strings. However, nylon is not just made into fibres. It has proved to be a very versatile material, and can be moulded into strong plastic items such as gear-wheels.

Nylon is a copolymer of two different monomers, a diamine and a dicarboxylic acid. Each monomer consists of a chain of carbon atoms (which are shown in the following diagrams simplified as boxes). At both ends of the monomers are **functional groups**. An amine group ($-NH_2$) on the first monomer reacts with a carboxylic acid group ($-COOH$) on the second monomer to make a link between the two molecules. Each time a link is made, a water molecule is lost:

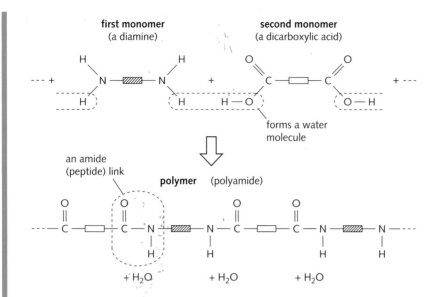

first monomer
(a diamine)

second monomer
(a dicarboxylic acid)

forms a water molecule

an amide (peptide) link

polymer (polyamide)

$+ H_2O$ $+ H_2O$ $+ H_2O$

rod is rotated

nylon fibre is pulled out

first monomer, dissolved in water

polymerisation occurs at the interface between the two liquids

second monomer, dissolved in an organic solvent

Figure 12.8 Nylon is a polyamide and can be made in the laboratory.

As a result, this type of polymer is known as a **condensation polymer**. Because an **amide link** (or peptide link) is formed during polymerisation, nylon is known as a **polyamide**. A version of nylon polymerisation can be carried out in the laboratory (figure 12.8).

Polyesters

Condensation polymerisation can also be used to make other polymers with properties different from those of nylon. **Polyesters** are condensation copolymers made from two monomers. One monomer has an alcohol group (—OH) at each end. The other monomer has a carboxylic acid group (—COOH) at each end. When the monomers react, an **ester link** is formed, with water being lost each time:

first monomer
has alcohol functional groups

second monomer
has carboxylic acid functional groups

forms a water molecule

an ester link

polymer (polyester)

$+ H_2O$ $+ H_2O$ $+ H_2O$

One such polyester has the trade-name 'terylene'. Like nylon, terylene can be turned into fibres and woven into clothing. Terylene clothing is generally softer than that made from nylon.

Thermoplastic and thermosetting polymers

Most of the plastics that we use, like poly(ethene) ['polythene'], poly(chloroethene) ['PVC'] and poly(phenylethene) ['polystyrene'], can be softened on heating and melted. They set again when cooled. Such plastics are useful because they can be re-moulded. These polymers are known as **thermoplastic polymers** (or thermoplastics or thermosoftening polymers).

Another, more restricted, group of polymers can be heated and moulded only *once*, for example melamine. Such polymers are known as **thermosetting polymers** (or thermosets). The chains in these polymers are cross-linked to each other (figure 12.9). These cross-links in the plastic are permanent chemical bonds. They make the structures rigid when moulded, and no softening takes place on heating.

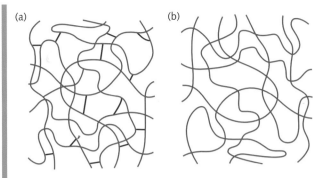

(a) (b)

Figure 12.9 (a) Thermosetting and (b) thermoplastic polymers have different properties.

12.6 The re-use, recycling and disposal of plastic waste

Plastic rubbish is a common but unwelcome sight around the world. Over the past 30 years, plastics have taken over as replacement materials in many applications. This is not surprising because they are light, cheap and corrosion-resistant, and they can be easily moulded and dyed bright colours. The problem arises from the fact that most plastics are not **biodegradable** – there are no natural micro-organisms that can break them down.

Some modern plastics are suitable for re-use. Soft-drinks bottles can be made from a plastic with the trade-name 'polyethylene terephthalate' (PET). These are sturdy and have several advantages for this particular use. In some countries, schemes for the re-use of these bottles are operated. However, such a re-use policy is not suitable for most plastics.

Figure 12.10 Different identification symbols help with the sorting of plastics for recycling. The symbols stand for the following trade-names: 1 = polyethylene terephthalate; 2 = high-density polyethylene; 3 = vinyl polymers such as PVC; 4 = low-density polyethylene; 5 = polypropylene; 6 = polystyrene; 7 = others such as multi-layer plastics.

So what *do* we do with our waste plastic? We must either recycle it or dispose of it. It is more economical and satisfactory to recycle than to use the alternative of depositing plastic waste in landfill sites. But there are problems with recycling because most plastic waste is a mixture of different types. Identification numbers and symbols (figure 12.10) have been introduced in the USA and are beginning to be used in Europe. Methods of sorting plastic waste by optical scanners or manually are being introduced. Once sorted, alternative treatments are available for recycling the different types of plastic waste.

Methods for **recycling plastic waste**:

- **thermoplastic** polymers – (i) heat at low temperatures; (ii) obtain molten or softened polymer; (iii) re-mould into new thermoplastic product(s),
- **thermosetting** polymers – (i) heat at high temperatures (700 °C) in the absence of air; (ii) obtain new monomers and other chemicals; (iii) re-polymerise into new product(s).

Incineration (**pyrolysis**) can be used to burn plastic waste, though care must be taken not to release toxic fumes into the air. Most of the products from pyrolysis can be used as fuels or separated by fractional distillation (figure 12.11). They can then be made into monomers

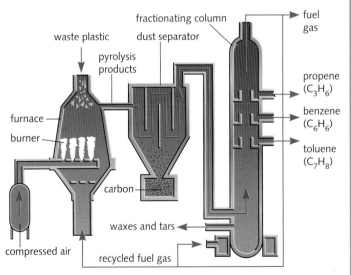

Figure 12.11 Pyrolysis of plastic waste can yield useful fuels and other products.

339

for making more plastics. Research is also being carried out to produce plastics that are **biodegradable** or **photodegradable**. One poly(ethenol) plastic has been developed that is soluble in hot water.

Biological polymers

This section covers the following ideas:

- biological condensation polymers
  - proteins
  - nucleic acids
  - carbohydrates
- enzymes and their use in industry
- food and food additives.

In 1953 the structure of **DNA** (deoxyribonucleic acid) was reported by Watson and Crick. Their work followed on from the X-ray diffraction results of Franklin and Wilkins. Their results opened up the new subject areas of molecular biology and genetics. The report on the DNA **double helix** (figure 12.12) was a great leap forward in scientific understanding. It showed how a biopolymer could store information and how that information could be faithfully copied from one generation to another. The Human Genome Project has as its target the complete mapping of human genes.

Nucleic acids (such as DNA) are condensation polymers, as are other biological polymers such as proteins and carbohydrates. Such biological

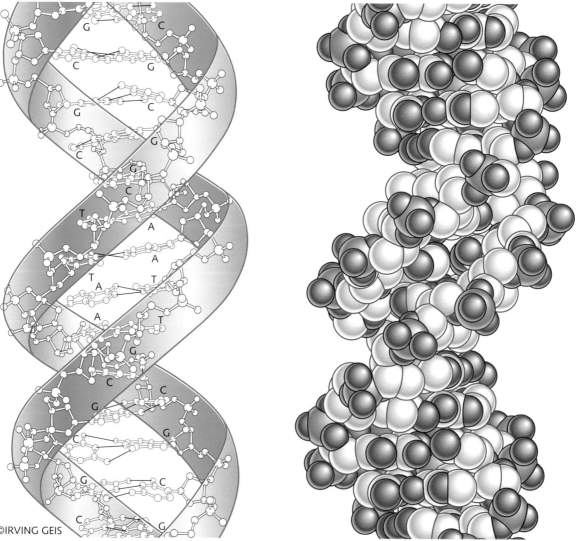

©IRVING GEIS

Figure 12.12 A computer graphic and a ball-and-stick drawing of the DNA double helix, showing the two interwoven strands of the giant polymer.

condensation polymers are very important in the human body:

- bones are made of minerals embedded in a protein (see below) called collagen,
- the tendons connecting muscles to bones are also made of collagen,
- the fibres in muscles are made of two other proteins,
- the surface layer of the skin is made of a protein called keratin; hair is made of keratin in the form of a fibre,
- haemoglobin in the blood and enzymes (see page 342) in cells are long-chain protein molecules,
- the molecules of DNA that carry genetic information are long-chain nucleic acids,
- energy is stored in the liver as a long-chain carbohydrate (see page 343) called glycogen.

Whenever monomers are linked together during the making of these polymers, water molecules are lost. Most of these polymers are copolymers, involving more than one monomer.

12.7 Proteins

Proteins are complex compounds that contain carbon, nitrogen, oxygen and, in some cases, sulphur. They fulfil a number of vital functions in the body.

- Proteins are the **structural molecules** from which tissues are constructed. When growth or repair of tissue occurs, new fibrous proteins are needed. Fibrous proteins have linear molecules and are insoluble in water. Collagen (in tendons, cartilage and bone), keratin (in nails and hair) and elastin (in arteries) are all long fibrous proteins.
- **Enzymes** are globular proteins that catalyse the reactions in living cells. Transport proteins such as haemoglobin are also essential to life.
- **Hormones** control body function, and **antibodies** are a defence mechanism against infection.
- Protein breakdown can be used as a source of **energy** in respiration.

Proteins are built from **amino acid** monomers. There are 20 different amino acids used, and they each contain two functional groups —NH_2 and —COOH. Glycine and alanine are two of the simplest amino acids. When they react together, an amide linkage (or **peptide linkage**) is formed to produce a **dipeptide** (two amino acids joined together):

forms a water molecule

a **dipeptide**

When this is repeated many times using the different amino acids, a polymer is formed. Short polymers (up to 15 amino acids) are known as **peptides**. Chains with between 15 and 100 amino acids are known as **polypeptides**. Chains involving more than 100 amino acids are called **proteins**. Some proteins, however, consist of more than one chain.

Insulin is a small protein made of two quite short polypeptide chains. It controls blood sugar levels. In 1953, Sanger reported the complete sequence of amino acids in the protein (figure 12.13 on page 342). This was the first protein sequence to be worked out, and Sanger was awarded the Nobel Prize. Protein sequencing is now done automatically using computers.

Protein analysis

Proteins can be **hydrolysed** (broken down) to amino acids by heating in concentrated hydrochloric acid. This is the reverse of the condensation process that formed them:

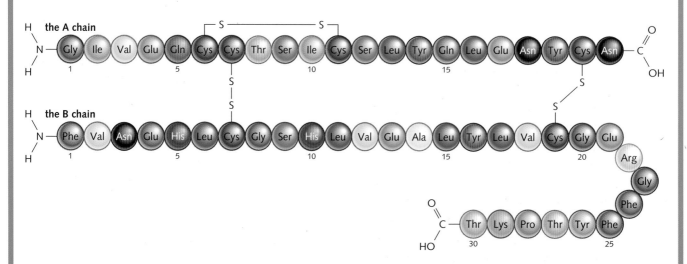

12.8 Enzymes

Enzymes are protein molecules that catalyse reactions in biological systems. They are very specific **catalysts** for a certain reaction, or for a particular type of reaction. Enzymes are unchanged at the end of a reaction and able to repeat the reaction many times over. Like all proteins, enzymes are three-dimensional structures. High temperatures or extreme pH destroy the structure and the enzyme's activity. We say that enzymes are **denatured** by heat and are sensitive to pH (figure 12.14).

The three-dimensional shape of an enzyme is crucial to it being a catalyst for a particular reaction. The arrangement of the protein folding means that only certain molecules can fit into the **active site**. This is the location on the enzyme where the chemical reaction takes place. The enzyme and the reacting molecule 'fit' together like a lock and key, and then the reaction can take place (figure 12.15). In medical disorders where an enzyme may be overactive, a drug 'key' may be found that fits the enzyme 'lock', but does not cause a reaction. In this way, the drug blocks the activity of the enzyme (see figure 13.11 on page 359).

Enzymes in industry

Enzymes can be extracted from organisms and used in a wide variety of ways. Proteases and lipases are now used in washing powders to digest

The mixture of amino acids can then be separated by **chromatography** (see page 37). Amino acids are colourless substances, but they can be seen if the paper is viewed under ultra-violet light. Otherwise a **locating agent** is used, which reacts with the amino acids to produce coloured spots.

The simple test for proteins, in food samples for instance, is the **biuret test**. Dilute sodium hydroxide is added to the sample and then a 1% copper(II) sulphate solution. The mixture is shaken and left to stand. A purple colour appears after about 3 minutes if a protein is present.

Figure 12.13 Finding the sequence of amino acids in human insulin won Sanger his first Nobel Prize. The different three-letter codes and colours represent different amino acids.

(a)

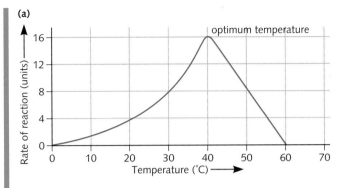

(b)

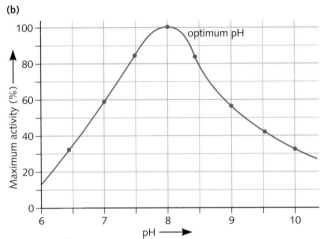

Figure 12.14 Enzymes are sensitive to changes in temperature and pH. Many work best at a temperature of 40 °C and a pH of 8.

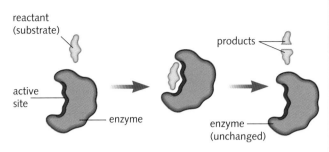

Figure 12.15 An enzyme and its substrate 'fit' together like a 'lock' and 'key'. The substrate is the molecule that binds to the enzyme. It is changed by the reaction that the enzyme is catalysing.

protein and fatty stains. Other uses of proteases include tenderising meat and skinning fish. Enzymes that break down carbohydrates are used in the food industry. Pectinase is used to clear the juices obtained from crushed fruit. Invertase is used in making the soft centres of chocolates. These are all examples of the use of biological materials in industry, that is biotechnology.

Whole organisms such as bacteria and yeast are used in biotechnology because they contain enzymes able to bring about specific reactions. The **fermentation** reaction of yeast is important not just in brewing and wine-making. The carbon dioxide released by the fermentation reaction is used to make bread rise when a mixture of dough and yeast is warmed. Bacteria are used in yoghurt and cheese-making. One new and unusual use of bacteria is in mining. *Thiobacillus ferrooxidans* is a sturdy micro-organism that has developed in a strange environment. It lives in the presence of acid and sulphur. Cultures of this bacteria are being used to extract copper and

other metals from mine waste and crushed ores that are poor in metal content. This approach is important environmentally. It helps to clean up the mine waste by removing heavy-metal ions, which cause damage to plants, animals and humans even in small **trace amounts**.

12.9 Carbohydrates

The sugar we use to sweeten our tea or coffee is sucrose ($C_{12}H_{22}O_{11}$). This is just one example of a **carbohydrate**; glucose ($C_6H_{12}O_6$) is another.

- **Carbohydrates** are an important source of energy in our bodies, and in all living organisms.
- A carbohydrate is a compound containing carbon, hydrogen and oxygen only. The ratio of hydrogen to oxygen is always 2:1.

All **polysaccharides** are long-chain condensation polymers of sugar molecules (**monosaccharides**). Condensation polymerisation of sugar monomers produces carbohydrates such as starch:

many **sugar monomers**
(e.g. glucose molecules)

H–O–🔲–O–H H–O–🔲–O–H H–O–🔲–O–H

⬇ elimination of water
between molecules

a **polysaccharide** (e.g. starch)

----O–🔲–O–🔲–O–🔲----

Starch and glycogen are two different polysaccharides of glucose, a monosaccharide. They store the glucose in an insoluble form in plants and animals, respectively. When energy is needed, cells break down the starch or glycogen back to glucose. The glucose is then oxidised by **respiration**. Cellulose is different polymer of glucose. It forms the fibrous structure of plant cell walls. These three polymers differ in the way in which the glucose monomer units are linked together.

Polysaccharides can be broken down in the laboratory by warming with hydrochloric acid (**acid hydrolysis**). The sugars present in the hydrolysis mixture can then be analysed by chromatography (see page 37). A locating agent must be used to detect the spots, because sugars are colourless. An interesting comparison is to analyse the products of the acid and enzyme digestions of starch. Acid hydrolysis breaks down starch to give glucose. However, the amylase present in human saliva only breaks starch down to give maltose. This is a molecule made of two glucose units joined together. The difference can be seen on chromatography of the products.

The presence of starch can be detected by testing with iodine solution; the solution turns a deep blue colour.

12.10 Food

Proteins, fats and carbohydrates are the main constituents of food. They are all digested by cells and organisms, and are converted back to their monomers. These monomers are then used as the building blocks for new molecular structures or as sources of energy. Our bodies can make a whole range of molecules necessary for our cells to function properly. However, some of these building blocks must come from our diet. For instance, there are some amino acids that we must obtain from our food. These are known as the **essential amino acids**.

Fats and oils are mixtures of large molecules that are the esters of long-chain acid molecules and glycerol. Fats that contain unsaturated acids are called unsaturated or **poly-unsaturated fats**, depending on the number of C=C double bonds in the chain. Fats that contain saturated chains are known as **saturated fats**. There is evidence that eating a lot of animal fat, which is higher in saturated fats, may increase the risk of heart disease.

Fats and oils (**lipids**) are an essential part of our diet:

- they are an energy source; lipids provide about twice as much energy per gram as do carbohydrates,
- they provide thermal insulation for the body,
- some vitamins, for example A, D and E, are insoluble in water but soluble in lipids; foods containing lipids provide these vitamins,
- lipids are an essential part of cell membranes.

Food additives

Food contains enzymes that can reduce its quality. Bacterial and fungal contamination may also occur. Various practical methods are used to protect food from decay. Salting and pickling are methods that have been used for a considerable time. More modern techniques include freeze-drying and refrigeration. Some food additives are used specifically to preserve food from chemical processes such as oxidation (**anti-oxidants**).

When apple slices are left open to the atmosphere, they go brown. This is the result of a reaction catalysed by an enzyme in the fruit. Soaking the slices in a dilute solution of vitamin C (ascorbic acid) prevents the browning. Vitamin C is a **reducing agent** (anti-oxidant). The number of additives in food has increased considerably over the years; they now exceed 3000 different substances.

In Europe, all additives must be declared on the packaging. They are listed with an E number. The substances are classified according to their use: colourings have E numbers in the range E100 – 180; preservatives are E200 – 290; anti-oxidants have E numbers between E310 and E321; and emulsifiers and stabilisers have some of the numbers in the range E322 – 494. The list includes around 350 substances that have been approved as safe. Individuals, though, must be careful for themselves as to what is safe for them. Some people, for instance, have allergic reactions to substances that do not affect others.

The purpose of various **food additives**:

- **alter taste** – flavourings, sweeteners and flavour enhancers (for example, monosodium glutamate, MSG),
- **alter colour** – colourings (for example, caramel),
- **alter storage life** – anti-oxidants (for example, butylated hydroxyanisole, BHA) and antibacterial agents (for example, sodium sulphite),
- **alter texture** – emulsifiers, stabilisers, thickeners (for example, starch), anti-caking agents, humectants and gelling agents (for example, pectin).

Summary of extension material

You should know that:

- there are natural and synthetic polymers that are made by a process other than addition polymerisation
- these polymers are produced by condensation polymerisation, and include nylons and polyesters
- different types of synthetic plastics and fibres can be made – some of these are thermosetting, but most are thermoplastic and can be re-moulded
- plastic materials are usually non-biodegradable and pose problems for waste disposal

- very important biological polymers are also produced by condensation polymerisation, for example DNA, proteins and carbohydrates
- a variety of different protein molecules occur naturally, but one important group is the enzymes – the biological catalysts that control metabolism
- proteins, carbohydrates and fats are the main types of food substances; vitamins, though needed only in small quantities, are important for good health.

12.6

(a) Ethene is an important industrial chemical produced from petroleum (crude oil) fractions by 'cracking'.
  (i) Give the structural formula of ethene. [1]
  (ii) Explain what is meant by 'cracking', and show how ethene can be formed from another hydrocarbon by this method. [2]

(b) Ethene is used in making poly(ethene) (polythene) by a process of addition polymerisation. Poly(ethene) is a thermoplastic material.
  (i) State what is meant by *addition polymerisation* and give an equation for the formation of poly(ethene) from ethene. [2]
  (ii) Describe the difference in properties between thermoplastics and thermosets and give a named example of a thermoset. [2]
  (iii) Explain, by means of a diagram, how the differences in properties between thermoplastics and thermosets are related to their structures. [3]

(WJEC, part question, 1990)

12.7 Hair is made up of long molecules of protein. The diagram shows part of a protein molecule.

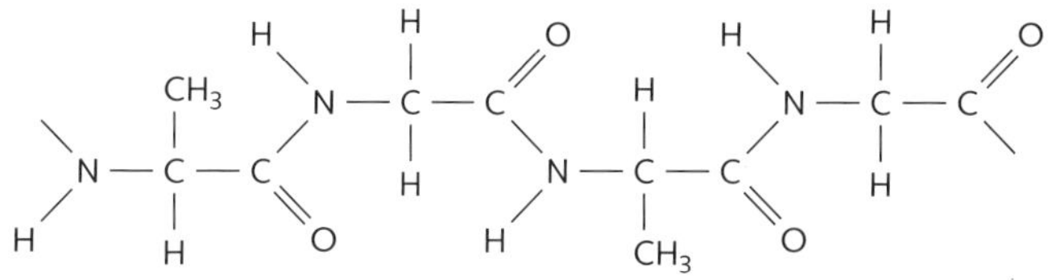

(a) Name the element in this protein which is not found in a carbohydrate. [1]

(b) The protein chain is made by joining together many smaller molecules such as **A** and **B**.

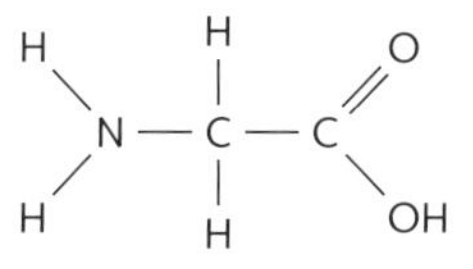

A 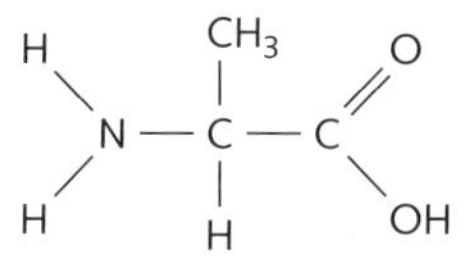   B

(i) What name is given to the type of small molecules, like **A** and **B**, that join to make protein chains? [1]

(ii) When these molecules join to make a protein chain, another substance is formed. Name this substance. [1]

(iii) Name the process in which molecules like **A** and **B** join to make a protein chain. [2]

(MEG, 1995)

12.8 Enzymes are 'organic catalysts'. They are proteins that can increase the rate of chemical reactions but remain unchanged once the reaction is over.

(a) What is meant by the term *organic*? [1]

(b) Describe *three* other ways by which the speed of chemical reactions can be increased. [3]

(c) Enzymes are used in washing powders. They operate in warm water in weakly alkaline or weakly acidic conditions. *Persil* is an example. (*Persil* is a registered Trade Mark.)

(i) What is the approximate pH range of a weakly alkaline solution? [2]

(ii) How could you obtain a sample of pure water from a solution of washing powder? [2]

(iii) *Persil* (*perborate* + *silicate* = *Persil*) is an example of a washing powder that often has enzymes added. Deduce the names of the *three* elements contained in perborate and silicate. [3]

(IGCSE, 1995)

12.9 Below is a scheme showing the reactions of some carbon compounds.

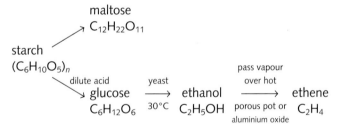

(a) Choose from the terms

fermentation   dehydration   hydrolysis

the type of reaction which occurs in each of the following: [3]

(i) starch → maltose,

(ii) glucose → ethanol,

(iii) ethanol → ethene.

(b) What does the '*n*' in the formula of starch $(C_6H_{10}O_5)_n$ tell you about the starch molecule? [1]

(NEAB, part question, 1991)

12.10

(a) Many foods contain a lot of starch. A number of chemicals can be produced from starch as shown in the flow chart below.

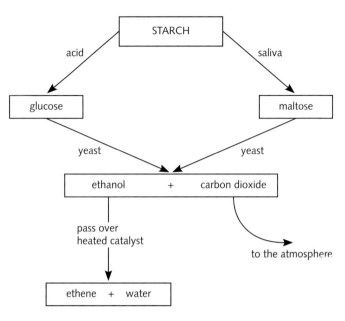

(i) Name *two* foods which contain a lot of starch. [2]

(ii) Maltose is a carbohydrate. Which *three* elements does it contain? [2]

(iii) Give a chemical change shown in the flow chart that is known as fermentation. State the starting material and the products. [2]

(iv) Give *two* major uses of ethanol. [2]

(b) Starch and protein are natural polymers. Starch can be hydrolysed to form sugars. Hydrolysis of starch in water is very slow.

(i) Explain what happens when starch is hydrolysed. [3]

(ii) How could you increase the rate of the hydrolysis of starch? Give *two* ways. [2]

(iii) Proteins are formed from amino acids joining together with the elimination of water. Draw a diagram to show how amino acids join to form a protein chain. [3]

(ULEAC, part question, 1991 and 1995)

12.11

(a) Amino acids are formed by the breakdown of protein molecules.

(i) Protein is one of the three main classes of compounds in food. Name the other *two*. [2]

(ii) Name the compound which reacts with proteins to form amino acids. [1]

(b) Nylon is a synthetic macromolecule which is held together by the same linkage as protein molecules.

(i) What is the name of this linkage? [1]

(ii) Draw a diagram of the structure of nylon. [2]

(iii) Name another synthetic macromolecule which, like nylon, is made by condensation polymerisation. [1]

(IGCSE, part question, 1989)

12.12 Recycling is an increasingly important process in modern industry. Plastics, however, are more difficult to recycle than glass, paper and metals.

One way of recycling plastics is to decompose them and to re-use the decomposition products to make plastics once more. This decomposition process is called 'pyrolysis'.

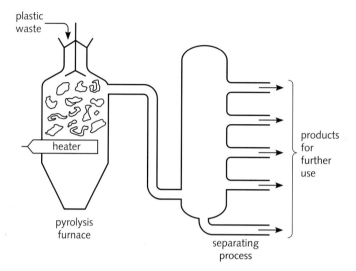

The equipment shown in the diagram can be used for this process. Plastic waste is heated to about 600°C, in the absence of air. It decomposes into a mixture of hydrocarbons. This mixture is then separated into useful raw materials for use in other processes.

(a) Explain why plastics are difficult to recycle. [1]

(b) What is meant by the term 'hydrocarbon'? [2]

(c) What feature of the pyrolysis process ensures that the plastic is decomposed but not burned? [1]

(d) What name is given to the process by which the mixture of hydrocarbons from the pyrolysis furnace is separated into its components? [2]

(e) If PVC is included in the recycled waste, it produces the pollutant gas, hydrogen chloride, HCl. This cannot be allowed to escape into the air. It can be removed by reacting it with slaked lime, Ca(OH)$_2$. What type of reaction occurs between slaked lime and hydrogen chloride? [1]

(ULEAC, part question, 1991)

12.13 *'Chemistry and Food'*

Natural foodstuffs differ from laboratory chemicals mainly in the complex mixture of substances that they contain; for example 42 chemicals have been identified in orange oil extracted from orange peel, including 12 alcohols, 2 esters and 14 hydrocarbons.

Preservatives are often added to food to make it last longer. There are some 47 preservatives which are permitted to be added to foods. They are mostly simple chemicals, often weak acids, for example vinegar (ethanoic acid). Sometimes metal nitrates are used for preserving cured meat products. This has given some cause for concern since a possible route exists by which nitrates can be converted by bacteria to chemicals which are known to cause cancers in animals.

One of the most widely used preservatives is sulphur dioxide. As a gas, this is very toxic in high concentrations, causing breathing difficulties. When used in foodstuffs, the gas is in solution and is present only in very small quantities.

If food doesn't look right, it doesn't taste right. There are only four basic tastes – sweet, sour, salt and bitter – and our appreciation of flavour is mostly due to smell and to a lesser degree visual appearance. Thus, colours are added to enhance natural colours and, in the case of canned foods, such as strawberries and peas, to replace colour lost in the processing. Without added colour, canned strawberries would be dull brown and peas khaki.

There are 46 colours which can be used by the food industry, of which 23 are plant pigments or simple derivatives of them. Artificial colours have great advantages over natural colours and are widely used. They are very rich in hue, which means that very small quantities can be used; they are also more stable than many natural colours. All permitted colours have been thoroughly tested and shown to be safe.

(a) Is orange oil an element, a mixture or a compound? Give a reason for your choice. [2]

(b) Name *one* other natural source of esters. [1]

(c) Why do you think only weak acids such as ethanoic acid, and not strong acids, are used as preservatives? [1]

(d) (i) Potassium nitrate is often used in preserving meats. Write a *word* equation to show how potassium nitrate may be formed from potassium carbonate. [1]

(ii) Write a balanced symbol equation for this reaction. [2]

(e) Write a balanced symbol equation to show what happens when sulphur dioxide dissolves in water. [2]

(f) (i) Describe briefly how the colours in a sample of peas may be identified to make sure that only permitted colours are present. [5]

(ii) What name is given to describe such an experiment? [1]

(NISEAC, part question, 1994)

Analytical chemistry

This section covers the following ideas:

- inorganic analysis
  - testing for negative ions
  - testing for positive ions
  - the tests for gases
- organic analysis.

Chemistry can be used in industry, medicine, agriculture and environmental science. Many of the uses in these areas depend on our ability to identify chemical substances. We need to know what we are dealing with. Analytical techniques, from the simple to the complex, help us to do just that. A drug company might need to analyse the drug paracetamol by infra-red spectroscopy (figure 13.1). A steel-making company must check the content of a batch of steel against the customer's requested composition. An environmental analyst might have to check river water for contamination with trace amounts of metal ions. Carefully established analytical methods are crucial to all of this, and more.

13.1 Inorganic analysis

There are certain important tests that we can use to identify gases and substances in solution.

Testing for metal compounds is important not just in itself, but because it introduces some of the strategy behind this type of analysis. In the first instance, we simply want to know *which* compound is present. This type of analysis is known as **qualitative analysis**. We need to find a reaction that clearly indicates that a particular ion is present. It must be a reaction in which only that ion takes part. The most useful reactions are **precipitation** reactions – where two solutions are mixed and an insoluble product is formed. The alternative to forming a characteristic precipitate is to produce a **gas** that can be tested.

Testing for negative ions

Before giving more detail of the tests for negative ions (anions) in solution, it is worth remembering the general pattern of solubility for inorganic compounds (figure 13.2). In this Venn diagram, soluble substances fall within the large circle. The circles for metal chlorides and sulphates overlap to a great extent with the large circle, because most chlorides and sulphates are soluble in water. The opposite is true for the carbonate and (hydr)oxide circles. The insolubility of silver chloride and barium sulphate (shown bold in figure 13.2) is the basis for the tests for chloride ions and sulphate ions, respectively.

The tests for the common negative ions are listed in table 13.1. For example, silver nitrate solution

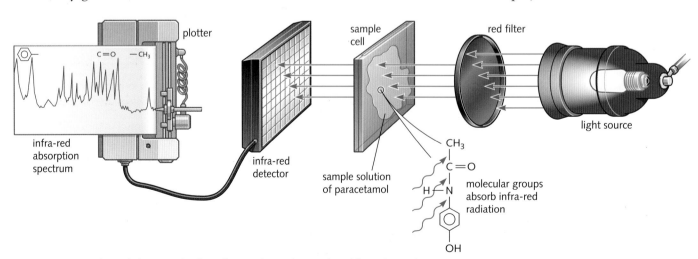

Figure 13.1 *Medicinal drugs and other chemicals can be analysed by infra-red spectroscopy.*

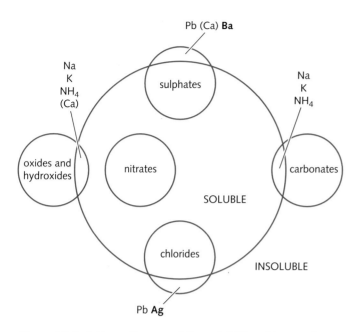

*Figure 13.2 A Venn diagram of the solubility of inorganic compounds. All the substances within the large central circle have a solubility greater than 1 g/dm³, and so are considered to be 'soluble'. The calcium compounds shown as (Ca) have solubilities of about 1 g/dm³. The **bold** letters show the insoluble compounds that are the basis of the tests.*

can be used to identify **halide** ions in solution. All chlorides will react with silver nitrate solution to give a white precipitate of silver chloride, AgCl. Bromides give a cream precipitate of AgBr and iodides a yellow precipitate of AgI.

Testing for positive ions

Once we have identified the negative ion present, the remaining part of the puzzle is to see which positive ion is present in the compound. The situation is more complicated, as there are more common alternatives, but the basic approach is the same.

We are helped in testing for positive ions by the fact that certain metal ions will give a characteristic colour in the **flame test**. If a clean nichrome wire is dipped in a metal compound and then held in the hot part of a Bunsen flame, the flame can become coloured (table 13.2 on page 350).

The **precipitation tests** for metal ions are based on the fact that most metal hydroxides are insoluble (figure 13.2). Some are also coloured and are therefore easily identified. Table 13.3 on page 350 lists the different tests used to identify positive ions

Table 13.1 Tests for negative ions (anions)

Negative ion	Test	Test result*
Carbonate (CO_3^{2-})	add dilute hydrochloric acid to solid	effervescence (fizzes), carbon dioxide produced (test with limewater)
Chloride (Cl^-) (in solution)	acidify solution with dilute nitric acid, then add aqueous silver nitrate	white ppt. of silver chloride formed: ppt. soluble in ammonia solution
Bromide (Br^-) (in solution)	acidify solution with dilute nitric acid, then add aqueous silver nitrate	cream ppt. of silver bromide formed: only slightly soluble in ammonia solution
Iodide (I^-) (in solution)	acidify solution with dilute nitric acid, then add aqueous silver nitrate	yellow ppt. of silver iodide formed: insoluble in ammonia solution
	OR	
	acidify solution with dilute nitric acid, then add lead nitrate solution	yellow ppt. of lead iodide formed
Sulphate (SO_4^{2-}) (in solution)	acidify solution with dilute hydrochloric acid, then add barium chloride solution	white ppt. of barium sulphate formed
	OR	
	acidify solution with dilute nitric acid, then add barium nitrate solution	white ppt. of barium sulphate formed
Nitrate (NO_3^-) (in solution)	make alkaline with sodium hydroxide solution, then add aluminium foil (or Devarda's alloy) and warm carefully	ammonia gas given off (test with moist red litmus)

* Note: ppt. = precipitate.

Table 13.2 Some flame test colours

Metal ion		Colour of flame
sodium	(Na^+)	yellow
potassium	(K^+)	lilac
calcium	(Ca^{2+})	brick red (orange-red)
lithium	(Li^+)	crimson
copper	(Cu^{2+})	blue-green
barium	(Ba^{2+})	apple green

using sodium hydroxide (a strong alkali) or ammonia solution (a weak alkali). The strategy to the tests is more clearly seen in the flow chart in figure 13.3.

When carrying out an analysis using these tests, try not to forget the background chemistry involved. The hydroxides of aluminium and zinc re-dissolve in excess sodium hydroxide because they are **amphoteric** hydroxides – they react with both acids and bases (see page 152). The hydroxides of the other metals in the table do not re-dissolve in excess sodium hydroxide because they are **basic** hydroxides – reacting only with acids in neutralisation reactions.

The tests for gases

Several of the above tests involve detecting gases produced by the test reactions. The **gas tests** are another important set of general analytical tests (table 13.4).

To study gases further, samples can be collected in a variety of ways, depending on their density and solubility in water.

Methods of collecting gases

There are four general methods of collecting gases – the apparatus used in each case is shown in figure 13.4 on page 352.

- **Downward delivery** is used for gases that are denser than air (a).
- **Upward delivery** is used for gases that are less dense than air (b).
- **Collection over water** is used for gases that are not very soluble in water (c).
- **Collection in a gas syringe** is useful when the volume of gas needs to be measured (d).

Table 13.3 Tests for positive ions (cations)

Positive ion (in solution)	Effect of adding sodium hydroxide*	Effect of adding ammonia solution*
Ammonium (NH_4^+)	ammonia produced on warming	–
Copper(II) (Cu^{2+})	light blue gelatinous ppt. of copper hydroxide; insoluble in excess sodium hydroxide	light blue gelatinous ppt.; dissolves in excess ammonia, giving a deep blue solution
Iron(II) (Fe^{2+})	green gelatinous ppt. of iron(II) hydroxide; insoluble in excess	green gelatinous ppt.; insoluble in excess
Iron(III) (Fe^{3+})	rust-brown gelatinous ppt. of iron(III) hydroxide; insoluble in excess	rust-brown gelatinous ppt.; insoluble in excess
Calcium (Ca^{2+})	white ppt. of calcium hydroxide; insoluble in excess	no ppt. (or only a very slight ppt.)
Magnesium (Mg^{2+})	white ppt. of magnesium hydroxide; insoluble in excess	white ppt.; insoluble in excess
Zinc (Zn^{2+})	white ppt. of zinc hydroxide; soluble in excess, giving a colourless solution	white ppt.; soluble in excess
Aluminium (Al^{3+})	white ppt. of aluminium hydroxide; soluble in excess, giving a colourless solution	white ppt.; insoluble in excess

* Note: ppt. = precipitate.

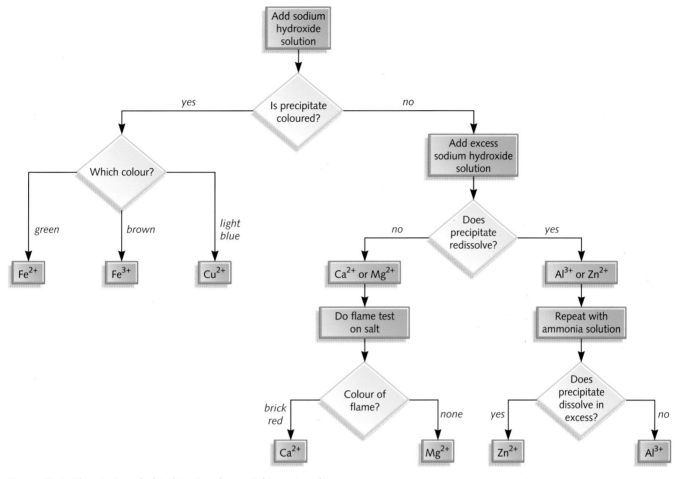

Figure 13.3 *The strategy behind testing for metal ions in salts.*

Table 13.4 Tests for gases

Gas	Colour and smell	Test	Test result
Ammonia (NH_3)	colourless, pungent smell	hold damp red litmus paper (or universal indicator paper) in gas	indicator paper turns blue
Carbon dioxide (CO_2)	colourless, odourless	bubble gas through limewater (calcium hydroxide solution)	white ppt. of calcium carbonate formed (solution turns milky)
Chlorine* (Cl_2)	pale green, choking smell	hold damp litmus paper (or universal indicator paper) in gas	indicator paper is bleached white (blue litmus will turn red first)
Hydrogen (H_2)	colourless, odourless	hold a lighted splint in gas	hydrogen burns with a squeaky 'pop'
Oxygen (O_2)	colourless, odourless	hold a 'glowing' wooden splint in gas	the splint relights
Sulphur dioxide* (SO_2)	colourless, choking smell	dip a piece of filter paper in potassium dichromate(VI) solution, hold it in gas	solution turns pale green (SO_2 is a reducing agent)

* These gases are poisonous, so test with care and use a fume cupboard.

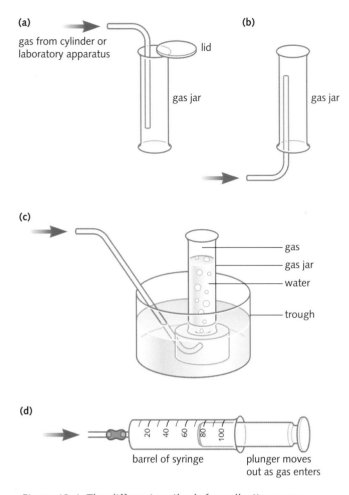

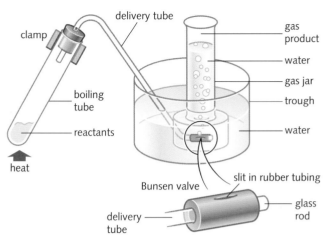

Figure 13.5 *Using a Bunsen valve to prevent 'sucking back'.*

Figure 13.4 *The different methods for collecting gases.*

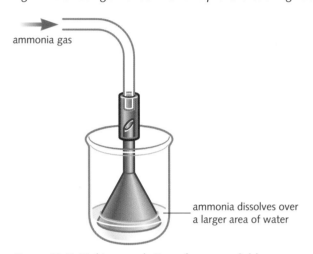

Figure 13.6 *Making a solution of a very soluble gas.*

Sometimes it is necessary to produce a gas by a reaction that requires heating. In such cases, there is a danger of 'sucking back' if the gas is collected over water. The problem arises if heating is stopped *before* the delivery tube is removed from the water. The reduced pressure in the reaction tube as it cools results in water rising up the delivery tube. In the worst case, the cold water can be sucked back into the hot boiling tube. The tube will crack and an explosion may occur. 'Sucking back' can be prevented by making sure that the delivery tube is removed first, before heating is stopped. Alternatively, a Bunsen valve (figure 13.5) can be fitted to the end of the tube.

One other useful adaptation for the delivery of gases is used for making a solution of a gas that is very soluble in water, for example ammonia or hydrogen chloride. The adaptation is shown in figure 13.6. The filter funnel increases the area over which the gas can dissolve, and prevents water rising up the delivery tube into the reaction vessel.

Methods of drying gases

Quite often we need to produce a *dry* sample of gas. This is done by passing the gas through a **drying agent**. Figure 13.7 gives the appropriate method for the three commonest drying agents. The agents are suitable for particular gases.

- **Concentrated sulphuric acid** is used to dry all gases except ammonia.
- **Anhydrous calcium chloride** is used for all gases except ammonia, which forms a complex with calcium chloride.
- **Calcium oxide** used to dry ammonia and neutral gases.

Tests for water and acidity

These are the two other useful general tests that we need to consider. Then our discussion of qualitative inorganic analysis is complete.

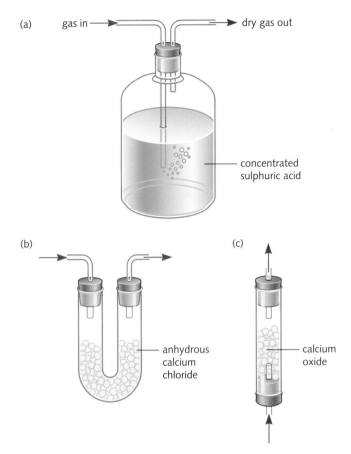

(a) gas in → dry gas out

concentrated sulphuric acid

(b) (c)

anhydrous calcium chloride

calcium oxide

Figure 13.7 The different methods of drying gases.

- *pH testing*
  The acidity or alkalinity of a solution can be tested using indicator papers (usually litmus or universal indicator see page 128). It is not very good chemical practice to dip the paper directly into the solution. Instead, a glass rod should be used to place a drop of the solution on the paper. For an accurate measure of pH, a pH meter can be used. Measurements of pH and other analyses are often carried out on soil samples. Soil is stirred with distilled water. The insoluble material settles out, but the solution above remains unclear because of fine suspended particles. These fine particles can be made to settle too by adding some barium sulphate to the suspension. The barium sulphate particles, themselves insoluble, physically drag the fine suspended material to the bottom of the container. The mixture can then be filtered and the solution tested in various ways for soluble ions, pH, etc.

- *Testing for the presence of water*
  Not all neutral colourless liquids are water. The *presence* of water can be detected using

anhydrous copper(II) sulphate or cobalt(II) chloride. Water will turn anhydrous copper(II) sulphate from white to blue; and it will turn anhydrous cobalt(II) chloride from blue to pink. To establish whether a liquid is *pure* water, you would need to test its melting point or boiling point. When testing a solid substance, the best criterion of purity is that it has a sharp melting point of the correct value.

13.2 Organic analysis

There are also tests to characterise certain organic compounds. You should be familiar with a few simple ones at this stage.

The test for unsaturated hydrocarbons

The simplest test for an unsaturated compound such as an **alkene** (for example ethene) is to use bromine water (see page 309). If the unknown compound is a liquid, then a small amount is mixed with bromine water and shaken. If the unknown compound is a gas, the gas should be bubbled through bromine water. The bromine water is initially an orange-brown colour. If the gas or liquid being tested turns it colourless, then that compound is **unsaturated** – it contains at least one double bond. Alkanes are saturated and would not react.

The test for ethanol and ethanoic acid

These two substances provide a simple test reaction for each other. They react with each other, with the addition of a few drops of concentrated sulphuric acid, to produce a sweet-smelling **ester**. The mixture is warmed gently, and the fruity smell of the ester can best be detected by pouring the reaction mixture into a beaker of water. This spreads the ester and disperses the distinctive 'pear-drop' smell.

Food tests

There are some simple tests for the many food chemicals (**nutrients**) – starch, glucose, proteins and fats. These are shown in figure 13.8 on page 354.

Chromatography

The individual monomers from proteins and carbohydrates can be separated by **chromatography** (see page 71). In both cases, the spots must be

(a) **Test for starch**
Add iodine solution

Blue-black colour
indicates presence
of *starch*

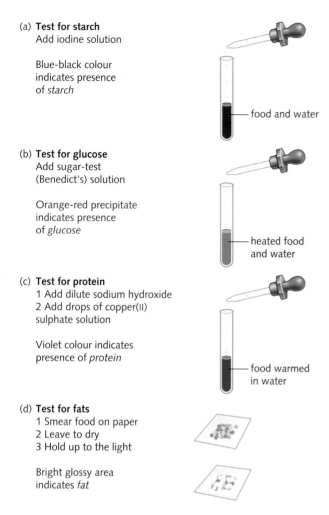

— food and water

(b) **Test for glucose**
Add sugar-test
(Benedict's) solution

Orange-red precipitate
indicates presence
of *glucose*

— heated food
and water

(c) **Test for protein**
1 Add dilute sodium hydroxide
2 Add drops of copper(II)
sulphate solution

Violet colour indicates
presence of *protein*

— food warmed
in water

(d) **Test for fats**
1 Smear food on paper
2 Leave to dry
3 Hold up to the light

Bright glossy area
indicates *fat*

Figure 13.8 *A summary of the simple chemical food tests.*

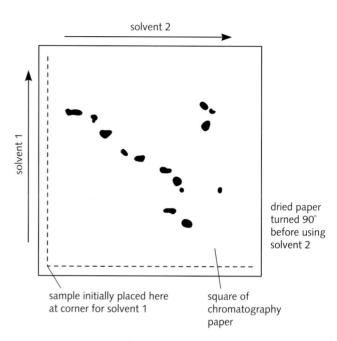

solvent 2 →

solvent 1

dried paper
turned 90°
before using
solvent 2

sample initially placed here
at corner for solvent 1

square of
chromatography
paper

Figure 13.9 *Amino acids can be separated by chromatography in two dimensions. So that they can be seen, the amino acids are stained by a locating agent.*

detected using **locating agents** because the compounds themselves are colourless. If a sample only gives a single spot, then this is an indication that it might be pure. It would be better to check, using different solvents, before being totally sure. One adaptation of this to separate more complex mixtures is to use two-dimensional chromatography. A square of paper is used and a single sample is placed in one corner. A chromatogram is run in the usual way. It is then dried and rotated through 90°. A second solvent is used to run the chromatogram in the new direction (figure 13.9).

The analyses described in this section are concerned with *which* compounds are present. That is, they are focused on detection and identification. They are **qualitative** tests. However, precipitation reactions can also be carried out to answer questions of *how much* of a substance is present. Titrations can also be carried out to

answer such questions in solutions. This type of analysis is known as **quantitative analysis**. Precipitation and titration have been discussed in sections 4.3 (page 104), 5.13 (page 141), 5.24 (page 151) and 6.9 (page 172). Precipitation reactions can be used to work out chemical formulas (try question 5.18 on page 153).

Summary of core material

You should know that:

- there is a series of tests that help us to analyse substances

- in inorganic chemistry these tests help us to find which positive ions (metals) and negative ions are present in an ionic compound

- there is also a series of tests for gases such as hydrogen, oxygen, etc.

- these analytical ideas can also be applied in organic and food chemistry

- quantitative experiments, such as titrations, which tell us how much of a substance we have (not just which substance we have), can be carried out.

13.1 This question is about testing a local water supply. Choose your answers from the following list. (An answer may be used once, more than once or not at all.)

A barium chloride   B dilute hydrochloric acid
C dilute nitric acid   D silver nitrate
E sodium hydroxide

A manufacturer needed to check what was contaminating the local water supply.

(a) Which solution should be added to a sample of the water to show that it contains sulphate ions?   [1]

(b) Which solution should be added to a sample of the water to show that it contains iron(II) ions (Fe^{2+})?   [1]

(MEG, 1992)

13.2 The table below shows the results of practical tests on substances A to E:

Substance	Action on universal indicator solution	Action on hydrochloric acid	Action on silver nitrate solution
A	stays green	no reaction	no reaction
B	goes red then bleaches	no reaction	no reaction
C	goes red	no reaction	white precipitate
D	goes blue	fizzes	white precipitate
E	stays green	no reaction	white precipitate

Choose, from A to E, the substance that is likely to be: [4]

(a) hydrochloric acid,

(b) distilled water,

(c) chlorine gas,

(d) sodium chloride solution.

(ULEAC, 1993)

13.3 Four test tubes of different gases A, B, C and D were tested using wooden splints and damp litmus paper. Copy and complete the table.   [4]

Gas	Name of gas	Test With splint	Test With litmus paper
A		no effect	bleached
B		small explosion with lighted splint	no effect
C	ammonia	no effect	
D	oxygen		no effect

(IGCSE, 1992)

13.4 Ammonia is produced when aqueous sodium hydroxide is warmed with an ammonium salt. Ammonia is less dense than air and very soluble in water.

The following apparatus was used to prepare a sample of dry ammonia gas.

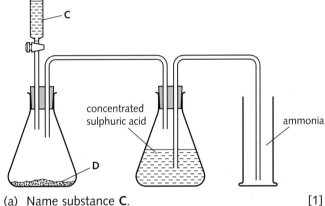

(a) Name substance **C**.   [1]

(b) Name substance **D**.   [1]

(c) What laboratory equipment necessary for the preparation of ammonia, is missing in the diagram? [2]

(d) Suggest why concentrated sulphuric acid should not be used to dry ammonia.   [1]

(e) There are *two* other mistakes in the apparatus shown in the diagram. Identify these mistakes.   [2]

(IGCSE, 1993)

13.5 Tests were carried out on a salt **C** which contained chloride ions.

Tests	Observations
(1) The appearance of salt **C**.	White crystals
(2) One spatula-measure of **C** was added to a test tube. The test tube was heated. Any gases given off were tested with universal indicator paper	Drops of water formed at the top of the tube. Indicator paper turned red.
(3) One measure of **C** was dissolved in water. The solution was divided into four equal portions.	
(i) To the first portion was added an equal volume of aqueous ammonia. Then an excess of aqueous ammonia was added.	White precipitate formed. In excess, no change.
(ii) To the second portion was added an equal volume of aqueous sodium hydroxide. Then an excess of aqueous sodium hydroxide was added.	White precipitate formed. Precipitate dissolved in excess.
(iii) To the third portion was added universal indicator solution.	Colour turned red. pH .... [1]
(iv) To the fourth portion was added a few drops of dilute nitric acid. Then aqueous silver nitrate was added.	.... [2]

(a) Write down what should go in the spaces in the 'observations' column in the table. [3]

(b) What does test (1) tell you about **C**? [1]

(c) What does test (2) tell you about **C**? [2]

(d) What does test (3) tell you about **C**? [2]

(e) Suggest an identity for **C**. [1]

(IGCSE, 1995)

13.6 A substance **G** contains three dyes. Two are water-soluble and one is insoluble.

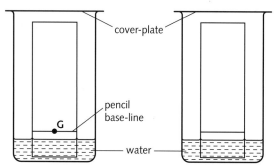

cover-plate

pencil base-line

G

water

At the start of the experiment   *At the end of the experiment*

(a) Copy the right-hand diagram. On your diagram, sketch the result you would expect if **G** were separated by paper chromatography. [2]

(b) Why was pencil used to mark the base-line instead of ink? [2]

(c) Why must the base-line be placed above the level of the water at the start? [1]

(IGCSE, 1995)

13.7 Two experiments were carried out on substance **H**.

Experiment 1
A white powder **H** was made by grinding some dry plant material. Some of the powder was heated in a test tube. The powder turned black and a vapour **J** was formed which turned anhydrous copper(II) sulphate blue. Carbon dioxide gas was also given off.

(a) Name suitable apparatus that could be used to grind the dry plant material. [2]

(b) (i) Suggest an identity for the black solid. [1]
    (ii) Suggest an identity for vapour **J**. [1]

(c) How would you test for the presence of carbon dioxide? [2]

Experiment 2
A fresh sample of **H** was dissolved in water and some yeast added to the solution. Fermentation took place.

(d) State a suitable temperature for the fermentation. [1]

(e) Give *two* expected observations during a fermentation. [2]

(f) What type of substance is **H**? [1]

(IGCSE, 1995)

EXTENSION
Medicinal chemistry

This section covers the following ideas:

- pharmaceuticals
- 'medicines by design'.

13.3 Pharmaceuticals, drugs and medicines

Pharmaceuticals are drugs that are prepared and sold with the intention of treating illness. A wide range of pharmaceutical products is available today. The pharmaceutical industry is one of the most important parts of the chemical industry. Many of its raw materials are produced by the petrochemical industry – one industry provides the feedstock for the other. The pharmaceutical industry is profitable, but its research and development costs are very high. For example, it costs more than £100 million to discover, test and release a single drug on to the market.

A **drug** is any substance, natural or synthetic, that in some way changes the way in which our body works. Most medicines contain drugs, but not all drugs are medicines. Some drugs are part of our everyday life. Caffeine is a drug present in tea, coffee and various soft drinks. A cup of tea contains 50–100 mg of caffeine. As a drug, caffeine affects the body in more than one way. It is a **stimulant**; there is enough caffeine in two cups of coffee to make you feel less sleepy. It can make you work faster and more accurately at practical tasks. However, over-use of caffeine can place stress on the heart. It is also a **diuretic**, which means that it stimulates the production of urine.

Some medicines are sold without a prescription. These include painkillers (such as aspirin and paracetamol), antacids and a variety of cold and 'flu remedies. Other medicines can only be obtained on prescription. These contain drugs that need to be taken under more controlled medical supervision. Table 13.5 shows the

Table 13.5 Some commonly available drugs

Name	Structure	Used for the treatment of
Aspirin	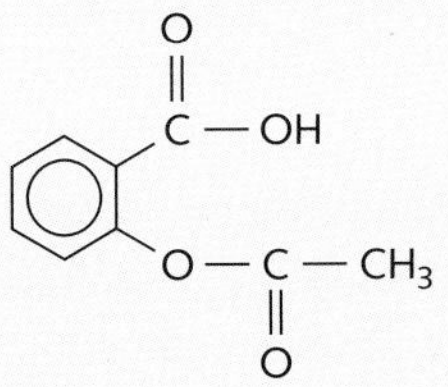	headaches, mild pain, heart disease
Paracetamol*	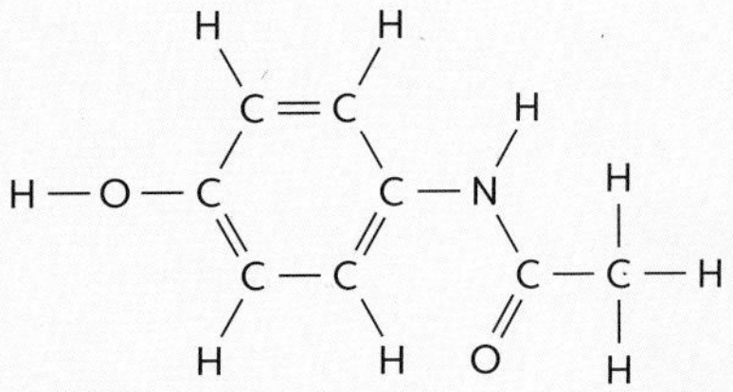	headaches, mild pain
Methyldopa	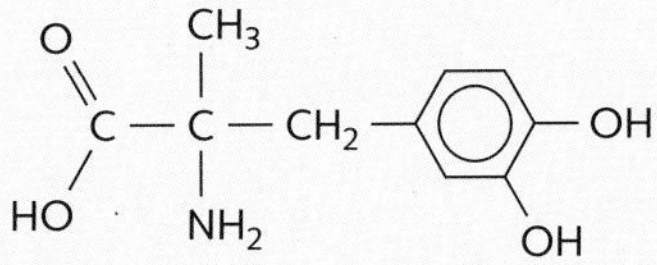	high blood pressure (hypertension)
Penicillin	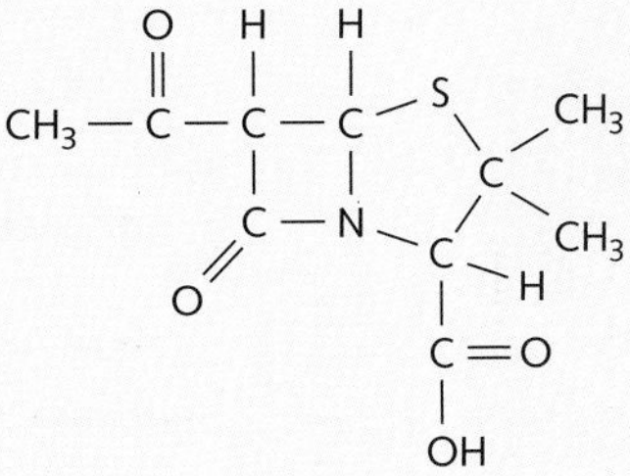	a variety of bacterial infections
Valium	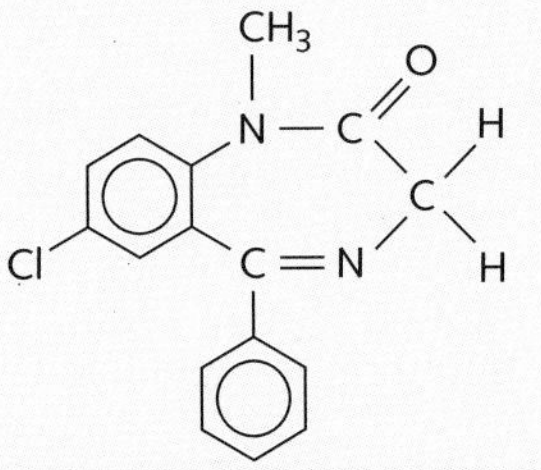	feelings of anxiety or depression

* The full structure of paracetamol is shown here. This shows the arrangement of the six carbon atoms in the benzene ring, and the hydrogen atoms attached to them. In the other structures shown here, and very often elsewhere, the benzene ring is drawn in an alternative way as

357

structures and uses of some common drugs available at the moment. These drugs are all complex organic molecules, many containing the benzene (C_6H_6) ring. (You do not need to know anything more about benzene at this stage.) Their complexity means that they have a particular and distinctive shape that affects their action in the body. Some drugs have a natural origin. Penicillin was originally produced by fungi, while aspirin was developed from a chemical originally found in willow bark (figure 13.10). Interestingly, one concern about the devastation of the tropical rainforests is the loss of the wide range of plants that may produce useful clues to other medicines.

In contrast to being developed from naturally occurring chemicals, many modern drugs are 'medicines by design'. The understanding of molecular shape is of crucial importance here, and powerful computer modelling programs are now available. A **binding site** is a particular place on the surface of an enzyme or a cell. When a chemical substance reacts with an enzyme or cell, it does so by attaching at a binding site. That binding site has a three-dimensional shape to fit the chemical with which it reacts. The body produces substances that match with binding sites and result in a chemical

reaction. Such a reaction might cause a muscle cell to contract, or a nerve impulse to move along a nerve.

Adrenaline is produced by the body. It interacts with different binding sites on muscle cells:

- in the air tubes leading to the lungs, adrenaline binds and causes them to open wider,
- in the heart, adrenaline interacts to make the heart beat faster.

Both these reactions prepare the body for intense activity. They are part of our built-in reaction to danger – the response being that of 'fight or flight'. The shape of adrenaline can be copied in two ways, as an agonist or as an antagonist. One way produces a molecule that acts like adrenaline and can be used to increase the body's natural response (an **agonist**). In contrast, a molecule can be produced that binds and blocks adrenaline. This stops the body's natural response (an **antagonist**). Both approaches are summarised in figure 13.11.

There are a wide range of medicinal drugs available for treatment. They can be categorised into different types, as follows.

- **Anaesthetics** induce loss of feeling and/or consciousness (for example halothane, see page 310).
- **Analgesics** relieve pain (for example aspirin, paracetamol and codeine).
- **Sedatives** induce sleep (for example barbiturates).
- **Tranquillisers** give relief from anxiety (for example valium).
- **Antibiotics** are substances that will kill bacteria, and so they fight diseases caused by bacteria (for example penicillin and tetracycline).
- **Anti-cancer agents** are drugs used in chemotherapy to kill off cancer cells.

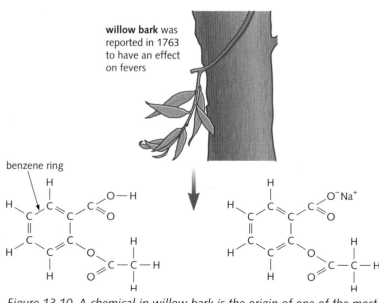

willow bark was reported in 1763 to have an effect on fevers

benzene ring

Figure 13.10 A chemical in willow bark is the origin of one of the most useful drugs.

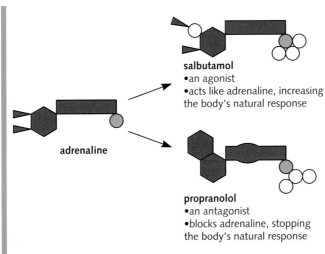

Figure 13.11 Molecules whose shape is similar to adrenaline can be used as agonists or antagonists to produce useful effects. Here the different shapes are used to represent different groups of atoms in the molecules. Salbutamol acts like adrenaline, and causes the air tubes leading to the lungs to open wider. So salbutamol is used in the treatment of asthma. Propranolol blocks adrenaline, and causes the air tubes to become narrower. So people with asthma should never use propranolol.

Chemotherapy is the treatment of disease (often cancers) by chemical compounds (drugs) without causing irreversible damage to healthy tissues. Chemotherapy is an alternative approach to treatment that can be used instead of or alongside **radiotherapy** (the use of targeted radiation).

Care must be taken when using drugs, as their use can become habit-forming. Even drugs, such as valium, that are not physically addictive can become psychologically addictive if used for long periods of time. Other drugs, such as nicotine, alcohol and the opiate drugs (morphine, cocaine and heroin), can become physically addictive.

All drugs, even those bought at the supermarket, can have side-effects on the body. These can be harmful. The medical use of drugs is often a delicate balance between the drug's useful effects and its side-effects. The harmful effects of illegal drugs can be very damaging and even lethal.

13.4 Vitamins and minerals

Henry VIII's ill-health at the end of his life had several causes. Modern analysis of his symptoms suggests that he suffered from scurvy (vitamin C **deficiency**). His diet suffered from a lack of fresh fruit and vegetables.

Vitamins and minerals are needed by the body, but in very small quantities. Although the amounts required are small, the effects that occur when they are missing are large. Our cells depend on a complex series of reactions that produce the biochemical compounds that the cells need. Without trace amounts of vitamins and minerals, enzymes cannot function properly and parts of this biochemical metabolism can fail. The symptoms of deficiency are relatively rare in the developed world. But in areas where food is short, thousands, if not millions, of people may be affected by diseases that are totally preventable.

A wide range of vitamin and mineral supplements is available at a pharmacy or in supermarkets.

Summary of extension material

You should know that:

- the production of pharmaceutical drugs is a major part of the chemical industry
- the way most medical drugs work depends on their molecular shape

- there are different types of medicinal drugs available – they can be categorised according to their effects
- our bodies require vitamins and minerals in trace, but significant, amounts to function properly.

359

13.8 In 1838 it was discovered that salicylic acid, extracted from the bark of a willow tree, had pain relieving properties. By the end of the century, the drug known as aspirin had been developed from it. *Aspirin works by preventing enzymes in the body from producing the compounds which cause pain.*

(a) Use diagrams to explain the sentence printed in *italics*. [3]

(b) (i) Why is aspirin considered to be a drug? [1]
    (ii) Suggest a reason why it was desirable to develop aspirin rather than use salicylic acid for pain relief. [1]
    (iii) Why would the developers of aspirin have expected it to have pain relieving properties? [1]

salicylic acid

aspirin

soluble aspirin

(c) When aspirin reacts with sodium hydrogencarbonate, the sodium salt of the aspirin forms. This is known as soluble aspirin.

$$C_9H_8O_4 + NaHCO_3 \rightarrow C_9H_7O_4Na + H_2O + CO_2$$

What is the minimum mass of sodium hydrogencarbonate which would be needed to produce 10.1 g of soluble aspirin? [4]

(MEG, 1995)

13.9 These labels are from bottles found in a medicine cabinet.

HEADEASE
Takes away the pain of headaches, rheumatism, neuralgia. Relieves the symptoms of colds and influenza.
Each tablet contains 500mg paracetamol.

INDICALM
For rapid relief from acid indigestion.
Each tablet contains 250mg calcium carbonate.

(a) For each of these medicines choose the word in the table that best describes it. [2]

Name	Type of medicine			
Headease	analgesic	antacid	antibiotic	antiseptic
Indicalm	analgesic	antacid	antibiotic	antiseptic

(b) If you put a tablet of *Indicalm* into a beaker of dilute hydrochloric acid, the tablet fizzes. The tablet dissolves to make a solution of calcium chloride. The gas given off is carbon dioxide. Write a word equation for this reaction. [2]

(c) The molecule shown below (labelled **X**) is used by bacteria to enable them to reproduce. It was discovered that the use of sulphanilamide could prevent the build-up of bacteria in the body.

X (compound used by bacteria)

sulphanilamide

Explain why sulphanilamide can be used to fight diseases caused by bacteria. [2]

(MEG, 1993 and 1995)

Experimental design and hypothesis testing

This section covers the following ideas:

- the nature of the scientific method
- hypothesis-testing and falsification
- the design of experiments
- planning an experimental investigation
- sources of error and experimental controls.

13.5 The scientific method

What makes science different from other ways of looking at the world? Science could be said to put forward a consistent and structured picture of the world. But the same might be claimed for other 'world views', from religious through to magical interpretations of the Universe and people's place in it. However, science does demand that ideas be tested against the real world. Experiments, where possible, are essential to the 'scientific method' – science is not a collection of 'X-files'.

The 'scientific method' is not a single structured procedure – an exclusive way of arriving at 'truth'. It is actually a collection of beliefs and activities, stressing at least three processes that interact with each other.

- *To explain*
  The first of these strands concerns the interaction between observation or experiment and theory. A theory grows out of an attempt to explain observed or experimental findings. Any theory is then tested by further experiments. This further testing can lead to an extension of the theory.

- *To quantify*
  The second strand concerns the wish of scientists to quantify their findings where possible. They wish to find a mathematical expression to account for the observed data. When tackling more complex problems involving many interacting factors, this usually means an extensive use of statistics.

- *To predict*
  The third strand introduces the element of prediction. If a theory is well established and tested, then it should be able to predict the results of future experiments.

Scientists are committed to the search for sensible answers to questions about the nature of life and the physical universe. There are different styles in pursuing these goals. Science can involve the creative and intuitive instincts of personality in making progress. Science is subject to social, political and economic forces, that is, forces from outside of science itself. The pressures placed on scientists such as Galileo and Darwin are evidence for that. These forces may apply even within the 'scientific community' itself. Boltzmann died in desperation at the lack of acceptance of his ideas by his fellow-scientists.

13.6 Revolutions in science

Sir Karl Popper has provided probably the most influential modern view of the scientific method. In this view, he emphasised that the purpose of experimentation is to prove theories false. A good theory will suggest several experiments that could disprove it. The strength of the theory is increased if it survives the testing. Any theory is always at the mercy of new evidence.

The normal progress of science is interrupted by '**scientific revolutions**' through which ideas in a particular area of science break new ground. This idea of the progression of science was suggested by Thomas Kuhn. He put forward the revolutions of Copernicus, Lavoisier and Darwin to illustrate his ideas. A similar revolution has taken place this century with the controversy that surrounded the acceptance of Wegener's plate tectonic theory. This revolutionised our ideas of the Earth's geology.

The influence of science extends beyond the boundaries of the scientific community. It produces knowledge and new possibilities that influence and create new moral choices. Scientists need to discuss with the general community how such discoveries should be used. They need to participate responsibly to make sure that scientific knowledge is used ethically and constructively. At its most influential, science can change the framework of a culture.

Women in science

However, the culture within a society can also affect science. The effects of social status and conditions are reflected in the emergence of women into scientific prominence relatively recently.

Francium would be a pretty exciting metal to experiment with! However, it has never been purified in enough quantity for anyone to have seen any – let alone see how it reacts with water. It is the most unstable of the natural elements, being highly radioactive. It was discovered in 1939 by Marguerite Perey while working in the Institut du Radium, whose director was Marie Curie.

Marie Curie, her daughter Irene Curie-Joliot and Marguerite Perey illustrate a growing trend in the twentieth century as more women entered science and made major contributions. Others since have included Rosalind Franklin, who worked out much of the detailed data involved in finding the structure of the DNA double helix, and Dorothy Hodgkin, who won the Nobel Prize in 1964 for establishing the structure of insulin.

The influence of human personalities in scientific discovery is shown very effectively in the award-winning BBC drama-documentary 'Life Story'. This traces the discovery of the DNA double helix and shows the different approaches to science of the people involved.

The 'human' mouse

The field of genetic engineering is one major area where science is presenting us with new moral choices. In June 1997, scientists reported the breeding of mice that carried human chromosomes. One leading genetics expert commented that: 'One wonders how many more genes you can put into these mice before they start complaining'. These experiments, along with the cloning of 'Dolly' the sheep, which made headlines earlier in 1997, pose radical questions about placing restrictions on scientific development. Are there experiments that should not be done?

13.7 Experimental design

Practical investigations are an essential part of GCSE coursework. They reflect the hypothesis-testing aspect of the scientific process. A **hypothesis** is not simply an idea picked out from nowhere. It attempts to find patterns in earlier tests or background research on a topic. In doing this, it makes predictions that can be tested experimentally. Figure 13.12 shows the possible stages involved in such an investigation. There are several feedback arrows on the flow chart. They stem from an evaluation of the results of the investigation.

- Repeating an experiment is always a good check on data, and is particularly valuable when numerical data are involved.

- The results may also suggest modifications to

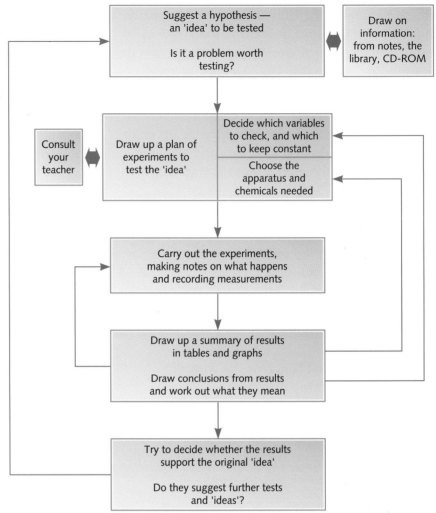

Figure 13.12 The stages involved in an experimental investigation.

the experiment in terms of the apparatus used or other parts of the design of the experiment.

- The final and over-riding feedback lies in how the experimental results might modify the original ideas behind the experiment.

There are points in the process where reference to library material and information on CD-ROM would help in designing the experiment. Your teacher will check your proposal before you carry out an investigation. IT spreadsheet packages should also be considered when presenting data. They give a variety of possibilities in terms of presenting results as graphs, and the use of bar-charts or pie-charts. Data-logging can help with the collection of experimental data. For example, a balance can be connected directly to a computer (figure 13.13a); and pH and temperature sensors can be used to follow a neutralisation reaction (figure 13.13b).

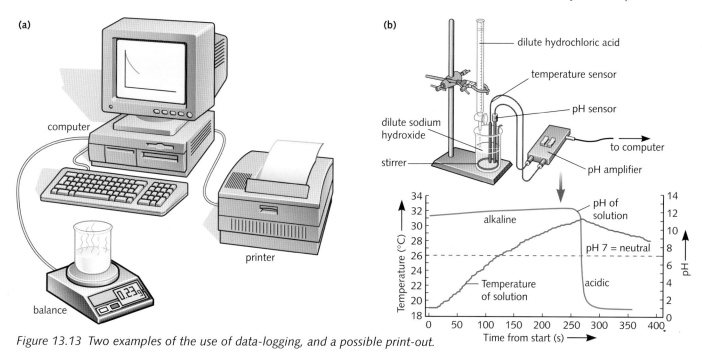

Figure 13.13 *Two examples of the use of data-logging, and a possible print-out.*

The following provides you with a check-list of ideas to bear in mind when planning your investigation.

Planning an **experimental investigation**.

- *Purpose of investigation* What is the hypothesis to be tested? What do you predict will happen and why?

- *Dependent and independent variables* Which variables are to be controlled (kept constant)? Which factors will be changed and compared? Which variables will be measured?

- *Plan of investigation* What are the basic details of the experiments? What will be changed, and how? How will the comparison be kept fair? What observations will be measured, and how? Is the experiment safe? Are there any dangers from the chemicals involved? What apparatus is needed?

- *Observations and results* What did you see happening? How can the results be compared and presented? Which is the best way to show the results: a table, a graph, a bar-chart or a pie-chart?

- *Conclusions* How can the results be interpreted? What was the pattern of the results? Can you explain the results in terms of chemical ideas? Did they fit the original hypothesis?

- *Evaluation of the results* Are there any improvements needed to the experiment? Is it necessary/useful to repeat it? Was it a fair comparison? Has the experiment produced any new ideas for further investigation?

Safety is of great importance in experiments, and you should be aware of those chemicals that can pose a risk. The meaning of the safety symbols and some chemical examples are shown in figure 13.14.

Irritant
Substances that can make your skin go red or blister – if they are dry powders, they can cause coughing
Examples: copper carbonate, calcium chloride

Highly inflammable
Substances that catch fire easily
Examples: ethanol, hexane

Oxidising
Substances that help others burn more strongly
Examples: ammonium nitrate, potassium manganate(VII)

Toxic
Substances that are poisonous and can kill you
Examples: chlorine, methanol

Harmful
Substances that may cause pain and discomfort
Examples: copper sulphate, barium chloride

Corrosive
Substances that will burn the skin and damage the eyes – they can damage wood and metal
Examples: sulphuric acid, sodium hydroxide

Figure 13.14 *Chemical safety symbols.*

When you plan your investigation, it is important to carry out a **risk assessment** for each part of the experiment. At the end of an experiment, be sure to clean up carefully and wash your hands.

Equally important for the safety and validity of your experiment is the apparatus you choose to use. You should be aware of the purpose and accuracy of the common pieces of experimental equipment (figure 13.15).

13.8 Sources of error in experiments

Almost every measurement has some degree of **error** or **uncertainty** in it. Some pieces of apparatus are more accurate than others. An awareness of **accuracy** and sources of error is important in evaluating the results of an experiment. Tables and graphs of results should be checked for results that do not fit the pattern. A typical graph is shown in figure 13.16. When plotting graphs, the line through the points should be a 'best-fit' line. Do not try to include points that are obviously out of place. The line you draw, after carefully plotting the points, should show up

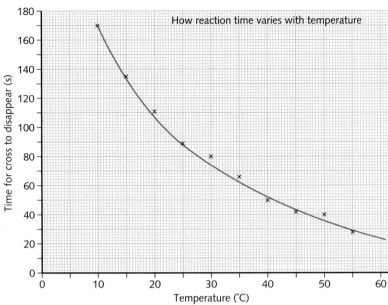

Figure 13.16 Plotting a graph is important to get the best from experimental data. This sample graph is from an experiment like the one in figure 7.11 (page 188).

the general pattern of the results. Very often this will be a straight line or a gentle curve. Try to draw the line so that the points are evenly scattered on either side. If a curve seems best, then make it as smooth as possible, avoiding sharp angles unless there is obviously a very sudden change in direction.

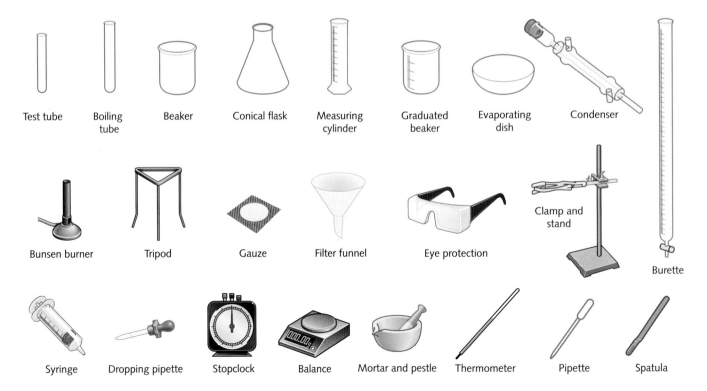

Figure 13.15 Common experimental apparatus.

When **plotting graphs**:

- plot the independent variable (here 'Temperature') on the horizontal (x) axis, with scale as large as possible,
- plot the dependent variable (here 'Time') on the vertical (y) axis, again with scale as large as possible,
- remember that the scales do *not* have to start at zero,
- label the axes clearly with the name of the variable and its units,
- give your graph a title,
- plot the points with a cross (or a small circle) using a *sharp* pencil,
- draw the best-fit line, which does not have to pass through *all* the points, and may be a straight line or a curve.

A point that does not fit the pattern is probably due to a **random error** in a particular reading. Measurements like this should be repeated where possible. There are errors that can be introduced in a different way. For instance, always reading a burette as shown in figure 13.17 would mean that the values given were always too high. This is an example of a **systematic error**. The presence of such an error can show itself when a graph is drawn. For example, a line that should pass through the origin does not do so.

- **Random errors** can be reduced by using apparatus that gives greater accuracy, by making measurements more carefully, or by making multiple measurements.
- **Systematic errors** can be eliminated by using accurate apparatus and improved technique.

13.9 Medical screening and experimental controls

The introduction of a new medical drug requires testing before the treatment can be made generally available. This is done by carrying out **clinical trials** of the drug, first on a small number of people and finally on a large number. This is an area of research that is an example of the

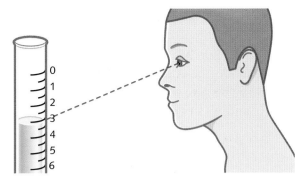

Figure 13.17 Poor experimental technique can result in systematic errors.

application of the scientific testing process to a large-scale problem in a complex system. Not all the variables can be controlled easily and so a *large sample* of the population must be used in the final trial. The sample must also be a *representative* one. Statistics must then be used to draw conclusions. A **control** must be introduced into the testing by comparing the sample with people who have not been given any treatment. A further control is to give a group a **placebo**. This group believe they are being given treatment, but in fact receive no active medicine.

Controls are important in any testing. Where possible, the relationship being tested must be isolated. Other variables must be kept constant so that they do not interfere. The matching of cause and effect in an experiment needs to be clear. The comparisons in an experiment must be fair for the results to be reliable.

Summary of core material

You should know that:

- in carrying out experiments it is important to control the situation so that not too many conditions are changing at once
- this develops into the ideas of a fair test and a controlled experiment – ideas central to any experimental investigation
- the scientific method is based in part on these ideas, so that any hypothesis can be properly tested
- these ways of thinking about experiments extend into medical research and methods such as clinical trials.

13.10 Malachite is an ore of copper. Malachite is a green substance which consists mainly of copper(II) carbonate which is insoluble in water. Copper metal may be extracted from malachite.

A student tried to obtain copper metal from malachite. This summary was taken from the student's notebook.

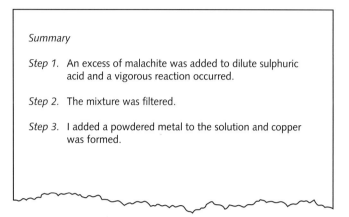

Summary

Step 1. An excess of malachite was added to dilute sulphuric acid and a vigorous reaction occurred.

Step 2. The mixture was filtered.

Step 3. I added a powdered metal to the solution and copper was formed.

(a) What would have been observed in Step 1? Explain. [1]

(b) Draw a labelled diagram of the apparatus used in Step 2. [2]

(c) Name a suitable metal that could be used in Step 3. Explain your choice. [2]

(d) Name a different method by which copper could be extracted from the solution. [1]

(IGCSE, 1995)

13.11 Your teacher gives you five different solutions, **A**, **B**, **C**, **D** and **E**. Each solution contains a different dissolved metal ion.

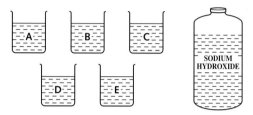

You can find out which metal ion is in each solution by following this plan:

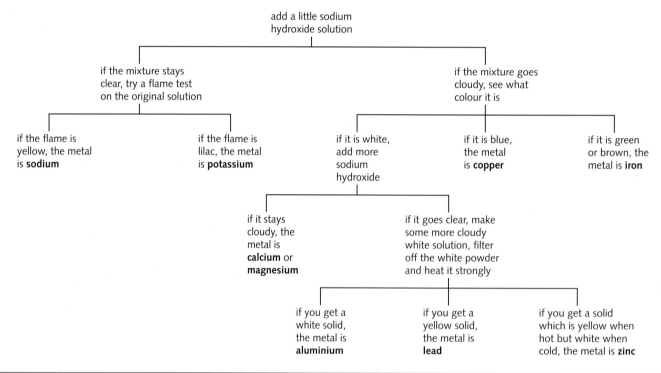

add a little sodium hydroxide solution

if the mixture stays clear, try a flame test on the original solution

    if the flame is yellow, the metal is **sodium**

    if the flame is lilac, the metal is **potassium**

if the mixture goes cloudy, see what colour it is

    if it is white, add more sodium hydroxide

        if it stays cloudy, the metal is **calcium** or **magnesium**

        if it goes clear, make some more cloudy white solution, filter off the white powder and heat it strongly

            if you get a white solid, the metal is **aluminium**

            if you get a yellow solid, the metal is **lead**

            if you get a solid which is yellow when hot but white when cold, the metal is **zinc**

    if it is blue, the metal is **copper**

    if it is green or brown, the metal is **iron**

Solution	Results of tests	Metal ion(s)
A	makes a blue cloudy solution when sodium hydroxide is added	
B	stays clear when sodium hydroxide is added; makes a flame go yellow	
C	goes cloudy and white when a little sodium hydroxide is added but goes clear again when more is added; the solid that remains after heating is white	
D	produces a cloudy solution however much sodium hydroxide is added	

(a) Read the information carefully. Then use it to complete the table by writing down what should go in the spaces in the 'metal ion(s)' column. [5]

(b) When you test solution **E** you think it contains lead. In fact, it does not contain lead, it contains zinc. Explain, in as much detail as you can, why it is easy to make this mistake. [3]

(NEAB, 1992)

13.12 Some students were investigating the rate of the reaction between sodium thiosulphate and hydrochloric acid:

$Na_2S_2O_3(aq) + 2HCl(aq)$
$\rightarrow 2NaCl(aq) + SO_2(aq) + H_2O(l) + S(s)$

A beaker containing 50 cm³ of 0.2 mol/dm³ sodium thiosulphate solution was placed on top of a black cross. Then 5 cm³ of 2 mol/dm³ hydrochloric acid was added and the clock started.

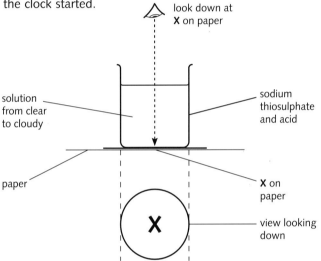

At first the cross could be seen clearly. When the solution became cloudy and the cross was no longer visible, the clock was stopped and the time recorded.

(a) Why did the solution go cloudy? [1]

(b) 50 cm³ of 0.2 mol/dm³ sodium thiosulphate solution contains 0.01 moles of $Na_2S_2O_3$.

5 cm³ of 2.0 mol/dm³ hydrochloric acid contains 0.01 moles of HCl.

(i) Explain how to calculate the number of moles of HCl in 5 cm³ of 2.0 mol/dm³ hydrochloric acid. [2]
(ii) Use the equation to work out which reagent, sodium thiosulphate or hydrochloric acid, is used up completely. [2]
(iii) What is the maximum volume of sulphur dioxide, measured at room temperature and pressure, that could be obtained in this experiment? [2]

(IGCSE, part question, 1996)

13.13 This question concerns three liquids **W**, **X** and **Y**.

Manganese(IV) oxide was added to 1 cm³ of **W**. If no visible reaction occurred, the liquid was heated and any gas given off tested with a glowing splint and with damp blue litmus paper. The experiment was repeated using **X** and **Y**. The results in the table below were obtained.

(a) (i) Name the gas produced from liquid **X**. [1]
     (ii) Name the gas produced from liquid **Y**. [1]

(b) Suggest a name for liquid **W**. Explain your answer. [2]

(c) (i) Which of the liquids is probably hydrochloric acid? Explain your answer.
     (ii) How could you confirm the identity of this liquid? [4]

	Observation with manganese(IV) oxide		Test on gases	
	In cold	When heated	Glowing splint	Blue litmus
W	no reaction	liquid boils – no reaction	extinguished	no effect
X	effervescence	vigorous effervescence	splint relit	no effect
Y	no reaction	effervescence	extinguished	bleached

(IGCSE, part question, 1990)

14 Study and revision skills

This chapter covers the following ideas and material:

- an introduction to revision methods, including
  - concept mapping, flow charts and mind maps
  - planned revision timing
  - practising examination technique
- a collection of past examination questions of various types covering a wide range of topics
- some pointers to tackling such questions and avoiding common errors, together with answers to the questions to help revision.

General techniques

14.1 Organisation of study time

The examinations are looming large. Suddenly you realise that you *do* need your notes and experimental work from the last year or two. Are they in good shape? Well...!

It is worth remembering that revision is just that. It shouldn't be the first time that you have tried to get to grips with a subject. Organisation of study habits over a whole course is a vital part of being successful. This certainly means practical things, such as making sure that your notes are intact and readable. But it also includes making sure that you have understood the ideas and connections as you have covered a topic. Nothing can be worse than trying to learn masses of material that you don't understand. The best preparation for an examination begins a long time before it! This spreads the load and lessens the tension as the examination approaches.

Figure 14.1 summarises various aspects of preparing for examinations. The coursework 'arm' emphasises not only the collection of good notes directly from class, but also the need to look at and use material from outside. Reading reference material and taking useful notes from it is a skill in itself. Table 14.1 outlines different methods of reading and their purpose. The first three methods are more appropriate to using books for reference. However, there are an increasing number of popular science books and magazines for which the last two methods are appropriate. There is an increasing amount of reference material now available on CD-ROM. You should find ways of using this material, as it provides a more interactive presentation of the material.

The ability to make notes and topic summaries as you work through a course is important, as they can then be used as a starting point for revision. You should not think of practical work in

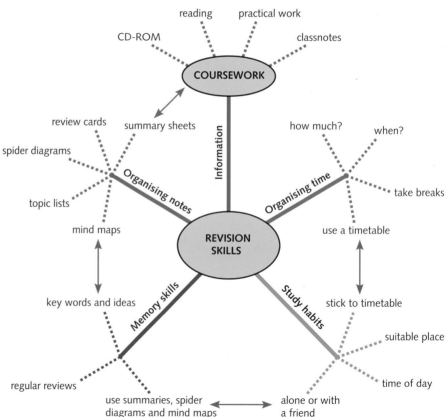

Figure 14.1 Revision involves organisation and the development of particular skills.

Table 14.1 Different methods of reading and their purpose

Type of reading	Method	Purpose
Skimming	looking for the main topics	to gain an overall impression
Scanning	looking for specific information	to find particular facts or conclusions
Reflective reading	reading carefully and thoughtfully, with attention to detail	to obtain a thorough understanding of a topic
Detecting bias	separating fact from opinion	to form a decided impression of a controversial area
Reading for pleasure	reading at own pace	to gain a feel for a subject, and for enjoyment

chemistry as separate from other classwork. The ideas and detailed information from the practicals is important in reinforcing your understanding of a topic. Indeed, a particular experiment may help you to remember and understand a crucial idea – giving you a visual clue on which to 'hang' the idea in your memory.

14.2 Organisation of revision study

The first aim of this organisation should be to provide a focused situation to help and direct your concentration. Plan out a timetable of revision that uses short blocks of time, say 45 minutes to an hour maximum, for each subject.

Your **revision timetable** should bear these points in mind:

- plan short sessions,
- take regular short breaks,
- change subject from one session to another,
- make sure your plan is realistic and achievable; it should stretch you, but not be so depressing that you are continually having to change it,
- make sure you tackle the areas of a subject you are weakest at, and target your revision to cover the whole course.

Studies suggest that such a pattern best suits our ability to concentrate. Make sure that you know the content of the syllabus you are taking, and that you have a selection of past examination papers to try.

14.3 Strategies of study

Your study sessions should use a variety of techniques to aid your understanding and learning of the material. Simply reading over your notes is not a particularly productive strategy. Try to summarise topics as you read, then shorten the summary down to a set of **key words**. Having learnt these, try to reconstruct notes on the topic. Your learning and understanding can also be checked and developed by answering questions from past examination papers. Keep the length of time taken to answer questions in mind when testing yourself. There is no point in preparing over-elaborate answers to short questions.

An important aspect in understanding a topic is to 'see the connections' between the ideas involved. Establishing these links makes it so much easier to remember the details of a topic. Pictorial methods of linking ideas can be very useful for this. The methods available include:

- flow charts,
- concept maps,
- Venn diagrams,
- mind maps.

The importance of all these methods is that they force us to sort out the material into key ideas, and then to establish the links between them. It is useful to draw up the diagrams for yourself. Remember that *your* 'maps' may well differ from other people's. Comparing notes with others, or even drawing them up together as a group, can also be very useful. Sharing ideas and comparing maps helps you to think things through. As you use these methods, you will develop greater skill in drawing them up.

Flow charts are linear in their approach and work down from a major idea by a series of subdivisions. They are useful for emphasising the different types of chemical substance, for example (see examples of charts in chapters 2 and 3).

Concept maps and mind maps are particularly useful in helping you to see the flow of ideas. In a concept map (figure 14.2), the inter-linking idea is written alongside the connecting arrow. Figure 14.3 shows a mind map covering aspects of the

nature of atoms and molecules. This particular map covers a wide range of ideas – radiating from the central idea that matter is made up of very small particles, atoms or molecules, depending on the substance being talked about. The inter-connections of ideas are emphasised. Putting the map on paper helps you to sort out your ideas! There are obviously overlaps between different topics. Figure 14.4 on page 372 shows how several 'storylines' can be linked together.

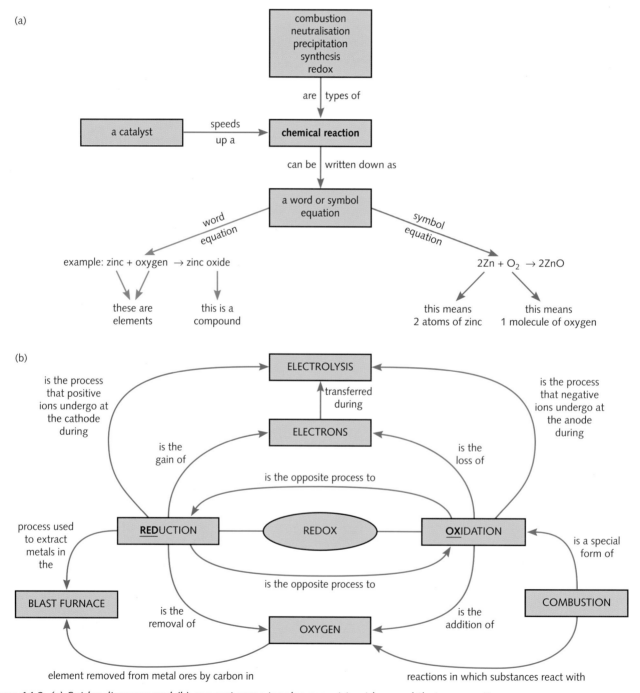

Figure 14.2 *(a) Spider diagrams and (b) concept maps involve organising ideas and their connections.*

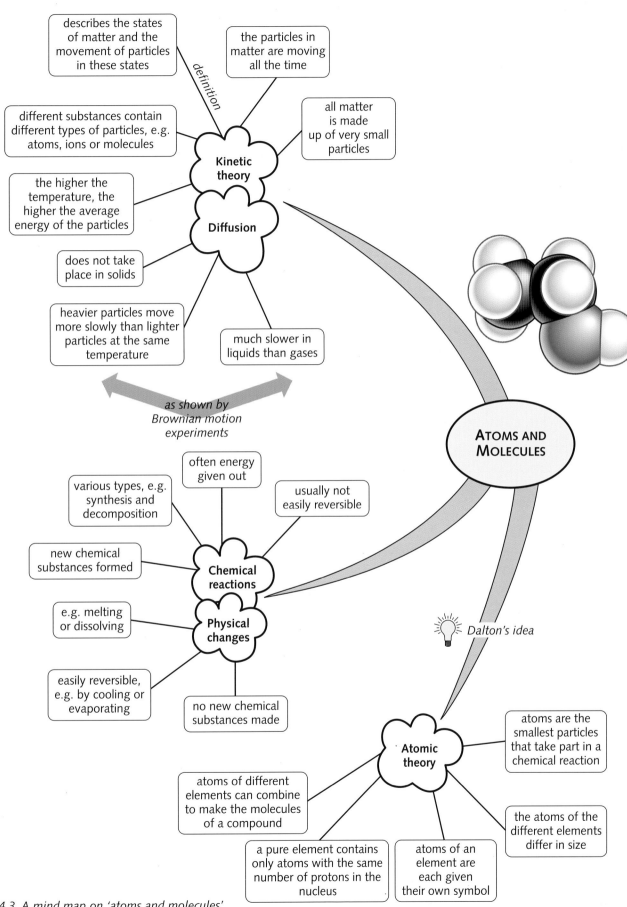

Figure 14.3 A mind map on 'atoms and molecules'.

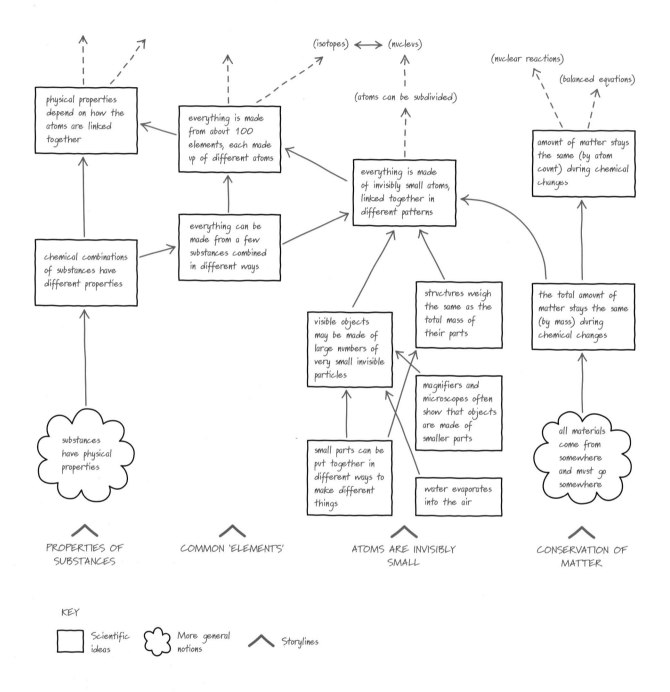

Figure 14.4 The different 'storylines' behind the maps branch into each other.

Venn diagrams are useful in helping to show where different categories overlap. For example, the different ways in which we categorise reactions can result in overlaps. Figure 14.5 shows this. It also shows how the term 'redox reaction' covers a wide range of reactions.

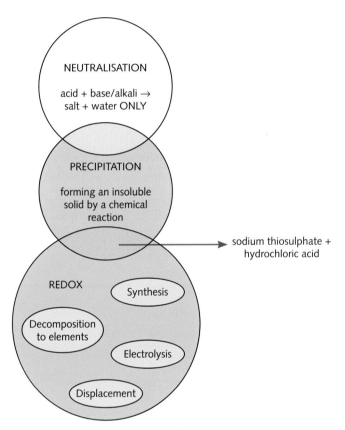

Figure 14.5 A Venn diagram showing various types of reaction. Can you think of examples to fill each space? (One has been done for you.)

14.4 Words are important

Chemistry can be said to have a language of its own. As for the other sciences, there are special terms that need to be understood and remembered – an 'atom' is not the same thing as an 'ion' or a 'molecule'. There are also some words that have a different slant on their meaning in chemistry. For example, saying that ethanol is 'volatile' does not mean that it is about to 'freak out', simply that it evaporates easily.

Throughout this book, you will find words that have been highlighted in **bold** type. It would be useful to make a note of these and make sure that you are clear about their meaning. A glossary of important chemical terms is also provided at the

end of the book. If your first language is not English – and possibly even if it is – it would be useful to keep your own 'chemical vocabulary' book to help you to learn and understand the terms used in this subject. This should help you to understand questions clearly and not get tied up in confusing 'waffle' in your answers.

14.5 Examination skills

As well as making sure that your knowledge and understanding of chemistry is good, it is certainly worth knowing your syllabus and examination(s) well.

- Make sure you know *which* examinations you are taking.
- Check *how long* each examination is.
- Check *how many* questions you will need to do.
- Study the *style* of questions you will have to answer. For example, will you need to write answers of longer than a few sentences?
- Make sure you have *practised* basic examination techniques, such as graph drawing.
- Make sure that you have the necessary *equipment*.

Knowledge of your particular syllabus and the examinations you are taking means that you can choose practice questions to cover the correct areas. You will also need to become familiar with the wording of questions. Certain standard words are used in the phrasing of questions – 'define', 'describe', 'predict' and 'suggest' are among those commonly used. Be sure that you understand the meaning of these words when they appear in questions. Be careful of two phrases in particular.

- '*State and explain*' Make sure that you *do* offer some explanation. Do not simply repeat the question in different words.
- '*State what you would observe (see)*' Such a question requires a visual description of what happens. Simply to state what chemical substances are formed in a reaction would not gain you marks.

Do take note of the number of marks carried by a question. It is a good indicator of how much detail you need in your answer. The mark scheme gives a clear indication of how many points you would need to make. In more complex questions that are testing your comprehension, be careful not to be put off by detail that may not be relevant to the precise question. You need to be able to pick out the relevant material from the other detail. This is one area where practising questions prior to the examination can be a great help. Do not let your answers be too brief and, in particular, remember to show your working in calculations. That way, if you make a simple error in the final answer, you may still gain marks for your method.

Remember, finally, that you are trying to communicate. Detail and sensible presentation – including good diagrams – can help you to succeed. The remaining sections of this chapter give you a series of questions of different types for you to practise. The more difficult questions are highlighted in the same way as the 'extension material' in the text.

Multiple-choice questions

14.6 Multiple-choice *not* multiple-guess!

Many students under-estimate multiple-choice questions. After all, the answer is there in front of them and might help them to remember the point in question. However, the questions can be a trap for those who haven't prepared well. The incorrect alternatives to the answer are technically known as **distractors**! They can seem very much like the 'right answer' if you rush at them. Think through each possibility carefully. Beware of questions phrased in the negative: 'Which property is *not* a characteristic of transition elements', etc. If you find yourself having to take a stab at an answer, then help yourself by first narrowing the field. Cut out the obviously wrong alternatives and take an educated guess.

In the selection of questions given here, question 14.9 is one where the wording must be read carefully. The *decrease* in mass asked about results from the escape of carbon dioxide through the cotton wool. The question requires the *best*

answer, so the distractor that talks of the cotton wool acting as a filter is not correct. This question also emphasises that the process of dissolving does not itself result in a change in mass. Likewise, loss of heat during an exothermic reaction does not mean that mass is lost. Question 14.6 requires careful reading too – if rushed, it is easy to put down the answer as 10 molecules (option D), missing the fact that the question says that only *one* molecule of butane is burnt.

Of these questions, 14.2, 14.5 and 14.16 have proved the easiest to answer. These questions are pictorial in presentation, and test basic, but essential, ideas. Questions 14.4 and 14.8 have been amongst the most consistently difficult to answer. They test difficult ideas such as ionisation (14.4) or a combination of ideas, for example, solubility and electrolysis (14.8). Knowing certain terms is important. Words that can prove difficult are 'constituent', 'reagent' and 'reactant' – so do check their meaning.

In some examination papers, you may be faced with multiple-response questions. Here you must *carefully* check through all the possible answers to the question. Grid questions are one possible type of multiple-response question. An example is shown in figure 14.6, and the questions that follow.

A sodium	B graphite	C molten zinc chloride
D hexane	E silver	F sulphur
G copper(II) sulphate solution	H sodium chloride crystals	I mercury

Figure 14.6 A typical multiple-response grid.

(a) Which *three* boxes represent *solids* that conduct electricity?
(Examine each box in turn to see whether it contains a correct answer. Boxes A, B and E would be correct; box I (mercury) is a good distractor because it is a conducting metal but a liquid.)

(b) Which *two* boxes represent conductors of electricity through which *ions* flow?
(Boxes C and G are correct; box H is a good

distractor as it contains ions but in the solid they cannot move.)

(c) Which box represents a liquid which conducts electricity by a *flow of electrons?*

(d) Which box represents an ionic *solid?*
(You should be able to do these last two parts from thinking through parts (a) and (b).)

Whether you will be taking an examination with multiple-choice questions is something you must find out well in advance and make sure you are well-practised for. Even if not, such questions are good for checking your revision of a wide range of material in a short time, so do use them. They can help you to pick out any basic errors of thought quite sharply.

The multiple-choice questions in this section are taken from the following sources: IGCSE, 1992 (questions 14.1–14.11 and 14.13–14.17); SEG, 1994 (question 14.23); MEG, 1992 and 1993 (questions 14.19, 14.20 and 14.22); and NEAB, 1991 and 1992 (questions 14.24–14.28). Questions 14.12 and 14.21 are based on a style of question used by the Scottish Examination Board (SEB).

14.1 What stages occur in distillation?

A condensation then evaporation
B condensation then filtration
C evaporation then condensation
D filtration then evaporation

14.2 Theobromine is a chemical found in cocoa beans. The diagram shows a chromatogram of theobromine and four different foods. Which food contains theobromine?

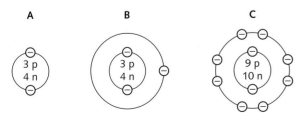

14.3 An element may be shown as $^{27}_{13}$Al. How many electrons does one atom of this element contain?

A 13   B 14   C 27   D 40

14.4 Which diagram shows a positively charged ion?

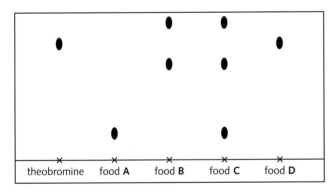

$\ominus$ = an electron
n = a neutron
p = a proton

14.5 The diagram represents a reaction.

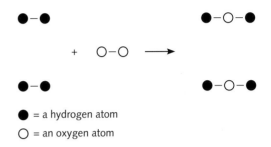

● = a hydrogen atom
○ = an oxygen atom

Which equation represents this reaction?

A $H_2 + O_2 \rightarrow H_2O_2$ B $H_2 + O_2 \rightarrow H_2O$
C $2H + O \rightarrow H_2O$ D $2H_2 + O_2 \rightarrow 2H_2O$

14.6 The equation for the burning of butane is shown below:

$2C_4H_{10} + 13O_2 \rightarrow 8CO_2 + 10H_2O$

How many molecules of water are formed when one molecule of butane burns completely?

A 4   B 5   C 8   D 10

14.7 The equation for the reaction of magnesium with hydrochloric acid is shown below:

$Mg + 2HCl \rightarrow MgCl_2 + H_2$

What mass of magnesium is needed to produce 2 g of hydrogen?

A 12 g   B 22 g   C 24 g   D 36 g

14.8 The table shows some of the properties of four compounds. Which compound could be aluminium oxide?

Compound	Solubility in water	Products of electrolysis of molten compound	
		Positive electrode	Negative electrode
A	soluble	metal	oxygen
B	soluble	oxygen	metal
C	insoluble	metal	oxygen
D	insoluble	oxygen	metal

14.9 Dilute hydrochloric acid is added to limestone chips as shown in the diagram.

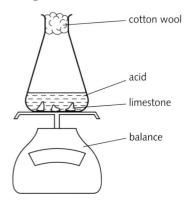

Why does the balance reading decrease as the reaction takes place?

A The reaction is exothermic.
B The reaction produces a gas.
C The marble dissolves in the acid.
D The cotton wool acts as a filter.

14.10 A rare plant has to be moved from a building site to a safer place. The plant only grows in a slightly acidic soil. What should be the pH of the soil at the safer place?

A 2   **B** 6   **C** 8   **D** 12

14.11 Acid + alkali → salt + ...

What is missing from the above equation?

A carbon dioxide   **B** hydrogen
C oxygen   **D** water

14.12 Using the chemicals in the boxes **A** to **I** as reactants:

A	B	C
NaCl(aq)	AgNO₃(aq)	HCl(aq)
D	**E**	**F**
Ba(OH)₂(aq)	H₂SO₄(aq)	CuSO₄(aq)
G	**H**	**I**
NaOH(aq)	MgCO₃(s)	Zn(s)

(a) Write a balanced equation for a reaction which would produce a soluble salt.

(b) Write a balanced equation for a reaction which would produce an insoluble salt and water.

(c) Give the letters of *two* boxes only, which, when reacted together, would produce hydrogen gas and a soluble salt.

(d) Give the letters of *two* boxes only, which, when reacted together, would produce carbon dioxide gas and a soluble salt.

14.13 The diagram shows the position of a period in the Periodic Table.

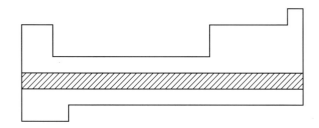

How does the type of element change across this period?

A	non-metals	→	metals	→	non-metals
B	non-metals		⟶		metals
C	metals	→	non-metals	→	metals
D	metals		⟶		non-metals

14.14 The diagram represents the manufacture of iron.

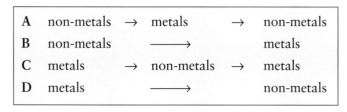

What is **X**?

A bauxite   **B** limestone
C mild steel   **D** sand

14.15 Four test tubes were set up to investigate the rusting of iron as shown in the diagrams. In which test tube will the nail rust most quickly?

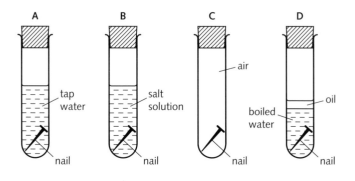

14.16 Which pair of compounds contains an alkene and an alkane?

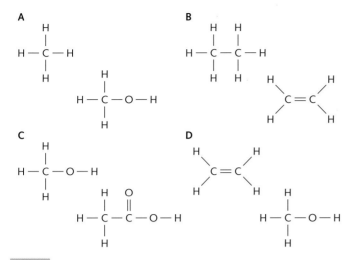

14.17 The diagram shows two ways of obtaining a substance **X**.

sugar $\xrightarrow{\text{fermentation}}$ $\boxed{\text{X}}$ $\xleftarrow{\text{steam}}$ ethene

What is **X**?

A   carbon   B   carbon dioxide
C   ethane   D   ethanol

14.18 Which one of the following molecules is produced when ethanol, C_2H_5OH, is dehydrated?

A CH_4 B C_2H_6 C C_2H_4 D CO_2

14.19 An organic compound **X** has a relative molecular mass between 40 and 50. On shaking it with bromine, the mixture quickly turns colourless. From this information, **X** could be:

A CH_3CO_2H B C_2H_4 C C_2H_5OH
D C_3H_6 E C_3H_8

14.20 Using fractional distillation, crude oil can be separated into its fractions. Which line gives the fractions in order of increasing boiling point?

Lowest boiling point $\longrightarrow$ Highest boiling point			
A	bitumen	diesel oil	paraffin	petrol
B	diesel oil	petrol	bitumen	paraffin
C	paraffin	diesel oil	bitumen	petrol
D	petrol	bitumen	diesel oil	paraffin
E	petrol	paraffin	diesel oil	bitumen

14.21 For each of the following questions, choose an answer (**A–F**) from the grid. There may be more than one answer to each question.

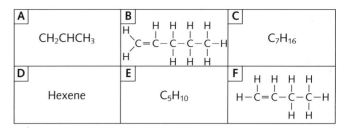

Which box represents:

(a) pentene?
(b) propene?
(c) a molecule which is not unsaturated?
(d) the fourth alkene?
(e) the fifth alkene?

14.22 The table below gives the results of six experiments involving the reaction between 0.2 g samples of zinc and $50\,cm^3$ samples of hydrochloric acid under different conditions.

Experiment number	Concentration of acid	Temperature of acid	Sample of zinc
1	$1\,mol/dm^3$	25 °C	granular
2	$2\,mol/dm^3$	25 °C	powder
3	$2\,mol/dm^3$	35 °C	granular
4	$2\,mol/dm^3$	35 °C	powder
5	$2\,mol/dm^3$	50 °C	powder
6	$3\,mol/dm^3$	50°C	powder

Which set of these experiments can be used together to show that the rate of a reaction changes with temperature?

A 1, 3 and 4   B 2, 3 and 4   C 2, 3 and 5
D 2, 4 and 5   E 2, 5 and 6

14.23 The decomposition of ammonium chloride to give hydrogen chloride and ammonia is shown by this equation:

$NH_4Cl \rightleftharpoons NH_3 + HCl$

Which of these statements are correct?

1 Ammonia and hydrogen chloride react to form ammonium chloride.
2 The change can reach equilibrium.
3 The change is reversible.

A 1 and 2   B 1 and 3   C 2 and 3   D 1, 2 and 3

In the next five questions, one or more of the responses is/are correct. Decide which of the responses to the question is/are correct and answer **A**, **B**, **C** or **D** as follows:

A   if all *three* are correct
B   if 1 and 2 only are correct
C   if 2 and 3 only are correct
D   if 1 only is correct

14.24 Which of the following substances when burnt in excess air would produce an acidic oxide?

1 sodium
2 sulphur
3 methane

14.25 The pH value of a solution of sulphuric acid could be increased by adding an equal volume of

1 the same sulphuric acid solution
2 sodium hydroxide solution
3 water

14.26 Which of the following react(s) with dilute sulphuric acid to form copper(II) sulphate?

1 copper(II) hydroxide
2 copper(II) carbonate
3 copper(II) oxide

14.27 A dilute aqueous solution of an acid would

1 react with many metals to give hydrogen
2 conduct electricity
3 produce a gas when added to a metal carbonate

14.28 $Ba(OH)_2(aq) + H_2SO_4(aq) \rightarrow BaSO_4(s) + 2H_2O(l)$

The above equation represents a reaction which could be classed as

1 acid–base
2 neutralisation
3 precipitation

Short-answer questions

14.7 Thinking clearly

You will meet the short-answer question at whatever level of GCSE examination you are entered for. You will need to be able to write precisely and to the point. In this area, the mark scheme for the question can be a useful guide as to the detail needed in an answer. A single-word answer is not going to gain the maximum marks where an answer worth, say, three marks is required.

You must always read the question carefully and answer the question asked. If, for example, you are asked to '*name* the gas given off when limestone reacts with acid', then give the name – carbon dioxide – not the formula – CO_2. If asked for a *word equation*, then do not make the question more difficult by trying to give a balanced chemical equation – you are making the question more difficult than the examiner intended!

Figures 14.7 and 14.8 show some examples of poor examination technique. In most cases, the student

(e) Methylated spirits is a mixture of ethanol (about 90%) and methanol (about 10%) together with a small quantity of purple dye.
Explain why the ethanol is treated in this way before being sold as 'meths'.

    to stop people drinking it.

Only 1 mark – more detail is needed on why the dye is added, and on why the mixture shouldn't be drunk.   (3 marks)

Figure 14.7 An example of poor examination technique.

The gas which is used for gas fires and Bunsen burners consists mainly of methane. When it is burnt in a Bunsen burner which gives a good supply of air, carbon dioxide and water vapour are formed.
(a) Methane is a hydrocarbon. What is a *hydrocarbon*?

    a hydrocarbon is a compound that contains carbon and hydrogen   [2]

1 mark – the word ONLY is missing. Many compounds contain carbon and hydrogen but are not hydrocarbons.

(b) Give the word equation for the complete combustion of methane.

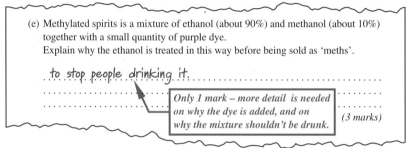

    $CH_4 + O_2 \longrightarrow CO_2 + H_2O$ [2]

You have not answered the question which asked for the WORD EQUATION. If you try to give the full equation you must get it fully correct to gain the marks – this equation is not balanced.

(c) Methane and ethane are saturated, other hydrocarbons are said to be unsaturated e.g. ethene. Describe a chemical test to distinguish between ethane and ethene.

    Ethene will decolourise bromine water

2 marks – this is the correct test and result for ethene, but you need to give full colour change AND state the negative result for ethane. NOTE THE SPACE PROVIDED AND THE NUMBER OF MARKS.   [4]

Figure 14.8 Bad technique will lose many marks.

is losing marks needlessly. Wherever comparisons are asked for in a question, always make a statement about both alternatives – even if one is a negative observation. Always mention the starting and finishing colours of a colour change.

Be careful not to overdo the word 'it' in your answers; be sure it is clear to what the 'it' refers (figure 14.9).

In an examination, your diagrams need not be works of art (figure 14.10). But you should remember the following points when drawing diagrams.

- Diagrams must be *realistic*.
- A *ruler* should be used for straight lines.
- Diagrams should be *labelled* properly.
- Most important of all, the reaction shown should *work safely*.

The majority of the marks central to your achieving a high grade will come from short-answer questions. They will be used to test your knowledge of the central ideas of chemistry and basic practical techniques, for example.

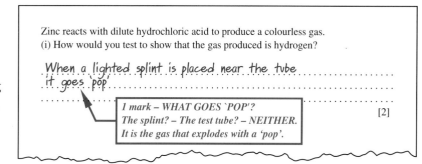

Zinc reacts with dilute hydrochloric acid to produce a colourless gas.
(i) How would you test to show that the gas produced is hydrogen?

When a lighted splint is placed near the tube it goes 'pop'.

*1 mark – WHAT GOES 'POP'?
The splint? – The test tube? – NEITHER.
It is the gas that explodes with a 'pop'.*

[2]

Figure 14.9 *Don't overdo 'it'!*

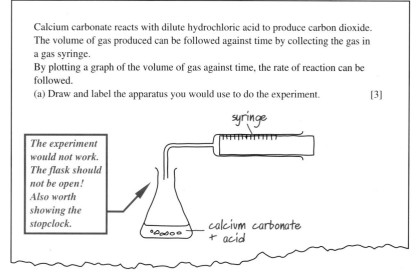

Calcium carbonate reacts with dilute hydrochloric acid to produce carbon dioxide.
The volume of gas produced can be followed against time by collecting the gas in a gas syringe.
By plotting a graph of the volume of gas against time, the rate of reaction can be followed.
(a) Draw and label the apparatus you would use to do the experiment. [3]

The experiment would not work. The flask should not be open! Also worth showing the stopclock.

syringe

calcium carbonate + acid

Figure 14.10 *A neat drawing – but the experiment wouldn't work!*

14.29 Magnesium reacts with water, steam and acids to produce hydrogen.

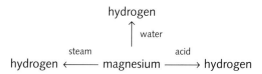

(a) The following diagram shows how the hydrogen gas produced from the reaction of magnesium with water may be collected.

(i) Copy the diagram and complete the labelling on it. [2]

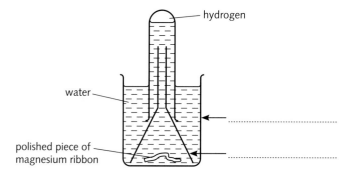

(ii) Describe how you could show that the gas collected is hydrogen. [2]
(iii) Suggest how the appearance of the magnesium would change after a week. [1]
(iv) Write a word equation for the reaction taking place between the magnesium and the water. [2]
(v) Suggest *two* ways by which you could speed up the reaction in this experiment. [2]
(vi) A few drops of universal indicator solution were added to the water in the beaker. What colour would you expect to see and what pH would this colour indicate? [2]

(b) Hydrogen may be produced more quickly by reacting magnesium with steam as shown below:
(i) Explain why the water turns into steam. [1]

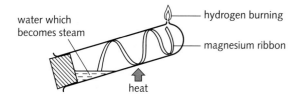

(ii) Name the substance produced when the hydrogen burns. [1]

(iii) How would you expect copper and zinc to behave, compared to magnesium, if they replaced magnesium in the test tube? [2]

(iv) Why would it be unsuitable to use sodium in this experiment? [2]

(c) Magnesium also reacts with acids to produce hydrogen. This reaction may be used to prepare hydrogen in the laboratory.

(i) Why does the first gas jar of gas collected not contain pure hydrogen? [1]

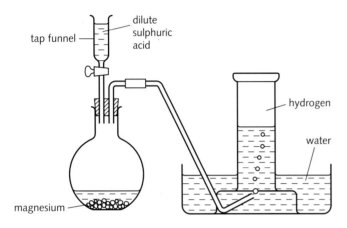

(ii) Write the word equation for the reaction taking place in the flask. [2]

(IGCSE, 1992)

14.30 Red lead, Pb_3O_4, is used in paints. It protects metal surfaces against corrosion. Red lead is made by heating lead(II) oxide, PbO, in air.

(a) Copy out and balance the following equation:

...$PbO + O_2 \rightarrow$ ...Pb_3O_4 [2]

(b) Red lead paint may be used to protect iron from rusting. Name *two* other ways of stopping iron or steel from rusting. [2]

(c) On strong heating, red lead decomposes to form oxygen and lead(II) oxide.

(i) How could you show that oxygen is given off in the decomposition? [2]

(ii) Suggest how you could show when the decomposition was finished. [2]

(d) Red lead reacts with concentrated hydrochloric acid to form lead(II) chloride, chlorine and water:

$Pb_3O_4 + 8HCl \rightarrow 3PbCl_2 + Cl_2 + 4H_2O$

(i) Describe how you could show that chlorine was given off during the reaction. [2]

(ii) Suggest how, using an electrical method, you could obtain lead from lead(II) chloride. [3]

(IGCSE, part question, 1994)

14.31 Aluminium compounds are used in water treatment. The table shows the solubility of an aluminium compound in water.

Temperature (°C)	Concentration of dissolved aluminium compound		
	pH 6.0	pH 7.2	pH 8.0
5	2.2	0.1	0.3
15	1.1	0.3	1.2
25	0.8	0.5	4.9

(a) When the temperature is 15 °C, at which pH is the aluminium compound least soluble? [1]

(b) How does the solubility of the aluminium compound change with temperature at pH 6.0? [1]

(c) Iron(III) compounds are also used in water purification. Describe how you could distinguish between a dilute solution of Fe^{3+} ions and a dilute solution of Al^{3+} ions. Outline the test and the result for both ions. [3]

(MEG, part question, 1995)

14.32 Quicklime, CaO, is made by heating limestone, $CaCO_3$, in a rotating kiln.

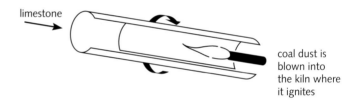

Limestone is added at the top of the kiln. Turning the kiln lets the limestone move slowly downwards as it is heated. Quicklime is formed and is taken from the bottom of the kiln.

(a) Give the chemical name for:
(i) quicklime, [1]
(ii) limestone. [1]

(b) Heat is required for the reaction to take place. What is the name given to reactions that take in heat? [1]

(c) Some students investigated this reaction. They heated a piece of limestone on the edge of a gauze. Describe what they would see. [2]

(d) Some limestone comes from a quarry in a National Park. This quarry is to be extended.
(i) Give *one* problem that may be caused by extending the quarry. [1]
(ii) Suggest *one* way in which the area may benefit from extending the quarry. [1]

(MEG, part question, 1995)

14.33 A student used the following apparatus to investigate the rate of reaction between zinc and hydrochloric acid.

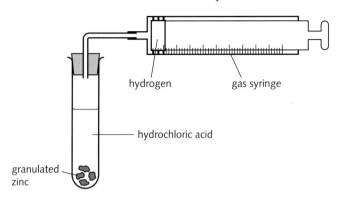

A student carried out two experiments. Information about these is given in the table.

	Experiment 1	Experiment 2
Granulated zinc	excess	excess
Hydrochloric acid	5 cm³ (1 unit concentration)	5 cm³ (1 unit concentration)
Temperature	20 °C	20 °C
Copper sulphate solution	none	few drops

The results are shown on the graph.

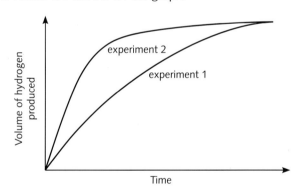

(a) (i) How do you know that experiment 2 has a faster rate than experiment 1? [1]
  (ii) Suggest why this happens. [1]

(b) Suggest why the rate of hydrogen production slows down towards the end of both experiments. [1]

(c) Copy the graph above. Sketch curves on your graph for the results of experiments using the following conditions. Clearly label your curves experiment 3 and experiment 4. [4]

	Experiment 3	Experiment 4
Granulated zinc	excess	excess
Hydrochloric acid	5 cm³ (0.5 unit concentration)	5 cm³ (1 unit concentration)
Temperature	20 °C	40 °C
Copper sulphate solution	none	none

(MEG, 1995)

14.34 This question is about a group of compounds called alkanes.

(a) Copy and complete table I. [4]

Table I

Name of alkane	Formula of alkane	Structure
(i)	CH₄	H–C–H with H above and H below
Ethane	(ii)	(iii)
Propane	C₃H₈	(iv)

(b) Copy the axes for graphs I and II. Use the information in table II on page 382 to complete your graphs I and II.

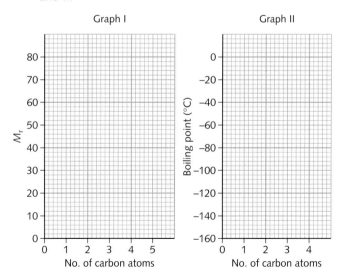

Table II

Number of carbon atoms in alkane molecule	Relative molecular mass of alkane (M_r)	Boiling point of alkane (°C)
1	16	–160
2	30	–90
3	44	
4	58	0
5		

(i) From graph I, estimate the relative molecular mass (M_r) of the alkane with 5 carbon atoms.

(ii) What information is needed, in the absence of the graph, to calculate relative molecular masses?

(iii) From graph II, estimate the boiling point of the alkane with 3 carbon atoms per molecule. [8]

(c) (i) Name *one* naturally occurring material which consists mainly of one alkane.

(ii) Name *one* naturally occurring material which consists of a mixture of many alkanes.

(iii) Name *one* alkane and give a use for it. [3]

(ULEAC, 1992)

14.35 Part of the Periodic Table is given below showing the position of *six* elements. All of those shown are present in air either as elements or in compounds.

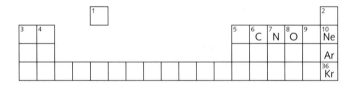

(a) Some of the boxes in the Periodic Table above contain a number.

(i) What is this number called?

(ii) What number should go in the box with argon (Ar)?

(iii) Give *two* pieces of information about the structure of an atom of argon which can be deduced from this number. [4]

(b) (i) Which of the elements shown are in the same group as neon (Ne)?

(ii) What is the name of this group of elements?

(iii) What is the symbol for *one* other element in this group. What box in the table does it go in?

(iv) State *one* property shown by all the members of this group.

(v) State *one* use for a named member of this group. [6]

(c) (i) Which of the six elements shown in the table is *not* found as an element in clean air?

(ii) Name the compound of this element present in unpolluted air.

(iii) State *two* ways in which this compound gets into the air.

(iv) State *one* way in which this compound is removed from air by natural processes. [5]

(d) (i) Which of the six elements shown in the table is the most reactive?

(ii) Write a balanced equation for the reaction of this element with magnesium showing state symbols. [4]

(e) Some older versions of the Periodic Table showed hydrogen above element no. 3 (lithium) and some showed hydrogen above element no. 9 (fluorine).

(i) State *one* similarity in electronic structure between an atom of hydrogen and an atom of lithium.

(ii) From your knowledge of the properties of the other elements in the group containing fluorine, state *two* similarities between hydrogen and fluorine. [3]

(ULEAC, 1992)

14.36 The table below shows the formulas, melting points and pH values of aqueous solutions (when soluble) of the oxides of some elements.

(a) (i) How many of these oxides are solid at a room temperature of 20°C? [1]

(ii) Why does the element with atomic number 18 not have an oxide? [1]

(iii) When sodium oxide is added to water, the solution formed has a pH of 14. Explain the reason for this. [2]

(b) Explain, in terms of the forces present, why chlorine(I) oxide has a low melting point. [2]

(c) Magnesium is manufactured by the electrolysis of molten magnesium chloride.

(i) Use the table to suggest why molten magnesium chloride is used as the electrolyte, rather than molten magnesium oxide. [2]

Atomic (proton) number	11	12	13	14	15	16	17	18
Formula of oxide	Na_2O	MgO	Al_2O_3	SiO_2	P_4O_6	SO_2	Cl_2O	no oxide
Melting point (K)	1193	3173	2313	1883	297	198	253	–
pH of aqueous solution (if soluble)	14	11	insol.	insol.	3	3	3	–

(ii) Name the product at each electrode. [1]

(iii) Write an ionic equation for the reaction that takes place at the cathode of the cell during the electrolysis. [2]

(ULEAC, part question, 1995)

14.37 This question is about metals and alloys. Zinc can be extracted from the ore, zinc-blende, which contains mainly zinc sulphide ZnS. After concentration to remove some impurities, the zinc sulphide is roasted in air to convert it into zinc oxide and sulphur dioxide. The zinc oxide is dissolved in dilute sulphuric acid. Zinc dust is then added to precipitate metal impurities such as cadmium, present as cadmium sulphate. Electrolysis of aqueous zinc sulphate solution produces zinc at an aluminium cathode and oxygen at a lead anode.

(a) (i) Write a symbol equation for the reaction between zinc sulphide and oxygen. [2]

(ii) What environmental impact might the emission of sulphur dioxide have? [1]

(b) Cadmium, atomic number 48, has the electron configuration 2,8,18,18,2 and reacts with sulphuric acid in the same way as does zinc.

(i) Write down the symbol of the cadmium ion. [1]

(ii) Is cadmium more reactive or less reactive than zinc? Give your reason. [1]

(iii) Deduce an ionic equation to show how zinc reacts with cadmium ions. [1]

(iv) Explain why the reaction in (b)(iii) is an example of a redox reaction. [2]

(c) A sample of brass was heated to 500 °C and then quenched by plunging it into cold water. The brass became harder and more brittle. A second sample of the same brass was heated to 500 °C but was then cooled very slowly. The brass became softer and more malleable. Explain why these heat treatments alter the characteristics of the brass. [2]

(MEG, part question, 1995)

14.38

(a) An all-metal Viking sword was discovered. The hilt was not corroded. The iron blade was badly rusted, especially near the hilt.

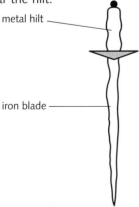

metal hilt

iron blade

(i) Name a metallic element that does not corrode. [1]

(ii) Suggest a reason why the rusting was greatest near the hilt. [1]

(iii) A modern sword blade would be made out of an alloy of iron that does not corrode. What is the name of this alloy and what *two* other elements are in it? [3]

(b) Metals are malleable and can be beaten into the shape of a sword. Why are metals malleable? [2]

(IGCSE, part question, 1994)

14.39 An important polymer is poly(acrylonitrile). The world consumption for this polymer has increased from 0.2 million tonnes in 1960 to 3.8 million tonnes in 1990. Its principal use is as a fibre for clothes and bedding. It is made by the polymerisation of acrylonitrile, $CH_2{=}CH{-}CN$. Acrylonitrile is made by the reaction:

$$2CH_3{-}CH{=}CH_2 + 2NH_3 + 3O_2$$
$$\rightarrow 2CH_2{=}CH{-}CN + 6H_2O$$

(a) Propene is made from the naphtha fraction of hydrocarbons in petroleum. The naphtha fraction is heated in the absence of air:

$$C_{10}H_{22} \rightarrow 2C_3H_6 + \text{hydrocarbon X}$$

(i) What technique is used to obtain the naphtha fraction from petroleum? [1]

(ii) Give the name and structure of hydrocarbon **X**. [2]

(b) The addition polymerisation of acrylonitrile forms poly(acrylonitrile). Draw the structure of poly(acrylonitrile). [2]

(c) The addition polymerisation of propene forms a different polymer.

(i) Name the polymer manufactured from propene by addition polymerisation. [1]

(ii) Suggest a use for this polymer. [1]

(d) Synthetic macromolecules have partially replaced natural products, such as the carbohydrate cotton, for bedding.

(i) Explain what is meant by the term *carbohydrate*. [2]

(ii) Why does the disposal, as rubbish, of a cotton sheet cause fewer environmental problems than the disposal of a poly(acrylonitrile) sheet? [2]

(e) Biomass is plant or animal organic matter. It contains carbohydrates such as glucose, starch and cellulose.
  (i) Name the process by which plants make glucose from carbon dioxide and water. [1]
  (ii) State the conditions necessary for this process to occur. [2]

(f) In plants, glucose molecules (M_r 180) are changed into molecules of starch (M_r 250 000).
  (i) What type of reaction is this? [1]
  (ii) By representing glucose molecules as HO–☐–OH explain how the molecules of starch are formed from the simpler glucose molecules. [2]

(IGCSE, 1994 and part question, 1988)

14.40

(a) Poly(alkenes) are made from petroleum (crude oil) by the following route:

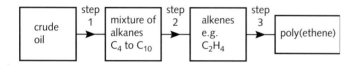

  (i) What is the molecular formula of the alkane which contains ten hydrogen atoms per molecule? [1]
  (ii) The mixture of alkanes contains isomers. Explain the term *isomer* and illustrate your answer by drawing the structural formulas of *two* compounds which are isomers. [4]
  (iii) What is the name of the process used in step 2 to make alkenes? [1]
  (iv) Name the type of reaction in step 3. [1]

(b) A poly(alkene) was decomposed in the apparatus drawn below. One of the products of this decomposition was the gaseous compound **X**.

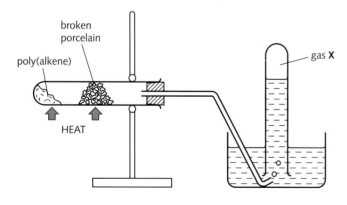

  (i) Gas **X** decolourised aqueous bromine. What is the functional group in this gaseous compound? [1]

(ii) A 10 cm^3 sample of gas **X** needed 45 cm^3 of oxygen for complete combustion and 30 cm^3 of carbon dioxide were produced. By copying out and completing the following equation, work out the formula of gas **X**, which is a hydrocarbon. [2]

…C…H… + …O_2 → …CO_2 + …H_2O

(iii) What is the name of the polymer which could be obtained by polymerising gas **X**? [1]

(IGCSE, 1990)

14.41 The rate of reaction between a metal and bromine can be studied using the apparatus shown below.

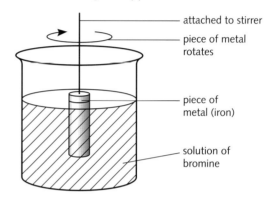

A piece of metal, for example iron, was weighed and placed in the solution as shown above. The metal was removed at regular intervals and each time it was washed, dried and weighed. It was then replaced in the solution and the reaction continued.

From the results (mass of metal and time), the rate of the reaction can be calculated.

(a) (i) How would the rate change if more of the piece of metal was in the solution? Explain your answer. [2]
  (ii) The experiment was conducted using different solutions of bromine. The following results were obtained.

Concentration of bromine solution	Rate
0.05 mol/dm^3	10 mg/minute
0.1 mol/dm^3	20 mg/minute

Explain the change in rate. [2]

(b) In a reaction between a solid and a solution, the rate may depend on the speed of stirring. Describe how you could find out if the rate of the reaction between solid iron and bromine solution depends on the speed of stirring.

(c) Iron has two oxidation states so it can form two ions: Fe^{2+} and Fe^{3+}.
  (i) How could you test a solution to find out which ion is present? Outline the test, and give the result for both ions. [3]

(ii) Copy out and complete the ionic equation for the reaction that forms Fe^{2+}: [2]

$Fe + Br_2 \rightarrow \ldots\ldots\ldots + \ldots\ldots\ldots$

(d) In the reaction between iron and bromine:

iron atoms change into iron ions;
bromine molecules change into bromide ions.

(i) Which of these changes is a reduction? Explain your choice. [2]

(ii) If iodine was used instead of bromine, predict how the rate of the reaction would change: increase, decrease or stay the same. Give a reason for your answer. [2]

(IGCSE, 1995)

Data-handling and comprehension questions

14.8 An eye for detail

Success in science means being able to pick out the detail of a question so as to probe further and understand more of the complex world around us.

Being able to grasp the detail of a topic can be tested by comprehension questions. Many of these questions may be quite long. When faced by such questions, it is essential to read carefully and not be put off by the detail being presented. Many of the answers can be drawn from the question itself, but a good general understanding is needed. Taking a highlighting pen into the examination and using it to pick out relevant points can be useful. Practice can give you a general approach that is not knocked off course by the new angles that come up in these questions. Figure 14.11 is a straightforward example (from MEG, 1995) of how answers are first drawn from the passage, but then built upon.

Also included here are questions that involve data-handling and working out information from flow charts. Some data-handling questions, such as the example in figure 14.12 on page 386 (from IGCSE, 1997), involve interpreting results from experiments.

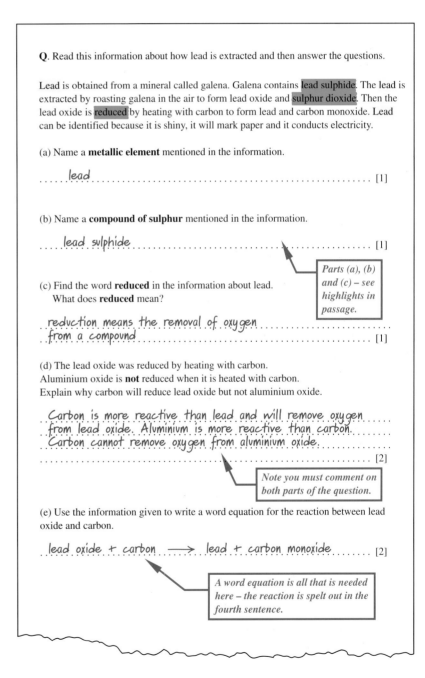

Q. Read this information about how lead is extracted and then answer the questions.

Lead is obtained from a mineral called galena. Galena contains lead sulphide. The lead is extracted by roasting galena in the air to form lead oxide and sulphur dioxide. Then the lead oxide is reduced by heating with carbon to form lead and carbon monoxide. Lead can be identified because it is shiny, it will mark paper and it conducts electricity.

(a) Name a **metallic element** mentioned in the information.

......lead.. [1]

(b) Name a **compound of sulphur** mentioned in the information.

......lead sulphide.. [1]

Parts (a), (b) and (c) – see highlights in passage.

(c) Find the word **reduced** in the information about lead. What does **reduced** mean?

..reduction means the removal of oxygen........
..from a compound.. [1]

(d) The lead oxide was reduced by heating with carbon.
Aluminium oxide is **not** reduced when it is heated with carbon.
Explain why carbon will reduce lead oxide but not aluminium oxide.

..Carbon is more reactive than lead and will remove oxygen....
..from lead oxide. Aluminium is more reactive than carbon......
..Carbon cannot remove oxygen from aluminium oxide...........
.... [2]

Note you must comment on both parts of the question.

(e) Use the information given to write a word equation for the reaction between lead oxide and carbon.

..lead oxide + carbon $\longrightarrow$ lead + carbon monoxide....... [2]

A word equation is all that is needed here – the reaction is spelt out in the fourth sentence.

Figure 14.11 Using a highlighter in a comprehension question can be useful.

Q. A student investigated the reaction of magnesium with dilute hydrochloric acid.

Experiment 1
A 10 cm³ sample of dilute hydrochloric acid was placed in a boiling tube. The initial temperature of the acid was measured. A 2.5 cm length of magnesium ribbon was added to the acid in the boiling tube. The maximum temperature reached was measured. The gas given off was tested and gave a pop with a lighted splint.

(a) Name the gas given off . . . . *hydrogen* . . . . [1]
[2]

(b) Record the temperatures in the space next to the thermometer diagrams.
Initial temperature of hydrochloric acid

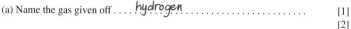

Read the temperature to the nearest first decimal place.

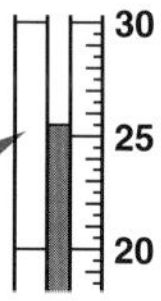

= . . . . *25.5* . . . . °C

Maximum temperature reached when magnesium was added

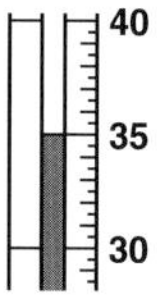

= . . . . *35.0* . . . . °C

Temperature rise produced by 2.5 cm of magnesium ribbon

= . . . . *9.5* . . . . °C

Experiment 2
A 10 cm³ sample of the same hydrochloric acid was added to a boiling tube. The initial temperature of the acid was measured. A 3 cm length of magnesium ribbon was added to the acid in the boiling tube and the maximum temperature reached was measured.

Experiment 3
Experiment 2 was repeated using a 4 cm length of magnesium ribbon.

Experiment 4
Experiment 2 was repeated using a 5 cm length of magnesium ribbon.

Experiment 5
Experiment 2 was repeated using a 6 cm length of magnesium ribbon.

(c) Record the temperatures in the spaces next to the thermometer diagrams shown and calculate the temperature rise in each case. [5]

Do not confuse the experiment number with the length of ribbon used.

experiment	length of ribbon	initial temperature of acid/°C	maximum temperature reached/°C	temperature rise/°C
2	3 cm	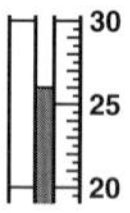 26.0	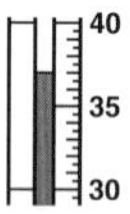 37.0	11.0
3	4 cm	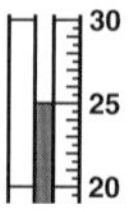 25.0	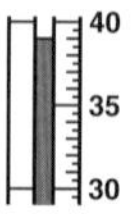 39.0	14.0
4	5 cm	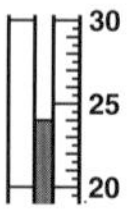 24.0	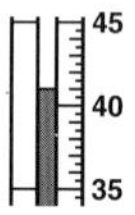 41.0	17.0
5	6 cm	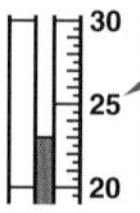 23.0	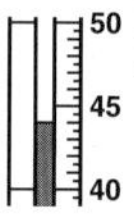 44.0	21.0

Read the temperature to the nearest first decimal place.

Figure 14.12 A typical data-handling question.

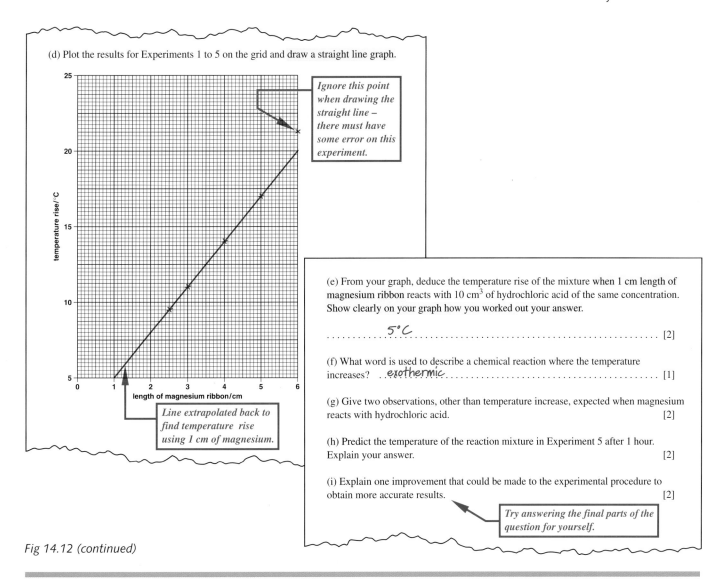

(d) Plot the results for Experiments 1 to 5 on the grid and draw a straight line graph.

Ignore this point when drawing the straight line – there must have some error on this experiment.

Line extrapolated back to find temperature rise using 1 cm of magnesium.

(e) From your graph, deduce the temperature rise of the mixture when 1 cm length of magnesium ribbon reacts with 10 cm^3 of hydrochloric acid of the same concentration. Show clearly on your graph how you worked out your answer.

.... *5°C* .... [2]

(f) What word is used to describe a chemical reaction where the temperature increases? ... *exothermic* .... [1]

(g) Give two observations, other than temperature increase, expected when magnesium reacts with hydrochloric acid. [2]

(h) Predict the temperature of the reaction mixture in Experiment 5 after 1 hour. Explain your answer. [2]

(i) Explain one improvement that could be made to the experimental procedure to obtain more accurate results. [2]

Try answering the final parts of the question for yourself.

Fig 14.12 (continued)

14.42

(a) Study the data below to help you to answer the questions that follow.
In each case give two reasons why:
  (i) the chain on a padlock is made of iron and not of aluminium; [2]
  (ii) deep-sea diving weights are made of lead; [2]
  (iii) silver coins are not made of silver; [2]
  (iv) tins cans are not completely made of tin; [2]
  (v) overhead electrical cables are made of aluminium and not of copper; [2]
  (vi) overhead aluminium electrical cables have a steel core. [2]

Metal	Density in g/cm^3	Melting point in °C	Relative tensile strength*	Relative electrical conductivity*	Reaction if left in air	Relative cost per tonne
Aluminium	2.7	659	☆☆	☆☆☆	corrodes slowly	750
Copper	9.0	1083	☆☆☆☆	☆☆☆☆	corrodes slowly	1 000
Iron	7.9	1540	☆☆☆☆	☆☆	corrodes quickly	130
Lead	11.3	328	☆	☆	corrodes slowly	290
Silver	10.5	961	☆☆☆	☆☆☆☆	corrodes very slowly	150 000
Tin	7.3	232	☆	☆	does not corrode	9 100
Zinc	7.1	420	☆☆☆	☆☆	corrodes slowly	500

* The greater the number of stars in the table, the higher the tensile strength or electrical conductivity.

(b) High purity copper is needed because it is used in electrical wires. You get high purity copper by electrolysis using a thin, pure copper cathode and a solution of copper(II) sulphate.

(The Faraday constant (F) is 96 000 coulombs per mole (C/mol). The relative atomic mass of copper is 64.)

A current of 200 amperes (A) is used for 12 hours. What mass of copper is formed at the cathode? Show clearly how you obtain your answer. [5]

(SEG, 1994)

14.43

(a) The map shows the site where a factory producing sulphuric acid is going to be built. The site for the factory is labelled 'X'.

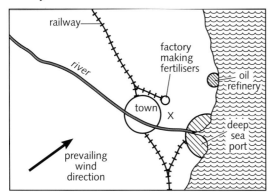

Use the map to help you to answer these questions.

Suggest an advantage of building a factory which produces sulphuric acid near to
   (i) a deep sea port, [1]
   (ii) a factory which produces fertilisers. [1]
   (iii) State and explain *two* other advantages of building the sulphuric acid factory at the site shown on the map. [4]

(b) Dilute sulphuric acid reacts with each of the substances listed in the first column in the table. Name the substances formed and state what you would see. [3]

| Substances | Reaction with dilute sulphuric acid | |
	Name of substances formed	Observations
copper(II) oxide	copper(II) sulphate and water	....
sodium hydroxide solution	.... and	no change seen
barium chloride solution	.... and	white precipitate

(c) Name the type of reaction taking place when dilute sulphuric acid is added to
   (i) sodium hydroxide solution,
   (ii) barium chloride solution. [2]

(d) The equation which represents the reaction between copper(II) oxide and dilute sulphuric acid is:

$$CuO + H_2SO_4 \rightarrow CuSO_4 + H_2O$$

   (i) Calculate the relative formula mass of copper(II) oxide, CuO.
   (ii) Calculate the relative formula mass of copper(II) sulphate, $CuSO_4 \cdot 5H_2O$.
   (iii) Use your answers to (i) and (ii) to calculate the maximum mass of copper(II) sulphate, $CuSO_4 \cdot 5H_2O$, which could be obtained from 8 g of copper(II) oxide. [3]

(NEAB, 1992)

14.44 The following table gives some information about several substances.

| | Melting point (°C) | Boiling point (°C) | Electrical conductivity | | |
			of solid	of liquid	in water
A	37	344	poor	poor	insoluble
B	−114	−85	poor	poor	good
C	614	1382	poor	good	good
D	−60 – −40	40 – 75	poor	poor	insoluble
E	−130	36	poor	poor	insoluble
F	29	685	good	good	good
G	1610	2230	poor	poor	insoluble
H	110 – 135	decomposes	poor	poor	insoluble

Answer the following questions using one of the letters **A** to **H**. Each letter may be used once, more than once or not at all.

Using the list, write the letter of a substance which at 20°C is a

(a) simple molecular solid;

(b) soluble ionic solid;

(c) metal which reacts with water producing ions;

(d) pure liquid containing simple molecules;

(e) gas containing simple molecules which produces ions when added to water;

(f) mixture of liquids. [7]

(NEAB, part question, 1993)

14.45 Two industrial processes (Haber process and contact process) are shown in the diagram. Each process uses air for one of the starting materials.

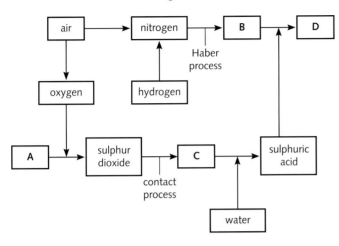

(a) (i) Give the name of the process by which air is separated into oxygen and nitrogen. [1]
 (ii) Give the name of *one* other important product of this process. [1]

(b) Name the substances which are represented by the letters **A**, **B**, **C** and **D**. [4]

(c) Name the catalyst used in
 (i) the Haber process, [1]
 (ii) the contact process. [1]

(d) Give *one* other important use for nitrogen and oxygen and in each case explain why air is not a suitable substance for that particular use. [4]

(WJEC, 1990)

14.46 An investigation was carried out into the energy changes that occur when different metals are added to copper(II) sulphate solution.

Tube	Thermometer diagram	Initial temperature of copper(II) sulphate solution in °C	Metal added	Thermometer diagram	Temperature of mixture after 1 minute in °C	Temperature rise in °C
1	25 / 20		magnesium ribbon	30 / 25		
2	25 / 20		magnesium powder	60 / 55		
3	25 / 20		zinc granules	25 / 20		
4	25 / 20		zinc powder	45 / 40		
5	20 / 15		iron granules	20 / 15		
6	20 / 15		iron powder	35 / 30		

$3\,cm^3$ of copper(II) sulphate solution was added to each of six test tubes and the temperature of each solution was taken. An equal amount of metal was added to each test tube, the contents stirred, and the temperature of the mixtures noted after one minute.

(a) Use the thermometer diagrams to write down the values that complete the results table. [6]

(b) Draw a bar chart on graph paper to show the temperature rise for each of the six metal samples.

You will need to work out a scale for the temperature axis.

[4]

(c) What *two* observations, apart from temperature changes, would be made when magnesium is added to copper(II) sulphate solution? [2]

(d) State *three* conclusions that you can draw from all the results to these experiments. Explain how you arrived at each conclusion. [6]

(SEG, 1992)

14.47 The reduction of silver bromide to silver is the basis of photography. A film can consist of a polyester base coated with gelatine. In the coating of gelatine there are crystals of silver bromide.

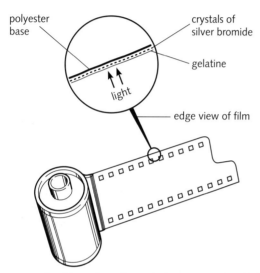

The places on the film which have been exposed to light change from white to grey to black. The unexposed silver bromide stays white. The reaction that occurs is:

$$2AgBr \rightarrow 2Ag + Br_2$$

white   black

(a) (i) Give the name and draw the structure of a polyester. [3]
   (ii) What is the name of the linkage that is found in all proteins, such as gelatine, and in the synthetic macromolecule nylon? [1]
   (iii) Name the type of compound formed when a protein is hydrolysed. Name the experimental technique that is used to identify these compounds. [2]

(b) In crystals of silver bromide, the ions Ag^+ and Br^- are arranged in a simple cubic lattice.
   (i) Draw the arrangement of ions in the lattice. [2]
   (ii) The overall reaction is thought to happen in two steps. In the first step, energy from the light brings about the change
   $$2Br^- \rightarrow Br_2 + 2e^-$$
   What type of reaction is this? [1]
   (iii) Write an equation for the second step which is the reduction of silver ions to silver. [1]

(iv) Explain why a film which has been exposed to dim light changes to grey and why, when the film is exposed to brighter light for the same time, it turns black. [2]

(c) Silver is recycled, as are most metals. Silver is recovered from aqueous solutions in film-processing laboratories. Zinc is added to the solution containing silver ions. Silver and unreacted zinc are filtered off. An excess of hydrochloric acid is added to this mixture of metals and, after filtering, silver is obtained.
   (i) Give an environmental reason for recycling metals. [1]
   (ii) Silver is below copper in the reactivity series. Explain the chemistry of this method of recovering silver using zinc and then an acid. [3]

(IGCSE, 1990)

14.48 Read the following passage and answer the questions which follow.

Until 1985 chemists believed that there were only two allotropes of carbon. In 1985 a third allotrope, buckminsterfullerene, was identified. The diagram shows the structure of a molecule of buckminsterfullerene. Each circle represents one carbon atom.

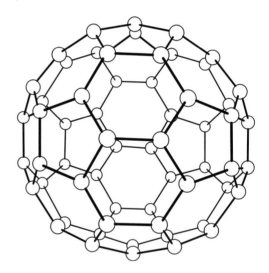

The molecule has 60 carbon atoms covalently bonded together, to give a structure with a shape similar to a modern football. The formula of buckminsterfullerene is C_{60}.

(a) (i) Explain what is meant by the word *allotrope*. [2]
   (ii) Name the other *two* allotropes of carbon. [2]
   (iii) State the name of *one* compound which could be produced by burning buckminsterfullerene in air. [1]

(b) (i) Calculate the relative formula mass of buckminsterfullerene. [1]
   (Relative atomic mass: C = 12)
   (ii) Use your answer to part (b)(i) to help you to calculate the number of moles of buckminsterfullerene in 3600 grams of the substance. [1]

(iii) Buckminsterfullerene vaporises at temperatures above 400°C. Suggest, in terms of structure, why buckminsterfullerene might be expected to vaporise at a much lower temperature than the other allotropes of carbon. [1]

(c) Buckminsterfullerene is soluble in an organic solvent unlike the other allotropes of carbon. What is meant by an *organic solvent*? [2]

(d) Suggest a reason why molecules like buckminsterfullerene might increase the lubricating ability of engine oil. [1]

(NEAB, 1992)

14.49 Read the following newspaper account about biofuels and answer the questions which follow.

Hot rod car enthusiasts may soon be screeching into garages and filling up with the latest super petrol – made from the humble potato.

Biofuels – produced from potatoes, sugar beet and oil seeds – are set to be given a big tax boost by European Community leaders.

EC experts say biofuels could mean less pollution from carbon dioxide emissions and a new outlet for the community's agriculture.

Bioethanol is produced by fermenting sugar from sugar beet or starch from potatoes and is already propelling a quarter of Brazil's cars. About one million vehicles are running successfully on petrol containing up to 20 per cent bioethanol.

If the new fuels take off experts predict a five per cent drop in the use of conventional fossil fuels in ten years, with a consequent reduction in carbon dioxide emissions – the major cause of the greenhouse effect.

Express & Star, Saturday, 14 March 1992

(a) Explain what is meant by
   (i) a fossil fuel, [1]
   (ii) the greenhouse effect. [2]

(b) Ethanol and bioethanol are the same substance. Suggest why the newspaper account uses the term *bioethanol*. [1]

(c) (i) Briefly describe how a solution of ethanol can be made in the laboratory from sugar by fermentation. [3]
   (ii) Name the method used to obtain almost pure ethanol from this fermented solution. [1]
   (iii) The equation which represents the fermentation reaction is
   $C_6H_{12}O_6 \rightarrow 2C_2H_5OH + 2CO_2$
   Calculate how many tonnes of ethanol can be made from 45 tonnes of sugar. [3]

   (Relative atomic masses: H = 1, C = 12, O = 16)

(d) Write the equation for the complete combustion of ethanol when used as a fuel in car engines. [2]

(e) Suggest why using plants to produce biofuels helps to maintain the carbon dioxide/oxygen balance in the atmosphere. [1]

(NEAB, 1993)

14.50 Over seventy of the known elements are metals. Only about half of them are of any great economic importance. The rest are either found in very small quantities or have no practical use at present. This position may change as further scientific development occurs. For example, before the Second World War the only use of uranium was in making yellow glass. Uranium is now in world-wide demand.

Only a few metal elements occur free in nature. Most metals occur in compounds. Metals like gold, silver and copper that occur free have been used for a very long time. Other metals, like tin, known in early times, were those that could be easily extracted from their compounds. Bronze, an alloy of tin and copper, was used so much that it gave its name to the Bronze Age. Iron was more difficult to extract from iron ore so that weapons and tools were not made from iron until later.

(a) (i) What was the main use of uranium before the Second World War?
   (ii) Why is uranium in considerable demand today?
   (iii) Suggest *two* reasons why about half of the known metal elements are not of economic importance.
   (iv) Why are metals like gold and copper found free in nature?
   (v) Suggest *two* reasons why iron replaced bronze as the major tool-making material. [7]

Metals high in the reactivity series, like aluminium, are obtained from their ores by electrolysis. Aluminium is a very useful element. It is the most abundant metal in the Earth's crust. The main ore is bauxite which is found in Africa, Australia and America. Bauxite (Al_2O_3) melts at 2045°C. In 1886 it was discovered that molten cryolite would dissolve bauxite. The melting point of this mixture is 900°C. This discovery enabled aluminium to be extracted on a commercial basis.

(b) (i) Why is it not possible to extract reactive metals like aluminium from their ores by simple chemical means?
   (ii) What discovery made it possible to produce aluminium on an economic basis?
   (iii) Suggest reasons why aluminium extraction plants are usually found near power stations or coalfields and deep water ports.
   (iv) Suggest *two* reasons why aluminium is preferred to copper for use in overhead power cables even though copper is the better electrical conductor.

(v) Suggest why aluminium is not obtained by the electrolysis of a solution of an aluminium compound in water. [9]

(c) Many drink cans are now made from aluminium. There are collection sites for used cans so that the metal can be recycled. What factors must be considered when deciding whether aluminium cans should be recycled? [5]

(d) Magnesium is extracted from molten magnesium chloride by electrolysis. The process is similar to the extraction of aluminium from bauxite.

In the extraction of magnesium:

(i) at which electrode will magnesium be produced?
(ii) which gas will be produced in the extraction process?
(iii) why are special precautions required to remove this gas?

It is dangerous to allow molten magnesium to come into contact with water.

(iv) What gas is produced when magnesium reacts with water?
(v) Why is this gas dangerous? [5]

(ULEAC, 1991)

14.51 Read the following passage before answering the questions which follow.

ZINC
(Modified from: *The Essential Chemical Industry*, The Chemical Industry Centre, University of York, 1989.)

Zinc is a common metal whose uses are given in the pie chart below. Annually throughout the world 6 000 000 tonnes are produced of which 200 000 tonnes are produced in the United Kingdom.

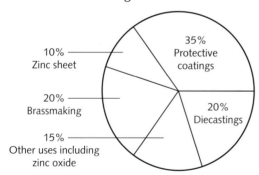

The main ore used for the extraction of zinc is zinc blende (ZnS). It is often found with the main ore for lead, galena (PbS), which also contains enough silver for extraction. In addition to silver both ores contain other metal impurities. The metals are separated during the extraction processes. Initially the mixture of both ores is heated strongly in air to produce the metal oxides:

$2ZnS + 3O_2 \rightarrow 2ZnO + 2SO_2$

$2PbS + 3O_2 \rightarrow 2PbO + 2SO_2$

The zinc is then extracted by either an electrolytic process or by a thermal process.

Electrolytic process
The metal oxides mixture is added to a hot solution of dilute sulphuric acid, allowed to react, and then filtered. Powdered zinc is added to the filtrate and this precipitates many metal impurities including cadmium and silver. Cadmium is also a valuable by-product from this reaction.

The zinc sulphate solution is then transferred to the electrolytic cell and electrolysed. Zinc is discharged at the cathode and oxygen at the anode:

$4OH^-(aq) \rightarrow 2H_2O(l) + O_2(g) + 4e^-$

Periodically the zinc is removed from the cathode, melted and cast into ingots. The zinc produced by this process is 99.96% pure. The liquid remaining in the cell at the end of the process contains a high percentage of sulphuric acid.

Thermal process
The roasted lead and zinc oxides, hot coke, and hot air are fed into a blast furnace, similar to that used for the extraction of iron. The lead and zinc oxides are reduced by carbon monoxide. The operating temperature of the furnace is between 1000°C and 1500°C.

(a) (i) What percentage of zinc is used to make an alloy with copper? [1]
(ii) What mass of the zinc produced in the United Kingdom is used in protective coatings? [2]

(b) Write a balanced symbol equation for the reaction which converts the zinc oxide into a soluble zinc compound used in the electrolytic process. [2]

(c) The lead and zinc compounds in the electrolytic process are separated by adding the oxide mixture to dilute sulphuric acid. Explain how this occurs. [4]

(d) What can you deduce about the position of cadmium compared with zinc in the reactivity series? Explain your answer. [2]

(e) The percentage of silver in galena is about 5%. Why is this extracted? [1]

(f) State whether the formation of zinc at the cathode is oxidation or reduction. Explain your answer. [2]

(g) Explain how carbon monoxide is produced in the thermal process. [3]

(h) Write a balanced symbol equation for the reaction to produce zinc in the blast furnace. [2]

	Lead	Zinc
Melting point (°C)	328	420
Boiling point (°C)	1751	908

(i) Using the above information suggest how the lead and zinc can be separated and removed from the blast furnace. [4]

(NISEAC, 1992)

14.52 You do not need to know anything about the extraction of sulphur in order to answer this question. Read the information carefully and then use it to answer the questions.

Sulphur is a yellow solid with a density approximately twice that of water and a melting point of 112 °C. It is insoluble in water.

Sulphur can be extracted from underground deposits. The process is similar to drilling for oil as the sulphur is brought up as a liquid. Very hot water is pumped down to the sulphur deposits. The water is under pressure so that its temperature can be made greater than 100 °C. Hot air is also blown down and the frothy mixture of air, water and sulphur is forced to the surface, as shown in the diagram. The mixture then goes to settling tanks where the sulphur separates and solidifies.

(a) The boiling point of water at different pressures, in atmospheres, is shown in the table:

Pressure (atm)	1	2	3	4	5	6	7
B.p. (°C)	100	121	134	144	152	159	166

(i) Plot a graph of boiling point (b.p.) against pressure. [4]
Use this graph, where necessary, to answer the questions which follow.

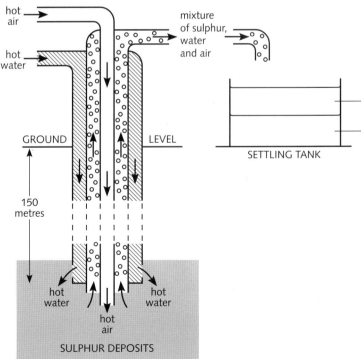

(ii) What is the lowest temperature at which the water could bring liquid sulphur up the pipe? [1]
(iii) What pressure must be applied to the water to bring its boiling point to this temperature? [1]

(b) The water is normally used at temperatures of at least 155 °C.
(i) What pressure must be applied to bring the boiling point of water to 155 °C? [1]
(ii) Suggest why such a high temperature is used. [2]
(iii) Suggest why the hot water is in the *outermost* tube. [1]

(c) The diagram shows a settling tank with two layers.
(i) Why are there *two* layers? [1]
(ii) Say what the two layers contain and explain your answer. [2]

(ULEAC, 1993)

14.53 *Polymers and plastics*

Polymers and plastics are made by joining together hundreds of small molecules called monomers into long chains. Poly(ethene) (polythene), which has an average molecular mass of 140 000, is made from the alkene, ethene, obtained from the thermal cracking of petroleum fractions. Polythene is a very long chain alkane and its many uses depend on its lack of reactivity. Poly(propene) (polypropylene) and PVC are two other common polymers made from petroleum fractions.

Their lack of reactivity makes polymers and plastics very difficult to recycle and also to separate from other materials such as metals. In the assembly of the average car 150 kg of plastics are used. This helps to reduce the overall mass of the car and improves fuel consumption but makes recycling of scrap cars more difficult.

The chemical industry is developing new methods of recycling plastics. For example, it is now possible to separate PVC from other plastics using a machine which includes an X-ray source to detect the chlorine present. However, most used plastics are still dumped in rubbish tips although some are burned in large incinerators where the energy produced is used for local heating schemes. The burning of PVC produces hydrogen chloride gas which dissolves in rain water.

(a) Why are polymers and plastics difficult to recycle? [1]

(b) Why is it important to find new methods for recycling polymers and plastics? [1]

(c) Give *one* advantage and *one* disadvantage of burning polymers and plastics in incinerators. [2]

(d) Give the advantage to the motorist of using plastics in cars. [1]

(e) Give *one* use of
   (i) polythene,
   (ii) PVC. [2]

(f) Explain the meaning of the term 'thermal cracking'. [2]

(g) (i) Draw the structural formula of ethene. [2]
   (ii) Calculate the relative molecular mass of ethene. [2]
       (Relative atomic masses: H = 1, C = 12)
   (iii) Calculate the number of ethene molecules, on average, which join together to form a polythene chain. [2]

(h) (i) What do the letters PVC stand for? [2]
   (ii) Draw the structure of the monomer used to make PVC. [2]
   (iii) Draw the structure of the polymer PVC. [2]

(NISEAC, 1993)

14.54 The flow chart below summarises a series of chemical reactions of sodium and its compounds.

(a) Which of the chemicals in the flow chart is used:
   (i) to make soap?
   (ii) in the production of glass?
   (iii) for de-icing roads?
   (iv) as an antacid?
   (v) as a fertiliser? [5]

(b) Describe what would be observed in reaction 1 on the flow chart. [3]

(c) (i) Name solution **A**. [1]
   (ii) Give balanced symbol equations for any *two* of the three reactions shown involving solution **A**. [4]

(d) Describe the method by which you would make a neutral solution of sodium chloride from sodium hydroxide solution in the laboratory. [4]

(e) Name the solid **B** on the flow chart. [1]

(f) Describe what would be observed in reaction 2 on the flow chart. [2]

(g) (i) Name the product **C**. [1]
   (ii) Give a balanced symbol equation for the reaction in which product **C** is formed. [2]

(NISEAC, 1991)

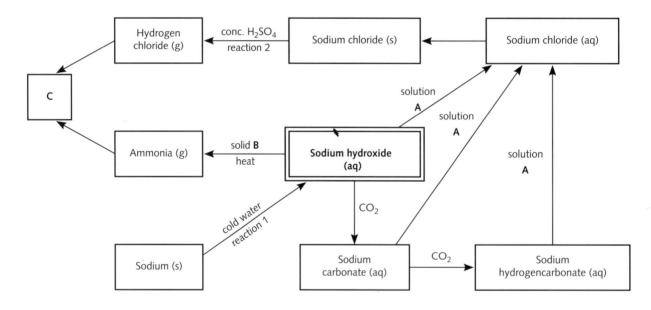

Flow Chart

Answers to questions

14.1 C   **14.2** D   **14.3** A   **14.4** A

14.5 D   **14.6** B   **14.7** C   **14.8** D

14.9 B   **14.10** B   **14.11** D

14.12 (a) Between G and C $NaOH + HCl \rightarrow NaCl + H_2O$
       (b) Between D and E $Ba(OH)_2 + H_2SO_4$
                   $\rightarrow BaSO_4 + 2H_2O$
       (c) I with C or E   (d) H with C or E

14.13 D   **14.14** B   **14.15** B   **14.16** B

14.17 D   **14.18** C   **14.19** D   **14.20** E

14.21 (a) B and E   (b) A   (c) C   (d) B and E   (e) D

14.22 D   **14.23** D   **14.24** C   **14.25** C

14.26 A   **14.27** A   **14.28** A

14.29 (a) (i) Beaker; inverted (upside-down) filter funnel
         (ii) Place a lighted splint in the gas, at the mouth of the test tube, and there should be a small explosion – a 'squeaky pop'.
         (iii) The magnesium would be tarnished. The metal would have lost its shine. The metal would have gained a white coating.
         (iv) Magnesium + water
                 $\rightarrow$ magnesium hydroxide + hydrogen
         (v) Break the magnesium into small pieces or powder it. Warm and stir the reaction mixture.
         (vi) The indicator turns blue, indicating that the solution is alkaline.
       (b) (i) Heat is conducted through the glass and causes the water to boil.
         (ii) Water vapour
         (iii) Zinc would be less reactive than magnesium but would still give hydrogen. Copper would not react.
         (iv) Sodium is too reactive. The reaction would be too dangerous to attempt.
       (c) (i) The first gas jar would contain the air pushed out of the flask and tubing.
         (ii) Magnesium + sulphuric acid
                 $\rightarrow$ magnesium sulphate + hydrogen

14.30 (a) $\underline{6}PbO + O_2 \rightarrow \underline{2}Pb_3O_4$
       (b) Any two from: galvanising the iron; tin- or chromium-plating; sacrificial protection using magnesium blocks.
       (c) (i) Place a glowing splint (spill) at the mouth of the tube. The splint should relight.
         (ii) A glowing splint applied to the mouth of the tube would no longer relight, showing that oxygen was no longer being produced.
       (d) (i) A piece of moist (damp) blue litmus paper placed in the gas would turn (first red and then) white. It would be bleached.
         (ii) The lead(II) chloride is placed in a crucible

and melted. Two graphite electrodes connected to a battery are placed in the molten salt. Silvery molten lead is produced at the cathode (negative electrode).

14.31 (a) pH 7.2
       (b) The solubility decreases with increasing temperature.
       (c) The test is to add sodium hydroxide solution (NaOH(aq)) to the solutions. With a solution containing Fe^{3+} ions, a red-brown precipitate of iron(III) hydroxide is formed – the precipitate does not redissolve in excess alkali. With a solution containing Al^{3+} ions, a white precipitate of aluminium hydroxide is formed – this precipitate will redissolve in excess alkali.

14.32 (a) (i) Calcium oxide
         (ii) Calcium carbonate
       (b) Endothermic reactions
       (c) The piece of limestone would glow and begin to crumble (become powdery).
       (d) (i) Increased damage to (scarring of) the landscape; or new access roads may need to be built; or increased amount of dust produced.
         (ii) More jobs to the area; or a better road network developed.

14.33 (a) (i) Early in experiment 2 more hydrogen is produced in a given time than in experiment 1.
         (ii) The copper sulphate acts as a catalyst. Other aspects of the two experiments are identical.
       (b) As the reaction goes on, the amount of reacting substances (reactants) present gets smaller. So the speed of the reaction slows down as the particles collide less often.
       (c) Experiment 3 – Line will be less steep than experiment 1 at the start, and will flatten out (plateau) at half the level of experiment 1. Experiment 4 – Line will be steeper than experiment 1 and will flatten sooner, but at the same level as experiment 1.

14.34 (a) (i) Methane;   (ii) C_2H_6;

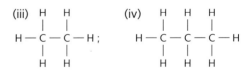

       (b) Complete the graphs to obtain two curves.
         (i) 72
         (ii) The general formula of the alkanes (C_nH_{2n+2}) and the relative atomic masses of carbon and hydrogen.
         (iii) Draw a line for three carbon atoms (C_3) up to meet the curve, then read across: $-42\,°C$.

(c) (i) Natural gas
(ii) Crude oil
(iii) Butane – bottled gas
Methane – gas heating
Hexane – solvent

14.35 (a) (i) The atomic number
(ii) 18
(iii) There are 18 protons in the argon nucleus; and 18 electrons in the argon atom.
(b) (i) Argon (Ar), krypton (Kr)
(ii) The noble gases
(iii) Put in helium (He) above Ne.
(iv) They are all unreactive gases.
(v) Helium – used in weather balloons. Neon – used in advertising lights.
(c) (i) Carbon
(ii) Carbon dioxide
(iii) Burning of fossil fuels, respiration
(iv) Photosynthesis by plants and trees
(d) (i) Oxygen
(ii) $2Mg(s) + O_2(g) \rightarrow 2MgO(s)$
(e) (i) Both hydrogen and lithium have one electron in the outer shell of their atoms.
(ii) Both hydrogen and fluorine exist as diatomic elements (H_2 and F_2). Both have a valency of 1 in covalent compounds (both can form an X^- ion).

14.36 (a) (i) Five: Na_2O, MgO, Al_2O_3, SiO_2, P_4O_6
(ii) This element is a noble gas and is unreactive.
(iii) Sodium oxide reacts with water to give sodium hydroxide, which is a strong alkali.
(b) In chlorine(ɪ) oxide there are strong covalent bonds in the molecules but only weak forces between the molecules. Not much heat energy is needed to break these weak forces and so the melting point is low.
(c) (i) Magnesium oxide has a very high melting point. A large amount of energy would be needed to melt it. Magnesium chloride has a lower melting point and needs less energy to melt it. It is less expensive in energy costs to use magnesium chloride.
(ii) Magnesium at the cathode; chlorine at the anode.
(iii) $Mg^{2+} + 2e^- \rightarrow Mg$

14.37 (a) (i) $2ZnS + 3O_2 \rightarrow 2ZnO + 2SO_2$
(ii) SO_2 is an acidic gas and one of the main causes of acid rain.
(b) (i) Cd^{2+}
(ii) Cadmium is less reactive than zinc. It is below zinc in the transition elements. These metals get less reactive towards the bottom of the Periodic Table.
(iii) $Zn(s) + Cd^{2+}(aq) \rightarrow Zn^{2+}(aq) + Cd(s)$

(iv) It is a redox reaction because electrons have been gained and lost: Zn has lost electrons and been oxidised; cadmium ions have gained electrons and been reduced.
(c) When the brass is cooled quickly, the crystals are small and there are more grain boundaries along which the metal can break. So this brass is hard but brittle. When the brass is cooled slowly, the grains are larger. There are fewer grain boundaries and the brass is more malleable and softer.

14.38 (a) (i) Aluminium (or chromium)
(ii) Water would collect at the joint between the hilt and the blade.
(iii) Stainless steel; chromium and carbon
(b) Metals are malleable because the layers of atoms can slide over each other when forced without the metallic bonding being broken.

14.39 (a) (i) Fractional distillation
(ii) Butane (C_4H_{10})

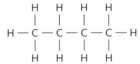

(b)

(c) (i) Poly(propene)
(ii) Crates and piping
(d) (i) A carbohydrate is a compound that contains only carbon, hydrogen and oxygen. The hydrogen and the oxygen atoms are in the ratio 2:1.
(ii) Cotton is a biodegradable condensation polymer. Poly(acrylonitrile) is a synthetic non-biodegradable polymer – when it is burnt there is the risk of poisonous fumes being given off.
(e) (i) Photosynthesis
(ii) The reaction requires sunlight and the presence of chlorophyll in green leaves. Chlorophyll is a light-absorbing molecule and captures the energy from sunlight.
(f) (i) Condensation polymerisation
(ii) See the text and diagram in the subsection on 'Carbohydrates' in section 12.9, page 343.

14.40 (a) (i) C_4H_{10}
(ii) Isomers are compounds with the same molecular formula but different structural formulas.
See the structures of 2-methylpropane and

butane in the subsection on 'Isomerism' in section 11.5, for example on page 309.

    (iii) Catalytic cracking

    (iv) Polymerisation

  (b) (i) A $C=C$ double bond is present.

    (ii) $\underline{2}C_3H_6 + \underline{9}O_2 \rightarrow \underline{6}CO_2 + \underline{6}H_2O$
        10 cm³   45 cm³   30 cm³

      Formula: C_3H_6

    (iii) Poly(propene)

14.41 (a) (i) The rate of reaction would be increased. A greater surface area of the metal would be in contact with the solution. This increases the chance of reaction.

    (ii) The rate of the reaction increases with the increased concentration of the solution. As the solution concentration is doubled, so is the rate of reaction.

  (b) All the conditions between the two experiments are kept constant – the solution concentrations, the depth to which the metal is dipped, and the temperature. The only change made is in the speed of stirring – one experiment is double the speed of the other. The rate of reaction is measured for the two experiments.

  (c) (i) The solutions are tested with sodium hydroxide solution. With Fe^{2+} in the solution, a dirty green, gelatinous precipitate is formed, which does not dissolve in excess alkali. With Fe^{3+} in solution, a red-brown, gelatinous precipitate is formed, which does not dissolve in excess alkali.

    (ii) $Fe + Br_2 \rightarrow Fe^{2+} + 2Br^-$

  (d) (i) Bromine molecules changing to bromide ions is a reduction because electrons are being gained.

    (ii) The reaction would be slower. Iodine is less reactive than bromine (iodine is a weaker oxidising agent than bromine).

14.42 (a) (i) Iron has a higher tensile strength and a lower relative cost than aluminium.

    (ii) Lead has a high density and only corrodes slowly.

    (iii) Silver would be too expensive and too heavy to carry.

    (iv) Tin is relatively expensive and not very strong.

    (v) Aluminium is less dense and less expensive than copper.

    (vi) The steel core strengthens the cable and conducts electricity better than aluminium.

  (b) Total charge passed is
$$Q = It = 200 \times (12 \times 60 \times 60)$$
$$= 8\,640\,000\,C$$
Number of moles of electrons
$$= 8\,640\,000/96\,000 = 90\,mol$$

$Cu^{2+} + 2e^- \rightarrow Cu$
2 mol electrons $\rightarrow$ 1 mol of Cu
Moles of Cu produced = 90/2 = 45 mol
1 mol Cu = 64 g
Mass of copper produced = 45 × 64 = 2880 g
(2.88 kg)

14.43 (a) (i) For the import of sulphur by tanker.

    (ii) The sulphuric acid produced could be used to make ammonium sulphate or phosphoric acid.

    (iii) Good rail links to other parts of the country are needed for transport of materials to and from the factory. The prevailing wind direction will carry any leakage of polluting gases out to sea and away from land and centres of population.

  (b) First row: black solid dissolves, blue solution formed.
Second row: sodium sulphate and water.
Third row: barium sulphate and hydrochloric acid.

  (c) (i) Neutralisation

    (ii) Precipitation

  (d) (i) M_r of $CuO = 64 + 16 = 80$

    (ii) M_r of $CuSO_4 \cdot 5H_2O = 64 + 32 + 64 + 90$
      $= 250$

    (iii) From equation:
    1 mol $CuO \rightarrow$ 1 mol $CuSO_4 \cdot 5H_2O$
    80 g $CuO \rightarrow$ 250 g $CuSO_4 \cdot 5H_2O$
    8 g $CuO \rightarrow$ 25 g of $CuSO_4 \cdot 5H_2O$ crystals

14.44 (a) A   (b) C   (c) F   (d) E
    (e) B   (f) D

14.45 (a) (i) Fractional distillation of liquid air

    (ii) Argon

  (b) A – sulphur; B – ammonia; C – sulphur trioxide; D – ammonium sulphate

  (c) (i) Finely divided iron

    (ii) Vanadium(v) oxide

  (d) Nitrogen – As a refrigerant. Air would not have a precise, well-defined freezing point.
Oxygen – In oxy-acetylene welding torches. Air would not give as hot a flame.

14.46 (a) See table below

Experiment	Initial temperature (°C)	Temperature after 1 minute of reaction (°C)	Temperature rise (°C)
1	20.0	29.0	9.0
2	20.5	56.0	35.5
3	19.0	25.0	6.0
4	21.0	41.0	20.0
5	18.5	20.0	1.5
6	19.5	34.5	15.0

(b) Draw a suitable bar chart with appropriate scales.

(c) The blue colour of the copper sulphate solution would fade. A brown precipitate would form on the magnesium.

(d) (i) All these three metals are more reactive than copper, as they all displace copper from copper sulphate. There is an exothermic reaction in each case.

    (ii) Powdering the metals produces a faster reaction. The temperature increase during the first minute is greater for each metal when they are powdered.

    (iii) The reactivity of the metals in order of increasing reactivity is: iron < zinc < magnesium. The temperature rise produced is greatest for magnesium and least for iron.

14.47 (a) (i) Terylene

$$\left(\!\!-O-\boxed{CH_2-CH_2}-O-\overset{\overset{\displaystyle O}{\|}}{C}-\left(\!C_6H_4\!\right)-C-O-\!\!\right)_n$$

    (ii) The amide (peptide) link

    (iii) Amino acids; chromatography

(b) (i) Draw alternating Ag^+ and Br^- ions in a lattice – similar to the arrangement for sodium chloride shown in figure 3.22 on page 91.

    (ii) Oxidation

    (iii) $Ag^+ + e^- \rightarrow Ag$

    (iv) The more light shines on a region of the film, the more silver (Ag) is produced, which darkens the film in that area.

(c) (i) The conservation of limited, non-renewable resources.

    (ii) Zinc is more reactive than silver and displaces it from a solution of silver salts. A precipitate of silver is formed on the zinc. After filtering, the unreacted zinc and silver are treated with acid. Silver does not react but the zinc does. The zinc forms soluble zinc chloride; the silver can be filtered off.

14.48 (a) (i) Allotropes are different structural forms of the same element in a particular physical state. They have different physical properties.

    (ii) Diamond and graphite

    (iii) Carbon dioxide

(b) (i) C_{60}, $M_r = 12 \times 60 = 720$

    (ii) 1 mol buckminsterfullerene = 720 g
Number of moles in 3600 g = 3600/720 = 5 mol

    (iii) Diamond and graphite are both giant molecular structures. Buckminsterfullerene is made up of smaller units, and is a simple molecular structure.

(c) An organic solvent is a liquid that will dissolve covalent substances. It is made up of covalent molecules, mainly containing carbon, hydrogen and possibly oxygen atoms.

(d) The small, bead-shaped molecules of buckminsterfullerene would be dispersed throughout the oil and would help the parts move over each other.

14.49 (a) (i) A fossil fuel is a carbon-containing fuel produced underground by the action of heat and pressure on dead organic material. It is produced over geological periods of time.

    (ii) This is the effect by which heat from the Sun is trapped in the Earth's atmosphere rather than reflected back out into space. Gases such as water vapour and carbon dioxide are responsible for absorbing this heat.

(b) The ethanol used was made from a biological source.

(c) (i) A solution containing carbohydrate material (sugars) is mixed with yeast at 35–40°C. Enzymes in the yeast convert the sugar into ethanol and carbon dioxide. The final solution contains about 12% ethanol.

    (ii) Fractional distillation

    (iii) M_r for glucose = 72 + 12 + 96 = 180
M_r for ethanol = 24 + 6 + 16 = 46
From equation:
1 mol glucose $\rightarrow$ 2 mol ethanol
180 g glucose $\rightarrow$ 92 g ethanol
180 tonnes glucose $\rightarrow$ 92 tonnes ethanol
45 tonnes glucose $\rightarrow$ (92 × 45)/180 = 23 tonnes ethanol

(d) $C_2H_5OH + 3O_2 \rightarrow 2CO_2 + 3H_2O$

(e) One is the reverse of the other. The burning of biofuels uses oxygen from the air and produces carbon dioxide. The growth of plants uses carbon dioxide and produces oxygen.

14.50 (a) (i) For making yellow glass

    (ii) It is used as a nuclear fuel for power stations.

    (iii) Some metals cannot be extracted in usable amounts. Other metals have no practical use.

    (iv) Because they are relatively unreactive.

    (v) Iron was harder and stronger. Iron ore was more abundant.

(b) (i) These metals are too reactive and chemical reducing agents are not strong enough to remove oxygen from the ores.

    (ii) Molten cryolite dissolves bauxite, reducing the working temperature of the cell.

(iii) The extraction requires a large amount of electrical energy so the extraction plants need to be near sources of cheap electricity.

(iv) Aluminium cables are stronger and less dense.

(v) Aluminium is too reactive and hydrogen, not aluminium, would be obtained at the cathode.

(c) Factors include the following.
- Can the aluminium cans be easily collected and separated from the other cans? Yes, if necessary, as most other cans are made of steel and can be picked out with a magnet.
- Can the cans be crushed and transported easily?
- Can the cans be melted easily and at a lower energy cost than making new aluminium?
- Is the aluminium easy to re-mould?
- Is the ore in sufficiently limited supply to be worth protecting in this way?
- Is the demand for aluminium high enough?

(d) (i) The cathode (negative electrode)
(ii) Chlorine gas
(iii) Chlorine is a toxic gas, damaging to the lungs.
(iv) Hydrogen
(v) Hydrogen burns and forms explosive mixtures with air.

14.51 (a) (i) 20%
(ii) $(35 \times 200\,000)/100 = 70\,000$ tonnes
(b) $ZnO + H_2SO_4 \rightarrow ZnSO_4 + H_2O$
(c) Both oxides react with the sulphuric acid to give metal sulphates. Zinc sulphate is soluble, but lead sulphate is insoluble and this stops the reaction. The zinc sulphate solution can be separated from the insoluble lead oxide by filtration.
(d) Cadmium is below zinc in the reactivity series. It is displaced from its salt solutions by the addition of zinc.
(e) The high selling price of silver covers the high cost of extraction.
(f) Reduction – because electrons have been gained.
(g) The carbon reacts with oxygen in the air to produce carbon dioxide. This is then reduced to carbon monoxide by reaction with more carbon.
(h) $ZnO + CO \rightarrow Zn + CO_2$
(i) Zinc can be distilled off, as its boiling temperature is below that of the furnace. Lead would run off as a liquid, as its melting point is below that of the furnace but its boiling point is above the furnace temperature.

14.52 (a) (i) Graph – plotted correctly
(ii) $112\,°C$
(iii) 1.5 atmospheres

(b) (i) 5.4 atmospheres
(ii) To make sure that there is no chance of local cooling causing the sulphur to solidify and block the pipe.
(iii) To keep the molten sulphur at an evenly high temperature, so it does not lose heat to the surroundings.
(c) (i) Sulphur and water do not mix.
(ii) Top layer is water; bottom layer is molten sulphur.
Sulphur has a density about twice (2×) that of water, so it forms the bottom layer.

14.53 (a) Plastics and polymers are very unreactive.
(b) Recycling would conserve our resources of crude oil (petroleum).
(c) Advantage – burning plastics produces energy, which can be used locally, and reduces litter on dumps.
Disadvantage – burning plastics can produce toxic or acidic waste gases, which pollute the atmosphere.
(d) Use of plastics reduces fuel consumption and reduces corrosion in parts of the car.
(e) (i) Plastic bags, kitchenware
(ii) Plastic bottles, raincoats, electrical insulation, drainpipes
(f) Thermal cracking is the splitting of large hydrocarbon molecules (chains) into smaller molecules by the action of heat.
(g) (i)

(ii) $M_r = (2 \times 12) + (4 \times 1) = 28$
(iii) $140\,000/28 = 5000$
(h) (i) Polyvinyl chloride
(ii)

(iii)

14.54 (a) (i) Sodium hydroxide
(ii) Sodium carbonate
(iii) Sodium chloride
(iv) Sodium hydrogencarbonate
(v) Ammonia
(b) The sodium melts into a ball and floats over the surface of the water. Bubbles of gas are given off, and the metal dissolves away.

(c) (i) Hydrochloric acid
     (ii) NaOH + HCl $\rightarrow$ NaCl + H$_2$O
          Na$_2$CO$_3$ + 2HCl $\rightarrow$ 2NaCl + H$_2$O + CO$_2$
          NaHCO$_3$ + HCl $\rightarrow$ NaCl + H$_2$O + CO$_2$

(d) Titration using a burette and pipette. 25 cm^3 of
    sodium hydroxide solution is placed in a flask
    using a pipette. An indicator (phenolphthalein)
    is added, and acid is run from the burette until
    the indicator just changes colour (pink to
    colourless). Note the volume and repeat the
    experiment without the indicator.

(e) Ammonium chloride

(f) Solid salt dissolves in the acid and steamy fumes
    of hydrogen chloride gas are given off.

(g) (i) Ammonium chloride
     (ii) NH$_3$ + HCl $\rightarrow$ NH$_4$Cl

Glossary

A

absolute temperature: a temperature measured with respect to absolute zero on the Kelvin scale – absolute zero is the lowest possible temperature that can be achieved.

acid: a substance which dissolves in water, producing $H^+(aq)$ ions – acid solutions turn litmus red and have a pH below 7. In their reactions acids act as proton donors.

acid rain: rain which has been made more acidic than normal by the presence of dissolved pollutants such as sulphur dioxide (SO_2) and nitrogen oxides (NO_x).

acid salts: salts formed when only some of the replaceable hydrogen of an acid is replaced by metal ions or the ammonium ion (NH_4^+).

activation energy (E_A): the energy required to start a chemical reaction – for a reaction to take place the colliding particles must possess at least this amount of energy.

addition polymer: a polymer formed by an addition reaction – the monomer molecules must contain a $C=C$ double bond; for example, poly(ethene) is formed from ethene.

aerobic decay: decay of organic matter which takes place in the presence of air.

alcohols (*alkanols*): a series of organic compounds containing the functional group —OH and the general formula $C_nH_{2n+1}OH$; ethanol is by far the most important of the alcohols and is often just called 'alcohol'.

alkali metals: elements in Group I of the Periodic Table, they are the most reactive group of metals.

alkalis: soluble bases which produce $OH^-(aq)$ ions in water – a solution of an alkali turns litmus blue and has a pH above 7.

alkanes: a series of hydrocarbons with the general formula C_nH_{2n+2}; they are saturated compounds as they have only single bonds between carbon atoms in their structure.

alkenes: a series of hydrocarbons with the general formula C_nH_{2n}; they are unsaturated molecules as they have a $C=C$ double bond somewhere in the chain.

allotropy: the existence of an element in two or more different forms (*allotropes*) in the same physical state; for example, diamond and graphite are both solid forms of carbon.

alloys: mixtures of elements (usually metals) designed to have the properties useful for a particular purpose; for example, solder (an alloy of tin and lead) has a low melting point.

amino acids: naturally occurring organic compounds which possess both an amino (—NH_2) group and an acid (—COOH) group in the molecule. There are 20 naturally occurring amino acids and they are polymerised in cells to make proteins.

amphoteric hydroxides: hydroxides which can react with both acids and alkalis to produce salts; for example, zinc hydroxide.

anaerobic decay: decay of organic matter which takes place in the absence of air.

anode: the electrode in any type of cell at which oxidation (the loss of electrons) takes place – in *electrolysis* it is the positive electrode.

artificial fertiliser: a substance added to soil to increase the amount of elements such as nitrogen, potassium and phosphorus (*NPK fertilisers*); this enables crops to grow more healthily and produce higher yields.

asthenosphere: the partially molten lower regions of the *mantle* in which there are convection currents.

atmospheric pressure: the pressure exerted by the atmosphere on the surface of the Earth due to the weight of the atmosphere.

atom: the smallest particle of an element that can take part in a chemical reaction. All atoms of the same element have the same number of protons in the nucleus.

atomic mass unit: exactly $\frac{1}{12}$ of the mass of one atom of carbon-12, the most abundant isotope of carbon.

atomic number (*proton number*) *[Z]*: the number of protons in the nucleus of an atom. It is also the number of electrons present in an atom and the position of the element within the Periodic Table.

B

balanced chemical (symbolic) equation: a summary of a chemical reaction using chemical formulas – the total number of any of the atoms involved is the same on both the reactant and product sides of the equation.

base: a substance which neutralises an acid, producing a salt and water as the only products. Common bases are the oxides and hydroxides of metals; in their reactions bases act as proton acceptors.

biodegradable plastics: plastics which are designed to be degraded (decomposed) by bacteria.

biopolymers: natural polymers such as starch and proteins.

blast furnace: a furnace for smelting iron ores such as haematite (Fe_2O_3) with carbon to produce pig (or cast) iron (in a modified form the furnace can be used to extract metals such as zinc).

boiling: a condition under which gas bubbles are able to form within a liquid – gas molecules escape from the body of a liquid, not just its surface.

boiling point: the temperature at which a liquid boils; a liquid boils when the pressure of the gas created above the liquid equals atmospheric pressure.

bond energy: the energy required to break a particular type of covalent bond.

C

carbohydrates: a group of naturally occurring organic compounds containing carbon, hydrogen and oxygen; the ratio of hydrogen to oxygen atoms in the molecules is always 2:1 and they have the general formula $C_x(H_2O)_y$.

carbonate test: if effervescence occurs when an acid is added to a substance and the gas produced tests positively for carbon dioxide, the substance is a carbonate.

carboxylic acids (alkanoic acids): a family of organic compounds containing the functional group —COOH (—CO_2H), they have the general formula $C_n H_{2n+1}COOH$. The most important and well known of these acids is ethanoic acid, which is the main constituent in vinegar.

catalyst: a substance which increases the rate of a chemical reaction but itself remains unchanged at the end of the reaction; the catalyst has a part to play in the reaction but is restored at the end.

catalytic converter: a device for converting dangerous exhaust gases from cars into less dangerous emissions; for example, carbon monoxide gas is converted to carbon dioxide gas.

catalytic cracking: the decomposition of long-chain alkanes into alkenes and alkanes of lower relative molecular mass. The process involves passing the larger alkane molecules over a catalyst heated to 500°C.

cathode: the electrode in any type of cell at which reduction (the gain of electrons) takes place. In *electrolysis* it is the negative electrode.

centrifugation: the separation of an insoluble solid from a liquid by rapid spinning during which the solid collects at the bottom of the sample tubes. The liquid can then be *decanted* off carefully.

ceramics: materials such as pottery made from inorganic chemicals by high-temperature processing.

chain reaction: a reaction which is self-sustaining because the products of one step of the reaction assist in promoting further reaction.

chemical formula: a shorthand method of representing chemical elements and compounds using the symbols of the elements.

chemical reaction (change): a change in which a new substance is formed.

chloride test: a chloride is present in a substance if a white precipitate is produced when dilute nitric acid and silver nitrate solution are added to a solution of the substance.

chlorofluorocarbons (CFCs): a group of substituted alkanes containing fluorine and chlorine atoms. They are generally unreactive but they can diffuse into the stratosphere where they break down under the influence of ultra-violet light. The products of this *photochemical process* then react with ozone, damaging the protective layer.

chromatography: a technique employed for the separation of mixtures of dissolved substances, which was originally used to separate coloured dyes.

colloid: a *suspension* of very small particles in a fluid. The particles cannot be seen and do not settle out, but they do scatter light.

combustion: a chemical reaction in which a substance reacts with oxygen – the reaction is exothermic. Burning is a combustion reaction which produces a flame.

composite materials: materials which combine the properties of two substances in order to get the exact properties required for a particular purpose.

compound: a substance formed by the chemical combination of two or more elements in fixed proportions.

concentration: a measure of how much solute is dissolved in a solvent. Solutions can be *dilute* (with a high proportion of the solvent), or *concentrated* (with a high proportion of the solute).

condensation: the change of a vapour or a gas into a liquid; during this process heat is given out to the surroundings.

condensation polymer: a polymer formed by a *condensation reaction*; for example, nylon is produced by the condensation reaction between 1,6-diaminohexane and hexanedioic acid. This is the type of polymerisation used in biological systems to produce proteins, nucleic acids and polysaccharides.

condensation reaction: a reaction in which a simple molecule (for example, water or ammonia) is produced when two reactant molecules join together.

contact process: the industrial manufacture of sulphuric acid using the raw materials sulphur and air.

continental drift: the movement of *tectonic plates* about the Earth's surface.

core: the central, densest, part of the Earth, composed mainly of iron and nickel. The outer core is molten and surrounds the solid, inner core which exists at very high temperature and pressure.

corrosion: the name given to the process that takes place when metals and alloys are chemically attacked by oxygen, water or any other substances found in their immediate environment.

covalent bond: a chemical bond formed by the sharing of one or more pairs of electrons between two atoms – such bonds are present in compounds involving non-metals. In addition to single covalent bonds, double and triple bonds can also exist in some elements and compounds.

cross-linking: the formation of side covalent bonds linking different polymer chains and therefore increasing the rigidity of the plastic – thermosetting plastics usually contain many cross-links.

crust: the solid, outermost, layer of the Earth. It is not continuous, but subdivided into plates of continental or oceanic crust.

crystallisation: the process of forming crystals from a saturated solution.

D

decanting: the process of removing a liquid from a solid which has settled or from an immiscible heavier liquid by careful pouring.

deliquescence: the process during which a substance absorbs water vapour from the atmosphere and eventually forms a very concentrated solution.

density: expresses the relationship between the mass of a substance and the volume it occupies;

$$\text{density} = \frac{\text{mass}}{\text{volume}}$$

diatomic molecule: a molecule containing two atoms, for example hydrogen, H_2, and oxygen, O_2.

dibasic acid: an acid which contains two replaceable hydrogen atoms per molecule of the acid; for example, sulphuric acid, H_2SO_4.

diffusion: the process by which different substances mix as a result of the random motions of their particles. Diffusion can only take place within or between fluids.

displacement reaction: a reaction in which a more reactive element displaces a less reactive element from a solution of its salt.

distillate: the liquid distilling over during distillation.

distillation: the process of boiling a liquid and then condensing the vapour produced back into a liquid. It is used to purify liquids and to separate liquids from solutions.

drug: any substance, natural or synthetic, that alters the way in which the body works.

ductile: a word used to describe the property that metals can be drawn out and stretched into wires.

dynamic (chemical) equilibrium: two chemical reactions, one the reverse of the other, taking place at the same time, where the concentrations of the reactants and products remain constant because the rate at which the *forward* reaction occurs is the same as that of the *back* reaction.

E

earthquakes: shock waves caused by the movements of the Earth's *tectonic plates* scraping past each other on a fault, or at margins where one plate is descending into the *mantle*.

efflorescence: the process during which a substance loses water of crystallisation to the atmosphere.

electrode: the point where the electric current enters and leaves a battery or *electrolytic cell*.

electrolysis: a process in which a chemical reaction is caused by the passage of an electric current.

electrolyte: an ionic compound which will conduct electricity when it is molten or dissolved in water; electrolytes will not conduct electricity when solid.

electrolytic cell: a system for converting chemical energy to electrical energy. The system is made by connecting two metals of different reactivity via an electrolyte; *fuel cells* are electrolytic cells capable of providing a continuous supply of electricity without recharging.

electron: a sub-atomic particle with negligible mass and a charge of –1; electrons are present in all atoms, located in energy levels outside the nucleus.

electron configuration (arrangement): a shorthand method of describing the arrangement of electrons within the energy levels of an atom.

electron energy levels: the allowed energies of electrons in atoms – electrons fill these levels (or *shells*) starting with the one closest to the nucleus.

electrostatic force of attraction: a strong force of attraction between particles with opposite charges – such forces are involved in *ionic bonding*.

element: a substance which cannot be further divided into simpler substances by chemical methods; all the atoms of an element contain the same number of protons.

empirical formula: a formula for a compound which shows the simplest ratio of atoms present.

emulsion: the apparent mixing of two immiscible liquids by the use of an emulsifier, which breaks down one of the liquids into tiny droplets. The droplets of this liquid float suspended in the other liquid so that they do not separate out into different layers.

endothermic change: a process or chemical reaction which takes in heat from the surroundings. ΔH has a positive value.

enzymes: protein molecules which act as biological catalysts; they are specific to certain reactions and are most effective within narrow temperature and pH ranges.

erosion: the removal and transportation of weathered rocky material by wind, streams and rivers, glaciers and the sea.

esters: a family of organic compounds formed by esterification, the reaction of an alcohol with a carboxylic acid. Esters are characterised by strong and pleasant tastes and smells.

evaporation: a process occurring at the surface of a liquid, involving the change of state of a liquid into a vapour at a temperature below the boiling point.

exothermic change: a process or chemical reaction in which heat energy is produced and released to the surroundings. ΔH has a negative value.

F

Faraday constant: the quantity of electricity transferred by one mole of electrons; it has a value of 96 500 C/mol.

filtrate: the liquid which passes through the filter paper during filtration.

filtration: the separation of a solid from a liquid, using a fine filter paper which does not allow the solid to pass through.

fluid: a gas or a liquid.

foam: a mixture formed between a gas and a liquid. The gas forms tiny bubbles in the liquid but has not dissolved in it.

fossil fuels: fuels, such as coal, oil and natural gas, formed underground over geological periods of time from the remains of plants and animals.

fossils: traces of prehistoric life which have been preserved by natural processes in rocks.

fractional distillation: a method of distillation using a fractionating column; it is used to separate liquids with different boiling points.

Frasch process: the process of obtaining sulphur from sulphur beds below the Earth's surface; superheated water is pumped down a shaft to liquefy the sulphur, which is then brought to the surface.

free radicals: atoms or groups of atoms with unpaired electrons and therefore highly reactive; they can be produced by high-energy radiation such as ultra-violet light in photochemical reactions.

functional group: the atom or group of atoms responsible for the characteristic reactions of a compound.

G

gel: a mixture formed between a solid and a liquid, in which the solid forms a network that traps the liquid so that it cannot flow freely.

geological time: very long, extended periods of time (over millions of years) during which the Earth was shaped.

giant ionic structure: a lattice held together by the electrostatic forces of attraction between positive and negative ions.

giant metallic lattice: a regular arrangement of positive metal ions held together by the mobile electrons moving between the ions.

giant molecular substances: substances where large numbers of atoms are joined by covalent bonds forming a strong lattice structure; for example, diamond and silica. The network of bonds extends throughout the crystal. These substances tend to have very high melting points.

glass: a supercooled liquid which forms a hard, brittle substance that is usually transparent and resistant to chemical attack.

grain boundaries: the boundaries between the grains in a metal along which a piece of metal may fracture.

grains: the small crystal areas in a metal. Controlling the grain size affects the properties of a piece of metal.

greenhouse effect: the absorption of reflected heat from the Earth by gases in the atmosphere such as water vapour, carbon dioxide and methane (*greenhouse gases*); increased emission of these gases by human activities leads to atmospheric warming (*global warming*).

group: a vertical column of the Periodic Table containing elements with similar properties. Atoms of elements in the same group have the same number of electrons in their outer energy levels.

H

half-life: the time taken for the radioactivity in a sample of a radio-isotope to fall to half its original value – the value is constant for a particular radio-isotope.

halogens: elements in Group VII of the Periodic Table – generally the most reactive group of non-metals.

hardness of water: caused by the presence of higher than usual concentrations of calcium or magnesium ions in water. It causes the production of limescale in water heaters, the blocking of hot water pipes and the inefficient use of soap. *Temporary* hardness (caused by calcium or magnesium hydrogencarbonates) can be removed by boiling, but *permanent* hardness (caused by calcium or magnesium sulphates) cannot.

heat of combustion: the heat change which takes place when one mole of a substance is completely burned in oxygen.

heat of neutralisation: the heat change which takes place when one mole of hydrogen ions is completely neutralised.

hydrated salts: salts containing water of crystallisation.

hydrocarbons: compounds which contain carbon and hydrogen only.

hydrolysis: a chemical reaction involving the reaction of a compound with water. Covalent bonds are broken during the reaction and the elements of water added to the fragments. Hydrolysis can be carried out with acids or alkalis, or using enzymes.

I

igneous rocks: rocks formed when magma cools and solidifies. Igneous rocks are usually crystalline and of two main types: *intrusive* (for example, granite) and *extrusive* (for example, basalt).

immiscible: if two liquids form two layers when they are mixed together, they are said to be immiscible.

indicator: a substance which changes colour when added to acidic or alkaline solutions; for example, litmus or phenolphthalein.

insoluble: term that describes a substance that does not dissolve in a particular solvent.

inter-molecular forces: the weak attractive forces which act between molecules; for example, van der Waals' forces.

intra-molecular forces: forces which act within a molecule; in other words, the covalent bonds which hold the molecule together.

ionic (electrovalent) bond: a strong electrostatic force of attraction between oppositely charged ions – this type of bonding exists in most metallic compounds.

ionic equation: the simplified equation for a reaction involving ionic substances. Only those ions which actually take part in the reaction are shown; *spectator ions* are left out of the equation.

ions: charged particles made from an atom, or groups of atoms (polyatomic ions), by the loss or gain of electrons – the gain of electrons produces negative ions; the loss of electrons produces positive ions.

isomers: compounds which have the same molecular formula but different structural arrangements of the atoms – they have different *structural formulas*.

isotopes: atoms of the same element which have different numbers of neutrons in their nuclei; they differ in their mass (nucleon) numbers. Some isotopes are radioactive because their nuclei are unstable (*radio-isotopes*).

K

kinetic theory: a theory which accounts for the bulk properties of the different states of matter in terms of the movement of particles (atoms or molecules) – the theory explains what happens during changes in physical state.

L

lattice: a regular three-dimensional arrangement of atoms, molecules or ions in a crystalline solid.

lava: molten rock material that surges from a volcanic vent or fissure.

law of conservation of mass: matter cannot be lost or gained in a chemical reaction – the mass of the reactants equals the total mass of the products.

law of constant composition: a particular compound always has the same elements joined together in the same proportions by mass.

lime: a white solid known chemically as calcium oxide (CaO), produced by heating limestone – it can be used to counteract soil acidity, to manufacture calcium hydroxide (slaked lime) and is also used as a drying agent.

limestone: a form of calcium carbonate ($CaCO_3$) – other forms include chalk, calcite and marble; limestone can be used directly to neutralise soil acidity and in the manufacture of iron and steel, glass, cement, concrete, sodium carbonate and lime.

lithosphere: the Earth's crust and the upper, rigid layer of the mantle.

locating agent: a compound which reacts with invisible, colourless spots separated by chromatography to produce a coloured product which can be seen.

M

magma: molten rock which includes dissolved water and gases.

main-group elements: the elements in the outer groups of the Periodic Table (Groups I to VII and 0).

malleable: a word used to describe the property that metals can be bent and beaten into sheets.

mantle: the thick layer of the Earth between the core and the crust – the lower mantle (*asthenosphere*) is partially molten and convection currents flow through it.

mass number (nucleon number) [A]: the total number of protons and neutrons present in the nucleus of an atom.

mass spectrometer: an instrument in which atoms or molecules are ionised and then accelerated; the ions are then separated according to their mass.

matter: anything which occupies space and has mass.

melting point: the temperature at which a solid turns into a liquid – it has the same value as the freezing point. A pure substance has a sharp melting point.

metal extraction: the separation of a metal from its ore; the method used depends on the position of the metal in the reactivity series. All methods are based on a reduction process. For the most reactive metals this is achieved by electrolysis where the metal is produced at the cathode. For less reactive metals the metal oxide is usually chemically reduced with carbon (or carbon monoxide) in a furnace.

metallic bond: an electrostatic force of attraction between the mobile 'sea' of electrons and the regular array of positive metal ions within a solid metal.

metalloid (semi-metal): elements which show some of the properties of metals and some of non-metals; for example, boron and silicon.

metals: a class of chemical elements which have a characteristic shiny appearance and are good conductors of heat and electricity.

metamorphic rocks: formed when rocks buried deep beneath the Earth's surface are altered by the action of great heat and pressure.

miscible: if two liquids form a homogeneous mixture when added together, they are said to be miscible.

mixture: a system of two or more substances that can be separated by physical means. Mixtures can be *homogeneous*: for example, solutions; or *heterogeneous*: for example, suspensions.

Moho (Mohorovicic discontinuity): the boundary between the Earth's crust and the mantle.

Moh's scale of hardness: a measure of the strength and rigidity of a substance based on scratching one material with another – diamond, the hardest natural material, is given the maximum value of 10.

mole: the measure of amount of substance in chemistry. One mole of a substance has a mass equal to its relative formula mass in grams – that amount of substance contains 6.02×10^{23} (*Avogadro's constant*) of atoms, molecules or formula units depending on the substance considered.

molecular formula: a formula which shows the actual number of atoms of each element present in a molecule of the compound.

molecule: a group of atoms held together by covalent bonds.

monomer: a small molecule, such as ethene, which can be polymerised to make a *polymer*; many monomers are joined together to make a polymer.

monosaccharides: a group of simple carbohydrates (simple sugars) – they are sweet to taste and soluble in water; for example, glucose.

N

neutralisation: a chemical reaction between an acid and a base to produce a salt and water only. The reaction can be summarised by the ionic equation
$$H^+(aq) + OH^-(aq) \rightarrow H_2O(l)$$

neutron: an uncharged sub-atomic particle present in the nuclei of atoms – a neutron has a mass of 1 relative to a proton.

nitrogen cycle: the system by which nitrogen and its compounds, both in the air and in the soil, are interchanged.

nitrogen fixation: the direct use of atmospheric nitrogen in the formation of important compounds of nitrogen. Most plants cannot fix nitrogen directly, but bacteria present in the root nodules of certain plants are able to take nitrogen from the atmosphere to form essential protein molecules.

noble gases: elements in Group 0 – a group of stable, very unreactive gases.

non-metals: a class of chemical elements that are typically poor conductors of heat and electricity.

non-renewable (finite) resources: sources of energy, such as fossil fuels, and other resources formed in the Earth over millions of years, which we are now using up at a rapid rate and cannot replace.

normal salt: an ionic substance formed when all the replaceable hydrogen of an acid is completely replaced by metal ions or the ammonium ion (NH_4^+).

O

oil refining: the general process of converting the mixture that is collected as crude oil into separate fractions. The fractions are separated from the crude oil mixture by *fractional distillation*. These fractions are the basis of the petrochemical industry and are used as fuels, lubricants, waxes, bitumen and as chemical feedstock for making a wide range of chemicals.

ore: a naturally occurring mineral from which a metal can be extracted.

organic chemistry: the branch of chemistry concerned with compounds of carbon found in living organisms.

oxidation: there are three definitions of oxidation: (i) a reaction in which oxygen is added to an element or compound; (ii) a reaction involving the loss of electrons from an atom, molecule or ion; (iii) a reaction in which the oxidation number of an element is increased. Oxidation is brought about by an oxidising agent.

oxidation state: a number given to show whether an element has been oxidised or reduced. The oxidation state of an ion is simply the charge on the ion. In a covalent molecule the number indicates the attraction that atom has for the electrons in the bonds – the numbers are worked out according to defined rules.

ozone (trioxygen): a colourless gas (O_3) which is an *allotrope* of oxygen. It is produced in the stratosphere by the action of high-energy ultra-violet radiation on oxygen gas, producing oxygen atoms. These oxygen atoms then react with further oxygen molecules to produce the ozone layer.

ozone depletion: the production of a 'hole' in the ozone layer by the action of certain compounds, most notably CFCs.

ozone layer: a layer of ozone in the stratosphere which prevents harmful ultra-violet radiation reaching the Earth's surface.

P

period: a horizontal row of the Periodic Table. Within a period the atoms of all the elements have the same number of occupied energy levels but an increasing number of electrons in their outer shell.

Periodic Table: a table of elements arranged in order of increasing atomic number to show the similarities of the chemical elements with related electron configurations. The elements are arranged in vertical *groups* and horizontal *periods*.

pH scale: a scale running from below 0 to 14, used for expressing the acidity or alkalinity of a solution. A neutral solution has a pH of 7.

photochemical process: a chemical reaction that occurs when light, usually of a particular wavelength, falls on the reactants.

photochemical smog: a form of local atmospheric pollution found in large cities in which several gases react with each other to produce harmful products.

photodegradable plastics: plastics designed to degrade under the influence of sunlight.

photosynthesis: the chemical process by which plants synthesise glucose from atmospheric carbon dioxide. The energy required for the process is captured from sunlight by chlorophyll molecules in the green leaves of the plants.

polar molecules: covalent molecules (for example, water molecules) in which the atoms bonded together show different strengths of attraction for the electrons making the bonds. The sharing of these electrons is not equal and therefore some atoms bear a slightly negative charge, while others are slightly positive.

pollution: the modification of the environment caused by human influence. It often renders the environment harmful and unpleasant to life. *Water* pollution is caused by many substances, such as those found in fertilisers and in industrial effluent. *Atmospheric* pollution is caused by gases such as sulphur dioxide, carbon monoxide and nitrogen oxides being released into the atmosphere by a variety of industries and also by the burning of fossil fuels.

polymer: a substance consisting of very large molecules made by polymerising a large number of repeating units or *monomers*.

polymerisation: the chemical reaction in which molecules (monomers) join together to form a long-chain polymer.

polysaccharides: a group of complex carbohydrates that are polymers of sugars. They can function as storage molecules (for example, starch) or as structural macromolecules (for example, cellulose).

precipitation reaction (double decomposition): a reaction in which an insoluble salt is prepared from solutions of two suitable soluble salts.

primary atmosphere: the original thick layer of gases, mainly hydrogen and helium, that surrounded the Earth's core soon after the planet was formed 4500 million years ago.

proteins: polymers of amino acids formed by a condensation reaction; they have a wide variety of biological functions.

proton: a sub-atomic particle with a relative mass of 1 and a charge +1 found in the nucleus of all atoms.

pure substance: a single chemical element or compound – it melts and boils at definite temperatures.

R

radioactivity: the spontaneous decay of unstable radio-isotopes. There are three possible products of radioactive decay –
α-particles, β-particles and γ-rays.

reaction rate: a measure of how fast a reaction takes place. Particular reactions may be affected by the following factors: the surface area of the reactants, the concentrations of the reactants, the temperature at which the reaction is carried out, light, and the use of a catalyst.

reactivity series of metals: an order of reactivity, giving the most reactive metal first, based on results from a range of experiments involving metals reacting with oxygen, water, dilute hydrochloric acid and metal salt solutions.

recycled metals: scrap metals that have been collected, sorted, re-melted and then cast again into useful objects. Scrap iron and steel can be separated from other metals magnetically. Such recycling often saves money and energy and also conserves valuable resources.

redox reaction: a reaction involving both *reduction* and *oxidation*.

reduction: there are three definitions of reduction – (i) a reaction in which oxygen is removed from a compound; (ii) a reaction involving the gain of electrons by an atom, molecule or ion; (iii) a reaction in which the oxidation number of an element is decreased. Reduction is brought about by a reducing agent.

relative atomic mass [A_r]: the average mass of an atom of an element, taking account of the isotopes of the element, on a scale where a carbon-12 atom has a mass of exactly 12.

renewable resources: sources of energy and other resources which cannot run out or which can be made at a rate faster than our current rate of use; for example, the wind is renewable and can be used to generate electricity.

residue: the solid left behind in the filter paper after *filtration* has taken place.

reversible reaction: a chemical reaction which can go both forwards and backwards depending on the conditions. This means that both forward and back reactions may occur and a *dynamic equilibrium* can be set up.

R_f value: in chromatography, the ratio of the distance travelled by the solute to the distance travelled by the solvent.

rock cycle: the natural cycle by which rocks are pushed upwards, then eroded, transported, deposited, and possibly changed into another type of rock by conditions of temperature and pressure – these rocks may then be uplifted to enter a new cycle.

rust: a loose, orange-brown, flaky layer of hydrated iron (III) oxide, $Fe_2O_3.xH_2O$, found on the surface of iron or steel. The conditions necessary for rusting involve the presence of oxygen and water. The rusting process is encouraged by the presence of electrolytes such as acid or salt.

S

saturated solution: a solution which contains as much dissolved solute as possible at a particular temperature.

secondary atmosphere: a mixture of gases, created by early volcanic activity, which included ammonia, nitrogen, methane, carbon monoxide, carbon dioxide and sulphur dioxide gases.

sedimentary rocks: formed when solid particles carried or transported by seas and rivers are deposited. Layers of sediment can pile up for millions of years and the sediment at the bottom of the pile experiences great pressure, causing the grains to become cemented together. Sedimentary rock deposits have definite layers or strata through them.

seismometer: an instrument used to detect and measure the size of earthquake waves.

simple molecular substances: substances made up of individual molecules held together by covalent bonds. There are only weak forces between the molecules. These substances tend to have low melting and boiling points.

soapless detergents: soap-like molecules which do not form a scum with hard water. These substances have been developed from petrochemicals. Their calcium and magnesium salts are water soluble and they are biodegradable.

soaps: substances formed by saponification; in this reaction, the oils or fats are hydrolysed by concentrated aqueous sodium hydroxide to produce the sodium salts of long-chain organic acids; for example, sodium stearate. Soap will dissolve grease because of the dual nature of the soap molecule.

soil: a mixture of mineral particles and organic matter or humus.

solubility: a measure of how much of a solute dissolves in a solvent at a particular temperature.

solubility curve: a graph showing how the solubility of a substance in a solvent changes with temperature.

soluble: term that describes a solute that dissolves in a particular solvent.

solution: formed when a substance (solute) *dissolves* into another substance (solvent).

spectator ions: ions that are present in a chemical reaction but take no part in it.

states of matter: solid, liquid and gas are the three states of matter in which any substance can exist, depending on the conditions of temperature and pressure.

strong acid: an acid that is completely ionised when dissolved in water – this produces the highest possible concentration of $H^+(aq)$ ions in solution; for example, hydrochloric acid.

strong alkali: an alkali that is completely ionised when dissolved in water – this produces the highest possible concentration of $OH^-(aq)$ ions in solution; for example, sodium hydroxide.

sub-atomic particles: very small particles – *protons*, *neutrons*, and *electrons* – from which all atoms are built.

sublimation: the direct change of state from solid to gas or gas to solid. The liquid phase is by-passed. Some simple molecular solids can do this at atmospheric pressure (for example, carbon dioxide, iodine).

substitution reaction: a reaction in which an atom (or atoms) of a molecule is (are) replaced by different atom(s), without changing the molecule's general stucture.

sulphate test: if a white precipitate is produced when dilute hydrochloric acid and barium chloride solution are added to a solution of a substance, a sulphate is present.

supercooled liquid: a liquid that has cooled below its freezing point without solidifying; for example, glass.

suspension: a mixture containing relatively large particles of an insoluble solid, or droplets of an insoluble liquid, spread (suspended) throughout a liquid.

tectonic plates: sections of the Earth's crust, the majority having continents sitting on top of them. They move very slowly about the Earth's surface (*continental drift*). The driving force behind this movement is thought to be convection currents within the mantle.

T

thermal decomposition: the breakdown of a compound due to heating.

thermoplastics: plastics which soften when heated (for example, polythene, PVC) – they can be re-moulded.

thermosetting plastics: plastics which do not soften on heating but only char and decompose (for example, melamine) – they cannot be re-moulded.

titration: a method of quantitative analysis using solutions. A volume of one solution is slowly added to a known volume of another solution using a burette until an end-point is reached. If an acid and alkali are used, then an indicator is used to show that the end point has been reached.

transition elements: elements from the central region of the Periodic Table – they are hard, strong, dense metals that form compounds which are often coloured.

troposphere: the layer of the atmosphere closest to the Earth, which contains about 75% of the mass of the atmosphere.

U

universal indicator: a mixture of indicators which has different colours in solutions of different pH.

V

valency: the combining power of an atom or group of atoms. In ionic compounds the valency of each ion is equal to its charge. In a covalent molecule the valency of an atom is the number of bonds that atom makes.

volcanoes: the holes (vents) or cracks (fissures) in the Earth's crust through which molten rock (magma) and hot gases escape to the surface during an eruption.

W

water cycle: the system by which water circulates around the Earth, involving various changes of state in the process. The driving force behind the water cycle is energy from the Sun.

water of crystallisation: water included in the structure of certain salts as they crystallise; for example, copper(II) sulphate pentahydrate ($CuSO_4.5H_2O$) contains five molecules of water of crystallisation per molecule of copper(II) sulphate.

weak acid: an acid which is only partially dissociated into ions in water – usually this produces a low concentration of H^+(aq) in the solution; for example, ethanoic acid. The acid molecules and the ions produced exist in *dynamic equilibrium* in solution.

weak alkali: an alkali which is only partially dissociated into ions in water – usually this produces a low concentration of OH^-(aq) in the solution; for example, ammonia solution.

weathering: the action of wind, rain and frost on rock, causing its break-up.

word equation: a summary of a chemical reaction using the chemical names of the reactants and products.

X

X-ray diffraction: a technique using beams of X-rays which is often used to study crystal structures.

Index

absolute temperature 49
absolute zero 49
accuracy 364
acid hydrolysis 344
acid rain 21
acid salts 150
acidic oxides 126–127, 152
acids 126–129, 132–136, 146–150
activation energy 182, 194
active site (of enzyme) 342
addition polymerisation 335–337
addition reactions 311–312, 335
adrenaline 358–359
adsorption 193
advanced water treatment (AWT) plants 211–212
aerobic bacteria 212, 294
aerosols 32, 311
agonists 357–358
air 217
alcohols 315–318
algae 23, 226, 294
algal bloom 294
alkali metals 68, 250–253
alkaline earth metals 253–258
alkalis 127, 129, 133–134, 147
alkanes 306–308, 310–311
alkenes 308–309, 311–312
alkenes (test for) 353
allotropes 94, 220–221
allotropy 94, 220–221
alloy steels 280
alloys 32, 65, 90–91, 255
alpha(α)-particles 53, 57–58
alternative energy sources 18–19
aluminium 116–117, 258–261, 281, 286–288
aluminium ions (test for) 260
aluminium recycling 302
aluminium smelters 116–117, 286–288
amide link 338, 341
amino acids 341, 344
ammonia 237–239
ammonia (test for) 351
ammonia production 201, 238, 291–292
ammonium ions (tests for) 137
ammonium nitrate 293–295
amorphous solids 96
amount of substance 162
amphoteric hydroxides 152, 260, 265, 350
amphoteric oxides 152, 350
anaerobic bacteria 212, 331–332
anaerobic respiration 316
anaesthetics 310, 358
analgesics 358
analytical tests 348–354
anhydrous salts 140, 198, 222
anions 115
anions (tests for) 136, 348–349
anode 115, 274–275
anode sludge 124
anodised aluminium 259, 290
antacids 132, 134, 149
antagonists 358
antibiotics 358

anti-cancer agents 358
anticline 10
antimatter 2
anti-oxidants 344
antiparticles 2
apparatus 364
argon 248
aspirin 357, 358
asthenosphere 5
atmosphere 15–17
atmospheric pollution 21–23
atmospheric pressure 29
atomic energy levels 60
atomic number (Z) 54–55
atomic spectra 60
atomic structure 52–55, 59–62
atomic theory 45
atoms 49–50, 52
Avogadro's constant 162
Avogadro's Law 167

background radiation 1
bacterial digestion 212
balanced (symbolic) equations 102
basalt 8
bases 133–134, 149
basic oxides 133, 152
basic oxygen process 279
basicity of acids 150
batteries 273–274
bauxite 116, 259, 286–287
best-fit lines 364–365
beta(β)-particles 57–58
Big Bang 1
binding sites 358
biodegradeable molecules 302, 324
biodegradeable waste 339
biogas 331–332
biological catalysts (enzymes) 190
biological polymers 340
biomass 195, 332
biosphere 15
biuret test 342
Blast furnace 278–279
Bohr's theory 61
boiling 28, 29, 31, 47
boiling point 29–31, 47
bond energies 180
brass 91
breathalyser 317
brine 295
bromide ions (test for) 349
bromination 311
bromine (extraction) 209
bronze 91
Brownian motion 48–49
Buchner funnel 34
buckminsterfullerenes 95
bucky-balls 95
bucky-tubes 95
Bunsen valve 317, 352
burette 141, 142
burning 105
butane 307
button cells 274

$C=C$ double bonds 308–309, 310
$C\equiv C$ triple bonds 310
caffeine 357
calcium 253–256
calorimeter 180–181
car batteries 274
carbohydrates 195, 340–341, 343–344
carbon 225–235, 305–306
carbon cycle 16, 225
carbon dioxide 227–228
carbon dioxide (test for) 351
carbon monoxide 23, 227
carbon steels 280
carbonate ions (test for) 136, 349
carbonates 228–229
carboxylic acids 320–324
cast iron 279, 280
catalase 190
catalysts 188–190, 193, 199, 292–293
catalytic converters 189
catalytic cracking 328–329
cathode 115, 274–275
cations 115
cations (tests for) 136–137, 349–351
cells 273–275
cement 296
centrifugation 35
ceramics 96–98
CFCs 22, 245, 311
Chadwick J. 53
chalk 255, 296
charge 54
chemical bonding 72–78
chemical change 44–45, 100–101
chemical equations 102
chemical 'footbridge' 166, 168, 173
chemical formulas 78–79
chemical names 80–81
chemical reactions 44–45, 100–101
chemical vocabulary 373
chemical weathering 10
chemotherapy 359
chlor–alkali industry 295–296, 300
chloride ions (test for) 349
chlorination 211–212
chlorine 242–245
chlorine (test for) 351
chlorine manufacture 96
chlorofluorocarbons (CFCs) 22, 245, 311
chlorophyll 195, 226, 255
chromatography 37–38, 342, 353–354
cirrhosis 317
clinical trials 365
closed systems 198
coal 226, 327, 331–332
collision theory 193–194
colloids 33
colours of transition metal ions 262
combining power (valency) 79–80 263
combustion 105, 218
common salt 139, 252
composite materials 97–98, 297
compound fertilisers 294
compound ions 76–77
compounds 44–45, 75, 78–79, 159
compressed natural gas (CNG) 331

concentrated solution 39, 130
concentration (effect on reaction rates) 186–187, 194
concentration (of solution) 39, 171
concrete 296
condensation 28
condensation polymerisation 337–338, 343
condensation reaction 342
conductivity titrations 151
conductors 112–114
conglomerate 9
conservation of mass 101–102, 165
contact process 201, 222, 295
continental crust 5
continental drift 6
continuous phase 33
controls 365
cooling curve 30
Copernicus 361
copolymer 335, 337
copper ions (test for) 264
copper refining 124, 284, 290
core (of Earth) 4
corrosion 107, 259, 280–281
coulombs 174
covalent bonding 73–75, 78
covalent compounds (properties) 78
Crick F. 89, 340
cross-links 338
crude oil 226, 327–330
crust (of Earth) 4, 5–7
cryogenics 236
cryolite 116–117, 287
crystallisation 36, 39
Curie M. 361

Dalton J. 45–46
Darwin C. 361
data-handling questions 385–387
data-logging 363
decantation 34
decomposition 44
dehydrating agent 222
dehydration 222
dehydration of ethanol 317
deliquescence 145
delocalised electrons 73, 89
denaturation 342, 343
density 87
dependent variable 363
descalers 132, 320–321
detergents 23, 24, 322–324
deuterium 56
diamond 92, 94
diaphragm cell 295
diatomic molecules 50, 73–74
dibasic acid 150, 222
diesel oil 328–331
diffraction pattern 88–89
diffusion 48–50
digestion 105
dilute solution 39, 130
dipeptide 341
diprotic acid 150
direct combination 145
dispersed phase 33
displacement reactions 105, 269
dissociation (into ions) 146–147, 148
dissolving 31, 38, 48, 212–213
distillate 36
distillation 36

diuretic 357
DNA (deoxyribonucleic acid) 89, 340, 362
double helix 89, 340, 362
Down's cell 289
downward delivery 350, 352
drugs 357
drying agents 352
drying gases 352–353
ductility 87, 89
duralumin 90
dynamic equilibrium 147, 199, 320
dynamite 295

Earth's core 4
Earth's crust 4, 5–7
Earth's mantle 4, 5–8
earthquakes 4–5
efflorescence 145
effluent control 301
elastic materials 88
electric arc furnace 280
electrical conductivity 88, 112–114
electrochemical cells 273–277
electrodes 115
electrolysis 45
electrolysis calculations 174–175
electrolysis of molten compounds 114–116
electrolysis of solutions 116–125
electrolytes 113–114
electrolytic cells 115
electrolytic conductivity 114
electrolytic extraction of aluminium 286–288
electrolytic extraction of magnesium 288–289
electrolytic extraction of sodium 288–289
electromagnetic radiation 57
electron arrangements 59–62, 66–68
electron orbits (energy levels) 60–62
electron pairs 84
electron shells 60
electrons 52–55
electroplating 119–120, 124, 281, 290
elements 44, 73, 78–79
empirical formulas 164–165
emulsifiers 33
emulsions 32
end point 141, 151
endothermic changes of state 47
endothermic reactions 101, 178–180
energy level diagrams (for reactions) 178–179
E-numbers 33, 344
environmental costs 301
enzymes 190, 316, 324, 341
epicentre (of earthquake) 4
equilibrium 198
erosion 11
errors 364–365
essential amino acids 344
ester link 338
esterification 317, 321
esters 321–322
ethane 307
ethanoic acid 317, 320–321
ethanoic acid (test for) 353
ethanol 312, 315–318
ethanol (test for) 353
ethyl ethanoate 321

eutrophication 23, 294
evaporation 28–29, 47
exothermic changes of state 47
exothermic reactions 101, 178–180
experimental controls 365
experimental design 362
experimental error 364
experimental investigations 363
explosives 296
extraction of copper 284–285
extraction of iron 278–279
extraction of lead 284–285
extraction of metals 268, 278–280, 284–285
extraction of zinc 278–279, 289–290
extrusive igneous rock 8

Faraday constant 174
fats (test for) 354
fatty acids 321
feedstock (chemical) 328
fermentation 315–316
ferromagnetism 263
fertilisers 237, 292, 293–295, 300
filtrate 34
filtration 34
finite resources 327
fire extinguishers 218
fire triangle 218
flame photometer 252
flame tests 60, 251, 254, 349–350
flash point 330
flue-gas desulphurisers 22, 301
fluids 48
foams 32
focus (of earthquake) 4
food 344
food additives 344–345
food chain 24
food colourings 38
food tests 353, 354
formulas 78–79
fossil fuels 327
fractional distillation 36
fractional distillation of crude oil 328–329
fractional distillation of liquid air 217
fractionating column 36–37
Frasch process 219
free radicals 16, 310, 311
freezing point 28
fresh water 17
froth flotation 284
fuel cells 207–208, 275
fuels 105, 316
fullerenes 95
functional groups 315, 337

galaxies 1
galvanisation 281
gamma(γ)-rays 57–58
gas collection over water 350, 352
gas giants 3
gas syringes 350, 352
gases 27–28, 47
gases (test for) 350–351
gasohol 316
gasoline 328–330
Geiger–Marsden experiment 53
gels 32
giant ionic lattices 75–76, 87, 90–91
giant metallic lattices 79, 87

giant molecular structures (lattices) 74–76, 87, 92
glass recycling 302
glasses 96–98
global warming 22, 226
glucose 343–344
glucose (test for) 354
glycerol 321
grain boundaries 90
grains 90
granite 8
graphite 92, 94
graphs 365
greenhouse effect 22, 226
greenhouse gases 22
ground water 211
Group 0 66, 68, 247–248
Group I metals 68, 250–253
Group II metals 253–258
Group VII 66, 68, 242–245
group trends in Periodic Table 256
Groups 64, 66
gunpowder 296

Haber process 199, 201, 238, 291–292
haemoglobin 23, 198, 227, 294
half-life 58
halide ions (tests for) 349
Hall–Heroult process 287
halogens 66, 68, 242–245
halothane 310
hard water 231–234
hardness 87–88
HCFCs 311
heat of combustion 180
heat of neutralisation 181
heat of reaction 180
heating curve 30
helium 247
heterogeneous mixtures 31–35, 44
HFCs 245, 311
Hofmann voltameter 120
homogeneous mixtures 31–33, 35–38, 44
homologous series 308, 315, 320
homopolymer 335
hormones 341
hot spots (volcanic) 7–8
humus 11
hydrated protons 152
hydrated salts 140, 165
hydration 312, 315
hydrocarbons 306–311
hydrochlorofluorocarbons (HCFCs) 311
hydrofluorocarbons (HFCs) 245, 311
hydrogen 70, 205–208
hydrogen (test for) 351
hydrogen economy 207
hydrogen fuel cell 207–208
hydrogen ions 129
hydrogen manufacture 296
hydrogenation 312
hydrogencarbonates 228–229, 231
hydrolysis 341–342, 344
hydrophilic regions of molecules 322–323
hydrophobic regions of molecules 322–323
hydroxide ions 129
hypothesis testing 362

igneous rock 8–10
ignition temperature 330

immiscible liquids 32
incineration 301
independent variable 363
indicators 127–128, 151
industrial catalysts 190, 263
industrial uses of radioactivity 58–59
infra-red spectroscopy 348
insulators 113
insulin 341–342
inter-molecular forces 84, 95
inter-molecular space (IMS) 47
intra-molecular forces 95
intrusive igneous rock 8
investigations 362
iodide ions (test for) 349
ion exchange 234
ion movement 115
ionic bonding 75–76, 78, 91
ionic compounds (properties) 78
ionic crystals 90–91
ionic equations 109, 144–145, 148
ionising radiation 57
ions 73, 115
iron production 278–279
iron salts (test for) 264
isomerism 309–310
isomers 310
isotopes 55–57, 157
isotopic labelling 59

kelvin 49
Kelvin scale 49
kerosine 328–329
kinetic theory 46–49
krypton 248
Kuhn T. 361

landfill sites 301
lattices 47, 74, 87
lava 8–9
Lavoisier A. 361
law of conservation of mass 101–102
Le Chatelier's Principle 200
lead–acid car battery 274
lead compounds (pollution) 23
leptons 1
lime 133, 202, 297
lime kiln 202
limescale 232
limestone 9, 202, 255–256, 278, 296
limestone cycle 256
limewater 104, 228, 256, 349
lipids 334
liquid petroleum gas (LPG) 307, 331
liquids 27–28, 47
lithium 250–251
lithosphere 5
litmus 127–128, 151
locating agents 37–38, 342
lock and key model (of enzyme) 343
long (L-)waves 4–5
lubricating oil 328–329

macromolecules 305
magma 8–9
magnesium 253–255
magnetic properties 263–264
magnetic separation 34–35, 302
main-group elements 66
malleability 87, 89
mantle (of Earth) 4–8
marble 9, 255, 296

margarine manufacture 312
mass 27
mass concentration (of a solution) 171
mass number (A) 54–55
mass spectrometer 52, 56, 156
matter 2, 27–28, 44
medical screening 365
medical uses of radioactivity 58–59
melting 28, 31, 47
melting point 28–31, 47
melting point determination 30
membrane cell 296
Mendeleev D. 64
mercury cathode cell 295
metabolic route (ethanol) 316–317
metal ions (tests for) 136
metal oxides 126–127, 218
metal reactivity 267–272
metallic bonding 73, 89
metallic conductivity 114
metallic lattices (crystals) 73, 87, 89–90
metalloids 65–66, 234
metals 65–66, 73, 89, 98
metamorphic rock 9–10
methane 22, 178, 306–307, 331–332
methanol 315
methods of extracting metals 268, 278–280, 284–285
methyl orange 128, 151
mid-ocean ridges 7
mild steel 91, 280
mineral acids 127
mineral resources 300
mineral waters 213
minerals 300
miscible liquids 31–32
mixtures 31–33
mobile electrons 73–89
Moho (Mohorovicic discontinuity) 5
Moh's scale of hardness 87–88
molar mass 163
molar volume (of a gas) 167
mole 162–168, 171–173
molecular formulas 164–165
molecules 49–50
monobasic acids 150
monoclinic sulphur 220
monomers 335–338, 341, 343
monoprotic acids 150
monosaccharides 343
mono-unsaturated oils 312
Montreal protocol 311
mortar 297
mudstone 9
multiple covalent bonding (double and triple bonds) 74, 76

naming compounds 80–81
natural gas 226, 327
nebula 3
negative ions (tests for) 136, 348–349
neon 248
neutral oxides 152
neutralisation reactions 104, 133, 148–149
neutrons 52–55
nitrate ions (test for) 349
nitrates 23, 237, 252, 293–295
nitric acid 239–240
nitric acid manufacture 292–293
nitro-chalk 294
nitrogen 236–242

nitrogen cycle 237
nitrogen-fixing bacteria 237
nitrogenous fertilisers 293–294, 300
nitroglycerine 295
nitrosamines 296
noble gases 66, 67–68, 95, 247–249
nodules 209
non-electrolytes 113–114
non-metal oxides 126–127, 218
non-metals 65–66, 73, 205–249
non-renewable resources 18, 327
normal salts 150
NPK compound fertilisers 294, 300
nucleic acids 305, 340
nucleon number 54–55
nucleus 54
nutrient overload 23, 294
nutrients 23
nylon 337–338

oceanic crust 5
oleum 295
open systems 198
optimum pH 343
optimum temperature 200, 343
ores 268, 300
organic acids 126–127
organic chemistry 305
organic solvents 37–39, 88, 212, 311
Ostwald process 292–293
oxidation 106, 110–111, 123, 274, 317
oxidation–reduction reactions 106
oxidation state (number) 85
oxides 126–127, 152, 218
oxidising agents 106, 111
oxidising agents (tests for) 111
oxygen 217–219
oxygen (test for) 351
ozone 16, 22, 211, 217
ozone 'hole' 22, 311
ozone layer 16, 22, 311
ozone layer depletion 22

Pangaea 6
paper recycling 302
paracetamol 357
paraffin 328–329
parent acid (of a salt) 135
penetrating power 57–58
penicillin 357–358
peptide link 338, 341
peptides 341
percentage purity 167
percentage yield 167
percolation 210–211
Perey M. 361
Periodic Table 64–65, 69
periodic trends 67, 256
periods 64, 68, 96
permanent hardness 232–233
pesticides 24, 245
PET 339
petrol 328–330
pH meter 128
pH of salt solutions 150
pH scale 128–129, 148
pH testing 353
pharmaceuticals 357
phase 31, 33
phenolphthalein 128
photochemical reactions 104, 195, 310
photochemical smog 23

photodegradable plastics 340
photography 195
photosynthesis 16, 195, 225–226
physical change 45, 100
physical weathering 10–11
pig iron 279–280
pipette 141–142
placebos 365
plastic waste 339
plastics 335
plate boundaries 7
plate tectonics 5–6
plotting graphs 365
polar molecules 78, 84
poly(chloroethene) (PVC) 329, 336
poly(ethene) 329, 335
poly(propene) 329, 335
poly(styrene) 329, 337
poly(tetrafluoroethene) (PTFE) 336
polyamides 338
polyatomic ions 76–77
polyesters 338
polymerisation 335–338
polymers 335, 337, 340
polypeptides 341
polysaccharides 343–344
poly-unsaturated oils and fats 312, 344
Popper K. 361
porous (unglazed) pot 317, 330
positive ions (tests for) 136–137, 349–351
potassium 250–252
potassium nitrate 252
precipitation reactions 104, 110, 136, 144, 348–351
preferential discharge (in electrolysis) 117, 123
preparation of salts 141–142, 144–145
pressure 49
primary atmosphere 15
primary cells 274
primary (P-)waves 4–5
primitive particles 1
primordial soup 305
propane 307
protein (test for) 354
proteins 190, 305, 340–343
protium 56, 215
proton number 54–55
protons 52–55
PTFE 336
pure substance 29, 38, 44
purity 38
PVC 336
pyrolysis 339

qualitative analysis 348, 354
quantitative analysis 354
quarks 1

R_f value 37
radioactive decay 57
radioactivity 57–59
radiocarbon dating 58
radio-isotopes 55–56
radiotherapy 58–59, 359
radon 248
rancidity 107
random errors 365
rate of reaction 185–196
rates of diffusion 50
reactivity series of metals 267–268

reclaimed land 288, 301
recycling 18, 287–288, 301
recycling plastic waste 339
redox reactions 106, 110, 259–260, 269–270
reducing agents 106, 111
reducing agents (tests for) 111
reduction 106, 110–111, 123, 268, 274
refinery gas 328–329
refractory bricks 278
re-inforced concrete 296–297
relative atomic mass 52, 55–56, 157
relative formula mass 157
relative molecular mass 158
renewable resources 18–19, 316
representative samples 365
residue 34
resources 15–19
respiration 16, 106, 218–219, 225–226, 344
reverse osmosis 209
reversible reactions 197–202
rhombic sulphur 220
risk assessment 364
rock cycle 8–10
run-off 23, 209, 211, 294
rust prevention 281–282
rusting 280–282
Rutherford, Lord 53

sacrificial protection 282
safety symbols 363
salt preparations 141
salts 135–142, 144–145
sandstone 9
Sanger F. 341–342
saponification 322
saturated fats 344
saturated fatty acids 321
saturated hydrocarbons 306–308
saturated solution 39
scientific method 360
scientific revolutions 361
sea salt 139, 212
sea water 208–209
secondary atmosphere 15
secondary cells 274
secondary (S-)waves 4–5
sedatives 358
sedimentary rocks 9–10
seismogram 4
seismometer 4
semi-conductors 234
semi-metals 66, 234
separating funnel 35
separation of mixtures 34–38
sewage treatment 212
shapes of molecules 84
shock waves 4–5, 328
silica 92, 234
silicon 234
simple molecular compounds 75, 77, 87
simple molecular lattices 77, 79, 87
siting a chemical plant 300
slag 278–280
slaked lime 297
slate 9
soap 233, 322–324
soap detergents 322
soapless detergents 322
sodium 250–252
sodium carbonate production 297

sodium chloride   139–140, 209, 252
sodium hydroxide production   296
sodium nitrate   252
soil   11–12
soil pH   133, 150–151
solar system   3
solder   91
solid solutions   32, 90
solids   27–28, 47
solubility   39–40, 88
solubility curves   39–40, 173
solubility of gases   39–40
solubility of salts   39, 140, 349
solute   38
solutions   31, 38–39
Solvay process   297
solvent   38, 212
solvent front   38
sources of error   364
specific heat capacity   181
spectator ions   109, 145, 149
spontaneous reactions   103, 182
stainless steel   90–91, 280
stalactites   232
stalagmites   232
standard atom (for atomic mass)   156
standard pressure   29
standard solution   172
starch   343–344
starch (test for)   354
states of matter   27–28
state symbols   109
steam re-forming   206
stearic acid   321
steel   91, 279–280
steel making   279–280
steel recycling   280, 302
stimulants   357
straight N fertilisers   294
stratosphere   16–17
strong acids   146–147
strong alkalis   147
strong electrolytes   114
structural formulas   306–310
structural proteins   341
structure of Earth   3–4
sub-atomic particles   53–55
subduction zones   7
sublimation   28–29, 36, 95
substitution reactions   310
sucking back   317, 352

sulphate ions (test for)   349
sulphates   223
sulphur   219–224
sulphur dioxide   220
sulphur dioxide (test for)   351
sulphur trioxide   221
sulphuric acid   221–223
sulphuric acid production   201, 222, 295
sulphurous acid   220
super-cooled liquids   96
super-heavy elements   69
supernova   2
surface area (effect on reaction rates)   185–186, 194
surface catalysts   193
surface tension   322
surface water   211
suspensions   32–33
symbols   46
syncline   10
synthesis   45, 103
systematic errors   365

tectonic plates   5–6
temperature (effect on reaction rates)   187–188, 194
temporary hardness   232–233
tensile strength   87
terrestrial planets   3
terylene   338
tests for gases   350–351
tests for negative ions (anions)   136, 348–349
tests for oxidising agents   111
tests for positive ions (cations)   136–137, 349–351
tests for reducing agents   111
tests for unsaturation   353
thermal conductivity   88
thermal decomposition   103, 270
thermal pollution   23
thermal titrations   151
thermit reaction   259–260
thermoplastic polymers   338–339
thermosetting polymers   338–339
Thompson J.J.   53
titration calculations   172
titrations   141–142, 151
trace elements   278
tranquillisers   358
transition metals (elements)   66, 261–267

transpiration   210
tribasic acid   150
trinitrotoluene (TNT)   295
triprotic acid   150
tritium   56
troposphere   16–17
types of reaction   103

universal indicator   128
unleaded petrol   23
unsaturated hydrocarbons   308–309
unsaturated hydrocarbons (test for)   309
upward delivery   350, 352

valency   79–80, 263
valium   357
van der Waals forces   93, 95, 306
vapour   29
Venn diagrams   373
vinegar   317
viscosity   221
vitamin C   344
vitamins   359
volcanoes   5, 7–9
volume   27, 28, 49

water   17, 208–214
water (tests for)   213–214, 353
water cycle   17, 209–210
water of crystallisation   140
water pollution   23–24
water softeners   234
water supplies   17, 210–212
Watson J.D.   89, 361
weak acids   146–147, 202, 320
weak alkalis   147, 202
weak electrolytes   114
weathering   10–11
Wegener A.   361
word equations   101

xenon   248
X-ray diffraction   88–89

yeast   316
yield   167

zinc ions (test for)   265
zone refining   234